Democratization

Democratization

Christian W. Haerpfer

Patrick Bernhagen

Ronald F. Inglehart

Christian Welzel

OXFORD
UNIVERSITY PRESS

OXFORD
UNIVERSITY PRESS

Great Clarendon Street, Oxford OX2 6DP

Oxford University Press is a department of the University of Oxford.
It furthers the University's objective of excellence in research, scholarship,
and education by publishing worldwide in

Oxford New York

Auckland Cape Town Dar es Salaam Hong Kong Karachi
Kuala Lumpur Madrid Melbourne Mexico City Nairobi
New Delhi Shanghai Taipei Toronto

With offices in

Argentina Austria Brazil Chile Czech Republic France Greece
Guatemala Hungary Italy Japan Poland Portugal Singapore
South Korea Switzerland Thailand Turkey Ukraine Vietnam

Oxford is a registered trade mark of Oxford University Press
in the UK and in certain other countries

Published in the United States
by Oxford University Press Inc., New York

British Library Cataloguing in Publication Data

Data available

Library of Congress Cataloging-in-Publication Data

Democratization / Christian W. Haerpfer . . . [et al.].
        p. cm.
   Includes bibliographical references and index.
   ISBN 978–0–19–923302–1
1. Democracy. 2. Democratization. I. Haerpfer, Christian W., 1952-
   JC423.D381357 2009
   321.8—dc22

                                                        2008049929

Typeset by Laserwords Private Ltd, Chennai, India
Printed in Great Britain by
CPI Antony Rowe, Chippenham, Wiltshire

ISBN 978–0–19–923302–1

10 9 8 7 6 5 4 3

Preface and Acknowledgements

Since the global wave of democratization peaked in the aftermath of the collapse of the Soviet Union, the subject has become of crucial concern for any attempt of understanding the contemporary political world. Consequently, over the past 10 years, courses on democratization have established themselves as core components of a large, and increasing, number of undergraduate and postgraduate curricula in politics and international relations. At the same time, the availability of high-quality textbooks in that field has been very limited.

The idea for a new book to fill this gap first surfaced in a conversation between the editors and Ruth Anderson at Oxford University Press in October 2006. They agreed that an introductory text that would introduce students to the theoretical and practical dimensions of democratization in an accessible and systematic way has been lacking for quite some time. Bringing together leading authors from diverse international backgrounds, including some of the best known names in the field, as well as younger scholars, they decided to produce the present book. The resulting text treats in a single volume all important aspects of contemporary democratization, including theories of democratization, critical prerequisites and driving forces of democratic transition, pivotal actors and institutions, and the conditions and challenges for the consolidation of new democracies, including the analysis of failed democratization. To demonstrate how all these factors have affected democratization around the world, we decided that all major world regions should be covered, and we included cases of successful democratic consolidation as well as countries in which the future of democracy remains highly uncertain.

In the process of writing and editing this book, we have incurred great debt to an even greater number of people—too many to list in detail. But we would like to particularly acknowledge the help of Ecaterina McDonagh, who has been responsible for creating the Online Resource Centre supporting the book. Of course we also thank all our contributors for fitting their expertise into the general framework of this book. Thanks are also due to Ruth Anderson, Suzy Armitage, and Thomas Sigel, who have been patient and supportive at different stages of the process.

The contribution of Christian W. Haerpfer to this volume has been supported by a Woodrow Wilson Fellowship of the Kennan Institute for Advanced Russian and Ukrainian Studies in Washington DC, and by the CINEFOGO network under the Sixth Framework Programme of the European Union. The University of Aberdeen has been very supportive of this project and facilitated the participation of five scholars from its Department of Politics and International Relations as editors and/or authors. We are also grateful to a considerable number of anonymous reviewers whose comments early on in the process were immensely helpful in improving the structure and content of this book. Needless to say, we are solely responsible for any remaining errors.

How to use this book

This text is enriched with a range of learning tools to help you navigate the text material and reinforce your knowledge of democratization. This guided tour shows you how to get the most out of your textbook package.

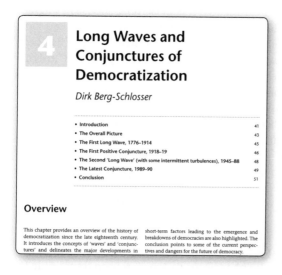

Overview

This feature at the beginning of every chapter sets the scene for upcoming themes and issues and indicates the scope of coverage within each chapter topic.

Introduction

Opening each chapter, the Introduction succinctly presents the main themes and issues, thus providing a framework as you work your way through the topics.

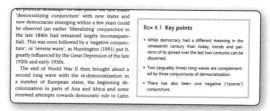

Key point boxes

Key point boxes summarize and drive home the key issues to reinforce learning.

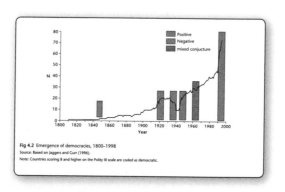

Figures

Figures help illustrate key principles and provide a variety of statistics and explanations related to democratization.

Table 9.2 Multi-level Model Explaining Emancipative Values

PREDICTORS:	DEPENDENT VARIABLE: Emancipative Values	
	Coefficient	T-Ratio
Intercept	.423	71.659***
Individual Level Effects (IL):		
- Education level	.127	25.945***
- Being Muslim	– .053	– 6.2 96***
- Being Protestant	.004	1.146
- Religiosity	– .031	– 6.543***
Country Level Effects (CL):		
- Action resources	.004	6.166***
- Democracy stock	____	n. s.
- Muslims (%)	– .000	– 1.742*
- Protestants (%)	____	n. s.
*Cross Level Interaction Effects (IL*CL):*		
- Education * Action resources	.003	4.257***
- Education * Democracy stock	____	n. s.
- Education * Muslim (%)	– .001	– 2.556**
- Being Muslim * Action resources	– .002	– 2.696***
- Being Muslim * Democracy stock	____	n. s.
- Being Muslim * Muslim (%)	____	n. s.
Explained variance (%): IL (% of total)	12% (8%)	
CL (% of total)	80% (24%)	

Source: World Values Surveys 1995–2006.
Notes: Number of individual level units (respondents) is 141,303. Number of country level units (nations) is 80.
Significance levels: * p < .10, ** p < .05, *** p < .01, n. s. (not significant).

Tables

Tables provide additional data to enrich your knowledge of democratization.

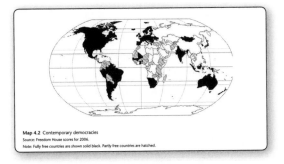

Map 4.2 Contemporary democracies
Source: Freedom House scores for 2006.
Note: Fully free countries are shown solid black. Partly free countries are hatched.

Maps

Maps show democracies before the last conjuncture and after.

Conclusion

Not all new democracies turned out to be stable, and there were some minor reversals, such as a military coup in Gambia in 1997—a country that until then had been among the longest-lasting democracies in Africa. Quite a few of the other new democracies in Central and Eastern Europe and, even more so,

Conclusion

Succinctly summarized, the Conclusion provides a re-cap of each chapter and reinforces the main points.

QUESTIONS

1. Does democratization proceed in waves?
2. How can social change be explained?
3. Is democratization inevitable?
4. What is the difference between waves and conjunctures of democratization?
5. How many waves of democratization have there been?
6. How many conjunctures of democratization have there been?

   Visit the Online Resource Centre that accompanies this book for additional questions to accompany each chapter, and a range of other resources: <www.oxfordtextbooks. co.uk/orc/haerpfer/>.

Questions

Questions at the end of each chapter test your understanding and help you to track your progress.

FURTHER READING

Coleman, J. S. (1990), *Foundations of Social Theory* (Cambridge: Harvard University Press). Introduces and explains the logic behind the 'bathtub' model of social science explanation used here.
Markoff, J. (1996), *Waves of Democracy. Social Movements and Political Change* (Thousand Oaks, CA: Pine Forge Press).

Further reading

This end-of-chapter feature provides reading lists as a guide to find out more about the issues within each chapter topic and to help you locate the key academic literature in the field.

IMPORTANT WEBSITES

<www.idea.int> International Institute for Democracy and Electoral Assistance (IDEA) in Stockholm.
<www.bertelsmann-transformation-index.de> Bertelsmann Transformation Index (2006), 'The Bertelsmann Transformation Index 2006', online.

Important websites

A selection of websites relating to democratization allows you to explore different subjects in more depth.

NOTES

1 In this chapter, the model is employed only in its most abstract sense, making no explicit assumptions of the 'rationality' (or otherwise) of the individual and collective actors.
2 Although improved Polity IV data are available for the period after the Second World War, consistency demands using Polity III data throughout.
3 Some applications concerning Eastern Europe and Sub-Saharan Africa can also be found in Berg-Schlosser (2004c, d).

Notes

This feature provides more details pertaining to in-text discussion to enrich student learning.

Guide to the Online Resource Centre

www.oxfordtextbooks.co.uk/orc/haerpfer/

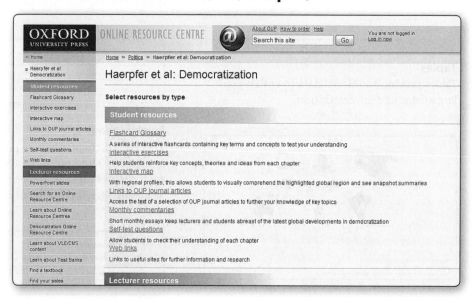

The Online Resource Centre that accompanies this book provides lecturers and students with ready-to-use teaching and learning materials.

STUDENT RESOURCES

Interactive map with regional profiles allows students to visually comprehend the highlighted global region and provides snapshot summaries.

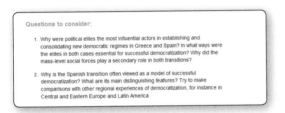

Interactive exercises help students reinforce key concepts, theories, and ideas from each chapter.

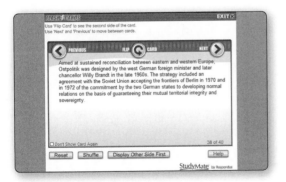

Flashcard glossary allows students to test their understanding of the terminology.

Web links provide links to selected sites allowing lecturers and students to easily research pertinent topics.

Monthly updates with questions keep lecturers and students abreast of the latest global developments in democratization and offer questions to reinforce key points.

Links to OUP journal articles allow lecturers and students further exploration of more in-depth articles about democratization.

LECTURER RESOURCES

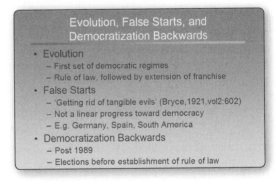

PowerPoints complement each chapter and are a useful resource for preparing lectures and handouts. These fully customizable slides include key concepts, ideas, and theories enabling teaching flexibility.

Brief Contents

Part Two: **Causes and Dimensions of Democratization**

Part Three: Actors and Institutions

Part Four: **Regions of Democratization**

Detailed Contents

Part One: Theoretical and Historical Perspectives

Part Two: Causes and Dimensions of Democratization

Part Four: Regions of Democratization

About the Editors

Christian W. Haerpfer is Associate Professor of Political Science at the University of Aberdeen, UK.

Patrick Bernhagen is Lecturer in Politics and International Relations at the University of Aberdeen, UK.

Ronald F. Inglehart is Research Professor in the Center for Political Studies at the University of Michigan, USA.

Christian Welzel is Professor of Political Science at Jacobs University Bremen, Germany.

About the Contributors

Mervyn Bain is Lecturer in Politics and International Relations at the University of Aberdeen, UK.

Dirk Berg-Schlosser is Professor of Political Science at Philipps University Marburg, Germany.

Matthijs Bogaards is Professor of Political Science at Jacobs University Bremen, Germany.

Michael Bratton is University Distinguished Professor of Political Science and African Studies Center at Michigan State University, USA, and former Executive Director of the Afrobarometer.

Francesco Cavatorta is Lecturer in the School of Law and Government at Dublin City University, Ireland.

Donatella della Porta is Professor of Sociology in the Department of Political and Social Sciences at the European University Institute in Florence, Italy.

M. Steven Fish is Professor of Political Science at the University of California at Berkeley, USA.

Richard Gunther is Professor of Political Science at Ohio State University, USA.

Natalia Letki is Assistant Professor at the Political Science Department of Collegium Civitas, Warsaw, Poland.

John Markoff is Professor of Sociology, History and Political Science at the University of Pittsburgh, USA, and Research Professor at the University Center for International Studies, University of Pittsburgh.

Ian McAllister is Professor of Political Science in the Research School of Social Sciences at the Australian National University.

Leonardo Morlino is Professor of Political Science at Istituto Italiano di Scienze Umane in Florence, Italy, and Director of the Research Centre on Southern Europe at the University of Florence.

Andrea Oelsner is Lecturer in Politics and International Relations at the University of Aberdeen, UK.

Pamela Paxton is Associate Professor in the Department of Sociology at Ohio State University, USA.

Gary Rawnsley is Professor of Asian International Communications at the University of Leeds, UK.

Richard Rose is Director of the Centre for the Study of Public Policy and Professor of Politics at the University of Aberdeen, UK.

Federico M. Rossi is Researcher in the Department of Political and Social Sciences at the European University Institute in Florence, Italy.

Doh Chull Shin is Professor of Political Science at the University of Missouri, USA.

Rollin F. Tusalem is a PhD student in the Department of Political Science at the University of Missouri, USA.

Katrin Voltmer is Senior Lecturer in Political Communications at the University of Leeds, UK.

Stephen White is Professor of International Politics and Senior Research Associate of the School of Central and East European Studies at the University of Glasgow, UK.

Jason Wittenberg is Assistant Professor of Political Science at the University of California at Berkeley, USA.

Hakan Yilmaz is Professor at the Department of Political Science and International Relations, Boğaziçi University, Istanbul, Turkey.

Introduction

Christian W. Haerpfer, Patrick Bernhagen, Ronald F. Inglehart, and Christian Welzel

IN 1989 the number of democracies exceeded the number of autocracies for the first time in history, apart from a brief period after World War I. Since the early 1970s, the number of democracies has risen steadily. Indeed, data from the Polity IV project indicate that the number of 'full democracies' in the world increased from 44 in 1985 to 93 in 2005 (see Figure 1.1). The number of democracies more than doubled in two decades, while the number of autocracies was cut in half. This dramatic development constituted a global wave of democracy.

For the first time in human history, a majority of the world population lives under freely chosen governments. Samuel Huntington (1991) calls it the 'third wave of democratization' and characterizes it as 'one of the most important developments in the history of humankind'. This statement is not exaggerated. Democracy improves people's lives in many ways. Compared with non-democracies, democratic countries are better at protecting and respecting their citizens' human rights (Poe and Tate 1994). Democracy seems to reduce the risk of civil war and (Gurr 2000) and even of terrorism (Li 2005). There is also evidence that democratic countries behave more peacefully internationally (Russett 1993). Democratic **states** also tend to be richer and economically more developed than non-democracies, although it is not clear whether wealth promotes democracy or democracy promotes wealth, or both. Democracy has been credited with providing a better environment for economic development and for distributing society's wealth more equitably (Reuveny and Li 2003) and reducing the most extreme levels of poverty (Sen 1999). The evidence supporting the last two claims is ambiguous, however. While Bruce Bueno de Mesquita *et al*. (2003) find that democracy reduces

infant mortality, a statistical analysis by Michael Ross (2006) produces more dubious results. Quan Li and Rafael Reuveny (2006) find that democracies are also better at protecting the natural environment, although there are reasons to fear that democratic institutions encourage ecologically irresponsible political behaviour (Gleditsch and Sverdrup 2003). Finally, there is evidence that democracy increases people's happiness and life satisfaction (Inglehart *et al*. 2008). Despite some skepticism, an array of positive outcomes is attributed to democracy.

Many of the positive aspects of democracy are weaker in the new democracies than in long-established ones (Rose 2001). As Figure 1.2 illustrates, human rights, prosperity, peace, and welfare spending are strongly correlated with a society's level of democracy. For example, the countries scoring highest on democracy have a mean income level about four times as high as the countries scoring at the lowest level. The columns in this figure reflect the strength of the correlations. When we control for how long a society has lived under democratic institutions, democracy's correlation with prosperity, peace, and human rights diminishes considerably, suggesting that long experience with democracy contributes to its positive correlates (Gerring *et al*. 2005). But the correlations do not vanish. They remain strongly positive and statistically highly significant: even new democracies rank substantially higher than non-democracies on human rights, prosperity, peace, and welfare spending. The rise of democracy seems to improve people's lives in many important ways.

Although democracies tend to perform better than dictatorships on these dimensions, these are statistical tendencies rather than iron laws. One can find cases in which autocracies perform well in meeting the expectations of citizens and consequently enjoying

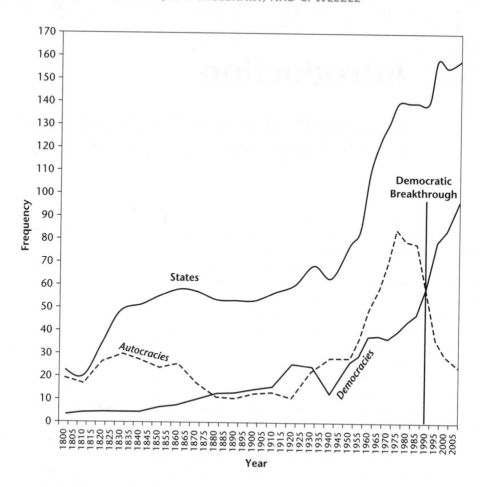

Fig 1.1 The global wave of democracy

Notes: Democracies are 'full democracies', defined as countries in the upper quartile of the Polity IV democracy-autocracy scale; full autocracies are those countries in the lower quartile. Intermediate or incomplete regime types are not included in the graph.

high levels of **legitimacy**. For example, Singapore is highly prosperous and well-governed although it has authoritarian government. And China currently has one of the highest economic growth rates in the world. Democracies tend to perform better than authoritarian states, but there is no guarantee that they will. But quite apart from the benefits people around the world have come to associate with democracy, there are ethical grounds for believing that human beings should decide their common political affairs in a democratic fashion. Democratic government maximizes the extent to which people attain individual autonomy and political equality, which are highly valued in most societies around the world. Autonomy allows people to choose how to live their own lives. It is consistent with the assumption that adults are normally the best judge of their interests and goals (Dahl 1989: 129–30). Without personal autonomy one cannot follow one's own will—a crucial requirement for moral behaviour. According to Immanuel Kant (1996), reason—a uniquely human capacity—enables people to have a free will. This free will can only be effective if it operates so that one's self-imposed imperatives could be accepted as universally binding laws. For Kant, being the subject of one's own laws—being autonomous—is the basis of human dignity and the supreme principle of morality.

Because autonomy is of such fundamental value it must equally apply to all persons in the highest possible way; any deviation or qualification would mean a reduction of human dignity. Thus the argument for autonomy is also an argument for equality. Robert

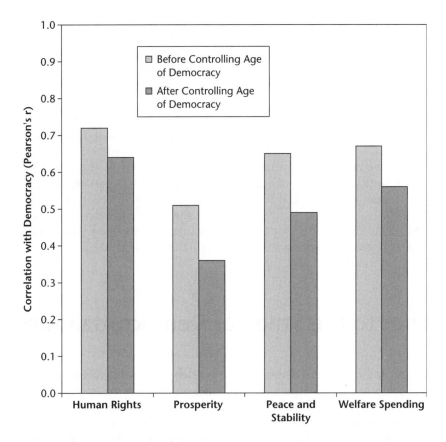

Fig 1.2 The linkage between democracy and humane, prosperous, and peaceful societies

Notes: Democracy is the combined and inverted Freedom House index, averaged over the period 2000–05. The human rights measure is the index of 'physical integrity rights' between 2000 and 2004 by Richards and Cingranelli (available at <http://ciri.binghamton.edu>). Prosperity is measured as per capita GDP in purchasing power parities in 2003, with data taken from the World Bank. Peace and stability is the World Bank's 'good governance' scores for 'political stability and absence of violence' in 2005. Welfare spending is measured with World Bank data on the percentage of government spending in health and education minus spending in military. The age of democracy is Gerring *et al.*'s (2005) 'democracy stock' index as of 1995.

Dahl holds that the principle of intrinsic equality is an integral part of the fundamental beliefs and values of Western society (Dahl 1989). Later in this volume, we will examine how this appeal to a common cultural heritage raises problems for democracy's universal appeal. Nevertheless, emphasis on equality has widespread appeal in many non-Western societies, and there is evidence that the desire for freedom and autonomy are universal human aspirations (Welzel *et al.* 2003).

For all these reasons, the recent dramatic expansion of democracy has been widely viewed as opening the way to a more prosperous, peaceful, and humane world. Political scientists have enthusiastically welcomed the democratic trend of recent decades and

Francis Fukuyama (1992) described the triumph of democracy as the 'end of history,' arguing that with the collapse of communism, there is no longer an alternative model that can credibly challenge the claim of liberal democracy to be the best form of society.

Nevertheless, there are good reasons for taking a critical view of the democratic trend. The first is that many of the new democracies show serious defects, especially in the extent to which they protect human rights, respect the **rule of law**, and in their **accountability** and transparency. 'Effective democracies', that is, democracies in which the rule of law effectively protects popular rights, still constitute a clear minority of the world's societies, accounting for about half of all democracies and a quarter of all states. Second, even though mass support for democracy has become almost universal, many citizens' support for democracy is shallow and lacks genuinely democratic motivations (Inglehart 2003). Particularly in new democracies, when people pay lip service to democracy, it is often supported because it is thought to be linked with prosperity rather than as a good in itself, and the meaning of democracy may be seriously misunderstood. Consequently—surprising as it may seem—there is only a weak relationship between the extent to which the public of a given society endorses democracy, and its actual level of democracy.

Nevertheless, the global diffusion of support for democracy and the expansion of democracies is an important turning point in history. Today, through-out most of the world, democracy has become the sole credible basis of political legitimacy. More than ever, governments around the world are evaluated and measured against democratic standards by international organizations, by international media outlets, by non-profit organizations and by international non-governmental organizations such as Amnesty International, Human Rights Watch, Journalists Without Borders, Transparency International, among many others. The growth of a transnational civil society that focuses on assessing and promoting democracy is a reflection of the global democratic trend. A major success of democracy is the fact that it has become the most widely accepted model of a legitimate human order.

Approaches to the Study of Democratization

The global democratic trend of recent decades has become subject of an ever growing literature. An enormous range of explanations and interpretations have been advanced for the global spread of democracy. Despite this variety, there are two relatively simple distinctions, defining four major approaches. The first distinction is between focusing on *how* democracy emerges, and focusing on *why* it emerges. The first approach focuses on what happens during a democratization process, emphasizing the role of elite pacts, mass **social movements** or international interventions. It focuses on proximate causes rather than long-term causes. In a strict sense, this situation-oriented approach does not explain democratization. It describes it, even if the description is highly formalized, as in game-theoretical models of transition processes. Its strength is illuminating the role of human agency, that is, how given decision-makers carry out democratization.

Another approach focuses on conditions that pre-date democratization processes. The aim is to identify the factors that make it likely for democratization to start and to succeed, rather than focusing on what takes place during the process of democratization itself. Using this approach, scholars have emphasized the role of economic development, social cleavages, class coalitions, international alliances or the structure of the world economic system. The emphasis here is on the *why* rather than the *how* of democratic transitions. The strength of this condition-focused approach is in highlighting the root causes and the circumstances within which democratic transitions typically emerge.

The strengths and weaknesses of the situation-focused and the condition-focused approaches are compatible, indeed they are perfectly complementary, and so there is no reason to view them as competing alternatives. Insights from both approaches must be integrated to attain a full understanding of democratization processes.

The second major distinction is between approaches focusing on domestic factors and those focusing on international factors. The early literature on transitions to democracy tended to treat each transition as an isolated national event. But when scores of democratization processes in clusters in international waves, as occurred in the broad wave of democracy that took place since 1970, the assumption that democratic transitions are primarily driven by domestic circumstances can only be part of the story. It is clear that international and transnational forces and actors are involved when democratization processes occur as international trends. Hence, a more recent approach has emphasized the role of changing international alliances; the liberalization of the global economic system; the diffusion of democratic ideas through **globalization** of information, global trade and tourism; international democracy promotion through national governments, and international organizations including international non-governmental organizations (INGOs); and decisive events that changed the international context in a pro-democratic way, such as the nullification of the **Brezhnev Doctrine**.

Like domestic factors, international factors cannot on their own account for democratization. When one examines what happened in Latin America, East Asia, Eastern Europe, or Sub-Saharan Africa, it is clear that many countries in the same region were exposed to similar international influences, but these countries differed greatly concerning whether, when, and how deeply they democratized. International factors may create an external opportunity structure that makes it relatively difficult or relatively easy for democratization to occur, exposing all countries in a given region to a new situation. But how these opportunities are used depends on domestic factors. Again, the two types of approaches are not mutually exclusive, but complementary.

The scholarly debate has often been marked by sweeping statements that have at times been accepted uncritically and at other times been fiercely disputed. For instance, Przeworski *et al.*'s (2000) claim that economic development does not contribute

to the emergence of democracy, but helps existing democracies to survive, was once widely accepted but has, more recently, been reappraised. Boix and Stokes (2003) and Inglehart and Welzel (2005) have criticized this claim, presenting strong evidence that economic development does help new democracies to emerge. Similarly, in an influential book, Acemoglu and Robinson (2006) argued that the main driver of democratization is the masses' interest in economic redistribution. But the most massive wave of democratization in recent history—that of the former communist bloc—does not seem to have been motivated by desires for more economic equality but rather by a desire to get rid of a system that provided relatively equal distribution at the cost of human liberty. This makes it seem likely that this widely-accepted thesis will also be reappraised. Indeed, it can be argued that the main motivating force behind democratization was inspired by a desire for freedom, rather than economic redistribution (Hofferbert and Klingemann 1999).

It is misleading to take any one explanatory factor as an absolute guide. This book examines a number of perspectives, approaches, and insights that have informed research on democratization. Several different analytical perspectives contribute to an understanding of this topic. Consequently, this book aims to provide a structured overview of the leading perspectives and insights concerning democratization.

Plan of the Book

Throughout the book, democracy and democratization—the process of attaining democracy—are discussed together. Our motivation for treating these two aspects together is the belief that the key factors that enhance and diminish democracy are at work in established democracies, in new democracies and in **regimes** that are in the process of democratizing. Beyond this common thread, each approach to democratization is presented by a leading scholar in the field. The sequence and ordering of chapters is based on four aspects of democratization: (1) theoretical and historical perspectives of democratization, (2) causes and dimensions of democratization, (3)

actors and institutions in democratization, and (4) geographical regions of democratization. The chapters are organized within these four sections.

Democracy means different things to different people, and just what distinguishes democracies from non-democratic regimes is not as clear as it might seem. Democracy has been on the rise (with intermittent declines) since the late eighteenth century. The first step is to make it clear what democracy is and how we know it when we see it. Moreover, to understand the recent global wave of democracy, we need to see it in its historical context. Part One (Theoretical and Historical Perspectives) discusses the difference between democratic and undemocratic states (Ch. 2) and how to determine whether a country is democratic or not, and to measure how democratic it is (Ch. 3). Chapter 4 provides an historical overview of democratization since the late eighteenth century, discussing 'waves' and 'conjunctures'. Chapter 5 focuses on the global wave of democratization from 1970 to the present. Chapter 6 provides an overview of the major theoretical explanations of democratization, from situation-focused approaches to condition-focused approaches, and assesses the relative explanatory value of various factors, within the framework of human empowerment.

Part Two (Causes and Dimensions of Democratization), explores the factors that facilitate and inhibit democratization and discusses the role of democracy beyond the narrowly political sphere. Starting with the international context of democratization, Chapter 7 examines the roles that supra-national, intergovernmental, and international non-governmental organizations play in democratization, and discusses the role of democratization in the foreign policies of major powers such as the USA and the European Union. Chapter 8 explores how economic factors affect transitions to democracy and discusses the problems involved in simultaneous transitions from communist systems to democratic and capitalist systems, and the role of business elites in democratization.[1] Chapter 9 deals with political culture, religion, and questions of legitimacy, examining the role of mass beliefs in democratization, particularly the role played by rising emancipative beliefs. Chapter 10 examines the extent to which women benefit from democratization, reinforcing the view that democratization is not only about electoral enfranchisement but also about other aspects of social, economic and political life, with **gender** equality being crucially important. Chapter 11 analyses the importance of civil society and social capital for successful democratization, reviewing the debates stimulated by Robert Putnam and examining problems of 'weak' civil society and its impact on democratization.

Democracy does not automatically emerge as soon as a number of favourable social and economic conditions are in place. It requires people to become active and demand and negotiate political reforms, within the arenas in which the struggle for democracy is carried out. Even when major conditions are favourable, democracy can break down if people make the wrong choices, or political institutions are inadequate. Part Three (Actors and Institutions) analyses the role of social movements, protest, and **transnational advocacy networks** in transitions to democracy (Ch. 12), and of elections and voter behaviour in democratizing and newly democratized systems (Ch. 13). Chapter 14 focuses on the role of political parties, while Chapter 15 scrutinizes the role of electoral systems and party systems, and the implications of parliamentary and presidential systems. Chapter 16 analyses the relationship between the mass media, democracy, and democratization. The last chapter in this section (Ch. 17) analyses failed and incomplete democratization processes and identifies key factors that make democratization go wrong.

The fourth section of the book (Regions of Democratizations) examines how the global democratic trend toward democracy manifested itself in various regions of the world. Most chapters follow a structure that starts with a brief historical overview, and then examines how the factors identified in Parts Two and Three influence the democratization processes encountered in the given region. The focus is on regions rather than single countries, which facilitates the discussion of international variables, contagion effects and other regional dynamics. The regions are examined according to the sequence in which the global wave of democracy travelled around the world. Analysing the democratization processes in Southern Europe in the 1970s, Chapter 18 examines the role of pre-transitional legitimacy crises of authoritarian regimes, elite pacts and mass mobilization, and international influences as exerted by the European Union. Chapter 19 examines democratization in Latin America, emphasizing the democratic transitions and democratic **consolidation** in Argentina, Chile, Mexico, and Venezuela. Chapter 20 deals with democratization in post-communist Europe and the former Soviet Union, the largest group of countries affected by the global democratic trend. It emphasizes the unique scope and pace of transitions in this area and explains why the process of democratization has been very successful in some countries but failed entirely in others. Successful democratization is rare in North Africa and the Middle East, which is the focus of Chapter 21. Political Islam, the

Israel-Palestine conflict, and the prevalence of rent-seeking economies based on oil wealth are uniquely important factors of this region. In Chapter 22, democratization in the poorest region in the world, Sub-Saharan Africa, is analysed. Though still ridden by severe economic problems, the region has nevertheless experienced a strong trend toward democracy, to the surprise of many observers. The chapter pays special attention to South Africa, Kenya, Rwanda, and Zimbabwe. Lastly, democratization in South-East Asia is the focus of Chapter 23. Here, we examine examples of successful mass-pressured democratization as in the Philippines and South Korea, and the contrasting example of elite-guided democratization in Taiwan. The chapter also deals with failed popular pressures to democratize, as in China; with democratization that was reversed by military rule, as in Thailand; and with the absence of any attempt to democratize, as in Vietnam or Singapore.

The concluding chapter (Ch. 24) draws together the themes of the book, summarizing the lessons learned for democratizers. On this basis, we attempt a cautious sketch of the future prospects for the expansion of democracy and for deeper democratization around the world. To do so, the chapter examines the global democratic trend of recent decades in a broader evolutionary perspective based on the process of natural selection of regimes, that reflects their relative likelihood of survival in given environments.

NOTES

1. Throughout this book, the terms 'political order', 'political system', and 'political regime' are used interchangeably.

Part One

Theoretical and Historical Perspectives

2 Democratic and Undemocratic States

Richard Rose

Overview

This chapter explains the difference between democratic and undemocratic **states**. It is not only about whether there are elections: it is about whether or not it there is the rule of law. When both conditions are met, elections are free and fair and the government is accountable to the electorate. When laws can be bent or broken, unfair elections represent the will of governors more than that of the governed. Less than one-third of the political systems in the world today are fully democratic states. Some are incompletely democratic because they hold elections without the rule of law; some are incompletely undemocratic because, even though they follow the rule of law they are not accountable to a popular electorate. Moreover, some **regimes** are fully undemocratic because they lack both free elections and the rule of law. To understand the process of democratization, we need to understand the changes that must occur to produce a change from an undemocratic to a democratic state.

Introduction

A state is democratic if there are free and fair elections that can hold government accountable; however, this can happen only if there is a state. A strong state is no guarantee of a strong democracy. The pyramids of Egypt are monuments to an ancient civilization that succeeded in wielding undemocratic authority for thousands of years. In today's world, while some states are fully democratic there are many that are incompletely democratic and some states actively repress their subjects. To label such regimes as 'failing' to democratize can be misleading. Middle East sheikdoms such as Saudi Arabia and the People's Republic of China have not failed to become democratic; they have succeeded in maintaining undemocratic regimes.

The history of the modern state in Europe is not about democracy; it is about authority. To view history as if it were the story of democracy expanding is to read history backwards, inferring purposes and goals from the unintended as well as intended consequences of wars and domestic events. Because the problems of governing are endless, the adoption of democratic institutions is not the end of history

nor does democracy assure economic growth, full employment and the absence of crime. The argument for democracy is not that it is perfect but that it is preferable to the alternatives. Democracy has spread across the world in the face of competition with undemocratic regimes. Over the last 100 years or so, European countries have tried many alternatives; most have been costly in human life and dignity. As Winston Churchill (1947) told the House of Commons shortly after the end of World War II:

Many forms of government have been tried, and will be tried in this world of sin and woe. No one pretends that democracy is perfect or all wise. Indeed, it has been said that democracy is the worst form of government, except all those other forms that have been tried from time to time.

Defining Democratic States

Democracy can be used as a noun or as an adjective. When it is used as a noun, it is an abstraction, an ideal of how a country ought to be governed. More than that, it is a highly valued symbol. However, abstractions are often vague. To make the idea of democracy concrete, it must be related to the political institutions of the state.

The state as the starting point

Within a given territory a **state** exercises a monopoly of the powers of coercion such as the police, courts and army. A state claims the right to order subjects within its territory to obey its laws, pay taxes, and risk their lives in military service. If it fails to meet these minimum requirements, it is no longer a functioning state. North and South America are exceptional in being continents in which the great majority of states have boundaries that are more than a century old. Most states were formed without granting subjects the right to vote or speak free of censorship.

The central institutions by which a state exercises its authority are called a **regime**. Regimes can come and go while the state remains. France is a state that is centuries old but as a consequence of events since the French Revolution of 1789 it has had more than

10 different regimes; its present regime dates from 1958. A regime does not change when a general election results in the change of the government of the day. As the British saying puts it, the Queen's Government must be carried on. In a stable undemocratic regime control of government changes hands through decisions of an oligarchic clique. The process of democratization is a change from an undemocratic to a democratic regime.

The **governance** of a state concerns the way in which its institutions relate to its citizens. In an era of big government, states impose many obligations on their citizens and they also distribute many social benefits. In a democratic state, citizens can give direction to government at free elections and governors are meant to do what the people want. In an undemocratic state, the government tells subjects what to do, and subjects are meant to comply. In an incompletely democratic state popular choices are distorted by unfree and unfair elections or by arbitrary actions of governors.

The authority of a regime can be maintained in different ways; in a modern state it is maintained by the **rule of law**. When a regime accepts limitations on its powers, it is what the Germans call a *Rechtsstaat*, a regime in which the law rather than might prevails. When the scope of government action is an object of dispute, courts have the power to strike down actions of government as unlawful. Governors cannot act according to their whims or interests. They are constrained by the law and by courts from acting arbitrarily, muzzling critics, and corruptly exploiting public office. Subject to legal regulation, civil society institutions such as business enterprises, churches or intellectual or cultural bodies can exist independently of the state. A rule-of-law state does not have to be a democratic state, for laws can restrict the right to vote and authorize censorship. The rule of law is not just a desirable addition to democratic governance but a necessary precondition for a fully democratic state. In a rule-of-law state the constitution not only sets out what governors can do but also what they cannot do—and it is enforced. In the words of Juan Linz (1997: 120-21), 'No state, no *Rechtsstaat*, no democracy'.

The rule of law is the foundation of political **accountability**. Elections cannot control government if governors are not accountable to the rule of law. If they are, power cannot be exercised absolutely; it is constrained by constitutional rules that set out what governors can and cannot do, such as the checks and balances of the US Constitution. A democratic government is accountable to its citizens through free and competitive elections. However, where the law rules the courts can also stop an elected government from invoking the will of the people as a justification for ignoring the law and the rights of its critics and of minorities.

The characteristics of a democratic state

A *literal definition of democracy* is 'rule by the people'. However, this abstract statement does not give any indication about how the people are meant to rule. Political theorists and advocates of political causes perennially contest what this ideal means in practice. Political scientists focusing on the complexities of governance in different parts of the world have offered dozens of different, albeit often overlapping definitions, of what it means for the people to rule a state.

The *minimalist definition* is that of Joseph Schumpeter (1943: 271); in a democratic state there is 'free competition for a free vote'. Instead of the people deciding what government does, the popular role is

to decide who governs. The first condition of democracy today is that all adult citizens have the right to vote. Second, elections are competitive, free and fair. Competition between parties distinguishes democracy from government by an enlightened monarch, a dictator or a one-party state. Third, voters decide who holds the principal offices in government.

The rule of law is needed to ensure that governors are held accountable through elections that are free and fair. Individuals must be free to exercise their rights to voice criticisms of government, organize political parties and compete for office in free and fair elections. If the government of the day 'manages' elections by banning opposition parties, harassing critics, intimidating electors and falsifying the count of votes, then the winners of an election will be chosen by the government rather than the electorate. Only if winners of an election are subject to the constraints of the rule of law will losers be protected from the abuse of governmental power. If a corrupt government is voted out of office and its successor equally abuses public office for private gain, then an election will simply produce a rotation of rascals. To ignore the fact that dozens of countries hold elections that are unfair and unfree is the 'fallacy of electoralism', that is, 'privileging elections over all other dimensions of democracy' (Karl 2000: 95-6).

Broader definitions of democracy emphasize multiple forms of **participation** in politics. Participation not only means that all adult citizens have the right to vote but that they are also free to advance their views by joining political groups, engaging in open discussions about how the country ought to be governed and protesting by writing letters to politicians or taking part in demonstrations. Whereas positivist political scientists argue that it doesn't 'pay' individuals to vote, democratic idealists respond that participating in politics is a citizen's obligation as well as a right. Devolving powers to local communities in which citizens can discuss issues face to face is recommended as a way of counteracting problems of scale in a European Union of 400 million European Union citizens or a land in which Americans can live 3,000 miles apart. Deliberative democracy is promoted on the principle of judgment by a jury of a representative sample of citizens that listen to and question statements about a complicated issue by experts and politicians and then state their views. Experiments have shown that such deliberations can raise the level of information and awareness of participants, but they do not resolve disagreements about what government ought to do (Fishkin 1991).

A leading theorist of democratic participation, Robert Dahl (1997: 74), regards a regime that is 'completely or almost completely responsive to all its citizens' as an unattainable ideal. Dahl describes a second-best solution as a **polyarchy**, a 'representative system with a widely inclusive adult electorate'. Dahl (1970) has recognized that considerations of efficiency and lack of expertise can also limit the scope of democratic decisionmaking. There is not the time or, for that matter the popular interest, to hold referendums every month and elections annually. Furthermore, some issues require technical knowledge that few people have, resulting in expert technocrats such as central bankers making many important decisions in a democratic state. Issues such as the state's role in the economy show disagreements between political parties and between economic experts about the best way to achieve economic growth without inflation. These disputes are not resolved in academic seminars but in competitive elections.

Because democracy is virtually everywhere a very positive symbol there is a tendency to stretch the concept by adding a variety of political goals that advocates think desirable (see Collier and Levitsky 1997). However, there is no agreement about what these goals should be. Communist states so valued the symbol of democracy that their one-party regimes were described as people's democracies. The goal of social justice, interpreted as a high degree of economic equality, is advanced as a logical corollary of equality in the right to vote, or even as a **necessary condition** of allowing all citizens to participate fully in a democratic society. However, many econo-

---

Box 2.1 **Key points**

- A viable state and the rule of law are prerequisites for democracy.
- There is no single definition of democracy.
- Definitions of democracy vary between minimalist and maximalist extremes.

---

mists postulate that maximizing individual choice free of state control is the most democratic form of government. The interest of incumbent governors is evident in Vladimir Putin's characterization of Russia as a sovereign democracy. The term 'sovereign' is used to reject criticism of its unfair elections by international bodies and foreign governments.

The European Union requires a state to practice democratic governance in order to gain admission. The multiple criteria it promulgated at a European Council meeting in Copenhagen effectively describe a state that is both modern and democratic. It not only practices the rule of law and holds free elections but also maintains a functioning market economy and has a bureaucracy that can effectively administer EU rules and regulations (Rose 2008).

Bringing the state back into the analysis avoids the reductionist assumption that political participation and elections are all that is needed to create a democratic regime. The fundamental problem of an incomplete electoral democracy is not due to deficiencies in the electoral system but that it is not governed by the rule of law. Moreover, focusing on the state is necessary to understand the dynamics of democratization, since it is a process of turning an undemocratic state into one that is democratic.

The State of States Today

To understand states today we need to think in two dimensions. The first dimension—governors are accountable to the constitution and courts—makes a state modern. The second dimension—governors are accountable to its citizenry through free and fair elections—is a necessary condition of being democratic.

There are different ways in which a regime can be autocratic or democratic (Table 2.1). A two-dimensional classification of contemporary states produces two familiar categories of regimes, one that is fully democratic and one that is an unaccountable autocracy. It also produces two mixed categories,

Table 2.1 Types of Governance—Democratic and Undemocratic

| | | Rule of law | |
		Yes	No
Elections	All can vote	Accountable democracy	Plebiscitarian autocracy
	Few or none can vote	Constitutional oligarchy	Unaccountable autocracy

each of which is incompletely democratic but in different ways. This avoids lumping together under the same heading regimes as different as Britain under King George III, Stalin's Soviet Union, and a Latin American military dictatorship.

Different kinds of accountable democracies

Although the defining principles of democratic states are fixed, there is no one best way to institutionalize accountability. Democratic systems differ in their electoral systems and in their institutions for maintaining the rule of law, and elections register disagreements about who should govern. The constitutions of democratic states set out fundamental rules for the practice of democratic governance, but the basic assumptions underlying these rules differ. In a majoritarian democracy governors make decisions in accord with the wishes of most citizens. A corollary of this approach is that their actions may be opposed by a minority of the electorate. By contrast, proportional theories of democracy endorse forms of governance in which all or nearly all citizens share in the making of decisions whatever party they vote for (Lijphart 1999; Powell 2000: Ch. 1).

The chief argument in favour of *majority rule* is that it provides effective government by concentrating power in the hands of a single party. In a parliamentary system, a government formed by a party with a majority in parliament can be confident that its actions will be endorsed by the legislature. If the parliament is elected by the first past the post system, seats go to the candidate who wins the most votes in a constituency, whether this is less or more than half. A party can win an absolute majority of seats with less than half the popular vote. Opposition parties have the right to criticize government's actions, but they lack the votes in parliament to prevent the

government getting its way. The opposition's lack of power is real but temporary; it is limited to a single term of parliament. At the end of that term, the governing party and opposition compete in a free and fair election in which dissatisfied electors can vote to turn out the government and those satisfied can vote to renew the government for another term. While no democracy exactly matches this idealized model, the British system of single party government is the best known approximation. Its most obvious shortcoming is that no British government has won as much as half the popular vote since the election of 1935. At the 2005 general election the electoral system manufactured an absolute majority of seats in parliament for a Labour Government that received only 35 per cent of the popular vote.

The power of a majority government is not absolute. It is constrained by the constitution and by courts that are empowered to annul actions of a government that are unconstitutional. Limits are normally placed on a government using its majority to amend the constitution by requiring approval by a referendum, a constitutional convention, or a two-thirds or three-quarters majority in parliament. Federalism introduces yet another limitation by dispersing power between two levels of government. Major policies can require a concurring majority at both levels before taking effect, or the endorsement of a second chamber, such as the US Senate or the German *Bundesrat*, that represents territories rather than people. In separation-of-powers systems such as the USA and France the direct election of both a president and a legislature can lead to divided government with different parties winning control of the two chief institutions of state.

The chief argument in favour of *proportional government* is that it is fair to all citizens. Rejecting the majoritarian bias of a first-past-the-post election, a proportional representation system of election awards parties seats in Parliament more or less in keeping with their share of the popular vote. Since the party with the most votes rarely has as much as half the popular vote, a government can usually be backed by a majority only if there is a coalition of two or more parties. Proportional government readily accommodates minorities, for the largest party in parliament can have less than one-third of the seats there, as is the case in the Benelux countries. Even if it is bigger than that, it will need a small party to join it in government if it is to have a majority, as is often the case in Germany. Whereas a majority system excludes opposition parties representing up to half or more of the electorate, a proportional system is inclusive with a multiplicity of parties participating in a coalition government.

The sharing of power is not 100 per cent proportional. Rules intended to prevent the extreme fragmentation of party competition can require that a party win at least five per cent of the popular vote to qualify for seats in parliament. Such a threshold can exclude a number of parties from parliament that collectively gain up to one-fifth of the popular vote. The absence of a majority party in parliament shifts responsibility for choosing a government from the electorate to party leaders who haggle with each other about who gets what offices in a coalition government. Even though a coalition government commands a much bigger share of the vote than a majority government, this does not eliminate differences of opinion about what government should do. Diverse views of coalition partners can lead to political instability and the break up of a coalition. The price of listening to many voices in search of a consensus can be delay or even indecisiveness, resulting in ineffectual government.

Different kinds of undemocratic states

A *constitutional oligarchy* is an incomplete democracy because the actions of governors are not constrained by a mass electorate. However, they are constrained by the rule of law. Courts have sufficient independence to void actions of governors inconsistent with the law and to protect subjects if the regime restricts their liberties unlawfully. Although the behaviour of the regime may not be popular, it is predictable. For example, laws and regulations about censorship and freedom of association set out what peo-

ple are allowed to do as well as what they are not free to do. Laws confer a degree of autonomy on civil society institutions such as the media, universities, business corporations and trade unions. An undemocratic assembly of oligarchs can call a government to account. An example is the case of an unrepresentative British House of Commons, in times before full (male) suffrage, petitioning the monarch to redress grievances before granting the supply of money that the King needed to govern.

In a *plebiscitarian autocracy* there are elections with mass participation and a choice of parties and candidates. However, it is an incomplete democracy because the weakness of the rule of law means that elections are not free and fair. If a referendum is held in which the government not only decides what the question will be but also what the result will be it is a plebiscite, in which the outcome represents the will of the regime. Plebiscitarian autocracies were frequent in twentieth century Latin America, where they are sometimes labelled delegative democracies, since the winner of an election claims the right to act without being constrained by the rule of law. In Argentina, for example, Juan Peron used popular election as president to establish personal rule and Carlos Menem, elected with the personalistic slogan *siganme* (follow me), led a government that was corrupt and repressive. A plebiscitarian autocracy can persist indefinitely but there is always the possibility that an election result can go against the government, as happened in the Orange Revolution in Ukraine in 2004.

In an *unaccountable autocracy* power is exercised arbitrarily at the will of the few without a pretence of legitimating power through elections. Decisions by rulers can override any provision of the constitution and judges are subservient to governors. An autocrat's wilfulness can be exercised through courtiers or household guards, for example, the *oprichniki* of Ivan the Terrible, rather than through bureaucrats. Those who have the confidence of the ruler may enjoy substantial discretion to exploit their offices for personal benefit, but the absence of the rule of law means that those close to the ruler are insecure and risk being purged or executed if the ruler becomes suspicious that his (it is rarely her) underlings are a threat.

As long as the scope of a despot's unaccountable power was limited to face-to-face communication with courtiers and trustworthy administrators, its impact on subjects was limited. The twentieth century saw the creation of totalitarian regimes that went beyond traditional unaccountable autocracies. Whereas traditional autocrats accepted that some areas of social life were of no concern of the state, totalitarian regimes systematically and pervasively sought to control the whole of its subjects' lives. The totalitarian regimes of Hitler's Germany and Stalin's Soviet Union are no more, but North Korea, established in 1948, is older than two-thirds of the regimes in the United Nations.

Most regimes are incompletely democratic or autocratic

To get a sense of which types of regime are most common in the world today requires measures of electoral democracy and of the rule of law. Freedom House annually compiles a global evaluation of the conduct of elections (see Ch. 3). It assesses whether a country gives its citizens political and civil rights, including the right to vote for the national government through free and fair elections. Its standards are high enough to rule out blatantly unfair contests without penalizing new democracies in which inexperienced governors and citizens sometimes stumble when learning how to conduct free elections. On these criteria, Freedom House credits 123 contemporary regimes as holding democratic elections.

Transparency International has developed an index of the extent to which public officials conform to the rule of law or behave corruptly. Its Perception of Corruption Index is compiled from expert assessments of bribery in allocating public resources and there are good theoretical grounds for expecting corruption in handling public money to reflect a lax attitude toward laws constraining political power. The index rates government on a scale of 1 for a regime that is totally corrupt to 10 for a regime that always acts within the law (<www.transparency.org>). In principle, every regime could be classified as law-abiding; in reality this is far from the case. Since the European Union requires its members to adhere to the rule of law, it provides a benchmark standard for labelling regimes as law-abiding. Among 27 EU member states Romania ranks lowest with an index score of 3.7, far below the top EU

countries of Scandinavia. Nonetheless, Romania is well above the median of the regimes that Transparency International evaluates around the world.

Combining the Freedom House and Transparency International ratings provides a two-dimensional profile of countries on every continent. This shows that the chief obstacle to democratization today is not the absence of elections but the failure of regimes that hold elections to govern by the rule of law (Figure 2.1). The median regime is a plebiscitarian autocracy; they constitute 30 per cent of all regimes in the world today. Among the regimes holding competitive elections without the rule of law are countries such as Indonesia and the Philippines, where control of the government can change hands but there is also a high level of corruption. In such a setting, opposition parties face an uphill battle to compete with the party of power, for the law offers critics of the regime and their supporters little protection from intimidation by government. Recent events in Ukraine have shown that even when the opposition has succeeded in winning an election new governors have not rid the state of the lawless corruption endemic under their predecessors.

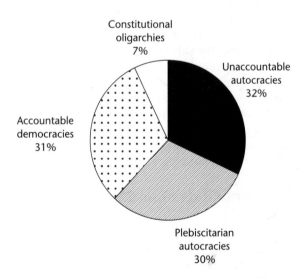

Fig 2.1 A global overview of regime types

Sources: a total of 180 states classified according to whether the regime is an electoral democracy, according to Freedom House 2007 and whether the regime's regard for the rule of law gave it a rating equal to or higher than Romania on the Perception of Corruption Index of Transparency International 2007 (<www.transparency.org>, accessed December 2007).

An additional 32 per cent of regimes are unaccountable autocracies, in which governors do not need to worry about elections and have little regard for the rule of law. Saudi Arabia is an extreme example of an absolute monarchy governed without elections. These autocracies differ in institutional form: some are personal dictatorships, others are controlled by a military or civilian clique, and a few use a party to mobilize a show of popular support. If elections are held rulers make sure that the result shows what it wants regardless of what the electorate wants. For example, in Turkmenistan Saparmurad Niyazov was initially elected President for an eight-year term with 99.99 per cent of the popular vote and the parliament then extended his term for life. After his death, a successor was elected president with almost 90 per cent of the vote. Together unaccountable and plebiscitarian autocracies govern more than three-fifths of the countries in the world today.

Accountable democracies constitute just under one-third of all regimes. They differ substantially in form: most are parliamentary democracies, a smaller proportion are presidential systems and some share power between a popularly elected president and representative assembly. The majority of accountable democracies are European and modern economies but many did not succeed in their first attempt at democratization but lapsed into autocratic rule. India is an outstanding example of a country demonstrating that it is possible to be democratic even if much of the population is poor and illiterate and there are developing countries on every continent that show that a high level of economic development is not a necessary condition of being an accountable democracy.

Only 7 per cent of regimes are constitutional oligarchies in which public officials act in accord with national laws but without the need to be accountable

---

Box 2.2 **Key points**

- Democracies differ in many of their political institutions.
- There are different types of non-democratic regimes.
- The rule of law is often more difficult to establish than elections.

---

to the electorate. Singapore is the best known example, for its rulers boast of 'good' (that is, honest) government and its Transparency International rating is higher than that of the USA and five-sixths of European Union member states. However, Singapore's leaders reject democratic government as an alien idea inconsistent with its definition of Asian values and the regime enforces laws that muzzle opposition. Hong Kong is another Asian political system that is rated more honest than the USA, France, or Germany, but its government is accountable to the communist regime in Beijing rather than to the Hong Kong electorate. A handful of states in the Middle East, such as Bahrain and Qatar, also have regimes that are constitutional autocracies.

To lump all regimes that are not accountable democracies under the heading of undemocratic states obscures major differences between regimes that are lawless and without elections and those that are plebiscitarian autocracies (Linz 2000). Among incomplete democracies, the big obstacle to democratization is not the absence of competitive elections but disregard for the rule of law. For every one constitutional oligarchy there are more than four regimes that are plebiscitarian autocracies.

Evolution, False Starts, and Democratization Backwards

By definition, the starting point for democratization is an undemocratic regime. The first modern states were neither democratic nor democratizing. In the seventeenth and eighteenth centuries the Prussian and French monarchies modernized post-feudal institutions in order to gain more power over their nominal subjects. The checks on a monarch's power did not come from elections but from the territorial power of aristocrats and from oligarchic assemblies that represented the estates of the few. The rule of law was made firm in seventeenth-century England by Parliament revolting against the King in order to enforce its will. The outcome was not a democracy but the restoration of a monarchy subservient to a parliament that represented the few not the many.

Evolution has characterized the first and oldest set of democratic regimes. They first of all established the rule of law. The powers of monarchs in Scandinavia, the Netherlands and England were gradually checked by assemblies of aristocrats, landowners, civic spokespersons and other estates. To describe such assemblies as undemocratic is to project today's values backwards in time. The institutions are best described as proto-democratic. They could evolve into democratic institutions because the law constituted a check on absolutist rule and there was competition between elites for political influence.

The process of democratization that followed was not a choice made at a specific point in time. It happened as a consequence of a series of actions. Rule of law regimes were capable of gradual and peaceful liberalization through the enactment of statutes granting more rights to individuals and institutions of civil society. First, restrictive franchise rights had to be abolished and the right to vote expanded until universal suffrage was achieved. Secondly, to exercise this right required freedom of speech and association and the right of political parties and interest groups to organize. The third step was the election of representatives with the power to control government; this meant the surrender of traditional powers in the hands of servants of the Crown and hereditary estates. In the UK, this process took more than a century after the 1832 Reform Act. A Bill of Rights was quickly added to the American Constitution signed in 1787 but it left clauses about slavery intact. All Americans were not effectively guaranteed the right to vote until the passage of the Voting Rights Act in 1965.

Getting rid of tangible evils

Evolution requires freedom from immediate external or internal upheavals. However, the majority of countries in Europe have not enjoyed sufficient isolation from war or sufficient domestic harmony to maintain a regime without interruption. The typical story of a European country is not the gradual evolution of democracy through many generations but the abrupt alternation between democratic and autocratic regimes due to military defeat, domestic upheavals or both.

Writing after the First World War, James Bryce (1921, vol 2: 602) characterized progress toward democracy as driven by 'the wish to be rid of tangible evils'. However, the process has often been that of trial and error, and along the way some states have produced great evils. Germany is the paradigm example of an oscillation of regimes. The modernization of Prussia created a constitutional autocracy with powers sufficient to dominate European neighbours as well as its own citizens. Free elections were introduced in 1871, but this did not make the state democratic for the government was accountable to the monarch and not to a popularly elected parliament. That regime collapsed in military defeat at the end of World War I in 1918 and was succeeded by the short-lived democratic Weimar Republic and then the Nazi Regime of Adolf Hitler. Thus, there were millions of Germans familiar with a democratic republic or a rule of law state when, after 12 years, the Hitler regime collapsed in military defeat. The post-1945 Federal Republic of Germany has succeeded in becoming an established democracy. After the communist state in East Germany collapsed in 1990 and Germans were united in the Federal Republic its oldest citizens had lived in five different democratic or autocratic regimes.

European states such as France, Spain, Portugal and Greece show that the experience of one authoritarian regime is insufficient to make politicians embrace democracy. In each country political change has been a process of trial and error alternation between democratic and autocratic regimes. This pattern is also familiar in Latin America. In each case big changes to and from democracy have occurred as the result of domestic political upheavals such as civilian dictators, military coups or popular protests.

Economic development has been no guarantee of political development. The modernization of Japan was accompanied by three major wars in the first half of the twentieth century, before military defeat in 1945 led to the establishment of a durable democratic regime. The Republic of Turkey began modernization in the 1920s under the leadership of its founding general, Kemal Atatürk, but the choice of government by free elections came three decades later and has been intermittently subject to military interference since. In China regime change has been a history of one undemocratic regime replacing another. The traditional monarchy in 1911 was succeeded by a military dictatorship in the 1920s and then by a communist regime in 1949. Today, the country is a major participant in international politics and markets as a one-party state without a pretence of governing democratically.

Democratization backwards characterizes the process of regime change that followed the fall of the Berlin Wall in 1989. The legacy of communist regimes was not a modern rule-of-law state but an anti-modern state in which the will of the party and of party leaders substituted for the rule of law. Immediately following the collapse of Soviet-imposed unaccountable regimes, elections were everywhere held to give public evidence of the end of that regime. However, institutionalizing the rule-of-law state has not always been easy. In Central and Eastern Europe the unequivocal rejection of imposed communist regimes plus a legacy of previous regimes with some respect for the rule of law supported rapid change. For example, Latvia simply re-enacted its 1922 constitution.

In 2004 the European Union admitted eight ex-communist countries as meeting its standards of democratic governance. After initial experiments with competitive elections in the early 1990s, post-Soviet states have established regimes that hold unfree elections and govern with limited regard to the rule of law. In successor states from Belarus to Uzbekistan leaders have succeeded in converting a regime that tried semi-free elections into a fully undemocratic state.

In much of the world today the critical issue is not whether a regime is democratizing but whether it will persist or be replaced by another. In India the persistence of a regime that has faced political and military emergencies as well as economic challenges is evidence of successful democratization. By contrast, Pakistan's history has been marked by false starts toward democracy and defaulting to military rule. In Latin America regime changes have tended to favour the replacement of a military dictatorship by a popularly elected president, some ruling with regard for the rule of law and others not. In many countries of Africa and the Middle East regime changes have often happened, but in many cases the rule of law is weak and consequently elections have not been free and fair. Thus, regime changes have demonstrated 'resilient **authoritarianism**' (Posusney 2004: 135).

Dynamics of Democratic and Undemocratic States

Governing is an unending process: the collapse of the Soviet Union was not the 'end of history' (Fukuyama 1992) but the end of a particularly repressive regime. The fourfold typology of states in Figures 1 and 2 shows that democratization is not the only path that regimes have followed. Relatively few countries have evolved without setbacks from a constitutional oligarchy to becoming a rule of law accountable democracy. Most democracies today have made at least one false step toward democracy and then relapsed into undemocratic rule, before subsequently succeeding in remaining democratic for at least two generations.

All regimes are subject to domestic pressures from social, economic and political changes and international pressures from an increasingly open international environment. This is true whether a regime appears to be a **consolidated** democracy or a consolidated autocracy. A consolidated regime is a regime that has sufficiently strong institutions so that the pressures for change that arise can be dealt with within its existing framework, whether by responses that maintain the regime unaltered, for example, changing leadership through an election or by agreement among a military junta or the central committee of a one-party state. An unaccountable autocracy may appear to be a steady state because it rests on the coercive power of governors whereas an accountable democracy may appear to be a steady state because it rests on the consent of its citizenry.

A consolidated regime can be reformed by changing one of its institutions, for example, a proportional representation system of election may be adopted or a military junta can choose a civilian leader, without disrupting the regime. In response to pressures such as the black civil rights movement in the USA in the 1960s, a successful reform resulted in a re-consolidation of a long-established regime. In the UK the electorate has reformed the two-**party system** by voting in substantial numbers for a third party, thereby strengthening rather than weakening the principle of competitive elections.

A consolidated regime is not necessarily an effective, strong state, for survival is the first priority of governors under pressure. A regime may be maintained indefinitely by playing off opponents against each other. For example, General Francisco Franco maintained a dictatorial Spanish regime for 36 years by balancing pressures from the army, a fascist party, an authoritarian church and defeated opponents in the Spanish civil war. In developing and low income countries a lack of administrative and economic resources can limit what any kind of regime can do. Geographical and ethnic divisions can add to these problems and create new ones. Consolidation requires recognizing the limits to what government can do.

Regime change not only registers the 'failure' of one set of rules but also the success, if only temporarily, of political leaders in charge of a new regime. Dramatic changes from unaccountable or plebiscitarian autocracies have characterized the past three decades. However, this is not the only type of change that can occur. A plebiscitarian autocracy may turn into an unaccountable autocracy by abandoning elections in which multiple parties compete or an unaccountable autocracy can introduce semi-competitive elections; each has happened in many successor states of the Soviet Union. Either type of autocracy may be succeeded by a newly democratic regime, as happened in the post-communist regimes of Central and Eastern Europe.

Dynamics of democratic regimes

Within democratic regimes there are continuing debates about reforms proposed with the intent of reducing the gap between existing polyarchies and the ideal democracy, for example, changes in party finance, in the electoral system and decentralizing governance or reducing or expanding its responsibilities. Proponents of reform are challenged by defenders of the status quo with the argument that it is the best that is possible in an imperfect world. Moreover, when the status quo supports the powers that be, for example, winners under existing election laws, leaders of a consolidated regime have incentives to keep things as they are.

Established democracies benefit from being path dependent, since what was done in the past influences what happens in the present and the future (cf. David 1985; Rose and Davies 1994). When an established democracy faces major economic problems, governors have cause to fear that they may lose the next election. However, this does not mean that the regime is threatened with repudiation, since these regimes have become consolidated because they have successfully dealt with economic challenges in the past. We might even describe such regimes as 'fool proof', for it would be difficult to imagine anything that could be done to destroy the long established democratic systems in Scandinavia.

The practice of government re-enforces electoral competition, because the longer a party is in government the more it is at risk of losing the next election due to the failure of its policies, neglect of its supporters, arrogance in exercising power, or just bad luck. A coalition government faces an additional risk: the need for endless discussion within a coalition can result in procrastination and the avoidance of important decisions, thus crippling its response to major challenges when prompt and hard actions are needed.

Dynamics of constitutional autocracy

In a constitutional autocracy the principal tension is not between those who favour and oppose the rule of law, but between those who want to reform it and those against change. In the evolution to democracy, reformers have advocated amending franchise laws so that more citizens could vote regardless of their birth, property or education. The challenge of reform remains today in a country such as Singapore, where the Government offers its subjects the advantages of living in a prosperous rule of law society, but laws make clear that governors are not properly accountable to the citizens.

Dynamics of plebiscitarian autocracy

The dominant influence in plebiscitarian autocracies is the will of those in power. Governors know what they want, and in pursuit of their goals are not constrained by the rule of law. However, the fact that elections are held requires the government to organize a show of support and gives opponents a window of opportunity to mobilize protests against their rule. If the minority of votes for the opposition increases, governors may treat this as a signal to introduce reforms to maintain their autocratic rule. Even though election laws are unfair and the opposition is subject to media neglect and intermittent harassment such elections make governors concede that there is a plurality of political views in society (cf. Schedler 2006).

Dynamics of unaccountable autocracy

An unaccountable autocracy need not worry about embarrassing election results, for either elections are not held or they are not at all competitive. However, the powers that such a regime uses to suppress feedback can create problems. The suppression of feedback means that unaccountable governors do not know what their subjects really think. The fact that subjects comply with the regime's demands does not mean that they are loyal but only that the regime has cowed them into the appearance of submission. The gap between submissive and real support is shown by comparing the vote for communist parties before and after the abolition of the one-party state. In Soviet times more than 99 per cent of the electorate voted for the Communist Party. In the first competitive election in the Russian Federation in 1993, the Communist Party won less than 12 per cent of the popular vote.

The first challenge facing unaccountable autocracies that want to maintain their monopoly of power is to find out what their subjects want and think. The People's Republic of China has responded by holding local elections in which multiple candidates can compete for local support. This puts pressure on party officials to satisfy their local population as well as to paint a rosy picture in reports to party superiors. While this is a significant first step in the direction of accountable government, as long as competitive elections are not held at national level it is only a short step. For many other unaccountable autocracies the idea of opening up their regime to popular feedback is a step too far. Most governors of unaccountable autocracies prefer to carry on imposing their will without regard for their subjects—and risk that doing so may lead their regime to be overthrown.

Conclusion

The variety of states in the world today shows that it is an over-simplification to divide regimes into those that are democratic and those that are not. Almost two in five of today's regimes are incomplete democracies, because elections are plebiscites on a government unconstrained by the rule of law or they are orderly but do not allow all citizens to participate. Moreover, the challenges facing regimes of all sorts show that democratization is not the only direction in which dynamic change can occur. Not only do regimes that Dahl describes as polyarchies fall short of the democratic ideal, but also unaccountable autocracies fall short of the totalitarian ideal of the complete

---

Box 2.3 Key points

- Early constitutional states were oligarchic rather than accountable to mass electorates.

- Democratization has more often come about by trial and error rather than through gradual evolution as in Britain.

- Democratic and non-democratic regimes have difficulties; democracy does not mean the end to problems.

- Autocracies have their own ways of dealing with the inevitable problems of governing. Sometimes, these set them on a path to liberalization and democratization.

control of their subjects. Whether incomplete democracies are heading toward consolidation as accountable democracies or unaccountable autocracies is problematic. A third alternative is that they persist as they are, not because they approximate a political ideal, but on the Churchillian principle that, however bad they are, the current regime is preferable to all the country's historical or prospective alternatives.

QUESTIONS

1. What is a democracy?

2. What is the difference between a state and a regime?

3. Why is a state necessary to make a government democratic?

4. What effect does the presence or absence of the rule of law have on a state's capacity to be democratic?

5. What is the difference between a plebiscitary and a despotic autocracy?

6. What has happened to the many constitutional oligarchies of Europe?

Visit the Online Resource Centre that accompanies this book for additional questions to accompany each chapter, and a range of other resources: <www.oxfordtextbooks. co.uk/orc/haerpfer/>.

FURTHER READING

Linz, J. J. (1997), 'Democracy Today: An Agenda for Students of Democracy: Lecture Given by the Winner of the Johan Skytte Prize in Political Science, Uppsala, September 28, 1996', *Scandinavian Political Studies*, 20/2: 115–34. This lecture offers an engaging and persuasive account of the importance of the rule of law for effective democracy.

Rose, R. (2008), 'Evaluating Democratic Governance: A Bottom-up Approach to European Union Enlargement', *Democratization*, 15/2: 251–71. When the EU evaluates countries applying for membership, they are examined with reference to a wider set of criteria than are covered by democracy indices. The implications of doing so are spelled out in this article.

Rose, R. and Mishler, W. (2002), 'Comparing Regime Support in Non-Democratic and Democratic Countries', *Democratization*, 9/2: 1–20. This article explains how different social, economic and political contexts influence regime support among citizens.

Rose, R. and Shin, D. C. (2001), 'Democratization Backwards: The Problem of Third-Wave Democracies', *British Journal of Political Science*, 31/2: 331–54. Arguing that recent democratization processes face major obstacles to consolidation because they introduced elections before the establishment of the rule of law, this article sets out possible trajectories of states that democratized 'backwards'.

IMPORTANT WEBSITES

<www.freedomhouse.org> This is a non-governmental organization based in Washington DC and New York that annually evaluates political and civil rights of member states of

the United Nations. Its website also includes detailed reports on political institutions and practices in each state.

<www.transparency.org> Transparency International is a non-governmental organization based in Berlin that promotes anti-corruption measures and annually reports the extent to which governments around the world are perceived as corrupt.

<www.ipu.org> The Inter-Parliamentary Union, Geneva, is an association of national parliaments. Its website contains detailed information about parliaments, including election results, in democratic and in autocratic countries.

3 Measuring Democracy and Democratization

Patrick Bernhagen

Overview

This chapter discusses problems of classifying countries as democracies and non-democracies and measuring how far a country has advanced on the path of democratization. Examining different concepts and dimensions of democracy, the chapter asks if democracy should be thought of as a property that is either present or absent, or, alternatively, a characteristic that can be present to a greater or lesser extent. Using well-known and publicly available quantitative indices of democracy, the chapter then illustrates the problems faced by researchers of translating these concepts into measures. Lastly, various hybrid **regime** categories are examined for their contribution to efforts of classifying and measuring political regimes.

Introduction

Researchers and policymakers frequently have to assess how democratic countries are—or whether they are democratic at all—for a variety of reasons. In social science research, testing claims that more democracy means more equality, less conflict, or greater economic prosperity requires researchers to put numbers on countries to gauge their democraticness. Policymakers wanting to make economic aid conditional on democratic performance or demanding certain thresholds of democratic **governance** before inviting countries to negotiations on EU accession need measures that allow them to say which country is democratic and which one is not, or which countries are more democratic and which ones less.

Democratization can be understood as the replacement of an undemocratic political system with a democratic one. Alternatively, it can be seen as the process of making a political system more democratic—regardless of whether that system should be classified as a democracy, an autocracy, or something in between. While these alternatives might at first appear to be different ways of expressing the same thing, they actually reflect fundamental differences in the way democracy is conceptualized. The first notion of democratization, replacing one type of regime with another, implies a *categorical* concept of democracy. Often this is a *dichotomous* concept, according to which a political system either is or is not democratic. The second notion corresponds to a *graded* concept of democracy, implying that political systems can be placed on a *continuum* stretching from more to less democratic countries. This will be discussed in the first part of the chapter.

Regardless of which of these perspectives is adopted, anyone wanting to compare democracy and democratization in different countries or analyse the causes or effects of democracy in a systematic manner requires some form of measurement to determine how democratic a political system is, or whether it is democratic at all. Because democracy cannot be as straightforwardly observed as, e.g. national income (for which simply every citizens' income is recorded and added up), indicators have to be used to enable measurement. The second part of the chapter discusses how democracy measures can be broken up into components and indicators.

Short of full democratization, transition processes can result in the establishment of intermediate regimes types. A bewildering number of terms have been put forward in the literature to characterize these in-between types, including 'delegative', 'illiberal', or 'electoralist' democracies, or 'competitive', 'electoral' or 'contested' autocracies, to name only the best known ones. These will be discussed in the last part of the chapter.

Is Democracy a Matter of Degree?

Conceptualizing democracy

Before we can attempt to measure something we must have an operationalizable concept of it. To say that a concept is operationalizable means that the potential strategies and techniques used for measuring the concept are already taken into account when defining the concept itself. At the same time, however, a concept should not be distorted by the desire to measure it: it should foremostly be theoretically sound. A good starting point is the definition of democracy given in the previous chapter, according to which a country is democratic to the extent that its government is held accountable to citizens by means of free and fair elections (see Ch. 2). This is of course still a fairly abstract notion which needs to be further fleshed out if it is to be measured: Who should count as a citizen and who should be excluded from political **participation**, and on what grounds?

Are elections supposed to be the primary, or even the only means through which leaders are held accountable, or are other modes of participation available to citizens? Does the fairness of elections refer to each contestant having a fair chance of winning or to each citizen being given an equal chance of affecting the outcome?

There is widespread consensus today that entitlement to participation in elections should extend to all adult citizens, save perhaps people in closed mental institutions or convicts—although these exclusions are debatable and some are in fact highly contested (see Manza and Uggen 2002). But what if people who are legally entitled to vote fail to do so because poverty or ignorance discourage them from realizing their democratic rights? And what does it say about a democracy if some citizens' political involvement is restricted to casting a vote at an election every few years, while others socialize with political leaders on a regular basis? Answers to these questions range from Joseph A. Schumpeter's minimalist position, according to which the role of citizens is largely restricted to electing representatives, to richer ones involving the active participation of citizens in decisionmaking, including the local level and the workplace (Pateman 1970), or by way of referendums (Cronin 1989) or deliberation in citizen juries or interactive polling (Fishkin 1991).

A distinction between minimalist and broader perspectives can also be made regarding the question of how far a concern with political equality should go. Minimalists tend to let formal voting equality suffice, insisting that every citizen should have either exactly one vote or, when the electoral or voting system provides for a plurality of votes, that all citizens have an equal amount of votes to cast. Yet one might go further and highlight a need to extend political equality beyond its formal provision, taking into account how differences in people's income, education, or occupation affect the extent to which they have an effective say in politics (Verba, Schlozman and Brady 1995). Lastly, the idea of equating democracy with competitive multi-party elections has been heavily criticized. Terry Karl (1986) argued that military domination and human rights abuses rendered many Latin American regimes of the 1980s and early 1990s less than democratic despite their holding regular and overall fair elections. To classify these countries nonetheless as democratic would mean falling prey to the 'fallacy of electoralism'.

While the substantive merits of minimalist and maximalist conceptions of democracy are discussed elsewhere (Barber 1984; Przeworski 1999), there are at least three pragmatic advantages to adopting a minimalist perspective when it comes to deciding whether or not a country is a democracy in the first place. First, it avoids the inevitable wrangling that would ensue if richer definitions of democracy are put forward, as the question of which additional attributes ought to be included in a definition of democracy will be connected to all sorts of normative concerns and ideological inclinations. For example, some might like to see social justice as part and parcel of a proper democracy, while others might argue that extensive private property rights are a constituent element of democracy. With socioeconomic background being a major determinant of

citizens' political participation, as well as a scarcity of democracies in which private property rights are not effectively protected, each side would have a strong case. But given that there is also a certain tension between unfettered property rights and policies aimed at decreasing socioeconomic and political inequalities, agreement between the two parties is not very likely. Indeed, a substantively enriched, maximalist concept of democracy would arguably be an 'essentially contested' one (Gallie 1964).

Second, many of the ingredients that are likely candidates for broader concepts of democracy may actually be factors that researchers suspect to be causally related with democracy. For example, there are good reasons to expect that democratic systems are better than non-democratic ones at promoting socioeconomic equality. Adopting a richer definition of democracy which already contains social justice as a criterion precludes the pursuit of this and a host of other important questions from the outset (Przeworski *et al.* 2000: 33).

Third, a minimalist definition enables us to deal in a constructive manner with a dispute that has busied students of democracy and democratization for quite some time—whether democracy is best thought of as a dichotomy or a continuum.

Sortal versus scalar concepts

The Italian political scientist Giovanni Sartori (1987) maintains that political systems are 'bounded wholes' and should be treated accordingly. Just like one would classify people as being either alive or dead, or married or single, he argues, so should one classify political regimes as being either democratic or non-democratic—with no room left for any intermediate state of affairs (1987: 182–4). This logic is shared by Adam Przeworski and his colleagues (2000), who apply a dichotomous concept in their attempt of measuring democracy. Adopting Schumpeter's minimalist view, these scholars define democracy as a 'regime in which government offices are filled by contested elections' (2000: 19). By 'government office' they mean the executive and legislative branches of government, while 'contestedness' requires that more than one party has at least in principle a chance of winning an election.

So far so simple, but many scholars disagree with the idea that democracy can or should be classified in such a simple, binary manner. At the level of conceptual logic, treating democracy as a 'sortal concept', i.e. something that enables us for any political system to say simply whether or not it is a democracy, is not compelling. Eddie Hyland (1995) argues that a 'scalar concept' implying the presence of a characteristic to a certain *degree* is just as plausible. This would enable us to place any political system on a scale of 'more or less' democracy. Such a scalar logic is applied by Robert Dahl (1989: 106–31). He identifies five criteria for a democratic process:

1. Effective participation: All citizens should have equal opportunities for expressing their preferences throughout the process of making binding decisions.

2. Voting equality: Every citizen must have an equal and effective opportunity to determine the outcome of political decisionmaking processes.

3. Enlightened understanding: Citizens must have adequate and equal opportunities to learn about relevant policy alternatives and their likely consequences.

4. Control of the agenda: Citizens must have the exclusive opportunity to decide which matters are placed on the public agenda, and how they get there.

5. Inclusion: All permanent adult residents must enjoy full rights of citizenship.

These criteria clearly go beyond the minimalist view of democracy outlined above. But rather than stipulating minimum requirements, they are ideal standards against which actual political systems ought to be evaluated. In the real world, countries vary in the extent to which their political systems meet these criteria. A scalar view is also taken by Kenneth Bollen (1980: 372), who defines democracy as 'the extent to which the political power of the elite is minimized and that of the nonelite is maximized'. This implies a continuum between two ideal points—one in which all power is concentrated in the hands of a monarch or dictator, and another in which all power is held by the people. Each country can then be located on some point on this continuum.

What criteria should be used for choosing between a scalar view of democracy and a binary classification rule? Recall that these conceptual issues are part of an effort to measure democracy, an effort for which we need an operationalizable concept. In general terms, operationalizable concepts should be able to perform two tasks. First, our operationalizations should allow us to measure the kinds of things we are actually interested in. In the methodology of the social sciences, this is referred to as *validity* and includes the extent to which a concept proves helpful when used to pursue interesting research questions (*construct validity*). Second, operationalizable concepts should allow us to classify, or 'code', actual countries on our classification or scale with minimal error. For example, they should serve to minimize the instances in which we end up classifying a country as democratic that is in fact non-democratic, and vice versa. This is referred to as *reliability*. It is good practice in the social sciences to settle conceptual issues first and only deal with issues of operationalization and measurement once a concept has been clearly defined (Lazarsfeld 1966). In the case of democracy, however, debates about concept formation and the task of finding appropriate ways of measuring the concept are often intertwined. Przeworski *et al.* (2000), for example, claim that erroneous coding decisions are minimized by using a binary concept. On the contrary, Bollen (1990) maintains that any measure of democracy becomes less error prone the more fine-grained it is.

In practice, the choice between dichotomy and scale is often a pragmatic rather than a logical one. Comparing how the different conceptualizations perform in research situations, Zachary Elkins (2000) found several advantages of applying a scalar concept of democracy. For example, a scalar measure reveals interesting causal relationships between regime type and military conflict that would not be detected when using a dichotomy. David Collier and Robert Adcock make a virtue out of necessity and suggest that the choice of a concept should be allowed to vary with the research question at hand. They recommend that research that focuses on democratization as 'a well-bounded event' use dichotomies, while scalar concepts might be more helpful in other contexts (1999: 562–3). Thus, rather than trying to find objective criteria that guide concept formation, the answer to the question, 'What is democracy?' should depend on why the question is being asked. The flexibility implied in this recommendation is appealing. But it comes at a price, namely to forgo the ability of defining what a thing is independently of why one is interested in it.

Shades of democracy in autocratic systems

An alternative way in which students of democracy can avoid getting bogged down in the debate about dichotomy versus gradations involves applying a scalar view of democracy only to countries already classified as democratic in the first place. This strategy is endorsed by Sartori (1987: 156), who proposes a two-step procedure. In a first step, regimes must be classified as democracies or nondemocracies. In a second step, a further set of criteria can be applied only to the democratic regimes to gauge just how democratic they are (1987: 182–3). Przeworski *et al.* (2000: 57) agree that, once regimes are found to adhere to a minimum condition (of electoral contestation of government offices), they can then be evaluated as 'more' or 'less' democratic. While, for example, most people would agree that Germany and the UK are both democracies, one could argue that the British political system is less democratic because the country's first-past-the-post electoral system deprives vast numbers of voters of an effective opportunity to influence the composition of parliament. But Sartori as well as Przeworski and colleagues remain strictly opposed to the idea of discerning degrees of democracy in countries that do not meet a minimalist criterion.

By contrast, Kenneth Bollen and Robert Jackman argue that democracy is *always* a matter of degree, even if dealing with countries below a threshold at which they would be deemed fully democratic (1989: 618). For example, while Mexico and Spain in the

> ### Box 3.1 **Key points**
>
> - Democracy can be thought of as one class of a dichotomy, or as a scalar property displayed by political systems to different degrees.
>
> - Most scholars agree that gradations of democracy can be meaningfully distinguished among countries meeting the minimum criteria required to qualify as a democracy in the first place.
>
> - The idea of distinguishing among nondemocratic regimes by the degree to which they display gradations and dimensions of democracy is logically coherent remains controversial.

1960s would both fail to qualify as fully democratic countries, Bollen and Jackman point out that the degree of political competition, and therefore of democraticness, was nonetheless higher in Mexico than in Spain at the time. Based on a statistical analysis of the validity and reliability of dichotomous and scalar measures of democracy, Elkins (2000: 299) concurs that 'looking for traces of democracy in seemingly "nondemocratic" regimes makes good theoretical and methodological sense'. The idea that we can find different degrees of democraticness among nondemocratic regimes might appear a contradiction in terms. But as was pointed out in the previous chapter, not all autocracies are alike. Among autocracies, there are vast differences regarding the selection of rulers, how rulers consolidate and sustain power, how much political mobilization and participation of citizens is tolerated, and even whether or not they hold elections. If democracy is about holding rulers accountable to citizens, it makes sense to say that a plebiscitary autocracy is more democratic than an entirely unaccountable autocracy.

Measuring Democracy

Dimensions of democracy

We have defined democracy as a political system in which the rulers are accountable to citizens through regular electoral participation. While this definition

refers to a single dimension—**accountability**—many democratic theorists think about democracy as a multi-dimensional phenomenon. Robert Dahl (1971) identified two dimensions of democratic government: citizens' participation in the political process, and competition among political groups for office. He subsequently fleshed these out further to arrive at his five criteria of the democratic process—effective participation, voting equality, enlightened understanding, control of the agenda, and inclusion. If these criteria are to be satisfied, Dahl argues (1989: 220–2), the following seven institutional guarantees must be in place:

1. Elected political officials

2. Free and fair elections

3. Inclusive suffrage (the right to vote for virtually all adults)

4. The right to run for public office

5. Freedom of expression

6. Alternative sources of information

7. Associational autonomy (the freedom to form organizations).

In this perspective, the relatively simple concept of democracy contains several dimensions which, in turn, depend on the provision of an even larger number of institutional safeguards. This multi-dimensional view of democracy is widely accepted among researchers seeking to measure democracy. Some draw direct inspiration from Dahl and orient their measurement of democracy on the two dimensions of competition and participation. Tatu Vanhanen's (2000) Index of Democratization, for example, adheres strictly to Dahl's two dimensions. Bollen's (1990) Index of Political Democracy also takes inspiration from Dahl. But instead of participation, Bollen places the notion of 'political sovereignty' alongside 'political liberty'. By the former, he means essentially free and fair elections, while the latter corresponds roughly to Dahl's notion of competition. Other measurement strategies also start out with a two-dimensional perspective, but then proceed to either restrict or expand the number of dimensions. Michael Coppedge and Wolfgang Reinicke's (1991) **Polyarchy** Scale, for example, despite taking its name from Dahl's two-dimensional concept, has contestation as its sole dimension. Likewise, Przeworski and his colleagues (2000) conceptualize democracy in a unidimensional way as the contestation of offices.

By contrast, Mark Gasiorowski's measure of democracy refers to three elements: competition, participation, and the guarantee of civil liberties required to ensure the first two. For Gasiorowski (1996: 471), a regime is democratic if

(1) meaningful and extensive competition exists among individuals and organized groups for all effective positions of government power at regular intervals and excluding the use of force, (2) a highly inclusive level of political participation exists in the selection of leaders and policies such that no major (adult) social group is excluded, and (3) a sufficient level of civil and political liberties exists to ensure the integrity of political competition and participation.

Note how this central role of civil and political liberties corresponds to the notion of the rule of law as a necessary precondition for a fully democratic **state** outlined in Chapter 2.

Some of the most widely-used measures of democracy are based on a multi-dimensional view. Monty Marshall and Keith Jaggers' Polity IV index, for example, captures three institutional dimensions—or 'authority patterns'—that organize the political process in modern states: the process by which governments are selected ('executive recruitment'), the extent to which nonelites are able to influence political elites in regular ways ('political competition and opposition'), and the relationship between the executive branch and other elements of the political system ('independence of executive authority') (Marshall and Jaggers 2007).

The popular Freedom House Index aims to capture political rights and civil liberties as two overarching dimensions, which are each composed of further sub-dimensions. Political rights are seen as enabling people 'to vote freely for distinct alternatives in legitimate elections, compete for public office, join political parties and organizations, and elect representatives who have a decisive impact on public policies and are accountable to the electorate' (Freedom House 2008a). The dimension of political rights is consequently broken up into the three sub-dimensions of the electoral process, political pluralism and participation, and the functioning of government. The civil liberties dimension encompasses freedom of expression and belief, associational and organizational rights, the rule of law, and personal autonomy and individual rights. While most of these sub-dimensions capture the classical liberal principles, the last one in particular also contains positive claims to personal security, socioeconomic rights, freedom from severe socioeconomic inequalities, property rights, and freedom from war.

The problem of conceptual overload

The Freedom House Index has been criticized for 'overloading' the concept of democracy with a host of characteristics that are all in one way or another related to democracy but are really facets of political liberalism, social justice, and security, which should not be confused with democracy as a characteristic of the political process (Schneider and Schmitter 2004). The distinction is extremely important. Democracy is about holding the government accountable to citizens, while liberalism is about minimizing the extent to which governments—no matter how accountable to the citizenry they may be—act arbitrarily and interfere in people's lives. Most of the main provisions demanded by the classic liberal tradition—above all the rule of law, freedoms of movement, expression and association—are preconditions of democracy. It is difficult to imagine how any democratic regime could be made to work in the absence of these. Furthermore, democratic regimes are on the whole much more likely than autocracies to maintain and observe these principles, as well as others such as *habeas corpus*, the sanctity of private home and correspondence, the right to a fair trial according to pre-established laws, or freedom of religion (Schneider and Schmitter 2004). But there is nothing in principle that prevents autocracies from guaranteeing any number of these liberal provisions, and many non-democratic regimes, from nineteenth century Britain to present-day Singapore, have been as respectable in their regard for civil liberties as some democracies. There is also nothing in principle that prevents democratic countries from interfering quite considerably with their citizens' private lives. Many model democracies dictate at astonishing levels of detail what and where their adult citizens should drink or smoke (UK, USA) or in what colour they should paint their houses (Germany). In recent years, democratic governments in the UK and USA have repeatedly attempted to suspend or severely curtail the right to petition for a writ of *habeas corpus*—one of the cornerstones of the liberal tradition. But while the practice in many democracies of restricting peoples' freedom to order their private lives in ways they see fit make these countries less liberal than others, they do not in themselves render them any less democratic.

For the same reasons, most human rights should not be treated as dimensions of democracy. Some human rights, such as freedom of speech and assembly, are of course indispensable for democracy to exist. Furthermore, where democracy rules, human rights tend to be respected more than in autocracies. But treating human rights as definitional ingredients of the concept of democracy would be a different matter altogether. The concept of democracy denotes a mode of political decisionmaking in situations where binding rules have to be established or costs and benefits distributed. Although it is tempting to equate democracy with a number of other, desirable features commonly encountered in democratic countries (e.g. wealth, stability, equality, human rights) it is important to maintain the distinction between democracies on the one hand and factors that might well be its causes or consequences on the other.

Philippe C. Schmitter and Terry Lynn Karl (1991) list four other factors that are frequently associated with democracy, often prompted by its positive normative connotations, but that should not be treated as dimensions of democracy. First, democracy does not include economic efficiency and growth. It may be the case that, on average, democracies fare better economically than non-democracies. But there are also powerful arguments for expecting that stable democracies develop 'institutional sclerosis' as powerful social groups enforce inefficient redistribution, thereby stalling capitalist economic performance (Olson 1982). At the very least, this points at highly interesting mechanisms by which politics and economics interact that should be subject to investigation.

Second, democracy does not mean political or administrative efficiency. As Schmitter and Karl (1991) point out, democracies' capacity to make and implement decisions may even be worse than that of dictatorships, where fewer actors are given opportunities for dragging their feet. At the very least, democracies share the same problems and irrational tendencies that afflict all methods of aggregating individual preferences into collective outcomes that are not either dictatorial or determined by the throw of a dice (Arrow 1963).

Third, democracy does not include domestic stability or civil peace. While democratic institutions and procedures may well serve to channel discontent and the resolution of major grievances away from the street and into more orderly modes of settling conflicts, episodes of civil strife in France, Northern Ireland, and Spain remind us that even consolidated democratic institutions guarantee neither a pacified populace nor temperance on the part of the authorities.

Fourth, political freedom is not synonymous with economic freedom. Democracy is not the same as capitalism and it certainly does not mean small government. The right to participate in collective decisionmaking does not include a right to private property. Political liberalization—the rolling back of autocratic regimes—does not by definition include economic liberalization—the rolling back of the state from the economy. Democratization may go hand in hand with the abolition of tariffs and other barriers to trade, privatization of state-owned enterprises, removal of price controls or currency restrictions, lowering of tax burdens, or the slashing of state subsidies to producers. But it may just not: throughout much of the post-war period, democratic institutions have processed popular demands for welfare state expansion, public economic activity, and proactive macro-economic management in all developed industrialized democracies (Franzese 2002). The relationship between democracy and the economy will be discussed in greater detail in Chapter 8.

In sum, it is important not to confuse democracy with its often desirable concomitants. Table 3.1 summarizes what is and what is not an essential ingredient to democracy.

Indicators of democracy

Once the logical structure of a concept, and its key dimensions have been identified, researchers face the problem that most of these dimensions are not easily observed. Worse, for some dimensions it may simply not be possible at all to be measured directly. In this situation, suitable indicators must be identified that have a reasonable relationship to the concept or dimension we are interested in. This is where the aforementioned criterion of validity becomes relevant. To find a valid indicator of a concept, we have to minimize the inevitable gap between the two (King *et al.* 1994: 110–1). Generally, this task becomes more difficult the more abstract the concept is. Fortunately, compared to more abstract concepts like postmaterialism or social capital, the concept of democracy turns out to be quite manageable. Identification of suitable indicators is facilitated by the recognition of its dimensions, and empirical democratic theorists have been quite imaginative in this task.

Perhaps the most straightforward strategy of identifying indicators is Vanhanen's. Vanhanen claims that his two basic dimensions—competitiveness and participation—are easily captured by official election data. First, his indicator of competitiveness is the combined vote share of the smaller parties and independents in elections (or their share of the seats in parliament if vote distribution figures are not available). Second, participation is simply voter **turnout**, defined as the percentage of the adult population that voted in elections. Vanhanen (2000) claims that

Table 3.1 Dimensions of Democracy

Democracy *is* a political system in which:	Democracy is *not*:	Democracy's *necessary preconditions* are:
• the government is held accountable to citizens • by means of free and fair elections	• socioeconomic equality • capitalism • small government • property rights • economic efficiency and growth • political or administrative efficiency • freedom of religion • stability • peace	• the right to vote for virtually all adults • the right to run for public office for virtually all adults • freedom of association • freedom of expression • freedom of the press.

his indicators have the advantage of being based on official statistical data on elections, which are generally exact and reliable, thus limiting the need for subjective judgements (which, in his view, is inherently error-prone).

Przeworski and his colleagues are less willing than Vanhanen to rely on readily available figures. Instead, they take more active coding decisions in assigning countries to the bins of democracy or non-democracy. Nonetheless, the step these researchers have to take from publicly available documents to coding decision is relatively simple, and Przeworski *et al.* (2000) are very clear in justifying and explaining their coding rules. They classify a country as democratic only if the chief executive and the legislature are elected in contested races. While this is obvious in cases in which an incumbent politician or party loses an election and relinquishes power, the situation is of course less easily identified when incumbents happen to win elections successively. Przeworski *et al.* deal with the potential ambiguity of these cases by insisting on an electorally induced change in government before considering a country democratic. While in some countries, such as Japan in 1993, it has taken an awfully long time to eventually disperse concerns that rulers might outstay their welcome, Przeworski *et al.* choose to err on the side of caution.[1]

By contrast, most other indicators of democracy rely primarily on expert coding, i.e. on interpreting countries' constitutions or on subjective evaluations of the political situation in a country on the basis of media reports or by people who know the circumstances more or less well. An example of this is Gasiorowski's Political Regime Change Dataset. Gasiorowski classifies countries on a case by case basis, interpreting various case studies and historical sources such as *Keesing's Record of World Events*. Although Gasiorowski's concept of democracy involves three distinct dimensions, no clearly separated indicators are used to arrive at the coding decisions. By contrast, Kenneth Bollen (1980) identifies three separate indicators for each of his two dimensions of democracy. He uses freedom of the press, the strength of the opposition, and level of government sanctions as indicators for his 'political liberty'

dimension, while the other dimension, 'political sovereignty', is supposed to be captured by the fairness of elections and the openness of the executive and legislative selection procedures. Like most other researchers constructing indices based on subjective evaluations, Bollen uses data already coded by others, chiefly a number of 'political variables' from Arthur Banks' Cross-National Time-Series Data Archive. A big improvement is achieved in the construction of Coppedge and Reinicke's Polyarchy scale, which uses multiple coders and conducts tests of intercoder reliability.

Such tests are also offered by the people behind the Polity IV scale, who are also very meticulous in spelling out their coding rules. Their three dimensions of democracy are broken further down into six sub-dimensions, or 'component variables', which serve as indicators for the coding process. The coding itself takes place on the basis of historical sources, including the countries' constitutions, and academic publications by country experts.

The Freedom House Index uses three to four different indicators for each of its dimensions. To assign scores, the researchers at Freedom House employ a broad range of sources, including foreign and domestic news reports, non-governmental organization publications, think tank and academic analyses, and individual professional contacts. Most of the Freedom House indicators for the dimension of political freedom overlap with indicators employed by other researchers. But the validity of some of the indicators, such as the absence of 'economic oligarchies' or the constraining effects on people's political choices of 'religious hierarchies' is at least debatable, as is the inclusion of the ability of ethnic and homosexuals, religious minorities and the disabled (Freedom House 2008a). These problems become exacerbated by the civil liberties dimension, whose aforementioned inclusion of socioeconomic rights and personal security leads to indicators that have little to do with democracy as a procedure for political decisionmaking. To summarize how the different concepts, dimensions, and indicators of democracy relate to each other in the measures used most commonly by researchers, they are arranged alongside each other in Table 3.2.

Table 3.2 Measurements of Democracy: Concepts, Dimensions, and Indicators

Researcher(s)	Concept	Dimensions	Indicators
Kenneth Bollen	Graded	• Political sovereignty • Political liberty	• Press freedom • Freedom of group opposition • Government sanctions • Fairness of elections • Executive selection • Legislative selection
Przeworski *et al.*	Dichotomous	• Contestation of offices	• Election to executive • Election to legislature
Vanhanen	Graded	• Competition • Participation	• Combined vote/seat share of the smaller parties • Voter turnout
Coppedge and Reinicke	Graded	• Competition	• Free and fair elections • Freedom of organization • Freedom of expression • Pluralism in the media
Gasiorowski	Graded	• Competition • Participation • Civil liberties	• (No separate indicators)
Freedom House	Graded	• *Political rights:* • Electoral process • Political pluralism • Participation	• Elections to executive • Elections to legislative • Fair elections • Pluralism of political parties • Strong opposition • Freedom from domination by the military, foreign powers, totalitarian parties, religious hierarchies, economic oligarchies, or other powerful groups • Full political rights for minorities • Agenda power of elected officials • Freedom from pervasive corruption • Open and transparent government
		• *Civil liberties:* • Freedom of expression and belief • Associational and organizational rights • Rule of law • Personal autonomy and individual rights	• Media pluralism • Freedom of religion • Academic and educational freedom • Freedom of opinion and speech • Freedom of assembly • Associational freedom • Trade union freedom and collective bargaining • Independence of the judiciary • Rule of law • Protection from political terror

continued

Table 3.2 Measurements of Democracy: Concepts, Dimensions, and Indicators (*continued*)

Researcher(s)	Concept	Dimensions	Indicators
			• Freedom from war and insurgencies
			• Freedom from discrimination
			• Freedom of abode, travel, employment and education
			• Protection of private property
			• Personal social freedoms (including gender equality, choice of marriage partners, and size of family)
			• Equality of opportunity and absence of economic exploitation
Polity IV	Graded	• Political competition and opposition	• Regulation of participation
			• Competitiveness of participation
		• Executive recruitment	• Regulation of chief executive recruitment
			• Competitiveness of executive recruitment
			• Openness of executive recruitment
		• Independence of executive authority	• Executive constraints

Aggregating dimensions and indicators into scales

With the obvious exception of Gasiorowski's uni-dimensional scale, the indicators used to assess the multi-dimensional aspects of democracy eventually have to be aggregated into a single scale representing democracy as a whole. Just how the individual components are aggregated can be as important as choosing which indicators to use. The need to create a composite index out of component indicators and dimensions raises important questions of how the individual dimensions relate to each other. Are some dimensions more important than others? Do all facets of democracy need to be present at least to a certain degree before we can speak of a democratic system? Or is it meaningful to say that a high score on one dimension of democracy can compensate for a low score on another? The German political system might be more democratic than the British system as its electoral laws grant effective influence to a higher proportion of voters. But it can be argued that this advantage is offset by the fact that Germany's citizenship laws deny democratic rights to millions of permanent adult residents.

Przeworski *et al.* (2000) insist that both their criteria, electoral contestation of the legislature *and* the chief executive have to be met simultaneously. Likewise, Tatu Vanhanen views both dimension of his index of democracy—participation and competition—as equally important and rejects the idea that the scores on each should be allowed to substitute for one another. To apply these rules when aggregating his indicators, Vanhanen simply multiplies one by the other and divides the product by 100, resulting in a scale ranging from 0 to 50. Finally, he defines three threshold values that must be met simultaneously for a country to be classified as a democracy. According to Vanhanen's rule, a country can be regarded as democratic if the combined vote or seat share of the opposition parties is at least 30 per cent (competition), if at least 10 per cent of the entire population voted (participation), and if the combined Index of Democracy has a score of five or higher.

The Polity IV autocracy-democracy scale is created by adding up scores on the various sub-dimensions, which leads to a 21-point scale, ranging from -10 to +10, where negative values denote autocracies. While this appears straightforward at first sight, the aggregation rule is in fact quite convoluted and has drawn a fair amount of criticism (Munck and Verkuilen 2002). The individual components are weighted differently by using different scales and assigning a different number of points for each attribute. While the practice of weighting scores can be seen as a legitimate way of

acknowledging that some attributes are more important than others, Marshall and Jaggers (2007) provide
no justification for the weighting scheme. To decide
which countries are to be considered fully democratic,
a threshold of seven on the scale of democracy is
stipulated. Countries scoring between one and six
are considered 'partial democracies'. The Polity IV
researchers do not explain why a country with a score
of seven is democratic why one scoring six is not.[2]

The Freedom House Index uses a simpler aggregation rule. Raw scores are generated by adding up the
scores assigned to each component. The raw aggregate
scores are then transposed into categories on a seven-
point scale according to a table drawn up by Freedom
House. But this seemingly straightforward method
has also met severe criticism, not least because no
theoretical justification for this choice of aggregation
rule is offered. Moreover, equal weighting of each
indicator achieved by aggregation through addition
might be inadequate considering what is actually
measured by the many different components (Munck
and Verkuilen 2002). Once values on the seven-point
index are assigned to countries, the Freedom House
researchers specify a threshold of 2.5 on the political
rights dimension as the minimum requirement for
being dubbed a liberal democracy ('free'). Countries
scoring 3.0 to 5.0 are considered 'partly free', while
those rated 5.5 or higher are classified as 'not free'.

Again, no justification is given for why these thresholds are chosen and not others.

In the light of the problems and ambiguities associated with aggregating indicators for individual
dimensions of democracy into summery scales, some
researchers have chosen a 'minimalist' path, selecting
only a few of a number of available indicators into
the aggregation procedure. Some even operationalize
democracy with a single indicator, seeing approaches
based on multiple indicators as insufficiently transparent (e.g. Ulfelder and Lustik 2007). However, this
practice too is open for criticism. As most scholars
agree that democracy is a multi-faceted concept, it
is unlikely that any single indicator will on its own
deliver a valid and reliable measure of democracy.

The spread of democracy according to the four major indices

Having discussed the major steps that researchers need
to take in order to construct quantifiable measures of
the democraticness of states, we will now look at the
way some of the democracy measures work in practice.
Figure 3.1 shows how the share of democratic countries in the world is tracked by four major indices of
democracy—the Freedom House Index, the Polity IV
autocracy-democracy score, Przeworski *et al.*'s Political

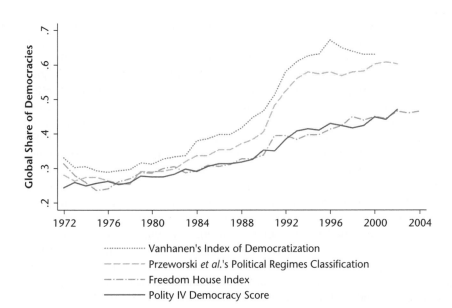

.... Vanhanen's Index of Democratization

– – – – –   Przeworski *et al.*'s Political Regimes Classification

–·–·–·–   Freedom House Index

———   Polity IV Democracy Score

Fig 3.1 The global share of democracies as tracked by four major indices

Regimes Classification, and Vanhanen's Index of Democratization. These indices are widely used in academic research as well as by political practitioners. They continuously cover the bulk of the world's countries over many decades and come in datasets that are freely available to the public (see the web links at the end of this chapter). Many more measures of democracy exist than the ones discussed in this chapter. Excellent overviews and critiques of these are provided by Foweraker and Krznaric (2000) and Munck and Verkuilen (2002).

The indices in the chart trace the percentage of democracies among the world's countries between 1972 and 2004. To make the different indices comparable with each other and with Przeworski *et al.*'s binary classification, we turned the Freedom House, Polity IV, and Vanhanen's indices into dichotomous measures by applying the thresholds for full democracy defined but these researchers. Despite their considerably different conceptualizations and measurement techniques, the four indices trail each other rather closely until about 1991.

The most distinctive feature throughout the entire period is displayed by Vanhanen's index, which consistently finds the share of democracies several percentage points above that indicated by the other three measures. This is a direct consequence of the very minimalist conceptualization underlying Vanhanen's measurement. As long as at least 10 per cent of the adult population turned out at the most recent election, the largest party gained no more than 70 per cent of the votes (or seats, as the case may be), and the score on combined index is no less than 5, Vanhanen awards the seal of democracy. It does not matter whether or not the election outcome affects powerful political offices, or if the incumbent parties have exerted undue amounts of pressure on opposition candidates, the media or the electorate. By contrast, the other three indicators use a variety of means to ascertain the extent to which an election has been truly free and fair before assigning the stamp of democracy. As a result, throughout the period covered in Figure 3.1, a country like Malaysia counts as a democracy according to Vanhanen's index, while being classified as nondemocratic and only partly free by the other three measures.

From about 1991 onwards, the measures behave more differently. The indices by Vanhanen and Przeworski *et al.* now classify more than half of the countries as democratic (over 70 per cent from 1994

onward in the case of Vanhanen's index). By contrast, according to the Freedom House and Polity IV measures, only about 40 to 45 per cent of the countries are democracies throughout the 1990s. These differences reflect the different dimensions ascribed to democracy by the various indices. The period between 1989 and 1991 witnessed a vast number of countries transitioning from strictly authoritarian and communist rule to some form of democratic regime. In addition, a number of countries that emerged from the former Yugoslavia and Soviet Union around that time quickly established some form of democratic constitution. For Przeworski and his colleagues, and even more so for Vanhanen, this has frequently been sufficient for coding a country as democratic in the minimalist sense of electoral contestation of offices (and, in the case of Vanhanen's index, some modicum of voter participation). But the gap between the Przeworski *et al.* and Vanhanen indices now also widens further—up to 11 percentage points in 1996. Among other things, this reflects the cautionary approach by Przeworski and his colleagues to wait until the first election-induced change of government before calling a country democratic.

Both Freedom House and the Polity IV researchers apply a number of additional criteria, making it more difficult for countries to qualify for the democracy label. Freedom House requires countries to adhere to a host of criteria more or less closely related to its dimensions of political rights and civil liberties. Countries with significant levels of civil unrest or severe socioeconomic inequalities, for example, can easily fall short of Freedom House's threshold for 'free' countries.

The coders on the Polity IV team ask tough questions about the degree of popular **accountability** of the country's executive and the extent to which a party's chances of success are independent from their relationship with the people in power. For example, since 1982 regular elections have been held in Honduras. As these have from time to time led to the peaceful transfer of power from one party to another, Przeworski *et al.* have classified the country as continuously democratic since the end of the last military regime in 1982. Likewise, reasonable voter turnout and electoral strength of opposition parties make Honduras a democracy in Vanhanen's eyes. But for a number of reasons, including the continuing traditionalist and paternalistic nature of Honduran politics and resulting doubts about the effectiveness of political competition, the country has failed to reach the Polity IV threshold for a full democracy until 1999. Throughout the same period, the country's Freedom House classification oscillated between 'free' and 'partly free', mainly due to the a precarious human rights record and ongoing threats to press freedom. Similarly, from 1991 to 2000 Nepal has been classified as democratic by both Vanhanen and Przeworski *et al.*, while failing to achieve the status of a full democracy according to Polity IV and being classified as only 'partly free' by Freedom House throughout most of the decade. As a result of these different conceptualizations, the number of democracies in the world is much lower when either the Freedom House or Polity IV indices are applied; while many more countries are deemed democratic by Przeworski *et al.*, and even more by Vanhanen.

Box 3.2 **Key points**

- Democracy is a multi-dimensional phenomenon, but care should be taken to not overload it with too many related, but conceptually distinct, characteristics of social and political life.

- Democracy's dimensions can aid the choice of indicators of democracy.

- Different aggregation rules give different emphasis to the various dimension of democracy.

- Despite their methodological differences, major democracy measures agree far more often than they disagree.

Hybrid Regimes and Sub-types of Democracy

The above overview of approaches to quantifying democracy has shown that qualitative, classificatory assessments also always play a role even when a graded view of democracy is adopted. Thus, the seven-point Freedom House scale is used to assign countries to the three groups of 'free', 'partly free', and 'not free' regimes, and the 21-point Polity IV scale serves to classify countries as democracies, autocracies and anocracies. The respective middle categories denote what is often referred to as 'hybrid regimes'. A bewildering number of terms have been suggested in the literature to characterize these in-between types. Labels like 'electoralist', 'populist', 'delegative' or 'illiberal' democracy refer to diminished forms of democracy, with the latter two being among the best known classifications. Guillermo O'Donnell's (1994) notion of 'delegative democracy' denotes a political system in which institutional checks and balances are weak or insufficient, allowing the executive to centralize power and abuse its authority to encroach upon domains of other institutions such as the legislative or the judiciary. By contrast, Fareed Zakaria's concept of 'illiberal democracy' refers to political systems where government formation is determined by popular vote but the rule of law is weak and civil liberties are severely curtailed.

In these systems, according to Zakaria (2003: 17), '[d]emocracy is flourishing; liberty is not'.

On the other side, classifications like 'competitive authoritarian' or 'semi-authoritarian' regimes, and 'electoral' or 'contested' autocracies take autocratic regimes as their point of departure and classify countries according to the mode or intensity of the authoritarian grip exerted by rulers. Various forms of 'enhanced **authoritarianism**' include 'electoral' or 'contested' authoritarianism as the most commonly cited types. While the motives behind the construction of these categories—above all a desire to avoid the pitfalls of 'electoralism'– are laudable, Ariel Armony and Hector Schamis warn that they may lead to conceptual ambiguity and empirical confusion. In these scholars' view, 'the resulting palette of qualified, yet improperly specified, regimes not only hinders differentiation among the cases but also clouds the basic distinction between democracy and autocracy' (Armony and Schamis 2005: 114). On the other hand, they point out, it is important to remember that old and new democracies alike are susceptible to illiberal practices or to power being accumulated by executives and technocrats. Indeed, democracy without some degree of delegation is widely considered unfeasible. At least all existing democracies entail 'a "chain of delegation", from voters to representatives and from representatives to experts' (Armony and Schamis 2005: 114). The longer, the more complex and the more intensive this chain is, the greater are the risks it entails regarding the quality and transparency of democracy.

Once we acknowledge that all political systems differ in the degree to which ordinary people are able to effectively hold their rulers accountable, much of the conceptual confusion highlighted by Armony and Schamis can be seen as coming down not so much to conceptual confusion but rather to disproportionate attention to detail and a proliferation of—often synonymous—words. No real world political system is ever likely to correspond perfectly to the ideal-typical properties that make up a theoretically sound class. And while it is tempting to create ever more precise classes to match reality more

closely, nothing will be gained if in the end there are as many classes as there are cases to fill them. Fortunately, most of the existing distinctions that spawned the various subtypes of democratic, autocratic and hybrid regimes can be subsumed under the fourfold classification offered in the previous chapter. If a given country's level of democracy is the extent to which it empowers people by means of democratic participatory rights and the rule of law, we can line all existing countries up on a continuum on which perfect accountable democracy is the one polar end and perfect unaccountable autocracy the other. While there are many shades of gray in between, sorting hybrid regimes into plebiscitarian autocracies and constitutional oligarchies is usually sufficient to capture the important dimensions of effective democracy. More fine-grained distinctions are better captured by quantitative scales.

Conclusion

This chapter has highlighted the main problems to which students of democratization should pay attention when measuring democracy across countries and over time. The issues raised here should also be taken into consideration by anyone planning to use existing indicators of democracy, including the ones discussed here. The comparison of four major indices of democracy highlighted the dangers of demanding too little of democracy as well as demanding too much. In demanding too little, Vanhanen is at times led to classify countries as democratic that would be deemed nondemocratic by other researchers. This is because Vanhanen (as well as, to a lesser extent, Przeworski et al.) ignores the different degrees to which electoral participation and party competition effectively render political leaders accountable to citizens. In demanding too much and capturing social and political aspects that are not necessarily ingredients to democratic regimes, Freedom House can at times end up denying the status of democracy to countries that would be correctly classified as democratic by other measures. By mixing elements of democracy with other aspects affecting individual, social and political life in a country, it is not always clear if what is measured by Freedom House is democracy or something

else relating to the quality of social life. In a sense, this criticism is unfair, as Freedom House do not actually claim to provide an index of democracy. It is rather that researchers frequently use this index as a proxy for democracy (Berg-Schlosser 2004a). Thus, several of the chapters in this book use Freedom House data to represent different degrees of democracy.

Researchers are often free to use individual components of existing indices rather than the finished product. They are then able to develop their own aggregation rules and manipulate democracy measures to suit their specific research needs or to best accord with their concept of democracy. This assumes that the democracy measures are provided in a way that allows others to disaggregate them—a property that is satisfied by all but the Freedom House Index. Lastly, the Polity IV and Freedom House measures have been methodologically improved. In particular, the underlying coder decisions have been made more transparent, heeding some implications from earlier criticism (e.g. Munck and Verkuilen 2002).

While this chapter has discussed the most fundamental problems encountered by students of democracy and democratization when classifying regimes and quantifying their democratic credentials, a number of other considerations have not been dealt with. Some of these are of a technical nature, but it is nonetheless important to pay attention to these issues when endeavouring to compare democracies. For example Kenneth Bollen and Pamela Paxton (2000) looked closer at the pitfalls associated with the human element in the coding process. Analysing widely used measures of democracy, including the Freedom House index discussed above, they found evidence that measurement error is often specific to individual judges. This has ramifications for the validity of the measures. It is questionable how Freedom House indicators of 'economic oligarchies', 'pervasive corruption' or 'religious hierarchies' regularly affect the ratings of countries in the developing world, the Middle East and the former communist world, while registering hardly at all in Germany, Ireland or the UK, where some of these problems have been present at a considerable scale for many years. Others have found considerable measurement error in the Polity IV score, identifying a bias that might have substantive consequences when the score is used as an independent variable in cross-national statistical analyses (Treier and Jackman 2008).

Finally, the discussion of hybrid regimes and subtypes of autocracy and democracy suggests that the old distinction between quantitative researchers who think in terms of 'degree' and qualitative researchers whose categories capture differences in 'kind' may have to be abandoned. As Collier and Levitsky (1997) point out, much qualitative research actually works with an implicit ordinal scale of degrees of democracy rather than with a large number of nominal distinctions. What matters is that classifications are grounded in theory and supported empirically by relating meaningfully to graded measures of democracy.

QUESTIONS

1. How can democracy be measured?

2. Does it make sense to distinguish degrees of democracy when comparing democratic systems?

3. What are the advantages and disadvantages of a minimalist concept of democracy?

4. What are hybrid regimes?

5. How many dimensions should a quantitative scale of democracy have?

6. Are some dimensions more important than others?

Visit the Online Resource Centre that accompanies this book for additional questions to accompany each chapter, and a range of other resources: <www.oxfordtextbooks.co.uk/orc/haerpfer/>.

FURTHER READING

Armony, A. C. and Schamis, H. E. (2005), 'Babel in Democratization Studies', *Journal of Democracy*, 16/4: 113–28; Collier, D., and Levitsky, S. (1997), 'Democracy with Adjectives: Conceptual Innovation in Comparative Research', *World Politics*, 49: 430–51. These two articles provide overviews and critical discussions of the proliferation of special types of autocracy, democracy and hybrid regimes.

Collier, D. and Adcock, R. (1999), 'Democracy and Dichotomies: A Pragmatic Approach to Choices About Concepts', *Annual Review of Political Science*, 2: 537–65. A very helpful clarification of the issue at stake in the debate on dichotomy versus gradations.

Goertz, G. (2006), *Social Science Concepts: A User's Guide* (Princeton, NJ: Princeton University Press). Highly insightful discussion of how concepts such as democracy are constructed in the social sciences.

Berg-Schlosser, D. (2004), 'The quality of democracies in Europe as measured by current indicators of democratization and good governance', *Journal of Communist Studies and Transition Politics*, 20/1: 28–55; Foweraker, J. and Krznaric, R. (2000), 'Measuring Liberal Democratic Performance: An Empirical and Conceptual Critique', *Political Studies* 48/4: 759–78; Munck, G. L. and Verkuilen, J. (2002), 'Conceptualizing and Measuring Democracy: Evaluating Alternative Indices', *Comparative Political Studies*, 35/1: 5–34. These three articles discuss the democracy measures that feature in this chapter alongside other ones in great detail.

Vanhanen, T. (2000), 'A new dataset for measuring democracy, 1810-1998', *Journal of Peace Research*, 37/2: 251–65. In justifying his own, contested, method, Tatu Vanhanen provides a useful and accessible discussion of democracy measurement.

IMPORTANT WEBSITES

<www.ssc.upenn.edu/cheibub/data/default.htm> José Antonio Cheibub's web site hosts the Political Regimes Classification data compiled by Przeworski *et al.* (2000).

<www.freedomhouse.org> Freedom House is a non-profit, non-partisan organization publishing the annual *Freedom in the World* surveys and the Freedom House Index of Political Rights and Civil Liberties.

<www.cidcm.umd.edu> The Polity IV project web site contains information on, and access to, the most recent update of the Polity data series.

<www.fsd.uta.fi> The Finnish Social Science Data Archive provides the data used for Tatu Vanhanen's Index of Democratization.

<http://ksghome.harvard.edu/pnorris/data/data.htm> Pippa Norris' web site provides an integrated dataset merging all four of the above democracy measures.

NOTES

1. Because the cases in which democratic countries may have been erroneously coded as autocratic are known, Przeworski *et al.* mark them with an identifier, enabling other researchers who use their data to err in the other direction if they so prefer.

2. Some scholars using the Polity IV data apply an even stricter threshold of eight when dichotomizing the democracy measure. See, e.g. Epstein *et al.* (2006), who provide a rationale for their choice.

4 Long Waves and Conjunctures of Democratization

Dirk Berg-Schlosser

Overview

This chapter provides an overview of the history of democratization since the late eighteenth century. It introduces the concepts of 'waves' and 'conjunctures' and delineates the major developments in this respect. In this way, the major long-term and short-term factors leading to the emergence and breakdowns of democracies are also highlighted. The conclusion points to some of the current perspectives and dangers for the future of democracy.

Introduction

Processes of worldwide democratization have been analysed and described with a great number of approaches and metaphors. Most common among the latter has been the concept of 'waves'. Samuel Huntington (1991) distinguishes three major ones, and two 'reverse' waves. These he dates as follows:

First, long wave:	1828–1926
First reverse wave:	1922–1942
Second, short wave:	1943–1962
Second reverse wave:	1958–1975
Third wave:	1974–

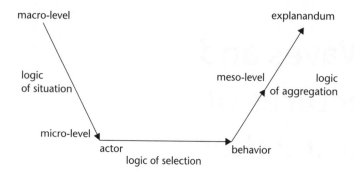

Fig 4.1 Linking levels of analysis
Source: Adapted from Coleman (1990) and Esser (1993).

Renske Doorenspleet challenges this periodization and, instead, speaks of a distinct 'fourth wave' beginning in 1989/90 with the fall of the Berlin Wall and concurrent and subsequent events in Central and Eastern Europe leading to the dissolution of the Soviet bloc, the end of the Cold War and its repercussions in many parts of the world. These classifications and the historical factors lying behind them thus have been disputed (Berg-Schlosser 2004a). Others speak of significant 'moments' (Green 1999), or 'pulses of isomorphic change' (Thomas *et al.* 1987). Each of these concepts remains relatively vague, but all imply a certain perspective (regularity, ups and downs, reversals, etc.) which may lead to a reification of reality rather than its more profound and theoretically and historically grounded analysis.

Here, we start first from a detailed observation of the occurrence of democracies (and their eventual breakdowns) in the course of time. On this basis, it is possible to identify some slower, long-term developments and certain periods of more abrupt changes. For the first phenomenon we use the term 'long waves' which is similar, but not identical, to ideas in economics (Kondratieff 1979) or world system theory (Wallerstein 1974). For the second phenomenon, we adopt the concept of 'conjuncture' which implies certain critical moments in which a series of related events can happen in a relatively short period of time, but which also become 'fluid' in the sense that possible outcomes can go in different directions (Dobry 1986).

In this way, both country-specific, longer-term social-structural and political-cultural developments can be accounted for, and actor-related aspects and influences of the international environment in moments of crisis can be incorporated as well. For this purpose, we find it useful to refer to James Coleman's

(1990) overall model of sociological explanation linking different levels of analysis (often nicknamed 'the bathtub'). This model is represented in Figure 4.1.

This model can integrate broader 'objective' geopolitical and social structural conditions on the upper left-hand side. These refer to the class structure and other social cleavages which historically have emerged in the course of time such as rural-urban, capital-labour, religious or linguistic cleavages which continue to shape political life (Flora *et al.* 1999; Moore 1966). These are the 'conditions of occurrence' (Mill 1974 [1843], Cohen and Nagel (1934) or the 'opportunity set' (Elster 1989) which are perceived on the micro-level of individual citizens and political actors. In this way, certain conceptual frames and distinct political-cultural sub-milieus may also be identified as the *subjective* dimension of politics. These perceptions and attitudes can then be translated into concrete political actions (behaviour) and further aggregated at the meso-level by **social movements**, interest groups, political parties etc. The *explanandum*, on the upper right-hand side is the type of political system (democratic or not) which can be observed. For example, the voting behaviour in elections of individuals and groups can be shaped by their *objective* social-structural position and *subjective* group identities which then translate into a particular **party system** which may be conducive or not (if extremist or fundamentalist forces prevail) for democracy. In addition, such a constellation of factors is, of course, also embedded in an international system of neighbouring **states**, regional and global powers, and international organizations. The international system interacts with an individual country at all levels through the media, trade, tourism, migration, foreign policy or military intervention.[1]

In the following, we will first present a diagram showing the emergence of democracies during the last two centuries based on the Polity III scores compiled by Jaggers and Gurr (1996). This is the democratization index available that is based on country-by-country assessments of constitutions and similar legal documents and covers the entire period from 1800 through 1998.[2] This graphical presentation already highlights some of the longer-term trends and more sudden ups and downs in these developments. In this way, two (and a possible third) long-term wave and three major positive (and one negative) conjunctures of critical periods of change can be identified. On this basis, then, these major phases will be inspected in closer detail discussing the major factors lying behind these developments. A concluding section will summarize these findings in the light of current empirical democratic theory.

The Overall Picture

To get a first glimpse at the overall course of events, Figure 4.2 shows the emergence of democracies over the last two centuries. In this way, major long-term trends ('waves') and briefer turmoils ('conjunctures') can be made more visible. However, a number of qualifications must be made. First of all, as mentioned before, the data base for these assessments are the available constitutions and similar legal documents for the countries considered. There may, however, be remarkable discrepancies between these texts and actual political reality which cannot be detected in this way. Furthermore, a certain (US-American) coder bias may also play a role for such assessments (see also Ch. 3).

Second, the very notion of 'democracy' for the largest part of the nineteenth century and beyond does not correspond to present-day, more demanding definitions. Thus, the dimension of 'inclusion' (i.e. who can vote in elections and participates more generally in politics), one of the key components of Dahl's (1971) concept of **polyarchy**, was severely restricted during this period. In the UK, for example, the franchise was based on criteria of property and education and was expanded only very slowly to reach (almost) universal equal suffrage after the First World War. Women were excluded from voting almost everywhere, New Zealand (1893), Australia (1902), and Finland (1904) being the first countries to introduce full women's voting rights. In the USA, Native Americans and Blacks were, at least de facto, excluded in many parts of the country until the Supreme Court decisions of the 1950s, the 'civil rights' movement of the 1960s and eventually the passage of the Voting Rights Act in 1965. 'Contestation' (i.e. open pluralist competition between candidates and parties), Dahl's second crucial dimension, was similarly confined to some nobles and honourables in the beginning and officially recognized political parties only emerged in conjunction with the labour and similar movements in a number of countries at a later stage. In the same way, civil liberties (e.g. freedom of speech, the media) and the rule of law (independence of the judiciary, fair legal procedures for all) were severely restrained or controlled by those in power during this time. Nevertheless, democratization as a *process* can clearly be observed during this period and gained momentum on all these dimensions in the course of time (for a more elaborate discussion of these concepts see also Chs. 2 and 3).

A third qualification concerning this diagram must also be kept in mind. The numbers presented here only show the overall 'net' situation for any given year. So it may very well be the case, and this has actually occurred during the 1960s for example, that a number of previous democracies broke down (as with the series of military coups in Latin America after 1964) whereas at the same time some new (at least initial) constitutional democracies emerged (for example in Sub-Saharan Africa). For this reason, the worldwide regional distribution of these developments distinguishes this picture more clearly. In the beginning, however, the occurrence of such fledgling democracies was largely confined to (Western) Europe, the USA, the British dominions in

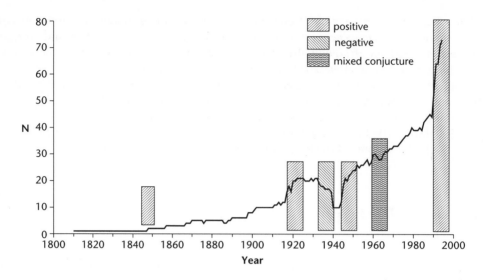

Fig 4.2 Emergence of democracies, 1800–1998

Source: Based on Jaggers and Gurr (1996).

Note: Countries scoring 8 and higher on the Polity III scale are coded as democratic.

Canada, Australia and New Zealand, and a few Latin American Republics (e.g. Chile with full male suffrage since 1874, Argentina 1912–1930 or Uruguay 1919–1933).

With these caveats in mind, a rough periodization of these developments becomes possible. We can date the first 'long wave' from the early beginnings in the late eighteenth century, the American (1776) and French Revolutions (1789) being the major watersheds accompanied by gradual developments in the United Kingdom and elsewhere, to the end of World War I which significantly changed the European political landscape. At that point, the first major 'democratizing conjuncture' with new states and new democracies emerging within a few years could be observed (an earlier 'liberalizing' conjuncture in the late 1840s had remained largely inconsequential). This was soon followed by a 'negative conjuncture', or 'reverse wave', as Huntington (1991) put it, greatly influenced by the Great Depression of the late 1920s and early 1930s.

The end of World War II then brought about a second long wave with the re-democratization in a number of European states, the beginning de-colonization in parts of Asia and Africa and some renewed attempts towards democratic rule in Latin America. This period also showed some intermittent turbulence, as already mentioned, in the 1960s with a series of military coups in Latin America but some new, if short-lived, democracies in Africa. In contrast to the periodization by Huntington (1991) we do not consider the coup in Portugal in 1974 which led to a democratization there and subsequent events in Greece and Spain to be the beginning of a new distinct wave. As the diagram shows, these events fit into a more continuous longer-term trend and, even more substantially, cannot, in our view, be considered to be *causally* related to the events in Central

---

Box 4.1 **Key points**

- While democracy had a different meaning in the nineteenth century than today, trends and patterns of its spread over the last two centuries can be discerned.

- Two (arguably three) long waves are complemented by three conjunctures of democratization.

- There has also been one negative ('reverse') conjuncture.

and Eastern Europe and beyond after 1989–90, the final major 'conjuncture' so far. Whether this will be followed by another 'long wave' or some reversals remains to be seen. According to this rough chrono-logical scheme the following sections have been organized to discuss in greater detail the various forces and factors at work.

The First Long Wave, 1776–1914

There have, of course, been precursors to today's large-scale democracies in other places and times. The Greek *polis*, the Renaissance city-states, but also 'acephalous' societies among Germanic, American Indian or Sub-Saharan tribes in former times can be mentioned here. All these have, however, been small-scale and not really inclusive (excluding, for example, slaves in ancient Greece and women in most societies). By contrast, larger political enti-ties (kingdoms, empires, etc.) were hierarchically structured and their (perceived, if at all) **legitimacy** based on some expression of a divine will, as up to the present day in the dynasties in Saudi-Arabia or Morocco which claim to be direct descendants of the successors of Mohammed, the sharifs. In actual fact, a greater number of such dynasties originated from military conquest, but some claim to a religious legitimization was usually maintained.

Only with what Robert Dahl (1989) calls the 'sec-ond transformation' did new ideas and social forc-es emerged which initiated the first 'long wave' of democratization in modern times. The major ele-ments of this transformation were a *republican* tradi-tion of appointed or elected rather than hereditary rulers (as in ancient Rome or the Renaissance city-states), the development of *representative* govern-ments in large-scale political units (beginning in England, USA, and France),and the idea of the *politi-cal equality* of all citizens which was strongly pro-moted by the American and French Revolutions but which had its earlier proponents in the writings of such authors as John Locke, and Jean-Jacques Rous-seau. The European enlightenment, as expressed in the writings of Immanuel Kant for example, also greatly contributed to a non-transcendental, secu-lar orientation of politics and a new legitimization based on 'the power of the people'.

The paths taken to more democratic forms of government varied somewhat and were either evo-lutionary (as in UK) or revolutionary as in the USA (breaking with the colonial past) or France (abolish-ing the inefficient 'ancien régime'). The factors at work were both highly motivating new ideas and slo-gans like 'no taxation without representation' in the North American colonies or 'liberté, égalite et frater-nité' in France and the basic human and civil rights derived from them as well as social movements and classes which became their main protagonists. Lib-eration movements of this kind were the anti-slavery movement in some of the colonial powers and former colonies, and (initially) national sentiments among 'late-comers' of European nation-states as Germany and Italy, and in the newly independent republics of Latin America (Markoff 1996).

At a later stage, the labour movement, newly founded trade unions and socialist or social-demo-cratic political parties, and the women's movement engaged for an extension of the suffrage became the main carriers. The urban bourgeoisie and mid-dle classes played a more ambiguous role. In early instances, they favoured liberal ideas and an exten-sion of the suffrage, for example in the movements leading to the (mostly failed) revolutions of 1848, when it served their own interests. Later, however, they sometimes formed alliances with the remaining aristocratic forces against the labour movements as in imperial Germany.

At the same time, this long wave which lasted more than a century was accompanied by increasing levels of literacy, urbanization, and significant tech-nological advances as railways, the telegraph, etc. which greatly facilitated communications over large areas. In terms of the international environment, the sovereign nation state became the universally accepted model, even though what a nation was, who was included and whether it corresponded with the demos of active citizens remained a subject of debate (Anderson 1991).

The major European states then clashed in their struggle for power which culminated in the World War I with its incredible violence and number of deaths, disruption of international trade and communications, which affected all corners of the world. It also unleashed new demands about social equality and political rights which had been in the making for many years.

> ### Box 4.2 Key points
>
> • The main ingredients to democratization have been republicanism, representation, and political equality.
>
> • The first long wave was kick-started by the US and French Revolutions and developed through incremental extensions of the franchise.
>
> • The labour movement and nationalist ideas played crucial roles in establishing mass democracy at the national level.

The First Positive Conjuncture, 1918–19

The war led to the first major 'conjuncture' of political forces, actors and events in a short period of time. As a result of the war the major continental empires (the Ottoman, the Habsburg, the Tsarist in Russia, and the German) were dismantled, and a new form of **regime**, a new international movement and (later) a major contender in international politics emerged: the communist Soviet Union.

The peace treaties at the end of the war also created a new political landscape with the newly independent states of Finland, Poland, Czechoslovakia, Hungary, Yugoslavia, the Baltic states, etc. which all, initially, had democratic constitutions, and democratized others, as Austria and Germany, or led to a significant extension of the suffrage as in Belgium, the UK, and the Scandinavian countries. On the international level, the newly founded League of Nations, following President Woodrow Wilson's proposals, should secure collective security, national self-determination and open economies.

As it turned out, however, not all was well with the new democracies. The territorial losses imposed by the peace treaties on the losers of the war, as for example in Germany or Hungary, created strong resentments and 'revanchist' demands. After the substantial losses of human lives and property the economic situation remained shaky and high 'reparations' were imposed as well. International peace was also far from secure and the Soviet Union and

newly founded communist parties in many countries began to constitute a new challenge.

In retrospect, only a few of these new democracies became sufficiently consolidated, and even some of the older ones were greatly shaken by subsequent events. In terms of major tenets of empirical democratic theory, the basic conditions of the democracies in Europe can be summarized in an analytic map (Figure 4.3).

In this diagram, the major factors considered to be favourable for democracy, or their absence, are listed. First, a secure statehood and pre-war existence of democracy (Rokkan 1975). Simply put: 'no (or a fragile) state, no democracy'. Second, the absence of a powerful landed upper-class or major feudalistic remnants as emphasized by Barrington Moore (1966: 418): 'No bourgeoisie, no democracy'. Third, a relatively high level of socioeconomic development as expressed by gross national product (GNP) per capita or various indicators of industrialization, urbanization, or literacy (Lipset 1983). Fourth, relative cultural, linguistic, or religious homogeneity or, if segmented along such lines, some elite consociational arrangement as in Switzerland to bridge such cleavages (Lijphart 1977). Fifth, a democratic political culture as opposed to more 'parochial' or 'subject' non-democratic and authoritarian orientations (Almond and Verba 1963). Sixth, the absence of high levels of political unrest and strong anti-system forces

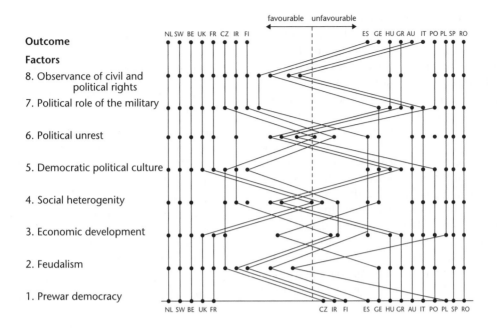

Fig 4.3 Analytical map of Europe

both from the political left and right or some fundamentalist groups (Linz 1980). Seventh, civil control of the violent means of coercion and subordination of the military and other armed forces to legitimate political authorities. Eighth, a respect for civil and political rights, the rule of law and the independence of the judiciary (Dahl 1989: 244–64).

It can be seen, that all of the pre-war democracies had mostly favourable conditions and remained stable, whereas in countries like Poland, Portugal, Spain, or Romania the recently created democratic systems met with very unfavourable circumstances and collapsed fairly soon, leading to military dictatorships or traditional authoritarian regimes.

Even more interesting are the cases in the middle where, in spite of mixed conditions, the new democracies in Czechoslovakia, Ireland, and Finland were sustained, whereas they broke down in Estonia, Germany, Hungary, and a number of others. Here, in addition, the impact of the great world economic crisis after 1929 was strongly felt, now leading to a negative conjuncture or reverse wave of democratization. This encouraged antidemocratic and fascist movements and distinctive moves by major actors which led to the downfall of more democracies, the Weimar Republic in Germany being the most spectacular one.

In such 'conjunctural' situations, major actors can turn events either way. This was most clearly demonstrated in the cases of Finland and Estonia which, overall, had very similar background conditions and were shaken by the economic crisis and relatively strong fascist-like movements, the Lapua movement in Finland and the Veterans' movement in Estonia. In Finland, however, the incumbent President Svinhufud actively turned against the Lapua and put its revolt at Mäntälä down with the help of the military. By contrast, President Päts in Estonia in a 'coup from above' pre-empted a possible surge of the Veterans, dissolved parliament, and created, in fact, an authoritarian regime with himself remaining at the top.

In Latin America, the deteriorating world economic situation also led to more protectionist authoritarian regimes as in Argentina and Brazil after 1930. In Turkey, the new republic founded by Kemal Atatürk, in spite of some secularizing and modernizing reforms, maintained an authoritarian regime. In the Japanese monarchy, some initial liberalizing reforms with universal suffrage for men after 1920, the 'Taisho democracy', were reversed by the military. The 'League of Nations' turned out to be ineffective, and the international situation became increasingly antagonistic. The Nazi regime in Germany with the attack on Poland in September 1939, and the Japanese military with the attack on Pearl Harbor in 1941, then unleashed an even more bloody and horrible war—now affecting practically the entire world.

With the final defeat of Nazi Germany, Japan, and their allies in 1945 a positive 'window of opportunity' was again opened for renewed and extended attempts of democratization, but also for the expansion of Soviet style communism. The victorious World War II allies, with the US, UK, France, and the Soviet Union as the major powers, created economic and political systems following their model in the defeated countries occupied by them. In this way, in Central and Eastern Europe 'people's democracies' emerged which, however, as this oxymoron already suggests, were democratic by name only. Renewed attempts of democratization in Austria, (West-) Germany, Italy, and Japan should, however, prove to be more fruitful.

> **Box 4.3 Key points**
>
> - Many new democracies came into being in the form of newly independent states, such as Finland, Poland, Czechoslovakia, Hungary, Yugoslavia, and the Baltic states.
>
> - Among the defeated powers, the outcome of the war discredited their old regimes and opened opportunities for democratization (e.g. in Austria and Germany).
>
> - As a result of the encompassing mobilization within the war parties, women and workers in pre-existing incomplete democracies were able to gain political representation (e.g. Belgium, the UK, and the Scandinavian countries).
>
> - The League of Nations was established to secure collective security, national self-determination and open economies.

The Second Long Wave (with some intermittent turbulences), 1945–88

In spite of being on the side of the victors, World War II had also shaken the dominance of the remaining colonial powers, in particular the UK and France but also, in a lesser role, the Netherlands and Belgium. In the inter-war period already, nationalist independence movements had emerged in a number of overseas territories, in particular in Asia. After the war, the European powers were not able to hold on to their colonies much longer, and India and Pakistan (now separated) became independent in 1947, Indonesia in 1949. French efforts to keep their territories by military force were in vain, and after protracted bloody wars they had to leave Vietnam in 1954 and Algeria in 1963. In Sub-Saharan Africa, Ghana and Sudan were the first countries to become independent in the mid-1950s, followed by a great wave of independence in 1960 or shortly thereafter for most of the former British, French, and Belgian colonies. Only Portugal held on to its territories until the mid-1970s, and South Africa, with its Apartheid regime ruled by a minority of European descent, remained a special case.

Initially, in most of the newly independent states democratic constitutions were adopted, usually crafted after the model of the previous colonial power, i.e. a 'Westminster' type parliamentary system for the former British territories and a presidential system not unlike the Fifth Republic in France in the francophone states. Only a few of these, however, actually became consolidated. This was most notably the case in India, still today the world's largest democracy, but neighbouring Pakistan and later, after another separation, Bangladesh soon succumbed to military regimes. In Africa, only Botswana and tiny Mauritius remained continuously democratic. Most of the other African states showed a mixed picture of military dictatorships and authoritarian single-party regimes.

In Latin America, in the early years after the war a number of countries, such as Argentina, Brazil, Bolivia, etc., re-democratized and suffrage was extended to women in most of them. Here, too, however, the situation remained precarious and many returned to (often quite bloody) military regimes in the 1960s and 1970s, most spectacularly in Brazil in 1964 and Chile in 1973. Only Costa Rica, after 1948, and Venezuela, after 1958, consistently kept their democratic constitutions (see also Ch. 19).

Elsewhere, in Turkey the first multi-party elections were also held after the war bringing the opposition into power. Here, too, the military later intervened, and similar situations were found in the Philippines, which turned into an authoritarian regime under President Marcos after 1966, and Greece, following a military coup in 1968. The entire North African and Middle Eastern region had remained untouched by democratic movements and maintained either, as in Saudi Arabia, Jordan and Morocco, traditional monarchies or had turned into military dictatorships, as in Iraq or Syria, or authoritarian single party systems, as in Egypt or Tunisia.

On the international scene, the first years after the war also had led to a renewed attempt to introduce a system of collective security with the founding of the United Nations in 1945 and, for the first time, an agreement on universal human (and democratic!) rights as embodied in the UN Charter of 1948. The charter has been signed by all member-states, including the clearly non-democratic ones. But these hopeful signs were soon overshadowed by what came to be called the 'Cold War' when the victorious World War II alliance broke apart and the Western powers now faced a reinvigorated Soviet Union, a victorious communist revolution in mainland China and similar movements in other countries. Attempts to 'contain' communism sometimes also turned into 'hot' wars as in Korea (1950–53) or Vietnam (1959–75). In all these cases and beyond the super-powers mostly followed their perceived strategic and economic interests rather than the newly agreed upon principles of international law, human rights, and democratic rule.

Nevertheless, in the course of de-colonization and the Cold War period the total number of democracies worldwide has steadily increased, with some of the ups and downs just mentioned. In Southern Europe, the authoritarian regimes in Portugal (by a coup in 1974) and Spain (by a negotiated transition after the death of Franco in 1975) democratized and military rule was ended in Greece in 1978. The 'bureaucratic-authoritarian' (O'Donnell 1973) military regimes in Latin America also felt increasing economic difficulties and resentment by growing numbers of their populations. Almost all of them returned to some form of democratic rule by the end of the 1980s (O'Donnell *et al.* 1986). This also applies to the Philippines, after the fall of Marcos, and South Korea (see also Ch. 23). The overall picture, before the latest major democratizing conjuncture, thus looked as follows (see Map 4.1).

The Latest Conjuncture, 1989–90

When the war in Vietnam turned into a stalemate, the USA realized that it would not win facing increasingly stiff opposition at home. In the early 1970s a period of 'détente' was initiated which led to an acceptance, more or less, of the geo-political status quo. In Europe, too, a rapprochement took place between East and West and a number of treaties were signed and economic cooperation increased in the course of the new **ostpolitik**. Most significant were the 1975 Final Act of the **Conference on Security and Co-operation in Europe** (CSCE) which led to the founding of the Organization for Security and Cooperation in Europe (OSCE). In these accords, the respect of basic human rights and civil liberties was guaranteed, a clause to which political dissenters in East European countries such as Czechoslovakia and Poland increasingly referred.

At the same time, with the oil crises of the 1970s and the over-centralized economies of Central and Eastern Europe and the Soviet Union reaching some of their inherent limits, living conditions deteriorated in a number of them, further fuelling the increasing political discontent. This was most strongly the case in Poland, where the 'Solidarity' union was

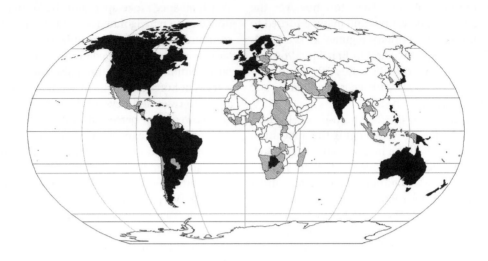

Map 4.1 Democracies before the last conjuncture

Source: Freedom House scores for 1987/88.

Note: Fully free countries are shown solid black. Partly free countries are hatched.

Box 4.4 **Key points**

- De-colonization and newly gained national independence led to a steady growth in the number of democracies.

- Some instances of re-democratization in Latin America, also South Korea.

- Autocratic regimes consolidated in much of North Africa and the Middle East.

founded in 1980, also supported by the Catholic church, which led to a series of strikes and, finally, with the support from Moscow, to a takeover by the Polish military.

In the meantime, after the occupation of Afghanistan by the Soviet Union in 1979, the arms race between the superpowers had resumed momentum, putting an additional strain on the economies of the Eastern bloc. When the Afghanistan invasion also turned out to be a failure, reformist groups in the Soviet Union realized that both militarily and economically the Eastern bloc had overstretched itself.

The new secretary general of the Communist Party of the Soviet Union, Mikhail Gorbatchev, therefore initiated a new period of détente and abandoned the doctrine of his predecessors concerning the 'limited sovereignty' of the Socialist countries vis-à-vis the Soviet Union which had been applied on several occasions, most notably in the case of the military intervention in Czechoslovakia in 1968.

These developments further encouraged dissident and reformist groups in these countries. But then, and still unexpected by most observers, another most dramatic 'conjuncture' unfolded which saw the downfall of practically all communist regimes in Central and Eastern Europe within a number of weeks—after the fall of the Berlin Wall on 9 November 1989. If ever a 'domino theory' was justified, there it really applied, exhibiting the economic 'implosion' and lack of legitimacy of these systems. This now meant the chance of a re-democratization of this part of the world and the definite end of the Cold War (see also Ch. 20).

The public execution of the former Romanian dictator Nicolae Ceauşescu and his wife Elena in December 1989 also showed dictators and authoritarian rulers elsewhere what their possible fate could

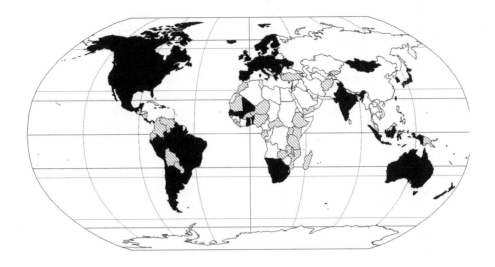

Map 4.2 Contemporary democracies

Source: Freedom House scores for 2006.

Note: Fully free countries are shown solid black. Partly free countries are hatched.

be. No longer able to rely on superpower support in either camp, many of them succumbed to increasing pressure from civil society movements from within and pressure from abroad. After the 'La Baule' agreements initiated by France for the francophone states in 1990 and with the increasing political conditionality exercised by the International Monetary Fund and the World Bank, relatively free and fair multiparty elections were held in a greater number of countries in Sub-Saharan Africa. In most of these, groups led by the former opposition prevailed and new democratic regimes were installed in a greater number. A 'second liberation' after independence, now from their own authoritarian rulers, thus had taken place (the most comprehensive account of these transitions can be found in Bratton and van de Walle 1997, see also Ch. 22).

The break-up of the Soviet Union led to a variety of new regimes. While some new democracies emerged, as in the Baltic states, a merely 'electoral' or façade democracy had taken hold in Russia. Outright authoritarian regimes were established in Belarus and most of Central Asia, in some cases with the previous leaders re-emerging in a new guise. Compared to 57 countries classified as 'free' by Freedom House before 1989, almost 80 were thus classified towards the end of the 1990s and another 40 could be regarded as 'electoral democracies', i.e. almost two-thirds of all states now claimed to be some kind of formal or effective democracy. This really now appeared to have become the 'only (legitimate) game in town' (Di Palma 1990). The present state of affairs is shown in Map 4.2.

Conclusion

Not all new democracies turned out to be stable, and there were some minor reversals, such as a military coup in Gambia in 1997—a country that until then

had been among the longest-lasting democracies in Africa. Quite a few of the other new democracies in Central and Eastern Europe and, even more so,

Sub-Saharan Africa cannot be considered fully consolidated, they still face possible antidemocratic threats, or are not fully supported by civil society. In other parts of the world, some stable but still in certain ways 'defective' democracies have come into being. Thus, Guillermo O'Donnell (1994) speaks of 'delegative' democracies in many Latin American states where, apart from regular elections, overall political involvement by the population has remained low, and where politics is largely 'delegated' to the, often populist and ineffective, leaders.

In a number of the longer-established democracies increasing discontent with political leadership and political parties, decreasing levels of voter **turnout** and similar signs of 'disaffection' have also been noted (Pharr and Putnam 2000). Thus, concerns with the overall 'quality' of democratic systems both in terms of their proper functioning and performance (Diamond and Morlino 2005), but also in a more demanding normative sense (e.g. Barber 1984) have increasingly come to the fore. Such qualities are now regularly assessed by institutions like the World Bank (Kaufman *et al.* 2006) or the International Institute for Democracy and Electoral Assistance (IDEA) in Stockholm, which attempts to apply a qualitative 'democratic audit' developed by David Beetham (1994) and his collaborators to many more countries in the world. At the same time, some new quantitative empirical measures such as the 'Bertelsmann Transformation Index' (2006) have also been developed.[3]

One possibility to further enhance the qualities of existing democracies may also lie in the more widespread introduction of 'direct' forms of democracy, opening more channels of involvement by the populations at large and, by doing so, enhancing their understanding of the necessity and relevance of widespread political and civil engagement (see, e.g. Pallinger *et al.* 2007).

Whereas these recent developments and their support on the international level seem to confirm an expectation of a new longer wave bringing about more and better democracies, and turning some of the purely electoral democracies into more substantive ones, as for example in Ukraine after 2005, there are other tendencies which are more disheartening. Above all, as was emphasized before, for democracies to emerge and to become sustainable a certain minimum level of secure statehood, both in terms

of undisputed territorial integrity and an effective state monopoly of the means of coercion, is required. In the words of Juan Linz: 'No state, no democracy' (Linz and Stepan 1996b: 14).

Thus, it is not surprising that the events which led to further democratization in some parts after 1990 also resulted in a number of 'failing' and even 'collapsed' states, in particular in countries where pronounced ethnic or religious heterogeneity could be instrumentalized for purposes of political secession, or the sheer plundering of resources by greedy warlords—as in Liberia, Sierra Leone, Afghanistan etc. (Zartman 1995). The disintegration of the Soviet Union and former Yugoslavia, where underlying ethnic, religious and regional tensions were no longer contained by a repressive regime are also cases in point. Democratic processes alone, e.g. referenda and majority vote, cannot be expected to solve such problems if important minorities feel left out or discriminated. Consociational arrangements in such situations presuppose at least a certain willingness to compromise and often require also an international consensus and pressure as in Bosnia or, possibly, Kosovo. The current war in Iraq is a telling example, where 'regime change' was attempted under circumstances where practically all of Dahl's basic conditions, listed above, have been lacking.

In a similar way, the events of September 11, 2001, and their aftermath, have shaken the prospects for a more peaceful and more democratic world. Not only that a new fundamentalist Islamist challenge has arisen, which denies some of the basic tenets of a universal normative theory of democracy, such as basic human rights and civil liberties, the dignity and political equality of all human beings regardless of **gender**, religion and similar characteristics. Some of the security measures taken to confront this challenge also threaten some of these values—such as freedom of expression, unhindered movement across borders by people and goods, etc. In this respect, the unilateralism of the USA as the only remaining superpower also tends to undermine the possibility to arrive at a more universally accepted, peaceful, and more democratic world order (Green 1999).

On the whole, the latest wave has not come to an end, but shows some signs of weakening and possible reversals. A number of major conditions of empirical democratic theory, as listed above, are not (yet?)

met in considerable parts of the world. The Islamist challenge and the future political development and international role of China will be major factors in this respect.

As this overview of the developments of modern democracies over the last two centuries has shown, there are many influences at work shaping today's (and tomorrow's) world. Some of these factors, like social-structural and political-cultural ones, are changing relatively slowly in the course of modernization and **globalization**. The revolution in communication technology, but also the industrial and cultural divide it entails so far, may further accelerate these processes. At the same time, global economic and environmental problems pose new challenges. Other factors, as in some of the conjunctures, are more actor- and situation-specific. There is no single coherent empirical theory of democracy which would integrate all these aspects and their respective internal and international interactions (but see Ch. 6).

But even if more stable democracies come about, their internal decision-making processes, by necessity, remain inherently conflictual and, within some institutional and normative limits, open-ended. This, however, should not be seen so much as a weakness, but as a potential strength necessary to adapt successfully to new internal and global challenges. Whether democratic feed-back mechanisms and basic values of human dignity really become universal thus remains an open question. The 'end of history' (Fukuyama 1992) or Immanuel Kant's (2006) 'eternal peace' are not in sight.

QUESTIONS

1. Does democratization proceed in waves?

2. How can social change be explained?

3. Is democratization inevitable?

4. What is the difference between waves and conjunctures of democratization?

5. How many waves of democratization have there been?

6. How many conjunctures of democratization have there been?

Visit the Online Resource Centre that accompanies this book for additional questions to accompany each chapter, and a range of other resources: <www.oxfordtextbooks. co.uk/orc/haerpfer/>.

FURTHER READING

Coleman, J. S. (1990), *Foundations of Social Theory* (Cambridge, MA: Harvard University Press). Introduces and explains the logic behind the 'bathtub' model of social science explanation used here.

Markoff, J. (1996), *Waves of Democracy. Social Movements and Political Change* (Thousand Oaks, CA: Pine Forge Press). Provides an introduction to democratization in historical perspective, setting developments in their international context.

Moore, B. (1966), *Social origins of dictatorships and democracy: lord and peasant in the making of the modern world* (Boston, MA: Beacon Press). This social-structural account of democratization is a classic.

Rueschemeyer, D., Huber Stephens, E. and Stephens, J. D. (1992), *Capitalist development and democracy* (Chicago, IL: University of Chicago Press). Arguing that industrial capitalism promotes democracy by empowering the urban working class, this book analyses how democracy has established itself better in some countries than in others.

Berg-Schlosser, D. and Mitchell, J. (2000) (eds), *Conditions of Democracy in Europe, 1919-39. Systematic Case-Studies* (London: Macmillan); Berg-Schlosser, D. and Mitchell, J. (2002) (eds), *Authoritarianism and Democracy in Europe, 1919-39. Comparative Analysis* (London: Palgrave Macmillan). These two volumes analyse in great detail the survival and failure of European democracies in the interwar years.

Beyme, K. v. (1996), *Transition to Democracy in Eastern Europe. Advances in Political Science* (London: Macmillan). Sets out and demonstrates an analytical framework for the analysis of democratization in post-communist countries.

IMPORTANT WEBSITES

<www.idea.int> International Institute for Democracy and Electoral Assistance (IDEA) in Stockholm.

<www.bertelsmann-transformation-index.de> Bertelsmann Transformation Index (2006), 'The Bertelsmann Transformation Index 2006', online.

NOTES

1   In this chapter, the model is employed only in its most abstract sense, making no explicit assumptions of the 'rationality' (or otherwise) of the individual and collective actors.

2   Although improved Polity IV data are available for the period after the Second World War, consistency demands using Polity III data throughout.

3   Some applications concerning Eastern Europe and Sub-Saharan Africa can also be found in Berg-Schlosser (2004c, d)

The Global Wave of Democratization

John Markoff (with Amy White)

Overview

In the early 1970s, there were several non-democratic countries in Western Europe, most of Latin America was under military or other forms of authoritarian rule, the eastern half of Europe was ruled by communist parties, much of Asia was undemocratic, and in Africa colonial rule was largely being succeeded by authoritarian **regimes.** By the early twenty-first century the picture had changed radically, although to different degrees in different places. A great wave of democracy had touched every continent. This chapter provides a brief tour of the regions of the world. It explores what was distinctive about each region's democratization and what they had in common as well. The chapter concludes with a quick look at challenges faced by democracy in the early twenty-first century.

Introduction

How wrong we social scientists can be! In the early 1970s many of us were extremely pessimistic about the future of democracy in the world. It would be hard to point to many serious students of politics who expected a global wave of democratization that would dwarf earlier ones. That moment's pessimism was rooted in disappointed expectations forged a quarter century back. At the end of World War II there had been considerable hope for a democratic future. The murderous Nazi regime and its European and Asian allies had just been decisively defeated by an alliance of the Western democracies, the Soviet Union, and China. In the Western half of Europe, the victorious democratic powers brought democracy back or supported its establishment on a firmer footing than before. The military occupation of the defeated countries was an opportunity to democratize them. A democratic Western Germany, Austria,

Italy, and Japan seemed a good barrier against a renewal of aggressive militarism. The USA, moreover, shielded by oceans from the war's devastation, emerged as the buoyant leader of the global economy, poised to spread its products, ideas, and institutions far and wide.

Equally important, the end of the European colonial empires was at hand. The war had deeply wounded these empires as Japan seized Asian colonies of Britain, France, the Netherlands, and the USA. Asians who had fought the occupying Japanese were not always eager to have their former European rulers back. And colonial troops who had fought to defend, let us say, French democracy against fascist aggression and returned home with military experience, were not always eager to see European rule continued in their own homeland. As for the post-war USA, it tended to see its own interests enhanced by dismantling, rather than restoring the empires of its wartime partners, and ended its own colonial rule in the Philippines. So, over the next generation, colonies attained self rule and many hoped for democratic government for these new Asian and African **states**.

As post-war social scientists turned to the study of the social conditions that promoted democracy, they often focused on economic development or appropriate cultural values as key (Lipset 1983). This led to a lively debate among those who thought one or the other more important. But either thesis had a variant that was very optimistic about the future. As economic development spread, so would democracy; as modern Western values spread, so would democracy. The USA and its Western allies could even actively help these processes through development aid programmes and diffusing their democratic values.

By the mid-1970s, however, students of politics were a great deal less optimistic. The eastern half of Europe remained firmly under Soviet-dominated communist rule. Not only did few foresee an imminent collapse of communism, but many thought that in the long struggle with the USA known as the Cold War, Soviet- or Chinese-allied communists were gaining ground because they seemed to many intellectuals in poorer and post-colonial countries to offer a plausible route out of impoverished misery. The democratic hopes of former colonies were dashed as some underwent military coups, while in others presidents successfully claimed expanded powers, and in still others antidemocratic revolutionary forces fought their way to power. Whether antidemocratic revolutionaries or antirevolutionary militaries came out on top, the prospects of stable democracy in many poorer countries looked dim.

Most dismaying of all, some of the more economically developed countries of Latin America underwent coups, including Uruguay and Chile, despite their own longstanding democratic traditions. Reflecting on coups in Brazil in 1964 and Argentina in 1966, Guillermo O'Donnell (1973), came to the disturbing conclusion that economic development in poorer countries might actually generate social tensions that would bring democracy to an end rather than promote it. As for the notion that the wealthy countries might help out by promoting their democratic values, the most powerful and wealthy among them, the USA, turned out with some frequency to support authoritarian rule, including coups in Brazil (1964) and Chile (1973). By the time the Argentine military staged a second coup in 1976, ushering in a period of extreme brutality, many social scientists were sceptical of the future of democracy beyond the already democratic rich countries. One eminent scholar in 1984 deployed his considerable expertise in an essay entitled 'Will More Countries Become Democratic?' and concluded that 'the prospects for the extension of democracy to other societies are not great' (Huntington 1984: 218).

Democracy Ascending

From a vantage point a generation later, in the early twenty-first century, we can see that the Chilean and Argentine coups of the 1970s were at the tail end of a global antidemocratic wave. From the mid-1970s, a new advance of democracy in the world had begun. We will first show something of the scale of this great wave, then describe it in more detail. Table 5.1 lists countries that became significantly more or less

Table 5.1 Countries with Significant Change in Democracy between 1972 and 2004

Countries Significantly More Democratic

Polity IV		Freedom House	
Albania	Mali	Albania	Philippines
Algeria	Mexico	Andorra	Poland
Argentina	Moldova	Argentina	Portugal
Armenia	Mongolia	Benin	Romania
Benin	Mozambique	Bosnia	Senegal
Bolivia	Nicaragua	Brazil	Serbia & Montenegro
Bosnia	Niger	Bulgaria	Slovakia
Brazil	Nigeria	Cape Verde	Slovenia
Bulgaria	Panama	Congo (Brazzaville)	South Africa
Croatia	Paraguay	Czech Republic	South Korea
Czech Republic	Peru	Estonia	Spain
Djibouti	Philippines	Georgia	Taiwan
Dominican Republic	Poland	Ghana	Tanzania
Ecuador	Portugal	Greece	Thailand
Estonia	Romania	Hungary	Uganda
Ethiopia	Russia	Latvia	Ukraine
Georgia	Senegal	Lesotho	Uruguay
Ghana	Sierra Leone	Lithuania	
Greece	Slovakia	Macedonia	
Hungary	Slovenia	Malawi	
Indonesia	South Korea	Mali	
Kenya	Spain	Moldova	
Latvia	Taiwan	Mongolia	
Lesotho	Thailand	Mozambique	
Lithuania	Ukraine	Namibia	
Macedonia	Uruguay	Niger	
Madagascar	Zambia	Panama	
Malawi		Peru	

Countries Significantly Less Democratic

Polity IV	Freedom House
Gambia	Lebanon
Zimbabwe	Maldives
	Swaziland

Note: A country is listed as being significantly more or less democratic if there is a change of at least 10 in the difference of the Polity IV autocracy and democracy scores or at least 2.5 in the mean of the Freedom House political rights and civil liberties scores. Countries that appear on one list only are indicated with italics.

democratic over the three decades since 1972. For this purpose, we employ the Polity IV data and Freedom House scores. Because democracy is such a complex phenomenon, a country might have democratized considerably as measured by one index but not the other. Using Polity IV, we construct an overall measure of Democratization by considering the change that had taken place in the difference of 'democracy' and 'autocracy', that is, how strongly a country had advanced toward the first and away from the second. Likewise, for the Freedom House scores we ask how much closer countries were to the free end in 2004 than they had been three decades earlier.

The list makes a number of things clear. First, a large number of countries—64—had moved significantly toward democracy since 1972 by at least one of these measures. This does not mean that all such countries were democratic by all measures, only *strikingly more democratic* by one or two measures. Second, a majority of those had done so by both measures, something that is telling us that they had become more democratic in many ways. Third, very few countries had become and remained significantly less democratic during the same period (and none by both measures). Fourth, democratization was occurring in Western Europe, Eastern Europe, Latin America, Asia, and Africa. We can see why one could summarize this as a 'worldwide' wave although this is in a sense an exaggeration since some countries are not included in these lists while in the case of others the tide was running in the other direction.

Most of the remainder of this chapter will describe this wave of democratization, and we will have many questions about why some countries democratized to a great enough degree to appear in the box, while others did not. Figure 5.1 presents the levels of democracy from 1972 to 2004 for major world regions. It shows quite a number of interesting things. First of all, let us look at the countries of Western Europe, North America, and Oceania. This was the world's most democratic region in 1972 and has remained so. We can also see that it the first region in which the democratic wave took off. Three Mediterranean states with authoritarian regimes underwent major democratizing change, starting with Portugal, and despite difficulties have remained stably democratic. So some of the very big questions about the history

of democracy are about why precisely this group of countries was mostly well ahead of most of the rest of the world on democratization and why and how Portugal, Greece and Spain began to follow suit in the 1970s.

In Latin America, the democratization began later. It was actually still declining into the 1970s, but then the tide of authoritarian rule in Latin America began to recede. The period of major change extended from the late 1970s for a dozen years. Not only did the militaries who had made coups in the 1960s and 1970s return to their barracks over the next decade in Argentina, Brazil, Uruguay, and Chile, but older authoritarian regimes began to open up as well. So Latin America saw not merely the 'restoration' of democracy, but moved to a general level of democratization beyond that which had ever characterized the region as a whole.

Asia began the 1970s with mean levels of democracy only slightly below Latin America's, but entered the twenty-first century much lower, despite significant democratizations. The timing in Asia resembles that in Latin America, with a dip in the mid-1970s followed by an ascent that ended in the early 1990s. At the beginning of the period, Asian authoritarian regimes were a very varied group, with little in common: some countries were ruled by communist parties, some by presidents who had shut down opposition parties and parliaments, some by militaries. But by the mid-1980s very significant democratic movements emerged in the Philippines, in Taiwan, and in South Korea that played major roles in effecting political transformation, while democratic movements were contained in Burma and China. The great variety of political regime types in Asia alone raises many questions about the roles of economics, culture and history in nurturing democratic institutions or other arrangements.

The Soviet bloc in 1972 was resolutely authoritarian, with average scores much less than Latin America or Asia—quite the lowest of any of our regional categories, in fact. But starting in 1989, in rapid succession one after another of the European communist regimes were swept into history's dustbin. What is most distinctive about the regional pattern is how closely clustered in time the changes occurred. If the communist regimes, despite some very interesting

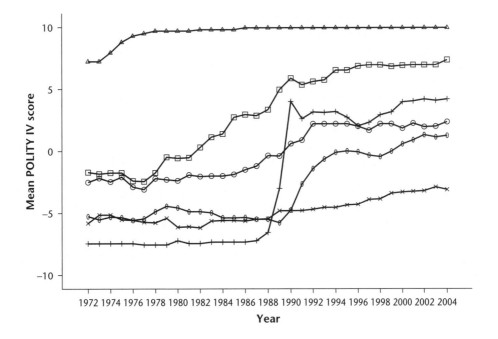

Fig 5.1 Mean level of democracy by world regions, 1972–2004

World region

Δ North America, Western Europe, and Oceania

☐ Latin America and Caribbean

+ Soviet/communist bloc

o Asia

0 Sub-Saharan Africa

X Middle East and North Africa

Sources: Polity IV Project (2007) and author's regional classification.

differences among them, were all deeply undemocratic political orders, the *post*communist regimes were varied indeed, with some in short order becoming about as democratic as their West European neighbours and others developing highly authoritarian regimes. Why did so much change happen so fast in so many places at more or less the same time? Why did countries that had for decades been organized in such similar ways move in such different directions?

Sub-Saharan Africa also started at an even lower mean level of democratization than Latin America or Asia, and its democratic upturn began later. But from 1990 into 1994 there were significant advances in a democratic direction in a wide array of countries, and more modest advances after that. In noting that the period of rapid change in Africa followed immediately upon the rapid change in the Soviet bloc, one asks whether this is simply a coincidence or whether there were some transnational processes taking place.

Finally, the Middle East and North Africa: Middle Eastern countries began the period with the same low mean level of democracy as much of Africa, but despite some democratization, ended it notably lower. Of the major geocultural regions shown on this graph, it had participated least in the democratic currents of the time. This raises fascinating questions, too.

But the big story revealed by these graphs is the combination of a global trend toward democratization, and great variety in the timing, and even occurrence of democratic change. Is there some common cause or causes underlying the global trend? Is there some process of mutual influence with earlier instances of democratization making later ones more probable? As subsequent chapters will make clear, the answers to these questions are far from obvious and are likely to be debated by scholars for some time to come. It is far from evident that the same answers will apply in all places and at all points within the general trend.

Other ways of organizing the data raise different questions. One of the best established of all generalizations about national differences in democracy has been that it is particularly characteristic of the richer countries. In Figure 5.2 countries of the world are divided into four groups according to their levels of gross national income (GNI) per capita. We do indeed see that the levels of democracy and the recent trend vary considerably by levels of wealth with the richest countries entering the 1970s as the most democratic group, the poorest countries as the least democratic, and the countries in between in wealth being in between in democracy as well. We can also see that democratization was taking place at all levels of national income, although the ascent began later among the 'low income' group.

Geography does not only suggest differences in wealth, but also in cultural traditions. Numerous scholars have argued that certain cultural traits favour, and others disfavour, democratic politics (e.g. Inglehart and Welzel 2005). We may very broadly

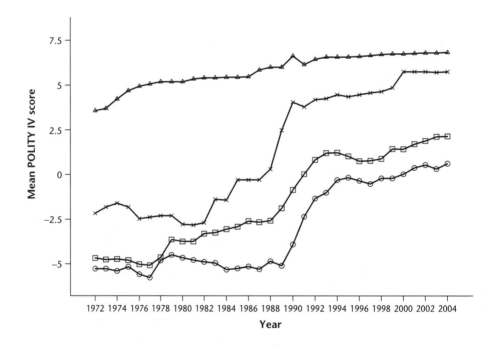

Fig 5.2 Mean level of democracy by gross national income per capita, 1972–2004

Income group (2006)

Δ High income (GNI per capita > US$11,115)

X Upper middle income (US$3,595 < GNI per capita ≤ US$11,115)

□ Lower middle income (US$905 < GNI per capita ≤ US$3,595)

o Low income (GNI per capita ≤ US$905)

Sources: World Bank (2007) and Polity IV Project (2007)

indicate cultural affinities by classifying countries by their historically dominant religious traditions, grouped into a few broad categories. This is far too crude for a fine-grained analysis of the richness and variety of cultures but adequate for posing some vital questions.

What Figure 5.3 shows plainly is that in the early 1970s it was historically Protestant countries that were especially likely to have high scores for democracy (but remember that some high-scoring countries like Japan, India in most years, and Israel are in our 'Other' group). The graph also shows that over the subsequent decades it was especially the countries with other Christian traditions that democratized, and Muslim countries were especially unlikely to have done so.

This graph is simple, but the very big questions it raises are not. Are there cultural traits that favoured early democratization, others recent democratization, and others still little democratization? Perhaps. But now consider that many other things are highly associated with these religious affiliations. A very large number of these Catholic countries were at one point colonies of particular places in Europe, Spain and Portugal, which also means that they were colonized at the heights of those countries' imperial expansion, beginning in the fifteenth century and continuing into the eighteenth. Similarly, a very large proportion of Muslim majority countries were until recently subject to imperial rule, for example, Pakistan by Britain, Morocco by France, Indonesia by the Netherlands, Libya by Italy, and Uzbekistan by

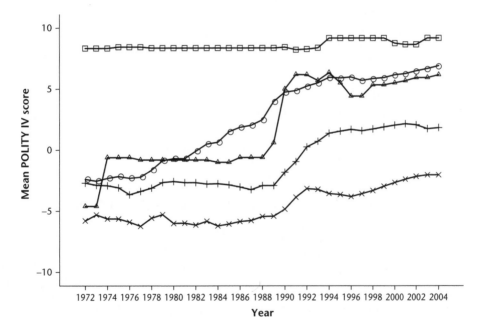

Fig 5.3 Mean level of democracy by historically predominant religious tradition, 1972–2004

Historically predominant religion

☐ Protestant

o Catholic

Δ Eastern Orthodox

+ Other

X Muslim

Sources: Author's classification of religious traditions and Polity IV Project (2007).

Russia. In consequence, there is a great deal of history countries with particular religious traditions have, that distinguishes them from other places—not just the way their citizens have learned to pray. And for a largely secular Europe one ought to speak of the way their citizens used to pray. So whether there is any connection of Protestantism, Catholicism, and Islam to democratization is a question demanding a good deal of thought. Subsequent chapters will explore this further.

Box 5.1 Key points

- Democratization has been on the rise on a global scale from the early 1970s onward.

- The growth of democratization is different in different geographic regions.

- Democratization is also different for poor and rich countries, respectively, and for countries with different cultural systems.

National, Regional, and Global Processes

The timing differences of major world regions suggests that democratization came about in different ways in Southern Europe, Latin America, the Soviet bloc, Asia, and Africa. A closer look will show important differences even in neighbouring countries: between Portugal's democratization and Spain's, Argentina's and Brazil's, Poland's and Czechoslovakia's, South Korea's and Taiwan's. To invoke specific places is to be reminded how idiosyncratic particular national experiences might be. Yet the fact that so many geographically distant places significantly democratized so close in time strongly suggests that processes came into play that were not simply nationally, or even regionally, idiosyncratic, but that operated on a truly trans-continental scale to move multiple countries in the same general direction. There are a variety of imaginable processes that might produce change in so many different countries in such a short space of time. For clarity, we will classify such processes into four kinds:

- *Internal* processes unfolding in similar ways in a number of countries, producing similar outcomes, without any coordinating mechanisms across those separate cases.

- *External* processes affecting in similar ways a group of countries, but not involving actions deliberately aimed at encouraging democracy.

- *Emulative* processes, in which changes happening in some countries have an impact on other countries later on.

- *Supportive* processes in which one or more countries or other powerful actors set out to encourage democracy elsewhere.

While later chapters will analyse the distinctive characteristics of the great wave of democracy in major world regions separately, we will now take a closer look at how these classifications work out in a comparative perspective. Note that these are not mutually exclusive categories. And as we shall see, particular processes were not equally important at all moments nor in all countries.

Mediterranean Europe, 1970s

To understand the transformations of Portugal, Greece, and Spain in detail, one must understand the very particular and distinctive unfolding of events in each. A colonial war going badly against revolutionary guerrillas in Portugal's still extensive African colonies led some officers, in emulation of their determined foes, to favour a revolutionary overthrow of the Portuguese state, an action carried out in 1974. A few months later, Greece's military rulers seemed likely to bring on a war with Turkey, a prospect that led frontline officers who anticipated disaster to prefer to drive their tanks to Athens and terminate military rule. The following year Spain's long-time ruler, Francisco Franco, died, which opened new possibilities for political party leaderships, for organized workers, and for rural people to work out new political arrangements. Such elements, and more, were deeply idiosyncratic.

But there were common *internal* and *external* processes, in play as well. All three Mediterranean countries were a lot poorer than their Western European neighbours and would have benefited mightily from full membership in the European Community (which later became the European Union), but the Community staunchly refused to countenance membership for avowedly antidemocratic states. So when these countries faced major crises, although each crisis was highly distinctive, their common poverty in comparison to wealthy neighbours gave those neighbours influence, and the pressure from those neighbours to democratize was strong.

There also was an element of *emulation*. Although some approved, for many it was an embarrassment to live in a country whose rulers tried to make one look different than the other Europeans one could see every day on television, as when Greece's colonels outlawed long hair or Spain's laws enforced dress codes. And once Portugal began its democratic journey, it was an extra embarrassment to many in Spain that Portugal, sometimes experienced as a sort of backwards country cousin, was actually moving faster to be more like the rest of Europe. For Greeks, resentful of their rulers' attempts to keep them from participating in contemporary European culture, the absence of democracy was all the more poignant in that Greeks could lay claim to their country having been the place that, a great while ago, coined the word the rest of Western Europe used to describe the only form of political life under which they would care to live.

Latin America, 1980s and early 1990s

At first glance, nothing connects Latin American and Southern European processes. Indeed the histories of antidemocratic politics in different countries in Latin America were different from each other. Mexico's early twentieth century revolution led to the congealed rule of the Institutional Revolutionary Party that dominated political life for decades. Central America and the Caribbean, except for democratic Costa Rica, and revolutionary but not democratic Cuba, were dominated by a variety of military or non-military strongmen, and prey to intermittent military intervention by the US Militaries which, with a variety of purposes, ruled most of South America (except for Colombia and Venezuela). Yet during the 1980s and early 1990s every military regime withdrew, and in the 1990s the Mexican system began to open.

Latin American countries had long been noted for oscillations between more or less democratic, and more or less authoritarian forms. Against that background, a big part of the story is not just that the political pendulum swung toward democracy but that it has swung back again so little. In 1974 only three countries in the region could reasonably be called democratic; a quarter century later all but Cuba could (although a closer analysis would want to take note of something of a democratic recession in some places in the early years of the twenty-first century). The non-Spanish speaking Caribbean was mostly democratic too, except for turbulent, troubled Haiti. Not only did most countries democratize but those democracies, while sometimes very troubled, did not collapse altogether, a great contrast with the past. By one measure, the likelihood of democratic breakdown in a given year had been 20 times greater in the years preceding 1978 than in the two decades that followed (Mainwaring and Pérez-Liñan 2005: 20).

What accounts for the new democratic durability? Let's look back a generation. Latin America is the world region with the most unequal distribution of income (Hoffman and Centeno 2003), generating great fearfulness on the political right about the potential appeals of leftist revolution, and leading the right repeatedly, often with the support of the USA, to foster military coups. In the 1960s and 1970s, Cuban-inspired threats, some real and some not-so-real, made such fears especially plausible to the Latin American right and to US governments as well. But by the late 1970s in much of the region, apart from Central America, a plausible revolutionary threat was fading for several reasons. Success in revolutionary guerrilla warfare had turned out to be far more difficult than proponents imagined (Wickham-Crowley 1992). In some countries, the Latin American revolutionary left had been decimated and demoralized by post-coup repression. And on a global scale, the appeals of revolutionary solutions were fading as the Soviet Bloc lost any lingering propensity to inspire. Finally, after 1989, in the wake of the collapse of European communist rule, military or other support for left revolution from that quarter—even for Cuba—dried up. In short, global *external* processes and parallel *internal* processes greatly weakened support for Latin American revolution on the left.

Reduced fear of a revolutionary left joined several forms of *supportive* change to weaken the cause of antidemocratic politics on the right as well, something even more important since it was the right that actually carried out the coups (Markoff 1997). First of all, beginning in the late 1970s the USA became a less reliable supporter of coups and authoritarian rule claiming the anticommunist mantle, which had been an extremely important element in the coups of 1964 and 1973 in Brazil and Chile. By the 1980s it became engaged in what was called 'democracy promotion'—through such organizations as the Agency for International Development and the **National Endowment for Democracy.** This policy combined support for certain democratic practices and economic liberalization, a body of policies known among its critics as 'neoliberalism' (Cox *et al.* 2000).

But it was not only the US Government that seemed less skittish about democracy in Latin America. The Catholic Church had undergone a dramatic transformation from a key moral support of right wing authoritarians, as in Portugal and Spain (and earlier in Italy), to a supporter of democratic politics, as signalled in the convening of a Vatican Council (known as Vatican II) in 1962. This shift was of considerable significance in helping stabilize Catholic Iberia's new democracies, and in easing the path for Catholic Latin America's as well.

There was another important cluster of parallel *internal* and *external* processes. The coups of the 1960s and 1970s had been justified not only as anticommunist defensive measures, but also to protect the nation against the corruptions of democracy itself—since the political class was seen as caving in to the irrational demands of those whose votes they sought, thereby bringing on economic disaster. The developmental programs of the 1950s and 1960s were financed by enormous foreign borrowing and often seemed to

be going nowhere. By the 1960s it was rather widely believed that getting rid of democracy would improve economic performance. Distinguished US economists advised Pinochet's brutal regime. But, apart from Chile, the 1980s were to show that antidemocratic state brutality was hardly a guarantee of hopeful patterns of economic progress. When criticism of economic affairs emerged again in the troubled 1980s, it was the generals who were accused of bungling and corruption. One of the causes of coups had been the mounting foreign debt in country after country. But under the military the debt generally grew even more. Democracy, by comparison, had come to look efficient.

That skyrocketing debt was embedded in another *external* process that unfolded on a transcontinental scale. In the early 1970s the oil-exporting countries radically raised the price of oil. Oil-rich countries then invested their vast new profits in Western banks. The Western banks in turn began to lend their new resources like crazy. In other words, the enormous debt expansion of Latin America happened not only because there were ready borrowers on a continental scale, but ready wealthy lenders as well. Sooner or later, there would be trouble as nervous banks sought to recover their investments and powerful financial bodies like the International Monetary Fund played a pivotal role. This took the form of demands on Latin American states for what were taken to be sound economic practices, which is one of the important mechanisms by which the political crises that ended military rule also led to the collection of policy shifts often labelled neoliberal: downsizing the public sector, controlling inflation, selling state-owned resources to the private sector, and reducing or ending tariffs.

Finally, there was a significant regional *supportive* process (Mainwaring and Pérez-Liñan 2005). As countries began to democratize, they joined together for collective action to keep their own recent democratizations in place and encourage others to join. The Organization of American States authorized intervention in the event of democratic breakdown and took action on a number of occasions. In addition, members of the important common trade area, the Mercosur, eventually embracing half a dozen countries, agreed to expel any of its members that broke with democracy. Moreover, the new practice of international election monitoring and the threat of UN-backed economic sanctions, have also helped to discourage antidemocratic revivals. In the judgment of Mainwaring and Pérez-Liñan (2005), without such supportive practices, no fewer than four countries would have experienced antidemocratic coups following initially shaky democratizations. This mutual support for democracy is without precedent in Latin American history.

Soviet/Communist Bloc, 1989 and beyond

Despite great differences in language and history the various states of Communist Europe in the early 1970s had much in common: similar institutional structures under the command of ruling parties making ideologically similar claims. This was even true of states with hostile relationships with the Soviet Union, like Yugoslavia or, later, Romania. When people meet for the first time who had lived before 1989 in different Soviet bloc countries, they swiftly discover how similar many aspects of daily life were. Even the same gray concrete housing blocs dominated urban landscapes throughout the region, widely taken by Soviet Bloc intellectuals as a material metaphor for a dreary political regime (although dreary urban vistas were hardly unknown in Glasgow, or the suburbs of Paris, or the south side of Chicago). Beyond the common institutional mould, a large part of the region was linked to the Soviet Union via economic specializations, largely organized for Soviet benefit and tied in militarily to the Warsaw Pact—the Soviet Union's response to the West's North Atlantic Treaty Organization. And the threat, or even actuality, of Soviet military action to rein in straying neighbours was palpable. Under its openly announced **Brezhnev Doctrine**, in fact, the Soviet Union would simply not permit any dilution of Communist rule.

One very important consequence of so much in common was that dramatic events in one country had ready resonance throughout the region, and the opening of some new opportunity anywhere might suggest there were opportunities everywhere. So there were many *emulative* processes at work, as patterns of dissent in one place quickly suggested possibilities or impossibilities elsewhere. Stalin's death

in 1953 and the denunciation of Stalin's crimes (in a supposedly secret but soon widely known speech by Soviet head of state Nikita Khrushchev) in 1956 helped galvanize revolt in East Germany, Poland, and Hungary, the latter taking an especially violent turn. The bloodily successful suppressions were taken by future dissenters to demonstrate the futility of armed resistance. When a reform movement inside the Czechoslovak ruling party in 1968 was also met by the Soviet occupation of that country, the message to future dissenters was that reform inside the ruling party was hopeless. Up to that moment some dissenters had acted in the name of Marxism against Soviet tyranny, and had hoped for a national and reformed socialism—as opposed to post-Stalinism backed up by Soviet tanks. After 1968 dissent was about creating a new social order.

In the Soviet Union itself, in Czechoslovakia, in Hungary, and in Poland, small groups of intellectuals mastered the art of evading censorship and circulated clandestine manuscripts, all in supportive contact with each other. A transcontinental *external* process provided some additional cover. Impelled by the limitations of its economic growth, the Soviet Union sought increased trade with the West. US manufacturers and farmers sought increased trade with the Soviet Union, something that was politically difficult for the US Government to support without the appearance of political concessions. The result was the Soviet Union's entry into the Helsinki Accords in 1975, providing for international monitoring of human rights abuses. This provided limited protection for some limited forms of dissent, especially if those dissenters campaigned for peace and disarmament, since the Soviet Union hoped for pressures against the US military presence in Western Europe. Other dissenters organized around religious institutions. Still others moved into environmental causes, avoiding overt head-on challenge to the regimes. But for many others, listening to Western radio, hanging out at basement jazz concerts, laughing at official statements that no one believed—not even the officials—dressing like Western young people, or joining a strolling crowd at precisely the hour the TV played the official news program, diffused a sense of widespread rejection, even if a positive course of action was unclear. In Budapest, or Prague, or Warsaw, things were similar.

In the economic realm, another *external* process played its part. Just as banks were eager to lend to Latin America in the 1970s and 1980s, but got skittish eventually, so they were eager to lend to the states of communist Europe, which faced the very real problems of maintaining standards of living while pursuing goals of socialist development through heavy industry. Apart from Romania, which rejected the path of national indebtedness (and thereby impoverished its people), East European governments borrowed heavily, leading down the road to the problem of how these loans were to be paid back, just as in Latin America. By the 1980s few believed any more that the Soviet bloc had some alternative path to economic growth that would eclipse the West, morally or materially, and extensive borrowing from Western banks or food purchases from Western farmers rubbed the failure in. So, despite the vast dissimilarity of their ways of not being democratic, part of what brought down communist rule in Poland and military rule in Brazil was being prepared unintentionally in the offices of Western banks.

As a general tactic Central and Eastern Europe's intellectuals had worked out the notion of reviving civil society through non-violent construction of a realm of freedom. In Poland, uniquely, this turned into a vast mass movement as a strike at the Gdańsk shipyard in August 1980 sparked the Solidarity movement in which millions participated, demonstrating how utterly the regime had lost the people, and emboldening countless everyday acts of routinized defiance even after the great mass displays were crushed under martial law and the threat of Soviet military action. All over Central and Eastern Europe, people had in Poland a model of a land of defiance, though how to move forward was not obvious, not even in Poland.

In the Soviet Union itself, the premier, Mikhail Gorbachev, confronted a sense of economic and political ossification and ruinous military commitment to a failing Afghan war. In the course of restructuring Soviet institutions and reordering priorities, Gorbachev was not only an important promoter of change at home, but an enabler of change elsewhere. In a UN speech in December 1988 he abandoned his predecessor Brezhnev's commitment to block change throughout the region by force. A

year later communist regimes had been brought to an end in Poland, Czechoslovakia, Hungary, East Germany, and Romania, followed over the next few years by the Soviet Union, Yugoslavia, and Albania.

Out of uniformity came diversity: ex-Communist states to the west of the ex-Soviet Union democratized; the Soviet Union disintegrated and some of its fragments, now separate states, also democratized, while others erected new forms of authoritarian rule. Poland, for example, is listed in Table 5.1, but Belarus is not. Yugoslavia fragmented, entered a period of warfare, and to some extent democratized. The divergent political histories since 1989 pose many very interesting questions about the sources of such different paths.

Asia, 1980s and 1990s

At the beginning of the 1970s, Asian patterns of government were an extremely diverse collection and its democratizations from the mid-1980s into the early 1990s correspondingly idiosyncratic (Diamond and Plattner 1998). India is frequently called the world's largest democracy but it entered a crisis in which democratic practice considerably contracted in 1975 ('the emergency'), a state of affairs that lasted until 1977. China was, and remains, the world's largest authoritarian state, with a ruling communist party that successfully suppressed enormous protests in 1989, and maintained its political domination while enacting major economic reforms. While in the Soviet Bloc 1989 stands for the year everything changed, in China it is the year the ruling party demonstrated its capacity to participate in the global economy without democratization when it crushed major protest in Beijing.

Other Asian states were ruled by communist parties in the early 1970s and, with one exception, they have not travelled any great length toward democracy since then. North Korea remains under the rule of its Great Leader. South Vietnamese revolutionaries and their North Vietnamese allies, at war with the USA and the government of South Vietnam, won their war, and the newly reunified country of Vietnam has remained under one-party rule. Cambodia's Khmer Rouge carried out killings on an extraordinary scale but was overthrown by the neighbouring Vietnamese. Despite a great deal of international attention, that country has not moved far toward democracy.

Located between China and Russia, Mongolia proved quite exceptional. Encouraged by the events of 1989, protest demonstrations were mounted in the capital, and the party leadership debated between following the Chinese or East European course. They chose the latter, rewrote the constitution, held multi-party competitive elections in 1990, did very well in electoral politics, surrendered parliamentary power peacefully after electoral defeat in 1996, but captured the presidency in elections in 1997 (Ginsburg 1995). Although its scores on various measures of democratization are less than those obtaining in Western Europe or North America, they are not only well ahead of China, North Korea, or Vietnam, but well ahead of the former Soviet Central Asian republics, too (Fish 2001).

Other places of Chinese heritage travelled different paths. Singapore was and has remained a wealthy former British colony whose undemocratic rule has been justified as being in accord with 'Asian values' that stress community over individual freedoms. Hong Kong was a British colony with little of a democratic character into the 1980s. As the date approached at which that prosperous coastal city was to be turned over to the People's Republic of China, as one of the very last dramas of terminating the formerly vast British Empire, the departing British rulers set up a democratic process. The first elected Legislative Council of the colony took office in 1985, and other posts became elected ones over the next several years. The result was that when China assumed sovereignty in 1997, it had acquired a small, rich place with significant democratic elements whose future was deeply uncertain.

Taiwan was under martial law until the late 1980s and ruled by the Kuomintang, a party still claiming itself the rightful ruler of all of China, despite US recognition of the People's Republic in 1979. Many Taiwanese experienced this as an alien occupation and the KMT sought to contain potential challenges by ending martial law in 1987, displaying symbols of Taiwanese culture, language and history, disbanding a legislature representing mainland provinces, organizing a multi-party contested election in 2000, and accepting electoral defeat that same year (Tien 1997).

Beyond the Chinese orbit, dramatic developments took place in the Philippines and South Korea. In the early 1970s, the Philippine government was headed by Ferdinand Marcos, who was elected President in 1965 and then went on to rule under martial law since 1972, justified as defence against Communists and Muslims. In the mid-1980s, as Marcos proved ineffective in fighting genuine insurgents and a mass protest movement formed around the widow of an assassinated opposition figure, military leaders removed him, initiating a period of democratization widely taken to demonstrate the effectiveness of 'people power'.

In South Korea military rule endured into the 1980s, long justified as a response to the threat from the North. Regional disparities and mobilized students fuelled protest movements and even insurrection. Korean politics were so turbulent that the current authoritarian period was the 'Fifth Republic'. In the face of an enormous anti-regime petition campaign of 1987 and losing US support, the government and opposition began to negotiate an opening of the system, inaugurating the Sixth Republic and a democratic process (Diamond and Kim 2000).

With democratic models all around, with a decreasing likelihood of enlisting US support for militaries claiming the mantle of anticommunism, with foreign sources of funds seeing in democracy an antidote for authoritarian corruption, and with the increasingly general acknowledgment on the international stage of democracy as the sole legitimate form of government, democratic currents took heart in other places as well—in Nepal, in Burma, in Pakistan, places where they faced considerable resistance—but the most spectacular development in the next decade was the collapse of the Indonesian regime in 1998 and its replacement by one with democratic claims.

As of the early twenty-first century, Asia was politically very varied, as it had been thirty years before. While there are some *external* and *emulative* elements in play that have made democratic outcomes more probable than in the past, the national political trajectories seem extremely idiosyncratic.

Africa, early 1990s

We saw in Figure 5.1 that from the 1970s until the end of the 1980s the mean democracy scores for sub-Saharan Africa were very close to those for the Middle East and markedly lower than for Asia or Latin America. Indeed, after a brief small ascent in the mid-1970s, the scores were actually declining slightly for the next decade. The early 1990s, however, were years of considerable change. By 2004, the mean democratization score had departed markedly from that of the Middle East. Bratton and van de Walle (1997) suggest that for much of the continent there was a typical sequence running from protest and political liberalization, through competitive elections and, sometimes, on to further democratization.

At the beginning of the 1970s much of the continent was ruled by what journalists were apt to call 'strongmen', academics 'neopatrimonial' rulers, and observers of official titles 'presidents for life'. South Africa had its distinctive system in which the great majority of its citizens lacked political rights. During the 1960s and 1970s, the region as a whole had experienced some economic growth and per capita national income had risen modestly. The 1980s, however, were disastrous, with average incomes falling. Widespread poverty led to overgrazing and deforestation, which in the worst-hit places generated massive famine. The decline in per capita income grew larger each year from 1990 to 1992, then eased off (while remaining negative) in 1993 and 1994 (Mkandawire 2005). So the local impact of the global economy helped bring about rising rates of protest in the early 1990s.

The protests, however, seem not to have been simply the direct consequence of local economic disaster. African governments, desperate for financial aid, signed numerous loan agreements with the World Bank and International Monetary Fund that came with a variety of harsh conditions. Bratton and van de Walle (1997: 132–3) have shown that the more such agreements a country negotiated, the more protests its government endured. On top of protests triggered by economic difficulty in themselves, or by the harshness of the loan conditions, it seems that entering into repeated humiliating arrangements with the world of international finance seriously sapped support for the governments in place. In coping with these crises, at once economic and political, governments moved to open up their political systems, and 29 African countries held contested multiparty elections for president, legislative office, or both between 1990 and 1994. Protests peaked in 1991, liberalizations in 1992, elections in 1993 (Bratton and van de Walle 1997: 4–5) and democratization, as we have measured it, was still rising a decade later.

For its part, South Africa, long an icon of racial exclusion, under pressure from **social movements** at home and condemnation abroad, and threatened with disinvestment by foreign sources of capital increasingly worried about social turbulence and decreasingly inclined to see antidemocracy as the best bet to protect investments, began its own democratization process leading to the elections of 1994, the first ever in which the black majority could vote. It didn't hurt that after 1989, it was hard to persuade Washington to prop up an ally in a global struggle against communism.

A parallel cluster of national cases were seen as failures *internally* and *externally*. They had failed to produce growth and they had failed to protect against the demands of foreign bankers. Parallel political processes of negotiation led to liberalization, both in national politics and economic policy in a large number of separate countries, to contested elections, and to increased but not unchallenged democratization since personalism and corruption proved durable. Democratization scores actually dropped, on average, late in the 1990s, but then resumed their upward climb.

We see *external* processes as well. Global financial institutions began to rethink their view of **authoritarianism** as a defence of investments against the irrationalities of democracy since autocrats were proving at least as corrupt as vote-seeking politicians. Latin America had democratized during the 1980s without threatening transnational finance. In addition, as in Latin America the US was less inclined to support tyrants with anticommunist claims and more inclined to the promotion of neoliberal democracy, especially after 1989. Finally, there is the effect of *emulation* as African movements and African governments learned from each other.

The movements saw the rising possibilities of challenge and the governments saw democratization as a way to manage the challengers.

In the decade and a half since 1990, African governments had moved very different distances from the authoritarianisms of the recent past, some significantly democratic like Cape Verde and some like Swaziland as authoritarian as ever. Most places were somewhere in between. Bratton *et al.* (2005: 17) call the modal African variant 'liberalized autocracy'.

Middle East and North Africa?

This region entered the 1970s with a very low mean democracy score and entered the twenty-first century with very little change, despite several very turbulent decades that included civil warfare, foreign occupations, interstate warfare and a lot of political upheaval. Although toward the end of our timeframe the USA claimed to be promoting democracy in the region, and had gone to war and occupied two countries, the results were not only unimpressive, but widely taken to be discrediting democracy-promotion and perhaps democracy itself. On the other hand, Turkey entered a new period in its long history of oscillation between more democratic and more authoritarian politics, as a new party both repudiated the long-dominant commitment to militant secularism and staved off the threat of military intervention.

> ### Box 5.2 **Key points**
>
> - Democratization in Southern Europe, Latin America, Central and Eastern Europe and Sub-Saharan Africa was driven by internal and external processes.
>
> - In addition, supportive processes played a part in Latin American democratizations.
>
> - East Asian democratization followed more idiosyncratic processes.
>
> - Democracy has made few notable inroads in North Africa and the Middle East.

Hopes of entering the European Union may have been playing something of the same role in Turkey as such hopes did in the democratizations of Southern Europe in the 1970s. But the general regional absence of effective democratization raises many very interesting comparative questions. When we listed democratizing countries in Table 5.1, few countries with majority Muslim populations appeared, but some did, like Mali. While some were inclined to attribute this to the legacy of a particular cultural tradition, others could point to a regional mix of recent colonial rule and anti-colonial struggle, poverty in some countries and oil-based wealth in others, each in its own way hampering democratic development.

Conclusion

By the early twenty-first century, more people in more countries lived under political arrangements with some reasonable claim to the label 'democracy' than ever before in human history. Figure 5.4 shows the number of people living in countries with differing levels of rights and freedoms, following the Freedom House classifications. Lower numerical scores indicate more extensive rights and freedoms. The countries at the far right, where rights and freedoms are most extensive, are places like Canada, Denmark,

Spain, Uruguay, and the US. But many more people are in countries scoring 2.5, places like Brazil, India, Senegal, and Thailand. And many more are at a very low 6.5, in places like Belarus, China, Haiti, Somalia, or Uzbekistan. It is evident after more than two centuries of democratization and even after the great wave explored in this book, that many people live under very undemocratic circumstances and many others under circumstances less than fully democratic by the standards of the day. Since many countries had

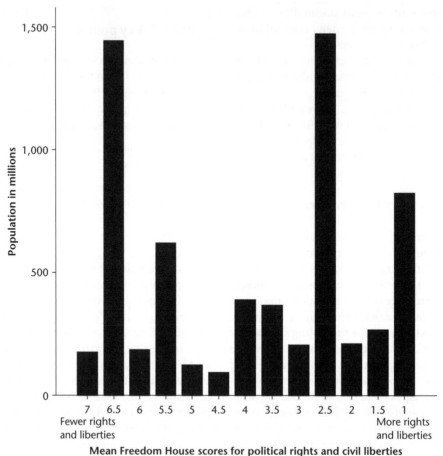

Fig 5.4 Population of countries with different levels of political rights and civil liberties, 2004
Source: Freedom House 2005.

not democratized, like China or much of the Middle East, significant scholarly attention was directed at understanding why not and at speculating about the future in such places.

But the very extent of the great wave was throwing into dramatic relief a new set of questions. In light of dashed hopes occasioned by past waves, the theme with which this chapter began, scholars wondered about a future antidemocratic counterwave and tried to understand the conditions under which democracy might not merely be brought into existence, but would endure, or as the literature would have it, be 'consolidated' (Diamond 1999). We have suggested, with special reference to Latin America, that the staying power of democracy could be as significant as getting it launched. One might wonder

whether new forms of polarization could or would emerge in large regions like Latin America (Seligson 2007) or whether the US-led 'global war on terror' might have some of the democracy-destroying consequences of the long confrontation with the Soviet Union that ended in 1989. And not just in poorer countries: some were noting with alarm the degree to which the rich countries were curtailing rights and freedoms in the name of security (Chebel d'Appollonia and Reich 2008).

Beyond durability, already by the mid-1990s the widespread achievement of significant democratization focused scholarly attention on the inadequacy of some of the newly democratized states. While many of these states were meeting accepted democratic standards, some were not, and yet others were disappointing in other ways. Were their democratizations complete or had they stalled somewhere on the way? Were they able to effectively provide the services citizens had come to expect of governments? Had they merely adopted the outward trappings of democracy, like elections, while avoiding some basics, like the rule of law? A new theme was emerging in the scholarly literature around the theme of 'the quality of democracy' (O'Donnell *et al.* 2004) as scholars variously identified such phenomena as 'illiberal' (Schedler 2006) or 'broken back' democracy (Rose *et al.* 1998).

These are complex issues and public opinion surveys in recently democratized countries of Latin America, the former Soviet bloc, Asia, and Africa revealed that citizens' judgments on the democracies that have emerged since the 1970s so far are also complex. Almost everywhere such surveys have been carried out (and these tend to be in the more democratic countries where such research is a lot easier), the majority—often the overwhelming majority—of citizens claim to favour democracy and reject authoritarian alternatives. At the same time, in some places significant numbers think some authoritarian variant is appropriate under some circumstances, very large numbers think democracy is not working well in practice, and enormous numbers are deeply critical of central political institutions like parliaments, courts, and parties. Indeed, deep reservations about democracy in actual practice turn out to be not simply a characteristic of democracies that are new, or illiberal, or broken back, but of the established wealthy democracies as well (Bratton 2007; Seligson 2007; Pharr and Putnam 2000). Some would argue that reservations about democracy in practice are part of the essential fabric of democracy.

The very extent of the new democratic wave, uneven as it has been, and incomplete as some of its democratizations have been, also raises some new

questions altogether. One of the reasons democrats at the end of World War II could hope for a more democratic world was the combination of democratic restoration in Western Europe, democracy promotion by military occupation of the defeated Axis powers, and the looming end of colonialism. With the demise of the globe spanning empires, one could anticipate that economic development or the spread of democratic values would ultimately mean the successive democratization of the new states, one by one. But in the twenty-first century, on the crest of the greatest wave of national democratizations in history, can we expect that future movements for democracy will continue to think of democratization within this framework? If the separate states are enormously different in their wealth and power, can we continue to think of a more democratic world as simply a further enlargement of the number of states that govern themselves in more or less the ways the Americans or British or French do? And if there are global institutions with which those states must engage (let us say, the World Bank or the International Monetary Fund) but which are not accountable to the citizens of those states, can we continue to think of a more democratic world as simply some sort of addition of the democracies of the separate states (Markoff 2004)?

Such questions have suggested to some that the early twenty-first century ought to be called the era, not of democracy, but of 'post-democracy' (Crouch 2005), to others that we need to consider the possibility of democracy beyond the states (Held 1995) and to others yet again that we need to rethink democratic institutions at various scales from the local community, through the national states, to the planet (Held and Pollitt 1986). One collection of essays triggered by the great wave was entitled 'Democracy's Victory and Crisis' (Hadenius 1997). But perhaps, as one of its leading students has it, democracy has always been in crisis (O'Donnell 2007).

QUESTIONS

1. How might you explain that in the early 1970s, just before the global wave of democratization, countries in different world regions were on average very different in how democratic they were (as shown in Figure 5.1)? Come up with at least two possible reasons.

2. How might you explain that since the 1970s, just before the global wave of democratization, countries in different world regions tended on the average to democratize to different degrees (as shown in Figure 5.1)? Come up with at least three possible reasons.

3. In what ways did countries that were already very democratic at the beginning of the 1970s contribute to the democratization of other countries in the years since then?

4. Are there ways in which countries that were already very democratic at the beginning of the 1970s hindered democratization in other countries?

5. Would you say that in any of the world regions external processes were much more important than in the other regions? Explain your answer.

6. Would you say that in any of the world regions internal processes were much more important than in the other regions? Explain your answer.

Visit the Online Resource Centre that accompanies this book for additional questions to accompany each chapter, and a range of other resources: <www.oxfordtextbooks. co.uk/orc/haerpfer/>.

FURTHER READING

Bratton, M. and van de Walle, N. (1997). *Democratic Experiments in Africa. Regime Transitions in Comparative Perspective* (Cambridge: Cambridge University Press). Shows why democratization occurred in the 1990s in some very poor countries and shows the limits of that democratization as well.

Held, D. (2006), *Models of Democracy*, 3rd edn (Cambridge: Polity Press). Thought-provoking account of different ways we might imagine democracy in the future.

Huntington, S. (1991), *The Third Wave. Democratization in the Late Twentieth Century* (Norman, OK: University of Oklahoma Press). Rich in ideas about how and why so many countries democratized in such a brief time span. Interesting speculation about the future.

Linz, J. J. and Stepan, A. (1996), *Problems of Democratic Transition and Consolidation. Southern Europe, South America, and Post-Communist Europe* (Baltimore, MD: The Johns Hopkins University Press). A broad, comparative treatment of transitions in three regions.

Markoff, J. (1996), *Waves of Democracy. Social Movements and Political Change* (Thousand Oaks, CA: Pine Forge Press). Sets the late twentieth century wave of democratization within the history of democracy over the centuries. Considers the role of social movements in pushing democratization forward.

Morrison, B. (2004) (ed.) , *Transnational Democracy in Critical and Comparative Perspective: Democracy's Range Reconsidered* (London: Ashgate Publishing). Essays commenting on the possibility of thinking about democracy beyond the national state.

Pharr, S. and Putnam, R. (2000), *Disaffected Democracies. What's Troubling the Trilateral Countries* (Princeton, NJ: Princeton University Press). Shows the range of discontents within the best-established democracies.

Robinson, W. (1996), *Promoting Polyarchy: Globalization, US Intervention and Hegemony* (Cambridge: Cambridge University Press). A critical look at deliberate efforts to promote democracy and the market.

IMPORTANT WEBSITES

<www.nipissingu.ca> This site provides a variety of fascinating materials on the world history of democracy.

Theories of Democratization

Christian Welzel

Overview

This chapter provides an overview of the factors that have been proposed as determinants when, where, and why democratization happens. Several of these factors are synthesized into a broader framework that describes human empowerment as an evolutionary force channelling the intentions and strategies of actors towards democratic outcomes.

Introduction

The question: which political **regime** prevails in which society, and why, has been at the heart of political science since Aristotle's first treatment of the problem. And so is the question as to when and why societies democratize.

Democratization can be understood in three different ways. For one, it is the introduction of democracy in a non-democratic regime. Next, democratization can be understood as the deepening of the democratic qualities of given democracies. Finally, democratization involves the question of the survival of democracy. Technically speaking, the emergence, the deepening, and the survival of democracy are strictly distinct aspects of democratization. But they merge in the question of *sustainable democratization*, that is, the emergence of democracies that develop and endure. Democratization is sustainable to the extent to which it advances in response to pressures from within a society.

There are many different explanations of democratization processes. Provided a grain of truth is in most of these explanations, researchers have too often tried to take sides, favouring one particular factor over all others. But the real challenge is to theorize about how different factors *interplay* in the making of democracy. This is what this chapter aims to achieve.

The Nature and Origin of Democracy

Before one can think about the causes of democratization one has to have an understanding of what democracy means—for one needs to have an idea of the nature of the phenomenon one wants to explain.

In its literal meaning, 'government by the people', democracy is about the institutionalization of people power. Democrat*ization* is the process by which this happens. People power is institutionalized through *civic freedoms* that entitle people to govern their lives, allowing them to follow their personal preferences in governing their *private* lives and to make their political preferences count in governing *public* life.

In the history of **states**, the institutionalization of people power has been an unlikely achievement. As power maximizing actors, power elites have a natural tendency to give as little power away as possible. There is a natural resistance among elites to grant civic freedoms to the wider public because such freedoms limit elite power (Vanhanen 2003). To acquire civic freedoms, ordinary people had usually to overcome elite resistance and to struggle for their cause (Foweraker and Landman 1997). This is no easy achievement. It requires wider parts of the public to be both *capable* and *willing* to mount pressures on power elites.

Quite logically then, the conditions under which democracy becomes likely must somehow affect the power balance between elites and masses, placing control over resources of power in the hands of the people. Only when some control over resources of power is distributed over wider parts of the public, are ordinary people capable to coordinate their actions and to join forces into **social movements** that are capable to

mount pressure on elites (Tarrow 1998). Under these conditions, bargaining power is vested in wider parts of the public as elites cannot access people's resources without consent. And if elites try to extract resources from people, they have to make concessions in the form of civic freedoms. Such was the case when the principle of 'no taxation without representation' was established during pre-industrial capitalism in North America and Western Europe (Downing 1992).

To be sure, no democracy in pre-industrial history would qualify as a democracy under today's standards because one defining element of *mature* democracies, universal suffrage, was unknown. All pre-industrial democracies were *nascent* democracies that restricted entitlements to the propertied classes. But nascent democracy was necessary to create mature democracy, encouraging yet disempowered groups to also push for civic freedoms, until universal suffrage created mature democracies early in the twentieth century in parts of the Western world (Markoff 1996). Since then people's struggles for empowerment have continued and expanded. Within established democracies, civil rights and equal opportunity movements did and do fight to deepen democracy's empowering qualities. Beyond established democracies, people power movements did and do pressure to replace authoritarian rule with democracy.

It is impossible to understand the driving forces of democratization without understanding why and where democracy first emerged. So we must have a closer look at the origin of nascent democracy in pre-industrial times and the factors giving rise to it. Without exception, all nascent democracies are found in agrarian economies of the freeholder type. Most freeholder societies organized defence in the form of a militia, the citizen-army (Finer 1999). In a freeholder-militia system, all men owning a slot of land provide military service and, in return, are entitled with civic freedoms. In pre-industrial times, a citizen army could only be sustained in a freeholder system. Only the yeoman who could sustain a family on his own could afford the armoury necessary for military service. In a freeholder-militia system citizens had bargaining power against central authorities—for citizens could boycott taxes and military service. Without a standing army at their exclusive disposal, rulers lacked the means to end such boycotts, disabling them to deny or abrogate civic freedoms (McNeill 1968).

Nascent democracy limited **participation** to the propertied classes. Still, compared to other pre-industrial regimes, nascent democracy is characterized by relatively inclusive civic freedoms. This constellation reflects relatively widespread access to basic resources, such as water, land, and armoury, and lack of central control over these resources. These conditions vest action capacities and bargaining power into the wider society and limit the state's repressive potential. The absence versus presence of democracy is about the absence versus presence of centralized control over resources of power (Dahl 1971).

Democracy and resource distribution

Freeholder systems not only gave rise to nascent democracy but also to pre-industrial capitalism. The combination of freeholdership, pre-industrial capitalism, and nascent democracy is hardly the result of an ingenious act of social engineering, such that some wise men decided at one point in history to create free-holdership, capitalism, and democracy. Instead, this constellation evolved in a cumulative process that was favoured by certain natural endowments. Freeholder systems only emerged where there was lack of centralized control over the resource that makes land valuable: water (Jones 1985). This was the case only where continuous rainfall over the seasons made water so generally available that a centrally coordinated irrigation system was unnecessary (Midlarsky 1997). Continuous rainfall over the seasons is only found in certain climatic zones, especially in North-West Europe, North America, and parts of Australia/New Zealand (Midlarsky 1997). These are the areas where we find the threefold constellation of freeholdership, pre-industrial capitalism, and nascent democracy.

Besides the continuity of rainfall, another natural endowment was conducive to nascent democracy. This condition, too, favours democracy by limiting centralized control over resources—in this case not over water but armoury. When a territory is, by means of its topography, shielded from the continuous threat of land war, there is no necessity to sustain a standing army at the exclusive disposal of a monarch (Downing 1992). With no standing army at hand, a ruler's control over coercion is limited. Hence, the proportion of sea borders (an island position in the optimal case) has been found to be positively related with the occurrence of nascent democracy (Midlarsky 1997). Iceland, the UK, and Scandinavia are examples. A functional equivalent of the shielding effect of sea borders are mountains. Shielded by the Alps from war with neighbours, Switzerland never needed a standing army. It sustained a freeholder-militia system, and is hence among the prime examples of nascent democracy.

Since democracy is about people power, it originates in conditions that place resources of power in the hands of wider parts of the populace, such that authorities cannot access these resources without making concessions to their beholders. But when rulers gain access to a source of revenue they can bring under their control without anyone's consent, they have the means to finance tools of coercion. This is the basis of absolutism, despotism, and autocracy—the opposite of democracy. The sixteenth-century Spanish monarchy turned more absolute after the crown gained control over the silver mines in South America. From then on, the Spanish Habsburgs did not have to ask for consent in the *cortes* to finance military operations (Landes 1998). This is a pre-modern example of what is today known as the 'resource curse'. It is a curse for democracy when a country is endowed with immobile natural resources that are easily brought under central control, giving rulers a source of revenue that requires no one's consent (Boix 2003). These revenues allow rulers to invest into the infrastructure of their power. Thus, 'oil hinders democracy' as Michael Ross (2001) put it.

So, we find both prosperity and democracy to be associated with climate. The more temperate the climate of a country, the more likely it is both to be rich and democratic (Landes 1998). According to Acemoglu and Robinson (2006), the geographic pattern of both prosperity and democracy simply reflects that white Europeans embarked early on a path of both capitalist and democratic development. They brought with them the institutions of capitalism and democracy wherever they could settle in larger numbers, that is, wherever they found a European-like climate. And when they settled in hotter climates, such as the Southern states of the USA or Brazil, they brought slavery and other exploitative institutions with them and resisted democracy. In this view, the global geographic distribution of capitalism and democracy simply reflects where climate 'required' European settlers to introduce slavery and exploitative plantation economies.

But why did Europeans embark on a path of capitalist-democratic development? Simply viewing this as a smart historic choice of Europeans is unsatisfactory. Following Jared Diamond (1997), the more likely reason why Europeans embarked on a course of capitalist-democratic development is that some unique natural endowments made this a more likely 'choice' in Europe than elsewhere.

Capitalism, industrialization, and democracy

One of the reasons why the duo of pre-industrial capitalism and nascent democracy emerged in Europe, is that, among the major pre-industrial civilizations, Europe was the only one that sustained rainfed freeholder societies on a larger scale (Jones 1985). But within Europe, this feature varies on a geographical gradient, becoming ever more pronounced as one moves north-westward, culminating in the Netherlands and England.

As one approaches Europe's north-west, the continuity of rainfall increases as a result of the influence of the Gulf Stream. In late medieval times, this led to an increasing agrarian surplus towards the north-west (Jones 1985). From this followed an entire chain of consequences, as shown in Figure 6.1: a larger urban population, a denser network of cities, a more commercialized economy, more advanced capitalism, and bigger and economically more powerful middle classes. Capitalism vested bargaining power in the wider

society. In the liberal revolutions and the liberation wars of the seventeenth and eighteenth centuries the middle classes used this bargaining power against monarchs to establish the principle 'no taxation without representation' (Tilly 1997). This is the birth of nascent democracy, and capitalism preceded it.

However, two qualifications of the claim that capitalism led to democracy are due (see also Ch. 9). First, capitalism led to democracy only where propertied groups, such as rural freeman and urban merchants, represented broad middle classes—not tiny minorities (Moore 1966). This condition was limited to the hubs of the pre-industrial capitalist world economy, centring on North-West Europe and its overseas colonial offshoots in North America (Wallerstein 1974). Colonies that were unsuited for large-scale European settlement were kept under an exploitative regime. Democracy was not imported by Europeans where the colonial interest was focused on extraction rather than settlement (Acemoglu and Robinson 2006). Second, pre-industrial capitalism only established nascent democracy, limiting civic freedoms to the propertied classes. The establishment of mature democracy with universal (male) suffrage was a product of industrialization and the working class's struggle for political inclusion (Huber, Stephens, and Rueschemeyer 1992). Yet, industrialization did not always lead to mature democracy, at least not to *enduring* mature democracy. Mature democracy in a stable form followed industrialization only where royal absolutism was prevented or abandoned and where nascent democracy was established already in pre-industrial times (Huntington 1968).

There is no uniform connection between industrialization and democracy. In fact, the fierce class struggles connected with the rising industrial working class often operated against democracy. Of course, industrialization almost always led to the symbolic integration of the working class by granting universal suffrage. But universal suffrage was as often organized in authoritarian ways as in democratic ones. Communist, fascist, and other forms of dictatorship all adopted universal suffrage in the industrial age. And while the working class almost always fought for universal suffrage, it often sided with populist, fascist, and communist parties that aborted the civic freedoms that define democracy (Lipset 1960).

Achieving mature democracy in a stable form at an early stage was neither the achievement of the middle

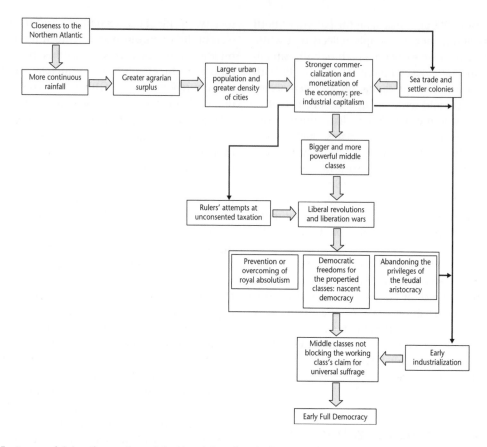

Fig 6.1 Factors explaining the northern Atlantic origins of capitalism and democracy

classes nor the working class alone. It appeared when the middle classes did not take sides against the working class (Collier 1999). This in turn only happened when the middle classes' victory over the aristocracy and royal absolutism was so decisive that neither an alliance with the aristocracy, nor reliance on state repression was an option in dealing with the working class. Partly for reasons originating in natural endowments, these conditions were historically unique to North-West Europe and its overseas offshoots (Moore 1966).

Social Divisions, Distributional Equality, and Democratization

Except under conditions found in North-West Europe and its overseas offshoots, the social class struggles associated with industrialization did not generally work in favour of democracy. This can be turned into a more general point. When class cleavages and group distinctions turn into enmity, political camps fight for the monopolization of state power in order to become capable of repressing the claims of rival groups. This pattern works against democracy (Dahl 1971).

Class cleavages turn easily into enmities when classes are segregated into separated milieus, when political parties are single-class parties, and when the distribution of economic resources between classes is extremely unequal. Under such circumstances, class coalitions and compromises are unlikely. Rivalry and enmity between groups will prevail (Lipset 1960). In European countries with a tradition of royal absolutism and continued privileges of the aristocracy, industrialization regularly produced such class divisions, polarizing an impoverished rural and urban working class against a privileged class of land owners, industrialists, bankers and office holders in the state apparatus and the army (Lipset and Rokkan 1967). Outside Europe, industrialization had the same effect in areas the Europeans colonized out of 'extractive interests' rather than for reasons of settlement (Acemoglu and Robinson 2006).

Wherever industrialization produced class polarization of this kind, the privileged classes would fear working class parties to be voted into office. Once in office, these parties might use their power to enforce land reforms and other redistributive measures that deprive the privileged classes of their privileges. Thus, the privileged classes would rely on state repression to prevent working class parties from gaining power. Confronted with state repression, working class activists would, in turn, radicalize and embrace revolutionary goals, aimed at a total reversion of the existing social order (Collier 1999). This is pretty much the pattern that explains Latin America's long lasting capture between right-wing military regimes and leftist guerrilla warfare (see Ch. 19).

Democratic countries in the 'centre' of world capitalism would often support the repression of working class interests in the 'periphery' in order to be able to outsource labour into cheap-wage regions and in order to prevent communism from taking over countries in the capitalist periphery. During the Cold War, and before the **Washington consensus**, the capitalist world system favoured democracy in the centres of capitalism, but authoritarian rule in its periphery (Wallerstein 1974). In any case, it can be said that extreme social polarization is detrimental to democracy because group polarization turns easily into violent fights for the monopolization of

the state (Dahl 1971). Peaceful power transfers from one group to another, as democracy foresees them, are not accepted under these conditions. Instead, military coups and civil wars that end up in the dictatorship of one group over others are the regular result of polarized societal cleavage structures (Huntington 1968).

The logic of group enmity does not only apply to social class. Societies can also be segregated into hostile groups on the basis of religion, language, and ethnicity, and the chances for this to happen increase with a country's religious, linguistic, and ethnic fractionalization, especially when fractionalization goes together with spatial group segregation (Rokkan 1983). Spatial segregation facilitates the stabilization of group identities, and this is an important precondition for the development of group hostilities. Sub-Saharan Africa, as the region with the highest ethnic fractionalization, exemplifies the latter type of group enmity and its negative effect on the chances of democracy to flourish (see Ch. 22). These insights can be turned into positive conditions for the emergence and survival of democracy. The presence of a large middle class, in whom economic differences do not go beyond a certain range, is a condition that eases group enmity, which in turn increases the acceptance of democratic power transfers between groups. Seen in this light, the transition of industrial to post-industrial societies is a positive development because it overcomes the sharp division between the working class and the privileged classes that characterized the industrial age (Bell 1973).

When resources are more equally distributed across socioeconomic, religious, ethnic, and other groups, this can diminish existential hostilities, making groups more inclined to accept each other as legitimate contenders for political power. If there is less at stake in the power game, all groups can be more relaxed about others winning the game for just one electoral round. Relative equality in the distribution of resources has thus a diminishing effect on hostilities for all sorts of groupings, be they class-related or ethnicity-related. In models explaining democratization, measures of income distribution are often used and have many times been found to significantly increase the chances of democracy to emerge and survive (Muller 1995; Vanhanen 2003).

Colonial Legacies, Religious Traditions, and Democracy

In its northern Atlantic origins, democracy is intimately connected to two traditions: Protestant religion and British descent (Lipset 1959). But this does not mean that Protestantism and British descent per se favoured democracy. They did so insofar as they were situated in the northern Atlantic centre of pre-industrial capitalism (Bollen and Jackman 1985). Neither Protestantism nor Britishness created pre-industrial capitalism. Countries such as the Netherlands, Iceland, and Denmark, were located at the northern Atlantic and so they embraced pre-industrial capitalism and nascent democracy, despite the fact that they were not British. Vice versa, Protestant Prussia was far off the northern Atlantic, so it neither embraced pre-industrial capitalism nor nascent democracy (Tilly 1997). Belgium, by contrast, was mainly Catholic but it is located at the northern Atlantic, so it adopted pre-industrial capitalism and nascent democracy. Contrary to Max Weber (1958 [1904]), who claimed that Protestantism created capitalism, it is just as plausible to argue that societies that were already capitalist adopted Protestantism as the religion granting the most **legitimacy** to the capitalist system (Landes 1998).

The relationship between Protestantism and capitalist democracy is as easily misunderstood as the fact that many of the early democracies are still monarchies today (e.g. UK, The Netherlands, Scandinavian countries). Monarchies survived until today in some of the oldest democracies because these monarchies did not insist on royal absolutism. Instead, they negotiated **social contracts** by which civic freedoms have been granted, creating constitutional monarchies that are anchored in society rather than being absolute from it (Lipset 1960).

Similarly misunderstood is the relationship between Islam and democracy. It has often been said that Islamic traditions are unfavourable to democratization (Huntington 1996). And indeed, the belt of Islamic countries from North-West Africa to South-East Asia is still the least democratized region in the world. However, this might not reflect a negative influence of Islam per se. Instead, for reasons of natural endowments, an unusual proportion of Islamic societies have based their economies on the export of oil. This places revenues in the hands of rulers without requiring anyone's consent, which is what explains the absence of democracy. As Michael Ross (2001; 2008) argues, Islam has little negative effect of its own on democracy, once one controls for oil exports. The same logic that explains why the capitalist development of Protestant societies favoured democracy explains why oil exports in the Islamic societies hinders democracy. Capitalist development tends to spread control over resources of power among wider parts of the society. Oil exports, by contrast, tend to concentrate control over resources of power in the hands of dynasties (see also Chs 8 and 21). On a more general note, explaining certain countries' affinity or aversion to democracy by criteria that simply group them into 'cultural zones,' 'civilizations', or 'families of nation' is inherently unsatisfactory as long as one cannot specify what exactly it is about these grouping criteria that creates these affinities and aversions.

Modernization and Democratization

Because of democracy's obvious link to capitalist development, 'modernization' has been most often championed as the decisive driver of democratization (Lerner 1958; Lipset 1959; Burkhart and Lewis-Beck 1994). The thesis that modernization favours democratization has been repeatedly challenged, but time and again it has been re-established against these challenges. Adam Przeworski and Fernando Limongi

(1997), for instance, thought to demonstrate that modernization only helps existing democracies to survive but does not help democracy to emerge. However, Carles Boix and Susan Stokes (2003) used the same data to show that modernization operates in favour of both the emergence and the survival of democracy. As of today, the fact that modernization operates in favour of democracy is beyond serious doubts.

The reasons as to exactly what it is about modernization that operates in favour of democracy are less clear. Modernization constitutes a whole bundle of intertwined processes, including productivity growth, urbanization, occupational specialization, social diversification, rising levels of income and prosperity, rising literacy rates and levels of education, more widely accessible information, more intellectually demanding professions, technological advancement in people's equipment and available infrastructure, including means of communication and transportation, and so on. Which of these processes does exactly what to increase the chances of a country to become and remain democratic is an unresolved problem, and most likely these effects are not isolable. Perhaps, it is precisely the fact that they are so closely intertwined that makes them so powerful.

One thing, however, seems clear that all these processes do together. They enhance the resources available to ordinary people, and this increases the masses' capabilities to launch and sustain collective actions for common demands, mounting effective pressures on state authorities to respond. Given that state authorities, by the nature of their positional interest, aim to preserve as much autonomy from mass pressures as possible, democratization is an unlikely result, unless the masses become capable to overcome the authorities' resistance to empower them (Vanhanen 2003). The major effect of modernization, then, is that it shifts the power balance between elites and the masses to the mass side. Democracy certifies this process institutionally.

Box 6.1 Key points

- Social divisions that foster group enmities hinder peaceful power transfers that are necessary for democracy to function.

- Democracy is anchored in social conditions in which resources of power are widely distributed among the population so that central authority cannot access these resources without their beholder's consent.

- Certain natural conditions have been favourable to a more widespread control over resources but modernization can happen everywhere and it is important because it tends to distribute the control over resources in the ways that favour democracy.

International Conflicts, Regime Alliances, and Democratization

The fact that scores of countries have democratized in distinctive international waves suggests that processes of democratization cannot be considered as isolated domestic events (see Chs. 4 and 7). They are influenced by international factors, especially the outcome of confrontations between opposing regime alliances. Therborn (1977) noticed that countries democratize as much as a consequence of wars as of modernization.

Whether, and when, countries democratize has often been decided by the outcome of international confrontations between the enduring alliance of Western democracies and shifting counter-alliances of antidemocratic empires. Thus, regime changes towards and away from democracy are not only a matter of power struggles between pro-democratic and antidemocratic forces *within* countries. Instead, power struggles between opposing regime forces take also place on the international stage, in confrontations between democratic and antidemocratic regime alliances. Indeed, three waves of democratization followed precisely such confrontations. Western democracies defeated the alliance of Germany, Austria-Hungary, and the Ottoman Empire in World War I; this led to a (later reversed) wave of democratization in Central and Eastern Europe. Western democracies again, together with the Soviet Union, defeated the fascist axis powers in World War II and this led to another wave of democratization, including, for the first time, countries outside the West, such as India and Japan. Finally, Western democracies triumphed over communism in the Cold War, leading to the most recent and massive wave of democratization throughout Eastern Europe and parts of Africa and Asia (Huntington 1991, McFaul 2002).

Part of the explanation as to why democracy has been spreading is the technological and military superiority of democracies, and their tendency to join forces against antidemocratic empires. Together, these two factors have enabled democracies to free societies from the tyranny of antidemocratic empires—when necessary, Western democracies have used their power to install democracy by military intervention, as in Grenada or Iraq. Since the 1980s, they have also used their economic power to press countries depending on Western credits to adopt electoral democracy.

This was a dramatic paradigm shift. During the Cold War, the capitalist world system was favourable to democracy in the centres of capitalism and to authoritarian rule at its periphery. But since the Washington consensus, Western countries promoted electoral democracy throughout the globe. Installing a system of electoral **accountability** seemed to be a better safeguard of investment security than the arbitrary rule of eccentric dictators, especially after communism and socialism lost their appeal. In addition, rich Western democracies dominate the global entertainment industry and images of the living conditions in Western countries spread around the planet. Consequently, people associate everywhere democracy with the freedom and prosperity of the West. And insofar as people find freedom and prosperity attractive, democracy has become the preferred type of regime in most populations of the world (Fukuyama 1990; Klingemann 1999; Inglehart 2003).

The economic, technological, and media dominance of Western democracies are important explanatory factors in the recent spread of democracy. Democratization is hence, to some extent, an externally triggered phenomenon. But whether externally triggered democratization leads to viable and effective democracy still depends on domestic conditions within a country. External influences can open important opportunities for democratic forces in countries where such forces exist. But external influences cannot create democratic forces where they do not exist. And without democratic forces growing strong inside a country, democracy will not be socially embedded. It remains a socially aloof, and hence, hollow phenomenon. Even if most people in a country associate positive things with the term democracy, this does not necessarily mean that people understand the freedoms that define democracy nor that they have the means and the will to struggle for these freedoms.

Externally triggered democratization has led to a spread of electoral democracy, but not necessarily effective democracy (Welzel and Inglehart 2008). Many new democracies have successfully installed competitive electoral regimes but their elites are corrupt and lack a commitment to the rule of law that is needed to enforce the civic freedoms that define democracy (O'Donnell 2004). These deficiencies render democracy ineffective. The installation of electoral democracy can be triggered by external forces and incentives. But whether electoral democracy becomes effective in respecting and protecting people's civic freedoms depends on domestic factors. Democracies have become effective only where the masses put the elites under pressure to respect their freedoms (Welzel 2007).

Elite Pacts, Mass Mobilization, and Democratization

Besides mass-level factors, actor constellations at the elite level are widely considered decisive for democratization processes. Considering transitions from authoritarian rule to democracy, scholars distinguish two opposing sets of actors: the regime elite and the regime opposition. The regime elite is usually not a monolithic bloc but a coalition of forces that can split under certain circumstances into an orthodox status quo camp and a liberal reform camp. The regime opposition, too, is often divided into a moderate bargaining camp and a radical revolution camp (Casper and Taylor 1996).

The early transition literature argued that a regime opposition in an authoritarian system cannot achieve a transition to democracy unless a split in the regime elite occurs and a liberal reform camp becomes visible (O'Donnell *et al.* 1986; Higley and Burton 2006). Such a split is likely to occur after a major economic crisis, a lost war or other critical events that undermine the legitimacy of the regime. Such critical events lead to the formation of a liberal reform camp that aims to regain legitimacy by initiating a liberalization process. If in such a situation the regime opposition is dominated by a moderate camp whose proponents are willing to bargain with the reform camp in the regime elite, a negotiated transition to democracy becomes

possible. This interpretation sees negotiated transitions via elite pacts as the ideal path to democracy. Mass anti-regime mobilization is not only unnecessary for democratic regime transitions from this point of view; it even endangers their success by prompting the regime elite to close its ranks and tempting it to issue repressive measures (Casper and Taylor 1996).

The recent democratization literature has altered these views rather decisively, emphasizing the positive role of non-violent mass opposition in knocking over authoritarian regimes and establishing democracy (Karatnycki and Ackerman 2005; Ulfelder 2005; Welzel 2007). These studies show that democracy is in most cases achieved when ordinary people struggle for it against reluctant elites. Democratization processes of recent decades have been most far-reaching and most successful where the masses were mobilized into democracy movements in such numbers and so ubiquitously that state authorities could not suppress them easily.

State Repression and Democratizing Mass Pressures

Recent studies on the positive role of mass opposition have altered our view on the survival of authoritarian regimes. Usually it was held that authoritarian regimes can use repression to silence opposition and that this allows them to endure, even if the masses find their regime preferences 'falsified' (Kuran 1991). However, most authoritarian regimes did not survive because of their ability to repress mass opposition (Wintrobe 1998). In fact, most authoritarian regimes did not have to deal with widespread mass opposition most of the time (Francisco 2005). This might partly be so because a credible *threat* of repression alone can keep people from opposing a regime. Yet, for the credibility of repression to become the key factor in stabilizing authoritarian rule, there must be a widespread belief in the illegitimacy of authoritarian rule in the first place. And this does not always seem to be the case. In fact, as Samuel Huntington (1991: 143) notes, most of the authoritarian regimes that were swept away by mass opposition movements late in the twentieth century, were initially 'almost always popular and widely supported'. It is only

when people come to find appeal in the freedoms that define democracy that they begin to consider dictatorial powers as illegitimate. Only then does the threat of repression become a relevant stabilization factor of authoritarian rule. And yet, there is ample evidence from the non-violent, pro-democratic mass upheavals of recent decades that when a population begins to long for freedoms, mass opposition does emerge—in spite of repressive threats (Karatnycki and Ackerman 2005; Schock 2005; Welzel 2007).

Once opposition becomes manifest, the success of attempts at repression does not only depend on the extent of coercion used; it depends as much on the size and scope of the mass opposition itself. Indeed, mass opposition can grow so wide that repression becomes too costly, overwhelming the power holders' repressive capacities. In such cases power holders are forced to open the way to a regime change. This happened quite often during the last three decades. Huge mass opposition swept away authoritarian regimes in scores of countries, including some strongly coercive regimes. The point here is that the desire for democratic freedoms and the corresponding belief in the illegitimacy of dictatorial powers are variables, not constants. When these variables grow strong, they provide a powerful motivational force for the mobilization of mass opposition in authoritarian regimes as soon as opportunities occur (Oberschall 1996). And no regime has the power to foreclose the rise of opportunities. Repression cannot isolate authoritarian regimes from the destabilizing effect of eroding legitimacy and rising mass demands for democracy.

Mass beliefs and democratization

Socioeconomic modernization and the emergence of mass democracy movements are not necessarily contradictory explanations of democratization. They are simply located at different stages in the causal sequence. By enhancing ordinary people's available resources, modernization increases collective action capacities on the part of the masses and thus makes mass democracy movements possible, be it to achieve democracy when it is denied, to defend it when it is challenged, or to advance it when it stagnates. But even if we link modernization with democracy movements, there is still something missing. As social movement research has shown, powerful mass movements do not simply emerge from growing resources among the population. Social movements must be *inspired* by a common cause that motivates their supporters to take costly and risky actions (McAdam 1986). This requires ideological 'frames' that create meaning and grant legitimacy to a common cause so that people follow it with inner conviction (Snow and Benford 1988). Successful frames are not arbitrary social constructions and not every frame is equally appealing in every population. Instead, frames must resonate with ordinary people's prevailing values to generate widespread and passionate support. This is why values are important. To advance democracy, people have not only to be capable to struggle for its advancement; they also have to be willing to do so. And for this to happen, they must value the freedoms that define democracy. This is not always a given, and is subject to changes in the process of value transformation.

Structural approaches implicitly assume that the masses do always anyways want democracy, so this is a stable and constant factor that does not vary across populations (Acemoglu and Robinson 2006). But ample evidence from the major cross-national survey programmes shows that the extent to which ordinary people value democratic freedoms varies widely across populations (Dalton, Shin and Jou 2007; Shin and Tusalem 2007). Hence, to make plausible that modernization favours democracy, one has not only to show that it increases people's capability to struggle for democratic freedoms but also that it increases their willingness to do so.

This seems unlikely from the perspective of **institutional learning theory**. Dankwart Rustow's (1970) 'habituation model', for instance, maintains that people learn to appreciate democracy's freedoms only if they have gathered experience with the practice of these freedoms. This requires democratic institutions *to be in place* for democratic values to emerge. In this view, people's valuation of democratic freedoms is endogenous to the presence of democratic institutions and does not cause them. Since an intrinsic valuation of democratic freedoms among the populace can only occur under enduring democratic institutions, modernization cannot give rise to pro-democratic values, unless it advances under democratic institutions.

By contrast, Christian Welzel and Ronald Inglehart (2008) argue that people's valuation of democratic freedoms reflects how much utility they see in these freedoms. And perceived utility is not only depending on first-hand-experience with the practice of these freedoms. It depends primarily on the resources that people command, for the more resources people have, the more they need freedoms to make use of them (Rostow 1961). Hence, growing and spreading resources increase the utility of democratic freedoms in ways that are easily becoming obvious. Accordingly, Figure 9.3 in Chapter 9 demonstrates that, under mutual controls, the endurance of democracy has no effect on people's valuation of democratic freedoms while modernization has. Emphasis on democratic freedoms is more driven by the utility of these freedoms than by the experience of them. This makes it possible that an intrinsic desire for democracy emerges in authoritarian regimes and that pro-democracy activists can create civic rights frames that resonate with people's emerging valuation of freedoms.

People's valuation of democratic freedoms becomes manifest in emancipative beliefs that emphasize the power, freedom, agency, equality and trustworthiness of ordinary people (Welzel and Inglehart 2008). As these values emerge, they motivate elite-challenging collective actions (Welzel 2007). In fact, emancipative beliefs motivate elite-challenging collective actions on every level of democracy (or lack thereof). And on all levels of democracy, emancipative mass actions operate in favour of democracy, helping to achieve democracy when it was absent and to sustain it when it is present.

Counter-intuitively, at first glance, the type of mass beliefs tapping public support for democracy in a most direct way is irrelevant to democracy, both to its survival and its emergence (Inglehart 2003). The percentage of people in a country who say they support democracy strongly and reject authoritarian alternatives to democracy strictly, has no effect whatsoever on subsequent measures of democracy, once one controls for the dependence of these attitudes on prior democracy (Welzel 2007). What matters is not whether people support democracy but *for what reasons* they do so (Schedler and Sarsfield 2006). Only when people support democracy for the freedoms that define it, are they ready to mount pressures on elites to introduce these freedoms when they are denied, to defend them when they are challenged, or to advance them when they stagnate. Thus, people's explicit support for democracy advances democracy if—and only if—this support is motivated by emancipative values. Devoid of these values, support for democracy has no effect.

Elite-conceded versus mass-pressured democratization

Two recent approaches link modernization to actor constellations and by doing so claim to have found the reason why modernization favours democratization. The two approaches are in direct contradiction to each other.

Acemoglu and Robinson (2006) interpret democracy as the result of a struggle over economic redistribution between propertied elites and impoverished masses. In this view, democracy is a struggle for universal suffrage in which both sides are motivated by conflicting interests in economic redistribution. The masses want democracy because universal suffrage would enable them to redistribute income from the elites, and the elites oppose it for precisely the same reason. Consequently, the elites will only concede universal suffrage if they have reason to believe it will not lead to extensive redistribution—otherwise, they will suppress mass demands for suffrage. The reason why modernization is important in this model is that it is assumed to close the income gap between the elites and the masses, tampering the masses' interest in extensive redistribution and the elites' fear of it. Suppressing the masses' demands for democracy becomes then more costly than conceding democracy and so the elites concede democracy. An additional reason why elites have less to fear from conceding democracy is when their capital is so mobile that they can move it out of the reach of taxation into other countries (Boix 2003).

Several strong assumptions underlie this model (these assumptions are not always made explicit but without them the model would not work). First, variation in mass demands for democracy cannot account for the emergence and survival of democracy, since the model assumes that the masses are always in favour of democracy. Second, the decision to democratize is always fully in the hands of the elites; they decide whether to repress mass demands for democracy or whether to concede democracy. Third, modernization increases the chances to democratize by changes in income equality and capital mobility that make universal suffrage more acceptable to the elites.

The human empowerment approach of Ronald Inglehart and Christian Welzel (2005) favours the exact opposite assumptions. First, these authors find a great deal of variation in the degree to which given publics desire democratic freedoms. Second, the decision to expand democratic freedoms

---

Box 6.2 **Key point**

- The global diffusion of democracy resulted partly from the military defeat of anti-democratic empires by allied democratic powers.

- Mass-pressured democratization is the more frequent and more successful type of democratization as compared to merely elite-conceded democratization.

remains exclusively an elite choice only as long as ordinary people's action resources are meagre. But this is precisely what modernization changes. It greatly increases ordinary people's action resources, enabling them to mount more powerful collective actions, putting increasingly effective pressure on elites. Third, the survival of authoritarian regimes is not simply a question of whether elites choose to repress the masses—it reflects the balance of forces between elites and masses, which tends to shift to the mass side with ongoing modernization. The recent waves of democratization were, in large part, a story of effective mass mobilization, motivated by strong emancipative beliefs among people who had become increasingly skilled and ambitious at organizing social movements. In this view, the major effect of modernization is not that it makes democracy more acceptable to elites. It is that modernization increases ordinary people's capabilities and willingness to struggle for democratic freedoms.

Institutional Configurations and Democracy

Beside socioeconomic modernization, social divisions, international regime alliances, elite constellations, social movements and mass beliefs, institutional factors have been claimed to influence democratization. Barbara Geddes (1999) argues that the type of authoritarian regime shapes the chances of democracy to emerge. She differentiates three types of authoritarian regimes: personalistic regimes, military regimes, and single-party regimes. By means of their institutional variation, these regimes are supposed to be vulnerable to different degrees to democratizing forces, as they offer different opportunities for regime opponents and command different resources to restrict their radius. Indeed, these three types of **authoritarianism** are vulnerable in different degrees to mass regime opposition (Ulfelder 2005). But the point is that all three of them are more likely to break down and to transit to democracy under the pressure of anti-regime mobilization.

The level at which regime type and other institutional variables operate is what is commonly called 'political opportunity structure' (Tarrow 1998). Any authoritarian regime, even the most powerful one, has some sort of a control deficit, depending on institutional structures. Depending on the nature and extent of these control deficits, authoritarian regimes offer democratic forces different opportunities to merge into a democratic mass movement. But one should not forget that opportunity structures do not by themselves create these mass movements and that no authoritarian regime has the power to foreclose opportunities forever. Once the resources and values that make people capable and willing to struggle for freedoms have emerged, people will find and create opportunities to join forces in mass democracy movements. Provided such movements grow strong enough, no authoritarian regime can resist them forever, regardless what institutional type of authoritarian regime it is.

Institutional variation plays also a role when it comes to existing democracy's malfunctions, which can be an important factor of their stability and survival. There is a large literature on the deficiencies of presidential democracies, as opposed to parliamentary democracies, and it is widely believed that presidential democracies are more vulnerable to antidemocratic challenges (Linz and Valenzuela 1994; Mainwaring and Shugart 1997; Lijphart 1999). Again, the argument is about opportunity structures. By means of their institutional structures, presidential democracies might offer antidemocratic challengers better opportunities to operate. But institutional opportunities do not create these challengers. Other, more deeply rooted societal factors are responsible for this.

The Human Empowerment Path to Democracy

Synthesizing the above discussion, we can now identify a 'master sequence' towards sustainable democratization. Modernization enhances the action resources of ordinary people, making them more capable to struggle for democratic freedoms in launching popular movements that sustain elite-challenging activities.

Fig 6.2 The human empowerment path towards democratization

By increasing people's action resources, modernization increases the utility of democratic freedoms and it does so in ways that are easily made perceptible through frames, so that people's valuation of these freedoms grows. This gives rise to emancipative values, making publics more willing to struggle for democratic freedoms.

Popular struggles for democracy become manifest in social movements whose activists frame democratic goals and mobilize the masses in support of these goals in campaigns that sustain elite-challenging actions (Foweraker and Landman 1997). If elites do not voluntarily give in, in anticipation of these mass pressures, these pressures can grow too strong to resist, forcing elites to give in, either by introducing democracy when they have denied it or by advancing it when they were to bloc its further advancement. This sequence is what Welzel and Inglehart (2008) call the 'human empowerment' path to democracy, as shown in Figure 6.2. It follows a sequence such that (1) growing action resources empower people *materially* by making them more capable to struggle for freedoms, (2) rising emancipative beliefs empower them *mentally* by making them more willing to struggle for freedoms, and (3) democracy empowers them *legally* by allowing people to practice freedoms.

The more human empowerment has advanced in its material and mental dimensions, making people capable and willing to practice democratic freedoms, the more sustainable the legal component of human empowerment—democracy—becomes. The human empowerment path to democracy is not the only path to democracy. But it is arguably the only path producing socially embedded and hence sustainable democracy.

Putnam's (1993) social capital theory of democracy represents a specific aspect of the general human empowerment framework (see also Ch. 11). As human empowerment advances in its material and mental dimensions, it makes people more capable and more willing to initiate and sustain collective action. In doing so, human empowerment creates social capital as a by-product.

A Typology of Democratization Processes

The human empowerment path to democracy is responsive to mass pressures for democracy. This path constitutes *responsive democratization*. This has been the dominant type of democratization in the emergence of nascent democracies and in the global wave of democratization of recent times. But there are other types of democratization processes that do not respond to mass pressures. These types can be classified as *enlightened democratization*, *opportunistic* *democratization*, and *imposed democratization*. In each of these types, the power elites' vested interest in monopolizing power is overcome by reasons other than mass pressures. In each of these types this leads to socially detached rather than embedded democracy, the latter of which can only result from mass responsive democratization.

One of the reasons why power elites might overcome their natural resistance to democratize is when negative historical experiences have discredited alternative forms of government. The adoption of democracy in post-World War II Germany, Italy, and Japan partly fall into this category. This type of *enlightened democratization* is the only type in which elites effectively respect democratic standards even in absence of mass pressures to do so. But this model is very rare in history as it is at odds with power elites' natural tendency to resist democratization.

Another reason why elites concede democracy even in the absence of mass pressures is when these elites depend on the will of external powers and when these powers are pushing for democracy. This case of *imposed democratization* is again typical of post-war democracies such as West Germany, Austria, Italy, and Japan after World War II. The US-led attempts to install democracy in post-war Afghanistan and Iraq fall into the same category of externally imposed democratization, though it is far from clear whether the latter cases will be successful.

Still another and increasingly widespread case in which elites concede democracy in the absence of mass pressures is when they believe they can easily corrupt democratic standards in practice and when the pretence of democracy is perceived as a useful means to open the doors to the international community, especially donor organizations. This case of *opportunistic democratization* has become more likely since the Washington consensus, as a result of which western credits have been tied to conditions of 'good **governance**.'

In the enlightened, imposed, and opportunistic types of democratization, elites concede democracy despite absent mass pressures to do so. Among these three types, elites respect democratic freedoms effectively only in the enlightened type but this type is rare. In the imposed and opportunistic types of democratization, elites do not effectively respect democratic freedoms. Responsive democratization is the only type of democratization in which democracy becomes socially embedded and hence socially sustainable.

Conclusion

Some approaches to understand democratization focus on societal *conditions*, such as modernization or distributional equality. Other approaches emphasize the role of collective *actions*, including elite pacts or mass mobilization. Conditions and actions are often portrayed as contradictory explanations of democratization when in fact a full understanding of democratization needs to highlight the interplay between conditions and actions.

It is self-evident that democratization is not an automatism that guides itself without agents. Instead, it is the outcome of intentional collective actions, involving strategies of power elites, campaigns of social movement activists, and mass participation. Thus, any explanation of democratization intending to illuminate the role of social conditions must make plausible how these conditions shape actor constellations. On the other hand, it is just as self-evident that actions leading to democratic outcomes are the result of choices that are socially conditioned. Thus, it is the task of action-centred approaches to illuminate how concrete actions respond to social conditions.

Figure 6.3 suggests *motivational mass tendencies* as the intervening force that helps translate *objective social conditions* into *intentional collective actions*. Motivational tendencies are based on shared beliefs and values. They are shaped, on one hand, by social conditions because what people believe and value is not a context-free given but reflects objective circumstances. On the other hand, motivational tendencies direct intentions towards goals that inspire actions.

The path in Figure 6.3 focuses on mass responsive democratization because this is the socially most sustainable type of democratization process. For this type of democratization to become possible, people must have the resources that enable them to act jointly for democratic freedoms, and this is where social conditions become relevant. Socioeconomic modernization, for instance, places more resources into the hands of ordinary people, enhancing their capacity for collective action. But in order to take the risks and costs to act jointly for democratic freedoms, people must passionately believe in these freedoms. This is where emancipative values become important. Where these values develop, they provide a

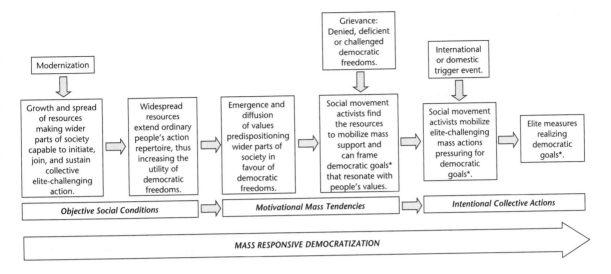

*Goals aiming at the introduction, deepening or defence of democratic freedoms.

Fig 6.3 Causal path toward mass-pressured democratization

motivational force that predispositions people in favour of democratic freedoms. If people have acquired both the capability and the willingness to join forces in struggling for democratic freedoms, and if there is reason for grievance because these freedoms are denied, deficient or challenged, at some point a critical event will prompt people to actually act together for these freedoms, be it to establish, to deepen or to defend them. Provided these actions grow strong enough, power elites will be forced to give in to their demands. When this happens we witness mass responsive democratization.

Mass responsive democratization is the joint result of objective social conditions, motivational mass tendencies, and intentional collective actions, triggered by critical events, in the context of enduring grievances. The role of objective social conditions in this causal interplay is that they determine a society's capabilities for collective action. The role of motivational mass tendencies is that they shape the intentions that inspire collective actions. The role of grievances is that they provide a reason to become active for the sake of given goals. The role of critical events is that they provide a trigger for collective actions. And the role of collective actions is that they constitute a challenge that, when becoming strong enough, leads to a political change.

Again, mass responsive democratization is not the only path to democracy. For democracy can be imposed by foreign powers or adopted by unilateral elite actions. But mass responsive democratization is the only path to democracy that creates socially embedded democracy. And only socially embedded democracy is sustainable democracy.

QUESTIONS

1. What is nascent democracy?

2. Which structural factors favour democratization?

3. Which structural factors impede democratization?

4. Why did democracy and capitalism co-evolve in Western Europe and North America?

5. Why did industrialization not always favour democratization?

6. What is the role of mass motivational tendencies in democratization?

Visit the Online Resource Centre that accompanies this book for additional questions to accompany each chapter, and a range of other resources: <www.oxfordtextbooks. co.uk/orc/haerpfer/>.

FURTHER READING

Acemoglu, D. and Robinson, J. A. (2006), *Economic Origins of Dictatorship and Democracy* (New York, NY: Cambridge University Press). Encompassing account of the origins of democracy from a political economy perspective.

Casper, G. and Taylor, M. M. (1996), *Negotiating Democracy* (Pittsburgh, PA: University of Pittsburgh Press). This book is the best on actor strategies, comparing failed and successful cases of democratization.

Dahl, R. A. (1971), *Polyarchy: Participation and Opposition* (New Haven, CT: Yale University Press). This classic provides the theoretically most comprehensive account of democracy until today.

Foweraker, J. and Landman, T. (1997), *Citizenship Rights and Social Movements* (Oxford: Oxford University Press). One of the best books on democratization from a social movement perspective.

Huntington, S. P. (1991), *The Third Wave* (Norman, OK: University of Oklahoma Press). The classic on waves of democratization and what causes them.

Inglehart, R. and Welzel, C. (2005), *Modernization, Cultural Change, and Democracy* (Canbridge: Cambridge University Press). Perhaps the most comprehensive account of democratization in a political culture perspective.

IMPORTANT WEBSITES

<http://repositories.cdlib.org/csd> This website links to downloadable publications of the Center for the Study of Democracy at UC Irvine.

<http://democracy.stanford.edu> This is the website of the Comparative Democratization project of Stanford University, directed by Larry Diamond.

<www.journalofdemocracy.org> This is the website of the Journal of Democracy. Some articles are free for download.

<www.tandf.co.uk/Journals> This is the website of the Taylor & Francis academic journal *Democratization*. Article abstracts can be read online.

Part Two

Causes and Dimensions of Democratization

7 The International Context

Hakan Yilmaz

Overview

This chapter discusses the major theoretical approaches to the issue of the international context of democratization. It also reviews the principal dimensions of the international context, namely, democracy promotion strategies of the USA and the EU, and examines the effects of **globalization** and the formation of a **global civil society**.

Introduction

Until recently, most analyses of democratization have treated their subject primarily as a national issue, by paying little or no attention to the influences coming from the international environment. Despite a variety of rich empirical analyses, the subject of external and internal linkages in the processes of democratization has remained an under-researched and under-theorized field. Transitions to democracy, whether in the distant past or in the more recent times, have almost always been accounted for by the operation of domestic factors. Thus, historical cases of democratization in early modern Europe were explained by underlining the legacy of separation of powers, church-state separation, independent towns, and by social contracts based on the principle of 'no taxation without representation' between the tax-paying citizens and the autocratic rulers of the state. More recent cases of democratization were studied by underlining sometimes the structural factors (e.g. the degree of national unity, the level of political institutionalization, economic development, and political culture) and sometimes the more intimately political factors (e.g. the nature of civil-military relations, the cracks within the ruling blocs, and the relative weights of the costs of suppression and toleration). Whether structural or political, in the historical and the more recent cases of democratization, the factors that were attributed primary explanatory power belonged mainly to the domestic social and political life, implying that democratization had little to do with the forces operating outside national borders.

The International Context of Democratization: Theoretical Approaches

In a famous essay on the interaction of domestic and international politics, Robert D. Putnam wrote that '[d]omestic politics and international relations are often somewhat entangled, but our theories have not yet sorted out the puzzling tangle' (Putnam 1993: 431). Putnam's critique has targeted the classical theories of international relations, but some scholars of comparative politics have expressed similar ideas concerning their own discipline. Douglas A. Chalmers observed that comparative political analysts frequently ignore international factors or relegate them to the contextual background. When attention is paid, it is usually restricted to intervention, dependency, subversion, or foreign aid (Chalmers 1993). For various intellectual, institutional, methodological, and historical reasons, examined in some detail by Andrew Moravcsik (1993) and Tony Smith (1994), theories of international relations and comparative politics have constructed two separate, independent, and self-contained political universes, domestic and international, with distinct actors and specific rules of the game. It was a rare exception for an analyst to refer to the developments in one of the political universes with the purpose of explaining an event that was taking place in the other universe.

Democratic transition has been one particular field of study in comparative politics in which the dismissal of the international factors was perhaps more pronounced than in the other fields. Geoffrey Pridham, writing on the Southern European democratizations in the 1970s, has argued that '[t]he international context is the forgotten dimension in the study of democratic transition. Growing work on this problem, both theoretical and empirical, has continued largely to ignore international influences and effects on the causes, processes and outcomes of transition' (Pridham 1991: 1). At the same time, a critical dimension of the international context affecting democratic developments in smaller countries, namely the efforts of the USA, EU, and other democratic powers to promote democracy worldwide, has also remained remarkably underresearched (Smith 1994: xiii–xiv).

By the early 1990s, influenced by the more obvious role played by the international environment in the Central and Eastern European transitions to democracy, theorists in the fields of international relations and comparative politics have made serious attempts to build approaches that would bridge the gap between the two political universes. In this connection, a number of interdisciplinary approaches have emerged, with the purpose of confronting the problem of external-internal linkages in the processes of democratic **regime** change. Important examples of the new approaches to the issue of external-internal linkages in democratization include Laurence Whitehead's concept of 'democratization through convergence' (Whitehead 1991), Geoffrey Pridham's idea of 'democratization through system penetration' (Pridham 1991), Douglas Chalmers' notion of 'internationalized domestic politics' (Chalmers 1993), and various theories of 'diffusion' in the vein of Samuel Huntington's 'snowballing' effects. Whitehead and Pridham developed their approaches from their analyses of the Southern European democratizations, while Chalmers based his theory on the Latin American cases. For now, it should be noted that such attempts have not yet produced widely accepted models of explanation. All such works are still at the level of initial reflections and explorations to be developed by further theoretical refinements and case studies. In fact, Putnam himself has called his two-level game approach a 'metaphor' that could at best serve as the starting point for building an 'algebra' (Putnam 1993: 437).

Whitehead's 'democratization through convergence' occurs in a process in which a non-democratic country joins a pre-existing democratic community of states without losing its sovereignty. Examples are the democratizations of Spain, Portugal, and Greece while these countries were being integrated with the European Community. According to Whitehead (1991: 45–6), the greatest puzzles in measuring the effects of the international factors arose in the intermediate cases of democratization through convergence where 'the key actors involved in regime change and democratization may have been overwhelmingly internal, [but] their strategies and calculations have often been strongly shaped by the pressure of externally designed rules and structures'.

Pridham's concept of 'system penetration' is similar to Whitehead's notion of 'regime convergence'. According to Pridham, long term external factors that 'penetrate' a given domestic system affect the background conditions of and prepare the way for regime transition. Hence, even if there is no immediate external factor at the time of the transition itself, the impact of the long-term external factors and the degree of 'system penetratedness' must be accounted for in the explanation of regime change (Pridham 1991: 21–5). The convergence approach of Whitehead and the penetration approach of Pridham are useful for understanding the impact of the international factors on the political regimes of countries which were not politically or economically dominated by a foreign power. The pitfall of both approaches is that they are not themselves theories. They are rather conceptual frameworks within which we can develop a model of explanation for the particular cases at hand.

A third approach to the role of the international factors in domestic politics has been developed by Douglas Chalmers, which he has called 'internationalized domestic politics'. Chalmers has formulated the concept of 'internationalized domestic politics' to account for the impact of the international factors on the cases of authoritarian breakdown and democratic transition in Latin America in the 1970s and 1980s. The author defines an 'internationally based actor' as any actor who stays involved in a country's domestic politics over a period of time, becomes built into the political institutions of the country, and is identified with international sources of power (Chalmers 1993: 1). When internationally based actors are a significant presence, then the political system that results is called 'internationalized domestic politics'—'internationalized' because of the presence of international actors, and 'domestic' because the problem at hand is not a question of foreign policy or interstate relations, but of decision-making on local issues. In contrast to a more conventional perspective that limited the international factors to the ones that arose solely from state-to-state relations and considered them as being external to a country's political system, Chalmers redefines political systems 'to include internationally based actors as normal parts of the system, not actors external to it' (Chalmers 1993: 35). Although Chalmers underlines the fact that internationalized domestic actors are not a novelty, he also says that internationalized domestic politics is a recent phenomenon. He attributes that phenomenon, on one hand, to the tremendous increase in the numbers, types, scope, and resources of internationally based actors, and on the other hand to the post-Cold War trend of globalization which is progressing through developments in communications, sales of national assets to foreigners by privatizations, liberalization of world trade, and a general decrease of a nation-state's control over social organization and production within its borders.

A fourth view on external-internal linkages in the processes of democratization centres on the idea of 'diffusion'. Diffusion refers to the various interactions and inter-linkages between two structures, one being the international context and the other one a single country that is situated in that context. Although various authors have later developed more focussed models of diffusion, Samuel Huntington's well-known theory of the three 'waves' of democratization can be taken as a predecessor of the diffusion approach. In his 1991 book, *The Third Wave: Democratization in the Late Twentieth Century*, Huntington refers to the 'snowballing' or demonstration effects, enhanced by new international communications, of democratization in other countries, as one of the factors that had paved the way for the third wave of transitions to democracy. In a later article, 'After Twenty Years: The Future of the Third Wave', Huntington has put the accent on the concept of diffusion for explaining the chances of electoral democracies to develop into liberal democracies. In that article Huntington argued that 'the extent to which non-western societies have proven receptive to either electoral democracy or liberal democracy tends to vary directly with the extent to which those societies have been subject to western influences' (Huntington 1997: 10). For Huntington, Western influence primarily meant being in the Western sphere of 'civilization', the latter being shaped by the norms and values of Christianity. Hence, in his view, among the non-Western countries, the Roman Catholic countries of Latin America and the Orthodox Christian countries of Central and Eastern Europe had the greatest chances for the transformation of electoral democracies into liberal democracies. Huntington went on to recommend the formation of a network or club of the liberal democratic nations of the world, in the form of a Democratic International, which he would baptize as the 'Demintern' in reference to the Communist International or Comintern. The primary function of this 'Demintern' would be 'expanding democracy on a global basis and enhancing the performance of democracy within countries' (Huntington 1997: 11–12). The 'Demintern' would in a sense institutionalize the mechanisms and channels of the diffusion of liberal democratic ideas and institutions across the nations and over the globe.

The idea of democratic diffusion has subsequently been elaborated in two analytical models. For these diffusion models, the international context for a country is formed mainly by its web of relations with the neighbouring countries in its own region. As such, it does not include the states, international organizations and other entities that are operating in the other, more distant parts of the globe. Daniel Brinks and Michael Coppedge (2006) examine the magnitude and direction of regime change in a set of countries between 1972 and 1996. They have found that countries tend to change their regimes to match the average degree of democracy or nondemocracy prevalent in their neighbourhood, with countries in the US sphere of influence being particularly prone to becoming more democratic. Brinks and Coppedge have also found that countries tend to follow the direction in which the majority of other countries in the world are moving.' (Brinks and Coppedge 2006: 463).

They insist that 'any model exploring the determinants of democratization that does not account for these spatial relationships is underspecified' (Brinks and Coppedge 2006: 482–3). A second diffusion model of democratization has been developed and tested by Kristian Skrede Gleditsch and Michael D. Ward (2006). These authors have found that the probability that an autocracy will become a democracy increases markedly as more of its neighbouring states are democracies or experience transitions to democracy' (Gleditsch and Ward 2006: 928). According to the authors, '[t]here is a marked tendency for cases to change in ways similar to their regional context over time, and transitions in one country often spill over to other connected states' (Gleditsch and Ward 2006: 929).

While diffusion models have quite convincingly shown that some sort of diffusion effect was in place in many recent cases of democratization, the models are unable to show just how diffusion works and through which channels democratic ideas and institutions spread among neighbouring states and societies. This weakness of the diffusion model has been noted by Brinks and Coppedge (2006: 482–3) who acknowledge that '[t]he nature of our testing precludes any empirical examination of the nature of the causal mechanisms; the best we can offer in that regard is a sketch of a theory that makes neighbour emulation plausible'. Similarly, Gleditsch and Ward (2006: 930) observe that 'it is difficult to fully specify the full range of possible micro-level processes of democratization and show how international factors influence these in a model at the aggregate level'.

Box 7.1 **Key points**

- Most analyses of democratization have treated their subject primarily as a national issue, paying little attention to the influences coming from the international environment.

- The international dimensions of democratization have been conceptualized as democratization by means of 'convergence', 'system penetration', 'internationalization of domestic politics', and 'diffusion'.

racy Promotion Strategies of the USA and opean Union

In most theories of democratization, the international context is portrayed as a 'structure', with no central logic, no overall design, no final destination, and no leading actor. Agency is usually ascribed to the militaries, political parties, elites, and other social groups within an individual country, that are reacting to the various, and in many cases conflicting, signals and influences coming from the international context surrounding it. In theories of 'democracy promotion', on the other hand, which have proliferated from the end of the 1980s onwards, the 'international context' has turned into a 'global agent', be it a single state like the USA, a supranational organization like the European Union, an international organization like the United Nations, or a transnational advocacy network like Amnesty International. This global agent, rather than being a passive or slow-moving structure, has been shown as consciously and deliberately trying to impart new mentalities, new institutions, and new codes of behaviour to a country for the openly declared purpose of promoting democracy in that country. According to Peter Burnell (2008: 38), '[t]he democracy promotion industry is multinational and its size at an all-time high. Current spending ranges somewhere between US $5 and $10 billion annually'.

The key terms of the democracy promotion literature are 'democracy promotion', 'democracy protection', and 'democracy assistance'. Philippe C. Schmitter and Imco Brouwer (1999) offer working definitions for these key terms. According to these authors 'democracy promotion' aims to contribute to the political liberalization of autocratic regimes and their subsequent democratization in specific recipient countries. 'Democracy protection', on the other hand, is implemented to consolidate a newly established democracy. Finally, 'democracy assistance' refers to specially designed programs and activities that are meant to raise the democratic performance of individuals and institutions in a democratic regime, such as training parliamentarians, educating citizens, or assisting local organizations in monitoring elections. Democracy promotion, democracy protection, and democracy assistance, regardless of their separate goals, are carried out by such activities as sanctions, diplomatic protests, threats of military intervention, activities to promote the observance of human rights, the acceptance of civic norms, and the transfer of institutional models such as electoral systems. Schmitter and Brouwer's definition excludes secret activities and covert operations, as well as activities (such as literacy campaigns or financial assistance) that might only indirectly promote democratization in a given country. The definition also excludes more objective factors of the international context that could positively influence democratization, such as imitation, contagion, or learning through contact with others.

What has been the driving logic behind the democracy promotion activities of the democratic powers, and what have been the achievements and failures of democracy promotion from its beginnings by the end of the Cold War until today? We will turn to an evaluation of the democracy promotion policies of the European Union, the USA and in the following section.

Democracy promotion by the USA

According to Tony Smith, liberal democratic internationalism is 'the American idea of a world order opposed to imperialism and composed of independent, self determining, preferably democratic states bound together through international organizations dedicated to the peaceful handling of conflicts, free trade, and mutual defense' (Smith 1994: 7). In this view, US support for the right wing dictatorships in various parts of the world in the post-war era was an exception rather than the rule, and it was caused by the need to prevent the more ominous prospect of letting these states turn into Soviet satellites. This view of the USA as a 'liberal internationalist' can be contrasted by the approach of James Petras and Morris Morley (1990), which portrays the USA as an 'imperialist power'. In their Marxist interpretation of the USA hegemony in Latin America, Petras and Morley make a distinction between the regime and the state. The state 'represents the permanent interests of class power and international alignments' while the regime 'represents the day to day policy decisions at the executive . . . level that can modify or negotiate the operations of the permanent interests but never challenge them without evoking a crisis' (Petras and Morley 1990: 111). If an authoritarian regime proves incapable to contain a social movement against the state, then the USA can 'sacrifice the dictators to save the state' (Petras and Morley 1990: 111). In order to prevent the anti-state movement of the masses, the USA can replace the former dictatorship by a more inclusive regime under the leadership of the moderate factions of the opposition. In this view, the driving force behind the US actions is not an idealist goal to promote democracy but the determination to protect the integrity of a client state, which is politically, militarily or economically subordinated to a more powerful state in international affairs, while remaining nominally sovereign. Thus, Petras and Morley argue that US policymakers' 'interpretations' of policy shifts from support for dictatorships to support for democratic regimes in terms of a White House commitment to promoting, or imposing, democratic values cannot be sustained.

In the aftermath of the Cold War, for the US policymakers, promoting democracy in the world was expected to serve two fundamental interests of the USA, the first one stemming from an **idealist** and the second one from a **realist** perspective (Gillespie and Youngs 2002: 8). First, democracy promotion would appeal to the underlying ethical concerns of US foreign policy, which adopted for itself the mission of spreading human rights and democratic norms across the world. This idealist position has been epitomized in the words of US President Woodrow Wilson's (1917) address to a joint session of Congress seeking a declaration of war against Germany:

The world must be made safe for democracy. Its peace must be planted upon the tested foundations of political liberty. We have no selfish ends to serve. We desire no conquest, no dominion. We seek no indemnities for ourselves, no material compensation for the sacrifices we shall freely make. We are but one of the champions of the rights of mankind. We shall be satisfied when those rights have been made as secure as the faith and the freedom of nations can make them.

The second, 'realist' drive behind the post-Cold War promotion of democracy stemmed from security concerns and it was meant to make the world safe for the USA. This reasoning has been influenced by the 'democratic peace' hypothesis, according to which war was unlikely between democracies. The origins of the democratic peace theory can be traced back to the German philosopher Immanuel Kant (2006), who, in his 1795 essay entitled 'Perpetual Peace: A Philosophical Sketch', argued that constitutional republics were a **necessary condition** for a perpetual peace in the world. Kant's idea was that a majority of the people would never vote to go to war, unless in self defence. Therefore, if all nations were republics, it would end war, because there would be no aggressors. Arguably, neither the idealist nor the realist logic fully dominated the US democratic promotion policies at any one point in time. As Robert Gates, the former head of the CIA and current Secretary of Defense, stated in a speech in 2007, 'from our earliest days, America's leaders have struggled with "realistic" versus "idealistic" approaches to the international challenges facing us. . . . We have at times made human rights the centrepiece of our national strategy even as we did business with some of the worst violators of human rights' (Gates 2007).

The record of US democracy promotion policies to date, particularly during the George W. Bush Administration, is at best mixed. The Middle East has taken the lion's share in the overall democracy promotion programmes of the Bush administration. Latin American countries, for instance, have not been paid a lot of attention in the last decade, though many democracies in the region have been shaken by political and economic crisis, which has paved the way for the coming to power of anti-American regimes in countries like Venezuela and Bolivia. Except for the heightened funds and efforts dedicated to the Middle East, the US democracy promotion activities in the other countries of the world, such as Indonesia, Nepal, and Liberia, remained unambitious. Even in the highly publicized 'colour revolutions' in Georgia, Ukraine, and Kyrgyzstan in the early 2000s, despite the claims that US government and institutions had been the prime movers of the revolutionary movements, the role of the US was at most modest (Carothers 2007: 10–11). With respect to the US democracy promotion activities in the Middle East, one can safely say that the returns on the increased funds and efforts remained marginal. First of all, much of the US funds and efforts have been consumed by the invasions and occupations of Afghanistan (since October 2001) and Iraq (since March 2003), both of which were far more related to the realist concerns of security, stability and oil rather than motivated by any idealist mission of bringing human rights and democracy to that part of the world. Except for its engagements in Afghanistan and Iraq, the USA has largely continued to do business as usual in the other countries of the Middle East. As US Secretary of Defense Robert Gates put it '[i]t is neither hypocrisy nor cynicism to believe fervently in freedom while adopting different approaches to advancing freedom at different times along the way – including temporarily making common cause with despots to defeat greater or more urgent threats to our freedom or interests' (Gates 2007).

Recently, many authors have observed a 'backlash' against democracy promotion by the USA. According to Peter Burnell, 'the current mood in and around the industry itself appears to be at an all-time low' (Burnell 2008: 39). What are the factors behind this backlash? Thomas Carothers identifies four main causes. In the first place, US invasion and occupation of Afghanistan and Iraq, and the rhetorical **legitimation** by the US Administration that these actions were taken for the sake of bringing democracy to these countries, have helped to associate democracy promotion with US military intervention. Second, conspiracy theories claiming that the 'colour revolutions' of Ukraine, Georgia and Kyrgyzstan were stage-managed by such US organizations as the National Democratic Institute (NDI), the International Republican Institute (IRI), Freedom House, and the Open Society Institute, have helped to associate democracy promotion with US covert operations. Third, the violation of human rights by and within the USA, symbolized by such incidents as Abu Ghraib, the practice of detaining people indefinitely at Guantanamo Bay, the undermining of fundamental civil liberties through the US Patriot Act, and discrimination

against Muslim Americans by such practices as terrorist profiling, has discredited the USA as the champion of democracy in the other parts of the world (Carothers 2006). Finally, a growing assertiveness of President Putin's international stance combined with Russia's improved financial prowess, as well as the wealth that is being accumulated by some commodity exporting developing world governments as a result of rising demand from the booming economies of China and India, have all served to reduce the leverage that Western governments could exert on behalf of democracy promotion (Burnell 2008).

What could be a more successful and sustainable regime of US democracy promotion? Edward Mansfield and Jack Snyder (2006) have argued that democratization has certain preconditions. These preconditions have to do with sufficient levels of state-building and nation-building. In other words, prior to launching democratization, a society must have established a mode of peaceful coexistence between the various ethnic groups that make it up, and it must have built the necessary institutions for interest representation and conflict resolution. If democracy, and particularly an externally imposed democracy, comes before these preconditions are met, then it will almost certainly lead that country to internal conflict and external aggression. Mansfield and Snyder recommend that a democracy promotion program should help a country to establish the preconditions of democracy, which consists of developing the economy, building an impartial and effective public bureaucracy, inducing the state to move away from patronage and repression as the basic instruments of government, and promoting a pro-democracy constituency within the civil society, the latter to serve as the internal push for democratization.

Democracy promotion by the EU

The term 'conditionality' has been coined to describe the democracy promotion strategy of the EU. Schmitter and Brouwer (1999: 15) have defined 'conditionality' as 'imposing or threatening to impose sanctions or providing or promising to provide rewards in order to promote or protect democracy'. Given the pace and depth of the democratic transformation of post-communist countries of Central and

Eastern Europe under EU conditionality, it would not be wrong to claim that in the last two decades the EU has been a far more successful democracy promoter than the USA. However, the main qualification of this claim to success is that it has only worked for countries that were on the way of joining the EU. These cases of democratization were, in the words of Peter Burnell (2008: 38), 'easy victories' for the EU. The countries of Central and Eastern Europe had just come out of Soviet domination, and EU membership was the best choice for them to secure themselves against Soviet power and to consolidate their newly won democratic regimes. Hence, they were ready to comply with the membership conditions that the EU set for them. From the perspective of the member states of the EU, on the other hand, Central and Eastern European nations were seen as part of a common European civilization, history, and geography. Therefore, enlargement to the East was viewed as the exercise of necessary solidarity with their kin.

For EU conditionality to be an effective catalyst of democratization, a number meta-conditions have to be met. First, in order to be effective political conditionality must involve a rightly balanced mix of conditions and incentives. The adoption of the political conditions by the receiving countries create serious adjustment costs, which can only be outweighed by substantial incentives. Thus, in the case of the Central and Eastern European transitions of the 1990s, the principal incentives involved a clear timetable for quick accession to the EU coupled with generous aid, credit, and direct investment flows from member states to the candidate countries. Those incentives helped the candidate countries to face the costs of political and economic transition, which was undertaken in line with the EU requirements. On the other hand, a situation of conditions with no incentives, instead of contributing to the promotion of democracy, might produce just the reverse effect and might play into the hands of the opponents of liberalization and democratization. Second, the EU must not change the conditions in the middle of the game (consistency of the conditions). Third, the EU must apply essentially the same conditions to all the candidates (fairness of the conditions). Finally, the candidate country must have an undisputable prospect for joining the club, when she meets all the conditions for membership (attainability of the prize).

If one or more of these meta-conditions are violated, conditionality might not produce the desired outcomes. What is more worrisome, violations of these meta-conditions by the EU might provoke a nationalist reaction within a candidate country and thereby produce the opposite outcome, in the form of a backlash against EU-driven democratization and liberalization.

The case of Turkish candidacy illustrates the point. Turkey has been a candidate state for the EU since December 1999 and it has started accession negotiations in October 2005. Turkey has been the only candidate country for which an accession date has not been specified. Not only has a date for joining the European club not been set, but many influential politicians from the EU member states, including French President Nicolas Sarkozy and German Chancellor Angela Merkel, have started to question whether Turkey is a European country and therefore has a right to join the EU. New membership conditions have also been created for Turkey, which make the accession process harder and longer, compared to the Central and East European countries. For example, for the case of Turkey, the EU has formulated a new concept, the so-called 'absorption capacity' of the EU, meaning that, even if Turkey met all the conditions, the EU could still refuse entry, if it judged that it was not ready to take in a new member. The impact of these and other violations of the meta-conditions of conditionality was to bring about in Turkey what may be called a 'reverse conditionality'. In other words, as the EU has started to disengage itself from Turkey, critically placed Turkish political actors and social forces have responded to this signal coming from the EU by either detaching themselves from the EU project or at least adopting a position of indifference with respect to it. The consequence of 'reverse conditionality' might be that European values might lose their support base in the Turkish political and civil society, with the outcome of an erosion of the reforms made in the area of democratization and liberalization. Ironically, to save the earlier democratization reforms that had been made under EU conditionality, Turkey might now need to de-link the project of democratization from the project of EU accession, because reversals in the latter process could seriously harm the advances made in the former.

As Antoaneta Dimitrova and Geoffrey Pridham (2004) observed, EU conditionality has not been very effective for countries with no prospect of membership. A case in point is the Mediterranean countries of North Africa. The Barcelona Process, which had been set in motion in the mid-1990s to bring the Mediterranean countries to a closer political and economic cooperation with the EU, and to socialize the political class and civil society in the region into a greater acceptance of European democratic ideals and values, has not produced tangible results (Gillespie and Youngs 2002). A closer analysis of the newly proposed 'Union for the Mediterranean', which had been put into the EU agenda by French President Nicolas Sarkozy, reveals that, unlike the previous Euro-Mediterranean Partnership (the Barcelona Process), this new EU-Mediterranean cooperation scheme would not have any political or democratic substance. Avoiding politics, the Mediterranean Union's focus would be on crime and terrorism, sustainable development, illegal immigration and energy security, and its key objective would be to establish a Euro-Mediterranean free trade area by the year 2010.

> ### Box 7.2 Key points
>
> - In 'democracy promotion', a global agent (the USA, the EU, the UN, or a transnational advocacy network) consciously and deliberately tries to impart new mentalities, new institutions, and new codes of behaviour to a country for the openly declared purpose of promoting democracy.
>
> - The term 'conditionality' has been coined to describe the democracy promotion strategy of the EU. 'Conditionality' is defined as imposing sanctions or providing rewards in order to promote democracy.
>
> - Recently, there has been a 'backlash' against democracy promotion by the USA. The association of democracy promotion with US military intervention; the violation of human rights by the USA; and a growing assertiveness of states like Russia and China have all served to reduce the leverage that the USA and other Western governments could exert on behalf of democracy promotion.

Globalization, Global Civil Society, and Democratization

Globalization and the decline of state power

The internalist understanding of democratization, prioritizing the role of domestic factors in paving the way to democracy, was relatively plausible until the onset of globalization in the 1980s. In a world where nation states could effectively control the movements of money, commodities, people and information through their borders, it made sense to take the state, with all that existed within its borders, as the basic level of analysis for political change. This closed-polity view of change in political science corresponded roughly to the closed-economy model of economics: in both,

the role of international factors was seen as secondary to explaining political or economic outcomes. In a world dominated by nation states, the kind of international factors that were significant enough to exert a lasting impact on domestic developments could only come from one state clashing with other, competing states, which typically took the form of war, invasion, occupation, economic domination, economic sanctions, and colonization. One likely consequence of such clashes was that, like defeat in war, they dramatically weakened state power at home, both physically and normatively, thus increasing the chances of the opposition forces to win the political struggle they were waging against the forces of the state. Theda

Skocpol (1979) underlined the role of such state-weakening international factors in explaining the French and Russian revolutions. Losing external wars was no doubt the primary cause of the collapse of fascist regimes of Germany and Italy after the Second World War. In the 1970s, the failure of the colonial adventures of the Portuguese army led to the downfall of the Salazar regime in Portugal, while the Turkish military intervention in Cyprus triggered the end of the 'colonels' regime' in Greece. More recently, the US-led NATO operations against Serbia and Afghanistan, and the US invasion of Iraq, helped remove the ultranationalist, Islamic fundamentalist, and Baathist regimes in these countries. Regime change, and in particular democratic regime change, as a result of the impact of state-weakening international interventions, will no doubt be with us for years to come. In fact, that has been the favourite method for 'democracy promotion' for the Bush Administration and the 'neoconservative' sections of the US foreign policy establishment in recent years.

By the end of the Cold War, however, state power has arguably been weakened by globalization. Globalization meant, particularly for the smaller states, that their control over the movements of money, commodities, people and information across their borders has entered a process of decline. This has been particularly the case for financial capital and information, whose cross-border movements are increasingly independent from regulation by individual states. The enormous progress in information and communications technologies, the spread of the internet, and the world-wide proliferation of the alternative markets for investing financial capital meant that state borders have become increasingly porous and permeable. Some authoritarian states, such as Iran and China, have been waging a quixotic struggle to slow down the penetration of their borders by banning the use of the satellite dishes or restricting the use of the internet. Some other semi-authoritarian states, such as Russia, have been trying to cleanse their societies from the 'infection' of globalization, by ousting international NGOs from their countries, nationalizing the assets of newly emerging capitalists, censoring the media, and persecuting journalists.

Positive and negative effects of global civil society upon democratization

Globalization has prepared a very different field for the game of democratization, involving both encouraging and discouraging facets. Global forces, whether they come in the form of superpowers such as the USA, **supranational** organizations such as the EU, or transnational companies, have acted like double-edged swords, sometimes cutting in favour of democratization and sometimes against it. In the process of globalization states have become more vulnerable to the demands of the global forces that control capital movements, investment decisions, technological innovation, and the production and dissemination of information, norms, and values. These global forces can and sometimes do use their power to further the cause of democracy. One example is no doubt the democratic transformation in the post-Communist countries of Central and Eastern Europe under EU conditionality. US-led NATO actions to prevent ethnic cleansing and to establish stable political regimes in former Yugoslavia is another example of the positive impact of global forces on the promotion of human rights and democracy. Yet a third example is the fact that human rights violations have gained an unprecedented visibility due to the widespread information networks of human rights organizations. This global visibility is no doubt a factor that has made authoritarian governments think twice before proceeding to suppress democratic forces. At other times, however, states, transnational companies and other globally operating entities have not shied away from backing utterly repressive regimes, such as the ones in the oil-producing countries in the Middle East and Central Asia, often in return for securing lucrative political or economic deals. Facing the increasing challenges of globalization, and in order to cope with rising internal dissent, states have resorted to extreme measures, which involved, primarily, anti-globalist mass mobilizations along the lines of populist, nationalist, religious fundamentalist ideologies. These are what can be called 'de-democratization' or 'authoritarian restoration' attempts in the age of globalization. In these processes of authoritarian restoration, dissenters are often tainted as foreign agents, imperialist lackeys, and enemies of the nation, and are persecuted under the charges of betrayal and subversion. Putin's Russia, Ahmadinejad's Iran, Chavez's Venezuela are all examples of this anti-globalist authoritarian backlash. Most states that take these de-democratizing measures against the forces of globalization can afford to do so because they are oil or natural gas exporting **rentier states** (see Ch. 8). As exporters of a highly demanded global product, their bargaining power vis-à-vis the global forces is high compared to the non-rentier states such as Turkey, Argentina, Chile, and Brazil. Rentier states also have access to financial resources to finance their anti-globalist restoration or preserve their authoritarian systems. The non-rentier states, on the other hand, have had to be more responsive to the liberalizing and democratizing conditions recommended to them by the outside world.

What impact has globalization had on the world's authoritarian regimes? On the positive side, globalization has spread democratic norms and values through the national boundaries and helped generate new ethical codes of behaviour for the states, international organizations, and multinational companies. The advances in the information technologies have greatly increased the visibility of the actions of the states and other powerful actors, thereby eroding secrecy, widening transparency, and exposing the states to the scrutiny of the global civil society. Under the circumstances of increasing transparency, states that are in search of global prestige and credibility have had to restrain their despotic actions. On the negative side, globalization has exacerbated economic and political inequalities in the world, further widening the gap between the richer and poorer nations and regions. Their growing wealth has made richer nations more self-centred, more conservative, and more indifferent towards the problems of the poorer nations. Richer nations' main concern for the more disadvantaged nations of the world has remained limited to aid, charity, and the prevention of migration. Poorer nations, on their part, having seen no way out of the cycle of poverty, have become more susceptible to the manipulations of religious fundamentalists, ultranationalists, terrorists, and human traffickers. Amy Chua (2002) pointed to another dangerous liaison between a country's insertion into economic globalization and the democratization of its political

regime. Chua argues that, if there was an economically dominant ethnic minority in that country, the initial impact of globalization would be to further enhance the dominant position of that minority. Economic globalization tends to exacerbate existing inequities insofar as the economically dominant minorities are better-positioned to take advantage of new economic opportunities, have better access to capital, and they are endowed with a cultural tradition of entrepreneurialism that other groups do not have to an equal extent. This can result in growing resentment on the part of an impoverished and marginalized majority. Hence, when democracy is introduced into such a tense domestic environment, a majority group or coalition of groups may be tempted to use its democratic powers for settling of scores, which can lead to many incidents of ethnic clashes and ethnic cleansing. As examples of democratization resulting in the majority's aggression against market-dominant ethnic minorities, Chua cites anti-Semitism in Weimar Germany and post-Communist Russia; hostility for the wealthy Chinese minority in the Philippines; Serbian assaults against the more affluent Croats in former Yugoslavia; violence against the more prosperous Tutsi minority by the Hutu majority; and seizures of white-owned farms in Zimbabwe.

A significant outcome of globalization has been the formation of transnational advocacy networks, defending global norms and values in the areas of human rights, minority rights, democracy, and the protection of the environment, which together have been paving the ground for the emergence of a global civil society. Transnational advocacy networks have brought together individuals and associations from all over the world in defence of certain highly valued issues. Some of those issues have been truly global in nature, such as global warming. In many cases, though, advocacy groups managed to 'globalize' certain essentially local issues, such as the massacres in Darfur (Sudan) or the mistreatment of the detainees at the Abu Ghraib prison in Iraq. When an issue found its way onto the global agenda, chances increase that it becomes the subject of some sort of 'humanitarian intervention' by the most powerful agents of globalization, including the UN, NATO, transnational companies, the USA, the EU, or INGOs .

We are, as yet, only at the beginnings of a global civil society, which exists mostly in the form of a virtual community enabled by the internet. However, even at this initial stage, a global civil society has played two very significant roles in democracy promotion. First, it has given an unprecedented global 'visibility' to the suppressive policies and atrocities committed by the governments. Secrecy and denial had traditionally been the Chinese Wall behind which authoritarian governments could hide their objectionable actions. New communication technologies, from the internet to cell phones, have made secrets much more difficult to keep. Sooner, rather than later, massacres, tortures, extrajudicial killings, electoral fraud, and other such practices, are likely to find their way onto the global agenda. Misinformation, disinformation, selective information, bad information, and manipulation of all sorts have always been, and probably will always be, with us. This does not, however, refute the fact that the age of secrecy is coming to an end. Governments and oppositions will increasingly have to operate in an environment of abundant information and will not be able to rely on secrecy.

What can we say about the impact of the global civil society on democratization? On this issue we can discern two contrasting views, one optimistic and the other one more cautious and pessimistic. From an optimistic point of view, the growth of a global civil society is seen as helping build social capital, trust and shared values across the globe, facilitating an understanding of the interconnectedness of global problems and their solutions. Global civil society is considered to be a vehicle that spreads ethical norms and values across national boundaries, and that acts as a deterrent for governments who might attempt to violate human rights and freedoms. Pessimists, on the other hand, would argue that transnational advocacy networks avoid the more important but politically sensitive causes, and they turn their attention to

> ### Box 7.3 **Key points**
>
> - A significant outcome of globalization has been the formation of transnational advocacy networks, defending global norms and values in the areas of human rights, minority rights, democracy, and the protection of the environment, which together have paved the ground for the emergence of a global civil society.
>
> - Global civil society is considered to be a vehicle that spreads ethical norms and values across national boundaries and that acts as a deterrent for governments who might attempt to violate human rights and freedoms.
>
> - Sometimes transnational advocacy networks avoid important but politically sensitive causes and restrict their attention to the less important but generally acceptable issues. If they do so, their efforts fall short of challenging the unfair distribution of political power and economic resources over the globe.

the less important but generally acceptable issues. As such, they do not make a real difference because they do not challenge the unfair distribution of political power and economic resources over the globe. This anti-political attitude of transnational advocacy networks stem from two factors. One factor is that they often ask for funding and understanding from the dominant actors of the global system, such as superpowers, supranational bodies, and multinational corporations, which leads them to compromise with their supporters' conservative agendas. The second factor is that they want to appeal to as broad an audience as possible, which forces them to choose mainstream discourses and overly general issues.

Conclusion

Is democracy possible within the borders of a single state? Or should democracy, if it is to survive in any country, become a transnational system, sustained by supranational agencies? A similar debate had been made in regard to socialism in the early twentieth century. Shortly after the Russian revolution, one hot topic of debate among the theorists of socialism of the day was 'socialism in one country' vs. 'socialism as a universal system'. A realist camp, among which were figures like Nikolai Bukharin and Joseph Stalin, were staunchly defending the idea of consolidating socialism in Russia only, even at the expense of revising some of the most well-known texts of Marxism, in which the founders of the movement talked of a universal, at least pan-European, proletarian revolution and socialism as a world-system. The idealist camp, first defended by V.I. Lenin himself, and then by Aleksandr Zinoviev and most notably by Leon Trotsky in his theory of Permanent Revolution, argued that unless the socialist revolution had been spread to at least the advanced countries of Europe, by the force of arms if necessary, and a socialist European and then world system had been established, a socialist regime could not survive in Russia or, for that matter, in any other single state.

The question that we are facing today in relation to democracy bears some resemblances to that historical question of the socialist revolution: Can an advanced democratic regime, fully equipped with influential participatory mechanisms, and based on a comprehensive array of individual or human rights, survive in any single country, unless democracy becomes the global norm, perhaps eventually supported by accountable and competent supranational authorities? In its early years, democracy was a rather simple system, involving the guarantee of basic rights and liberties and **participation** in free and fair elections at the level of the nation state or below. Democracy today has become a much more complex system. One dimension of its complexity has to do with an immensely widened and detailed system of rights, going far beyond the basic rights and liberties of the early days. Rights today cover individuals, ethnic groups, age groups, **gender** groups, foreigners living in a country, animals, and the eco-system, and encompass a whole array of political, economic, social and cultural matters. Parallel to the widening and deepening in the area of rights, participation too grew far more advanced than its rather uncomplicated early meaning of free and fair elections. Today, democratic participation covers many more areas, including decision-making at the work place, in schools, local communities, political parties, and various civic associations. What is more, direct democracy, which had been in the past not feasible but for very small polities, has now become manageable for large populations, thanks to the advances in information and communications technologies. What we are observing is the evolution of democracy to a deepened, advanced and complex political system. As a result, one can argue that a single country, however large and rich it may be, might not possess the economic resources, political institutions, social capital, and cultural traditions required to sustain such a regime. Hence, disciplinary mechanisms of international or supranational bodies, to which individual democratic states would pool part of their sovereignties, may be necessary for the democratic regime in each state to have the best chances to survive at its most highly developed stage.

QUESTIONS

1. By the early 1990s, theorists in the fields of international relations and comparative politics began taking into account the international dimensions of democratization. What were the important changes in the international arena that led the theorists to pay more attention to the international dimensions of democratization?

2. Is a supranational global authority needed to promote and sustain democratization at a global scale?

3. Various authors have shown that the diffusion of democratic ideals and institutions across the nations in a world region has been one of the most effective international dimensions of democratization. What could be the specific ways and means of the diffusion of democracy?

4. Imagine an authoritarian country being surrounded by democratizing neighbours. What could be, for this country, the economic, political, and security costs of remaining authoritarian in an increasingly democratizing regional environment?

5. The state in country C faces charges of human rights violations while trying to keep radical opposition forces under control. C's interests in the international system incentivize it to forge an alliance with democratic states. However, such an alliance is made conditional upon C's improvement of its human rights record. Under these circumstances, what kind of policies can C follow in the domestic and international arenas?

6. How do superpowers such as the USA and transnational unions such as the EU behave when their particular political, economic or military interests come into conflict with the outcomes of democracy promotion abroad? How should they behave?

Visit the Online Resource Centre that accompanies this book for additional questions to accompany each chapter, and a range of other resources: <www.oxfordtextbooks. co.uk/orc/haerpfer/>.

FURTHER READING

Grugel, J. (1999) (ed.), *Democracy without Borders: Transnationalization and Conditionality in New Democracies* (London: Routledge). This book analyses the transnational dimensions of democratization, by putting the emphasis on the role of civil society and non-state actors. The chapters examine selected cases from Europe, Africa, and Latin America.

Yilmaz, H. (2002), 'External-Internal Linkages in Democratization: Developing an Open Model of Democratic Change', *Democratization*, 9/2: 67–84. This article presents an open model of democratization for the semi-peripheral states of the international system. It introduces two new external variables: the expected external costs of suppression and toleration. It then applies the open model to the cases of political change in Spain, Portugal and Turkey in the aftermath of the Second World War.

Pevehouse, J. C. (2002), 'Democracy from the Outside-in? International Organizations and Democratization', *International Organization*, 56/3: 515–49. This article explores the linkages between membership in regional international organizations and democratization. It discusses which organizations should be expected to be associated with democratic transitions. It also presents a statistical test of the major arguments it has developed.

Munck, R. (2006), 'Global Civil Society: Royal Road or Slippery Path?', *Voluntas - International Journal of Voluntary and Non-profit Organisations*, 6/3: 325–32. This article offers a critical discussion of the dominant views that global civil society has become an important mechanism for global democratization. It argues that these approaches depoliticize global civil society and make it the social wing of neoliberal globalization. It calls for bringing progressive politics back in the global social movements.

Carothers, T. (2007), *US Democracy Promotion During and After Bush*. Washington, D.C.: Carnegie Endowment, Carnegie Endowment Report, September 2007. Available at <www. carnegieendowment.org>. This report offers a critical discussion of the US democracy promotion under President George W. Bush. It argues that Under George W. Bush, US democracy promotion has been widely discredited through its association with American military intervention. It also claims that beyond the Middle East US foreign policy is primarily driven by economic and security interests. It argues that the success of US democracy promotion requires ending the close association of democracy promotion with military intervention and by strengthening the core institutional sources of democracy assistance.

Dimitrova, A. and Pridham, G. (2004), 'International Actors and Democracy Promotion In Central And Eastern Europe: The Integration Model And Its Limits', *Democratization*, 11/5: 91–112. This article focuses on the influence of the European Union in the process of democratization in Central and Eastern European states. It argues that the EU model of democracy promotion through integration has been more successful in fostering democracy than the efforts of other international organizations in other parts of the world. The weakness of the model is that it has limited potential when encountering defective democracies with little chance of becoming EU members.

IMPORTANT WEBSITES

<www.carnegieendowment.org> The web site of the Carnegie Endowment publishes important articles on US democracy promotion.

<www.brookings.edu> The Brookings Institution website includes many useful commentaries on the successes, as well as failures, of the US democracy promotion in the Middle East and other regions of the world.

<http://usinfo.state.gov> The website of the US State Department offers the official US views on democracy promotion.

<www.alde.eu> ALDE stands for the Alliance of Liberals and Democrats for Europe. It brings together liberal and democratic members of the European Parliament. This website includes many useful articles on the European democracy promotion.

<www.fride.org/publications> FRIDE is a think tank based in Madrid that aims to provide innovative thinking on Europe's role in the international arena. Its research interests cover the areas of peace and security, human rights, democracy promotion, and development and humanitarian aid.

<http://ec.europa.eu> The website of the European Commission's department of External Relations and European Neighbourhood Policy offers the official EU views on democracy promotion.

8 Democracy, Business, and the Economy

Patrick Bernhagen

Overview

This chapter explores the relationship between democratization and the economy. After an historical overview of the emergence of capitalist democracy the chapter introduces some general problems of the relationship between democracy and capitalism, drawing out the main areas in which the two systems condition each other. This is followed by an analysis of the role of business in democratizing countries. Lastly, the intricacies of combining major political and economic reforms are discussed.

Introduction

With the demise of the Soviet Union and the communist **regimes** in Central and Eastern Europe in the late 1980s and early 1990s, capitalist democracy has virtually become the only game in town except in most countries around the world. The atrocities, human rights abuses, economic inefficiencies, and numerous other failings of these systems that were gradually uncovered was such that almost any other politico-economic system would be deemed preferable. With feudal and kinship-based economic structures restricted to all but the most primitive agrarian societies, capitalism remains the sole contender. For the foreseeable future at least, there seems to be no alternative to some form of market economy.

How has it come to this? In Central and Eastern Europe and the former Soviet Union, dual transitions have taken place. Political dictatorships, usually under the leadership of communist parties, were replaced with democratic institutions. Simultaneously, planned economies were replaced with the capitalist institutions of private property and the market. The communist countries thus faced a comprehensive transformation of their entire political-economic edifice. But in other regions too transformations have not been restricted to a narrowly conceived political realm. While many of the countries that have recently undergone a democratic transformation have already had capitalist market economies in place when embarking on the process of democratization, transitions in Southern Europe, Latin America, and East Asia have also taken place in the context of economic restructuring. The reforms have overwhelmingly tended to be in a neoliberal direction aimed at marketization, privatization, and free trade. Thus, both political and economic reform appear to be part and parcel of the global wave of democratization.

This conjuncture of democratization and marketization is not new. In historical perspective, democratization and the rise of capitalism have accompanied each other. But their common path has been far from smooth and the relationship between the travelling companions is frequently not a very harmonious one. The main reason for this is that the two systems operate according to distinct mechanisms and embody different normative ideals. Democracy has already been defined in Chapter 2 as a political system in which rulers are held accountable to citizens by means of free and fair elections. Following Adam Przeworski (1991: 101), capitalism is defined as 'any economic system in which (1) the optimal division of labour is so advanced that most people produce for the needs of others, (2) the means of production and the capacity to work are owned privately, and (3) there are markets in both.'

While capitalism and democracy equally rest on the enlightenment principles of individual freedom, rationality and equality, capitalist democracy entails a fundamental tension between the property rights of owners and the personal rights of citizens—owners and non-owners alike (Bowles and Gintis 1986: 32). This is evident with respect to democracy's normative principles of equal **participation** and the **accountability** of leaders (see Ch. 3). First, democracy entitles citizens to equal political rights by virtue of their being citizens. In democratic doctrine, it does not matter if someone

---

Box 8.1 **Capitalism**

Like democracy, capitalism has been defined in many ways. Some conceptualizations emphasize private enterprise, while others highlight production for competitive markets. Marxists focus on the separation of labour from the means of production. While all of these elements are important, they all also constitute ideal types that will never be perfectly matched in the real world. All existing capitalist systems allow for some role of public enterprise, deliberately restrict competition in some markets, or have room for some form or another of collective employee ownership. But none of these deviations from the ideal type mean that the respective systems are not primarily capitalist in orientation. The emphasis on 'orientation' is captured by

Charles Lindblom's (1977: 94–5) term, 'private enterprise market-oriented systems', which encapsulates all the above elements without insisting on perfection. The terms 'business' and 'business actor' denote firms, their owners and senior managers, their public affairs representatives and in-house lobbyists, as well as trade associations and peak organizations. Of course, in reality no two businesses are the same, and neither business associations nor individual firms are usually unitary actors. Moreover, researchers sometimes need to distinguish between business associations, firms, their owners, and their managers. In this chapter as well as elsewhere in this book, such distinctions will be made only where the context requires them.

is male or female, black or white, or rich or poor. All that matters for the entitlement to effective and equal democratic participation is for a person to be a citizen and, usually, to be above a certain minimum age. Entitlement according to capitalist doctrine is also independent of race or sex. But it is fundamentally linked to money and private property, which in capitalist systems are unequally distributed as a matter of principle: if income, wealth, and ownership in productive assets were to be kept as equal as the right to vote, any capitalist economic system would instantly grind to a halt.

Second, democracy demands that leaders are held accountable to citizens, typically through some form of free and fair elections. Capitalism makes no such pretence. With very few exceptions, decisions in business enterprises are made by the owners or by their appointed managers. At most, leaders of business enterprises are accountable to shareholders. But unlike in the democratic **state**, the subjects to managerial decisions, employees, are not normally entitled to elect the decisionmakers. Similar to leadership change in stable autocracies, control of business enterprises changes hands through decisions made by an oligarchic clique. This leads to the paradoxical situation that political democracy is occupying new territory in more and more countries around the globe, while business enterprises continue to be governed like 'command economies in miniature' (Moene 1993: 400).

These contradictions between the way political and economic matters are organized in capitalist democracies have important implications for political, economic and social life in general and for the success of democratic transformation and **consolidation** in particular.

Capitalism and Democracy: The Historical Connection

According to a central claim of modernization theory, economic development and democratization are both part of the advance of modernity (see Ch. 6). Once a society reaches sufficient levels of wealth, technology, education, bureaucratic capacity, and a proliferation of individual social and political skills, its citizens become dissatisfied with paternalistic political authority and demand popular sovereignty (Rostow 1961). This leads to the erosion of traditional political institutions and, eventually, to democratization. In this view, the global spread of democracy is an historical inevitability; its driving force is capitalist development. This relationship between the two is depicted in Figure 8.1.

Evidence that higher levels of democracy are associated with higher economic development is shown in Chapter 5 (Figure 5.2). Indeed, historically, when market economies have been successful over a period of time, pressure for democratization has often followed soon. And if newly democratized countries continue to prosper economically, democracy is likely to survive. In the words of Seymour Martin Lipset (1959: 75): 'the more well-to-do a nation, the greater the chances that it will sustain democracy.' This assigns capitalism a pivotal role in the global spread of democracy, as no other socioeconomic system appears to be equally capable of producing social wealth.

According to Adam Przeworski *et al.* (2000: 88–92), the real contribution of economic development is not so much that it causes democratization, but that it increase the survival chances of political regimes. In this view, regardless of what prompts democratization, if more and more countries continue to develop economically, and economically developed democracies are more stable than other countries, over time the world should become increasingly populated by wealthy democracies Przeworski *et al.* (2000).

While modernization theory suggests a rather harmonious relationship between the expansion of economic liberties and democratic political rights, others have emphasized the importance of

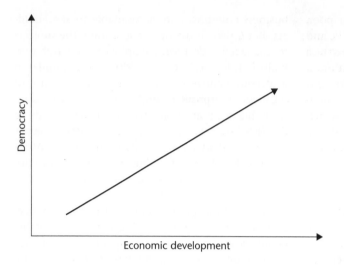

Fig 8.1. The relationship between economic development and democracy according to modernization theory

class conflict in the connection between capitalism and democracy. For Rueschemeyer, Stephens and Stephens (1992), capitalist development favoured democratization primarily because it transformed the class structure, strengthening urban labourers, small business owners, and middle-class professionals, while weakening the landed upper class. But of the former, the working classes were the last to gain political representation, and they had to wrest it of the more privileged groups in protracted and often violent struggles. Sometimes these were related to inter-state conflict. According to Göran Therborn (1977: 17–23), both world wars offered the politically excluded classes opportunities to gain political representation, either in the form of external allies or because the ruling elites traded political concessions to the lower classes in exchange for support for the national war effort.

Constitutional and republican forms of government were originally developed to meet the political demands of aspiring commercial classes. In England, the Glorious Revolution of 1688–89 established the Bill of Rights, greater parliamentary authority, and judicial independence. It also put the Whigs, who later developed into the political party of the ascending bourgeoisie, in a position to break up the monopoly rights of chartered trading cartels—a crucial step in the establishment of market capitalism in England. But while the revolution thus broadened access to political power from monarchs to aristocracies and then to propertied citizens and removed

barriers to the development of modern commerce and trade, it did not actually implement democracy. Rather, it kick-started a process of the gradual widening of participation in politics to the majority of the adult population. In Britain, and elsewhere in Europe, this process took another two centuries to eventually secure the expansion of civil and political rights for the benefit of substantial groups of the population. All along, capitalist entrepreneurs and liberal philosophers and statesmen have watched with scepticism, and often with outright hostility. And they had good reasons to be sceptical. The gradual extension of the franchise from propertied men to all adults went hand in hand with significant curtailments of capitalist property rights, redistribution, and the emergence of the welfare state (Macpherson 1973: 148).

Nonetheless, capitalist development ultimately contributed to democratization, if only to de-radicalize the lower classes and avert violent revolution and threats to private property. In this view, capitalist elites traded political concessions for continued control over the economy. Daron Acemoglu and James Robinson (2000) demonstrate how wealthy elites in Britain, France, Sweden, and Germany acceded to extensions of the franchise to ordinary people, even though doing so led to higher taxation of their wealth and incomes. In this view, conceding democratization was a price elites found worth paying to ward off the threat of a more violent overthrow of the still nascent capitalist order.

While the positive relationship between capitalist development and democracy is quite robust, there are a number of notable exceptions. First, countries like Botswana and India, as well as more recently Ghana and Namibia, sustain consolidated democracies without significant capitalist development. India, for example, has enjoyed stable democracy for over half a century but has only recently begun to develop a more advanced capitalist economy. The majority of the workforce in India is still employed in agriculture, poverty is endemic, and for much of the post-war period the economy has been under tight government control. This exception is sometimes being explained by reference to the British colonial history. While the colonial rulers at times relied heavily on the physical repression of national liberation movements, at other times their reaction to colonial discontent involved the establishment of institutions of representative democracy and partial self rule (Smith 1978). The Government of India Act of 1919 created a parliamentary assembly for the country; and a follow up legislative act in 1935 laid the foundations for what later became India's federal system of government.

Thus, it can be argued that former British colonies were institutionally better prepared for democratic rule than territories controlled by other colonial powers such as France, Portugal or Spain (Bollen and Jackman 1985: 444–5). Moreover, British colonialism may have contributed indirectly to democratization on a global scale. While French, Portuguese, and Spanish colonial empires transplanted their own feudal and absolutist structures into their colonies, British colonialism was inextricably interwoven with the country's own transition to capitalism (Wood 2003). The settlers, merchants, and traders who colonized North America were entrepreneurs, for whom self-government and parliamentary representation were ideal means of protecting their markets and property from the arbitrary rule of colonial governors and rulers in the metropolis. The slogan, 'no taxation without representation' was coined to express the North American colonists' frustration with their lack of participation in political decisions—a frustration that eventually led to the American Revolution. Thus, whether it was through the installation of representative institutions or the export of capitalist entrepreneurs,

British imperialism likely has had a positive effect on democratization around the world.

Second, there are numerous countries that combine highly successful capitalist economies with the partial or complete absence of democratic institutions. The famous economic tigers of the 1980s—Hong Kong, Singapore, South Korea and Taiwan—are cases in point, as are the Brazilian dictatorship between 1964 and 1985, or China from the 1990s onward. Brazil, South Korea, and Taiwan eventually became democracies, although democratization did not follow smoothly on economic development. In fact, political liberalization in Brazil only set in when economic development began to slow down. However, in the light of modernization theory it makes sense that countries first modernize economically. Only when economic development has generated sufficient levels of educated, urban-dwelling citizens will pressure for democratization build up and eventual come to the boil—an image that has been projected vividly on to TV screens around the world by South Korean student protesters in the 1980s.

But the successful combination of authoritarian rule and market capitalism in some countries also suggests that the relationship between economic development and democratization implied by modernization theory, although overall positive, may not be linear. Among other things, this has to do with the triangular relationship between economic development, inequality, and democracy. According to Robert Dahl (1971), democratization is inhibited by high economic inequality for two reasons. First, economic resources can be translated into political resources. Concentrated economic power may thus enable elites to prevent political reforms that extend rights and liberties to others. Second, economic inequalities can generate resentment and frustrations among the disadvantaged, thereby eroding the sense of community and **legitimacy** upon which democracy is often thought to rest.

According to the Kuznets (1955) hypothesis, inequality increases in the initial phase of the development process and only starts to decrease again once a critical average income is attained. This non-linear shape of the effect of development on inequality is represented by the inverted U, or 'Kuznets curve' depicted in Figure 8.2. The resulting increase in inequalities can lead to class conflict that is too severe to be accommodated within democratic institutions,

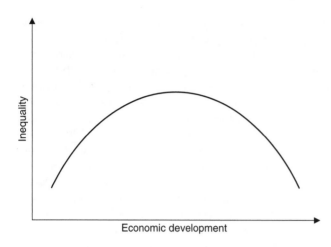

Fig 8.2 The Kuznets curve of economic development and inequality

giving rise either to revolution or to military intervention and conservative **authoritarianism** protective of the property rights of the dominant classes. It is also plausible that people find improvements in their material well-being to be of overarching importance, and that demands for more wide-ranging political and civil freedoms associated with democratic government do not arise until higher levels of income and education are reached.

There is some empirical evidence for a relationship between economic inequality and democracy, but the evidence points into conflicting directions. On the one hand, a certain degree of inequality might be required for the initiation of democracy (Midlarsky 1997). If everybody was more or less equally well off under autocracy, few people might expect to improve their lot if the country became more democratic. On the other hand, very large income inequality affects democracy negatively, and often to such an extent as to counteract any positive influence on democracy of economic development (Muller 1995). At any

> ### Box 8.2 **Key points**
>
> - At present, alternatives to capitalism appear discredited.
>
> - Capitalism emphasizes property rights, while democracy emphasizes personal rights.
>
> - Historically, capitalism and democracy evolved together, but it is not clear how exactly development of the one affected the other.
>
> - Capitalism produces inequality, which can both stimulate and hamper democratization.

rate, introducing the Kuznets relationship between economic development and inequality into the association between capitalist development and democracy is compatible with the claim of modernization theory that democratization is most closely associated with mature capitalist societies.

What Capitalism Does for Democracy

The economist Milton Friedman (1962: 9) insisted that there has been no society 'that has been marked by a large measure of political freedom and that has not used something comparable to a free market to organize the bulk of economic activity.' This, Friedman suggested, is because in a market society

the means for production, and hence for people's livelihoods, are owned privately. The ability to maintain a livelihood independently of the state is an essential precondition for citizens to critically confront the state—and hence to participate freely in politics. Moreover, capitalist entities themselves—

above all firms and trade associations—are organizations of civil society in which people pursue common objectives and work out solutions to common problems. A particular role is played by **business associations**. According to Wolfgang Streeck and Philippe C. Schmitter (1985: 15), these associations can bolster democracy by enlarging a country's 'repertoire of policy alternatives', enabling it to respond flexibly to new problems without having to undergo dramatic changes. The role of business associations is in an area of **governance** 'between' states and markets. Markets frequently fail to provide collective goods necessary for economic growth and development. It is up to governments to rectify these failures, but they too can be deficient in their efforts to do so. Business associations can help to overcome this dilemma by providing self-regulation of industries and securing the provision of collective goods such as industry standards, collective bargaining, technology transfer, training or market information to members. On behalf of their members, associations also attempt to influence the political process by means of election campaigning, lobbying, and consultative functions in state-sponsored policy fora. In **corporatist** systems, they often take on quasi-public functions in areas such as industry regulation or training.

While business associations form part of civil society, their activities are not restricted to democratic countries. In Singapore, as well as in pre-democratic South Korea and Taiwan, business associations played considerable roles in the formulation of government policy (Doner, Schneider and Wilson 1998: 135–6). In the context of newly democratized countries, business associations can contribute to political openness, enhance government effectiveness, and weaken antidemocratic alliances. Furthermore, to the extent that business associations are engaged in sectoral self-regulation and the resolution of disputes, they can unburden the political system by depoliticizing distributional conflicts between capital and labour—which can be vital for young democracies struggling to respond to a plethora of urgent tasks (Doner, Schneider and Wilson 1998: 137).

The capitalist way of running the economy also bestow on businessmen and women a considerable amount of political power and influence. As in capitalist societies their number is relatively small compared to consumers or workers, capitalists' political clout can be disproportionate. From the vantage point of democratic governance, which envisages political power to be held by the many and not the few, this is highly problematic. Although the problem is not new—Karl Marx and Friedrich Engels claimed in the middle of the nineteenth century that '[t]he executive of the modern state is but a committee for managing the common affairs of the whole bourgeoisie' (Marx and Engels 1977 [1848]: 223)—it has not yet been satisfactorily resolved. Contemporary democratic theorists such as Robert Dahl (1989: 324–8) continue to be concerned that capitalists' political power might undermine political equality, democratic accountability, and the legitimacy of public policy. But just how are business people supposed to achieve disproportionate influence in democratic political systems? After all, in a democracy, public officials must respond to a variety of demands, which constrains the ability of business actors to translate their economic power into political power. At least seven different mechanisms can be distinguished that provide the owners and managers of firms with political influence not equally available to other people.

First, substantial disparities in income and wealth are inevitable in a capitalist system. This leads to political inequalities at the level of the individual. In every liberal democracy, people with higher income and better and longer education are significantly more likely to vote in elections or contact politicians than people of less income and education (Verba, Schlozman and Brady 1995). As businesspeople are also more likely to be on the advantaged end of unequal distributions of income and wealth, they tend to be better able to make effective use of their democratic rights.

Second, a majority of people have to work for business people in order to make a living. In doing so they subject themselves to the latter's authoritative power over decisionmaking within the firm. C. B. Macpherson (1973: 10) claims that this amounts to a continuous net transfer of part of the powers of some people to others, and thereby to a diminution of the human essence of those from whom power is being transferred. It also contradicts the enlightenment principle that individual freedom is preferable to authoritative allocation of work and reward (Macpherson 1973: 19).

Third, as a numerically relatively small group, business can be more effective than others to organize politically. According to Mancur Olson (1965), a relatively small number of group members combined

Box 8.3 **The Politics of the Revolving Door**

The revolving door between business and politics can swing in both directions. In the UK, there is an established revolving door between the Foreign Office and petroleum firms such as Shell. In Peru, several business leaders gained cabinet posts in the time of the Fujimori administration, including the portfolios of industry, economy and finance, and foreign relations; two former leaders of the Peruvian Confederation of Private Entrepreneurial Institutions even made it to prime minister (Durand 1995). Some travel the revolving door full-circle: Starting out as Defence Secretary in the George H.W. Bush administration, the US Vice-President Richard Cheney later became chief executive of the transnational energy company Halliburton in 1995, only to find his way back into the federal administration in 2000 under his former boss' son, George W. Bush. After Mexican business leaders played a significant role in renewing the country's political elite, some businessmen-turned-politician–turned-businessmen now ride the revolving door on a global scale. For example, the former vice-governor of the Central Bank of Mexico, Francisco Gil Díaz, became CEO of telecommunications firm Avantel before returning to public service as Secretary of Finance in the cabinet of Vicente Fox. He has recently found a new professional home as a corporate director of HSBC in London.

with a concentration of benefits from collective action gives business much stronger incentives to organize for political action than larger groups, such as consumers or taxpayers, over whom both costs and benefits are more widely dispersed. In a pluralist society it is open to all organized interests—business or not—to try and advance their political goals by legal means of lobbying, campaign contributions, or advertising. Because of the logic of collective action, business is often more effective in this respect than other groups. This imbalance of group power may induce politicians to set up government agencies to look primarily after business interests. The result is a 'captured' bureaucracy that implements policies—including subsidies, barriers to market entry, or price guarantees—which are designed for industry's benefit (Stigler 1975: 114).

Fourth, in capitalist democracies there is plenty of social interaction between business leaders and political leaders. As a result, political and economic elites share a common outlook and preferences on many political issues (Domhoff 1998). These communalities are often forged from an early age, for instance in the elite preparatory schools and the Ivy League universities in the USA, in the 'public' schools and the Oxbridge colleges in the UK, or in the Ecole Nationale d'Administration in France. The ties between economic and political elites are further reinforced by the politics of the 'revolving door' (Salisbury *et al.* 1989). This involves private firms hiring former senior civil servants, regulators, or cabinet ministers for their technical expertise and social connections. Once in their new private sector positions, the former policymakers use their connections and influence to further their new employers' political interests as well as using their expertise to advise them on government relations and regulatory matters.

Fifth, to advance their political ends, business actors can attempt to influence public opinion (Page, Shapiro and Dempsey 1987). The public is inclined to listen to their messages because in a capitalist society matters concerning business and the economy are potentially of great concern to everyone. Expertise and policy advice is often produced by business-friendly think tanks such as the Heritage Foundation and the American Enterprise Institute in the USA, or the Centre for Policy Studies and the Adam Smith Institute in the UK (Smith 2000: 189–96). This enables business to manipulate public opinion in such a way that business interests will seldom be vitally challenged in politics. But even though, business actors like other political actors too, have been known to lie on occasion, the notion of manipulation should not be misconstrued to mean conscious deceit. Rather, it is important for the credibility of business-friendly political messages that they are genuinely believed by those that produce them.

Sixth, the capitalist organization of the economy imposes structural constraints on the ability of elected officials to deliver policies. In liberal democracies, voters tend to rely on economic evaluations more than on other signals in assessing the competence of politicians and deciding which party or candidate to vote for (Lewis-Beck and Stegmaier 2000). If a government presides over a declining economy, voters are more likely to support the opposition. This is referred to as economic voting and plays a crucial part for the structural power of business. According to Mitchell (1997: 62),

[e]conomic voting ensures that governments are acutely sensitive to variations in the major macroeconomic indicators. The significance to political leaders of the signals from the economy places business institutions and membership groups in a very strong position in the policy struggle.

Governments are well advised to anticipate the logic of economic voting in their policy decisions. But the strength of this mechanism can vary according to a number of contextual factors. For example, voters might find it more difficult to assign blame or praise for deteriorating or improving economic conditions when institutional responsibilities are blurred. This might make economic voting in the presidential or semi-presidential systems in many Latin American or Central and East European countries less likely. Moreover, in new democracies it may take some time for stable patterns of voting behaviour to emerge. Following a profound institutional shock—the end of the Franco dictatorship—it took nearly two decades for Spanish opposition parties to gain sufficient credibility to give leverage to the economic vote (Fraile 2002). However, recent research suggests that citizens in Latin American presidential democracies as well as voters in new democracies of Central and Eastern Europe use their economic assessments to evaluate the performance of incumbent governments (Gélineau 2007; Tavits 2005).

Because investment decisions in a capitalist system are mainly private, public officials cannot risk a capital strike by proposing policies that threaten the owners of capital. Aware that businesspeople can effectively veto policies that they perceive as harmful, governments carefully avoid such policies. As a result, business leaders enjoy a structurally privileged position that enables them to secure favourable political outcomes even if they abstain from political action (Lindblom 1977: 170–88). Most government

policies require funds and are thus ultimately contingent on the availability of sufficient tax receipts. Policies that make investment less attractive may eventually reduce the tax base and undermine the government's chances to achieve its various other policy goals. At its most fundamental level, the very existence of the state depends on the economy and its performance. This structural dependence of the state on capital is particularly significant for young democracies, as economic performance is one of the most important correlates of consolidation (Diamond, Hartlyn and Linz 1999: 46–8).

Seventh, business enjoys first-hand access to a range of information that is crucial to the successful designing of public policy, e.g. technical data, information on production costs, or company strategy. As much of this information is not directly available to governments, business actors can use their informational advantage to affect politicians' beliefs about the consequences of policy. These informational privileges add to capitalists' ability of obtaining desired political outcomes through lobbying. But such information asymmetries cannot be used without caution. Business actors are often prevented from abusing their information privileges as doing so might undermine their credibility—an important resource in politics (Bernhagen 2007).

To the extent that these factors provide business actors with disproportionate political power, they undermine democratic equality and legitimacy. Furthermore, they may thwart the efficiencies of the market economy and hamper society's economic development (Olson 1982). While business associations can perform a positive role in addressing problems of both market and state failure, the same associations can and do support rent-seeking behaviour of their members, facilitate price-fixing and other anti-competitive behaviour, raise entry barriers to new competitors, and lobby policymakers on behalf of a group that is already more powerful than others in society.

No matter what disproportionate political power businesspeople may enjoy in capitalist democracies, their political influence may grow even stronger with economic **globalization**. Increasing global integration of markets may further limit the range of policy choices available to democratically elected leaders.

From the 1980s onwards, increasingly unrestrained movement of capital between nations has the potential to reduce the policy autonomy of governments while strengthening the political bargaining power of capitalists. Under these conditions, political parties find it more difficult to respond to citizens' preferences in a consistent manner; their policies become increasingly similar, depriving citizens of an essential tool for making meaningful choices at elections.

Coping with globalization might also make social-democratic welfare policies or demand-side management less feasible. Because large companies and transnational corporations have the option to shift or outsource production to low-wage countries, union bargaining power relative to employers is weakened, undermining an important countervailing force to business interests. The need for nation states to create profitable environments for investors may induce them to forgo necessary but costly policies, thus affecting the 'quality of democracy' (Morlino 2004) by leading to a 'race to the bottom' of social, environmental, and health and safety-related standards between countries.

A rolling-back of the welfare state due to sharpened constraints on governments' ability to raise revenue would make it increasingly difficult for governments to compensate globalization's losers. To the extent that in this way globalization leads to the erosion of

> ### Box 8.4 **Key points**
>
> - Market capitalism enables citizens to be economically independent from the state.
>
> - Firms and business associations are civil society organizations that fulfil a number of useful social tasks.
>
> - Business actors avail of a plethora of power resources that are not, or not equally, available to non-business interests, enabling business to dominate politics.
>
> - Economic globalization can restrict political choice and erode the capacities of states.

the power and capacity of the state, democracy itself is imperilled, because the state is the primary locus of democratic arrangements in the modern world (Cerny 1999: 19). In extreme cases, these problems can lead to a reversal of democratization. 'Flight of capital' has been blamed for contributing to the overthrow of the liberal governments of France in 1925, and again in 1938, as well as playing a role in the development of a successful fascist movement in Germany in the 1930s (Polanyi 2001 [1944]: 25).

What Democracy Does for Business

Every state has to create an institutional environment for private economic activity. And every state also has to interfere with that activity to a greater or lesser extent. The only exceptions are communist systems in which the bulk of economic assets are either owned directly by the state or organized in some other form of public ownership. But where markets and private property provide the building blocks of economic activity, they do so because a political authority exists that grants, respects and protects these rights and thereby creates the institution of the market. Markets are not part of some 'natural' order of affairs that arises spontaneously in the absence of political authority. Without authority, including some form of judicial authority or arbitration, markets are virtually inconceivable. For

them to exist and operate, effective rights of private property have to be in place. The origins of these rights cannot be found in moral principles or natural law; they are the outcome of political decisions (Sened 1997). Institutions and the rights they promote are unlikely to survive unless they are designed and enforced by central agencies with some monopolistic power over the use of force—i.e. by governments. As Thomas Hobbes (1996 [1651]: 101) wrote 350 years ago, 'where there is no coërceive Power erected, that is, where there is no Common-wealth, there is no Propriety'.

But governments cannot be counted upon to produce and uphold property rights unless they can expect political and economic benefits in return. Every government, democratic or authoritarian, depends on some level of popular support and on economic resources in the form of surplus revenues (in non-communist systems, this means tax receipts).[1] Governments grant property rights to induce more efficiency and productivity. They hope to make tangible benefits from excess productivity through increased tax revenues and enhanced political support from citizens made better off through these rights. To maximize incentives for investment and production, political leaders have to make credible commitments that investments will not be expropriated in the future. The mechanism by which rulers can make the necessary commitment to constraining their powers is constitutional government (Brennan and Buchanan 1980).

Even with property rights guaranteed, investment and production can still be discouraged below optimal levels if their fruits are taxed too highly. The specific constitutional arrangement to address this problem is parliamentary representation. This is particularly appropriate if societal interests are heterogeneous. The members of a diverse constituency require some form of representative body to bargain with the government on their behalf over rights and tax rates. According to Douglass North and Barry Weingast (1989), the Glorious Revolution in England implemented just these changes. By limiting the Crown's legislative and judicial powers, it not only constrained its ability to alter rules at will, it also removed the Crown's power to set tax rates unilaterally. In this way, democratic institutions can protect capitalist entrepreneurs from excessive taxation.

Parliamentary lawmaking, competitive elections, and the expansion of the franchise all lead to a broadening of the socioeconomic basis of the government. This reduces the likelihood that a narrow set of interests will be able to seize control over legislation and markets. Special interest groups might be able to get around this by forming coalitions to aid each other in rent-seeking, but in no other political system will they find this as difficult as in a democracy. Moreover, the rule of law and judicial autonomy prevent government agents and bureaucrats from undermining or circumventing the decisions of parliament. Thus, majority rule and the rule of law provide strong barriers to the degeneration of capitalism into a corrupt network of state-sanctioned monopolies and political patronage. In addition, the civil liberties required for the effective functioning of democratic government, in particular freedom of speech and assembly, are also part of the canon of civil liberties essential for free commercial activity (Olson 1993). As a consequence, liberal democracy provides a uniquely favourable institutional setting for market capitalism.

All of this suggests that investors should flock to democracies. A good indicator of the extent to which a country provides a welcoming context for doing business is the inflow of foreign direct investment (FDI). Indeed, many of the countries where democratic reform has stagnated (Belarus, Cambodia, Egypt, Jordan, Malaysia), become entangled in instability or ethnic violence (Pakistan, Kenya) or failed to take off in the first place (Tunisia, Uzbekistan, Vietnam) have seen FDI inflows decrease or stagnate in recent years (UNCTAD 2002). Thus, globally active capitalists seem to prefer to invest in democracies rather than in autocracies. But they would not shy away from engaging in autocracies if they had good reason for it.

A number of non-democratic states have done extremely well in recent decades. Algeria, Sudan, and Kazakhstan have all enjoyed substantial rises in FDI despite their failure to implement democratic institutions. This can be explained by their considerable wealth in natural resources—above all oil. Natural resource abundance favours the development of **'rentier states'**, i.e. states that are highly dependent on external rents produced by a relatively small number of economic actors (Beblawi and Luciani 1987). When rents can be generated from the exploitation of natural resources rather than from production or investment, states are in a position to skim the revenues from resource extraction with relative ease or even to undertake the extracting operations themselves. In either case, they can dispense with the need to tax a wide and diverse constituency of producers. Democratization is a response to popular aspirations summarized in the slogan 'no taxation without representation', and rentier states can do without either (Huntington 1991: 65). This logic can partly explain the persistence of autocracies in very wealthy countries in the Middle East and North Africa, where autocrats are able to finance their rule with oil revenues (see also Ch. 21), but also the democratic shortcomings in Nigeria, Russia and Venezuela. In a statistical analysis, Michael Ross (2001) finds evidence of a negative

correlation between natural resource exports and democracy.

Closely related to the problem of taxation is the problem of redistribution. While democracies may be less likely to extract excessive taxes from producers than autocracies, the fact that democratization empowers the masses may lead to higher taxation of the rich—and hence of capitalists. In all capitalist societies, the actual distributions of income and wealth are skewed in such a way that the person with the median income earns less than the mean income. In democratic societies, policy tends to be dictated by the voter with the median preference (Downs 1957). With respect to income distribution, that voter is of course the one with median income. As a country democratizes and extends political inclusion from the few to the many, the position of the median voter shifts downward in the income distribution. In a full democracy, the median voter will favour a higher tax rate in particular for high income earners and more economic redistribution. Thus, democratization brings more people with below-average incomes to the polls who can then collectively force the government to redistribute income from the rich to the poor (Meltzer and Richard 1981).

This logic is quite compelling. Indeed, the fact that via redistribution democracy can be expected to reduce economic inequality could mean that the Kuznets curve itself is actually caused by democratization, rather than democratization being facilitated by decreasing inequality in the right half of the curve. Analysing the histories of democratic and socioeconomic reform in Britain, France, Germany and Sweden, Acemoglu and Robinson (2000) find that democratization has indeed led to reductions in income inequality. On a wider scale, however, the evidence is more mixed. Recently, Michael Ross (2006) found that democracy may not actually benefit the poor as much as this model suggests. In particular, the bottom 20 per cent of the population in capitalist democracies seem to gain no material benefits at all from democracy. Although unmatched in numbers and equipped with the right to vote, the poor have generally not decided to take away from the rich. This is sometimes referred to as the 'paradox of redistribution'. A number of theories have been put forward to explain the paradox, including some of the mechanisms outlined above by which business interest can dominate the political process in capitalist democracies.[2]

Taxation and redistribution are of course not the only way in which governments interfere with business activities. They regulate a host of areas including environmental outputs, labour rights, corporate governance, consumer rights, and many more. These activates cause both costs and benefits for business. Moreover, governments frequently constitute an important consumer of business products, ranging from paper clips used by government bureaucrats to expensive and technologically advanced weapons systems. In many of these areas of regulation, dictatorships could potentially outperform democracies, which have to respond to the political preferences of consumers, environmentalists and workers. Yet, although autocracies lack these constraints, they generally fail to provide more attractive regularity frameworks for business. The reason for this lies in the distorted information flows in authoritarian systems: Unless ruler receive more or less sincere information from across the spectrum of businesses, they are unable to create a regulatory environment in which diverse commercial activity can flourish.

Box 8.5 Key points

- Liberal democracy provides a favourable institutional setting for market capitalism.

- States that rely heavily on natural resource extraction face fewer demands for democratization.

- Although democracy equips the poor with the right to take away from the rich, they have not done so to an extent that would eradicate existing inequalities.

The Role of Business Actors in Democratic Transition

Having established the advantages and disadvantages that democracy entails for business actors, we are now in a position to analyse the role of economic actors in the context of democratization. In the transitions from communism in Central and Eastern Europe and the former Soviet Union, property rights had to be created where previously there had been none or only a few. But even democratization in countries that already have some form of capitalist market economy can lead to existing property rights being altered, expanded or curtailed. This will generally affect the way in which businesses operate. In the process of democratization, interests other than business gain political leverage that had been suppressed by the *ancien régime*. These include organized labour, as well as consumer groups or environmental activists. The interests of these groups will frequently clash with those of business. Extending political representation to these sectors of society involves the risk that they use their new found political influence to expropriate the wealth of the old elites or regulate business to such an extent that investment and production become less profitable. As a consequence, business leaders have incentives to oppose democratization. This is particularly the case in situations of high levels of income inequality or when investments cannot easily be moved to other countries or sectors.

By definition, the most successful businesses in non-democratic countries have benefited from the autocratic regime. As a result, business actors have frequently opposed democratic transitions or helped to undermine young democracies. For example, business leaders provided the primary bases of civilian support for the authoritarian regimes that replaced democratic governments in Argentina and Chile in the 1960s and 1970s. When Chilean industry leaders and business associations felt they were unable to influence government decisionmaking in the conventional ways outlined above they did not hesitate to support the overthrow of the democratic government by military insurgents in 1973. Likewise, Argentinean business leaders supported the 1976 military coup. Ironically, the ensuing military government's economic policy with its emphasis on economic liberalization and deregulation actually decreased the political influence of Argentine industrialists. According to Carlos Acuña (1995), the emasculation of organized business by the Videla government was a central factor in a process of reorientation, at the end of which Argentine business came to perceive democracy as the lesser evil.

By contrast, Carles Boix (2003) argues that democratic transition is supported by business in countries with moderate levels of economic inequality and in sectors of high asset mobility. Both factors mean that business has only limited threats to face from empowered masses. If inequality is moderate, so will be demands for redistribution. And if firms can credibly threaten to pull their capital out of a country and redeploy elsewhere, voters and politicians alike might quickly realize the structural constraints on how far redistribution is allowed to go. More sceptically, Guillermo O'Donnell and Philippe C. Schmitter (1986: 27) argue that Latin American business actors can be expected to tolerate democratization when they view the authoritarian regime as 'dispensable'.

Some business actors may have suffered various disadvantages when autocracy and would hence be genuinely supportive of democratization. Latin American businesses have at times taken a proactively positive view of democracy (Payne and Bartell 1995: 267–71). This has especially been the case when the authoritarian regime displayed economic incompetence, disregarded the rules of the capitalist game by nationalizing private enterprises, or failed to offer sufficient channels of political influence to business. Thus, in Bolivia and Mexico, business leaders played a significant role in the transition from authoritarianism and one-party rule to democracy. Business actors have also played a proactive part in democratic transitions elsewhere. For example, in the Philippines, the business sector supports the National Movement for Free Elections (NAMFREL), a non-partisan organization which, as its name suggests, works to ensure that elections in the country are free and fair (Villegas 1998: 158).

Thus, business can end up on either side of the struggle for democracy. In the words of Eva Bellin (2000), business leaders in late developing countries are 'contingent democrats' who consistently defend their material interests. They are likely to support democracy when their economic interests put them at odds with the authoritarian state and vice versa. Further, business does not constitute a monolithic bloc. The political preferences of business actors depend on numerous context conditions, including the sector of their activity. This can lead some business actors to oppose authoritarian systems and support opposition parties and civil society organizations while others support the incumbent authoritarian regime. For instance, most Brazilian businesses tended to support the 1964 military coup. But Brazilian auto assemblers opposed the military regime, as its leanings toward foreign capital effectively destroyed their hitherto protected status and undermined their relationship with domestic suppliers (Addis 1999: 108).

Of course, in our globally integrated world, domestic business elites are not the only actors that matter. Democratization can create opportunities as well as challenges for foreign capitalists. To the extent that democratization results in greater protection of private property rights, it can increase the inflow of foreign direct investment (Li and Resnick 2003). While domestic capitalists frequently bear many of the costs of democratization, having to face competition where they enjoyed cosy protection under the old regime, their multinational and foreign counterparts are more often set to benefit from democratization. But the political role of transnational business actors too is more ambiguous. According to Guillermo O'Donnell (1988), transnational businesses in tandem with domestic technocrats and military officers were the main actors in bringing down democratic regimes in Latin America in the 1960s and 1970s. Domestic business leaders were seen mainly as playing only a minor role, perhaps choosing to support the installing of an authoritarian system if they believe that this would protect them from organized labour and left-wing political parties. In the other direction, more recently both transnational businesses and the domestic business community in Mexico supported Vicente Fox's centre-right National Action Party in its successful attempt in June 2000 to end over 70 years of single-party rule by the Institutional Revolutionary Party.

Business is neither intrinsically opposed to democracy nor fundamentally in favour of it. Its preferences with respect to democratic reform are contingent on a variety of factors, including the expected policies of the democratic system and the relative power granted to business actors and countervailing interests, above all organized labour. But even strong labour movements and policies perceived as inimical to business interests do not necessarily trigger an antidemocratic reflex. Rather, the way business actors react to unfavourable circumstances depends to a great extent on their capacity to defend their interests in a peaceful manner by using the channels of interest group influence outlined above. In this sense, business interests can pose a threat to democracy if they are too weak *and* if they are too strong. According to Leigh Payne and Ernest Bartell (1995: 272–80), if business actors are too weak, they may be unable to defend their interests within a pluralist polity or compete in a neoliberal global economy. They may then be tempted to look to a more authoritarian system for protection. The threats to democracy from a private sector that is too strong are of a different nature. If a democratic system offers too many opportunities for business actors to advance their interests, it is likely to enjoy the sustained support of business. But a politically powerful business community can thwart economic development through rent-seeking and induce policymakers to forgo necessary programmes to alleviate poverty, ameliorate severe inequalities, or effectively protect the environment, thereby reducing the quality of democracy.

Assessing the experience with democracy of Chilean business leaders, Ernest Bartell finds that, while content with the prospect that democracy in the country is likely to endure, business continues to maintain strong opposition to any attempts at redistributing wealth by political means in a more equal fashion. Thus, business seems to prefer a restricted scope of democratization (O'Donnell and Schmitter 1986: 69) and consequently a restricted version of democracy. This concerns both the extent of citizen control over political decisionmaking as well as the content of the decisions that are made and thereby the quality of democracy. Moreover, with a view to Latin America, O'Donnell and Schmitter caution that business actors may always reserve the option of supporting an authoritarian solution if democratic politics went too far in contravening their interests. The attempted coup by Venezuelan business leaders in 2002 suggests that this threat has not completely disappeared.

Political and Economic Reform

The global wave of democratization has transformed countries with vastly different politico-economic systems. In Latin America and East Asia, economic reform meant the liberalization of existing capitalist economies. In the postcommunist setting, capitalist economies have been constructed with 'capitalism's opposite in principles and operation' as the point of departure (Bunce 2001: 45). Despite their differences, the economic transformations in these three groups of countries share an essential commonality. They have all been aimed at macroeconomic stabilization, microeconomic liberalization and institutional reforms such as privatization of state-owned firms and changes in the tax, banking, and finance systems. They also have in common a tension between economic and political reform.

Two strategies have been offered to deal with this tension. A radical approach, referred to as the **Washington consensus**, recognizes that voters may not support necessary reforms because of individual uncertainty about the payoffs from restructuring socialist, subsidized or protected economies. While such reforms might be sustained once implemented, they would likely be rejected if subjected to a popular vote in advance. The alternative, known as the 'gradualist' approach, demands that reform programmes be carefully embedded in an effective net of social protection and negotiated within the widest possible framework of social groups and representative institutions including trade unions and opposition parties. Otherwise political conditions for the successful continuation of reform may become eroded. It was feared that the potentially ensuing technocratic style of policymaking associated with the Washington consensus might weaken the nascent democratic institutions and lead to economically inferior reform measures (Przeworski *et al.* 1995, 67–70). Most countries chose a middle route somewhere between the two strategies. To see how this has worked out in practice, we will explore the reform processes for each of three types of politico-economic systems.

Reforming systems with a history of export-led development

South Korea and Taiwan are classic examples of countries pursuing a strategy of export-led development. This strategy focused on adjusting domestic economies to production for global consumer goods markets. This meant that many social, economic and political aspirations of citizens had to be neglected, if arguably only temporarily so. To prevent a majority of citizens from reversing the strategy by voting for parties offering an alternative, an authoritarian regime was required (Evans 1987). This led not only to political repression but also to economic problems in the long term. While the strategy may have been suitable for fast-tracking the development of industrial production, it has not led to the creation of a sustainable capitalist economy. Although the tiger economies were hailed as miraculous successes in the 1970s and 1980s, the 1997 East Asian financial crisis was partly the result of their deep-seated structural problems. In the Korean case, these included a dysfunctional financial system and extremely poor labour relations. The crisis' effects on the South Korean economy and society and the democratic government's response were perhaps just as harsh as the social and political realities of the population under the authoritarian regime. Aimed at an opening of the economy and financial disengagement of the state, the reforms succeeded partly in fixing some of the economy's structural problems but led to a further deterioration of labour relations.

Reforming systems based on import substitution industrialization

After World War II many Latin American countries pursued a strategy of state-led growth known as import substitution industrialization (ISI). The idea was to replace imports, mostly of finished goods from more advanced economies, with locally produced substitutes. To achieve this, strong protective measures had to be in place to shelter domestic producers of finished products from foreign competition until their productive capacities were sufficiently developed. The problem with this strategy was that it failed to propel developing economies beyond the production of non-durable consumer goods and relatively low-tech intermediate goods at satisfactory standards. In many countries, the use of inflationary development finance, complex systems of import and price controls, and a lack of market incentives for efficient production led to disappointing results and spiralling foreign debts. The oil crises of the 1970s only exacerbated these problems. As if these difficulties had not been enough to lead Latin American governments to reassess their economic development strategies, the need to serve foreign debt forced them to improve their balance of payments by liberalizing markets and privatizing state-owned enterprises.

When ISI finally lost its credibility, democratic as well as autocratic regimes have embarked on reforming their economies. In many cases, these reforms

have led to improved macroeconomic performance and development. But the successes have come at the price of considerable increases in inequality throughout the region, which polarizes societies, affecting the quality of the often still young democratic regimes as well as undermining their legitimacy. Many Latin American economies converged on a neoliberal model exemplified in the pluralist politico-economic systems of the UK and USA. One aspect of this convergence has been the establishment and consolidation of business associations (Payne and Bartell 1995: 267–71). Increasingly, Latin American business actors are taking on the roles of their counterparts in advanced industrialized democracies outlined above, i.e. lobbying policymakers and negotiating labour relations.

Reforming collectivist economies

A distinctive feature of the transitions from communism in Central and Eastern Europe and the former Soviet Union is the fact that they have involved fundamental and simultaneous changes on both the political and economic dimensions of social life.[3] With the exception of the successor states to the former Yugoslavia, which had its own brand of socialism in place, the countries in the region had fairly uniform politico-economic systems imposed on them after World War II by the Soviet hegemon in collaboration with local communist parties. During 40 years of communism wide areas of social, political and economic life were organized according to designs established in the Soviet Union in the 1930s.[4] In 1989/90, these systems 'all died from the same disease' (Elster, Offe and Preuss 1998: 51), which can be summarized as the conjuncture of economic inefficiency, erosion of ideological legitimacy, and a structural incapacity to adjust to new problems and developments.

In many countries, comprehensive economic reform measures were swiftly pushed through while initial popular enthusiasm lasted. In most of the Central and East European countries the pace and determination of economic restructuring seems to have aided the democratic project. On the other hand, while the creation of capitalism has also gone a long way in many of the successor states of the former Soviet Union, the prospects for democracy there remain uncertain (Åslund 2007). Everywhere, economic liberalization has come at the price of sharp increases in inequality, including alarming deteriorations of living standards for large groups of citizens in some countries. But in the countries that have democratized, this does not seem to impinge much on the new regimes' legitimacy. Lastly, like in Latin American interest groups systems, businesses associations have been established and are increasingly active, both at home and in Brussels, as many of the former communist countries have either joined the European Union or hope to do so in the future.

Box 8.7 Key points

- Democratization in southern Europe, Latin America, and to some extent East Asia, has taken place in the context of profound economic restructuring.

- The reforms have mainly been aimed at marketization, privatization, and free trade.

- Two contending strategies of economic reform were advocated at the outset of the reform processes: the shock therapy approach of the Washington consensus and its gradualist alternative. Neither has been implemented in its pure form.

Conclusion

More often than not, democracy and capitalism go hand in hand. They do so for a reason: each creates a set of conditions that are favourable to the development and sustainability of the other. What business needs most to flourish—the inviolability of contracts, protection from expropriation, predictable lawmaking, stable taxation, and, in the case of transnational corporations, convenient avenues for repatriating profits—could in principle be provided by autocratic as well as democratic regimes. But these features are strongly linked to liberal democracy, which entails constitutionalism and the rule of law.

Capitalist development has in turn created immense opportunities for democratization. But the co-existence of the two systems is also riddled by problems. Capitalism generates inequalities in many dimensions of life, which can compromise the quality of democracy, undermine democratic principles, and in extreme cases may even threaten the very existence of a democratic regime. Experience over the past 20 years has cast doubt on both the hopes and the fears attached to the Washington consensus and its gradualist alternative. In particular, there seems to be a remarkably strong linkage between successful democratization and economic reform in many countries in Central and Eastern Europe as well as in East Asia—although in the latter case that linkage has a considerable temporal gap. The picture is much less optimistic in the former Soviet Union, where a new form of **bureaucratic authoritarianism** seems to be taking hold. Lastly, the relationship between democratization and economic reform seems to be most uncertain in Latin America.

QUESTIONS

1. How does economic development cause countries to democratize?

2. What are the normative underpinnings of democracy?

3. What are the normative underpinnings of capitalism?

4. Why are democracies attractive to investors?

5. Are the poor better off under democracy?

6. How do business actors pursue their political goals?

Visit the Online Resource Centre that accompanies this book for additional questions to accompany each chapter, and a range of other resources: <www.oxfordtextbooks. co.uk/orc/haerpfer/>.

FURTHER READING

Acemoglu, D. and Robinson, J. A. (2006), *Economic Origins of Dictatorship and Democracy* (Cambridge: Cambridge University Press). Encompassing account of the origins of democracy from a political economy perspective.

Boix, C. (2003), *Democracy and Redistribution* (Cambridge: Cambridge University Press). This book deals with many of the questions raised in this chapter, including how stable democracy is achieved, why authoritarian regimes manage to survive, and how different regimes distribute societal wealth.

Olson, M. (2000), *Power and Prosperity: Outgrowing Communist and Capitalist Dictatorships* (New York, NY: Basic Books). Mancur Olson's book emphasizes the importance of well-defined and protected property rights for market capitalism. It compares how democracies as well as communist and capitalist dictatorships extract revenue from citizens and how special interest groups can stall reforms.

Rueschemeyer, D., Stephens, E. H. and Stephens, J. D. (1992), *Capitalist Development and Democracy* (Chicago, IL: University of Chicago Press). Arguing that industrial capitalism promotes democracy by empowering the urban working class, this book analyses how democracy has established itself better in some countries than in others. It is essential for an understanding of the relationship between capitalist development and political reform.

Åslund, A. (2007), *How Capitalism Was Built: The Transformations of Central and Eastern Europe, Russia and Central Asia* (Cambridge: Cambridge University Press). A thorough and insightful analysis of the reform processes of all the former communist countries that emerged from the Soviet bloc. While the author makes no secret of his opinions on the various reform strategies, the book is very useful for anyone wanting understand how communist economies can be transformed into their opposite in the space of a few years.

Bellin, E. (2002), *Stalled Democracy: Capital, Labor, and the Paradox of State-Sponsored Development* (Ithaca, NY: Cornell University Press). Eva Bellin analyses why capitalists and workers have been reluctant to press for democratization in late-developing countries. While the theoretical argument is developed mainly in the context of the Tunisian political economy, the empirical analysis covers the relationships between the state, business and labour in Brazil, Mexico, South Korea, Egypt, and Zambia.

Bowles, S. and Gintis, H. (1986), *Democracy and Capitalism: Property, Community, and the Contradictions of Modern Social Thought* (London: Routledge & Kegan Paul). This book is important for an understanding of the normative dimensions of the relationship between capitalism and democracy. It highlights the political nature of economic activities that are often portrayed as apolitical.

Lindblom, C. E. (1977), *Politics and Markets: The World's Political-Economic Systems* (New York, NY: Basic Books). This classic should be read by anyone wanting to understand the relationship between politics and economics and the role of private enterprise in democracies. Thirty years after publication the book has only gained in relevance.

IMPORTANT WEBSITES

<www.corpwatch.org>; CorpWatch is an NGO that investigates and exposes corporate violations of human rights, environmental crimes, fraud and corruption around the world.

<www.lobbywatch.org> This UK-based NGO tracks public relations activities involving lobbyists, public relations firms, think tanks and political networks.

NOTES

1. Taxes are also raised in communist economies. But as the income of the state in communism is usually extracted directly from production, the primary purpose of taxation is not to generate income for the state but to regulate consumer purchasing power.

2. A good, concise overview is given by Przeworski 1999: 40–3.

3. In some cases, territorial changes have to be added as a third dimension of transformation.

4. An exception is Hungary, where comprehensive economic liberalization started in 1982. That year, a new set of regulations defined and granted private property rights in much of an already vibrant second (i.e. non-state controlled) economy, thus leading to the development of what Linz and Stepan (1996: 11) phrased an *economic society*—a supportive condition for a consolidated democracy.

9 Political Culture, Mass Beliefs, and Value Change

Christian Welzel and Ronald F. Inglehart

Overview

This chapter examines the role of mass beliefs and value change in democratization processes—something that is generally underestimated. Building on one of the central assumptions of political culture theory—the congruence thesis—we argue that mass beliefs are of critical importance for a country's chances to become and remain democratic. For mass beliefs determine whether a political system is accepted as legitimate or not, which has a major impact on a regime's likelihood of surviving. As the motivational source of opposition or support for a regime, mass beliefs play a crucial role in deciding whether a regime flourishes or is overthrown.

Introduction

The idea that a society's political order reflects its people's prevailing beliefs and values—that is, its political culture—has a long tradition. Aristotle (1962 [350 BC]) argued in Book IV of *Politics* that democracy emerges in middle-class communities in which the citizens share an egalitarian participatory orientation. And many subsequent theorists have claimed that the question of which political system emerges and survives in a country depends on the orientations that prevail among its people. Thus, Charles-Louis de Montesquieu (1989 [1748]: 106) argued in *De L'Esprit des Lois* that the laws by which a society is governed reflect its people's dominant mentality: Whether a nation is constituted as a tyranny, monarchy or democracy depends, respectively, on the prevalence of anxious, honest or civic orientations. Likewise, Alexis de Tocqueville (1994 [1835]: 29) postulated in *De la Démocratie en Amérique* that the flourishing of democracy in the USA reflects the liberal and participatory orientations of the American people.

In modern times the most dramatic illustration of the fact that a political order requires compatible orientations among its people was the failure of democracy in Weimar Germany. Although on paper, the democratic constitution adopted by Germany after World War I seemed an ideally designed set of institutions, it never took root among a people who were accustomed to the authoritarian system they had previously experienced. When the new democracy failed to provide order and prosperity, Hitler came to power through democratic elections. The failure of democracy in Germany had such catastrophic consequences that it troubled social scientists, psychologists, and public opinion researchers for many decades. And the research inspired by this disaster seemed to indicate that democracy is fragile when it is a 'democracy without democrats' (Bracher 1971 [1955]).

In this vein, Harold Lasswell (1951: 473, 484, 502) claimed that whether democratic regimes emerge and survive largely depends on mass beliefs. Similarly, when Seymour Martin Lipset (1959: 85–9) analysed why modernization is conducive to democracy, he concluded that modernization changes mass orientations in ways that make people supportive of democratic principles, such as political pluralism and popular control over power. More recently, Samuel Huntington (1991: 69) argued that rising mass desires for freedom provide the intervening mechanism that explains why modernization has given rise to democratizing movements in scores of countries in recent decades.

Gabriel Almond and Sidney Verba (1963: 498) and Eckstein (1966: 1) introduced the term 'congruence,' claiming that political regimes become stable only in so far as their authority patterns meet people's authority beliefs—'regardless of regime type', as Eckstein (1998: 3) notes. According to this congruence thesis, authoritarian regimes are stable when the people believe in the **legitimacy** of dictatorial powers, just as democratic regimes are stable in so far as people believe that political authority ought to be subject to popular controls.

Ronald Inglehart and Christian Welzel (2005: 187) have extended these propositions to suggest that in order to endure, political regimes must supply democracy at levels that satisfy the people's demand for it. In support of this claim, they provide empirical evidence demonstrating that, at the peak of the global wave of democratization, those countries in which mass aspirations for democracy exceeded the extent to which democratic institutions actually existed before that peak, subsequently made the greatest progress in democratization; while those countries in which the supply of democracy exceeded the level of mass aspirations for democracy, actually tended to become *less* democratic during the subsequent decade.

The Role of Mass Beliefs in Democratization Literature

Most of the recent democratization literature has paid surprisingly little attention to the role of mass beliefs in democratization. This applies to both of the two dominant types of approaches in the democratization literature: structure-focused approaches and action-focused approaches.

Structure-focused approaches emphasize structural aspects of society, such as modernization, income equality, group divisions, class coalitions, religious composition, colonial heritage, or world system position (Doorenspleet 2005). Advocates of these approaches perform sophisticated statistical analyses to demonstrate how much given structural factors increase or decrease the likelihood that a country will become and remain democratic. But these analyses specify no mechanism by which these structures translate into the collective actions by which democratization is initiated, accomplished, consolidated, and further pursued. But structural factors, such as high levels of education or GNP, can not in themselves bring about democratization—this requires action by human beings.

The second type of approach focuses on such actions. It describes democratization processes through the elite actions and mass actions that make democratization happen (Casper and Taylor 1996). But describing, reconstructing, classifying, and simulating these actions, does not explain them. An object, such as democratization, can only be explained by causes that are exogenous to it, or the explanation is tautological. Action-focused approaches enrich our understanding with telling narratives and **thick descriptions**. They clarify how democratization was attained. But fail to explain *why* it came about, which requires identifying the link that ties democratizing actions to the conditions that make them likely. This failure is all the more glaring when it is clear that there are structural configurations under which democratizing actions are significantly

more likely than under others. For example, virtually all of the countries that democratized in the global wave from 1986 to 1995 were middle-income countries; very few of them were low-income countries.

Structure-focused and action-focused approaches have a common blind spot: How to get 'from structure to action'. Structure-focused approaches are unable to tell us how the structures they emphasize translate into the actions that accomplish democratization. Action-focused approaches, on the other hand, leave us uninformed about how the actions accomplishing democratization grow out of structural features. The problem is that neither structure-focused approaches nor action-focused approaches take mass beliefs into account—when mass beliefs constitute the missing link between these two types of approaches.

Mass beliefs are needed to translate 'structure into action'. All collective actions, including those that bring about democratization, are inspired by shared goals (Tarrow 1998). Hence, if structural aspects of society play a role in making democratizing actions more likely, these structures *must* give rise to orientations that make people believe in democracy as a desirable goal. People's beliefs are thus the intervening variable between social structure and collective action. Ignoring this, democratization processes cannot be adequately understood.

Box 9.1 **Key points**

- The democratization literature is dominated by structure-focused approaches and action-focused approaches.

- Both approaches tend to neglect mass beliefs as a potential source of democratizing pressures, even though these beliefs help translating structures into actions.

Mass Demands for Democracy

There is a tendency in the political culture literature to equate popular preferences for democracy with actual mass demands for democracy (Seligson 2007). But popular preferences for democracy do not automatically translate into mass pressures to democratize.

Preferences for democracy are often superficial or purely instrumental (Schedler and Sarsfield 2006). At this point in history, most people in most countries say favourable things about democracy simply because it has become socially desirable and has positive connotations. Preferring democracy for these reasons is a *superficial* preference for democracy (Inglehart 2003). Because Western democracies are obviously prosperous, some people believe that if their country becomes democratic, it will become rich. This is an *instrumental* preference for democracy (Bratton and Mattes 2001): people seek democracy for other reasons than the political freedoms that are its defining qualities.

Mass preferences for democracy are widespread almost everywhere, but if these preferences are superficial or instrumental, they will not motivate people to struggle or risk their lives to obtain democracy. People are most likely to do so if they give high priority to the freedoms that democracy provides. Only when democracy is valued as a good in itself, are strong mass pressures likely to be brought to bear on elites—whether to attain democratic freedoms when they are absent, or to defend these freedoms when they are endangered.

But how do we know that people support democracy for its defining freedoms? Democracy is an emancipative achievement that frees people from oppression and discrimination and empowers them 'to live the lives they have reason to value' (Sen 1999). Thus, the values motivating democracy emphasize equality, liberty, tolerance and empowering people to govern themselves, in both private and public life. People who value these goals over others, emphasize emancipative values. If they support democracy (as most people do), they are more likely to be motivated by the fact that democracy provides freedoms, than by the belief that it provides prosperity or other instrumental motivations. The beliefs that motivate people's preference for democracy are as important as the fact that they say they prefer it (Bratton and Gymiah-Boadi 2005).

Mass pressures for democracy do not necessarily emerge simply because a large share of the public says they prefer democracy to its alternatives. People may give lip service to democracy for shallow or instrumental reasons. Only if people's preference for democracy reflects the fact that they place a high value on freedom and self-expression, they are relatively likely to pursue democratization actively. Hence, in order to know whether people prefer democracy *intrinsically*—that is, for its defining freedoms—one needs to find out how strongly they emphasize emancipative values. People's responses to the questions shown in Table 9.1 enable us to measure the extent to which they emphasize emancipative values.

Emancipative values give priority to equality over patriarchy, tolerance over conformity, autonomy over authority, and expression over security, as shown in Table 9.1. Emancipative values are closely related to self-expression values as described by Inglehart and Welzel (2005), who demonstrate that their measure of self-expression values has an inherently emancipative impetus and use the terms self-expression values and emancipative values interchangeably. Since these values cover a broad syndrome of interrelated beliefs, representing a coherent worldview, they can be measured in a number of different ways, all of which tap the same underlying dimension. The measure of emancipative values used here is conceptually more coherent and focuses more explicitly on the theme of emancipation than does self-expression values. Although they use different indicators and are operationalized in different ways, the two measures correlate very strongly (at r=.90), an indication of how robust the underlying dimension is. The theoretical explanation of the factors that give rise to self-expression values applies equally to emancipative values.

Table 9.1 An Index of Emancipative Values

Under-lying dimension	EMANCIPATIVE VALUES (correlation with self-expression values: r = .90)			
Factor loadings*	.76	.72	.63	.54
Belief in	Equality over Patriarchy	Tolerance over Conformity	Autonomy over Authority	Expression over Security
Items	Agree that woman can live by herself	Agree that abortion can be justified	Autonomy chosen as a goal to teach	Priority to giving people more say in government over order and stable prices
	Disagree that men make better political leaders	Agree that homosexuality is justified	Imagination chosen as a goal to teach	Priority to giving people more say in local affairs over strong defence and fighting crime
	Disagree that education is more important for boys	Agree that divorce is justified	Obedience not chosen as a goal to teach	Priority to protecting freedom of speech over order and stable prices
	Disagree that men have more right to a job		Faith not chosen as a goal to teach	

* Factor analyses of over 340,000 respondents from 90 countries in the 5 waves of the World Values Surveys 1981–2007. Subindices are the arithmetic means of their respective component variables, each normalized to a scale with minimum 0 and maximum 1.0. The Emancipative Values Index is the arithmetic mean of the four subindices. If one subindex is missing, the Emancipative Values Index is the arithmetic mean of the remaining three components.

Countries of different cultural zones around the world differ surprisingly little in the extent to which the public says they prefer democracy. At this point in history, democracy has become the most widely preferred system around the world, even in countries governed by authoritarian institutions (Klingemann 1999). But countries differ considerably in the extent to which their people prefer democracy *intrinsically*—and the difference is important: if intrinsic preferences for democracy are weak, the actual level of democracy is low; but if intrinsic preferences for democracy are strong, the actual level of democracy is generally high (Welzel and Inglehart 2006).

Regime Legitimacy

Some scholars assume that autocracies are always illegitimate, as far as the general public is concerned, and that overwhelming majorities of ordinary people almost always prefer democracy to autocracy (Acemoglu and Robinson 2006). In this view, autocracies lack legitimacy and are able to survive only because they are able to repress opposing majorities. Historically, this is inaccurate: autocracies of the past and present were not always considered illegitimate.

Unfortunately, people do not always support democracy, because they inherently value its defining freedoms. Evidence from the World Values Surveys and other cross-national surveys indicate that emancipative mass beliefs vary dramatically cross-nationally, and when these beliefs are weak, people give priority to authority and strong leadership over freedom and expression. This does not prevent people from becoming dissatisfied with an incumbent authoritarian regime's policies and representatives when they perform poorly. But disillusionment about policies and authorities does not mean that people view dictatorial powers as inherently illegitimate. Even dissatisfied people can continue to prefer strong leaders and authoritarian rule. They might wish to have one dictator replaced by another without rejecting authoritarian rule. In fact, when emancipative values are weak, people are more likely to accept limitations on democratic freedoms for the sake of national order or other goals.

Another important factor is that the absence of emancipative values biases people's understanding of democracy in an authoritarian direction. As evidence from the World Values Surveys demonstrates, when emancipative values are weak or absent, people may consider authoritarian regimes to be democratic: their underlying values emphasize good economic performance and order, rather than political rights and civil liberties.

It is not true that the publics of authoritarian regimes always value democratic freedoms and that authoritarian regimes survive simply because of their repressive capacities. But intrinsic preferences for democracy can and do emerge in authoritarian regimes when they experience a modernization process that changes ordinary people's value priorities and action repertoires.

The theory of intergenerational value change advanced by Inglehart and Welzel (2005) holds that virtually everyone likes freedom, but they do not necessarily give it top priority. People's priorities reflect their socioeconomic conditions, placing the highest subjective value on the most pressing needs. Since material sustenance and physical security are the first requirements for survival, under conditions of scarcity, people give top priority to safety goals; while under conditions of prosperity, they become more likely to emphasize self-expression and freedom. During the past 50 years, rising economic and physical security have led to a gradual intergenerational shift in many countries placing rising emphasis on emancipative values. At the same time, rising levels of education and changes in the occupational structure have made mass publics increasingly articulate and increasingly accustomed to thinking for themselves. Both processes encourage the spread of emancipative values that give priority to equality over patriarchy, tolerance over conformity, autonomy over authority, and expression over security. As these beliefs spread, dictatorial regimes tend to lose their legitimacy.

Implicitly, much of the literature assumes that whether people consider a given regime legitimate or not only matters for democracy but not for autocracy (Easton 1965). It matters for democracy because when a majority rejects democracy, antidemocratic forces can become sufficiently widespread to gain power and abandon democratic institutions. Autocracies, in this view, do not need legitimacy, since they can repress even widespread opposition. Hence, as long as an authoritarian regime stays in control of the army and secret police, it can survive despite mass opposition.

This is inaccurate. Recent cases of democratization demonstrate that when mass opposition grows strong enough, even rigidly repressive authoritarian regimes can be overthrown (Schock 2005). Repression does not necessarily cause mass opposition to break down as soon as it faces repression—indeed,

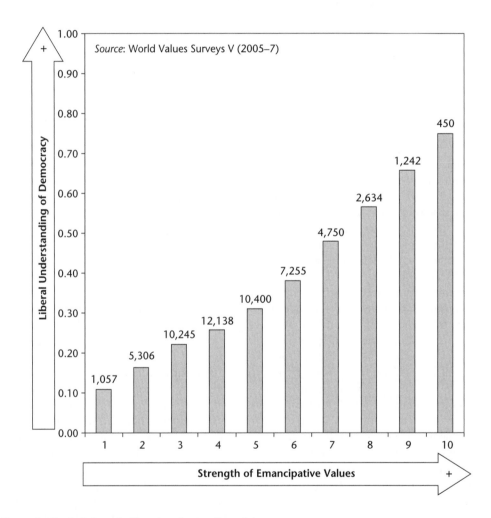

Fig 9.1 Emancipative beliefs and a liberal understanding of democracy

Notes: Emancipative values are measured as shown in Table 9.1 but broken down into ten categories of increasing strength. Based on a scale from 0 to 1, category 1 measures emancipative beliefs of strength from 0 to .1, category 2 measures strength from .1 to .2 and so on, until category 10 measures strength .9 to 1. The liberal understanding of democracy measures how much people place their definition of democracy on civil rights, free elections, free referenda votes and equal rights for both sexes. The scale has a minimum of 0 for the least liberal and 1 for the most liberal understanding.

repression has sometimes increased and intensified mass opposition (Francisco 2005). Moreover, the characteristics of the mass opposition itself are important too. Mass opposition has usually failed when it was driven by relatively small and clearly identifiable groups, making it easy to isolate them. But emancipative values tend to become widespread at high levels of economic development, as people gain higher levels of education, material resources, intellectual skills, and connecting networks. When this happens, large segments of the public have both the resources and ambitions to oppose **authoritarianism** (see Figure 9.2). Expanding action repertoires and emancipative values empower ordinary people to mount effective pressures on elites.

Human empowerment nurtures emancipative mass movements in any regime. In autocracies, emancipative movements oppose the regime, attempting to replace autocracy with democracy. In democracies, emancipative mass movements attempt to make their governments more responsive. In both situations, emancipative values tend to transform political institutions.

Figure 9.1 shows how rising emphasis on emancipative values tends to transform people's understanding of what democracy means. With low levels of emancipative values, people tend to view democracy as meaning that the economy prospers, unemployed people receive **state** aid, criminals get punished, and other instrumental views. With rising emphasis on emancipative values, they increasingly come to define democracy as meaning that people choose their leaders in free elections, civil rights protect people's liberties, women have equal rights, and people can change the laws. With each additional step on the ladder of progressing emancipative values, people's understanding of democracy takes on a more liberal character, focusing on the freedoms that empower people.

Neither people's understanding of what democracy means, nor the extent to which people give high priority to obtaining democratic freedoms, are constants as is implied in the models proposed by such writers as Boix or Acemoglu and Robinson. Both the meaning of democracy and the priority it holds, reflect mass values that vary according to a society's level of socioeconomic development. Mass beliefs matter, as the political culture school has long claimed: for mass beliefs help determine whether a given regime is accepted as legitimate.

Economic Performance and Regime Legitimacy

Many scholars have argued that any regime, whether autocracy or democracy, will have mass support as long as it is economically successful (Haggard and Kaufman 1995). On the contrary, we argue that this depends on people's value priorities. The impact of economic success on regime legitimacy is contingent on mass values.

Rising emphasis on emancipative values make people value civic freedoms increasingly highly. This happens regardless of whether a country has democratic or authoritarian institutions: emerging emancipative values lead people to place increasing value on civic freedoms. Accordingly, as Figure 9.1 demonstrates, rising emphasis on emancipative values is linked with a shift toward an increasingly liberal understanding of democracy—and this takes place among both democratic and authoritarian countries.

Rising emphasis on emancipative values make people judge the legitimacy of a regime less and less on the basis of whether it provides order and prosperity, and more and more on the basis of whether it provides freedom. Thus, as emancipative values grow stronger with rising levels of development, legitimacy increasingly depends on whether a regime provides liberty and democracy; with strong emancipative values, economic performance has little effect on people's acceptance of a regime (Hofferbert and Klingemann 1999).

In the long run, this poses a dilemma for autocracies. If they perform economically well over long periods of time, they move toward higher levels of socioeconomic modernization. By increasing people's material means, intellectual skills, and connecting networks, modernization widens people's actions repertoires. Widened action repertoires make the value of freedoms more obvious, as people increasingly recognize that they need freedom in order to make use of a wider action repertoire. Sustained economic development thus transforms the criteria by which people evaluate regimes, and leads to increasingly skilled and articulate publics that become increasingly effective at challenging authoritarian elites. While economic success legitimizes authoritarian regimes in the early stages of development, it no longer does so at higher levels of economic development.

The Congruence Thesis

Congruence theory argues that, in order to be stable, the authority patterns characterizing a country's political system must be consistent with the people's prevailing authority beliefs (Eckstein 1966). Thus, authoritarian systems tend to prevail where most people believe in the legitimacy of absolute political power, while democracies should prevail where most people endorse popular control of political power. This claim could not be demonstrated empirically when it first was formulated, since representative survey data measuring people's authority beliefs was only available then for a small number of countries, most of which were rich Western democracies. Congruence theory remained a plausible but unproven theory for many years. Accordingly, doubts were expressed about the empirical validity of the congruence thesis and its claim that people's legitimacy beliefs are an important determinant of the type of regime that governs them.

One reason for these doubts is the fact that political science has an inherent tendency to emphasise institutional engineering. This viewpoint has many adherents because it implies that one can shape a society by shaping its institutions—which means that political scientists can provide a quick fix for most problems. This encourages a tendency to treat institutions as the explanatory variable *par excellence* and a tendency to reject the idea that culture matters—or that institutions are shaped by cultural factors, since culture reflects deep-seated orientations that are relatively difficult (though not impossible) to reshape (Eckstein 1998). Accordingly, there is widespread resistance to cultural explanations of political institutions, including the idea that mass beliefs determine what level of democracy is likely to be found in a country (Hadenius and Teorell 2005). The fact that mainstream political science has a deep-rooted tendency to reject the idea that culture matters, does not prove that it does not. This question can only be answered by empirical tests.

Doubts that mass beliefs influence a country's level of democracy have taken two main forms. First, it has been questioned that there is any systematic relationship between mass beliefs and levels of democracy. For example, Seligson (2002) argued that the relationship Ronald Inglehart (1997) found between mass beliefs and democracy is an 'ecological fallacy'. Seligson based this claim on his finding that civic attitudes, such as interpersonal trust, have no significant effect on the extent to which people say they prefer democracy. But as Ronald Inglehart and Christian Welzel (2003) demonstrate, Seligson's finding simply confirms that mass preferences for democracy are not necessarily inspired by deep-rooted civic orientations: they may say they prefer it for shallow or instrumental reasons or because of social desirability effects. Only when preferences for democracy are motivated by emancipative values do they lead to the emergence of democracy in a country.

Since this debate, the World Values Survey has gathered sufficient data to demonstrate that there is a strong and systematic relationship between mass beliefs and levels of democracy. Over a global

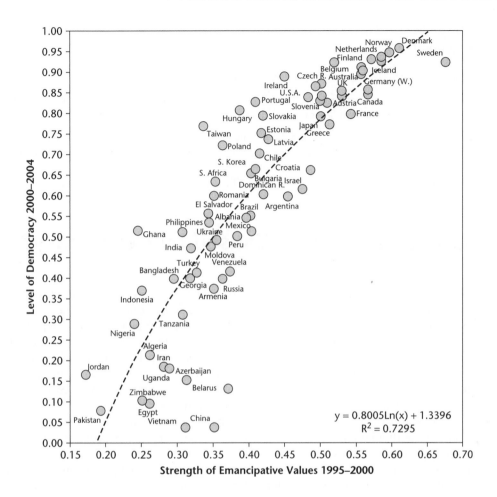

Fig 9.2 The relationship between emancipative values and levels of democracy

Notes: The horizontal axis measures emancipative beliefs as shown in Table 9.1. The vertical axis measures democracy levels as an average over four different indices of democracy, including the Freedom House index, the Polity IV autocracy-democracy scores, Vanhanen's index of democratization, and the Cingranelli and Richards (CIRI) ratings for integrity and empowerment rights. The scale is standardized to a minimum of 0 (democracy completely absent) to 1 (democracy fully present).

sample of more than 70 societies, the extent to which a public holds emancipative values correlates at r=.85 with a country's subsequent level of democracy, using the broad measure of democracy shown in Figure 9.2. The measure of democracy used here is the average of four of the most widely-used ways of measuring democracy: using this broad measure, one finds a strong relationship. As the strength of emancipative values in a society rises, the level of democracy also rises—and the relationship is remarkably strong and statistically highly significant.

Correlation is not causation, so the correlation shown in Figure 9.2 does not demonstrate what is causing what. Emancipative mass beliefs might cause high levels of democracy to emerge and persist, or it might work the other way around. It is even possible that there is no causal relationship between the two, with the relationship being due to some third factor such as economic modernization, which causes both emancipative values and democracy to reach high levels (Hadenius and Teorell 2005). We will discuss these possibilities further in the next section.

Box 9.2 Key points

- One can differentiate superficial, instrumental, and intrinsic mass preferences for democracy.

- Intrinsic mass preferences for democracy are inspired by emancipative beliefs and these preferences are the most likely to translate into powerful popular pressures to attain, sustain or deepen democratic freedoms.

- Sustained economic development tends to give rise to emancipative beliefs, but when these beliefs have grown strong in a population, a regime's momentary economic performance becomes less important for people to consider it legitimate.

Are Emancipative Values Caused by Democracy?

Advocates of **institutional learning theory** argue that people learn to value democracy by living under democratic institutions for many years (Rustow 1970). If this theory is correct, these beliefs can only emerge in countries that have been democratic for many years. And this implies that emancipative values cannot cause democracy to emerge—since they would only appear long after democracy has been established. It also implies that if mass preferences for democracy arise in authoritarian regimes, they must be instrumentally motivated, by goals other than democracy itself such as prosperity. Intrinsic mass preferences for democracy would only emerge through long experience under democratic institutions. Proponents of this view claim that emancipative values are 'endogenous' to democratic institutions (Hadenius and Teorell 2005).

But, as Inglehart and Welzel (2005) demonstrate, high levels of intrinsic support for democracy had emerged in many authoritarian societies *before* they made the transition to democracy. High levels of existential security and growth of action resources had contributed to making emancipative values widespread in such countries as Czechoslovakia, Poland, Hungary, Estonia, South Korea, and Taiwan before they democratized. An intrinsic valuation of freedom can emerge even in the absence of democracy, provided modernization takes place. By providing rising incomes and other resources, modernization raises ordinary people's sense of agency and this leads to growing emphasis on emancipa-

tory values. Rising education, information levels, opportunities to connect with people and other resources, broaden people's action repertoires, and this increases the perceived utility of freedom. In this view, emancipative values emerge and diffuse as a function of growing action resources, rather than as a function of long-term experience under democratic institutions.

Whether emancipative values emerge from growing resources or from experience with democracy can be tested by a statistical technique called multivariate regression analysis. Using an indicator of a society's accumulated experience with democracy and an indicator of action resources, we can examine which of the two has a stronger effect on emancipative mass beliefs measured subsequently. The first indicator, called 'democracy stock', has been developed by John Gerring *et al.* (2005) and measures a country's accumulated experience with democracy.[1] The indicator of resources is Tatu Vanhanen's (2003) 'index of power resources', which we prefer to call action resources.[2] The result of this regression analysis is graphically depicted in Figure 9.3 below. It shows that, controlling for each country's democratic experience, action resources explain 28 per cent of the cross-national variation in emancipative values. By contrast, controlling for each country's level of action resources, the democratic experience explains virtually none of the variation in emancipative values. Another 36 per cent of variation in emancipative values is explained by the inseparable overlap of action resources and the democratic experience, reflecting the fact that people in countries with a longer democratic history tend to have more action resources. Thus, while democratic experience strengthens emancipative mass beliefs only in so far as it goes with action resources, action resources strengthen emancipative mass beliefs on their own, independent of the democratic experience. Clearly, emancipative mass beliefs are not endogenous to democratic institutions. The idea that the rise of emancipative values is driven by growing resources finds far more empirical support than the idea that it is driven by experience under democracy.

It is possible for democracy to survive even in low-income countries—as India demonstrates. India has a long experience with democracy but the average Indian's level of resources is still limited—and mass emphasis on emancipative values is also relatively weak in India. Moreover, India's overall level of democracy is lower than some indicators suggest. Figure 9.2 demonstrates this point, using a broad measure of democracy, averaging four different indicators: the Freedom House political and civil liberties ratings, the Polity autocracy-democracy scores, the CIRI (Cingranelli and Richards) ratings of empowerment and integrity rights,[3] and Vanhanen's electoral

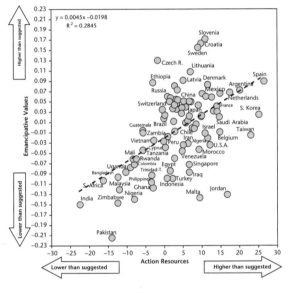

Diagram 9.3a

Vertical axis measures 'residuals' in emancipative values, indicating the extent to which these values exceed (in case of positive numbers) or the extent to which they fall short (in the case of negative numbers) of what a country's 'democracy stock' suggests. Horizontal axis measures 'residuals' in action resources, indicating the extent to which these resources exceed (in case of positive numbers) or the extent to which they fall short (in case of negative numbers) of what a country's 'democracy stock' suggests. The residuals in both variables are significantly positively related. This means: a population's emancipative values exceed (fall short of) its 'democracy stock' to the extent its action resources exceed (fall short of) its 'democracy stock'. In other words, action resources have an effect on emancipative values independent of 'democracy stock'.

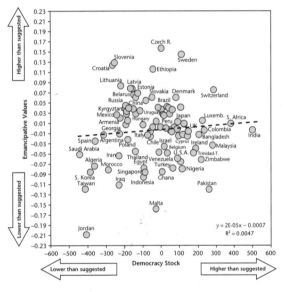

Diagram 9.3b

Vertical axis measures 'residuals' in emancipative values, indicating the extent to which these values exceed (in case of positive numbers) or the extent to which they fall short (in the case of negative numbers) of what a population's action resources suggest. Horizontal axis measures 'residuals' in 'democracy stock', indicating the extent to which this stock exceeds (in case of positive numbers) or the extent to which it falls short (in case of negative numbers) of what a population's action resources suggest. The residuals in both variables are *not* significantly related. This means: a population's emancipative values do *not* exceed (fall short of) its action resources to the extent its 'democracy stock' exceeds (falls short of) its action resources. In other words, 'democracy stock' has *no* effect on emancipative values independent of action resources.

Fig 9.3 The effects of action resources and level of democracy on emancipative values, controlling for the other variable

(a) Impact of resources on values, controlling for each country's level of democracy.

(b) Impact of a society's level of democracy on values, controlling for its level of action resources.

democracy data. Across these four indicators, India's democratic performance is moderate, particularly because of its low scoring on the Vanhanen index (reflecting low voter **turnout**) and its high degree of violations of citizens' rights, as documented in the CIRI data. Taking these indicators of Indian democracy into account provides a more balanced picture of its actual democratic performance than if one focuses solely on the Polity and Freedom House data.

Analysing the direction in the relation between emancipative values and levels of democracy depicted in Figure 9.2, Inglehart and Welzel (2005: 182–3) find that, after controlling for the action resources available to the average person in a society, prior democracy has no significant effect on subsequent mass beliefs; but, controlling for resource levels, mass beliefs prior to democracy *do* have a strong and statistically significant effect on subsequent levels of democracy. The causal arrow apparently runs from values to institutions, rather than the other way round.

Using this broad measure of democracy, it can be shown that the relation between emancipative mass beliefs and democracy is not a statistical artefact of a third factor, such as modernization, which might cause both emancipative values and democracy to reach high levels. Instead, Christian Welzel (2007) demonstrates that the effect of emancipative values on democracy remains significant when one controls for modernization, even using the very broad measure of modernization used by Hadenius and Teorell (2005). Considered in isolation, modernization explains about two-thirds of the variation in subsequent levels of democracy. This effect drops to less than half of the explained variation, taking into account modernization's own dependence on prior democracy. And when one controls for the effect of emancipative mass beliefs, the impact of modernization on subsequent democracy drops drastically—explaining only 14 per cent of the variance in subsequent levels of democracy. On the other hand, emancipative values alone account for almost three-quarters of the variation in subsequent levels of democracy, and still account for more than half of the variance when one controls for the extent to which these beliefs are shaped by prior levels of democracy. This effect drops further to 24 per cent when one controls for the effects of modernization.

What do these results indicate? The impact of both socioeconomic modernization and emancipative mass beliefs drop considerably when one controls for the effect of the other variable. This is so because these two phenomena overlap considerably, and the overlapping variance has a stronger effect on subsequent democracy than either of its parts. Thus, socioeconomic modernization is conducive to democracy mainly insofar as it is conducive to emancipative values among the public. Conversely, emancipative values are conducive to democracy mainly insofar as they are rooted in socioeconomic modernization. Socioeconomic modernization gives people the action resources that enable them to struggle for democratic freedoms; and emancipative values give them the motivation that makes them willing to do so. And both variables have their greatest impact when they act together, making people both motivated to seek democracy and able to exert effective pressures to obtain it.

Explaining Democratic Change

The global wave of democratization, and its subsequent reversal in some countries, brought changes to many countries' level of democracy. These changes constitute gains when a country climbs from a lower to a higher level of democracy, and losses when a country falls from a higher to a lower level of democracy. If emancipative mass values have a causal effect on democratization, they should be able to explain both gains and losses in levels of democracy from *before* the global wave of democratization in 1984–1988, to the period afterward in 2000–04.

Moreover, if congruence theory is correct in its assumption that incongruence between mass demands for democracy and given levels of democracy is a major source of regime instability, changes towards and away from democracy should be a

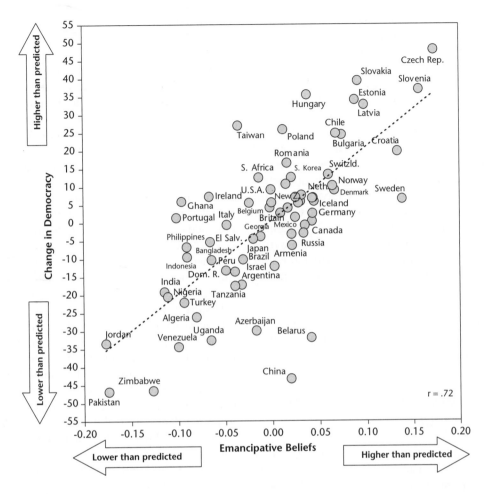

Fig 9.4 The effect of emancipative values on changes in democracy, controlling for each country's initial level of democracy

Notes: The horizontal axis measures emancipative values in around 1990 controlling for the level of democracy in 1984–88 (i.e. before the climax of the global democratization wave). Positive numbers show how much emancipative values exceed what the prior level of democracy predicts. Negative numbers indicate how much they fall short of it. The vertical axis measures changes in the level of democracy from 1984-88 (i.e. before the global democratization wave) to 2000–04 (i.e. after the global democratization wave), controlling for the level of democracy in 1984–88. *Interpretation*: The more a population's emancipative values exceed the prior level of democracy, the more this level increases over what the prior level predicts.

function of both the direction and the amount of incongruence. If mass demands for democracy are *lower* than is usual at a given country's level of democracy, a country's level of democracy should *fall* subsequently. And it should fall roughly to the extent to which mass demands fall short of the prevailing level, bringing the level of democracy in line with people's demands. Conversely, if mass demands for democracy are *higher* than a country's

level of democracy would predict, a country's level of democracy should *rise*. And it should rise approximately to the extent to which mass demands exceed a given democracy level, making mass preferences congruent with the country's political institutions.

Figure 9.4 confirms these expectations. Comparing the levels of democracy found in given countries during the period 1984–88 (before the peak of the democratization wave) with the levels on which we find them over the period 2000–04 (after the peak of the global wave), incongruence between mass demands for democracy and the initial democracy level explains about half of the changes in levels of democracy. Levels of democracy fell in most countries where they exceeded mass demands, while they increased in almost every country where they fell short of mass demands. Hence, the global wave of democratization can be seen as a major shift towards greater congruence between mass demands for democracy, as measured by emancipative values, and actual levels of democracy. China is the most prominent outlier in one direction, where the country actually became somewhat less democratic after 1988, despite mass demands for more democracy; and Taiwan is an outlier in the opposite direction, where the shift toward higher levels of democracy was even greater than the amount predicted by mass demands. But on the whole, changes toward or away from democracy tended to reflect unmet mass demands rather closely (r=.72), acting to reduce incongruence between mass demands and political institutions.

Emancipative values and human empowerment

These findings suggest that democracy is based on empowering human conditions in a society. It includes empowering cultural conditions that *motivate* people to struggle for democracy and empowering economic conditions that make people *capable* to do so. As an institutional means to empower people, democracy is inherently linked to empowering economic and cultural conditions. Democracy empowers people in *allowing* them to practice democratic freedoms. Human empowerment as a whole then is a syndrome of empowering economic, cultural, and institutional conditions.

Emancipative values constitute the cultural component in the human empowerment process and as such are the intervening variable between action resources, and democratic freedoms, as shown in Figure 6.2 (see Ch. 6).

Seeing mass beliefs in a mediating role between economic modernization and political democracy is consistent with Lipset's (1959) classic discussion of modernization. When Lipset asked why modernization is conducive to democracy he argued that this is true because modernization tends to generate beliefs and values that are favourable to democracy. Lipset thus understood that *objective* social conditions impact on political changes, such as democratization, through their tendency to nurture *subjective* orientations that inspire these changes. When he proposed this view of modernization, the survey data that would be needed to test it did not exist so, Lipset was unable to explore it any further, but this was his basic causal argument.

More than 30 years later Huntington (1991) followed a similar line of reasoning, arguing that the rise of modern middle classes in developing countries was conducive to beliefs that dictatorial powers were illegitimate, and there was a growing valuation of freedom, concluding that these changes in mass orientations provided a major inspiration of democratizing pressures.

Despite its focus on mass beliefs, the political culture approach has little to say about the role of mass beliefs in the process of democratization. While there is a widespread consensus that mass beliefs are important for the **consolidation** of existing democracies (Rose and Mishler 2001), the role of mass beliefs in transitions to or away from democracy is generally neglected. This reflects the type of mass beliefs that most of the political culture literature assumed were conducive to democracy.

Influenced by David Easton (1965), Gabriel Almond and Sidney Verba (1963), and Robert Putnam (1993), most political culture studies focus on allegiant orientations, including overt support for democracy, confidence in political institutions, interpersonal trust, and norms of cooperation and so forth. Allegiant orientations may indeed be helpful in consolidating existing democracies. But when one wants to explore the role of mass beliefs in *transitions* from authoritarian rule to democracy, one must identify orientations that motivate people to oppose authoritarian rule and struggle for democratic institutions. Emancipative values constitute precisely this type of orientation. Emancipative values give priority to tolerance over conformity, autonomy over authority, equality over patriarchy, and expression over security. If these beliefs arise in an authoritarian regime, the very legitimacy of authoritarian rule is undermined and mass regime opposition that topples these regimes becomes more likely.

But emancipative values do not only help to undermine authoritarian regimes. They also help to consolidate and deepen existing democracies. For people who are inspired by emancipative values are motivated to struggle for democratic freedoms, whether to attain them when they are absent, or to defend them when they are challenged, or to advance them when they stagnate. Accordingly, Welzel (2007) shows that emancipative values motivate peaceful elite-challenging mass actions and that they do so regardless of a country's level of democracy. The absence of democracy is thus no safeguard against the mass mobilizing effects of emancipative values. Emancipation-inspired mass actions, and only emancipation-inspired mass actions, have a democratizing effect, both in making democratic gains where the initial democracy level is low and in preventing democratic losses where the initial democracy level is high.

The kind of communal, supportive, and allegiant orientations emphasized in most of the political culture literature does tend to place power elites in a stable cultural context where they face little resistance. These orientations do not motivate people to put pressure on elites to establish, retain, or deepen

> ## Box 9.3 Key points
>
> - Emancipative mass beliefs arise when growing action repertoires among ordinary people increase the perceived utility of democratic freedoms. These beliefs are not the product of enduring democracy.
>
> - The further countries moved towards democracy the more people's emancipative beliefs were above the level suggested by the respective country's initial democracy level. Likewise, the further away countries moved from democracy, the more people's emancipative beliefs were below the level suggested by the country's initial democracy level.
>
> - Emancipative beliefs are a central component in a wider process of human empowerment, mediating the economic component of human empowerment (i.e. action resources) and its institutional component (i.e. democratic freedoms).

democratic freedoms. Emancipative orientations, by contrast, do serve this purpose. These beliefs are an important mass orientation for democracy, operating in favour of its emergence, survival, and deepening.

The Role of Religion

Besides the beliefs discussed so far, religiosity, religious denomination, and a society's religious demography have all been identified as important cultural factors influencing democracy (Inglehart and Norris 2003). A demographic dominance of Protestants, in particular, has been said to be favourable to democracy, whereas a Muslim dominance has been claimed to be detrimental to democracy (Huntington 1996). Inglehart and Welzel (2005) find that the percentage difference between Protestants and Muslims in a society strongly affects its subsequent level of democracy: the more Protestants outnumber Muslims, the higher the level of democracy. However, when one takes into account a population's overall emphasis on emancipative values, the effect of religious demography becomes weak, accounting for only a minor part

of the variation in levels of democracy. Protestant countries tend to be rich, have high educational levels and a high proportion of people employed in the knowledge sector. And a demographic dominance of Protestants is favourable to democracy largely because it is linked with socioeconomic conditions that strengthen emphasis on emancipative values.

This can be demonstrated by analysing the determinants of the strength of people's emancipative values, using World Values Survey data. As the multi-level model in Table 9.2 shows, if someone has a high level of education, this factor strengthens this person's emancipative values. The same is true for people living in countries where the average person's action resources are large. This contextual factor, too, strengthens people's emancipative values. Living in a country with

Table 9.2 Multi-level Model Explaining Emancipative Values

PREDICTORS:	DEPENDENT VARIABLE: Emancipative Values	
	Coefficient	T-Ratio
Intercept	.423	71.659***
Individual Level Effects (IL):		
- Education level	.127	25.945***
- Being Muslim	− .053	− 6.296***
- Being Protestant	.004	1.146
- Religiosity	− .031	− 6.543***
Country Level Effects (CL):		
- Action resources	.004	6.166***
- Democracy stock	——	n. s.
- Muslims (%)	− .000	− 1.742*
- Protestants (%)	——	n. s.
Cross Level Interaction Effects (IL*CL):		
- Education * Action resources	.003	4.257***
- Education * Democracy stock	——	n. s.
- Education * Muslim (%)	− .001	− 2.556**
- Being Muslim * Action resources	− .002	− 2.696***
- Being Muslim * Democracy stock	——	n. s.
- Being Muslim * Muslim (%)	——	n. s.
Explained variance (%): IL (% of total)	12% (8%)	
CL (% of total)	80% (24%)	

Source: World Values Surveys 1995–2006.

Notes: Number of individual level units (respondents) is 141,303. Number of country level units (nations) is 80. Significance levels: * p < .10, ** p < .05, *** p < .01, n. s. (not significant).

a rich democratic experience, however, does by itself not strengthen people's emancipative values, as is evident from the insignificant effect of the 'democracy stock' variable shown under country level effects.

Islam tends to depress people's emancipative values in various ways. To begin with, living in a country dominated by Muslims tends to lower one's emancipative values, whether one is a Muslim or not. But being a Muslim depresses emancipative values even more than living in a Muslim society. Moreover, living in a Muslim society diminishes education's generally positive effect on emancipative values, as is indicated by the negative sign of the interaction between education and the percentage of Muslims shown under cross-level interaction effects.

Nevertheless, the anti-emancipative effect of Islam can be alleviated, as is evident from the negative interaction between being a Muslim and the action resources of the average person in a country shown under cross-level interaction

Box 9.4 Key points

- Islam, independent of religiosity, and religiosity, independent of Islam, have modest but robust negative effects on emancipative beliefs.

- In depressing emancipative beliefs, religiosity in general and Islam specifically weaken the cultural foundation of democracy.

- With action resources growing throughout a society, Islam depresses emancipative beliefs less.

effects. This interaction means that the negative effect of being a Muslim on emancipative values shrinks as the action resources of the average person grows. Hence, Muslims are not immune to the logic of human empowerment: as a country's resources increase, being a Muslim becomes less and less of a hindrance to a shift toward emancipative values.

Conclusion

In the process of democratization, mass beliefs play a central role. Growing action resources increase people's sense of agency and this gives rise to emancipative values that emphasize freedom. These values inspire the collective actions that lead to democratization. Emancipative mass beliefs appear to be the single most important cultural factor in helping to attain, consolidate, and deepen democracy. As a system designed to empower people, democracy is an emancipative achievement, driven by emancipative forces in society.

Emancipative values are *not* endogenous to democracy. These beliefs emerge in authoritarian societies as well as democracies, provided they experience socioeconomic modernization. And sheer experience under democratic institutions by itself does not give rise to these values. Emancipative values are part of the human empowerment process because they lead people to give high priority to freedom of choice, and make them more willing to struggle for democratic freedoms.

If emancipative values arise in authoritarian regimes, mass pressures to democratize become more likely, increasing the chances of a transition from authoritarian rule to democracy. If emancipative values arise in democratic regimes, mass pressures to deepen their democratic qualities and make them more responsive become increasingly likely. Emancipative values constitute a major selective force in the rise and fall of political regimes, conferring a selective advantage on democracy.

QUESTIONS

1. What is the meaning of political culture?

2. What does congruence theory say?

3. In what regard do mass beliefs play a mediating role?

4. What are emancipative mass beliefs?

5. Why are emancipative values important for democratization?

6. Are emancipative values endogenous to democracy?

Visit the Online Resource Centre that accompanies this book for additional questions to accompany each chapter, and a range of other resources: <www.oxfordtextbooks.co.uk/orc/haerpfer/>.

FURTHER READING

Almond, G. A. and Verba, S. (1963), *The Civic Culture* (Princeton, NJ: Princeton University Press). This book is the classic of the political culture paradigm. It lays the conceptual groundwork and introduces many concepts still used today.

Dalton, R. J. (2004), *Democratic Challenges, Democratic Choices* (Oxford: Oxford University Press). This book analyses mass attitudes related to democracy throughout postindustrial societies.

Eckstein, H. (1966), *A Theory of Stable Democracy* (Princeton, NJ: Princeton University Press). This book elaborates congruence theory, the political culture school's most fundamental theoretical assumption.

Inglehart, R. and Welzel, C. (2005), *Modernization, Cultural Change, and Democracy* (Cambridge: Cambridge University Press). This is the most encompassing study on the influence of mass beliefs on democracy and democratization, covering some 70 societies and 25 years.

IMPORTANT WEBSITES

<www.worldvaluessurvey.org> This is the homepage of the World Values Survey Association. It presents and offers for download survey data from some 80 societies covering a period from 1981 to 2001.

NOTES

1. John Gerring *et al.*'s (2005) democracy stock measure adds up for each country the democracy rating points it accumulated on the Polity IV democracy scale over time. However, points for particular years are depreciated by one percent for each year this year falls into the past of the respective base year of the measure. We thank John Gerring and his team for giving us access to the data with base year 1995.

2. Vanhanen's index of 'power resources' is a composite measure of the economic, intellectual, and social resources available to the average person in a country. A precise description is available in Vanhanen (1997, 2003).

3. The CIRI data by Richards and Cingranelli are part of the human rights project located at Binghamton University. Based on reports by Amnesty International, Human Rights Watch and other sources, CIRI measures effective respect of several dimensions of human rights. Two scales, integrity rights and empowerment rights, summarize these ratings. Integrity rights measure several freedom-from-oppression rights (such as freedom from torture), while empowerment rights measure several rights entitling people to participate in and exert control over power (such as the right to a free vote).

10 Gender and Democratization

Pamela Paxton

Overview

This chapter addresses **gender** aspects of democracy and democratization. It begins with a discussion of gender in definitions of democracy, stressing that while women may appear to be included in definitions of democracy, they are often not included in practice. Explicit attention to gender (and other minority statuses) in democracy is aided by making a distinction between formal, descriptive, and sub-stantive representation. Women's formal political representation is explored by introducing the fight for women's suffrage. Following that, the chapter focuses on women's descriptive representation with detailed information on women's **participation** in politics around the world. Finally, the chapter turns to a discussion of women's role in recent democratization movements around the world.

Introduction

Generally, little attention is paid to gender in discussions of democracy (Pateman 1989; Waylen 1994; Paxton 2000). Theorists use gender-neutral language when defining democracy and measure democracy with seemingly universal concepts such as the people's right to vote. But as pointed out by numerous feminist theorists, the appearance of 'neutrality' toward gender in political theory or 'equality' between men and women in government actually hides substantial gender inequality. If gender-neutral language is used in principle, but in practice only men appear, then women are not equal in our theories or measures, but invisible.

A cursory look around the world suggests that women are highly underrepresented in democracies, implying that gender may be more important to democracy and democratization than typically understood. At the turn of the twenty-first century, there is little overt discrimination against women in politics. Almost every country in the world provides the legal right for women to participate in politics. Women can vote and women can run for office. But the lack of visible women in the political life of most nations suggests that veiled discrimination against women remains. In some countries, such as Sweden, Argentina, and Rwanda, women have made remarkable progress in their numbers. In many other countries, the struggle for equal representation proceeds slowly.

This chapter will address gender aspects of democracy and democratization. I begin by discussing gender in definitions of democracy. It becomes clear that a lack of direct attention to gender in discussions of democracy, rather then including women under universal concepts such as citizen, removes them from theory and measurement. As Navarro and Bourque (1998: 175) point out: 'philosophical discussions of political democracy have been carried on largely in the absence of a discussion of women's rights or the impact of gender inequities on the function of a democratic political order.' If women are not typically included in our understanding of democracy, how can they be? The second section of this chapter introduces the distinction between formal, descriptive, and substantive representation. Distinguishing between these three types of representation opens the door for the inclusion of gender (and other minority statuses) into theory on democracy. To introduce women's formal political representation, the next section of the chapter briefly introduces the fight for women's suffrage. Following that, we focus on women's descriptive representation by presenting detailed information on women's participation in politics around the world. This section highlights both women's generally low levels of representation around the world and the substantial variation that exists in women's achieved levels of representation. Finally, the chapter turns to a discussion of women's role in recent democratization movements around the world.

Gender in Definitions of Democracy

Almost all definitions of democracy derive from Dahl's (1971: 4) classic distinction between competition (contestation) and participation. Competition requires that at least some members of the political system can 'contest the conduct of the government' though regular and open elections. Competition is concerned only with the procedures used to determine leaders and not with the numbers of individuals who participate. Participation, Dahl's second dimension, relates to the numbers of people that can participate in politics. A democratic **regime** must be 'completely or almost completely responsive to all its citizens' (Dahl 1971: 2). Following this lead, contemporary scholars' definitions of democracy typically involve some discussion of universal suffrage, or the right to vote. Democracy requires inclusive political participation where all adults of a certain geographic area have political privileges. As an example consider Diamond, Linz, and Lipset's (1990: 6–7) definition of democracy:

democracy . . . denotes . . . a 'highly inclusive' level of political participation in the selection of leaders and policies, at least through regular and fair elections, such that no major (adult) social group is excluded.

A third common dimension, civil liberties, can be described as the freedom to express a variety of political opinions and the freedom to form and to participate in any political group.

Does the definition of democracy include women? On the surface it would appear so, as women should be able to contest elections and are included in the term 'major (adult) social group.' But feminist political theorists warn against the assumption that neutral language signifies inclusion. Indeed, theorists such as Anne Phillips, Carol Pateman, and Iris Young have shown that the abstract terms used in political theory, such as 'individual' or 'citizen', while having the appearance of being gender-neutral, actually signify white males (Pateman 1989; Phillips 1991; Young 1990).

So do women count as 'adults' or 'citizens' and are therefore included in these definitions of democracy? Or does the neutral language actually mask the exclusion of women? To answer this question we have to dig a bit deeper into various writers' definitions of democracy. Consider, for example, Samuel Huntington's (1991) definition of democracy. Huntington claims a government is democratic when 'its most powerful collective decision-makers are selected through fair, honest and periodic elections in which candidates freely compete for votes and in which virtually all the adult population is eligible to vote.' Huntington goes further, explicitly stating:

to the extent, for instance, that a political system denies voting participation to part of its society—as the South African system did to the 70 per cent of its population that was black, as Switzerland did to the 50 per cent of its population that was female, or as the USA did to the 10 per cent of its population that were southern blacks—it is undemocratic (1991: 7).

Far from rendering women invisible, it appears that Huntington explicitly includes them. In fact, in explicitly mentioning women and minorities, Huntington is almost unique. Most definitions use generic terms such as 'adults' or 'the people' without being explicit about who might be excluded.

But turning a few more pages in Huntington's book reveals that women can be excluded after all. Huntington (1991: 16) continues by giving 'reasonable

major criteria for when nineteenth-century political systems achieved minimal democratic qualifications in the context of that century'. One of these operational criteria is that '50 percent of adult males are eligible to vote'. Huntington's working definition using this criterion leads to a voting population made up of only 25 per cent of a typical adult population. And—at least in earlier historical contexts—it allows countries to be defined as democracies even if women do not have the right to vote.

The removal of women in practice from a definition that ostensibly includes them is also apparent in the work of Rueschemeyer, Stephens, and Stephens (1992). Rueschemeyer, Stephens, and Stephens begin with a fairly typical definition of democracy—'regular, free and fair elections of representatives with universal and equal suffrage' (1992: 43). Indeed, they state: 'however we define democracy in detail, it means nothing if it does not entail rule or participation in rule by the many' (1992: 41). But again turning a few additional pages sees women excluded from the definition of 'the many.' Rueschemeyer, Stephens, and Stephens explain that they 'choose for our historical investigations universal male voting rights, rather than truly universal suffrage, as a critical threshold that allows us to speak of democracy' (1992: 48). Thus, countries are considered democratic when universal male suffrage is achieved. Huntington's and Rueschemeyer, Stephens, and Stephens' definitions of democracy are hardly the only ones to include women in principle but exclude them in practice. See Paxton (2000) or for a variety of other examples.

If women are often overlooked in traditional theories of democracy, what about the newer trend to talk about the quality of democracy (Diamond and Morlino 2005)? Rather than distinguishing democracies from nondemocracies, theorists of the quality of democracy focus on determining what makes a 'good' democracy. And definitions of the quality of democracy are more likely to explicitly mention gender. Diamond and Morlino argue that eight dimensions help differentiate democracies by quality: the rule of law, participation, competition, vertical and horizontal accountability, respect for civil freedoms, greater political equality, and responsiveness. Equality is the relevant dimension for the inclusion of women. Diamond and Morlino (2005: xii) define this dimension as 'progressive implementation of greater political (and underlying it, social and economic) equality.' They further explain that the equality condition of democratic quality 'entails the prohibition of discrimination on the basis of gender, race, ethnicity, religion, political orientation, or other extraneous conditions' (xxvii). A focus on democratic quality therefore opens the door for the explicit discussion of gender in political theory. However, to this point, assessments of the quality of democracy have not explicitly considered the participation or representation of women (e.g. Altman and Peréz-Liñan 2002).

A particularly nice feature of a focus on equality is the acknowledgement that social and economic inequalities shape political inequalities. As Dietrich Rueschemeyer (2005: 47) explains:

Dominant groups can use their social and economic power resources more or less directly in the political sphere. And they can use their status and influence over education, cultural productions, and mass communications—their 'cultural hegemony,' in short—to shape in a less direct way the views, values, and preferences of subordinate groups. If these effects of social and economic inequality are not substantially contained, political equality will be extremely limited.

Although most current discussions of political equality focus on economic power, wealth, or socioeconomic inequality, the arguments easily apply to gender inequality. Think of males as the dominant group under gender stratification and re-read the quote above. To see how gender stratification might influence the views of the subordinate group,

> ### Box 10.1 Key points
>
> - Women may appear to be included in definitions of democracy but are often not included in practice.
>
> - Focusing on the quality of democracy opens the door to the explicit inclusion of women.

consider recent research by Richard Fox and Jennifer Lawless (2004). These researchers found that in a sample of *equally qualified* men and women, men were substantially more likely to express ambition toward political office. When the women were asked why they did not aspire to political office, they explained that they did not feel qualified. Such research suggests that women are socialized to believe that they are not qualified to participate in politics (see also Wolbrecht and Campbell 2007).

Assessing the quality of democracy raises the question: if a government chronically underrepresents women, are we positive the 'rules of the game' are fair? Certainly, the same question can be asked about any historically marginalized or oppressed group, for example a racial or ethnic group, and about economic groups. Understanding the quality of democracy requires going beyond a simple understanding of participation to understand the *factual representation* of such traditionally marginalized groups. It follows that to understand the way that gender can be incorporated into our understanding of democracy, we must better understand the concept of representation.

Women's Democratic Representation: Formal, Descriptive, and Substantive Representation

If the representation of women and other marginalized groups is central to democracy, what does 'equal representation' mean? When discussing democracy and women, theorists usually often make a distinction between formal, descriptive, and substantive representation. The most basic formulation of equal representation is *formal representation*—that women have the legal right to participate in politics on an equal basis with men. Achieving formal representation requires the removal of any barriers to women's participation in politics. Women must have the right to vote and the right to run for office. The goal of formal representation is the absence of direct and overt discrimination against women in politics.

The idea that women should have the right to vote has become nearly universally accepted over the last 100 years. Women's rights are now seen as human rights, and statements about women's political participation are set out in the resolutions, codes, and formal conventions of most international bodies as well as in the law of many individual countries. For example, at the 4th UN World Conference on Women held in Beijing in 1995, 189 countries agreed to a Platform for Action stating, 'No government can claim to be democratic until women are guaranteed the right to equal representation'. This is the type of representation at least overtly exemplified in most definitions of democracy—democracies must grant adult citizens the formal right to political participation.

But formal representation does not necessarily result in substantial numbers of women in positions of political power. Even though in most countries of the world women have the equal opportunity to vote and to participate in politics, women remain significantly underrepresented in positions of political decision-making. Over 98 per cent of countries in the world have granted women the formal right to vote and the formal right to stand for election. But few countries have more than 20 per cent women in their legislative bodies. Equal opportunity does not appear to automatically produce equality in the numbers of men and women participating in politics.

For this reason, feminist political theorists have argued that we need a different conception of equal representation. Equal representation can also require *descriptive representation*—descriptive similarity between representatives and constituents. If women make up 50 per cent of the population, they should also make up roughly 50 per cent of legislative and executive bodies.

Arguments for descriptive representation suggest that it is not enough to have formal political equality in politics. Rights alone do not remedy the social and economic inequalities that prevent women from taking advantage of their political opportunities. Instead, their past and continued exclusion from political elites reinforces the idea of women's inferiority (Phillips 1995).

To address this problem, feminist political theorists argue that something more is required: 'Those who have been traditionally subordinated, marginalized, or silenced need the security of a guaranteed voice and . . . democracies must act to redress the imbalance that centuries of oppression have wrought' (Phillips 1991: 7). That is, action must be taken, for example, electoral laws changed or gender quotas introduced, to ensure that women are represented in politics in numbers more proportionately similar to their presence in the population.

The case for descriptive representation hinges on the notion that racial, ethnic, and gender groups are uniquely suited to represent themselves in democracies. In principle, democratic ideals suggest that elected representatives will serve the interests of the entire community and be able to transcend any specific interests based on their own characteristics such as sex, race, or age. But in practice, 'while we may all be capable of that imaginative leap that takes us beyond our own situation, history indicates that we do this very partially, if at all' (Phillips 1991: 65). Because social groups (gender groups, ethnic groups) have different interests due to varied economic circumstances or histories of oppression, representation by groups other than ones own is not assured.

If groups cannot be well represented by other groups, each group needs to be represented among political elites. In the case of women, theorists argue that due to different socialization and life experiences, 'women bring to politics a different set of values, experiences and expertise' Phillips (1995: 6). Because of women's historically marginalized position, their general relegation to certain economic roles, and their primary responsibility for child and elder care, they have shared experiences and therefore common interests. Women have different interests than men, those interests cannot be represented by men, and therefore women must be present themselves in the political arena.

Even if we accept that women can best represent themselves and need to be numerically represented in politics, a question remains: Can *women* represent women? This question leads to a third type of equal representation: *substantive representation*, that women's interests must be advocated in the political arena. Substantive representation requires that politicians speak for and act to support women's issues.

Going even further than the numerical representation of women outlined in descriptive representation arguments, advocates of substantive representation point out that 'standing for' is not the same as 'acting for' (Pitkin 1972). Getting higher numbers of women involved in politics is only a necessary but not **sufficient condition** for women's *interests* to be served. For women's interests to be represented in politics, theorists argue that female politicians must be willing to and able to represent those interests. Some advocates of substantive representation argue that rather than simply electing women to political office, we should elect feminists, either women *or* men, who are more likely to be directly supportive of women's interests (Tremblay and Pelletier 2000). Others advocate mechanisms such as women's caucuses to support women who speak on heretofore unarticulated issue topics.

Box 10.2 **Key points**

- Formal representation is the legal right to participate in politics. For women this means having the right to vote and stand for office.

- Descriptive representation requires numeric similarity between legislative bodies and the electorate they represent in terms of gender, race, ethnicity, or other demographic characteristics. For women this means achieving a high percentage of representation in a legislature.

- Substantive representation requires that the interests and issues of a group be advocated in the political arena. For women this means ensuring that politicians speak for and act to support women's issues.

Women's Suffrage as an Aspect of Democratization

If we take the arguments in the previous section seriously, then understanding women's suffrage (formal representation) and women's legislative representation (descriptive representation) is critical to any understanding of democracy. This section will provide a brief review of the expansion of women's suffrage around the world while the next will present detailed information on women's political representation around the world.

Today we often take for granted that women have the right to vote almost everywhere, but this was not the case until the last century. From the world's first democracy in ancient Greece through the mid-1800s, political thinkers excluded women from notions of citizenship. Politics was the domain of men, and women were thought to lack the qualities and capabilities necessary for equal citizenship. Furthermore, religious doctrine and cultural traditions about women's proper place in society served as barriers to women's political participation. In the Third World, these beliefs were often reinforced by European Colonialism, which carried notions of separate spheres backed by political philosophers of the Enlightenment.

Against these powerful barriers, the fight for the formal representation of women in politics was long, difficult, and occasionally bloody. It was only following decades of struggle that women in many countries achieved suffrage. The enfranchisement of women was the primary goal of first-wave feminism. The term 'first wave' is used to distinguish early women's movements (covering the time period of the late nineteenth through the early twentieth century) from the women's liberation movements of the 1970s. Although women in many countries won the right to vote during feminism's first wave, in parts of the world the struggle continued for many years afterward.

Compared to fights for male suffrage, women's suffrage movements faced unique obstacles. Often a woman's movement in a particular country had to address distinctive cultural, political, or religious circumstances. In Latin America, for example, traditional values and machismo served to hinder women's progress (Lavrin 1994). In Uruguay, one opponent to suffrage invented a new term, *machonismo*, to describe the desire to copy men and divert women from their natural path (Hannam, Auchterlonie, and Holden 2000). Authoritarian regimes and conservative parties tended to oppose democratization and the extension of voting rights. Direct government suppression of independent women's organizations occurred at various times in France, Russia, China, Japan, Indonesia, Iran, Brazil, and Peru (Randall 1987). And, in the Middle East, Islam was (and is) used to justify women's continued exclusion from political participation.

Across the world, women's suffrage movements differed in many ways. For example, some women's movements developed earlier than others. Ann Knight, a British Quaker, produced the first recognizable women's suffrage pamphlet in 1847. And the first formal demand for women's right to vote in the USA was made only a year later at the Seneca Falls Convention in New York. By 1893, when New Zealand became the first country to introduce universal suffrage, movements in many Western countries were in full swing. The first-wave of the women's movement had begun in France and Germany in the 1860s, followed by the Nordic Countries in the 1870s and 1880s. Women's movements in Asia, Latin America, and the Middle East often lagged behind, developing in the first decades of the twentieth century.

Another factor that varied both within and across suffrage movements is women's use of militant tactics. Militant tactics, used first by suffrage organizations in the United Kingdom, can be distinguished from more conventional tactics such as lobbying, petitioning, and letter writing. Militancy can include the disruption of meetings, tax resistance, breaking windows, arson attacks on public buildings, imprisonment, and hunger striking. For example, on 1 March 1912 British suffragettes made coordinated stone-throwing attacks to break windows throughout London at 15-minute intervals (Jorgensen-Earp 1999).

Women used militant tactics, organizing demonstrations and attacking legislatures, in a wide range of countries (Jayawardena 1986). For example, in 1911, the Chinese Suffragette Society went to the first meetings of the National Assembly. When they were refused the vote they launched an attack and, by the third day, the Assembly had to send for troops for protection. Similarly, in Guangdong, the Provisional Government had promised women the vote, but retracted it, and women invaded the legislature (Hannam, Auchterlonie, and Holden 2000). Women also used militancy in Japan (1924), Egypt (1924), Iran (1917), and Sri Lanka (1927). In other countries women were reluctant to use militant tactics, afraid of being called unwomanly or too radical.

Just because women were fighting for the right to vote does not mean they achieved it quickly.

From the 1848 Seneca Falls Convention demand for female suffrage, it would take the USA 72 years—until 1920—to grant women that right. Table 10.1 presents dates of women's suffrage around the world for a select list of countries.

Over time these varying national debates about women's rights gave way to an internationally-recognized universal belief in women's enfranchisement (Paxton, Hughes, and Green 2006), and most countries of the world had granted women suffrage by the 1960s. It was sometimes countries with longer histories of democratic principles that held out—continuing to deny women rights. In Switzerland, for example, women gained the right to vote nationally only in 1971 and in local elections as late as 1990. Another group of countries with late suffrage rights

Table 10.1 Dates of Women's Suffrage in Selected Countries

1893	New Zealand
1902	Australia (aboriginal women excluded)
1906	Finland
1913	Norway
1915	Denmark
1918	Austria, Estonia, Germany, Hungary, Poland, United Kingdom (women over 30)
1920	United States of America
1930	South Africa (Whites), Turkey
1931	Chile (municipal elections), Spain, Sri Lanka
1932	Brazil, Thailand
1937	Philippines
1939	El Salvador
1942	Dominican Republic
1944	France
1945	Indonesia, Italy, Senegal
1947	Pakistan
1949	China, Costa Rica, Syria
1952	Greece
1956	Egypt
1959	Madagascar, Tunisia, Tanzania
1963	Afghanistan, Iran, Kenya
1971	Switzerland
1972	Bangladesh
1974	Jordan, Solomon Islands
1976	Portugal
1980	Iraq, Vanuatu
1994	South Africa (Blacks)
2005	Kuwait

were in the Middle East. In 1999 women secured voting rights in the country of Qatar, followed by Bahrain in 2001, Oman in 2003, and United Arab Emirates in 2006. One of women's most recent successes took place in Kuwait when, following a drawn out battle and several failed attempts, women were finally granted the right to vote in May 2005.

Despite these recent victories, women's equal citizenship is not yet universal. In Lebanon proof of education is required for a woman to vote, while a man is not subject to any education restrictions. Women's vote is optional, while men are required to vote by law. In Bhutan only one vote per family is

---

Box 10.3 Key points

- Women's fight for the right to vote was long, difficult, and sometimes bloody.

- Women achieved suffrage only recently in some places and still do not have the full right to vote in a few countries.

---

allowed at the village level, meaning that women are often excluded. As of 2007 Saudi Arabia still refuses to allow women the right to vote.

Women's Representation as an Aspect of Democracy

After the fight for formal representation was largely won, women needed to fight for *descriptive representation*. Slowly over the course of the twentieth century women began to make inroads into areas of power typically held by men: women began to hold political office, a few led the way as presidents and prime ministers, and women began to fill cabinet positions and advise leaders on public policy. But despite important landmark gains, women today are not well represented in politics. The worldwide average percentage of women in national parliaments is only 16 per cent. Of the over 190 countries in the world, a woman is head of government (president or prime minister) in only eight.

However there is substantial variation around the world in women's political representation. In some countries, women have become commonplace as members of parliament, reaching 20, 30, and even 40 per cent of legislatures. In many other countries, however, the struggle for descriptive representation proceeds slowly and women remain barely visible in political life. The pace of women's access to positions of power was also very different from country to country. In some countries women appeared in politics in significant numbers by the 1970s, while in others it would take until the 1990s to gain a political presence.

Figure 10.1 provides a way to understand the growth in women's descriptive representation over time. Figure 10.1 demonstrates that while women have reached important milestones, such as 20 per

cent of national legislatures in an increasing percentage of countries, women's overall representation remains low. Although over 60 per cent of countries have reached at least 10 per cent women in their national legislature, fewer have crossed the 20 per cent barrier.

There is substantial variation across regions of the world, and many highly developed Western countries fall far behind developing countries in their representation of women as political leaders. For example, Table 10.2 presents the top 20 and bottom 20 countries ranked by their percentage of women in national legislatures. As of April 2008, the USA placed 85th of 185 countries, falling behind Vietnam, Ecuador, and Ethiopia. Britain falls 69th, behind Mexico, Namibia, and Singapore. France, Italy, and the USA have never had a female president while Sri Lanka, the Philippines, and Indonesia have. It is also

---

Box 10.4 Key points

- Women have made substantial gains in representation in some countries, reaching 30 or 40 per cent of a legislature.

- In many countries women still make up only a small minority of legislators.

- Western countries do not necessarily lead the world in the representation of women.

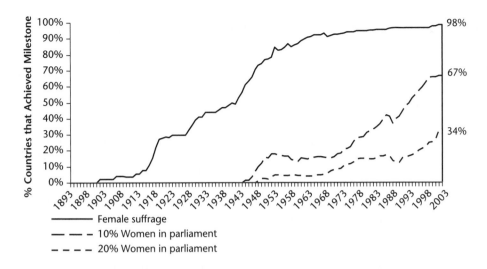

Fig 10.1 Countries Achieving Political Milestones for Women, 1893–2006

important to recognize that the top 20 countries are not that typical. Generally, 66 per cent of countries have fewer than 20 per cent women in their national legislatures. And looking at the bottom of Table 10.2 reminds us that seven countries have no women in their parliaments at all (see Paxton and Hughes 2007 for more information).

Table 10.2 Per cent Women in National Legislatures: Top 20 and Bottom 20 Countries

Rank	Country	Per cent	Rank	Country	Per cent
1	Rwanda	48.8%	...	...	.
2	Sweden	47.0%	124	Haiti	4.1%
3	Cuba	43.2%	124	Iran	4.1%
4	Finland	41.5%	125	Vanuatu	3.8%
5	Argentina	40.0%	126	Tonga	3.3%
6	Netherlands	39.3%	127	Comoros	3.0%
7	Denmark	38.0%	127	Marshall Islands	3.0%
8	Costa Rica	36.8%	128	Bhutan	2.7%
9	Spain	36.6%	129	Bahrain	2.5%
10	Norway	36.1%	130	Egypt	1.8%
11	Belgium	35.3%	130	Sao Tome and Principe	1.8%
12	Mozambique	34.8%	131	Kuwait	1.5%
13	Iceland	33.3%	132	Papua New Guinea	0.9%
14	New Zealand	33.1%	133	Yemen	0.3%
15	South Africa	33.0%	134	Belize	0.0%
16	Austria	32.8%	134	Micronesia	0.0%
17	Germany	31.6%	134	Nauru	0.0%
18	Uganda	30.7%	134	Palau	0.0%
19	Burundi	30.5%	134	Saudi Arabia	0.0%
20	Tanzania	30.4%	134	Solomon Islands	0.0%
...	...	.	134	Tuvalu	0.0%
...	...	.			

Women and Democratization Movements

Are there gender aspects to democratization movements? This section will explore how women and women's organizations have mobilized against authoritarian **states**. For example, women have used their roles as mothers to protest human rights abuses. An important feature of this section of the chapter will be women's use of **social movements** to enact change. Since women have traditionally been excluded from mainstream political activities, women can be particularly effective in pushing for democracy in situations where such traditional political activities are repressed by the state. The end of the section will also point out that even when women help achieve democracy, they may find it difficult to translate their participation in democratization movements into tangible gains in actual political power in the new democratic regime.

Women and women's organizations have mobilized against the human rights abuses of authoritarian regimes. Perhaps the most famous example of women fighting for democratization is the 'Mothers of the Plaza de Mayo', a group of mothers who protested the 'disappearance' of their children by the Argentinean military. Beginning in 1977, mothers gathered on Thursdays on the Plaza de Mayo, wore distinctive white headscarves, and processed in front of the Presidential palace carrying pictures of their kidnapped children. The Mothers also published demands in newspapers requesting information on the whereabouts of their children and worked with international agents to expose human rights abuses. Over time the number of women participating in the weekly demonstration grew, and drew international attention to human rights abuses in Argentina. Other women's groups fighting against authoritarian regimes across Latin America followed the lead of the Mothers and framed their protests as mothers, daughters, sisters, and grandmothers rather than individuals (Jacquette and Wolchik 1998).

The example of the Mothers of the Plaza de Mayo illustrates two important points about women's activism in democratization movements more generally. First, because women have been traditionally excluded from mainstream political activities such as political parties or unions, women have unique opportunities to mobilize precisely when mainstream activities are being repressed (Noonan 1995). Women's and other social movements are an important source of political activism when political parties, for example, are banned (Jaquette and Wolchick 1998). The opportunity for women presents itself because, in contrast to men, women's sources of power are often informal and non-traditional (Jaquette 1991). If women are 'invisible' in the public sphere, then they can be political actors during times when political action is dangerous (Chuchryk 1991). For example, when the government of Chile cracked down on street demonstrations by unions, women's human rights groups continued to protest (Noonan 1995: 102).

The second unique feature of women's activism exemplified by the Mothers of the Plaza de Mayo is the use of gender in the fight for democratic principles. The Mothers felt that they had the right to protest, as mothers, about their concern for their children and how their families were profoundly impacted by a disappearance (Fisher 1989). Similarly, housewife organizations in Latin America demonstrated and held purchasing strikes against the high cost of living, arguing that their children were going hungry because of economic crises and the regime's economic policies. These housewives organizations were responsible for helping organize larger urban protests against deteriorating living standards (del Carmen Feijoo and Gogna 1990).

Using gendered frames can be a particularly effective strategy against regimes that use gendered imagery to consolidate power. For example, the military had difficulty dealing with the Mothers in Argentina and in other countries such as Chile because it had claimed moral authority to defend family values (Noonan 1995). Across Latin America, regimes reinforced traditional views of a woman's place, co-opted traditional symbols of feminine morality, spirituality, and motherhood, and made 'Family, God, and Liberty' the cornerstone of the militaristic authoritarian regime (Alverez 1990: 5–8). When women in turn used this same imagery to protest, regimes had little recourse. As explained by Jo Fisher (1989: 60), the presence of 'silent, accusing' mothers on the Plaza de Mayo exemplified the very things the regime claimed to protect. In short, women can strategically challenge state power by seeming to act within traditional gender roles.

Women may also be safer than other groups when they use their gender against an authoritarian regime. It is difficult for a regime to retaliate against women who are only fulfilling their duties as 'good' mothers. Women themselves stated that they felt safer than other family members when protesting. In the words of a Mother of the Plaza de Mayo, 'a mother always seems more untouchable' (quoted in del Carmen Feijoo and Gogna 1990: 90). By using a maternal frame for their activities, women's activism meshed with state discourse and was therefore safer than a more oppositional frame (Noonan 1995). But safer does not equal safe; the first President of the Argentinean Mothers was one of many women that disappeared during the authoritarian period.

It is worth noting that women's activism for democracy was often linked to more general feminist

> ## Box 10.5 **Key points**
>
> - Because women often work outside traditional politics women may have unique opportunities to mobilize when regimes repress traditional politics.
>
> - Women can use gender to help them protest against repressive regimes.
>
> - Even though women may help in the fight for democracy they do not always achieve representation once democracy is achieved.

activism. As women gained political experience, they attempted to influence the state for a variety of causes that would help mothers and women. Consider a slogan of the Chilean women's movement, 'We want democracy in the nation and in the home' (quoted in Noonan 1995: 81). But although women help to resist authoritarian rule, they may find it hard to convert their activism into political representation once democracy resumes (Waylen 1994). The sobering statistics presented in the previous section remind us that women's participation in democratization movements does not always result in their equal representation once democracy is consolidated. Instead, women's movements continue to fight for the inclusion of women in all aspects of democracy.

Conclusion

This chapter addressed gender aspects of democracy and democratization. It began by pointing out that although women may appear to be included in definitions of democracy, they are often not included in practice. Beyond the simple inclusion of women's suffrage in discussions of democratization, attention to gender (and other minority statuses) in democracy is aided by making a distinction between formal, descriptive, and substantive representation. Both descriptive representation and substantive representation suggest that women's numbers matter. But women's participation in politics around the world shows a general lack of descriptive representation. Women's underrepresentation in democracies around the world implies that gender may be more important to democracy and democratization than typically understood.

QUESTIONS

1. Should measures of democracy explicitly include gender?

2. Is it reasonable for democracy to be measured differently for different time periods (e.g. male suffrage in the nineteenth century, female suffrage in the twentieth)?

3. What are the possible implications of excluding women's suffrage from the measurement of democracy? Does women's suffrage have implications for the history of democracy? For the causes of democracy? For the consequences of democracy?

4. Discuss the costs and benefits of taking descriptive representation seriously in democracies.

5. Is substantive representation an attainable goal? Is it a reasonable one? What are women's interests?

6. In what ways was the fight for women's suffrage different than the fight for male suffrage?

Visit the Online Resource Centre that accompanies this book for additional questions to accompany each chapter, and a range of other resources: <www.oxfordtextbooks.co.uk/orc/haerpfer/>.

FURTHER READING

Paxton, P. and Hughes, M. (2007), *Women, Politics, and Power: A Global Perspective* (Thousand Oaks, CA: Pine Forge Press). Provides a clear and detailed introduction to women's political representation across a wide range of countries and regions. Using broad statistical overviews and detailed case-study accounts, the book documents both historical trends and the contemporary state of women's political strength across diverse countries.

Phillips, A. (1995), *The Politics of Presence: The Political Representation of Gender, Ethnicity and Race* (Oxford: Clarendon Press). Does the identity of representatives matter? Does the fair representation of disadvantaged groups require their presence in legislatures? This text contributes to democratic theory by addresses problems of representative democracy with regard to gender and ethnic composition.

Paxton, P. (2000), 'Women's Suffrage in the Measurement of Democracy: Problems of Operationalization', *Studies in Comparative International Development*, 35/3: 92–111. Provides documentation of the disconnection between definitions of democracy and their use in practice.

Noonan, R. K. (1995), 'Women Against the State: Political Opportunities and Collective Action Frames in Chile's Transition to Democracy', *Sociological Forum* 10/1: 81–111. Jaquette, Jane S. and Wolchik, S. (1998) (eds) , *Women and Democracy: Latin America and Central and Eastern Europe* (Baltimore, MD: Johns Hopkins University Press). Two of many books and articles addressing women's role in democratization movements.

IMPORTANT WEBSITES

<www.idea.int/gender> The International IDEA Women in Politics page provides information on women's political participation and gender quotas.

<www.ipu.org> The IPU Parline Database archives data on women's representation in parliaments.

<www.un.org> The UN Fourth World Conference on Women Platform for Action: Women in Power and Decision-Making.

Social Capital and Civil Society

Natalia Letki*

Overview

This chapter focuses on the role of civil society and social capital in the process of democratization. It reconstructs the definitions of these terms in the context of political change and analyses the ways in which civil society and social capital are functional for the initiation and **consolidation** of democracies. It also recalls main arguments cast against the idea that civic activism and attitudes are a necessary precondition for a modern democracy. It concludes stressing that: (1) civil society and social capital may perform a number of vital functions for the introduction and consolidation of democracy, are neither a necessary nor a **sufficient condition** for a successful democratization, and (2) civil society and social capital and their relation to political and economic institutions are context specific.

Introduction

Democratization literature is plentiful and offers numerous explanations for why, how and when democracies emerge and consolidate or fail. It presents a long list of factors that are important in the process of 'making a democracy' (see Ch. 6), but it has been appreciated for several decades now that one of the most important among them are cultural predispositions of a given society (Almond and Verba 1963). Even the definition of democratic consolidation refers to the degree to which democratic government and liberal values are embedded in the minds of citizens (Linz and Stepan 1996b). This chapter will focus on the phenomena that are thought to contribute to the emergence of such a democratic political culture: social capital and civil society. In particular it will try to establish what functions social capital and civil society perform in the process of democratization. It will also point to a number of issues that make the relationship between civil society and social capital on one hand, and democracy on the other, much less obvious than it is widely believed.

Numerous accounts of the relationship between civil society and/or social capital, and democracy present the benevolent effects of the former on the latter. It has been argued that civil society and social capital contribute to the emergence of participatory civic culture, dissemination of liberal values, articulation of citizens' interests, and to creating mechanisms for influencing institutional responsiveness (Putnam 1993). As a result, both civil society and social capital have attracted an immense amount of attention in social sciences and beyond, among practitioners and the general public. They have also become part of the development strategies designed for democratizing and developing countries by international institutions.

At the same time, there exists a parallel stre. of research proposing that while both concepts are intellectually and emotionally appealing, their usefulness for analysing political and economic change in contexts other than stable Western democracies is limited. Decision on what type of organizations are included in civil society and contribute to social capital are context-insensitive, measures of the quality of democracy based on the strength of civil society are inadequate, and attempts to impose Western-born ideas on non-Western societies are myopic (Burnell and Calvert 2004). Moreover, arguments about the importance of civil society and social capital for democratic transitions are empirically unsustainable (Encarnación 2003).

The purpose of this chapter is therefore to present both accounts of the debate about the role of civil society and social capital in transition. Below, we define the key terms: social capital and civil society. Later, we will focus on their functionality in the context of democracy and democratization. After that we will turn to the main paradoxes linked to the role played by social capital and civil society in the new and old democracies.

Defining Civil Society and Social Capital

Both terms—civil society and social capital—are extremely popular, and as frequently happens with popular concepts, they have various definitions. Historically, the term 'civil society' came to designate the sphere of autonomy from the **state** in late eighteenth–early nineteenth century (Keane 1988). Since then, it has been used to mean a sphere of unrestrained activism of groups and associations of all sorts, free from intervention of the state. Because of this requirement for the self-limiting state, civil society has been linked exclusively with democracy. But the 'rebirth' of interest in the term 'civil society' is linked to the events in the authoritarian and totalitarian **regimes** of Latin America and Southern and East-Central Europe in the 1970s and 1980s. In these regions voluntary activism was severely restricted, if not outlawed, and citizens' activities were organized outside the official public space. As

a result, once the term 'civil society' was 'brought back in', it was stretched to also encompass protest activities and **social movements**, as the only possible manifestations of civic attitudes and engagement in non-democratic regimes (see Ch. 12).

'Civil society' refers therefore most often to the sphere of free, unrestricted social activism, in particular through voluntary groups and associations (Edwards *et al.* 2001). Some insist that civil society should be defined more broadly, including political parties and social movements, in particular in the context of democratic transformation (Kopecký and Mudde 2003). Expanding the definition of civil society to grass-root protest actions and social movements significantly changes how we understand the link between civic activism and various stages of democratization process. For example, Foley and Edwards (1996) described two main models of civil

serves as an ancillary to a demo-
another that represents liberal social
esting the non-democratic regime.
in the 1990s, the term 'social capi-
remely popular to designate links
and connections among people that result in the
creation of norms of cooperation and trust, and altogether constitute a resource which individuals and
communities can use for their benefit. It was during this period that the work of Robert Putnam on
democracy in Italy connected the concepts of social
capital and civil society (Putnam 1993). One of his
key indicators of social capital was membership in
voluntary associations, which customarily had been
used to capture civil society. Social capital, as mentioned above, builds directly on the notion of civic
associationalism as a key element shaping democratic attitudes and civic culture, but foremost—attitudes of trust and reciprocity that are only indirectly
related to politics. Social capital is usually defined
as consisting of two elements: behavioural (such as
networks), and attitudinal (such as trust and reciprocity). Various studies imply various types of links
between these elements (does trusting result from
meeting and socializing, or the other way round?),
but the key premise is that all types of networks are
relevant for civic attitudes and behaviour, as trust
and reciprocity can be generated by both formal
(group membership) and informal (e.g. spontaneous
sociability) networks.

Both civil society and social capital refer therefore
to social activism. The terms are often used interchangeably, especially in political science, where the
notion of social capital has been introduced as a direct
continuation of the thought of Alexis de Tocqueville
and his vision of participatory, deliberation-based
democratic society (Putnam 1993). From this short
review we may conclude that while 'civil society'

describes activism in voluntary organizations or, in
the context of third wave democratizations also in
social movements, 'social capital' refers also to the
product of this activism, i.e. norms and networks,
that can be used for further, individual or collective,
benefit. Civil society is a politically relevant sphere of
activism, but it is only one of several possible sources
of social capital. Others include informal sociability,
which is much more difficult to capture empirically,
thus is much less often present in empirical research,
and other types of interactions and exchanges, e.g.
within work or school context.

The above discussion is unlikely to disperse the
'acute definitional fuzziness' that both terms—civil
society and social capital—suffer from (Edwards and
Foley 2001: 4). It should be remembered, for example, that the definitions of these terms are highly
culturally specific and 'what the Poles have in mind
when they analyse civil society is only loosely comparable to what the Mexicans or the South Africans
take the term to mean' (Whitehead 2002: 71). However, it should help to achieve some clarity as to what
we mean when we talk about civil society and social
capital in the following sections.

Box 11.1 Key points

- In the context of democracy 'civil society' is defined
  as the sphere of free, unrestricted social activism,
  in particular through voluntary groups and associations. In non-democratic regimes this term refers to
  protest activities and social movements.

- Social capital is defined as consisting of two elements: behavioural (networks), and attitudinal
  (trust and reciprocity).

Civil Society and Social Capital in Democratization

While both civil society and social capital are
appealing concepts, as much as they refer to turning
every-day contacts and interactions into politically
relevant and important resources, it is the purported

functionality of both of them for how political and
economic institutions work that has put them in the
forefront of debate about the influence of social and
cultural factors on democracy and market economy.

In particular, high levels of social capital and a lively civil society have been considered prerequisites of democratic and economic consolidation. In contrast, societies with low levels of social capital and weak civil society are said to be unlikely to either initiate transformation or to consolidate a new democratic system. In their classic book on dimensions and challenges of democratization Linz and Stepan list civil society as one of five key spheres (next to political society, rule of law, state apparatus, and economic society) necessary for the modern democratic system to emerge and function (Linz and Stepan 1996). More recently, Whitehead widely discussed both civil society and social capital as 'condensed analogies that may help structure and simplify our thinking about the complex and untidy long-term changes involved in democratization' (Whitehead 2002: 67).

Democratization is a complex process, and has several stages; they vary depending on the type of transition. If it is a gradual, negotiated process, during the initial phase of liberalization civic organizations and popular movements may begin to emerge and they should strengthen as the building of democracy progresses. However, in a majority of transitions citizens' involvement manifested itself in the form of a rapid protest movement (as in the majority of transitions in Sub-Saharan Africa, democratizations in South-East Asia in the 1990s, recent 'revolutions' in Ukraine and Georgia). Also the 'regime of departure'—a type of non-democratic regime prior to the introduction of democracy—influences how and in what form civil society and social capital will manifest themselves. Totalitarian (such as those in Bulgaria or Romania in the pre-1989 communist Europe) and restrictive authoritarian regimes (e.g. pre-1987 South Korea) strictly outlawed any non-state linked citizens' activity, while authoritarian ones (e.g. Poland or Taiwan) reluctantly allowed some scope of civic freedoms, so that citizens' organizations and civic movements could emerge prior and during the liberalization and mature later on. African neopatrimonial authoritarian regimes allow for free associations, as long as they do not have a clearly political dimension (Bratton and Van de Walle 1994). Therefore, in transitions from more restrictive and closed regimes rapid protest movements are more likely to be the main manifestation of civic activism, while in more liberal ones more conventional forms of civic engagement will be permitted.

Networks as sources of information

Social relations are the key source of information, often acquired casually and effortlessly (Coleman 1988). **Participation** in networks of voluntary organizations, such as those that are part of civil society, but also more informal interactions, form channels citizens can—and do—use for information gathering and dissemination. Political discussion, exchange of opinions and preferences, as well as information about political issues provides citizens with powerful resources that can be used to aid preference formation, to vet politicians' activities, and to learn about opportunities for cooperation related to political matters. This is why formal and informal interactions are linked to increased institutional responsiveness, more frequent and more sophisticated political participation, and higher mobilization capacity (Claibourn and Martin 2007).

Such an important role of associations and groups as discussion forums has been stressed by researchers investigating democratization process in Southern and East-Central Europe and Latin America. It seems that while groups linked to the Catholic church in countries such as Brazil or Poland were indeed forums for 'critical discourse', that allowed groups and movements to 'organize antistate activity and promote democratization' (Paxton 2002: 258), in most authoritarian and totalitarian states voluntary activism was strictly outlawed, and the sphere of civil society could hardly exist (Bernhard 1993). This is where the notion of social capital is more useful: even when formal activism is restricted or forbidden, citizens form networks they rely on for information and dissemination of democratic ideals and opposition materials. Most often, these networks are not necessarily linked to the public sphere, they may originate at the workplace or within the local community. Where formal participation is suppressed, its functions are taken over by informal organizations. Even if these activities are not directly political but, e.g. welfare focused, they are likely to have political consequences (Bratton and Van de Walle 1994).

Associations as schools of democracy

Associations have long been called, in the Tocquevillian tradition, 'schools of democracy'. Taking part in their activities socializes citizens into other forms of participation, such as voting, campaigning or joining a political group, even if these groups are not directly aimed at politics and exercising political influence. 'Organizations teach citizens the civic virtues of trust, moderation, compromise, and reciprocity and skill of democratic discussion and organization' (Newton 2001: 229). The positive consequences of participation in organized activities are therefore threefold: they (1) socialize individuals into cooperative behaviour; (2) provide them with a number of skills necessary to effectively shape politics at the local and national level; and (3) expand their formal and informal networks, which they may use for other, political or social, purposes.

The absence of civil society prior to transition is therefore highly problematic for democratization: countries with no recent history of unrestrained civic activism will have problems forming an active civil society. This, in turn, will lower their chances for consolidation of democracy. Some authors, using examples from East-Central Europe and Africa, concede that certain key functions of civil society, such as spreading information and disseminating liberal attitudes can and have been performed by informal networks, but nevertheless to sustain a liberal democracy liberal civil society will be necessary (Howard 2002).

The relevance of membership in voluntary associations for political involvement has been demonstrated empirically using an example of the new democracies of Central-Eastern Europe. In the same manner to established democracies, where individuals involved in voluntary associations and groups are more likely to participate in politics (Verba *et al.* 1971), in new democracies citizens who have been mobilized into group activities and networks of some sort are more likely to be interested in politics, to vote, join political parties and join protest actions (Letki 2004). Voluntary activism and informal networks therefore aid not only information dissemination, but also interest articulation—two factors crucial for citizens' participation in democratic government.

Trust and democracy

It is only natural to expect that the publics in more liberal regimes will have more liberal social and political views than those living in non-democracies. However, other attitudes are less obvious. For example, trust in other people ('generalized trust') has been linked to democratic **governance**; citizens living in countries with longer histories of democracy are more likely to express trust in others, and those who are more trusting, are also more liberal and tolerant, which in turn aids the development of political and social pluralism (Inglehart and Welzel 2005). Whether this is a democratic institutional setup that leads to greater trust, or simply trust being conducive to democracy is yet unclear. What is clear is that interpersonal trust benefits democracies in a number of ways.

Dense trust networks make it possible to solve community problems at a community level, without institutional intervention and expenditure of institutional resources. Not only does this make institutions cheaper to run, but also it reinforces the ideal of self-government. Sense of community and connectedness with others, trust that extends beyond the immediate circle of family and friends, contribute to social order and liberal values. Trust and reciprocity aid contract enforcement and increase predictability and stability of cooperation. They allow individuals to overcome the classic dilemmas of collective action, and transform individual preferences into collective interests. In short, they aid all cooperation-based activities (Boix and Posner 1998).

The positive effects of interpersonal trust and reciprocity reach beyond politics, to the economy. There exists evidence linking levels of interpersonal trust and economic development, both in new and stable democracies. Since trust and reciprocity assist market exchange and contact enforcement, countries with high levels of interpersonal trust have more innovative and dynamically growing markets (Fukuyama 1995). And since there is a strong relationship between level of economic development and success of democratization (Przeworski *et al.* 1995), by contributing to the economic growth and human development, social trust and related attitudes also indirectly aid development and consolidation of democracy.

Scarcity of generalized trust is thought to be one of the main legacies of totalitarian and authoritarian regimes, where lack of political openness and pluralism led to the fragmentation and 'privatization' of society. Inability to trust those who are not members of the closest circle of family and friends is frequently quoted as the key obstacle to forming a strong liberal democracy, well anchored in mass values and attitudes. Societies undergoing a transition from non-democratic regimes are believed to be short of interpersonal trust, which in turn is considered to be one of the most serious obstacles to consolidating democracy (Inglehart 1997).

Similarly, social capital is perceived as highly functional for democracy, especially in the context of transition. All types of networks may potentially contribute to the development of civic attitudes and behaviour, all types of interactions outside the immediate circle of friends and family fuel the emergence of trusting and accommodating attitudes. Faith in those positive consequences of civil society and social capital for new democracies has made academics and practitioners believe that the weakness of civil society and low levels of social capital prior to transition are highly problematic for democratic consolidation. As a result, investing in social capital and the creation of interpersonal trust to promote development of democracy and market economy around the world has become one of more popular strategies applied by international institutions, such as World Bank and the IMF (Harriss 2002).

Reprise

Summing up, both social capital and civil society are regarded as highly functional for democracy prior, during and after the transition. They constitute networks than can be used to disseminate information, popularize democratic ideals, and mobilize citizens. They enable transformation of a segmented, distrustful society into a community with shared norms and objectives. In non-democracies, they help to bring the state down, in new democracies—they assist the development of a democratic, participatory political culture. Although formal civil associations are usually absent in authoritarian regimes, their functions are performed by protest movements.

> ### Box 11.2 **Key points**
>
> - Both civil society and social capital are regarded as highly functional for democracy and democratization: they aid dissemination of information and mobilization of citizens, and make political and economic cooperation possible.
>
> - Civil society and social capital are necessary for the emergence of a civic community and democratic, participatory culture.
>
> - Scarcity of social capital and weakness of civil society are considered to be among the key obstacles to introducing and consolidating democracy.

Paradoxes of Civil Society and Social Capital in New Democracies

The relevance of the functions of civil society and social capital, as discussed above, varies depending on the social and political context. Observing how civil society and social capital are generated and used in countries undergoing a democratic transition or consolidating a new democratic regime allows one to note some paradoxes which highlight that the relationship between civil society and social capital on one hand, and democracy on the other is not as straightforward as one might expect.

Are civil society and social capital necessary for democratization?

Ironically, there is no clear relationship between the type and strength of civic activism prior to transition, and the subsequent strength of civil society and social capital and—more generally—success of democratization. Although it would be logical to expect a direct link between the degree of social pluralism and civic mobilization prior to transition and the levels and quality of civil society in a new democracy, in fact this relationship is not very strong. Brazil and Poland are frequently quoted as countries that developed wide and active networks of civic activism before the transition yet faced serious obstacles when establishing civil society in a liberal democracy, while Spain democratized successfully despite a weak civil society prior to and after the transition (Whitehead 2002). Also numerous African democratizations were initiated as a result of mass civic action, yet after the transition even those African societies that managed to democratize (like Benin, Malawi, South Africa, and Zambia) notoriously suffer from low levels of civic and political engagement (Gyimah-Boadi 1996). Therefore, the patterns of presence or absence of civil society in transitions and success of democratization are not consistent with the cross-national relationship between social capital and civil society and democracy.

'Civil society against the state'?

The strength of civic activism prior to a transition may, ironically, become its weakness afterwards. High levels of mobilization against the authoritarian or totalitarian regime may be important for the initiation of the transition process or to demonstrate support for elite-led liberalization, but this type of civic participation is not sufficient for the development of stable democratic attitudes and participatory behaviour in the new, democratic order. Some authors present protest activities in new democracies as a specific version of a 'rebellious' civil society (Ekiert and Kubik 1999), but others stress their dysfunctionality in the context of a new, unstable regime (Edwards and Foley 2001). Protest activities do not fit with the consultation and feedback process

necessary to enhance the responsiveness and transparency of political institutions. Unless at least some parts of the popular movements evolve towards more conventional participation or conventional patterns of participation emerge as a part of the consolidation phase of democratization process, protest movements are more likely to destabilize than aid political situation (Mudde 2003).

Social capital, civil society, and democracy: what comes first?

Even in the context of stable democracies the causality of the relationship between social capital and the institutional setting is not a clear one, and this issue is even more complex in the case of new democracies. For a democracy to consolidate some degree of civic activism and social connectedness is necessary, but a certain degree of pluralism is also an indispensable pre-condition for the formation of a web of voluntary groups and associations. Survival of a new democracy is believed to hinge on mass attitudes and predispositions that form democratic political culture (Inglehart and Welzel 2005). At the same time, non-democratic regimes form conditions under which interpersonal relations atrophy, which leaves democratizing societies with a strong legacy of mistrust (Offe 1999). If one assumes that cultural characteristics are very stable, it seems that new democracies are doomed to fail because of the lack of required attitudinal preconditions among the public. However, this is clearly empirically wrong: democracies have been introduced and stabilized in countries that prior to transition had very weak civil society and very low levels of trust and reciprocity (e.g. Mexico, Chile, Spain or, more recently, Romania and Bulgaria).

In her analysis of the link between social capital (associational membership and interpersonal trust) and democracy Paxton has demonstrated empirically that the relationship between civic attitudes and behaviour and democratic government is reciprocal (2002). Others have shown that trust and related attitudes are as likely to be generated under non-democratic conditions as in democracies. In particular, East-Central European cases have provided evidence of trust and informal connections being resources essential for survival under the conditions of economic scarcity and political unpredictability (Letki and Evans 2005). There also exist studies presenting evidence for the causality flowing from a democratic and economic context to mass attitudes rather than the other way round (Muller and Seligson 1994). Overall, there is a large volume of research promoting links flowing from democracy to social capital and civil society as well as vice versa, with supporters of both sides holding strong onto their arguments.

Are all forms of social capital conducive for democracies?

So far we have focused on the desirable features of social capital and civil society, which are important for initiating democratization and for consolidation of democracy. It seems, however, that not all forms of associationalism and networks are equally compatible with democracy. First, following a recent distinction between 'bridging' and 'bonding' networks, where 'bridging' networks connect people of different groups/backgrounds, and 'bonding' networks form the intra-group structure, it should be noticed that all forms of 'tribalism', ethnic or religious loyalties represent strong bonding relationships. Associations and groups of that kind are thought to be generally incompatible with the principles of liberal democracy (Stolle and Rochon 2001). They promote patronage and corruption, and weaken pluralism and equality (Berman 1998). Movements and groups based predominantly on bonding ties (e.g. religious groups), which under the non-democratic regime may have generated high levels of civic mobilization aimed at liberalization and democratization, after transformation are likely to become a force undermining rather than stabilizing the new order (Paxton 2002).

Therefore, strong civil society does not necessarily mean strong democracy. A classic example of this paradox is the Weimar Republic, where a strong civil society led to the emergence of the Nazi regime (Berman 1997). Less extreme, but nevertheless dramatic, are the recent examples of Latin American states (Ecuador, Venezuela, Guatemala, and Bolivia), where strong popular forces were linked to attempts to overthrow a democratic regime or to the return of the authoritarian leaders (Brysk 2000). These observations are complemented by the recent findings that voluntary associations do not contribute to building a democratic political culture. They merely reflect the dominant 'cultural traits' of the time, thus any deficiencies in terms of liberal values and democratic predispositions are likely to be reflected and multiplied in the nature and activities of civil society (Rossteutscher 2002).

Also other, non-ethnicity based loyalty networks, may be detrimental to new democracies. For example, nomenklatura networks in East-Central Europe are frequently blamed for slowing down political and economic reforms through blending private and public interests, distorting resource circulation, limiting access to information, abusing the law and generally engaging in activities aimed at capturing the state. At the descriptive level nomenklatura networks are a very good example of informal social ties that are used as a resource for the economic advancement of individuals or even groups. Yet due to the network members' privileged position in the social and economic structure, the power of their networks is likely to become a serious burden

---

Box 11.3 Key points

- There is no clear empirical relationship between the type and strength of civic activism prior to transition, and the subsequent strength of civil society and social capital and success of democratization.

- Strength of anti-state civic movements prior to transition may destabilize politics in new democracies.

- Although higher levels of social capital and stronger civil society are associated with higher levels of democracy, it is not entirely clear whether this is social capital and civil society that strengthen democracy or democracy that generates social capital and promotes civil society.

- There are dark dimensions to social capital: strong intra-group links and loyalties (e.g. ethnic and religious, but also networks among political and economic elites) weaken pluralism and equality, and promote patronage and corruption.

on the new state, while their activities are aided by the uncertainty of the transition period (Stark and Bruszt 1998).

Paradoxically, the very movements that sparked renewed interest in civil society and its role in the modern democracy, like independence movements that led to a transformation in East-Central Europe, are likely to be now perceived as xenophobic, nationalistic, and populist. Independence movements, mobilizing citizens around the strive for freedom, lose their impact once freedom is introduced. Their appeal, based on calls for the freedom of expression of clearly defined national identities, weakens once conditions for political pluralism are achieved. If they choose to strive to attract followers around their original appeal, they are now likely to be perceived as antidemocratic, destabilizing elements in the society. The best examples are nationalistic movements in post-communist Europe (e.g. Slovakia, Bosnia), who were included in virtuous civil society for opposing communist regime, and excluded from it for using the same appeal to protest against the new democratic state (Mudde 2003).

Civil Society, Social Capital, and Democracy: A Western Perspective?

Much has been said about various types of networks and attitudes that accompany them, and their relevance for introduction and consolidation of democracy. However, this debate has been very strongly biased towards the models of society-state relations that have evolved in Western liberal democracies, including Western-style class structure and stress on liberal values. Patterns of transition and their outcomes around the world are analysed through the lens of Western academics and international institutions. Scholars dealing with political and social changes in Africa and Asia frequently point to this limited comparativeness of scholarship on transitions. They stress that the Western model of liberal democracy, promoted by Western societies in cooperation with international institutions, such as the IMF or **USAID**, is not compatible with the social, political and economic reality of African or Asian countries. In particular, the relations between the state and civil society, and the definitions of these two terms in these contexts diverge significantly from a celebrated 'Hegelian tradition'. Religious tradition of Confucianism forms a different basis for the relations between individuals, and their relations with the state in Asia than individualistic patterns found in Western societies. Pre-capitalist, personalistic social and economic relations dominant in Africa form a major challenge to the society-state relations rooted in the corporatist tradition of the West (Burnell and Calvert 2004).

A further example of such limited applicability of Western paradigms to analysing social phenomena outside of the Western context is post-communist East-Central Europe. Serious weakness of formal activism in groups and associations is accompanied by very strong interpersonal networks which, although politically largely irrelevant, have a very high social and economic capacity (Howard 2002). These networks are a direct legacy of communism, when they were a key resource used to 'get things done' (Rose 2001).

Lack of understanding of the specificity of social relations in various regions of the world will obscure

---

Box 11.4 **Key points**

- Concepts of social capital and civil society are biased towards the models of society-state relations that have evolved in Western liberal democracies. Therefore, their applicability to other contexts is limited.

- Lack of understanding of the specificity of social relations in various regions of the world limits the impact of international efforts to promote democracy.

their relationship with political institutions, and with democracy in particular. This observation is relevant beyond purely academic discourse: one of the key ways of promoting democracy around the world by an international community is through investing resources in building a strong civil society. However, research shows that the amounts spent on strengthening democracy through promoting liberal values and civil society are not linked to democratic survival. Organizations strongly sponsored by foreign aid do not hold on once the support programmes have been phased out for two main reasons: they are not well anchored in the local community and they focus on issues and activities preferred by the donors, but not necessarily most suitable or beneficial for the societies they are part of (Knack 2004).

Conclusion

The first part of this chapter re-examined the long-established relationship between civic attitudes and behaviour, and democracy. However, apart from discussing functionality of civil society and social capital for introduction and consolidation of democracy, it has also focused on certain shortcomings of the explanations offered by the social capital and civil society theory. The overall conclusion must therefore be that the relationship between social capital and civil society on one hand, and democracy on the other, is far less straightforward that has been hitherto postulated.

First, we argued that although voluntary associations and functions performed by them may fuel democratization and democratic consolidation, they are neither a sufficient nor a **necessary condition** for building democracy. It is true that prior to transition initiation, they may contribute to the emergence and dissemination of liberal values and attitudes among the mass public, socialize citizens into participatory behaviour, and allow to demonstrate popular support for political changes and oppositional elites that promote them. It is also true that afterwards civil society and grass-roots organizations serve as a consultation sphere that contributes to the policy-making **accountability** in new democracies. They promote self-government and civic-mindedness, help to improve standards for institutional accountability and transparency. Their benefits spill over the political sphere, and reach the market. Where individuals act on the assumption that others are trustworthy and inclined to cooperate, formal and informal economic exchange is more likely to happen, involve lower transaction costs, thus engaging fewer formal resources and institutional intervention.

However, most democratizations are elite-driven and based on elite-pacts, and most non-democratic regimes do not even allow for the emergence of, however limited, civil society. Its place is then taken by protest and independence movements, but their functionality for building a pluralistic, liberal society and participatory civic culture has been questioned as well. Empirical observation of the presence of civil society (either in the form of voluntary organizations or social movements) in democratizations around the world suggests that there is no significant relationship between the strength of civil society and social capital prior and after transition. Also, the strength of civil society may contribute to the institutional quality, but it may also destabilized new democratic institutions.

Second, we argued that there are some dark aspects of social capital and civil society which are usually overlooked when the functionality of these concepts for democracy and market economy is discussed. We pointed to the potential threat that strong bonding, in-group loyalties carry for the development of pluralism and equality. Also elite-based loyalty networks, although perfectly functional from the point of view of their participants political and economic situation, are one of the key obstacles slowing down political and economic reforms.

Finally, we presented arguments for the limited usefulness of the concepts of social capital and civil society for academics analysing transitions and practitioners supporting democratizations through grants and programs. Civil society, even if expanded to include protest movements in order to account for the specificity of third wave democratizations, is not a universal analytical or policy tool. It presupposes the existence of Western-style social structure, clear delineation of society from the state, corporatist style of government, and preference for liberal values and self-expression among the mass public. For cultural and economic reasons, these assumptions are unlikely to be true for most societies outside of the Western circle, making the classical model of civil society hardly compatible with the political and economic realities of Asian or African societies.

The appeal of civil society and social capital is based largely on their functionality for institutional quality, both in the sphere of politics and economics. In this chapter we have argued that they may maintain their functionality only if applied in the sensitive and context-conscious manner.

QUESTIONS

1. What are civil society and social capital?

2. What are the two types of civil society? Where do they come from? What is their relation to the state?

3. What is the relationship between civil society and attitudes of trust and reciprocity?

4. What is the relationship between the type of transition and civil society?

5. In what ways are networks functional for democratization?

6. Why are associations called the 'schools of democracy'?

Visit the Online Resource Centre that accompanies this book for additional questions to accompany each chapter, and a range of other resources: <www.oxfordtextbooks. co.uk/orc/haerpfer/>.

FURTHER READING

Burnell, P. J. and Calvert, P. (2004) (eds), *Civil Society in Democratization* (London: Frank Cass). This book is a collection of case-studies of civil society and social capital in transition. It provides relevant and context-sensitive examples of functionality and dysfunctionality of social organization for democratization.

Edwards, B., Foley, M. W. and Diani, M. (2001) (eds), *Beyond Tocqueville. Civil Society and the Social Capital Debate in Comparative Perspective* (Hanover, NH: Tufts University). This book brings together the most distinguished scholars dealing with the issue of social capital to present multi-disciplinary accounts of various functions of social capital and civil society.

Harriss, J. (2002), *Depoliticizing Development. The World Bank and Social Capital* (London: Anthem Press). This book provides a careful reconstruction of the origins of the concept of social capital, followed by its powerful critique in the context of international development.

Paxton, P. (2002), 'Social Capital and Democracy: An Interdependent Relationship', *American Sociological Review*, 67, 254–77. A widely-cited article presenting a careful and detailed empirical analysis of the relationship between social capital and democracy.

Warren, M. E. (1999) (ed.), *Democracy and Trust* (Cambridge: Cambridge University Press). An important, multi-faceted collection of essays by various authors analysing the link between trust and democracy.

IMPORTANT WEBSITES

<www.socialcapitalgateway.org> Social Capital Gateway is a website devoted to social capital. Apart from up-to-date information about social capital related events and publications and other social capital websites, it contains the most exhaustive social capital reading list.

NOTES

*   I would like to thank Adrienne LeBas and Christopher Garner for their helpful suggestions.

Part Three

Actors and Institutions

Social Movement, Trade Unions, and Advocacy Networks

Federico M. Rossi and Donatella della Porta

Overview

This chapter looks at the relationship between **social movements, cycles of protest**, waves of strikes, and **transnational advocacy networks** of resistance to non-democratic regimes in the global wave of democratization. It will present: (a) views from social movement studies within the democratization literature; (b) views of democratization within the social movement literature; (c) illustrations of the diverse roles played by movements, depending on the type of democratization process and the stage in which mobilizations emerge (resistance, liberalization, transition, **consolidation**, expansion).

Introduction

Social movements have not been prominent in the literature on democratization. Attention to social movements also varied within the main explanations of democratization. *Modernization theory* and the *historical class perspective*, as structural approaches mainly concerned with the preconditions for democracy, recognize a central role to economic conditions and social classes, but disregard social movements.

Transitology conceives democratization as an elite transactional process, presenting a more dynamic and contingent perspective of democratization, but recognizing a limited role for movements, unions and protest.

Social movements scholars, until recently, have paid little attention to democratization processes, mostly focusing their interest on democratic countries, where conditions for mobilization are more favourable. When addressing the role played by movements and **contentious politics** in democratization, they mainly apply two perspectives. First, the *new social movements* approach emphasizes the innovative, post-materialist dimension and non-state centric characteristic of movements during democratization. Second, the *political process* approach considers democratization as a product of the interaction between elite negotiations and mobilization processes.

In this chapter we will review these different perspectives, and finally propose an analytic organization of the different roles that social movements,

trade unions, advocacy networks, and **cycles of protest** play in the *dynamic, contingent* and *contentious* shaping of democracy. In doing this, we are of course not pleading for an exclusive focus on democratization 'from below'; we are convinced that the path and speed of democratization processes are influenced by the strength and characteristics of several social and political actors. The combination of protest and consensus is in fact a main challenge for democratization processes. We are however convinced that social movements are often important actors in all stages of democratization. In our discussion of these topics, examples will be drawn especially from Southern Europe, Eastern Europe, and Latin America.

Social Movements in Research on Democratization

This section will briefly review the limited role assigned to social movements and protest in democratization studies prior to the emergence of a more systematic interest on the issue by social movement students. We will begin with the structural approaches (*modernization theory* and the *historical class perspective*), and move then to the elite transactional process approach (*transitology*).

Structural approaches: modernization theory and historical class perspective

The first studies of democratization emerged in the aftermath of the massive destruction produced in Europe by World War II, and the reconfiguration of world politics linked mainly to the expansion of the Soviet Union's area of influence and decolonization in Africa and Asia. Within this context, two predominantly structural perspectives developed with the intention of explaining political regime change in peripheric countries (democratic, authoritarian or totalitarian). The intention generally was: (a) to identify the prerequisites for democracy to emerge and survive, and/or (b) to discover which social class is the key actor in promoting and sustaining a democratic regime.

Within modernization theory, Lipset's (1959) pioneer work associated the chances for the emergence of a democratic regime to economic development. This approach tended to recommend economic supports (such as Marshall Plans) as a precondition to political democratization, and accordingly considered the emergence of democracy in low-income countries improbable and its survival as precarious. Sustainable democracy required structural prerequisites, among them the development of a pro-democratic middle class. This perspective, however, does not take in much account agency and thus cannot explain why poor countries, such as Portugal (1974), Greece (1974), Ecuador (1979), Peru (1980), and Bolivia (1982), democratized before more industrialized countries such as Argentina (1983), Brazil (1985–1990), Chile (1991), and South Korea (1987–88). Although powerful in explaining the survival of already established democracies, modernization theory ignores the role of social actors in *crafting* democracy, and therefore cannot explain the different tempo (i.e. from decade long transitions to abrupt changes) and the quality of democratization (i.e. from procedural to substantive democracy).

Although some modernization scholars examined the role of the organized and mobilized actors in society, the most prominent one, Huntington (1965; 1991), rejects mobilization (in particular of the working class) as a source of democratization 'from below', defining as 'praetorian societies' those with high levels of mobilization. In his view, the potential disruption produced by claims for inclusion needs to be limited and controlled. Approaches such as Huntington's led to an additional, though inconsistent, conclusion that characterizes his version of modernization theory: that democracy needs low levels of mobilization and unionization, and that even these low levels can only be allowed after a relatively high level of industrialization has been achieved.

Several authors from diverse analytic traditions—among which Nancy Bermeo (1997), Ruth Collier (1999), Charles Tilly (2004a, b), and Doug McAdam *et al.* (2001)—have instead convincingly demonstrated the crucial role played by the mobilized actors in the emergence of democracy, and in its preservation or expansion. Especially within historical sociology, research singled out the role of 'the masses' in the first and second waves of democratization, as well as of resistance movements in the fall of authoritarian regimes at the end of World War II. A central question became: *Which is the democratizing social class?* In his historical approach Barrington Moore (1966), although agreeing with Lipset on the importance of some socioeconomic conditions, also stresses the role played by social classes (in particular, the urban bourgeoisie) in explaining first democratization in England (1642–49), France (1789–1848) and the USA (1861–65). Moore's hypotheses have been specified by Dietrich Rueschemeyer *et al.* (1992) who found that—given certain levels of economic development—the working class has been the key actor promoting democratization in the last two waves of democratization in southern Europe, South America, and the Caribbean. More recently, in another cross-national comparison, Ruth Collier (1999) suggested that the role of working class—although not so important in the nineteenth- and early-twentieth-century transitions in Western Europe as was suggested by Rueschemeyer *et al.*—was crucial in the most recent wave of democratization in Southern Europe and South America. Finally, John Markoff (1996) emphasizes the role of women's movements in demanding democratic rights in the first long wave of democratization, starting in the late eighteenth century.

Elite transactional process approach: transitology

While in the historical class perspective there is more concern for interactive historical paths than in classic modernization theory, both perspectives tend to overlook the role played by contentious actors, and the interactive mechanisms associated with democratization.[1] Agency is instead central in the so-called 'transitologist' approach, which however did not pay much attention to social movements as potential actors of democratization.

After the 1970s wave of democratization in southern Europe, political science approaches to the construction of political institutions have privileged parties as main democratic actors (Higley and Gunther 1992). Even the more dynamic approaches to democratization (O' Donnell and Schmitter 1986; Linz and Stepan 1996), that took into account the timing of the different steps of democratization, tended to perceive the *'reforma pactada/ruptura pactada'* in Spain (1977) as the model for successful democratization. This stressed a necessary de-mobilization of 'mass politics' (or at least their channelling within institutionalized political parties) for an effective consolidation of democracy.

Within this tradition, the most influential work on democratization is by O'Donnell and Schmitter (1986). In the theoretical volume concluding their broad research project, O'Donnell and Schmitter dedicate a section to what they call the 'resurrection of civil society', which means the short disruptive moment when movements, unions, churches and the society in general push for an initial liberalization of a non-democratic regime into a transition towards democracy. For the authors, this is a moment of great expectations when 'the people' emerges, but:

In any case, regardless of its intensity and of the background from which it emerges, this popular upsurge is always ephemeral. Selective repression, manipulation, and cooptation by those still in control of the state apparatus, the fatigue induced by frequent demonstrations and 'street theatre', the internal conflicts that are bound to emerge over choices about procedures and substantive policies, a sense of ethical disillusionment with the 'realistic' compromises imposed by pact-making or by the emergence of oligarchic leadership within its component groups are all factors leading toward the dissolution of the upsurge. The surge and decline of the 'people' leaves many dashed hopes and frustrated actors (1986: 55–6).

Thus, civil society short life is not only inevitable, given the re-channelling of **participation** through the political parties and the electoral system, but also desirable, as it is considered the only way to avoid frightening authoritarian soft-liners into abandoning the negotiation process with the pro-democracy moderates. In this vein, elites are not only the source of the democratization process, but also the ones who control its outcome. While for O'Donnell and Schmitter contentious politics favours the move from the liberalization of a non-democratic regime to a transition to democracy, for the authors in Higley and Gunther's (1992) volume, any kind of social movement, protest or strike must be controlled and demobilized in order to assure a consolidated procedural democracy. While in O'Donnell and Schmitter's view democratization is made possible by a division between (authoritarian and democratic) elites, in Higley and Gunther's analysis it is the consensus among negotiating elites that allows for consolidation. Transitology, thus, emphasizes the contingent and dynamic nature of the democratization process, but tends to reduce it to a bargaining among political elites in a context of uncertainty.

Within transitology Linz and Stepan (1996) present a model of extended transition, where not only the immediate liberalization/transition bargaining process is important, but also the characteristics of the previous non-democratic regime (i.e. authoritarian, totalitarian, post-totalitarian, sultanistic), the way the non-democratic elites exit from **state** power, the historical characteristics of the political parties and the elites, and when it ends the uncertainty climate. Their model of democratization pays explicit attention to 'civil society', defined in contrast to the 'political society' (i.e. the elites and institutionalized actors):

A robust civil society, with the capacity to generate political alternatives and to monitor government and state can help transitions get started, help resist reversals, help push transitions to their completion, help consolidate, and help deepen democracy. At all stages of the democratization process, therefore, a lively and independent civil society is invaluable (1996: 9).

Though recognizing its role in theory, the authors do not yet give much empirical space to civil society. They however reflect on the relationship between the characteristics of the previous authoritarian regime and the chances for the emergence of pro-democratic mobilizations (Linz and Stepan 1996: Ch. 3). Totalitarian regimes are those that, by eliminating any pluralism, jeopardize the development of autonomous organizations and networks that could then be the promoters of democracy. Sultanistic regimes, due to the high personalization of power, have a manipulative use of mobilization for ceremonial purposes and through parastate groups, discouraging and repressing any kind of autonomous organization that could sustain resistance networks. Authoritarian regimes, mainly when they were installed in countries with previous (semi) democratic experience, are the ones which generally experienced the most massive mobilizations, and the best organized underground resistance based on several networks that either pre-existed the regime or could be formed later, thanks to the higher degree of pluralism.

Linz and Stepan add another ideal-typical regime, post-totalitarian, but this seems to be more an intermediate step in the democratization of totalitarian regimes, than a regime type per se. Two sub-types of **authoritarianism**, not mentioned by these authors, are important for our purpose: (a) bureaucratic-authoritarianism, where a technocratic civic-military elite commands the de-politization of a mobilized society for capital accumulation (O'Donnell 1973), and (b) populist-authoritarianism, where the elites mobilizes the society from above for legitimating the regime while incorporating the lower classes. While some South American and South-East Asian countries (Argentina, Brazil, Chile, South Korea, Taiwan, etc) were bureaucratic-authoritarian; the predominant model in some Middle East and Northern African countries (Egypt, Algeria, etc) was the populist-authoritarian. Linz and Stepan hypothesize an interesting relationship between the type of non-democratic regime, and the potential for the emergence of movements, protests, strikes and underground resistance networks that antecedent liberalization, and accompanies democratization. This might offer not yet fully developed explanations for the differences that tend to appear in the degree and pace of protest emergence in democratization periods.

Linz and Stepan (1996: Ch. 2) also stress the need to consider multiple simultaneous transitions (e.g. simple, with only regime change; dual, with a change in regime plus economic system; triple, with change also in the nation-state arrangement). In this sense, it is not only important if the previous regime was authoritarian or totalitarian, but also if it was a capitalist or a communist one. Additionally, when there is a triple transition, the problem of nation-state building appears when nationalist movements mobilize in the name of contending visions of which should be the *demos* of the future democracy. Thus, while in the Soviet Union (1991) regional mobilization led to the dissolution of the political unit, in Spain it did not. Basque and Catalan nationalist movements undermined the **legitimacy** of Francisco Franco's regime, but were unsuccessful in achieving independence. Czechoslovakia (1989–92), for instance, experienced a peaceful dissolution of the polity along with a democratic and capitalist transition. These changes can only be explained through the intertwined role played by regime elites, democratic elites, mobilized groups, and international pressures. Within social movement literature, the role of movements was emphasized in the analysis of the moderation or radicalization of the claims for autonomy/ independence, and how this has favoured or jeopardized the transition to democracy (see Oberschall 2000; Glenn 2003; Reinares 1987).

Even though the dynamic, agency-focused approach of transitology allowed for an interest in the role played by movements in democratization to develop, it did not focus on them. In addition to its 'elitist bias', some other assumptions of transitology have been criticized. As Ruth Collier and James Mahoney (1997) argue, transitologists tend to emphasize the role of individuals over collectives, which reduces the process to strategic instrumental thinking, ignoring class-defined actors such as unions and labour/left-wing parties, and it is state-centric, subordinating social actors to state actors. As Gideon Baker (1999) contends, transitology tends to consider movements and protest actors as manipulated by elites and focusing on very instrumentally defined purposes. While an inevitable and desirable 'elitization' of the democratization process might be considered as the 'iron law' of transitolo-

gists, further research by the new social movements scholars and later by the political process students showed the important interplay between elites and the mobilized social actors as the necessary (though not sufficient) condition for a democratization process, questioning the elite-led/elite-ended logic that previously dominated democratization studies. A general agreement among scholars that have analysed democratization in non-elitist perspectives is that not even the Spanish transition model can be considered a purely elite-controlled bargaining process. Massive strike waves, terrorist attacks by nationalist movements, and an ascending cycle of protest characterized the transition (see Maravall 1982; Reinares 1987; Foweraker 1989), being better defined as a destabilization/extrication process (Collier 1999: 126–32) or as 'a cycle of protest intertwined with elite transaction' (McAdam *et al.* 2001: 186). In sum, transitology is accused of ignoring the long term, dynamic, contingent and contentious process associated to the creation of the conditions for the breakdown of non-democratic regimes. The next section addresses this question.

Box 12.1 **Key points**

- Modernization approaches have given little attention to agency (in general) and social movements in particular, focusing on the economic conditions for democratic stability.

- Other scholars have focused on the social classes that led democratization processes, paying however more attention to their structural conditions than to their mobilization.

- The dynamic study of democratization has considered social movements as short-lived relevant actors in the liberalization stage only, focusing research on the institutional actors specially when addressing transition and consolidation.

- Even though some authors mention a robust civil society as facilitating democratization process, transitology approaches have traditionally paid little empirical attention to its characteristics and development.

The Role of 'Democratization from Below': Perspectives from Social Movement Studies

With few exceptions (e.g. among Latin American scholars), the literature on social movements has shown little interest in democratization processes. Only recently the concept of contentious politics, as opposed to routine politics, has been proposed in order to link research on phenomena such as social movements, revolutions, strike waves, nationalisms and democratization (McAdam *et al.* 2001). Even those who accord an important role to social movements disagree on the positive versus negative effects of their intervention. Sometimes people mobilize against democratic regimes, demanding authoritarian solutions to political or economic crisis, providing the non-democratic actors with a popular source of legitimacy (e.g. middle class women's protests against Salvador Allende's government in Chile), and some actors seek restrictions of democratic rights in democratic regimes (e.g. European anti-immigration and xenophobic movements). In other cases, movements trying to promote democratization might have the unintended consequences of increasing state's repression, or facilitate the emergence of undemocratic actors (e.g. collapse of the Weimar Republic in Germany).

In many cases, however, a correspondence between social movements and the promotion of democracy can be found. Among others, Charles Tilly (2004b: 131) said,

What causes the strong but still incomplete correspondence between democratization and social movements? First, many of the same processes that cause democratization also independently promote social movements. Second, democratization as such further encourages people to form social movements. Third, under some conditions and in a more limited way social movements themselves promote democratization.

As the relationship between social movements and democratization is not simple, the main question for social movements' scholars has been: *When and how do movements promote democratization?* This section reviews the two main approaches in social movements' studies that have tried to answer this question:

the *new social movements*, and the *political process* approaches. We will begin with a brief overview of these standpoints, and then analyse the role of social movements in each stage of democratization.

The social movement literature has been very much focused on the Western European and North American experiences and only recently has systematic attention been paid to relations between social movements and democratization. In Europe the *new social movement* approach has looked at the emergence of a new actor in post-industrial society. Alain Touraine (1981), the most prominent exponent of this perspective, argued that the capital-labour conflict has been surpassed by new conflicts related to the self representation of the society and the types of actions related to its transformation. Thus, the new conflicts developed outside of the factory and the labour movement, and the claims for taking state power were abandoned by the women's, students and environmental movements of Western Europe. Although its original aim was to explain a very different phenomenon, the new social movements approach was widely applied in the 1980–1990s Latin American transitions, emphasizing the cultural and social democratization exercised by movements, de-centring the state as their main interlocutor (Slater 1985; Jelin 1987; Escobar and Álvarez 1992).

As interest in Latin American democratizations and the new social movements approach decreased, the *political process* approach became more prominent in studies of regime transformation as a result of the emergence of new democracies in Central and Eastern Europe and the former Soviet Union. Developed initially in the USA, but then rapidly spread in Europe, the political process approach devotes more systematic attention to the institutional context than the new social movements approach, highlighting the interrelationship amid governmental actors, political parties, social movements and protest. Trying to elucidate what favours the emergence of contention in liberal democracies, scholars within this perspective have proposed a curvilinear relation between the emergence of protest and the openness of political opportunities (Eisinger 1973). Recently, however, some North American scholars within this approach proposed the reformulation of transitology's perspective, taking into account the role played by contentious politics (McAdam *et al.* 2001; Schock 2005; Tilly 2004b). While social movements are not necessarily promoters of democracy, the elitist dynamic model does not fully explain democratization processes. Social movements play in fact different roles in each specific stage of the democratization process.

Cycles of protest and waves of strikes during democratization

Democratization is, in general, linked to two contentious dynamics: (a) a pro-democratic **cycle of protest**, and (b) an increasingly massive and non-syndical wave of strikes. According to Joe Foweraker (1995: 90, n. 2) '[d]emocratic transitions express a wide variety of trajectories and outcomes. The role of social movements within them is conditioned by the specific rhythm of the "protest cycle", the shape of the political opportunity structure, and the contingency of strategic choice'. In Spain, Brazil, and Peru, for instance, strike waves were very important during the entire or part of the democratization process (Maravall 1982; Sandoval 1998; Collier 1999). While Peru's democratization is very much associated with a strike wave (1977–80) against a highly unpopular authoritarian regime (Collier 1999), Brazil experienced a strike wave (1974–79), followed by a cycle of protest (1978–82) mainly mobilized by **urban movements** (Mainwaring 1987). Sometimes cycles of protest and strike waves converge, in many other occasions strike waves are stronger in the first resistance stages, decline later and, then, re-emerge during liberalization and transition in coordination with the upsurge of a cycle of protest originating from underground resistance networks.

As Table 12.1 shows, the role of social movements and other contentious actors varies in different stages of the democratization process. The rest of this chapter will illustrate this point with empirical cases.

Resistance to the non-democratic regime

Democratization as a process starts much earlier than transitology generally acknowledges. The elites begin a bargaining process because something happens that pushes some of them to withdraw their support for the non-democratic regime. One of the causes that undermines the legitimacy and the (national and international) support for the regime, is the role played by the *underground networks of resistance*. Latin American new social movements scholars were the first to study the role of the cultural and political *resistance to the authoritarian regimes* and the construction of alternative democratic networks (e.g. Jelin 1987). Human rights movements, trade unions, and churches promote the delegitimation of the authoritarian regime at international forums such as the United Nations, and in clandestine or open resistance to the authoritarian regime at the national level. The resilience of resistance networks under the impact of repression plays a decisive role in this stage, as they can lead to splits in the ruling authoritarian/totalitarian elites and force even unwilling elites to initiate liberalization (Schock 2005).

In countries with a majoritarian Roman Catholic population the Catholic Church played an important active role. In some countries, church-related actors played a pro-democratic role. The *Vicaría de la Solidaridad* in Chile condemned the repression, persecution and assassinations ordered by Augusto Pinochet, while helping coordination of the unions, parties and grassroots activists that organized protests against the regime in the 1980s (Lowden 1996). In Brazil, with the incorporation of liberation theology, the church helped recreate grassroots empowering spaces through the *Comunidades Eclesialis de Base* (CEB) (Burdick 1992). The role played by the CEB was central in the struggle for democratization, and the church worked as a broker in a pro-democratic coalition with the trade unions and urban movements. Similarly, in the Basque Countries, the local clergy supported the opposition against the Francoist regime, helping preserve the *Euskera* language (della Porta and Mattina 1986). And in Poland a

Table 12.1 The Role of Social Movements, Trade Unions, and Contentious Politics in Different Stages of Democratization

Stage	Role of social movements	Examples
Resistance	• Underground networks of resistance and cooperation among activists • International delegitimizing campaigns, denouncing of human rights violations	• Human rights movements and transnational advocacy networks • Anti-apartheid movement • Church-based networks
Liberalization	• Promoters of the expansion of the transition towards procedural democracy, or for the resistance to the process • Essay of new democratic practices (i.e. cultural [re]democratization)	• Trade unions strikes • Religion movements • Urban movements • Military led or controlled counter-movements
Transition	• Mobilization intertwined with elite pacts: Claims for justice and for the elimination of the reserved powers that limit the emerging democracy, or support to the authoritarian elites	• Human rights movements • Women's movements • Trade unions strikes • Right wing solidarity networks
Consolidation	• Movements introduce demands for a consolidated and inclusive substantive democracy, or claims for recovering the lost 'order' by limiting political or social rights	• Land-reform movements • Indigenous movements • Employment movements • Anti-immigration movements • Security protests
Expansion	• Campaigns for the democratization of international governmental organizations • Essay of local/national post-representative democracy	• Global justice movements

pro-democratic alliance developed between the Catholic Church and *Solidarność* union, which proved to be crucial in the network of resistance that helped to create the necessary resources for the massive mobilizations during liberalization and transition (Glenn 2003; Osa 2003).

In other countries, such as Argentina, the authorities of the Catholic Church played the role of the supportive bystander, and in some cases became an active participant in state terrorism (Verbitsky 2005), while civic networks played the delegitimizing roles (Wright 2007). The *Madres de Plaza de Mayo*, the *Servicio de Paz y Justicia* (SERPAJ), and the *Asamblea Permanente por los Derechos Humanos* (APDH), among other organizations of the human rights movement in coordination with human rights **transnational advocacy networks**, initiated national and transnational campaigns for 'truth and justice' in order to learn the fate of the 30,000 'disappeared'—kidnapped and killed by the military. By 'naming and shaming',

social movement organizations contribute to damage the image of authoritarian regimes in international forums such as the United Nations and the Organization of American States (Brysk 1993; Keck and Sikkink 1998). Although authoritarian regimes are closed to any kind of political opposition, Margaret Keck and Kathryn Sikkink (1998) have shown that a 'boomerang pattern' develops when human rights networks sensitize third countries and intergovernmental organizations to generate political pressure on an authoritarian regime:

Governments are the primary 'guarantors' of rights, but also their primary violators. When government violates or refuses to recognize rights, individuals and domestic groups often have no recourse within domestic political and judicial arenas. They may seek international connections finally to express their concerns and even to protect their lives. When channels between the state and its domestic actors are blocked, the boomerang pattern of influence characteristic of international networks may occur: domestic NGOs bypass their state and directly search out international allies to try to bring pressure on their states from outside (1998: 12).

Resistance to authoritarian regimes also developed inside non-religious cultural groups. In the Czech Republic, the main organization in the democratization movement, the Civic Forum, emerged from the action of a network of artists and theatres constructing a space for autonomy and expression after strong state repression of students' protests (Glenn 2003). During the resistance stage, social movements and their allies may be effective promoters of democratic values and understandings that erode a non-democratic regime and set the **necessary conditions** for liberalization to take place.[2]

Liberalization and the upsurge of mobilization

Democratization needs an acceleration of certain dynamics in order to occur. That produces the perception among the authoritarian elites that there is no other choice than opening the regime if they want to avoid an imminent or potential civil war or violent takeover of power by democratic and/or revolutionary actors. This was the case in the failed civic-military socialist revolution in Portugal in 1974 that started the transition into a democratic (although capitalist) regime; and the effect produced by protracted insurgency in El Salvador (1994) and in South Africa (1994) (Wood 2000). The intensity of the protests and strikes plays a crucial role in shaping the regime elite chances of pursuing a long and controlled transition or a short extrication from state power. Therefore, during the *liberalization* stage, organized society publicly (re)emerges in a much more visible fashion after the elimination of some restrictions in what has been called a 'resurrection of civil society' (O'Donnell and Schmitter 1986). During this stage movements may promote the expansion of the transition towards effective democracy, or resist the democratization process. In fact, trade unions, labour/left-wing parties and urban movements, mainly in shantytowns and industrial districts have been presented as main actors seeking democracy (Collier 1999). In Chile, shantytown movements organized by members of the Communist Party in Santiago were among the

main promoters of a 1983–87 cycle of protest that—though not fully effective—made clear for Augusto Pinochet that some source of legitimacy was necessary in order to stay in government, and so led to the initiation of a controlled transition (Schneider 1995; Hipsher 1998).

Transition to procedural democracy

During the *transition* to democracy, social movements may seek democratization, social justice, and the elimination of the reserved powers that limit the emerging democracy. Although political opportunities for mobilization open up due to the high uncertainty of this stage, nothing is yet defined, and cycles of protest may push in opposite directions. In fact, 'Mobilization strengthens the ability of challengers and elites to make claims yet also limits the range of acceptable outcomes because of the conditional nature of popular support' (Glenn 2003: 104). Old (labour, ethnic) movements and new (women's, urban) movements participate in large coalitions asking for democratic rights (Jelin 1987). Generally speaking, the transition stage is characterized by the mobilization of a pro-democracy coalition of trade unions, political parties, churches and social movements. Without this coalition democracy is usually not achieved because contending countermovements are likely to push for restoration of the authoritarian/totalitarian regimes. Some right wing or military networks might also resist transition or try to violently produce a democratic breakdown. This is exemplified by the *Carapitanda* military group in Argentina in 1987, 1988, and 1990, which tried to end the trials against the military who had tortured and assassinated during the 1976–83 authoritarian regime. In other cases the reaction comes from the regime *nomenklatura*, with an increase in repression, as in the case of the 1989 crush down of the Chinese students' movement, or the request of external support for controlling the situation, as it happened in Poland in 1981 (Ekiert and Kubik 1999; Zhao 2000).

The bargaining dynamic among elites and the increased radicalization of contention in the streets intensify the reciprocal relationship between elites and movements. Glenn (2003: 104) argues that the intertwined logic of the transition is manifold: (a) mobilizations affect elite negotiations: they introduce new actors to the political arena, alter the power relationships among the contending parties, and insert new demands into the process reshaping the course of action; and (b) elites' negotiations affects mobilizations: the bargaining itself changes the degree of openness of the political opportunities for movements by modifying part of the claims and acceptable interlocutors of the process.

The moment at which the society is demobilized and politics is channelled into party politics is considered by transitologists as the end of the transition period. This outcome, however, is only one of many possible ones in actual transitions. While in Argentina, Bolivia and the Andean region demobilization did not occur after the transition, in countries such as Uruguay and Chile politics was quickly institutionalized through the party system. While not yet fully studied, demobilization does not seem essential to consolidation, which depends instead on the presence of a relatively institutionalized **party system** in centralized and strong states, with parties that have historically monopolized the decision-making process and that were not fully dissolved by the authoritarian regime (Rossi 2007). Moreover, Adrian Karatnycky and Peter Ackerman (2005) argue that keeping elites under continuous popular pressures after transition is a major mean to a successful consolidation.

While in many cases traditional parties monopolized politics again, in a few others the leaders of the pro-democracy movements won the first free and open elections. This happened mainly in those countries where the party system was redone from a one-party system to a multi-party one as in Central and Eastern Europe, or where parties were historically weak, or were weakened by the military regime. The quantity of pro-democratic movement leaders that later occupied important institutional positions is larger than usually acknowledged. Some of the better known examples of social movement leaders who then assumed relevant institutional roles are: (a) Lech Walesa, the main leader of *Solidarność* who became the first post-soviet President of Poland; (b) Nelson Mandela, the leader of the anti-apartheid movement, who became South Africa's first democratic and black President; (c) Václav Havel, who was twice elected President (first of Czechoslovakia and then of

the Czech Republic) after organizing the successful Civic Forum that took Czechoslovakia to democracy and a peaceful division of the country; and (d) Raúl Alfonsín, who gained the presidency as a leader of the *Unión Cívica Radical* (UCR), one of the historical parties of Argentina, but also due to being a well-known human rights activist and the Vice President of the APDH organization. These examples show that the distinction between civil and political societies is artificial and that the assumption of a necessary monopoly on mobilization by classical parties in order for a democracy to consolidate is misleading.

Consolidation of a procedural (or substantive?) democracy

In the political science literature, *consolidation* is generally linked to the end of the democratization process as signalled by the first free and open elections, the end of the uncertainty period and/or the implementation of a minimum quality of substantive democracy (Linz and Stepan 1996; O'Donnell 1993). Democracy, however, cannot be consolidated without the universal and effective application of citizenship rights, which transcend voting. In this stage, movements in many countries claim for the rights of those who are excluded by 'low intensity democracies' and ask for a more inclusive democracy (i.e. land reform, employment, indigenous and women movements) and the end of the authoritarian legacies. Claims framed by movements in the name of 'rights', 'citizenship', and their political practices play a crucial role in creating citizenry (Eckstein and Wickham-Crowley 2003). As Joe Foweraker (1995: 98) observed, 'The struggle for rights has more than a merely rhetorical impact. The insistence on the rights of free speech and assembly is a precondition of the kind of collective (and democratic) decision-making which educates citizens'. In brief, social movements usually produce long term impacts that are not only institutional, but also cultural and social. These transformations are developed through the movements' alternative practices and values which help to sustain and expand democracy (Santos 2005). Furthermore, movements' networks play an important role in mobilizing against persistent exclusionary patterns and authoritarian legacies (Eckstein 2001).

Expansion to post-representative democracy

Finally, social movements may play important roles in the *expansion of democracy* (a not yet fully studied stage in democratization), addressing both the democratic reform of the international system of **governance** and the transcending of representative democracy in the national level, thorough experiments of participatory and deliberative democracy (Baiocchi 2005). There are at least two main perspectives on this issue. First, the **global civil society** perspective (Kaldor 2003) emphasizes the democratizing role played by a worldwide organized civil society, located between the state and the market (Cohen and Arato 1992), in the democratization at a supranational scale. Second, research on the **global justice movements** (della Porta and Tarrow 2005) and transnational advocacy networks analysis (Keck and Sikkink 1998) notes the role played by human rights, indigenous, women and alter-**globalization** groups in the promotion and expansion of national democratic regimes, as well as in the reformulation of the not so democratic procedures of the international governmental organizations, such as the World Bank and the International Monetary Fund (IMF). In the case of the global justice movements, proposals for reform

are especially oriented towards a broader transparency of decision-making in international governmental organizations, increased controls by the national parliaments, as well as the opening of channels of access for social movement organizations.

> ## Box 12.2 **Key points**
>
> - Protest cycles and waves of strikes play an important role in democratization processes.
>
> - The role of social movements tend to vary in the different stages of democratization:
>
>   1. Underground networks of resistance undermine internal and international supports for authoritarian regimes;
>
>   2. The intensity of the protest might accelerate processes of liberalization;
>
>   3. Social movements are often important allies of political parties and other collective actors in pro-democracy coalitions during the transition phase;
>
>   4. Also during and after democratic consolidation alternative praxis of democracy are practiced within social movements.

Conclusion

Though movements have played important roles in promoting democracy, they have not always been effective. In 1984 in Brazil, the large mobilization campaign called *Diretas Já* for the reformulation of the electoral system and the inclusion of direct elections had no impact on the authoritarian elites. This and other cases such as China's student protests in 1989, show that mobilization for democracy *alone* does not produce democratization.[3] A combination of several factors is necessary for effective democratization to take place. The main reason for the need to combine perspectives from above and from below is that the 'mode of transition', the context of the democratization process, the types of actors involved in the process, and their strategic interactions, all influence the kind of democracy that is established'

(Pagnucco, 1995: 151). The literature discussed in this chapter shows that the following combination of elements produces the most favourable setting for democratization: (a) a non-syndical strike wave and/or a pro-democracy cycle of protest; (b) increased political organization in urban areas, and a relatively dense resistance network; (c) in Roman Catholic countries, a church that is actively involved in the struggle for democratization; (d) international pressure from human rights advocacy networks; (e) a division among the authoritarian/totalitarian elites concerning whether to continue the non-democratic regime, and (f) the existence of pro-democratic elites able to integrate the demands for democracy coming from below (at least until transition is well initiated).

There are also configurations that can negatively influence democratization. Difficulties emerge: (a) when the transition must deal with simultaneous contending movements demanding national independence and alternative exclusionary *demos* views; and (b) when terrorist attacks and/or guerrilla movements develop during the democratization process rejecting democracy as a plausible immediate outcome. These two elements do not make democratization impossible, but may put the process at risk of never consolidating or of only bringing limited liberalization of authoritarianism. This leads us to the most intriguing regional failure to democratization—apart from China—that is the Middle East and North Africa (see Ch. 21). A partial explanation for the absence of democratization struggles in these countries may be related to: (a) the lack of support for democracy among strong and state-independent religious institutions, (b) an unorganized urban poor, (c) the corporativism of unions in claims that are just syndical (or the lack of them), and (d) the local weakness or inexistence of human rights movements (though the big pressure of transnational advocacy networks, and intergovernmental organizations). Though not a closed answer, the still ongoing important accumulation of research on twentieth-century democratization may well help us to improve our understanding of a *dynamic, contingent* and *contentious* shaping of alternative paths toward democra*cies.*

QUESTIONS

1. How do structuralist approaches define the role of social movement in democratization processes?

2. Who are the main authors that approach the role of social classes in democratization processes within a historical comparative approach and what do they suggest?

3. Which role do transitologists assign to social movement in the different steps of democratization?

4. What is the potential for social movements in different types of non-democratic regimes?

5. Are social movements always favourable to democracy?

6. How do cycles of protest and waves of strikes interact with democratic processes?

Visit the Online Resource Centre that accompanies this book for additional questions to accompany each chapter, and a range of other resources: <www.oxfordtextbooks. co.uk/orc/haerpfer/>.

FURTHER READING

Boudreau, V. (2004), *Resisting Dictatorship: Repression and Protest in Southeast Asia* (Cambridge: Cambridge University Press). This book is one of the few comparative research published in English about resistance movements against the recent authoritarian regimes of Burma (Myanmar), the Philippines and Indonesia within the contentious politics approach.

Collier, R. B. (1999), *Paths toward Democracy: The Working Class and Elites in Western Europe and South America* (New York: Cambridge University Press). This book presents a comparative analysis of the role played by unions and labour/ left-wing parties in the nineteenth- and early-twentieth-century democratizations.

Eckstein, S. (2001) (ed.), *Power and Popular Protest: Latin American Social Movements*, 2nd edn (Berkeley, CA: University of California Press). This book shows the different roles played by urban movements, human rights movements, guerrilla movements, women's movements and the Catholic Church in the 1970–1980 democratizations in Latin America.

Escobar, A. and Álvarez, S. (1992) (eds) , *The Making of Social Movements in Latin America. Identity, Strategy and Democracy*, (Boulder, CO: Westview). This book is the most prominent example of the new social movement approach applied to Latin American transitions and struggles for consolidation of democracy, includes chapters about urban movements, human rights movements, women's movements, unions and the Catholic Church.

Foweraker, J. (1989), *Making Democracy in Spain: Grassroots Struggle in the South, 1955–1975* (Cambridge: Cambridge University Press).This is one of the main books on grassroots resistance movements and networks to the authoritarian regime of Franco in Spain.

Keck, M. and Sikkink, K. (1998), *Activists beyond Borders: Advocacy Networks in International Politics* (Ithaca, NY: Cornell University Press). This book comparatively analyses the role of human rights transnational advocacy networks in the delegitimizing of authoritarian regimes and the aftermath prosecution of human rights violators. It includes an important theoretical argumentation about advocacy networks role and its distinction with movements.

McAdam, D., Tarrow, S. and Tilly, C. (2001), *Dynamics of Contention* (Cambridge: Cambridge University Press). This book proposes a series of mechanism that—if combined in a specific way—may produce democratization processes, thus presenting an ambitious theoretical proposal that redefines the role of contentious politics in major regime transformations.

Pagnucco, R. (1995), 'The Comparative Study of Social Movements and Democratization: Political Interaction and Political Process Approaches', in M. Dobkowski, I. Wallimann and C. Stojanov (eds), *Research in Social Movements, Conflict and Change* (London: JAI Press), 18: 145–83. This article is the first work in English that tried to combine the political process approach with transitology with the intention of finding theoretical cross-fertilization.

Tilly, C. (2004a), *Contention and Democracy in Europe, 1650-2000* (Cambridge: Cambridge University Press). This book presents a major social and historical analysis of the role played by contentious politics in the creation of democracy in Europe, and its impact in subsequent de-democratization, and re-democratization.

IMPORTANT WEBSITES

<www.amnesty.org> Amnesty International is the first and main worldwide human rights organization. Created in 1961 in the UK, it struggles for the universal application of civic and political rights through the defence of those individuals who suffer the violations of their rights by democratic or authoritarian states.

<www.civicus.org> CIVICUS is an international alliance of trade unions, faith-based networks, NGOs, etc. based in South Africa that works on the empowerment of organized citizens' activism, especially in areas where participatory democracy and citizens' freedom of association are threatened. Since 2000 it develops The Civil Society Index Program to assess the state of social organizations around the world.

<www.abuelas.org> Abuelas de Plaza de Mayo is one of the main organizations of the human rights movement of Argentina. Since 1976 integrated by the mothers and mothers-in-law of 'disappeared' women that were pregnant during the 1976–83 dictatorship of Argentina.

Since democratization they have been looking for the appropriated children of their sons and daughters and taking to court those individuals responsible for human rights violations.

<www.forumsocialmundial.org.br> World Social Forum is a global open meeting space of individuals, organizations, networks and social movements to debate ideas and coordinate actions with the purpose of expanding democracy in the promotion of a more equitable and with solidarity world. It met for the first time in 2001 in Porto Alegre (Brazil) and since then meets regularly in all the continents and every year or two in a worldwide scale.

NOTES

1. Collier (1999) develops a dynamic analysis of democratization processes, but concentrates her analysis on working class actors (i.e. unions and labour/left-wing parties) with the intention of finding empirical answers to Moore's puzzle.

2. For a comparative research of the role played by resistance movements and state repression in the struggles for democratization in the authoritarian regimes of Ne Win (1958–81) in Burma (Myanmar), Ferdinand Marcos (1965–86) in the Philippines and Thojib (Raden) Suharto (1967–98) in Indonesia, see Boudreau (2004).

3. This complex relationship had been extensively studied in recent works by Tilly (2001; 2004a and b)

We would like to thank Amr Adly, Leonardo Morlino, Philippe Schmittes and the book's editors for their useful suggestions.

Conventional Citizen Participation

Ian McAllister and Stephen White

Overview

Widespread conventional political **participation** across a population is essential for the successful transition from **authoritarianism** to democracy. This chapter explores the most visible and politically important act of conventional participation: turning out to vote in a national election. Patterns of political participation are influenced by an array of institutional factors, such as the type of electoral system and the number of political parties in a country, and by individual socioeconomic factors such as a person's educational attainments or income. A particular problem in many previously authoritarian societies is the absence of a diverse civil society, so that the social trust upon which a healthy democracy depends is often absent. Levels of political participation are usually high during the founding elections, but decline when democratic **consolidation** is underway, as the new **state** grapples with numerous economic and political challenges to its **legitimacy**.

Introduction

Political participation has a crucial role to play in the successful transition from authoritarian society to fully-fledged democracy. In countries that have successfully navigated this transition, political partici-pation has been central in acculturating democratic norms and values across the population, in generating trust in political institutions, and in promoting free, competitive political behaviour. The transition from authoritarianism to democracy is always a period of high risk for any society. Following the collapse of communism, the societies of Central and Eastern Europe had to undertake the economic transition from a command to a market economy, as well as the transition from totalitarian political institutions to democratic ones. Almost all of these economic transitions were accompanied by high levels of unemployment, rampant inflation, and rapidly declining living standards. Inevitably, these difficult conditions resulted in widespread calls for a return to authoritarian government to restore living standards. Democratic political participation has been one component in resisting these calls (Kostadinova 2003).

To some degree, the legitimacy of democracy in the immediate post-authoritarian period is achieved by the act of overthrowing the *ancien régime*. The initial enthusiasm for democracy in the founding elections usually ensures high levels of political participation, as well as widespread support for the new political parties that emerge to contest those elections (O'Donnell and Schmitter 1986). But the most serious risks to the new system come in the period of democratic consolidation, immediately after the founding elections, when the challenge is to ensure that democratic governments remain responsive to citizens' demands, and representative of the broad electorate. Once again, the key to successfully overcoming these challenges is to ensure widespread conventional political participation, so that democracy becomes the political norm rather than the exception. Participation also sends important signals to government about what citizens require and what concerns them.

The mainsprings of political participation are complex, as we describe in the sections that follow. At the aggregate level it is influenced by the type of political institutions that operate within the country, and at the individual level by the socioeconomic and cultural resources that a person possesses. During the period of democratic consolidation, participation depends on the diversity and complexity of civil society (Przeworski 1991). However, in many former totalitarian societies, most notably those ruled by communism, this is exactly what is absent. So after the initial euphoria generated by the collapse of communism, there was the realization that civil society would have to be re-created, and that the process would take decades rather than years. The situation has been further complicated by the uneven state of civil society in many former authoritarian societies. In Czechoslovakia and Hungary, for example, memories of democracy in the pre-war years still existed and both countries sustained an active pro-democracy movement in the 1960s and 1970s. In Russia, by contrast, the legacy of communism from 1917 onwards was the effective suppression of these values. This uneven inheritance has impacted on the patterns of democratization and participation across the postcommunist states.

This chapter examines the role of political participation in the transition from authoritarianism to democracy, with a particular emphasis on the period of democratic consolidation, following the initial founding elections. We define participation as conventional acts aimed at influencing government, and the next section discusses the nature and scope of political participation in detail. Section 3 discusses the particular case of election **turnout**, which is the most visible and important act of participation. Sections 4 and 5 examine institutional and social explanations for turnout, respectively, while the sixth and final section analyses the importance of participation for satisfaction with democracy. The countries covered in the empirical analyses are drawn from the newly emerging democracies of Central and Eastern Europe, but the discussion applies equally to the emerging democracies of Latin American, Africa and Central Asia.

Dimensions of Political Participation

The first major survey-based study of political participation, conducted by Sidney Verba and Norman Nie, defined participation as 'those activities by private citizens that are more or less directly aimed at influencing the selection of government personnel and/or the actions they take' (Verba and

Nie 1972: 2). Although the goal of participation is unambiguous, the methods by which citizens seek to exert political influence are many and varied. A citizen joining a political party, writing to his or her elected representative, or marching in a street demonstration, is seeking to influence political decision-making, but by very different means. Until the 1960s, political participation was usually conceptualized in terms of voting, party political activism, and by involvement in interest groups. These modes of democratic participation are collectively referred to as conventional political participation. During the 1960s, other means of participation began to emerge, ranging from peaceful street demonstrations to threats (and sometimes acts) of physical violence (Barnes and Kaase *et al.* 1979). Although the goal remained the same, these new methods were vastly different from the traditional ones and are usually referred to as unconventional political participation or political protest. This chapter is restricted to examining conventional forms of political participation.

The most common mode of conventional participation is the act of voting. In most democracies, voting involves a majority of citizens, and is a direct method of influencing the political process. Yet despite its ubiquity in democracies, voting is not necessarily the most effective means of exercising influence on political decision-making. Verba and Nie (1972; see also Verba, Nie and Kim 1978) identified three forms of participation in addition to voting: (a) campaign activity, involving active participation in election campaigns; (b) communal activity, which is concerned with organizational involvement within the local community; and (c) personal contacts with government officials on matters of personal or family concern. These four methods of conventional participation are outlined in Table 13.1, together with an evaluation of the influence that each places on decision-makers, the resources required to utilize them, and the consequences of each of them for the society as a whole.

The act of voting places high pressure on decision-makers, since the result will determine which party occupies government and is therefore in a position to implement its legislative program. However, voting conveys only minimal information to decision-makers about the nature of citizen demands and requires relatively little in terms of citizen resources. Voting also involves conflict and has collective implications for the society. The next two methods of participation in Table 13.1, campaign and communal activity, are broadly comparable across the three criteria. Both methods can place high pressure on decision-makers and deliver high levels of information, depending on the particular circumstances. Moreover, both require reasonable levels of initiative and cooperation and their outcome is likely to be collective in nature. The fourth form of conventional participation in Table 13.1, personal contact with officials about issues of personal concern, results in low pressure on decision-makers but it is not conflictual in nature and has implications only for the person who initiates the contact.

Table 13.1 Types of Conventional Political Participation

	Voting	Campaign Activity	Communal Activity	Personal Contacts
Political Influence				
Pressure	High	High	Low-High	Low
Information	Low	Low-High	High	High
Resources Required				
Initiative	Little	Some	Some-Much	Much
Co-operation	Little	Some-Much	Some-Much	None-Little
Results				
Conflict	Yes	Yes	Depends	No
Outcome	Collective	Collective	Collective	Particular

Sources: Adapted from Verba, Nie, and Kim (1978: 55) and Dalton (1988: 36)

To what extent did similar forms of political participation exist under authoritarian rule? Voting was clearly seen to be important in communist systems, for example, since it represented an affirmation of the system. However, since elections were not competitive or free, there was little or no campaign activity associated with them and the outcome was totally predictable. Studies of participation under communism have shown the existence of various other forms of political participation. For example, during the Brezhnev era, Bahry and Silver (1990) used interviews with Russian émigrés to identify four types of political participation: unconventional political activism, involving such activities as the distribution of *samizdat*; compliant activism, mainly concerning party-initiated work; social activism, involving residential and neighbourhood groups; and contacting public officials. Similarly, DiFranceisco and Gitelman (1984) identify three forms of political participation which distinguish between symbolic participation, such as voting, and contacts with public officials. Clearly, then, the level of communal activity was low, since the Communist Party undertook many of the functions of civil society. However, contacting public officials to seek the redress of grievances was evidently a widely used method of political participation.

Some of these pre-democratic patterns of participation are reflected in the current patterns of participation across six of the new democracies shown in Table 13.2. The estimates are all based on surveys conducted post–2000 in the new democracies, so reflect the experiences of at least three democratic elections. Turnout will be examined in more detail in the next section, but the results (based on self-reported voting) show a significant disparity between turnout in the new and established democracies. In the new democracies, turnout averages 70 per cent, with the highest—77 per cent—occurring in Hungary, and the lowest, 66 per cent, in Poland and Russia. By contrast, turnout in the established European democracies averages 81 per cent. Election campaign activity, however, varies little between the two groups of democracies, with just a slight advantage for the latter, as we would expect. However, both indicators show considerable variation across the five countries for which we have estimates: in Russia, for example, 28 per cent of the survey respondents said that they had persuaded someone about how to vote at the last election, compared to just 8 per cent in Bulgaria and Slovenia. Similarly, 11 per cent of the Hungarians interviewed said they had attended a political meeting, compared to just 4 per cent of Russians.

Communal activity represents the degree to which individuals will cooperate together in order to influence decision-makers and requires a reasonable level of cooperation and initiative; as such, we would

Table 13.2 Political Participation in New and Established Democracies (per cent)

	Voted	Campaign activity		Communal activity		
		Persuade others	Attend meetings	Work for party	Work for others	Contact official
Bulgaria	68	8	8	3	1	4
Hungary	77	18	11	2	1	12
Poland	66	11	6	2	4	6
Russia	66	28	4	3	5	9
Slovenia	76	8	7	4	2	15
Slovakia	68	-	-	3	8	9
Mean, new democracies	70	15	7	3	4	9
N	9,743	5,110	5,121	10,252	10,243	10,246
Mean, established democracies	81	16	8	4	19	16
N	20,811	22,704	20,515	20,797	22,793	22,787

Notes: See Box 13.1 for details of questions and countries.

Sources: Comparative Study of Electoral Systems, Module 2; European Social Survey, Round 3

Box 13.1 **Data Box**

The data used here are from the Comparative Study of Electoral Systems (CSES) survey, module 2, collected between 2001 and 2006 (<www.cses.org>) and the European Social Survey (ESS), round 3, collected in 2006/07 (<www.europeansocialsurvey.org>). The new democracies are Bulgaria, Hungary, Poland, Russia, Slovenia, and Slovakia and the reported means are based on those countries. The established democracies are Austria, Belgium, Britain, Denmark, Finland, France, Ireland, the Netherlands, Norway, Portugal, Spain, Sweden, and Switzerland and again the reported means are based on those countries. The choice of countries was dictated by those which were common between the CSES and ESS surveys. The CSES data are used to estimate campaign activity, and the ESS data the other indicators.

The CSES campaign activity questions were as follows. 'Here is a list of things some people do during elections. Which if any did you do during the most recent election? . . . talked to other people to persuade them to vote for a particular party or candidate? . . . showed your support for a particular party or candidate by, for example, attending a meeting, putting up a poster, or in some other way?' The CSES questions on political parties are as follows. 'During the last campaign did a candidate or anyone from a political party contact you to persuade you to vote for them?' 'Thinking about how elections in [country] work in practice, how well do elections ensure that the views of voters are represented by majority parties: very well, quite well, not very well, or not well at all?' 'Would you say that any of the parties in [country] represents your views reasonably well?' 'Regardless of how you feel about the parties, would you say that any of the individual party leaders/presidential candidates at the last election represents your views reasonably well?'

The ESS questions were as follows. 'Some people don't vote nowadays for one reason or another. Did you vote in the last [country] national elections in [month/year]?' 'There are different ways of trying to improve things in [country] or help prevent things from going wrong. During the last 12 months, have you done any of the following? Have you . . . contacted a politician, government or local government official? . . . worked in a political party or action group? . . . worked in another organization or association?' 'Using this card, please tell me on a score of 0–10 how much you *personally* trust each of the institutions I read out. 0 means you do not trust an institution at all, and 10 means you have complete trust. Firstly. . .'

expect to find higher levels of communal activity in the established democracies where there is a more developed and complex civil society. That expectation is confirmed by the survey estimates, which show that 19 per cent of those interviewed in the established democracies said that they had worked for a non-political organization or association in the 12 months prior to the survey, compared to just 4 per cent in the new democracies. That level was lowest in Bulgaria and Hungary at 1 per cent, and highest in Slovakia at 8 per cent. However, in both groups of countries, the likelihood of working for a political party or action group is uniformly low at between 3 and 4 per cent. This reflects the decline of party membership and partisanship generally across the established democracies (Scarrow 1996). Finally, contacting a public official in the previous 12 months involved about one in 10 citizens in new democracies, but substantially more—16 per cent— in the established democracies. The level is highest in Hungary and Slovenia, both of which maintained civil societies under communism, and lowest in Bulgaria, which had only a very primitive civil society.

Levels of political participation are therefore lower in the new democracies compared to established

Box 13.2 **Key points**

- Citizens can influence the political process in several ways, all of which require different resources, exert different types of political influence, and can have different results.

- Voting existed under communist rule, and although there was no free competition, turnout was generally high.

- Pre-democratic patterns of participation and the diversity of civil society impact on participation during the democratic transition.

ones, as we would expect, although the differences between the two groups of countries are not substantial. Indeed, election campaign activity—reflected in persuading others about how to vote and in organizational involvements—is very similar across the two types of democracies. The main difference that emerges between the two groups is in political activity which is predicated on the existence of a well-developed civil society. In this context, countries that managed to retain some of their pre-authoritarian social relations while under communist domination have fared better with the restoration of democracy. Most of these countries maintained a thriving civil society under authoritarian rule and that in turn has sustained a liberal political culture that has greatly facilitated the democratic transition during the 1990s.

Election Turnout

Authoritarian **regimes** that conduct elections generally record high levels of turnout. Under communism in Russia and eastern Europe, for example, election turnout was traditionally high, in order to deliver a message of unequivocal approval for the regime. In the last Soviet elections under communism, conducted in March 1984, the official reported turnout was 99.99 per cent.[1] Similarly, in the whole of Turkmenistan, there were 1.5 million voters at the national elections in 1984, but only one was officially recorded as absent. Comparable, though not quite as dramatic, results were recorded across many of the former Soviet states during the 1970s and 1980s. There were even occasions recorded when the turnout exceeded 100 per cent, as was the case when Stalin stood for election in 1937. So predictable were the elections that even as late as the 1980s, the Politburo could approve the final communiqué including all of the election results two days before the polls had even opened (White, Rose, and McAllister 1997).

One obvious explanation for results of this kind is fraud, particularly the widespread practice of voting for family members. Another explanation is the widespread use of 'absentee certificates', which allowed potential nonvoters to be removed from the register if they were thought likely to be away from home on polling day. However, it is also true that election officials went to considerable lengths in the communist years to ensure a high turnout, with ballot boxes being taken into hospitals, and even carried into people's own homes if they were unable to attend the polling place in person. 'Genuine' levels of turnout in communist Russia and indeed in several of the Central and East European states,

was in fact high. In Russia, independent estimates suggested that no more than 3 per cent of registered voters failed to record their vote in the early 1980s, although the proportion was steadily increasing (Roeder 1989: 474–5).

With the collapse of communism in 1989, turnout began to decline, but initially remained high, at least by the standards of the established democracies. In March 1989, when the first largely competitive elections took place throughout a democratizing Soviet Union, Figure 13.1 shows that turnout was at 87 per cent. Turnout had declined a year later, when elections took place in each of the Soviet republics (including Belarus and Ukraine as well as the Russian Republic). Turnout fell even more sharply in Russia in December 1993, when the first-ever elections took place to a newly-formed State Duma, in what was by then an independent Russian Federation. The reported figure was 54.8 per cent, but this was the proportion that had 'taken part in the election' by receiving a ballot paper, not the slightly smaller number that had actually cast a vote,[2] and there was in any case considerable administrative pressure to ensure a turnout of at least 50 per cent in order that the new constitution, which was being put to the vote on the same day, could be confirmed. Independent estimates suggested that turnout, in fact, was unlikely to have exceeded 43 per cent.

The patterns in the Belarusian and Ukrainian parliamentary elections shown in Figure 13.1 are very similar to Russia. Turnout in the Ukrainian parliamentary elections in 1989 was 93.4 per cent and in the Belarusian parliamentary elections 92.4 per cent—figures that would be regarded as exceptional

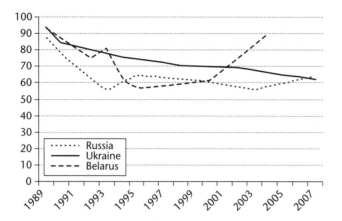

Fig 13.1 Election turnout in Belarus, Russia, and the Ukraine (per cent)

Source: McAllister and White (2008), White and McAllister (2007)

in the established democracies. By 1993, followed the founding elections, turnout in Belarus had declined dramatically, to just 56.4 per cent, and in the Ukraine, to 75.8 per cent in 1994. Since then, turnout in the Ukraine has further declined, dropping to 62.0 per cent in the 2007 parliamentary election. In Belarus, the 1995 parliamentary election represented the lowest point, and since then turnout has begun to rise, although the figure of 90.1 per cent for the 2004 parliamentary elections reflects the unusual circumstance of combining the election with a constitutional referendum to decide if the incumbent president, Alexander Lukashenko, should be able to serve a third term. The referendum was passed by an overwhelming majority.

Analysing turnout rates across many of the former communist states—Russia, as well as Armenia, Azerbaijan, Belarus and the Ukraine—is complicated by the existence of the 'against all' option on the ballot paper. In Russia, for example, until recently voters had the additional choice of voting 'against all' of the candidates and parties, rather than abstaining from voting altogether—the only option that voters in the established democracies possess if they dislike all of the choices on offer. In the 2003 Duma elections, the last before the 'against all' option was abolished, nearly 13 per cent voted 'against all' in the single member constituencies, making it the second largest group of voters, surpassed only by the vote for the Kremlin-sponsored United Russia. Generally, 'against all' voters tend to be more Western oriented than other voters, but are less satisfied with democracy in Russia.

There is some evidence to support the view that the founding or transitional elections in previously authoritarian societies have attracted much higher levels of turnout than later, consolidating, elections. In a study of four consecutive elections across 15 Central and East European countries Kostadinova (2003) finds much higher levels of turnout in the founding elections, and much lower turnout in later elections. This is attributed to the erosion of the initial popular euphoria for democracy by persistent economic problems, an ineffective and often corrupt political system, unfamiliar political institutions, and by a fragmented **party system**. However, the magnitude of the effects are greater than those found in post-authoritarian societies in other parts of the world, and are perhaps explained by the precipitous drop in living standards experienced by

---

Box 13.3 **Key points**

- In general, founding or transitional elections attract higher levels of turnout compared to later, consolidating elections.

- Election turnout in the new democracies has declined in line with that of the established democracies, although the explanations for the decline appear to be different.

- Economic challenges and difficulties in the new democracies soon erode the euphoria that accompanies the collapse of authoritarianism.

the former communist societies as they navigated the difficult transition from a command to a market economy. As a consequence, post-1990 turnout across the postcommunist states is now significantly below the average for the established democracies (Siaroff and Merer 2002).

Institutions and Political Participation

The institutional arrangements that exist within particular political systems have been shown to have a significant effect on levels of political participation. In general, studies show that parliamentary systems are associated with higher levels of electoral participation than presidential systems and this is particularly the case when parliamentarism is wedded to an electoral system based on proportional representation. Other institutional factors which increase turnout are small electoral districts and regular but not too frequent national elections (Lijphart 1999). Electoral rules that increase turnout include registration procedures that make it easier to enrol to vote; polling places that facilitate easier attendance; and, of course, compulsory voting (Franklin 2004). And not least, the more competitive the electoral race is seen to be by the electorate, the more motivated voters are to turnout to vote and to be seen to have their say in the outcome (Gray and Caul 2000). The competitiveness of the race is also related to the type of electoral system in the country, so that in proportional representation systems, competitiveness is more uniformly distributed across electoral districts than is the case in majoritarian systems (Powell 1980).

The role of political parties and the party system are a second set of institutional factors that influence turnout, and are generally regarded as central to effective electoral participation. The two major functions of political parties are, first, the mobilization of citizens to turnout to vote and, second, the conversion of voters to the party cause. The effectiveness of parties in fulfilling these two functions is obviously going to be crucial to electoral participation and, more indirectly, to the health of political system in general. Mainwaring (1999) argues that the institutionalization of the party system is a major factor shaping mass political behaviour in new and old democracies, with older systems exhibiting stable partisanship, low volatility and long-established parties that are not dominated by personalities or factions. By contrast, when the party system is fluid and lacks legitimacy, as is often the case in new democracies, parties are unable to fulfil their basic role of mobilization, and the lack of entrenched party loyalties means that relatively large proportions of voters will change their vote from election to election.

A central problem for political parties in new democracies is the lack of resources, which means that many of them are often dominated by personalities or factions. As a consequence, most rarely remain in existence for long enough in order to gain any enduring loyalty among voters and therefore to secure their long-time survival (Dalton and Weldon 2007). And because many parties are ephemeral, they are unlikely to attract the sorts of resources and funding that would enable them to create the sophisticated party organizations that would effectively mobilize voters (Birch 2005). A related problem is the low levels of party membership that are common in the new democracies, so few parties have a sufficiently large mass base that can be utilized for election canvassing, or used to raise funds and to shape party policy. These problems are reflected in the low levels of contact that voters report having with parties, and Karp and Banducci (2007) show that parties are less likely overall to contact voters in new democracies, though there are several notable exceptions, such as Brazil and the Czech Republic, where contact levels are higher. However, Karp and Banducci also find that parties in new democracies are more likely to target voters, which suggests that they are more parsimonious with their resources, and more likely to try and use their scarce resources to best effect.

The weakness of the party systems in the new democracies, viewed from the perspective of voters, is shown in Table 13.3. The first column shows the proportion of respondents who reported having

Table 13.3 Contact with and Views of Political Parties (per cent)

	Per cent who say....			
	Had contact with party	Views rep'ed in elections	Party rep's views	Leader rep's views
Bulgaria	9	55	45	51
Hungary	9	54	21	86
Poland	8	56	48	50
Russia	7	44	57	67
Slovenia	16	30	67	39
Mean, new democracies	9	48	54	60
N	5,116	4,097	4,668	4,690
Mean, established democracies	24	63	79	73
N	15,359	12,843	12,821	11,039

Notes: See Box 13.1 for details of questions and countries. 'Had contact with party' is the per cent who said they had contact with a party or candidate at the last election. Views represented in election combines 'very well' and 'quite well'.

Source: Comparative Study of Electoral Systems, Module 2

contact with a candidate or party in the last national election in their country. Confirming the findings of Karp and Banducci (2007), the figures show that just 9 per cent of the voters in the sample of new democracies reported such contact, compared to 24 per cent of voters in the established democracies. Voters in new democracies are also much less likely than their counterparts in the established democracies to see their views as being well represented in elections (48 per cent, compared to 63 per cent) and to identify a party that represents their views effectively (54 per cent, compared to 79 per cent). And the gap left by political parties is also not filled by leaders; 60 per cent of voters in the new democracies identified a leader as representing them, compared to 73 per cent of voters in the established democracies. The figures, then, show the weakness of the parties in newly democratizing countries, with detrimental consequences for electoral participation, stability and satisfaction with the democratic process.

How do political parties become institutionalized in new democracies? The transition from authoritarianism to democracy is an incremental process, during which elites and mass publics must come to trust their new democratic institutions. Political parties facilitate this delicate transition, by providing choices for voters and by acting as guardians of the 'democratic creed' (McAllister and White 2007). The very fragility of the transition from authoritarianism to democracy provides multiple opportunities for failure. The process by which political parties become institutionalized takes place through electoral experience, which builds confidence, and by the transmission of parental loyalties from generation to generation, which embeds parties within the mass political culture. Building these mechanisms is obviously difficult in a new democracy, but Russell Dalton and Steven Weldon (2007) show that an important component in new democracies is the latent socialization which is carried over from the authoritarian regime. They argue that the strong support for democracy that has been shown in these countries during the founding elections will assist in the process of democratic consolidation.

Box 13.4 Key points

- Institutional arrangements, particularly election rules, the type of electoral system, and the party system, all influence political participation.

- The weakness of the party systems in many of the transitional democracies is a particular factor undermining participation.

- Building strong, mass-based political parties that act within a competitive electoral framework with agreed rules is one of the most effective mechanisms for promoting democratization.

Citizens and Political Participation

The extent of conventional participation varies greatly between citizens within democracies. Some social groups are more influential in the political process than others, despite institutional rules and procedures designed to mitigate differences and provide equal access. These inequalities have been explained in terms of differences in socioeconomic resources, such as education, occupational status or income. Differential access to these resources helps to determine the lifestyle, social networks and motivations of individuals; it shapes, indirectly, different levels of political participation and ultimately determines the ability of ordinary citizens to influence government policy (Brady, Verba, and Schlozman 1995). More recently, social learning theories have identified cultural factors as potentially significant influences on political participation. Citizens absorb certain values from the political culture within which they are socialized and this, in turn, influences political participation. In this view, individual patterns of political participation are the product of a person's cumulative democratic experiences.

Both the resource and social learning explanations have important implications for political participation. In the resource model, levels of participation depend on the socioeconomic status of the electorate so that an economically underdeveloped society, or one in which a significant section of the population has lower levels of socioeconomic status, will find it difficult to sustain the levels of participation necessary to maintain democratic procedures. Moreover, it implies that efforts to increase political participation are largely dependent on improving socioeconomic conditions. The social learning model, by contrast, implies that participation is a consequence of learning certain values from the political culture. Absorbing these values is, in turn, a lengthy process and change only occurs over an extended, political stability, period.

Education is often regarded as the primary indicator of socioeconomic status, since it directly shapes career opportunities and personal wealth. Educational levels in the new democracies of Central and Eastern Europe are similar to those found in the established democracies, and the education systems were well developed under communism in order to provide open access and vocational training. Access to tertiary education was lower in many of the communist states than in the established democracies since the economies required fewer graduates. For example, among the new democracies examined here, 16 per cent of the electorate possessed a tertiary education, compared to 25 per cent in the established democracies. However, more persons in the new democracies—68 per cent, compared to 56 per cent in the established democracies—possessed a secondary education, emphasizing the economic importance placed on vocational education by the communist authorities.[3]

Education is important in shaping the main types of political participation in both the new and established democracies. In line with their counterparts in the established democracies, Table 13.4 shows that citizens in the new democracies are more likely to participate politically if they possess more education. There are, however, some significant differences. Most notably, education is less important in shaping whether or not a person votes in the new democracies, but it is more important in shaping campaign activity. This may be because voting is a familiar activity, while the types of activities that flow from free, competitive elections tend to be unfamiliar. Education is also less important among voters in the new democracies in determining communal activity, and in promoting contacts with public officials. One possible explanation for these patterns is that education is not as directly related to status and wealth in the former communist states as it is in stable market-oriented economies, although we would expect this to change as the economic transition progresses.

Reflecting the political culture of a society, social learning represents a person's cumulative experiences with society, which in turn helps to shape their political participation. Civil society is defined as the sphere of free, unrestricted social activism, in particular through voluntary groups and associations (see Ch. 11); as a consequence, civil society is usually regarded as the basis for representative democracy. In most

Table 13.4 Level of Education and Political Participation (per cent)

	Voted	Campaign activity			Communal activity		
		Persuade others	Attend meetings		Work for party	Work for others	Contact official
New democracies							
None, primary	66	11	5		1	1	10
Secondary	68	15	7		3	4	9
Tertiary	68	21	14		5	8	15
Established democracies							
None, primary	79	12	7		2	9	9
Secondary	78	16	8		4	17	14
Tertiary	88	23	10		7	30	25

Notes: See Box 13.1 for details of questions and countries.

Sources: Comparative Study of Electoral Systems, Module 2; European Social Survey, Round 3

authoritarian societies, particularly where there has been little or no experience of democracy for most of the population, civil society may effectively be non-existent; that was certainly the case in Russia in the 1980s, and in several other communist societies (Bernhard 1993). In these societies, social memberships usually revolved around the Communist Party, and to a lesser extent the trade unions, which were of course closely associated with the party.[4]

One measure of the complexity of civil society is social trust, and the extent to which individuals exhibit confidence in the basic institutions of the society. We have already observed the low levels of communal activity in the new democracies, reflecting the absence of any tradition of non-political collective action. To what extent is this also seen in the absence of social trust across these societies? Table 13.5 shows the extent to which there is trust in five basic state institutions across these six former communist countries. Three of the state institutions are political (parliament, politicians and political parties) and two of them are non-political (the legal system and police). As predicted, the citizens in the six new democracies have significantly lower levels

Table 13.5 Trust in Institutions in New and Established Democracies

	Trust in... (0 to 10 scale)				
	Parliament	Legal system	Police	Politicians	Political parties
Bulgaria	2.2	2.4	3.8	1.8	1.8
Hungary	3.4	4.4	5.2	2.6	2.6
Poland	2.7	3.8	5.0	2.1	2.1
Russia	3.3	3.7	3.3	2.9	2.8
Slovenia	4.2	4.2	5.0	3.2	3.3
Slovakia	4.2	4.2	4.7	3.6	3.6
Mean, new democracies	3.3	3.8	4.4	2.7	2.7
N	9,869	9,733	9,992	9,847	9,758
Mean, established democracies	5.1	5.6	6.4	4.1	4.2
N	22,193	22,377	22,657	22,448	22,308

Notes: See Box 13.1 for details of questions and countries.

Source: European Social Survey, Round 3

of trust across all five institutions compared to those in the established democracies. Most notable is the lack of trust in politicians and political parties, but there are also substantially low levels of trust in parliament and the legal system as well. There are also large variations across the six new democracies, with Bulgaria, Poland and Russia having much lower levels of trust than are found in Hungary, Slovenia or Slovakia, the latter usually considered as the countries that maintained some semblance of civil society under communism.

The patterns of social trust are an important predictor of political participation. For example, in the six new democracies, the **correlation** between turning out to vote and trust in parliament is .16 (significant at p < .000); there are similar, albeit not as strong, relationships with the other measures of participation.[5] Social trust, then, generated by learning and experience from an active and vibrant civil society, is an important component of political participation. To the extent that participation in the new democracies depends on social learning, progress towards achieving the levels found in the established democracies will necessarily be slow and dependent on the

---

Box 13.5 **Key points**

- The resources that citizens possess—especially educational attainments and wealth—are a major influence on whether or not they participate in politics.

- Norms and values that are absorbed from the political culture of a society are also important incentives to participate.

- The weakness of civil society within many formerly authoritarian societies is a problem in building social learning and developing the social trust upon which democracy rests.

- One factor affecting satisfaction with democracy is maintaining widespread political participation, particularly voting in national elections.

---

accumulation of trust over successive generations. To the extent that it depends on resources, progress is likely to be faster, since the education systems in the countries will more rapidly adapt to the economic transition.

Conclusion

Democracy is based on the assumption that all citizens participate equally in political affairs and that their decisions have equal weight. Without active citizen involvement in politics, democracy would cease to be meaningful, both in a literal and in a practical sense. Yet there is general agreement that democracy fails if there is too much citizen participation in politics; indeed, it is often argued that democracy is most likely to prosper when there is a balance between widespread political apathy and widespread citizen involvement. The challenge for newly emerging democracies, particularly in the immediate post-authoritarian period, is to ensure that there is sufficient participation to generate support for democratic norms and values, while moderating the types of political activities—such as protests and demonstrations, what are sometimes called 'moments of great drama' (O'Donnell and Schmitter 1986)—that

might undermine the fragile democracy. This is, of course, a delicate balance as these societies experience major economic transitions that depress living standards at a time when popular expectations are high.

This chapter has argued that widespread political participation, in its various forms, is crucial for a successful transition from authoritarianism to democracy. In turn, the institutional arrangements that exist in any particular society will mould patterns of participation, and the resources that voters possess will also influence the type and extent of their participation. So far we have assumed that political participation enhances democracy and makes it makes it more stable and enduring. But do we have any direct evidence that participation does, indeed, influence views of democracy among the mass electorate? Figure 13.2 shows that surveys show very different levels of

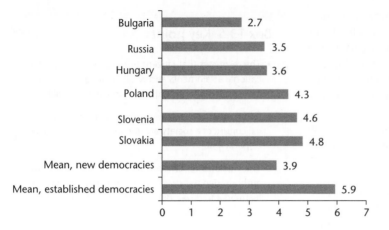

Fig 13.2 Satisfaction with Democracy (means)

Notes: See Appendix for details of questions and countries. Satisfaction with democracy is measured on a 0 to 10 scale.

Source: European Social Survey, Round 3

satisfaction with democracy by country, which would appear to be related to the length of time that the democracy has existed. Among the new democracies, the mean, on a 0 to 10 scale, is 3.9, while in the established democracies the same figure is 5.9. Among the new democracies, satisfaction is lowest in Bulgaria and highest in Slovakia.

Levels of participation have a strong and positive relationship with satisfaction with democracy. Table 13.6 shows that all forms of participation are significantly related to satisfaction with democracy. Most important is voting, which has a correlation of .12 with democratic satisfaction in the established democracies, and .08 in the new democracies. As the theories of democracy predict, then, regular attendance at the polls makes voters feel more positive about their democracy. The influence of the other forms of participation is more modest, although working for others in the established democracies has a notable influence, as does persuading others about whom to

vote for in the new democracies. Overall, the relationship between participation and satisfaction with democracy is stronger in the established than in the new democracies, as we would expect, since participation is more entrenched and related to democratic norms and values.

Widespread conventional political participation is crucial to the health of any democracy, regardless of its age. However, as we have argued here, it is particularly important in the immediate post-authoritarian period, when popular participation and involvement helps to cement support for the new democratic institutions. Longer-term, the new democracies can expect to see declining levels of participation, particularly in elections, as their systems come to more closely resemble those of the established democracies. There has been a long-term decline in electoral participation across almost all of the advanced democracies, starting in the early 1970s, with little indication that the trend has reached its nadir

Table 13.6 Political Participation and Satisfaction with Democracy (correlations)

	Voted	Campaign activity		Communal activity		
		Persuade others	Attend meetings	Work for party	Work for others	Contact official
New democracies	.08	.07	.04	.00^{ns}	.04	.02
Established democracies	.12	.02^{ns}	.01^{ns}	.03	.10	.02

Notes: See Box 13.1 for details of questions and countries. N = 10,176 new democracies, N = 22,731 established democracies. ns, not statistically significant at $p < .01$.

Sources: Comparative Study of Electoral Systems, Module 2; European Social Survey, Round 3

(Dalton and Wattenberg 2000). Ultimately, such a decline in electoral participation has the potential to harm democratic stability, but the expectation is that by then, the newer democracies will have accumulated sufficient resilience in order to meet this new challenge. For these countries, the challenges of democratic politics must seem to be almost as profound as those of their authoritarian past.

QUESTIONS

1. What are the main challenges to democracy in the immediate post-authoritarian period and how can they be overcome?

2. How does conventional political participation differ from other types of political participation?

3. What are the main types of political participation and what potential influence can they exert on political leaders?

4. Which types of political participation are most important in ensuring a smooth transition from authoritarianism to democracy?

5. How and in what ways do political institutions influence levels of political participation, particularly the act of voting in national elections?

6. What are the main functions of political parties and why are they so important for ensuring widespread political participation?

Visit the Online Resource Centre that accompanies this book for additional questions to accompany each chapter, and a range of other resources: <www.oxfordtextbooks. co.uk/orc/haerpfer/>.

FURTHER READING

Conge, P. J. (1988),'The Concept of Political Participation: Toward a Definition', *Comparative Politics*, 20/2: 241–9. Provides a review of some of the issues involved in defining political participation.

Kostadinova, T. (2003), 'Voter Turnout Dynamics in Post-Communist Europe', *European Journal of Political Research*, 42/6: 741–59. Examines patterns of voter turnout across four successive elections in fifteen postcommunist societies.

Bernhagen, P. and Marsh, M. (2007), 'Voting and Protesting: Explaining Citizen Participation in Old and New European Democracies', *Democratization*, 14/1: 44–72. Examines voter turnout alongside protest activities in nine postcommuinist countries and compares patterns with those found in West European countries.

White, S. and McAllister, I. (2007), 'Turnout and Representation Bias in Postcommunist Europe', *Political Studies* 55/3: 586–606. Examines a more limited range of postcommunist societies to evaluate the political consequences of differential turnout.

A special symposium in *Electoral Studies* (Volume 27 Part 1 2008) entitled 'Public Support for Democracy: Results from the Comparative Study of Electoral Systems Project' and edited by Ian McAllister, includes several papers examining support for democracy in countries at different stages of the democratization.

IMPORTANT WEBSITES

<www.idea.int> The International Institute for Democracy and Electoral Assistance website contains a variety of indicators of political participation, as well as monographs and debates concerning the promotion of democracy.

<www.cses.org>; <www.europeansocialsurvey.org> The two main comparative politics data projects, the Comparative Study of Electoral Systems and the European Social Survey both have their data available for download, as well as details of papers and publications using the datasets.

NOTES

1 Six other communist-ruled nations, and a few in Africa, had already attained the magical 100 per cent.

2 The Central Electoral Commission in Russia, and its counterparts in the other post-Soviet countries, conventionally report turnout in terms of the number who 'took part in the election' as a percentage of the registered electorate; this represents the total number who received ballot papers, but not the total number of votes cast. In the December 2003 Russian Duma election, by way of example, 60,712,300 were reported to have 'taken part in the election' (55.75 per cent of the registered electorate) but only 60,633,171 ballots were cast (55.67 per cent), a figure that was not separately reported, and of these nearly a million (948,409) were invalid ballots. We have sought wherever data are available to employ ballots cast as our standard measure.

3 Estimates are from the 2006–07 European Social Survey.

4 For example, in a 1990 Russian survey, 10 per cent of those interviewed had been party members, and 76 per cent members of trade unions. By 2005 that had declined to 1 per cent and 12 per cent respectively (White and McAllister 2007: Table 1).

5 We can only make these estimates for the European Social Survey since the trust questions were not asked in the CSES.

Political Parties

Leonardo Morlino

Overview

The first topic to be discussed is the definition of a party within the processes of democratization. Next we show how parties can be indispensable for the actual working of democracy. The subsequent three sections consider the actual role of parties during the processes of transitions towards democracy as well as during democratic **consolidation**, and in different types of crises. However, when such a role is more closely scrutinized, the empirical evidence shows a more complex picture where parties are not always present and, if they are, other actors can complement their action.

Introduction

In a large number of empirical analyses on the processes of democratization during the last four decades, the actual role of political parties, as key actors in that process, has been taken for granted, and, consequently, never explicitly singled out. In several cases scholars were in a difficult position on this matter: democratizations were taking place at a time of party weakening, if not vanishing, and in areas where those actors had never been strong or, when strong, were an undistinguishable part of an authoritarian **regime** that experienced a profound crisis and breakdown, especially in a key area, such as Central and Eastern Europe.

This chapter tries to fill this gap by addressing a few salient questions. However, we will start with a broad definition of a party, that is, our key actor. Here, we need neither a discussion on the best theoretical definition nor an overview of the literature on the topic, as these can be found in a number of previous studies (see, e.g. Mair 1997, Diamond and Gunther 2001b, Katz and Crotty 2005). For our purposes it is sufficient to refer to the classic definition by Downs (1957:25): 'a political party is a team of men seeking to control the governing apparatus by gaining office in a duly constituted election' as it allows us to encompass in this notion a variety of different political entities that were and are present in the processes of democratization. This definition can be adequately complemented by another that depicts the party in connection with the components it interacts with. In this perspective, a party is a 'central intermediate and intermediary structure between society and government' (Sartori 1976: ix), that is, an institution with a connecting role vis-à-vis the other regime institutions, on the one hand, and the people, on the other.

With such definitions in mind the key question to address, is: What are the various roles that parties, alone or with other individual or collective actors, play during the processes of democratization, that is, during the transition, installation, and consolidation, and the possible phases of democratic crisis? To achieve a clearer answer to such a broad issue, we will break it down into four specific questions: (i) Are parties an essential component of democracy? (ii) If so, are they a constant component of democratization processes, in particular of transition, and how do they interact with other actors? (iii) What is the key role performed by parties in the consolidation process? (iv) Can parties be the origin, or even the main 'authors', of failures of transition, consolidation, or even the beginning of a crisis at different points in time? We will start by addressing the first question.

Are Parties an Essential Component of Democracy?

An explicit reply to this question allows us to understand from the very beginning the possible role of parties within the specific processes of democratization. To do so we have to explore two of the different facets of the question: How are the parties an essential component in the working of every democracy and what kinds of party play what role? If we accept the empirical evidence that modern democracies are always representative and the related possibility that installing them mirrors this aspect, a number of consequences follow with regards to the key salient mechanisms in the working of every democracy. In this perspective King (1969: 120–40) singles out six functions of parties: *vote structuring*, which encompasses every aspect related to elections; *integration* and *mobilization*, related to citizen participation and its organization; *leadership recruitment*, which refers to a key, monopolistic function of parties with regards to elected people and those non-elected but appointed by parties to authority positions; *organization of government*, or party government, where there exists a relationship between the executive and the legislative and a number of other connections, implying the activity of coordination; *policy formation*, related to the party activity in problem solving and in influencing the entire policy-making process; *interest aggregation*, where parties transform societal needs into policy proposals. Strom (1990) also follows the same approach when stressing the role of parties as *vote-seeking, office-seeking* and *policy-seeking*.

In a not too dissimilar perspective, but with stronger focus on interactions and links, I prefer to stress the following five processes. First, there are the elections and their related aspects (election participation and its organization, recruitment of candidates, electoral lists, and electoral campaign). Second, there is the decisional process and the voting procedures in the parliaments for laws to be passed. Third, there is a need to make explicit and translate into the decisional process the needs and wants of (civil) society, be it organized or not, structured along the lines of pressure or interest groups, or more or less formally developed. Fourth, there is public debate and some steering from that on general or more specific policies to be decided, and the shaping of the decisional agenda. Fifth, there is the need to coordinate and implement the decisions made and to monitor that implementation. When the minimal democratic characteristics of civil rights, political rights and consequent political competition are added, then the essential presence of more than one 'team of (wo)men that is an intermediary structure between society and government and control the governing apparatus' is obvious: Who can perform all the connections and coordination necessary for a proper, or even not so proper, working of a democracy within more and more complex realities? Or, more precisely, who will recruit candidates, create electoral lists, run the electoral campaign, coordinate the vote in the parliamentary arena, decide the agenda to lead public discussion, and monitor policy implementation, if not those political teams that we call parties?

Let it be explicitly stressed that here we are not considering the functions or role parties should ideally perform in the way King, Strom, and others conceptualize that activity. Here, the key question is what kind of parties we actually have in the transitions to democracy, to the possible related consolidations and beyond. Within the expression 'political team', which only refers to the fact that there is a group of people working together with similar purposes, a large variety of realities can be accommodated. If we also consider the democratizations in Southern Europe, Latin America, Central and Eastern Europe and South-East Asia, we find almost the entire set of party models discussed by Diamond and Gunther (2001a: 9–13): from elite clientelistic parties to socialist, nationalist, religious mass-based parties, ethnicity-based parties, personalistic and programmatic electoralist parties, and movement parties; or—to adopt the simplified perspective of Raniolo (2006: 36–42)—elite parties, mass parties, and electoralist parties.

Moreover, the relevant phenomenon to emphasize is that, except in some earlier transition to democracy, such as for example the Italian and German after World War II, the socialist, nationalist, and religious mass-based parties are basically absent and the most commonly recurring models are elite parties, especially clientelistic parties, and electoralist parties, with strong personalization or sometimes strong territorial, but limited presence. The clientelistic parties are characterized by small membership, light—if any—organization, role of notables or of a restricted group, and patronage; the electoralist parties are characterized by open, not large membership, poor

party identification, light or very light organization, publicly financed, neutral relationships with interest groups, and a possibly key role of leader in the personalistic version.

In addition to the organizational dimension, when considering the model of parties that are present in the democratization processes, we cannot avoid taking into account the 'family' the parties belong to. In one of the best known classifications (von Beyme 1987; Ware 1996: 21–43) those 'families' include: 1. conservatives, 2. liberals and radicals, 3. social democrats and socialists, 4. agrarians, 5. ethnics and regionalists, 6. Christian-democrats and protestants, 7. communists, 8. fascists, 9. bourgeois protest, 10. ecologist movements. Let it be recalled that this well known and widely accepted classification refers to the Western European experience. This implies that when we consider other democratizations and new democracies in other areas of the world, we assume that more party 'families' should be added. This is only partially so. In fact, it is mainly the fifth category, ethnic and regionalist parties, that has to be enriched with nationalist parties and, more generally, parties with a strong territorial background. At the same time, some additional considerations should be made: some families have disappeared, such as fascists and communists; the class conflict characterized by the left-right alignment, if it still exists, is much less relevant; Christian and protestant parties are usually weak, where they are found; bourgeois protest parties are unknown; however, mixed realities, such as conservative and liberal, are still active.[1]

In order to pay attention to the key aspects presented in this section, we conclude the discussion on the parties as essential components of democracy by emphasizing one of the most salient paradoxes of contemporary transitions to democracy: the more the country is varied and the more complex it is, and

---

Box 14.1 **Key points**

- Political parties are an essential component of democracy.

- There is a large variety of parties, including some involving a minimal kind of organization.

consequently the more essential is the need of parties, the weaker the party organizations—be they elite or electoralist, where a small group often takes the lead. Such a paradox came out, more clearly, in the cases where either a modern society or a modernizing society already existed when the transition started unfolding. The first and most emblematic case was the Spanish one. But also some Central and Eastern European cases are very relevant in this perspective as in some cases, such as Poland or Czech Republic, societal modernization was complemented by a failure of mass parties, be they in a non-democratic context. We will now explore the consequences of this paradox for democratic changes complemented by other important additional aspects.

Are Parties the Key Actors of Transition? Are there Alternative Actors?

Variations in transitions to democracy

In a very effective and widely quoted analysis of transition to democracy, Dahl (1971)[2] singles out two basic dimensions (competition and participation) and three paths (competition takes the precedence on inclusiveness; inclusiveness comes first; the two phenomena go hand in hand in the transition to democracy). The existence and salience of a party role is taken for granted by him in the developments of both phenomena. If for simplicity's sake we could maintain such a theoretical framework and take into account a number of cases, such as those of southern Europe, Latin America, Central and Eastern Europe, some areas of Africa and East Asia, there would be a wide range of variations. However, this is not the best way to shed light on the role of parties in the processes of transition to democracy. We need to go through two related steps: first, singling out the key dimensions of variation when focusing on partisan actors; second, developing the main patterns of transition when the analysed dimensions are put together.

As shown in Figure 14.1, the main dimensions of variation are: continuity or discontinuity of party actors; the key characteristics of the basic democratic agreement; the number and range of development of actors along basic cleavages; the extent of participation; and the extent of violence during the transition and institutional installation. These five main dimensions do not cover the full range of aspects that characterize transitions to democracy. For example, the presence and role of the army is very important; and the continuity or discontinuity of the judiciary and bureaucracy are also important elements. Here, however, we only take into consideration the dimensions more closely related to the role of parties.

The extent of violence that characterizes the period of change is fairly easy to assess as it is sufficient to consider the number of deaths and of the injured in sit-ins, strikes or illegal occupations of public buildings or properties, and other illegal acts of radical parties or movements. This dimension is a salient one as the role of radicalism is taken into account and this carries a number of consequences for the democratic transition that may evolve into failure and the return to some authoritarian regime. The extent of peaceful participation with regards to elections, party memberships, and a number of other forms of participation is another salient dimension of every analysis of transition, but with a totally different meaning. If the extent of violence displays the measure of existing radical opposition to democracy, the legal forms and extent of participation show the explicit support actually existing for the transition and its end result. Consequently, both aspects are very important in showing which actors are against and which are for democracy.

The third and fourth aspects in Figure 14.1 are also related. Regarding the third aspect, it is important to analyse the transition and the resulting democratic arrangement focusing on the main conflicts or key issues that characterize the political arena, such as class conflict between left and right, religious

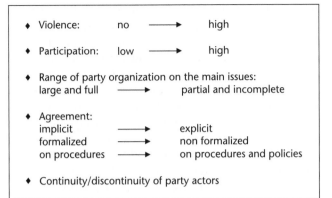

Fig 14.1 Dimensions of Variation in Transitions to Democracy

differences, ethnic, language or cultural differences, and, more recently, environmental conflict. These conflicts or cleavage are also the organizing criteria for parties that promote one or other side of the cleavage and, in doing so, structure the political arena inside and outside the democratic institutions, above all the parliament and the cabinet.

The emergence of the organized conflict is complemented by the fourth relevant aspect, the basic agreement that is at the grassroots of a democracy, if it becomes stable. Such an agreement can be explicit, for example, when the Constitutional Charter is discussed, and eventually approved by party elites in Parliament. It can be implicit when a previous Constitution is quickly resumed and enforced. Moreover, that agreement is more often on the constitutional design, that is, on the procedures to be followed for peaceful resolution of the conflicts or for the peaceful accommodation of interests and positions. In some cases, the agreement can encompass some policies, especially foreign policy or regional integrative policies. They become accepted and external to the arena of debate.

On the whole, on this aspect those authors who had analysed Southern European and Latin American transitions—especially Spain, Brazil, and Chile—emphasized the role of the 'pacts' in the transition phase and in establishing stable democracies (see, e.g. O'Donnell and Schmitter 1986: 37–47), whereas those who conducted research on Central and Eastern Europe—especially the Czech Republic, Estonia, Hungary, Latvia, Lithuania, Poland, Slovenia, and Croatia—glossed over that (see, e.g. McFaul 2002). The key point seems to be the success of actors in creating some sort of founding coalition,

not necessarily formalized or explicit, but such as to support the new democratic institutions: at least the new institutions have become accepted by elite and people, to a large extent, and are no longer challenged by most people. By itself this is not a relevant aspect of the transition to democracy. Transitions can be carried out for sheer imitation only, as again a few Central and Eastern European cases show, but it becomes relevant for a subsequent stabilization of the regime (see next section).

The fifth and last dimension we consider is the most important in analysing the transition, that is, continuity versus discontinuity of party actors. This dimension is easy to understand and assess. It refers to the persistence of the same elite, in case of similar political relationships, or to the change of elite and linkages between elite and people before and after the transition. But when we try to explore this dimension at greater depth, we immediately realize that this is the main dimension *vis-à-vis* the other four. In fact when we combine the extent of violence, participation, organization of conflicts and basic agreement with continuity or discontinuity of party elite, we have three basic dominant patterns of change: elite continuity, party continuity, and elite and party discontinuity.

Elite continuity, party continuity, and elite and party discontinuity

When continuity is explored, two main patterns emerge. The first one, *elite continuity*, is characterized by the existence of elite actors who were active during the non-democratic—often authoritarian—regime (see Linz 2000) and went on being active in all the phases of change until the end of democratic installation, on a few occasions persisting even later on, during the consolidation. These elite actors were not present as a party in the previous regime, but were present in the government at different levels, often in subordinate roles. When the regime is in crisis and later on during the transition and the installation, they are able to convert themselves into democratic, usually rightist, parties that become either opposition or incumbent parties, sometimes going through subsequent internal transformations.

When elite continuity is strong, violence and participation during the transition are low, if they occur at all. A limited number of conflicts are activated and the basic agreement, known as the 'pact'—very important for some authors (see above)—is explicit and mainly concerns procedures. Moreover, elite continuity entails the continuity of the old legal framework. This allows a controlled change and an easier **legitimation** of the institutional changes inside the social groups that are still loyal to the previous regime and frightened by the change. We can find good examples of such a pattern in Spain, Chile and Brazil. In more general terms, this is a possible pattern in all areas where an authoritarian regime or even a traditional one is the starting point, and this may happen not only in Southern Europe or Latin America, but also in South-East Asia.

The second main pattern, *party continuity*, regards those parties that were active, present and totally identified with the previous non-democratic, often mobilizational,[3] regime. During the phases of change they were able to adapt and become fully consistent with democratic mechanisms. Here, the continuity concerns not only the party elite—even if middle level elite—but also people used to participating and being linked to the non-democratic mass party. A mixture of ideology, clientelism and suppression accounted for those asymmetric relationships[4] during the authoritarian period. In the new democratic context, although profoundly transformed because of the disappearance of ideology and suppression, those relationships went on, often complemented by personal connections, especially in small towns and villages. This pattern is characterized by little or no violence, low participation in different domains, the emergence

of class cleavages as the main organized conflict and difficulties in achieving a basic agreement, and also by the constitutional design. Several Central and Eastern European transitions saw the transformations of communist parties into democratic leftist parties with a change of name, which were able to continue old allegiances, with the highest party continuity during the first years of democracy in Hungary and Lithuania, fairly strong continuity in Romania, Slovakia, and Slovenia, and strong continuity in Bulgaria, Estonia, and Poland (see also Morlino 2001).[5]

When considering the opposite, a third pattern emerges—*elite and party discontinuity*. In this case, the crisis and breakdown of a non-democratic regime brings about the fading away of actors who were active and supported the regime. Of course, such a discontinuity is the result of some kind of break, such as that caused by a war or by a colonial defeat with consequent loss of the colony. This pattern is characterized by a very broad turnover of the political elite, usually no previous experience of democracy, and a previous regime with no mobilization characteristics. Violence, participation, more developed party organization around the cleavages and a formalized basic agreement are, or can be, additional characteristics to this pattern. To trace good examples of such a pattern we have to go back to the democratization processes that followed the World War II, especially in Japan, Italy, and Germany—which we should remember was divided into two parts and later on separated by the Berlin wall—but also Poland and the Czech Republic, Argentina, and South Africa.

In addition, in complex realities as those we attempt to capture here, we never find the patterns sketched above in a 'pure', plain form. If they exist, they are dominant or quasi-dominant patterns. More explicitly, the elite continuity is always complemented by the involvement of new democratic elites, who were part of the opposition or in exile during the authoritarian period. During its transition and installation, Spain, which can be considered the best example of elite continuity, had the presence and key role of Socialists and Communists over those phases. The same applies to most of the transitions in Central and Eastern Europe when the other pattern, which we labeled 'party continuity', is considered; they are not 'pure' either. On an analytical level, it could be claimed that the third pattern characterized by discontinuity could present itself in a 'pure' form. But this is not so. Even when we consider the older cases of Germany, Italy, and Japan or, much more recently, the Portuguese case with the military coup (April 1974) and the 'carnation revolution',[6] the old elite and the old political relationships partially return. They might sometimes do so at a later stage, but return they do.

These three proposed patterns are consciously focused only on the role of party elites and parties. However, on the one hand, a few additional features provide the necessary context allowing the structuration of **party system** and party to happen and, on the other hand, the role of parties as actors usually is the key element that characterize the transition. More precisely, the pattern of elite continuity is possible in a **state** with a fairly developed bureaucracy and judiciary that accept adaptation in order to perform their roles; party continuity is possible when the basic relationships and human memories are still there, otherwise that kind of continuity is more superficial than real. In addition, elite and party discontinuity is possible if there is a breaking event that entirely shapes the context of transition. If there is a pattern of elite or party continuity, then the transition and installation are continuous and the issue can be how that continuity can be specified; the same applies to the third pattern. On the basis of what was illustrated in the previous section on the essential role of parties in a democracy, the simple point is that those actors play the key roles during the change.

International and external factors

Up to now the institutional context we have considered has been only the domestic one. Especially in the most recent transitions, the international context has become more and more relevant (see Pridham and Vanhanen 1994, Whitehead 2001 and, more recently, Magen and Morlino 2008). Consequently, the role of a number of international actors, such as political parties active in other countries, European and non-European governments (e.g. USA), and international organizations (from the UN to the World Bank, the European Union, the Council of Europe, the Organization for Security and Cooperation in Europe, OSCE) is becoming more and more relevant in helping one or other pattern of transitions and in connection with those domestic actors who are in favor of democratic change. International agents often cooperate between themselves, for example, the European Union and the Council of Europe, although others sometimes do not, for example, the European Union and the USA. The end result of this is that whereas the beginning, development and successful ending of democratic transition can be explained by the role of international actors, the first two continuous patterns are necessarily defined by domestic factors. However, the third discontinuous pattern, where a breaking event is a characterizing feature, can be heavily influenced by external actors.

An analysis that only stresses the three patterns described above would conceal and ignore the large differences among the cases that we allocate under those patterns, as well as in a mixed position. Thus, here the additional question to address concerns the singling out of the main factors that are relevant when we would like to understand better the role of the party elite in the transition and installation beyond those more general patterns. Although we have to set aside, if not exclude, every sort of determinism, several factors seem relevant in analysing the transitions in more detail. They are presented in Figure 14.2, where we stress above all the most relevant explanatory factors.

The Figure suggests that there are at least seven sets of different variables to explain the process of regime change towards democracy. They include: the institutional and, more generally, political traditions of the country with regard, for example, to the existence of a monarchy, the experience of previous internal conflict and colonial rule; the existence of previous mass politics, with parties already active in the past that can be revitalized in the new situation; the type of previous authoritarian regime, with or without some degree of people mobilization (see above); the duration of the regime: in the case of long elapsed memories the chances of reviving old links become more remote; the reasons for breakdown or crisis of the previous non-democratic regime, such as economic bankruptcy, which characterized the group of Central and Eastern European countries, where the imitation or, rather, demonstration effect was also relevant; the division inside the previous non-democratic coalition, as in Southern Europe and some Latin American countries; and an

- ◆ Political Traditions:
    government: monarchy/republic
    conflict: poor and far away ⎯⎯→ recurrent and close
    colonial rule
- ◆ Previous experience of mass politics
    intensity and diffusion
    duration
- ◆ Type of previous regime:
    competitive oligarchy
    military authoritarianism
    civil-military authoritarianism
    civil authoritarianism
- ◆ Duration of previous regime:
    short (less than ten years) ⎯⎯→ long (more than forty years)
- ◆ Reasons of breakdown/change of previous regime:
    deep socio-economic transformation
    economic bankruptcy
    divisions inside the dominant coalition
    military defeat
    external intervention
    imitation
- ◆ Extent of organization of the opposition in previous regime:
    low ⎯⎯→ high

Fig 14.2 Main Explanations for Party Role in Democratic Transition and Installation

external intervention like those already mentioned at the end of World War II; the existence and degree of organization of party opposition.

Party role in democratic transition

On this last factor, a common sense hypothesis is that if there is well-organized democratic opposition present during the crisis of a non-democratic regime, the role of that opposition is a major one later on in the transitional phase. Consequently, the expected pattern is *elite or party discontinuity*. In this context, common sense is not supported by the empirical evidence, to the extreme point that two of the cases with relatively strong organized and even well-rooted opposition (Spain and Chile) are also the best examples of elite continuity. Without going into unnecessary detail in this chapter, the key explanation is the combination of a past of radical conflict, a learning process, and a conscious moderate choice of opposition that left space to the actors of the regime who switched to a democratic choice, of course, under the non-explicit threat of the opposition. In a sense, nothing works as expected, as the memory of the past deeply influences every behavior: a strong opposition able to mobilize thousands

of people decides not to engage in an open conflict, a sector of the authoritarian elite plays a key role in the transitional phase by deciding to lead the process of change, and the opposition accepts this despite the institutional continuity to be accepted.

This analysis of the factors relevant to the change towards democracy brings us to the final question of this section: Ultimately are the party elites and their organization so salient in the transitional processes? More and more, it seems that people's distrust and lack of confidence are recurrent attitudes towards the elite who are so often conflictive, divisive and unable to solve the difficult problems present during the transition and later on. Even more, according to some authors (e.g. Schmitter 2001), parties have lost their pre-eminent role in the representation and aggregation of interest, that is, in some of their key functions (see above). In addition, della Porta and Rossi (see Ch. 12 in this book) analyse in more detail the role of movements during the transitional phases.

On this, two aspects seem worthy of attention. The first is that the presence and role of mass movements are more effective in provoking or in deepening the crisis of the non-democratic regime, as the demonstrations and strikes carried out during the last years of authoritarian crisis and before the transitions in Spain, Greece, Brazil, Chile, and Peru very clearly suggest. Second, if during transition and later there is mass participation and mobilization with or without violence, there is some room for actors other than parties to play a complementary role. On the whole, however, while movements played a role in some Central and Eastern European and Latin American transitions, especially for example in Brazil, Argentina, and Bolivia, the key role of the party elite remains dominant in all the cases we analysed. If we look for an example of a role played by party organization, it is virtually impossible to find, but if we consider a movement that is the 'weapon' adopted by a political leader or a small group of leaders to carry out the change, then there are a few examples, the first of which is characterized by the pattern of discontinuity (see above). In some cases, particularly in the past, organizations only emerged during the final period of transition and became established in the subsequent consolidation. However, during transitions and installations party elites are in the foreground, although their action can be complemented by the open intervention and support of party members

---

Box 14.2 Key points

- There are three basic patterns of transition: elite continuity, party continuity, and elite and party discontinuity.

- Parties are dominant in the process of transition, even if not always hegemonic.

---

and sympathizers. People are in the background as a threat and ready to intervene if the elite is not able to achieve their objectives. At the same time those same elites make a serious effort to keep people, and particularly radical movements, quiet and out of the arena, as they fear not being able to control those movements once they are set in motion. It is this complex interconnection between different moments of change and different roles and attitudes of people and elite that explains why the debate on the role of other actors rather than the party has created opposite opinions on the same empirical phenomena.

How do Parties Anchor a Democracy?

When analysing the process of consolidation, the first necessary step is to establish whether such a process is actually taking place. This is not as obvious as in the transitions where a number of dramatic events happen. In our perspective, which is focused on parties, the stabilization of electoral behavior, the emergence of recurring patterns of party competition, and the stabilization of the leadership are the three phenomena to be closely scrutinized: they give an immediate picture of the stabilization of the relationships between parties and civil society, i.e. the key, basic element in the whole process.

Electoral stabilization

Electoral stabilization involves the establishment of relationships between parties and the public and among the parties themselves. Following the initial phase of transition, which is accompanied by considerable fluidity, mass behavior may begin to follow more predictable and recurring patterns. The key indicator of stabilization in voting behavior is total electoral volatility (TEV) (Bartolini and Mair 1990). To this another qualitative indicator can be added, namely, critical elections (see Key 1955). As stabilization proceeds, a trend of declining volatility is expected: there will be a progressive shift from high electoral fluidity and uncertainty to more predictable patterns of voting behavior. In addition, when critical elections occur, there is a realignment of voting patterns, but also a relative freezing of those alignments. The decline of TEV and critical elections indicates that party-voter relationships have become more stable; that parties have established definite images; that the range of effective electoral competition is restricted to some sectors of the electorate; and that a party system crisis is unlikely.

The establishment of definite patterns of partisan competition

The second aspect concerns the establishment of definite patterns of partisan competition: the party system assumes its main characteristics. The index of party fractionalization (PF) or the number of 'effective' parties (NEP), in addition to the qualitative analysis of the non-emergence of new parties and movements, provide the best available indicators to test whether patterns of competition among parties are established and may remain stable for some time, or are changing. The usefulness of both indices is limited if they are not integrated with a qualitative analysis. The indices, in fact, mask differences among the countries and changes over time. The reference to new parties or movements also encompasses the possibility of party splits or party fusion, which should no longer occur in consolidation. Indeed, during a transition towards a new democratic regime, a large number of new parties can be expected to present lists for the first one or two elections. At a certain point, however, the regime's electoral system should at least begin to contribute to party system stabilization. To be sure, the differing electoral systems will have varying impacts on the prospects for the viability of new parties. In this context a crucial variable affecting the extent of stabilization is the level of the threshold set by each electoral system. These diversities notwithstanding, there will be a clear difference between the first one or two elections, when hundreds of party lists are presented, and the subsequent electoral contests, when a process of natural selection has already begun, and a stable leadership, organization, identity, image, and programmatic commitments are also set up. The creation of new parties and movements becomes a more and more unusual event when there is a process of consolidation. On the whole, the initial impact of the electoral threshold and the simple development of competition allow a few, definite parties to dominate the electoral and political arenas and to prevent the entry of new forces for a few years or decades. The party systems achieved a definite structure of party competition, their own competitive logic and some degree of stabilization. More serious problems may remain at an intra-party level, but this is a minor element in the consolidation when the other indicators provide definite evidence of stabilization. Of course, those developments can always be interrupted and reversed because of a change to some basic aspect, such as limited crises and deliberate action by party leaders. A different way of exploring the patterns of competition is to see if there has been a stabilization of cleavages. If the party system is divided into two camps in accordance with the left-right cleavage, and other cleavages, such as center-periphery, ethnicity and language, and religion, and have emerged and become stable, then there is additional empirical evidence of consolidation.

Stabilization of party leadership

Stabilization of electoral behavior and the emergence or change of patterns of party competition are focused on the mass level. The elite level is also highly relevant, especially with regard to the stabilization of party leadership and, more generally, of the political class. This is the third dimension to be analysed if the processes under scrutiny are more carefully detected.[7]

Once the evidence of the process has been gathered, then the subsequent analysis should explain better what lies behind those forms of stabilization. As soon as we reach this second step, we immediately understand how the contention that 'political parties must play a key role in democratic consolidation' is wrong. Although this is a starting point recalled by several authors, as Randall and Svasand (2002: 30) correctly remind us, empirical research pointed to a more complex reality, where even maintaining a focus on parties requires us to acknowledge how other actors concur to achieve that result within the frame of two key sub-processes, legitimation and anchoring.

Legitimation

Legitimation, or the process of developing legitimacy, is the unfolding of a set of positive societal attitudes towards the democratic institutions that are considered the most appropriate form of government. In other words, legitimation occurs when citizens generally believe that, in spite of shortcomings and failures, the existing political institutions are better than possible alternatives. As Linz (1978: 18) has written, '[u]ltimately, democratic legitimacy is based on the belief that for that particular country at that particular juncture no other type of regime could assure a more successful pursuit of collective goals'. Therefore, the objects of legitimation are rules and institutions, in their working, and its actors are still either parties or sectors of a more or less organized civil society.

The empirical analysis of legitimation, through survey data and documents in a number of countries (see, e.g. Morlino 1998), affords clear evidence that a continuum that concerns either elites or citizens can be identified. For simplicity's sake, at one end of the continuum, one can consider a partial or *exclusive* legitimation, which (i) is unable to attract positive attitudes and support of major sections of elites—sometimes very important ones in terms of economic resources and influence, or simply because of their numbers—and (ii) is characterized by a narrow consensus, where at least a political alternative is present in people's minds and values, and there are parties which consider themselves outside the democratic arena and which are also considered by others as such (that is, excluded). At the opposite end, there is widespread or *inclusive* legitimation, where all existing parties and other political organizations support democratic institutions, and there is a large consensus and no support for an alternative regime.

Anchoring

An exclusive or inclusive legitimation is complemented by anchoring. Whereas an anchor is an institution or more simply a mechanism, entailing organizational elements and vested interests, that is able to perform a hooking and binding effect on more or less organized people within a society, anchoring refers to the emergence, shaping, and adaptation of anchors that hook and bind and, consequently, may even control civil society in general or specific sectors. The metaphor of anchors and anchoring is intended to highlight the asymmetrical relationships between elites who are at the centers of those anchors and people; it also conveys the idea of the hooking and binding mechanism

where elite actors and people interact, and of the adaptive possibilities involved in the top-down direction of anchoring. Asymmetrical relationships and a binding mechanism imply the development of connections with people who may be educated and informed, but are very often in weaker positions in terms of power relations, knowledge, information, and time to devote to politics.

The most important anchors belong to the twin circuits of territorial and functional representation in their connections with the democratic regime, that is to parties and societal groups. As suggested by the classic analyses of party organization and elections, and strengthened by the results of several empirical studies, parties with their organization deserve special attention. Even in non-strongly ideological contexts, democratic competition forces parties to develop more efficient and functional organizations to run effective electoral propaganda, to be present and active in the inter-electoral period, and to create and project some alternative policy choice to the electors, also through their parliamentary activity. After some elections and the consequent application of the same electoral system, among the non-explicitly declared side effects of their competition, parties acquire some measure of direction over civil society through the stabilization of party 'supply' and of its leadership (also at a parliamentary level), and through the organization of the parties themselves and the creation of binding collective identities (see also Mair 1991). Electoral norms are well known and include the public financing of parties, the setting of limits and constraints on electoral propaganda, the existence of higher or lower thresholds for access to electoral competition and allocation of seats, and the adopted electoral formula.

In several countries, however, party organizations have never really developed. In the best cases parties were or are, to varying degrees personalized or very lightly structured, and mainly at a local level. For example, in his analysis of the role of parties in the processes of consolidation in Latin America, Espindola (2002) finds that only in Chile has party organization been a salient reality in that process. Also among the African countries, such as Benin, Botswana, Cape Verde, Ghana, Mali, Mauritius, Namibia, South Africa, where by 2008 there had been some relative consolidation, only Ghana and South Africa display stronger party development (see Mattes and Gyimah-Boadi 2005).[8]

Thus, again with reference to Southern Europe, as well as to a number of Latin American, Central and Eastern European and African consolidations, three other anchors and anchoring effects within the functional circuit of representation should be taken into account. They are related to: (i) organized associations, such as business elites, unions, and also religious associations and other structured interest groups in policy making (gate-keeping); (ii) non-organized, but active elites, such as large and small, but widespread, private businesses, intellectuals, or even individuals bound in a patronage or clientelistic relationship; and also (iii) organized interest bound in some form of neo-corporatist arrangement. Within this picture the organized and unorganized interest groups and the movements may be complex, rich, and multifaceted.

The clientelist relationships that characterize a few precise social and cultural contexts make non-organized, atomized people dependent on the incumbent elite, above all the partisan one which allocates benefits and resources of different kinds. Thus, those relationships create and shape a specific, strong process of anchoring that is characterized by specific formal institutions and informal rules deeply embedded in the political culture of the country or specific regions. Neo-corporatism, characterized by stable agreements and a more or less developed network of unions and other kinds of interest associations and interest intermediation committees, is also a potentially very strong anchor. In this case no specific formal institution performs the binding effect imposed from above, but it is the indirect result of agreements complemented by associations that may even be organizationally weak, although they always maintain a leading role in the specific sectors of society where they are active. The main consequence of this is the possibility of encapsulating conflicts, protest and a possible process of delegitimation. Another important anchor emerges out of the relationships between parties and economic elites, unions and other economic associations. This is the gate-keeping role that party elites and the party system are able to perform towards interest groups. That is the role performed by the incumbent and opposition parties, or also by the party system as a whole, in controlling the access of interest groups and economic elites to the decision-making arena, in settling the agenda of decision-making by creating priorities among different demands, and possibly in trying to solve problems that affect the everyday life of citizens. Consequently, for interest associations and other elites, party leaders and, in some cases, party organizations become the necessary gate-keepers to protect their interests and gain access to the decision-making process.

To better understand such a specific anchoring mechanism, different relationships between parties and interest groups can be considered. Two of them will be discussed here. The first, *dominance*, envisages a situation where the parties and the party system virtually control civil society in general, and interest groups in particular. The groups, although bearers of their own identifiable and given interests, become mainly ancillary organizations for the parties, which have autonomous sources of power in terms of ideology, internal organization, and a large membership. This is the case where unions, other associations and weak business elites are subordinate to parties. In such a situation there is usually a large or very large public sector in the economy, and party appointments fill all the positions in that sector. The second, almost opposite scenario, *neutrality*, foresees no definite dependency between groups and parties. Interest groups are more or less organized and politically active with their own economic and social bases and resources. Similarly, parties have their autonomous power bases and maintain control of the decision-making process, which mainly resides in the opportunities that the rules of the democratic regime give to party elites and in the characteristics of the party system. Parties are still able to perform a gate-keeping role: groups and people are compelled to appeal to parties and party leaders to promote and protect their interests. The essentiality of the parties and party elites is emphasized by their ability to perform their institutional role as proponents of policy alternatives by coping with the main current issues and problems, possibly as problem-solvers by choosing or accommodating different conflicting interests, and by having their decisions accepted by most of the people who are affected by them. Groups are in a more independent position *vis-à-vis* parties. No especially strong relationship exists or is established between a group and a particular party. Business groups are often in a more independent position vis-à-vis parties, and in spite of their possible links with parties, unions also have their own domains and autonomy.

Interaction between legitimation and anchoring

On the whole, the four anchors described here emerge out of Southern European cases (see Morlino 1998) and cases from other areas, but it is also possible to find anchoring effects in those same geo-political areas. For example, an important TV channel, a widely read newspaper, but also a supranational actor, such as the European Union, and the rules resulting from one or more international treaties, such as those on human rights or those on the accession process to the Union, can exert an anchoring effect on political elites and citizens of a country. Even if only for a short time, a movement can perform an anchoring effect as well. Direct participation and collective sense of identity, which are characteristics of political movements, may also have a powerful, if temporary, anchoring effect. In addition, one could also think how in a highly unstructured social and political context with little or no tradition of democratic institutions, even a governing institution, such as the head of the state or the prime minister, may actually have anchoring effects with several related consequences for the consolidation process.

There are obvious connections between the aspects sketched here and the existence of a more or less articulated civil society with different kinds of autonomous, non-political elites as well as networks of associations, including interest groups. They are two sides of the same coin. Moreover, it is not particularly difficult to check the existence of a civil society empirically: an active and participating public, different kinds of elites together with independent press and TV networks, a rich tapestry of associations, more or less highly organized—in other words, a high level of associability—are fairly easily empirically detected. In such a case the gate-keeping

relationship with party elites will be one of neutrality or even of direct access. On the other hand, if civil society is poorly organized without autonomous resources, dominance is more probable.

Here, some additional consideration is useful to connect anchoring and legitimation. First, one can have a poor process of exclusive legitimation, but at the same time some consolidation and a relatively stable democracy as a result. This is because there has been the development of a strong democratic anchoring. With an exclusive legitimation and weakly developed domestic anchors, some consolidation is still possible, if limited sovereignty is accepted by the governing elites of the country through some international agreement that keeps the regime democratic, that is, an external anchoring is achieved.

When there is an inclusive, widespread legitimation from the beginning, or when a successful sub-process of legitimation develops to the point that anti-regime and disloyal groups or parties are or become a tiny, unimportant minority, the anchors can be considered no longer essential for consolidation. In other words, the more widespread the legitimation, the weaker the anchors can be to achieve consolidation. However, they are still important for defining the characterizing aspects of the consolidation process, the existing democracy and also – even more relevant—for maintaining the democratic institution in case of a crisis of an economic or other origin.

Box 14.3 **Key points**

- Stabilization of electoral behaviour, emergence of recurring patterns of party competition, and the stabilization of leadership are the key elements of consolidation.

- Legitimation and anchoring are two key sub-processes.

- The main anchors are party organization, gate-keeping, clientelism, and neo-corporatism.

- Anchoring and legitimation are connected and can even complement each other.

When do Parties Fail?

There is a tradition of analysis that considers parties the main causes of divisions, deeper conflicts and ultimately the actors responsible for the crisis and breakdown of a democracy. Especially in the past in Europe and Latin America we can find empirical support for such an analysis, as parties have magnified deep conflicts that are present and often widespread within a society and, if complemented by widespread antidemocratic attitudes, could bring about the breakdown of the democratic regime. In this perspective, after World War II, one of the most debated cases has been that of Chile, characterized by the coup d'état led by Pinochet in 1973, but caused by the stark contrasts between the parties at the time, Christian Democrats and Socialists, and the plan of political change in a Socialist direction followed by Salvador Allende. In other countries and areas rather than the conflict over a socialist change, there have been ethnic, language or religious conflicts which, when radicalized to the extreme of jeopardizing the democratic institution or stopping and reversing a transitional process, can lead to breakdown, authoritarian reconsolidation, civil war, or stalemate. In every stage party leaders and parties play a role. However, within such processes **social movements**, illegal forms of participation and, above all, the adoption of violence almost always complement the divisive action of parties. Army and police often become involved in this 'destructive game'.

By contrast, even though radicalized the conflicts do not reach the point of casting doubt on democratic institutions, as they are largely and deeply legitimated, then there can be a crisis within the democracy with change or disappearance of some parties and the merging of others. The profound economic crisis in Argentina and the political crisis in Italy are two good examples of crisis within the democratic regime that did not at all affect the widespread beliefs in democ-

racy, per se, by the Argentinean or Italian people. Under such a hypothesis, the key aspect is a process of de-anchoring, that is, precisely the opposite of what happens during the consolidation process. Thus, the unfolding of a crisis is related to an expansion and deepening dissatisfaction at a mass level, which brings about a delegitimation and at the same time leads to internal and external changes that cause the destructuration of anchors. This may mean the fading away of party organization in the context of de-ideologization, such as the disappearance of a Communist threat; or the heavy undermining of clientelist connections in the context of a strong economic crisis; or it may mean the fading away of the gate-keeping role of incumbent parties, when there is fragmentation of the decision-making process; and even the possible end of neo-corporatist arrangements, when other policy directives and goals become prominent and break the cooperation and the agreements among the unions, entrepreneurs and government.

Moreover, we should remember that the unfolding of the crisis is related to the extent and characteristics of the previously achieved legitimacy, but even more to the transformations of the main existing anchors. This carries two analytical consequences. First, the crisis is indirectly related to the previous process of consolidation and how it occurred, with or without a strong anchoring. Second, if there were weak mechanisms of anchoring from the beginning, then the crisis unfolds in a different way, and the entire problem is the kind of dissatisfaction achieved and whether it raises doubts over democracy per se. Finally, the possible fading away of international constraints, for example the end of the Cold War, and the emerging of specific, contingent incentives have to be incorporated into any more detailed analysis of the crisis.

Conclusion

On the whole, an overview of the empirical evidence shows that clientelist and electoral parties are the most recurrent models of such a political organization in the

processes of democratization. The reason for this is well known. The alternative represented by organized mass parties is no longer relevant. They were the peculiar result of a specific historical period in a few European countries, where within well-defined nation states profound economic transformations and ideological tenets strengthened each other achieving that effect. Consequently, in most of the cases only lighter parties more focused on the elections with strong leaders seem feasible during the democratization processes.

Moreover, it is not surprising to find the three patterns of continuity and discontinuity described above, that is, elite continuity, party continuity, elite and party discontinuity. At the same time, it seems counterintuitive to see that empirically the cases of elite continuity encompass a covert, but effective role of anti-authoritarian opposition, often identified in the phases of authoritarian crisis. When the role of parties and party leaders are analysed within the broader transitional process, at least two aspects should be firmly pointed out. The first concerns the enormous variation in the transitions, which is such that the most that one can do is to single out the main dimensions of variations in the modes and the explanations of the process. The second is to recognize the role of other actors, together with that of the parties, be they institutional ones related to the previous regime, such as the army, police, bureaucracy and judiciary, or in varying degrees, organized groups and movements.

If we have those models of parties, and if party and party leaders share their role with other actors in the transitions towards democracy, it is no wonder that anchoring mechanisms such as clientelism appear stronger and more recurrent than party organizations or gate-keeping and neo-corporatism, which imply the existence of well-structured actors (see also Kitschelt and Wilkinson 2007). Of course, there can be a consolidation with stabilization of electoral behavior, the emergence of recurring patterns of party competition, and the stabilization of the leadership, but these are characterized by weak or very weak anchors. The key complementing point is the achievement of democratic legitimation that can even allow change to a specific democracy to take place, but not a change in democracy in general by preferring alternative non-democratic regimes.

Finally, especially where there has been some degree of consolidation during these years, parties no longer activate profound, radicalized internal divisions that can bring about a democratic breakdown. They basically seem to have learned the lesson of moderation, as a consequence of tough experiences, such as that of Chile with Pinochet. Consequently, most of the present crises are inside the democratic regime. But in some cases this cannot avoid party failure and even disappearance when civil society—often helped by political leaders—sees a party unable to solve the problems of the moment and shift their loyalty to other parties or even merely to leaders.

QUESTIONS

1. How do we define a party within the democratization processes?

2. What are the prevailing party models in recently established democracies?

3. What are the main patterns of party continuity or discontinuity during the transitional phases?

4. What are the main dimensions of variation in transitions to democracy?

5. What are the main explanations of party role in democratic transition and installation?

6. How can we detect the party and party system consolidation?

Visit the Online Resource Centre that accompanies this book for additional questions to accompany each chapter, and a range of other resources: <www.oxfordtextbooks.co.uk/orc/haerpfer/>.

FURTHER READING

Diamandouros, N. P. and Gunther, R. (2001) (eds), *Parties, Politics and New Democracy in the New Southern Europe* (Baltimore, MD: Johns Hopkins University Press). This is an in-depth comparative review of elections, parties and party systems in the four Southern European countries (Italy, Spain, Portugal, and Greece) during their phases of democratization. Moderation, centripetalism, and changes in the so-called anti-system parties are complemented by the richness of the different models of democracy that emerge.

Diamond, L. and Gunther, R. (2001b) (eds), *Political Parties and Democracy* (Baltimore, MD: Johns Hopkins University Press). With the help of a number of colleagues the two editors address the main topics that are relevant to the understanding of the parties in the processes of democratization. In doing so they cover several areas of the world, such as Latin America, post-communist Europe, and a few individual countries (Italy, Japan, Taiwan, India, and Turkey) that are particularly meaningful for the party change they underwent.

Katz, R. S. and Crotty, W. J. (2006) (eds), *Handbook of Party Politics* (Beverly Hills, CA: Sage). Despite the focus on USA and Europe, this is one of the most recent, authoritative and exhaustive surveys of theory and empirical findings on the topic.

Kitschelt, H., Mansfeldova, Z. Markowski, R. and Tóka, G. (1999), *Post-Communist Party Systems: Competition, Representation, and Inter-Party Cooperation* (Cambridge: Cambridge University Press). This book analyses the development of political parties in four Central and Eastern European countries: Bulgaria, Czech Republic, Hungary and Poland. However, the relevance of the topics covered by the book—the analysis of pre-communist conditions, communist rule, transition modes, institutional choices as well as party competition, representation and collaboration in those countries—extends beyond those cases.

Kitschelt, H. and Wilkinson, S. I. (2007) (eds), *Patrons, Clients, and Policies: Patterns of Democratic Accountability and Political Competition* (Cambridge: Cambridge University Press). This book covers different areas and countries where there have been processes of democratization and show the saliency of the clientelistic mechanisms. Moreover, it shows how the interactions among economic development, party competition, governance of the economy and ethnic heterogeneity determine the choices of patrons and clients.

Mainwaring, S. and Scully, T. (1996) (eds), *Building Democratic Institutions: Party Systems in Latin America* (Stanford, CA: Stanford University Press). The processes of party institutionalization in several Latin American countries are analysed using well-developed indicators.

Salih, M. M. A. (2003) (ed.), *African Political Parties: Evolution, Institutionalisation and Governance* (London: Pluto Press). Among the very few pieces of research on African political parties, this book stands out as it covers a number of cases, such as Ethiopia, Ghana, Kenya, Botswana, Namibia, South Africa, Tanzania, Zambia, and Zimbabwe. The party functions, ideology and structure, as well as evolution and institutionalization of parties, are analysed in addition to the relationship between parties and government, parties and representation, parties and electoral systems, and parties and parliament.

Two special issues of academic journals use the Comparative Study of Electoral Systems datasets to examine various aspects of democratization from the perspective of mass political behaviour. *Political Parties and Political Development: A New Perspective*, edited by Russell J. Dalton and Ian McAllister (a special issue of *Party Politics*, 13/2, 2007) includes papers focusing particularly on the contribution of parties to democratization. In this special issue, the articles by Russell J. Dalton and Steven Weldon ('Partisanship and Party System Institutionalization', pp. 179–96), Jeffrey A. Karp and Susan A. Banducci ('Party Mobilization and Political Participation in New and Old Democracies', pp. 217–34) and Ian McAllister and Stephen White ('Political Parties and Democratic Consolidation in Postcommunist Societies', pp. 197–216) are particularly useful.

IMPORTANT WEBSITES

<www.broadleft.org> Leftist Parties in the World: This online database contains summary information and on virtually every single political party, organization or group which considers itself to be leftist or has origins in leftist movements.

<www.psr.keele.ac.uk> Political Parties and Movements: this website lists political parties and their weblinks for every country in the world as well as international groups. Unlike Leftist Parties in the World, it covers the entire political spectrum but is not as detailed and comprehensive.

<http://psephos.adam-carr.net> Adam Carr's Election Archive, contains election statistics from 176 countries.

NOTES

1. To my knowledge no scholar has carried out a thorough scrutiny of party families in the new democracies outside Europe.

2. It is well known that Dahl labels existing democracies as polyarchies, but his label was ignored by subsequent studies and most of authors have continued to use a term ('democracy') that is an empirical and a normative one at the same time. No problem if we are well aware of this.

3. The expression 'mobilizational' refers to regime characterized by non-democratic participation controlled from above (see Linz 2000 and Morlino 2003).

4. To understand this point better, see also below the section on parties during democratic consolidation.

5. In that area the only two cases of weak party continuity and consequently discontinuity are the Czech Republic and Latvia.

6. The symbolic flower of the Socialist Party.

7. Mainwaring (1998, 67–81) points to similar aspects: stability in patterns of inter-party competition, party roots in society, legitimacy of parties and elections, party organization (see also below).

8. Ghana and South Africa have, respectively, a two-partyism and a dominant party system and are also the two largest countries of all. Botswana, Cape Verde, Mauritius, and Namibia all have a population of under two million. Mali (two-partyism) and Benin (moderate pluralism) are in between: a population of a little more than ten million in the former and of almost seven million in the latter.

Electoral Systems and Institutional Design in New Democracies

Matthijs Bogaards

Overview

This chapter looks at electoral systems and institutional design in new democracies. It summarizes the main insights from the literature on electoral systems in established democracies and examines the evidence from new democracies. The chapter focuses on the impact of the electoral law on the type of **party system** and its role as intermediary between society and government in plural societies.

Introduction

The relationship between electoral systems and party systems is a classic topic in comparative politics, which has been given new impetus by the recent wave of democratization. There is by now a sophisticated literature on the political consequences of electoral laws in established democracies. However, it is not clear whether what we know about electoral system design also holds true for emerging party systems in new democracies.

In new democracies, electoral system design is seen as the main lever to achieve a whole range of objectives, from fair representation, strengthening voter-candidate relations, helping to institutionalize and nationalize the party system, limiting polarization, and keeping the number of parties down, to social peace and **democratic consolidation**. The opening sentence of the International IDEA Handbook for Electoral System Design (Reynolds *et al.* 2005: 1) reads: 'The choice of electoral system is one of the most important institutional decisions for any democracy. In almost all cases the choice of a particular electoral system has a profound effect on the future political life of the country'. This chapter summarizes the knowledge of the political consequences of electoral laws, focusing on impact on party system, and reviews the emerging evidence from Eastern Europe, Latin America, and Africa.

Institutional Design

The choice of electoral systems is not made in isolation and the debates about electoral system design are part of a broader concern with institutional design that also includes, among others, the form of government (presidential versus parliamentary) and the territorial organization of government (unitary versus federal). Underlying these decisions is the belief that institutions matter and that institutional choices can have profound effects on the prospects for new democracies.

The institutional approach has a long tradition in configurative-descriptive studies, also known under the ironic label of 'grandpa's institutionalism' (von Beyme 1999: 297). Institutions can be defined here as 'organized patterns of socially constructed norms and roles, and socially prescribed behaviors expected of occupants of those roles, which are created and re-created over time' (Goodin 1996: 19). The study of institutions gained new popularity with the rise of the so-called **'new institutionalism'** in the 1980s (Hall and Taylor 1996). Originating in organization theory, new varieties of institutional and process-oriented analysis quickly spread to comparative politics and the study of democratization. With it came a shift in attention from contextual variables and structural determinism towards actors and an emphasis on choice.

The choice of electoral system is often formulated as a trade-off between **representativeness** and **governability**. Representativeness is thought to be maximized through the electoral system of proportional representation (PR) in multi-member electoral districts leading to a multi-party system and coalition cabinets, while governability is promoted by the electoral system of plurality in single-member districts, a two-party system and single-party governments. Especially in agrarian societies, constituency service and **accountability** are an additional dimension. In Arend Lijphart's (1999) typology of democracies, the choice of electoral system is tied to two fundamentally different types of democracy: consensus versus majoritarian democracy.

Traditionally, electoral system design is motivated by two main concerns. First, fragmentation, that is, a very high number of parties in parliament. The second concern is with the political organization of ethnicity in diverse societies, because ethnic parties are feared to lead to ethnic conflict. Lijphart (1985) and

Donald Horowitz (1991) wrote entire books outlining their (very different) blue-prints for South Africa after apartheid. Samuel Huntington (1991) throws in 'guidelines for democratizers' at regular intervals and Rein Taagepera (2007) starts every chapter with advice 'for the practitioner of politics'. The recommendations differ, but all these studies address the same underlying question: 'How can we intervene *politically* in steering and shaping a process of political development?' (Sartori 1968: 272). And most often, such intervention is through the electoral law, 'the most specific manipulative instrument of politics' in Giovanni Sartori's (1968: 273) famous words. Sartori (1968: 271) proclaims that 'to restrict political science to a science of *laissez faire* is not only anachronistic but useless and, by implication, harmful'. The case for **political engineering** as such is virtually undisputed among political scientists, despite complaints about the 'dissemination of designer democracies' (Nodia 1996: 23).

Electoral laws are cause and consequence. The electoral system helps shape the party system, but it is parties that determine the electoral law. They do so for a variety of reasons, ranging from the self-interest of politicians in winning office or adopting their favored policies to normative conceptions of how political systems should function. Sociological accounts claim that both the electoral law and parties are determined by underlying structural, cultural and historical variables in society (Rokkan 1970). However, the literature on institutional design shows that 'good' institutions are not necessarily in harmony with the rest of the social order. Cass Sunstein (2001) even argues that constitutions should be designed to counteract the most threatening tendencies in that nation and in this sense should be 'countercultural'. Actually, many electoral systems were not designed, but inherited from predecessor **regimes**, especially in newly independent countries.

Duverger's and Sartori's Electoral Laws

Maurice Duverger (1954) was the first scholar to conduct a systematic empirical investigation of the political consequences of electoral laws in comparative perspective. A whole literature developed around Duverger's laws (1964: 217, 239), which state, in the English translation, that 'the simple-majority single-ballot system favor the two-party system' and 'the simple-majority system with second ballot and proportional representation favor multi-partyism'. In fact, Duverger soon extended the number of laws to three, distinguishing between the effects of PR and majority systems. The laws then become: '1) proportional representation tends to lead to the formation of many independent parties, . . . 2) the two-ballot majority systems tend to lead to the formation of many parties that are allied with each other, . . . 3) the plurality rule tends to produce a two-party system' (Duverger 1986: 70). Although Sartori (1986) praises this formulation as the best Duverger ever provided, it was not picked up by the international, English language political science literature because it was only available in French. Duverger explained

the observed political consequences of electoral laws through their mechanical and psychological effect. The mechanical effect refers to the technical procedure through which votes are translated into seats. The psychological effect refers to the effect that the perception of the working of the electoral system has on the strategic behaviour of voters, candidates and parties (Blais and Carty 1991).

Building on Duverger, Sartori (1968) developed his own set of laws. These are constructed as social science laws, that is, 'generalizations endowed with explanatory power that detect a regularity' (Sartori 1994: 31). Explanatory power is what distinguishes an electoral law from statistical laws, which merely quantify a well-confirmed frequency. If social-science laws are seen as probabilistic rather than deterministic, a single exception is not enough to kill the law. Exceptions can be dealt with 'by entering a **necessary condition** that restricts the applicability of the law . . ., or by incorporating the exception(s) into a reformulation of the law that subsumes them.' (p. 32.) Sartori pursues both paths.

The result is a set of four main 'laws', comprising the most detailed, elaborate, and comprehensive predictions about the political consequences of electoral laws available (Sartori 1986). In addition, there is a separate set of 'rules' to capture the political consequences of the double-ballot electoral system (Sartori 1994).

Sartori's laws are formulated in terms of necessary and **sufficient conditions**. Plurality elections in single-member districts cause a two-party system, but only in the presence of a structured party system and only when electoral support is dispersed across constituencies. Sartori (1994: 40) warns that a 'two-party format is impossible—under whatever electoral system—if racial, linguistic, ideologically alienated, single-issue, or otherwise incoercible minorities (which cannot be represented by two major parties) are concentrated in above-plurality proportions in particular constituencies or geographical pockets'. When minorities are geographically concentrated, even two-party competition at the district level will not result in a national two-party system, since politics will differ from one district to another. In other words, the precise consequences of electoral laws become a matter of political geography.

Proportional representation (PR) is a permissive or 'weak' electoral system. By itself, it has no reductive effect on the number of parties. However, in most countries using PR, several features reduce the proportionality of the system, including electoral thresholds, small district size, and the precise formula used for converting votes into seats. Taking into account these differences, Sartori predicts that the less proportional PR is, the higher its reductive effect will be.

Majoritarian or double-ballot electoral systems have not attracted as much scholarly attention. Although Taagepera's (2007: 133) claim that 'if the

> ## Box 15.1 **Key points**
>
> - Institutions matter.
>
> - Institutions, including the electoral system, can be designed to achieve particular objectives under particular circumstances.
>
> - While research has mainly focused on Duverger's electoral laws, Sartori's electoral laws are the most precise social science laws available.
>
> - The political consequences of electoral systems should always be understood in context.

choice is Two-Rounds, anything can happen' is an exaggeration, it is true that a second round with a reduced number of candidates opens up all kinds of possibilities for maneuverings and exchanges that are difficult to model. Still, some predictions can be made, taking into account access to the second round (only the top two candidates or any candidate which passes a certain threshold of support), the decision-rule in the second round (majority or plurality), and the size of the district (single-member or multi-member). On this basis, Sartori (1994: 66–7) provides four 'rules'.

The effect of the double-ballot on the *kind* of party is more clear-cut than the effect on the *number* of parties: 'The double ballot strongly penalizes the anti-system parties' (Sartori 1994: 67). Anti-system parties are a mixed bag: revolutionary parties that reject the political system, extremist parties on either side of the political spectrum, and isolated parties that are ostracized by the prevailing opinion. Unless anti-system parties are able to win a majority by themselves, they will not obtain representation, as they fail to attract support from moderate voters.

The Party System as Independent Variable

Like the electoral system, the party system can be both consequence and cause. Sartori (1968) introduced the party system itself as an explanatory variable, predicting that the political consequences of electoral laws will be different for 'structured' and 'unstructured' party systems. Structured or strong party systems are what in contemporary terminology would be called 'institutionalized' party systems. Scott Mainwaring and Timothy Scully (1995: 15) identify four criteria for institutionalization: (1) patterns of competition manifest regularity; (2) parties develop stable roots in society; (3) citizens and organizations perceive parties and elections as the only legitimate means to determine who governs; (4) party organizations must be 'relatively solid'. Compared with party systems in long-established democracies, those in new democracies consequently tend not to be very institutionalized. The distinction between structured and unstructured party systems explains why under different circumstances the same electoral law can have different political consequences. Indeed, in their study of post-communist Eastern Europe, Jon Elster *et al.* (1998: 129) conclude that 'given programmatically diffuse parties, their weak organizational basis, an unsatisfactorily structured party system, and volatile voter alignments, electoral rules are unable to reduce the number of parties and to structure the party system'. Unstructured party systems are not limited to new democracies. The weakening of ties between voters and parties in the post-industrial Western countries, known as de-alignment, may also weaken the effect of electoral laws there.

Mixed Electoral Systems

The increasingly fashionable mixed electoral systems require special attention. Following Louis Massicotte and André Blais (1999), they come in basically three types: coexistence (PR and plurality/majority used at the same time, but in different parts of the country), combination (coexistence at the national level), and correction (a PR tier compensates for the distortions generated by plurality or majority elections). The best-known mixed electoral system, the German, elects half the members of parliament in multi-member PR districts corresponding to the German **states** and the other half in single-member districts. Basically, the PR elections are used to allocate the seats among parties, while the plurality elections are used to determine whether those seats are taken by candidates from the districts or the regional lists. Because the overall effect is proportional, the German electoral system is known as 'mixed-member proportional' and frequently classified as a PR system.

Matthew Shugart (2001) explains the popularity of mixed-electoral systems by arguing they maximize what he calls the effectiveness of the electoral system and are in a way the best of both worlds. On the other hand, Renske Doorenspleet's (2005) test of the empirical relationship between type of electoral system and governance indicators finds some confirmation for Sartori's (1994) prediction that mixed electoral systems combine the worst of both worlds. However, since mixed electoral systems are adopted especially by new democracies and by older democracies facing some kind of crisis of **legitimacy** and/or government, such as Japan, Italy, and Venezuela, this association may be due to other factors than the electoral system. In any case, the political consequences of electoral laws are more difficult to predict in mixed systems than in electoral systems following a single logic.

Box 15.2 **Key points**

- Electoral systems are expected to have different consequences in structured versus unstructured party systems.

- Party systems in new democracies are weakly institutionalized.

- It is important to understand the precise mix in mixed electoral systems.

- The more complex the mix, the more difficult it is to predict the consequences.

The Dependent Variable I: Counting Parties

The dependent variable for Duverger was *dualisme des partis* versus *multipartisme*, whereby party dualism could mean a classic two-party system as well as two blocs of parties. However, Duverger never specified how these tendencies should be empirically verified. The empirical study of the impact of electoral systems crucially depends on a method for counting parties. Quantitative approaches to the analysis of the relationship between votes and seats have adopted mathematical formulas that aim to capture the relative size of parties. The first one was the 'index of fractionalization' devised by Douglas Rae (1971). The standard in the literature by now is Markku Laakso and Taagepera's (1979) index of the **effective number of parties**, which is one divided by the sum of the squared fractions of the vote or seat shares of all parties. The index can be used for determining the effective number of electoral parties (using vote shares) or parliamentary parties (using seat shares).

Because more than one distribution can generate a particular value of the index, the effective number of parties risks to underestimate change and to hide diversity. Mogens Pedersen (1980) shows how Rae's index fails to detect party system change and even Taagepera (1999; 2007) has acknowledged the problem of misrepresentation of his index, which in his view becomes especially urgent when one party has an absolute majority. For example, since 1994, South Africa has had between 2.2 and 2.0 effective parties in parliament. On the face of it, this indicates a British or American style two-party system. However, since the end of apartheid, the country has been ruled by the ANC which obtained never less than 63 per cent of the votes and seats and since the 2004 elections even has the two-third majority necessary to change the constitution.

Sartori provides an alternative method for counting parties. Only those parties are **relevant** which have either coalition potential or blackmail potential. A party has coalition potential when, regardless of its size, it 'may be required as a coalition partner for one or more of the possible governmental majorities' (Sartori 1976: 122). A party has blackmail potential 'whenever its existence, or appearance, affects the tactics of party competition' (p. 123). The classic example was the Italian Communist Party, which because of its size forced the pro-system parties to form coalition governments against it. These counting rules apply to parliamentary systems. For presidential systems 'the counting criteria must be reformulated and relaxed, for the parties that count are simply the ones the make a difference in helping (or obstructing) the president's election, and that determine his having (or not having) a majority support in the legislative assemblies' (Sartori 1994: 34). With Sartori's counting rules, it is easy to identify one-party dominance as there is only one relevant party. Another advantage of Sartori's counting rules is that they are linked to his typology of party systems.

The Dependent Variable II: Party Systems

Duverger's interest was never in the number of parties as such or their relative size, but in the dynamics of party competition and the nature of the **party system**. We therefore need a typology of party systems. Sartori (1976) distinguishes between party systems on the basis of two factors: the number of parties and the level of polarization. Polarization is operationalized in terms of ideological difference between parties competing on a common left-right spectrum.

Sartori (1976) identifies five types of structured party systems: predominant (one relevant party), two party system (two relevant parties), moderate pluralism (2 to 5 relevant parties), polarized pluralism (6 or more relevant parties) and segmented party systems (moderate number of relevant parties representing linguistic, religious or regional communities). The distinction between moderate and polarized multiparty systems allowed Sartori to break through the equation of multi-party systems with instability, immobilism and a heightened potential for democratic breakdown. It showed that the main problem was with ideological distance and especially the presence of anti-system parties.

There has always been a debate in political science how far concepts and theories devised for the study for Western industrialized polities and societies can 'travel' (Sartori 1995). Does it make sense to use the notion of party and party system in countries where most 'parties' are little more than the personal vehicle for politicians, and should one talk about a party 'system' when parties come and go and politicians and voters alike show little loyalty to parties? Better than simply assuming universal applicability or stressing the uniqueness of the particular case or region, is to examine more closely how an existing framework of analysis can be applied to new settings. Driven by the desire to extend his party system typology to Africa, but appreciating the different conditions there, Sartori (1976) added a separate chapter with a simplified party system typology.

Sartori distinguishes four types of unstructured multi-party systems: dominant authoritarian, dominant, non-dominant, and pulverised. The non-

> ### Box 15.3 Key points
>
> - The number of relevant parties and the effective number of parties contain different information and serve different purposes.
>
> - Sartori developed different typologies for structured and unstructured party systems.
>
> - Most party systems in new democracies are unstructured.

dominant party system is described as a situation of 'relatively few parties that actually counterweight one another' (Sartori 1976: 258). The pulverised party system speaks for itself. A dominant party system is the equivalent of the 'predominant' party found in structured party systems (Sartori 1976: 261). This means an absolute majority over at least three consecutive elections. In a dominant *authoritarian* party system, one-party dominance is maintained by extra-democratic means. The authoritarian dominant party does not allow for competition on an equal basis and alternation in power is only a theoretical possibility. This category is of special interest for students of 'electoral **authoritarianism**' (Schedler 2006) and 'competitive authoritarianism' (Levitsky and Way 2002). These terms were coined to capture the increasingly common phenomenon of authoritarian regimes that organize multi-party elections.

Additional Variables: Cleavages and Presidentialism

Institutional approaches focus on the electoral system and the form of government, whereas the *sociological* approach focuses on the importance of pre-existing social cleavages to explain the number of parties. Although it is common to view Duverger as an institutionalist, closer reading suggests that he located the root determinant of the number of parties in the number of social cleavages, with the electoral system

as an intervening variable. Sartori (1968) specifies that the key factor is the permissiveness of the electoral system: the more permissive the electoral system, the more the party system will depend on factors other than the electoral system. In short: the weaker the electoral institutions, the stronger the impact of social factors on the party system. This can be deliberate. Stein Rokkan (1970) observed how the introduction of mass politics and the extension of the suffrage in the early 1900s in Western Europe was accompanied by electoral reforms in which proportional representation replaced the double ballot to allow for the more accurate representation of social cleavages.

The form of government is important for two reasons. First, because of its alleged consequences for the quality of democracy and the prospects of democratic consolidation, and secondly because of its impact on the number of parties. Presidential government has two key features: direct election and a fixed term of the head of government. In a presidential system of government, the number of parties cannot be explained exclusively by the electoral law for parliamentary elections. For Latin America and also for Africa, it has been shown that a presidential system of government, plurality elections for president, and concurrent elections all serve to depress the number of parliamentary parties (Shugart and Carey 1992; Mozaffar *et al.* 2003).

Ever since Juan Linz warned about the 'perils of presidentialism' and extolled the 'virtues of parliamentarism', there has been a lively debate about the best form of government for new democracies (Lijphart 1992; Cheibub 2006). The problem with presidents is that they can be either too weak or too powerful. When presidentialism is combined with a proportional electoral system for parliamentary elections and a multi-party system, as is common in Latin America, this weakens presidents, possibly triggering a crisis of governability (Mainwaring and Shugart 1997). Presidents can also be too strong, leading to the weakening of democracy. Guillermo O'Donnell (1994) has coined the term 'delegative democracy' for the phenomenon of a president who concentrates powers into his own hands and is unaccountable to parliament and the judiciary. According to Wolfgang Merkel (2004), delegative democracy is one of four types of defective democracies that are the most common outcome of the so called 'third wave' of democratization.

The State of the Art

Although Sartori's *Parties and Party Systems* made Duverger's work seem 'little but a relic', much of the scholarship continues to take its lead from Duverger's 'battered classic' (Daalder 1983: 12, 10). Characteristically, William Riker (1982) and Shugart (2005), in publications that purport to show the accumulation of knowledge on the political consequences of electoral laws, do not even include a reference to Sartori. Research has mostly concentrated on attempts to quantify Duverger's laws. The 'generalized Duverger's rule', formulated by Taagepera and Shugart (1989: 145) goes like this: 'the effective number of electoral parties is usually within plus or minus 1 unit from $N = 1.25\ (2 + \log M)$, whereby M stands for average district size. 'Duverger's Generalized Rule' is a statistical law, which 'represents an empirical fit strengthened by some theoretical plausibility (a hypothesis, if you will) and saddled with many deviating data points' (Taagepera and Shugart 1989: 146).

Taking also into account the size of the assembly (S), Taagepera (2007) offers the following formula: $N = (MS)$ to the power 1/6. This formula does not reflect an empirical pattern, although it is claimed to fit very well, but predicts an expected value based on no other information than the variables entered and some

> ## Box 15.4 Key points
>
> - Social factors, in combination with the electoral system, affect the party system.
>
> - The rules for and the timing of elections for an executive president affect the party system.
>
> - There is a trend towards quantification of the relationship between electoral system features and the (effective) number of parties.
>
> - Little attention is paid to the party system as the dependent variable.

mathematical deductions. It is valid only for simple electoral systems, meaning plurality in single-member districts and PR in multi-member districts of fairly uniform magnitude. It is valid only for stable democracies. It predicts the 'world average' and is deliberately blind to those features, including a country's political culture, that can make a country 'deviate'.

Taagepera (2007) claims that the mechanical aspects of Duverger's laws are by now so well understood that this part of the research agenda is closed, leaving scholars to study the strategic or psychological impact of electoral systems. One could also say that we know by now a lot about electoral systems, but not nearly as much about their impact on those variables that informed the interest of political scientists in the first place: political parties, the party system, and the dynamics of party politics.

The Evidence from New Democracies

Because of low party system institutionalization we expect, following Sartori, electoral laws to be less predictable in new democracies. In the case of geographically concentrated groups, moreover, and again following Sartori, we expect that plurality elections will not be associated with a two-party system. This is indeed what many studies have found. In the new democracies of Eastern Europe, plurality and majoritarian elections in single-member districts have returned independent candidates and small, local parties to parliaments (Moser 2001; Birch 2003). Studies on Africa have demonstrated the importance of the spatial distribution of ethnic groups for the impact of electoral laws (Mozaffar *et al.* 2003; Brambor *et al.* 2007).

The question then is: to what extent is the party system the same across the country's electoral districts? In the literature on electoral systems, this is known as 'electoral linkage' (Cox 1997). In the literature on party systems, this phenomenon is studied as 'the nationalization of party systems (Caramani 2004). Especially interesting is the question whether and how the electoral system can contribute to the nationalization of politics (Chhibber and Kollmann 2004).

In Africa the political consequences of electoral systems do not completely conform to expectations. There are three surprises. First, higher district magnitudes by themselves do not go together with a higher effective number of parties. Second, the electoral system with the highest effective number of parties is not proportional representation, but the majoritarian double-ballot. Third, the effective number of parties is low across different electoral formulas and district magnitudes. This number is even lower for those countries in which multi-party elections cannot be considered free and fair, signaling the importance of the regime variable. In Africa, arguably the most diverse continent, a concentration of power in a dominant or dominant authoritarian party is much more common than a pulverized party system, irrespective of the electoral system used.

None of this means that electoral systems are inconsequential or that their consequences are unpredictable in Africa. Lesotho is a case in point. The plurality system prevented the opposition from winning any seats, despite attracting 25 per cent of the vote nationwide, in the first free and fair multi-party elections of 1993. In 1998, the opposition won a single seat with 39 percent of the vote. The resulting riots and breakdown of order led to international intervention and agreement on the necessity of electoral reform. The new mixed-member proportional system, first used in the 2002 elections, finally provided the opposition with a share of the seats corresponding to its share of the votes, resulting in increased satisfaction with democracy among voters. In general, however, surprisingly little systematic research has been done on the relationship between electoral system and the survival/consolidation of democracy. Better documented is the link between the quality of elections and the quality of democracy (Lindberg 2006).

If classic authoritarian regimes organized elections at all, these were so-called 'elections without choice' in which voters could 'confirm' the official candidate or, more rarely, 'chose' between different candidates from the ruling party (Hermet *et al.* 1978). With one exception, the only countries still practicing the old communist system of majoritarian elections are the authoritarian post-Soviet republics. Eastern Europe after communism has witnessed electoral reform in the direction of more PR. Electoral reform in new democracies is quite common, despite exhortations by political scientists to allow voters and parties time to learn about the electoral system and to adjust their behavior accordingly. In general, the logic of electoral system choice in new democracies follows Josep Colomer's (2004b: 3) 'micro-mega rule', which holds that the 'large prefer the small and the small will prefer the large'. Thus, communist elites preferred majoritarian electoral systems in single-member districts in the hope of capitalizing on their local organization and candidates, whereas the democratic opposition advocated a more proportional electoral system with

---

> ### Box 15.5 **Key points**
>
> - Electoral systems can be designed to perform certain functions.
> - The main party system functions are blocking, aggregation, and translation.
> - The working of the electoral system depends on electoral geography.
> - Very different choices have been made in different times and places.

---

multi-member districts. The ultimate choice of the electoral system therefore depended on the balance of power between the two and the mode of transition to democracy.

Electoral System Design and Ethnic Conflict Management

What is the most appropriate electoral law for (new) democracies with heterogeneous, plural or divided societies, societies in which socio-cultural differences such as race, ethnicity, language, religion and region are politically salient? Electoral system is understood here in the broad sense, including also the regulations for party registration and candidate nomination, whose importance is beginning to get recognized. Despite all their differences, the two leading scholars of democracy in divided societies, Arend Lijphart and Donald Horowitz agree in their counsel against plurality elections in a plural society. At present, according to Reynolds (1999: 93), 'for ethnically divided states, the prevailing academic wind clearly blows in favour of proportional representation and against plurality'.

The longstanding juxtaposition of plurality elections and proportional representation loses much of its relevance when socio-cultural groups are geographically concentrated, as is often the case. Rather, the menu of choice is between electoral systems that promote *aggregation* of socio-cultural divisions, facilitate the political *translation* of ethnic differences, or *block* the political organization of socio-cultural cleavages. The challenge of socio-cultural diversity has provoked electoral designs not easily incorporated in traditional classifications of electoral systems. Table 1 gives a summary overview of how the **party system functions** of blocking, aggregation, and translation correspond with electoral systems.

In a democracy, the blocking function can be achieved through ethnic party bans. In an attempt to prevent ethnic conflict by preventing its political organization, the majority of African states have adopted a prohibition of ethnic parties, broadly understood to encompass parties organizing on a whole range of socio-cultural differences. The constitution of Senegal, for example, specifically prohibits parties based on ethnicity, faith, language, region, race, sect, and, surprisingly, **gender**. In Eastern Europe, out of a concern with national integrity, Albania and Bulgaria adopted constitutional bans on ethnic parties,

Table 15.1 Choosing an Electoral System in Plural Democracies

Role of party system	Electoral system	Illustrative cases
Blocking	Ban on ethnic parties	Bulgaria
		Albania
		Most contemporary African countries
Aggregation	Alternative vote	Fiji
		Papua New Guinea
	Single Transferable Vote	Northern Ireland
	Constituency pooling	Uganda 1970
	Spatial distribution requirement for presidential elections	Kenya
		Nigeria
		Indonesia
Translation	Reserved minority seats	Colombia
		Venezuela
		Several East European countries
	List PR	South Africa
	Any type of electoral system as long as groups are geographically concentrated	Switzerland

Source: Bogaards 2004; 2007

although both countries ultimately refrained from enforcing them. Irrespective of the effectiveness of ethnic party bans, such a basic limitation of the freedom of political organization, prohibiting the kind of parties that play a vital and legitimate role in many established Western democracies, is highly problematic from a normative point of view.

Aggregation can be achieved through a variety of electoral systems. The exact choice depends on two factors: the number and relative size of social groups and their geographical distribution or concentration. The classic idea of a moderate two-party system with broad-based parties that converge toward the centre, stimulated by plurality elections in single-member districts (Downs 1957), only holds for homogeneous societies. In societies with voting along ethnic lines, plurality elections will not produce aggregation. Three types of electoral system can: preferential voting in the form of the alternative vote or the single transferable vote, vote distribution requirements, and constituency pooling.

The alternative vote (AV) is a preferential majority voting system with strong incentives for vote pooling

given the right circumstances. Vote pooling occurs when political leaders seek support outside their own group to win elections and voters exchange votes across group boundaries. Papua New Guinea, a highly diverse society, recently reintroduced AV. In 1996, the Constitutional Review Commission in Fiji recommended the adoption of AV after a careful review of the alternatives and consultation with leading scholars (Lal and Larmour 1997). Its success is strongly contested (Fraenkel and Grofman 2006a, 2006b; Horowitz 2006).

AV only leads to vote pooling in heterogeneous electoral districts, which are difficult to draw when groups are geographically concentrated. In that case, constituency pooling is an alternative. Constituency pooling means that a candidate runs simultaneously in multiple constituencies that are far apart. To decide the winner, the total number of votes for a candidate across all districts is calculated. The successful candidate thus has to pool votes from different parts of the country inhabited by different groups. Constituency pooling was invented in Uganda in 1970 but never put to the test.

Among PR systems, only the single-transferable vote (STV) encourages vote pooling. STV is a proportional electoral system with preferential voting. Because STV works with multimember districts, it is somewhat easier to draw the necessary heterogeneous districts. However, because the threshold for winning a seat is lower, the incentives for vote pooling are also weaker. For Southern Africa, Andrew Reynolds (1999) has advocated its adoption.

A more unusual feature that promotes aggregation is a distribution requirement. In Nigeria, Kenya, and more recently Indonesia, the successful presidential candidate not only has to win an overall majority or plurality respectively, he/she also has to draw a minimum percentage of votes from a minimum number of regions.

The party-system function of translation can be ensured through the adoption of reserved seats for minorities. In Eastern Europe, several countries have reserved seats for minorities. In Kosovo, 10 of the 120 assembly seats were set apart for the Serbs and another 10 seats for other communities. The electoral system was designed for parliament to mirror society. In Latin America, Colombia and Venezuela have reserved some seats for indigenous peoples. This practice is contested as it relies on the predetermination of socio-cultural groups and the identification of candidates and/or voters as belonging to designated groups.

More commonly, translation is best served by list proportional representation although it can also be achieved with plurality and majority elections in case of geographically concentrated minorities, as demonstrated by cantonal elections in Switzerland. PR facilitates the political organization of small dispersed social groups, which do not have to be geographically concentrated to have a chance of parliamentary representation.

Consociational Democracy

If blocking simply aims to keep ethnicity out of politics and aggregation reconciles conflicting interests and values within parties, a party system based on the faithful translation of ethnic cleavages into political cleavages does little to accommodate them. The problems are simply projected onto the state's decision-making bodies, where additional arrangements are required in the form of **power-sharing**. The best-known model of power-sharing is **consociational democracy** (Lijphart 1977). Elite cooperation takes the form of grand coalitions in which the leaders of all main social groups are represented; proportional representation in assemblies and proportional allocation of offices and resources; segmental autonomy for social groups in the spheres important to them; and a mutual veto for groups that see their vital interests at stake.

Power-sharing arrangements have become the standard recommendation for post-conflict societies, leading Lijphart (2002) to observe a 'wave of power-sharing democracy'. However, there is a long list of critics and criticism of consociational democracy (see Andeweg 2000; O'Leary 2005). Especially common are complaints about elitism, inefficiency, and for treating the symptoms instead of the underlying causes. The Dayton-agreement that ended the war in Bosnia-Herzegovina has put into place elaborate power-sharing arrangements that are coming under increasing criticism for their failure to ease tensions and promote cross-ethnic politics. Instead of fixing ethnic identities and loyalties, the electoral system should permit fluidity in ethnic identification and encourage the politicization of different majorities on multiple dimensions.

> ### Box 15.6 **Key points**
>
> • For divided societies, PR is one element of the broader package of consociational democracy.
>
> • Consociational democracy is popular, but controversial.

For these reasons, consociational democracy is increasingly seen as a short-term solution to be followed by other, presumably more democratic and lasting arrangements. For some, these are 'integrative majoritarian' institutions propagated by Horowitz (1991), including voting pooling, presidentialism, and federalism. However, Philip Roeder and Donald Rothchild (2005) warn against federalism in divided societies, especially ethno-federalism in which federal units are drawn to reflect population boundaries, claiming this rewards ethnic politics and paves the way for secession.

Conclusion

This chapter has surveyed the state of the discipline with respect to the political consequences of electoral laws, focusing on the party system. It found that Sartori's laws are still the most useful, especially for new democracies. Sartori's distinction between structured and unstructured party systems helps to explain why electoral systems in new democracies with unstructured party systems may not have the same consequences as in established democracies. Sartori's insight about 'incoercible minorities' highlights the importance of geography for the impact of electoral systems and helps explain why plurality elections fail to produce a two-party system.

Let us conclude with four general lessons. First, if the scholarship on electoral system design has shown one thing, it is that, in the words of Reynolds (2005: 66), 'plainly there is no "one-size-fits-all" form of constitutional therapy. Particular circumstances and sound case-by-case judgments will always matter'. Second, the choice of electoral system is not limited to PR or plurality. The most innovative electoral designs have come from political practitioners, while political scientists have usually promoted existing formulas, adapting them to local circumstances. Some of the most interesting experiments are going on in places we know least about, such as the South Pacific. Third, the choice of electoral system is not an end in itself but an instrument in shaping the party system. This implies an understanding of the kind of party system that is desired and its role as an intermediary between society and government. Finally, the electoral system should not be considered in isolation. Ideally, the choice of electoral system should be part of a broader understanding of a country's political institutions and the way in which they reinforce or contradict each other.

QUESTIONS

1. What factors affect the adoption of an electoral system?

2. Do institutions matter?

3. How are Sartori's electoral laws different from Duverger's?

4. What factors determine the number of parties in a country?

5. Why should we expect electoral systems to have different consequences in new compared to established democracies?

6. How does political geography affect the outcome of electoral laws?

Visit the Online Resource Centre that accompanies this book for additional questions to accompany each chapter, and a range of other resources: <www.oxfordtextbooks. co.uk/orc/haerpfer/>.

FURTHER READING

Colomer, J. (2004a) (ed.), *Handbook of Electoral System Choice* (London: Palgrave Macmillan). This edited volume contains comparative analyses and case studies of electoral systems from all the regions of the world, including many new democracies.

Gallagher, M. and Mitchell, P. (2005) (eds), *The Politics of Electoral Systems* (Oxford: Oxford University Press). The bulk of this edited volume consists of case studies of electoral systems, electoral reform, and electoral performance, in mostly established democracies.

Lijphart, A. (1994), *Electoral Systems and Party Systems: A Study of Twenty-Seven Democracies, 1945–1990* (Oxford: Oxford University Press). A systematic analysis of the political consequences of electoral laws in established democracies, which combines a thorough discussion of the theories, the methodology, and the empirical evidence.

Reilly, B. (2001), *Democracy in Divided Societies: Electoral Engineering for Conflict Management* (Cambridge: Cambridge University Press). This book provides the most complete overview so far of the theory and practice of electoral system design in divided societies.

Reynolds, A., Reilly, B. and Ellis, A. (2005), *Electoral System Design: The New International IDEA Handbook* (Stockholm: IDEA). This book provides an easily readable guide to electoral systems around the world, their consequences, plus several case studies.

Sartori, G. (1976), *Parties and Party Systems: A Framework for Analysis* (Cambridge: Cambridge University Press). This is *the* classic work on political parties and party systems. The European Consortium for Political Research republished the book in 2005 in its ECPR Classics series.

Sartori, G. (1994), *Comparative Constitutional Engineering, An Inquiry into Structures, Incentives and Outcomes* (London: Macmillan). In this book, Sartori presents his most complete statement on the political consequences of electoral laws in combination with his recommendations for institutional design.

Shugart, M. and Wattenberg, M. (2001) (eds), *Mixed-Member Electoral Systems: The Best of Both Worlds?* (Oxford: Oxford University Press). This edited volume consists mainly of case studies analysing the reasons behind the adoption of mixed electoral systems and the consequences in selected countries, including some new democracies.

Taagepera, R. (2007), *Predicting Party Sizes: The Logic of Simple Electoral Systems.* (Oxford: Oxford University Press). In this research monograph, Taagepera brings together many of his earlier publications and makes a forceful plea for a natural science approach to the study of electoral systems.

IMPORTANT WEBSITES

<www.idea.int> International IDEA (Institute for Democracy and Electoral Assistance) is a very active intergovernmental organization promoting democracy around the world. The website has a lot of information on its programs and links to its many publications on democracy related topics, including electoral systems and political parties.

<www.aceproect.com> On its website, the 'electoral knowledge network' provides information from and links to eight partner organizations in the field of democracy promotion, good governance, and electoral assistance.

<www.electionguide.org> A guide to election results around the world.

<www.ipu.org> The website of the inter-parliamentary union. Its 'parline' database has information on the most recent parliamentary elections in many countries.

16

The Media

Katrin Voltmer and Gary Rawnsley

Overview

In this chapter we give an overview of the role of the media in processes of democratization. We will analyse the degree to which the media have transformed from an instrument in the hands of autocratic political elites to an independent institution in democratic life. We also consider the factors that facilitate, or impede, the media's ability to fulfil their democratic role. For this purpose we will discuss the media's political, economic, and social environment both in their domestic and international contexts.

Introduction

The media are a dominant actor in political and social life across the world. They are the main source of information from which people can learn about the world that lies beyond their immediate everyday experience, and they are the link through which the divergent parts of society can communicate with each other—political leaders with citizens, producers of goods with consumers, and individuals with each other. Due to their ability to reach and influence the masses the media are of crucial importance for both authoritarian and democratic **regimes**. However, the particular role of the media in both types of political order differs fundamentally.

From a normative point of view the media fulfil two main functions in democratic life. First, they provide a forum where all voices can be heard and engage in a dialogue with each other. As a forum of political public debate the media are expected to not only give access to the government and other officials, but equally to oppositional groups and the wider civil society. The idea of the media serving as a public forum goes back to John Stuart Mill's notion of a 'marketplace of ideas'. In his essay 'On Liberty' (1974 [1859]) Mill defends the freedom of the press by arguing that the public competition of different ideas helps to detect their strengths and weaknesses and, thus, eventually brings about the truth. Dahl (1989) therefore includes the media in his theory of procedural democracy as one of the preconditions (or 'standards' in his terminology) that are necessary for democratic institutions to work properly. Most importantly, the media enable the citizens to make informed choices by seeking out information about the political alternatives at hand.

The second function of the media is often described as a 'watchdog' role. This is what is usually referred to when the media are labelled the 'fourth estate'. In this role the media assume the position of adversary in their relationship with government officials and other powerful figures in politics, giving the media the responsibility of monitoring the actions of political actors and bringing any misconduct or abuse of power to public scrutiny. The understanding of the media as part of a system of checks and balances is deeply rooted in liberal thought which views the **state** as a potential threat to individual freedom. This is why Kelley and Donway (1990) regard the watchdog role as the media's key democratic function: it protects the citizens from the state and enforces government **accountability** and transparency.

It is all too obvious that these ideas are in sharp contrast to the media's role under authoritarian rule where they are primarily seen as instruments of the ruling elites rather than serving the general public interest. Hence, access to the media is often restricted to official voices while criticism of the government, not to mention the regime in general, is suppressed, sometimes with draconic means.

Given the fundamental differences between the role of the media in authoritarian and democratic politics, their transformation in the process of democratization is often one of the most disputed areas of change. It involves altering the media's regulatory framework, their organizational structure and the professional practices of journalists who are actually producing the information conveyed to the citizens. Due to the complexity of the relationship between governments and the media, and because any change affects the degree of control either side has on what

is communicated, many new democracies have not yet succeeded in transforming the media into fully democratic institutions. This coincides with a general weakness of the group of newcomers to democratic rule who have been labelled 'delegative', illiberal, or 'electoralist' to indicate the numerous flaws that impede the democratic process in these countries (see Chs 2 and 3 above). It can be argued that many of these deficiencies are linked to the insufficient transformation of the media. For example, lack of electoral fairness has been attributed to the manipulation of campaign coverage in favour of the incumbent candidate or political party. Further, corruption remains endemic in many new democracies either because the media are still too entangled with the power structure or because journalists lack the skills and resources to engage in investigative journalism. In other cases, the media have been accused of being over-critical and excessively negative which allegedly leads to political cynicism and the erosion of fragile governments that are struggling for **legitimacy**. Bennett (1998) maintains that the media might play a positive role in bringing down the old regime, but regards them as rather obstructive for the **consolidation** of the new order.

The media's role in processes of democratization is not constant over time, but varies according to the different phases of the democratization process. For example, during the open and highly dramatic period of the breakdown of the old regime and the subsequent creation of new institutions the media often become a driving force. They use the power vacuum of the transition to expand their own power to set the agenda and to interpret what is going on. In many new democracies the early years of transition have been something like a honeymoon for the media with journalists addressing issues that have never been covered in public before and dozens and hundreds of new outlets being launched. The Soviet Union during the era of Mikhail Gorbachev is an example for this (Mickiewicz 1999). However, market constraints and political pressures soon limit the open, sometimes chaotic space of public debate to give way to negotiations and day-to-day conflicts between political officials and the media that characterize the consolidation period.

Further, the way in which the media operate in the new democratic environment is to a large degree constrained and shaped by the specific role they had under the old regime (Voltmer, 2008). Hence, the pattern of political reporting and the media's relationship with the government differs significantly between post-communist democracies in Eastern Europe and those that emerged from military dictatorship, especially in Latin America, and from the authoritarian one-party regimes in Asia and Africa. Like most other institutions, media organizations are not created from scratch after the breakdown of the old regime. Instead, the existing ones are transformed and reshaped, but still carry elements of the logic and constraints of their predecessors. Journalists operating in the newly transformed media organizations still hold values and assumptions that are rooted in their professional life under the old regime and apply similar patterns of interaction when dealing with politicians. These forces of inertia merge with new values and practices adopted in the course of transition often leading to hybrid forms of journalism and political communication that in many respects differ from those in established Western democracies.

In the remainder we will discuss the relationship between the media and democratization in more detail. The main focus will be on traditional media (printed press, broadcasting) with their one-to-many logic of communication and high degree of editorial control over the disseminated content. But we will also consider the new media, in particular the Internet, that allow for many-to-many communication and are in principle open to everybody. We begin with an analysis of the relationship between international communication and political change, after which we move on to the structural aspects of the media that dominate domestic media policy, in particular the media's relationship with the state and media markets. This will be followed by a discussion of journalistic practices and the quality of political reporting in emerging democracies.

International Media, Communications Technologies, and Democratization

Throughout the global wave of democratization the international media have played an increasingly significant role in processes of political transition. Developments in information and communications technologies have coincided with the forces of **globalization** to allow political actors, media and now civil societies to impart, circulate and receive information faster and more efficiently than at any time in the past. Modern communications technologies mean that authoritarian governments find it ever more difficult to hermetically seal their borders and prevent their people from receiving often uncomfortable news, information and opinion from overseas sources. Moreover, we are only just beginning to comprehend the political consequences of new information technologies such as SMS, internet blogging, and web-based social networking which not only allow news to seep out from countries where the media are under tight political control (the so-called Saffron Revolution in Burma in 2007 was witnessed by an international media audience thanks to images captured on mobile telephones with cameras which were then uploaded to the Internet) but also help create and mobilize a distinctly transnational civil society, as the synchronized worldwide demonstrations in 2003 against the Iraq war demonstrated. In other words the international media and systems of communications are facilitating both the democracy process itself (implying transparency, accountability, dialogue and **participation**) and transitions to democracy around the world.

International broadcasting and the Demonstration Effect

During the Cold War shortwave radio broadcasts were the principal vehicle for communicating with audiences behind the Iron Curtain, and Western radio stations such as the BBC Overseas Services, the Voice of America, Radio Free Europe, and Radio

Liberty were a constant source of comfort and hope for listeners, and of irritation for Communist regimes (Rawnsley 1996). By the mid-1980s, the rapid expansion in communications technology, allowing for the global circulation of television broadcasts, meant that 'the image of a "worldwide democratic revolution" undoubtedly had become a reality in the minds of political and intellectual leaders in most countries of the world' (Huntington 1991: 102). In this way, audiences witnessed and experienced the global wave of democracy swelling on their television screens, adding sustenance and momentum to the idea that democratization was or could be a global phenomenon. Hyug Baeg Im (1996) has even referred to a 'tele-revolution' to describe the significance of communications on events in Central and Eastern Europe at the end of the 1980s.

Yet despite the sanguine tone that characterizes much of the literature, it is difficult to identify a direct relationship of cause and effect between the international media and democratization. We are offered only anecdotal evidence, currently beyond the possibility of rigorous empirical testing, to support the claim that the international media have inspired democratic change or revolution. This less than satisfactory situation has motivated researchers to concentrate principally on the 'demonstration effect', allowing them to bypass the problematic issue of direct **correlation** and focus instead on what is essentially a political 'side effect' of international communication.

In the context of democratization the demonstration effect refers to a process whereby media-users in one society observe political change in another. Populations become informed about and encouraged by changes elsewhere and begin to press for change at home as well; elites become panicky over the downfall of autocrats abroad and in response become more conciliatory or reactionary, either of which may spark mass mobilization (O'Neil 1998: 12).

Audiences may consume their international news from local media sources, but in recent democratizations the demonstration effect was more pronounced when audiences could (legally or illegally) receive news and information directly from foreign media. This usually happened when audiences received a regional 'spill-over' of TV signals, making the demonstration effect most noticeable when countries experiencing democratization were geographically

and/or culturally proximate. Thus at the end of the 1980s Albanians watched the East European revolutions unfold on television broadcasts from neighbouring Yugoslavia and Italy. Student demonstrators in Seoul in 1987 watched on their televisions the dramatic events that brought down the corrupt regime of Ferdinand Marcos in the Philippines in 1986. While it is impossible to state with any certainty that media coverage of events in one country led to political change in another, the demonstration effect may contribute to democratization by inspiring hope and motivation among audiences in authoritarian societies: they may learn from foreign broadcasts what is absent in their lives, be it political freedom or economic affluence. This may possibly stimulate specific aspirations for similar outcomes, and therefore undermine attempts by the authoritarian regime to maintain legitimacy based on performance, e.g. in **governance** and delivery of services. Thus, the transnational flow of information can lead to a dramatic 'revolution of rising expectations' among audiences and expose the 'credibility gap' between propaganda and reality. The Berlin Wall was not impervious against radio and television signals from the West passing into the East, giving East Germans news and entertainment that contradicted the official portrait of life on both sides of the Iron Curtain (Gunther and Mughan 2000).

However, we must also be mindful that while the demonstration effect may have positive consequences, it can also work against substantial change. The political transition that began in the Soviet Union convinced the leadership of the Chinese Communist Party of the dangers of the European model of transformation, and with hindsight the Chinese felt justified in suppressing the demonstrations in Beijing in June 1989 after seeing the fall of communism in Central and Eastern Europe (Nathan and Link 2001).

Agenda-setting function of international media

In addition to their contribution to the demonstration effect the international media may also influence the process of democratization in other less direct ways. One of the most significant examines the relationship between the media and political change from the perspective of international news flows and media agendas. The international media have the capacity to direct the attention of foreign political elites, audiences and other media towards a particular country and its problems. The potential political consequences of this 'agenda setting' function are considerable. The so-called 'CNN effect' (Livingston 1997) suggests that foreign policy may be created in part because of the images that are broadcast around the world by the media. The effect highlights how, in the glare of media attention and public opinion, it is increasingly difficult for governments to ignore international problems such as the repression and poverty of Zimbabwe, genocide in Darfur, the famines and droughts of Northern Africa, and the brutal suppression of the pro-democracy movement in Burma.

However, we must be careful not to ascribe too much influence to the CNN effect: in addition to the serious criticism of forcing a reactive foreign policy that is inspired by the need to placate public opinion, media coverage can also ignore the complexities of democratic change and overlook the fact that the process of political transition can be slow-burning and peaceful and not always dramatic, disorderly or violent. The CNN effect can therefore present an inaccurate picture of democratization and inspire the quick achievement of outcomes that are not necessarily desirable. Nevertheless, it can be important

> ### Box 16.1 **Key points**
>
> - New communications technologies have made it increasingly difficult for authoritarian regimes to hermetically seal their borders to prevent the flow of information in and out of the country.
>
> - The most noticeable influence of international communications in the process of democratization is the 'demonstration effect'.
>
> - The transnational flow of information has also encouraged a 'revolution of rising expectations' in many authoritarian and transitionary societies.
>
> - The media may draw attention to problem areas and have the capacity to influence global public and political opinion—the so-called 'CNN Effect'—though it is important not to exaggerate this.

for those struggling for democracy to know that their cause is receiving international media attention (hence the proliferation of signs written in English seen in television coverage of protests throughout the world), even if the actual impact of external forces is indeterminate (Shelley 2005).

Media-State Relationships

While the international media usually withdraw their attention from countries that undergo transitions to democracy once the dramatic events of the collapse of the old regime are over, transforming the relationship between political power and the media is a long and often painful process that seldom reaches the headlines outside the domestic realm.

The liberal model of democracy assumes an inherent antagonism between the interests of the state on the one hand and society and the media on the other. Indeed, the notion of the media acting as a watchdog is based on the assumption that political power poses the main threat to liberty and therefore has to be kept at bay. However, the relationship between the state and the media is highly ambivalent, in particular in processes of democratizing. There is no doubt that since under the old regime the state has been the principle violator of media independence, freeing the media from the influence of the state is of paramount importance. At the same time, it is only the state which has the legitimate authority to provide a regulatory framework that protects the media from undue external influences, be they political or economic. Hence, an all-powerful state that is unwilling to give up control over the media is as much an impediment to the development of democratic media as a weak state which is unable to implement the necessary policies.

Media regulation and media laws

The transformation of the regulatory framework in which the media operate takes place on two levels. On the constitutional level, the guarantee of communication freedoms (freedom of expression and freedom of the press) is rarely disputed and has been implemented in virtually all new (or revised) constitutions. However, it is the level of subsidiary media legislation, such as libel law and access to information that determines how effectively communication freedoms are put into practice. These pieces of regulation set the boundaries for interference in the operation of media organizations and journalistic reporting by political actors while defining the discretionary power of the media to investigate political issues. For example, strict libel laws are one of the main factors that stifle critical reporting. Especially when libel laws fall under the jurisdiction of the criminal rather than the civil code they pose a serious threat to journalists who frequently face severe charges and even imprisonment when their news stories are deemed offensive to the political authorities. Access rights to official information, or freedom of information legislation, allows journalists—as well as citizens in general—to view any information held by public bodies that affect the public interest. Freedom of information rights generate an enabling environment that helps journalists to investigate critical issues, even though it has to be said that political authorities usually learn very quickly how to curb the potential damage that might result from unwanted releases of information.

Media regulation below the constitutional level remains one of the most disputed policy areas even in democracies that are regarded well on their way towards consolidation. For example, Slovakia, part of the European Union since 2004, passed a press law in April 2008 that allowed the Ministry of Culture direct control over media coverage in a range of issues and introduced an automatic right of reply with no possibilities of editorial intervention in terms of content and space. The law triggered widespread protest from both international and domestic observers (Reporters Without Borders 2008). Romania, another new EU member state, reinstated libel and defamation in the penal code in 2007 after these offences had been

decriminalized the previous year, hence reducing the independence of the media that had already been achieved (Freedom House 2008: 6). Meanwhile, in May 2008 the Nigerian parliament delayed again the passage of its Freedom of Information Act that is being discussed since 1999 when the country returned to democratic rule. Nigeria is regarded one of the most corrupt and secretive states. A more open access to official information would obviously impair the vested interests of the political class, hence the attempt to prevent the law from being put into effect (International Federation of Journalists 2008). These cases illustrate the close interdependence of democratic development and an independent press that often resembles a 'Catch-22' dilemma: For the media to take on a democratic role they depend on a protective regulatory framework provided by political legislators—the very same actors that might come under scrutiny once the media gain more independence to cover political issues.

The conflict between political power holders and the media frequently culminates over issues of the regulation of broadcasting. Since television is believed to be particularly influential in shaping public opinion, most authoritarian regimes keep tight control over the main television channels, usually by state ownership and direct political supervision. By and large, the transformation of the main broadcasters into independent outlets has been largely unsuccessful in most new democracies. In many Asian and African countries the government, in some cases even the military, continues to own the main television channel, thereby preventing opposition voices a fair access to the airwaves.

The Internet and mobilization

In this situation the Internet has the potential to become an important medium that enables civil society actors to circumvent the political control imposed on mainstream media. For example, in the 2002 Korean presidential election the Internet played a crucial role in bringing the outsider candidate Roh into power in spite of his difficulties in presenting himself in the mainstream media. His supporters, mainly young, urban, well educated citizens, set up a discussion forum that quickly became the most popular political site and effectively used online networking to mobilize **turnout** of Roh supporters. Since then, all Korean parties have engaged in e-campaigning, but the new facilities of Web 2.0 and citizen journalism remain political forces that are unpredictable and difficult to control (Park and Lee 2008). While Korea is one of the wealthiest countries in Asia with one of the most advanced communication infrastructure worldwide, the Internet plays a lesser role in poorer countries, for example in Africa. However, mobile phone technology is significantly changing the media environment here as well. Due to the low cost of mobile phones they are the fastest spreading communication technology in the region and have been instrumental in mobilizing support in recent elections. Citizens have also used mobile phone cameras to detect and publicize electoral fraud. Further, the development of the technology into a general platform to receive and send information is an increasingly important source of citizen empowerment in countries where traditional media reach only small parts of the population.

Some new democracies have tried to adopt a public service broadcasting model as a regulatory framework that intends to keep the broadcaster equally distant from both political and economic influences. In Central Eastern Europe, for example, media policymakers turned to the various versions of public service broadcasting that exist in Western Europe as blueprints for transforming their own broadcasting systems. However, the outcome is mixed at best and most public service broadcasters remain vulnerable to political interference. For example, the dispute over the terms of operation of public service broadcasting in Hungary went on over five years and was appropriately dubbed a 'media war' (Sükösd 2000), indicating the intensity of conflict both between the parliamentary parties and between the legislators and the broadcaster. The main issue of the controversy was related to the appointment of the management of the broadcast organization. As in most other countries of the region, the final compromise is highly politicized as the majority in parliament, or even the executive, has the right to appoint and/

or dismiss the top personnel of the public service broadcaster. As a consequence, with every new government the leadership of the broadcaster, often even individual journalists, are being exchanged with figures that are close to, or members of, the governing party (Paletz and Jakubowicz 2003). Furthermore, government officials continue to interfere in the actual programming by replacing or cancelling particular programmes or pressuring journalists to cover an issue in a particular way. In some countries, especially in Eastern Europe, bribery—or so-called envelop journalism—is a common tool to buy favourable news coverage, resulting in the media becoming part of a system of mutual dependency and corruption rather than helping to fight it (Lovitt 2004).

Politicians and media in new democracies

The extent to which politicians in new democracies interfere with the independence of the media might come as a surprise, especially as the problem is not confined to members of the old elites but equally includes those who once mobilized opposition against the old regime and fought for freedom of expression and free media. One explanation for this apparent disregard of democratic rules can be seen in the particular circumstances in which electoral politics in new democracies takes place. Since authoritarian regimes tolerated only a minimum of pluralism (if any) the newly emerging political parties and political leaders find themselves in a situation where they have to win their majorities without the support of efficient party organizations. Even years after the regime change party organizations are often still weak, especially at the grassroots level, thus limiting the parties' ability to mobilize electoral support, not to mention long-term loyalty among voters. The extreme electoral volatility in post-communist countries is highlighted by the Polish case, where since the first democratic elections in 1989 no single government has been able to get re-elected. The absence of organizational efficiency and mass support leaves the media as the only channel through which political parties and candidates can communicate to voters. Controlling the media is therefore imperative for political survival in post-communist (and indeed most new) democracies. Paradoxically, the instrumentalization of the media also increases the media's influence on the political process because using the media for one's own purposes inevitably requires adherence to their logic of operation and adaptation to their way of covering political issues. As Oates puts it in view of Russian parties, 'the institution of television has come to dominate the institution of political parties' (Oates 2006: 153).

Another reason for the frequent clashes between political actors and the media lies in the fact that abstract concepts such as press freedom—and democracy for that matter—are much more open to interpretation than textbook knowledge might imply. Establishing these values in day-to-day political life requires a collective, potentially open-ended process of negotiating meaning—in the literature referred to as **social constructivism**—which involves controversies about first principles and their application (Whitehead 2002). One of the key issues surrounding the debates about the democratic role of the media touches upon the balance between freedom on the one side and responsibility on the other. However, these debates do not take place in an ideal Habermasian (1984) context of **rational discourse**. Rather, they are linked to the interests and strategies of the involved participants. As a consequence, references to the common good are frequently used as a Trojan horse to disguise one's own stakes, or to endow them with an aura of unselfishness. For example, Wasserman and De Beer (2006) describe the conflict between the post-apartheid government and the media in South Africa as a debate over the ultimate purpose the media should serve within the new democratic order. The government employed the concept of the 'national interest' as defined by the democratically elected officials to describe the role of the media, who in turn claimed to act in the 'public interest'. In a similar vein, Asian governments have discovered so-called Asian values to commit the media to a less adversarial, more consensual and deferential mode of reporting, and thus reinforce and justify through cultural references authoritarian-style politics.

Even though claims of 'national interest' or traditional values can be dismissed as attempts to give particularistic goals universal appeal, there are situations where unrestrained media can exacerbate violent conflicts and undermine the complex process of state and nationbuilding, for example in numerous African countries and currently in Iraq (Price and Thompson 2002). An example of limited press freedom in the process of transition is Spain, a case often regarded as a model transition. During the years immediately following Franco's death and in the face of immanent military take-over, the media joined the general elite consensus and committed themselves to promote the political goals of the new government, namely democratic values, amnesty for the supporters of the old regime and national unity in the face of separatist movements. It was only after a couple of years that the press gradually moved towards a more independent and adversarial stance vis-à-vis the government (Barrera and Zugasti 2006). The crucial point in this case is that the media committed themselves to adhere to these goals rather than having them imposed by external powers.

Box 16.2 **Key points**

- The media's main functions in democratic life are to provide a forum for public debate and to act as a watchdog which holds political officials to account.

- In many new democracies the media's ability to fulfil these functions is restricted by continuous government interference in editorial policy.

- Restrictive libel laws and the absence of freedom of information rights are major impediments for free and independent media.

- One of the main reasons why governments are reluctant to give up control over the media is the lack of alternative communicative links with the citizens, such as effective party organizations.

The Media and the Market

Besides the state the market is the other external force that affects the media's ability to fulfil their democratic role. The fact that the media are part of the market—and indeed an immensely dynamic global industry—is often seen as a way of liberating them from undue political interference. Liberal theorists (see for example Fowler and Brenner 1982) go further by taking John Stuart Mill's metaphor of a 'marketplace of ideas' as an economic prescription of media entrepreneurs competing with each other for audiences thereby generating the plurality of voices that Mill regarded necessary for a viable democracy. However, neither in established nor in new democracies have market forces proven to be the benevolent 'invisible hand' that brings about independence and diversity. On the contrary, more often than not the media find themselves, as Waisbord (2000) puts it with regard to the media in Latin America, 'between the rock of the state and the hard place of the market'. Rather than creating a space of open debate marketization and globalization have contributed to a highly problematic fusion of private ownership and political power which makes it difficult for individual journalists to challenge the dominant power structure (Curran and Park 2000). However, the effects of market conditions on the democratic performance of the media differ widely across countries. One factor that shapes the economic structure and performance of the media after regime changes are the economic conditions of the industry under the old regime.

Media in post-communist Europe

To begin with, the transformation of the media in post-communist countries has to cope with a double challenge—to simultaneously de-couple the media from the political power structure and to introduce a competitive media market. The latter was necessary because communist regimes had nationalized all significant industries, including the media, in order to eradicate private capital and to exploit the media as instruments of mass indoctrination under the direct control of the communist party. Commercialization after the breakdown of communism hit most of the media organizations completely unprepared

and drove many of them into bankruptcy (Splichal 1994). With the withdrawal of generous state subsidies people cancelled their subscriptions to newspapers resulting in a dramatic decline of newspaper circulation. Ironically, the former official state organs managed best because they had sufficient resources, managerial know-how and name recognition to position themselves in the new market. Even though the first couple of years after transition saw a blossoming of new media outlets most of them closed down very quickly. One of the few examples of surviving opposition papers is the Polish *Gazeta Wyborsza*.

Since there were usually no investors in the country to buy, not to mention to run a newspaper or television channel, governments in Central Eastern Europe had to sell the media to foreign conglomerates who were more than happy to expand their empires to the East. For example, Hungary sold its regional newspapers for the symbolic price of one German Mark (approximately 63 US cents at the time). While foreign conglomerates were quick to buy into countries where economic growth promised profitable returns, countries with weak economies such as Romania and Bulgaria had difficulties finding investors. As a consequence of the continued dependency of the media on state subsidies they remained in their old role as mouthpieces of the government. The course of privatizing the media was most problematic in Russia where super-rich oligarchs used their assets from the financial and energy industries to buy up virtually all national newspapers with the aim to use them as an instrument for exerting influence on government policies (McNair 2000). The almost impenetrable fusion of political and economic power has seriously stifled public debate in post-communist Russia. Contract-style murders of journalists—only few of which have resulted in conviction—has made Russia one of the most dangerous countries for critical journalists today.

Media in Latin America

In Latin America, the trajectory of media markets under authoritarian and democratic rule differs markedly from the situation in post-communist countries. Unlike communist regimes, military dictatorships left the capitalist structure of the economy largely intact. Hence, with the exception of a few official government organs, newspapers and television stations remained in private hands. In many countries, for example in Chile under Pinochet, the media industry flourished and the communication infrastructure of the country was brought to a high standard (Tironi and Sunkel 2000). This did not prevent the government from exerting strict censorship on political issues. But as long as the media confined themselves to entertainment they could operate largely on their own terms. In this environment, the media industry of the subcontinent developed into one of the strongest globally, and, in a rare example of 'reverse cultural imperialism', Brazil's media company Globo is now one of the top exporters of soaps and television dramas.

The commercial structure of the media in Latin America saved them from the dramatic changes that characterized the transformation of the media in post-communist countries. In fact, the lack of change can be regarded as one of the main problems since policymakers did not see the necessity to put the regulation of the media and their ownership structure high on their agenda. On the contrary, the lack of regulation created a media environment that is predominantly supportive of the incumbent political elite. Many media outlets are actually owned by political officials or their relatives who make sure that unfavourable opinions do not find a platform. What is worse, since in most Latin American countries there is no requirement to disclose the ownership structure of the media, the flow of influences remains opaque and beyond public control (Waisbord 2000).

> ## Box 16.3 **Key points**
>
> - Because of the fusion of ownership and political power, privatization of formerly state-owned media has often failed to ensure independence of the media.
>
> - In many developing countries where consumer and advertising markets are weak, the state remains the main source of revenue for the media, in particular broadcasting.

Media in Africa

Meanwhile, in poor developing countries commercialization of the media is hardly a viable option. Especially in most parts of Africa consumer markets are too limited to provide sufficient revenues through advertising (Hyden, Leslie, and Ogundimu 2003). Due to the weakness of the market, governments usually own both the main national newspapers and the main television channel. Even in wealthier countries like South Africa the state remains the main advertiser, and hence the main source of income in a media environment that on the surface of it appears as a commercial market. While the national media remain largely under political control, independent media are thriving on the local level with community radio playing a key role in creating an open space of debate from below (Myers 1998). International organizations involved in media development are therefore increasingly turning to the local media to promote democracy and development (Global Forum on Media Development 2007).

Journalistic Professionalism and the Quality of Reporting

As outlined in the introduction of this chapter, democratic media are expected to provide an open forum where a plurality of voices can be heard, and to hold government officials accountable by acting as a public watchdog. In this section we will turn to the question whether the media in new democracies are actually meeting these expectations in their day-to-day reporting of political matters.

Notwithstanding the specific legacies of their old regime, their level of economic development or their cultural context, political reporting throughout the recently democratized countries is highly opinionated and politicized. Nearly all media, whether print or audiovisual, are taking side in favour of particular political parties, candidates, societal groups, or ideologies whereas neutral, or balanced, news coverage is clearly the exception. Many observers therefore regard journalism in new democracies as deficient, lacking the professional values of objectivity and detachment that are guiding western news reporting. However, this view presumes a universality of journalistic standards which is neither supported by the historical development nor by normative media theories.

Historically, objectivity is a relatively late achievement in the development of western journalism. In the USA it emerged at the beginning of the last century as a market response to a diverse mass audience. In Europe the 'old' model of partisan journalism persisted and continues to dominate the print media (Chalaby 1998). Newspapers, including the national quality press, in Britain, France, Germany, and Italy, to name but a few countries, can easily be located within the ideological space of partisan conflict. The choice to support a particular case is not only an accepted part of press freedom, but also one of several possible ways of achieving diversity in the 'marketplace of ideas'.

McQuail (1992) in his normative theory of media performance distinguishes between internal and external diversity both being legitimate ways of representing the diversity of viewpoints in the public sphere. Internal diversity refers to a situation where a single media outlet comprises all relevant viewpoints without favouring a particular position. The BBC with its commitment to balance and neutrality is an example for this model. External diversity establishes the representation of all viewpoints through the aggregation of individual media each promoting a particular cause or ideology. Internal diversity is usually regarded as the superior model as it ensures that the reader or viewer is exposed to all relevant alternatives in a political debate and on the basis of this information is put in a position to make an informed choice. The downside of internal diversity is that the balancing of viewpoints provides little, if any, cues as to the value and validity of a position leaving it entirely up to the individual audience member to make up their mind. This might correspond to the ideal of a rational citizen, but it hardly meets the

need for orientation that is in particular short supply in periods of transition, which can cause an acute sense of disorientation and anomy in the individuals who have to find their way in dramatically changing circumstances. External diversity offers this orientation. It has also the potential to strengthen political alignments, to support group loyalties and to encourage political participation.

Since both internal and external diversity have their advantages and drawbacks, it is important to consider the political and cultural context when judging their implications for political life. External diversity might be a beneficial influence in contexts of high electoral volatility and weak party alignment because of its potential to contribute to developing links between political parties and their constituencies. As we have shown in the discussion of the relationship between the state and the media, the lack of party membership and partisan loyalties is one of the reasons for the attempt of governments, political parties and political leaders to instrumentalize the media for their own purposes. However, it is difficult to draw the line between a lively political contest on the one hand and unbridgeable hostility between adverse political camps that undermines cohesion and mutual tolerance on the other hand. External diversity of the media can be a detrimental, even dangerous, force in situations where no mechanisms have been found to moderate conflicts between antagonistic groups. This is often the case where ethnic or religious differences are the salient markers for the definition of group membership and political interests. For example, the media played a devastating role in the genocide in Rwanda (Thompson 2006), but they have also fuelled hatred in the aftermath of the 2008 election in Kenya.

Another consequence of a strong partisan press is that there is never a shortage of adversarialism. However, since the main aim of this criticism is to damage the political opponent it frequently takes on an aggressive and shrill tone and might even twist the truth in order to achieve its political goals. An extreme form of partisan adversarialism is the spreading of *kompromat*. The Russian word denotes unproven allegations and rumours and has been successfully employed in election campaigns. The timely revelation of details from a politician's private life, alleged dubious business deals or views that have been said in private have destroyed quite a few political careers regardless of whether or not the allegations turned out a hoax after the (lost) election (de Smaele 2006). Especially in highly commercialized market conditions, media partisanship often results in a journalistic culture of scandal where the hunt for sensational headlines becomes more important than scrupulous investigation of facts.

The apparent shortcomings of news reporting give rise to the question whether the media are to be blamed for the widespread lack of trust in political institutions and disenchantment with the democratic project that plagues many new democracies (Klingemann, Fuchs, and Zielonka 2006). To date there are only very few empirical studies that investigate the relationship between the media and citizens' democratic orientations in new democracies. Contrary to the assumption that the media contribute to political apathy (Patterson 1993), existing empirical evidence suggests that the media in new democracies have an overwhelmingly positive effect on the acquisition of political knowledge, participation in public affairs and support for democracy (Schmitt-Beck and Volt-

---

Box 16.4 **Key points**

- In most new democracies political reporting is highly opinionated and biased towards particular groups, parties or ideologies.

- It is questionable whether the Anglo-Saxon model of objective journalism is universally applicable. However, the effects of partisanship on the political process depend on the nature of the cultural and political divisions in society and the degree of polarization.

- Empirical evidence suggests that the media in new democracies have a positive effect on citizens' political involvement and support of democracy.

---

mer 2007). It seems that after decades of suppression, controversy and debate, even if it does not meet the highgrounds of normative theories of public communication, the media stimulates citizens' cognitive involvement in politics rather than alienating them.

Conclusion

Unlike earlier instances of democratization, the global wave of democracy takes place in a media-saturated environment, with global information flows reaching even the remotest places of the globe. The media have therefore not only been a driving force in recent regime changes, but they continue to affect the structure and functioning of the newly established institutions. In fact, it would be impossible to fully understand the dynamics of democratization without taking the media into account. Because of the pervasiveness of the media all politics, whether democratic or non-democratic, has become closely intertwined with processes of mass communication. It is therefore safe to say that new democracies are 'leapfrogging' into what has been labelled 'media democracies' (Meyer 2002) where political processes are mediated and, thus, shaped by the way in which the media portray political events and how they are consumed by mass publics.

This chapter set out to illustrate the complex relationship between the media and processes of democratization. As our survey of recent transitions has demonstrated, the media have been both a beneficial and an obstructive force in transitions from authoritarian to democratic rule. In particular, international communication and the demonstration effects of the transnational flow of information can accelerate, but in some instances inhibit attempts to bring down dictatorship and autocratic leaders. Further, in almost all new democracies the transformation of the structures and practices of mass communication has been extremely contested among the political elites involved in institution building, and even years after transition to democratic rule this issue continues to ignite conflicts between governments and the media. This is particularly the case where, due to the lack of alternative resources, political actors are highly dependent on the media to mobilize popular support.

Meanwhile, market conditions and commercialization have not always been effective in minimizing political interference. On the contrary, large numbers of newspapers and television stations are owned by political figures resulting in an alarming fusion of economic and political power. In other cases underdeveloped national economies and weak consumer markets have made it necessary for the state to run or subsidize the main national media. As a consequence of political and economic constraints, the media's ability to fulfil their democratic functions is often restricted in spite of individual journalists trying to maintain their independence from external pressures. Across virtually all new democracies political coverage is characterized by a high degree of partisanship which contradicts journalistic standards and has frequently led to intolerance and hostility between groups. However, as we have argued, depending on the circumstances advocacy media may contribute to an effective representation of divergent voices and can provide valuable cues to citizens seeking for orientation in a complex and insecure world.

Overall, the role of the media during transitions to democracy demonstrates the extreme contingency of democratization processes. While they are a crucial precondition for the proper working of democracy, the media are also dependent on political institutions to provide the regulatory conditions for their independence. In other words, democracy needs the media, and the media need democracy.

QUESTIONS

1. Discuss why the successful transformation of the media is a crucial precondition for the consolidation of new democracies.

2. How does the role of the media under the old regime affect their performance after the regime change?

3. Discuss the view that the media may help promote a political transition but are unlikely to initiate one.

4. Discuss the argument that international communications provide a positive contribution to democratization. How do they contribute to a 'revolution of rising expectations'?

5. Assess the 'CNN effect' as an influence on democratization.

6. How do libel laws affect the media's ability of independent reporting?

Visit the Online Resource Centre that accompanies this book for additional questions to accompany each chapter, and a range of other resources: <www.oxfordtextbooks. co.uk/orc/haerpfer/>.

FURTHER READING

Curran, J. and Park, M.-J. (2000) (eds), *De-Westernizing Media Studies* (London: Routledge). This volume takes a fresh look at the role of the media both in established and emerging democracies. The chapters present a broad range of case studies from Asia, Africa, North and South America, Europe and the Middle East. The conclusions drawn from these studies challenge accepted assumptions about free markets, the role of the state and globalization.

Ferdinand, P. (2000) (ed.), *The Internet, Democracy and Democratization* (London: Frank Cass). This book explores the potential of the Internet to change the way in which citizens participate in politics and ultimately how political institutions operate. The volume brings together studies that illustrate the democratizing power of the Internet, but also how antidemocratic and anti-modern groups (neo-Nazis, Taliban) use the technology for their own purposes.

Gunther, R. and Mughan, A. (2000) (eds), *Democracy and the Media: A Comparative Perspective* (Cambridge: Cambridge University Press). This volume compares and contrasts the impact of the media on politics, and the impact of politics on the media in authoritarian, transitional and established democracies. Individual contributions provide rich insights into individual countries. Altogether the book highlights the contingent interaction of political, economic, legal and cultural factors on the role of the media in democratic politics.

Mickiewicz, E. (2008), *Television, Power, and the Public in Russia* (Cambridge: Cambridge University Press). This book is one of the few that focuses on media audiences during periods of transition. The author conducted a large range of focus groups with television viewers in Russia to explore 'the other side of the screen', i.e. how ordinary citizens perceive and interpret the political messages they receive.

Price, M. E., Rozumilowicz, B., and Verhulst, S. G. (2001) (eds), *Media Reform: Democratizing the Media, Democratizing the State* (London: Routledge). This volume focuses on the transformation of the legal and regulatory framework of the media in new democracies. Some of the case studies compiled in this book include countries that are rarely covered in the literature, such as Uzbekistan, Uganda, Jordan and Uruguay. The book aims to draw conclusions for more effective ways of media reforms that promote the development and consolidation of democratic practices.

Rawnsley, G. D. (2006), *Political Communication and Democracy* (London: Palgrave). This book provides an accessible general introduction to the relationship between politics and the media. Particular emphasis is laid on recent developments such as globalization, international communication and terrorism.

Voltmer, K. (2006) (ed.), *Mass Media and Political Communication in New Democracies* (London: Routledge). This volumes looks at the media as part of a system of interactions and interdependencies in which journalists and political actors compete and cooperate with each other in order to gain control over the public agenda. The volume discusses contested normative issues, election campaigns, and media effects on citizens in new democracies. Case studies include countries from Eastern and Southern Europe, Latin America, Asia and Africa.

Waisbord, S. (2000), *Watchdog Journalism in South America: News, Accountability and Democracy* (New York, NY: Columbia University Press). An excellent comparative study of four Latin American countries (Argentina, Brazil, Columbia, Peru) on the interplay of press partisanship and investigative reporting. The empirical material is drawn from interviews with journalists and editors and shows the changing journalistic culture on the continent.

IMPORTANT WEBSITES

<www.freedomhouse.org> As well as political and civil liberties, this organization also monitors the development of press freedom around the world. Scores are given that rank-order the degree of press freedom alongside detailed country reports.

<www.gfmd.info> The Global Forum for Media Development brings together more than 300 international NGOs involved in supporting media, journalists and media activists.

<www.oecd.org> The Organization for Economic Cooperation and Development reports regularly on media developments in its member states. International Development Statistics are available online.

<http://rsf.org> Reporters Without Borders: This NGO monitors press freedom and the working conditions of journalists around the world. Like Freedom House, Reporters Without Borders provide detailed annual country reports and scores to classify the degree of press freedom in individual countries.

<http:web.worldbank.org> The World Bank has launched a Communication for Governance and Accountability Program that aims to promote communications to develop a democratic public sphere and to promote good governance.

Failed Democratization

M. Steven Fish and Jason Wittenberg

Overview

This chapter identifies key factors that lead to democratization 'going wrong'. After explaining why some new democracies slide backwards while others flourish, the chapter considers how the hazards of democratic reversal can be reduced.

Introduction

The early 1990s were a time of high spirits for democrats. Much of Latin America had recently shaken off authoritarian **regimes** that had become symbols of Ibero-American despotism, with their abysmal human rights records and farcical rhetoric of national grandeur. They had seemed rock-solid in the 1970s, but in the 1980s they yielded to movements for open rule. In some countries in East and South-East Asia a similar trend was evident, with military-backed regimes that had appeared impregnable submitting to popular movements. The very symbol of robust twentieth-century despotism, the Soviet Union, as well as authoritarian Yugoslavia, had disintegrated. The 10 **states** that had formed the Soviet or Eastern bloc became 28 separate states, many of which were racing headlong toward political freedom. In Africa, broad national conferences were calling strongmen to public account and neo-colonial racial oligarchies were headed toward demise. Even in some countries that did not democratize, the winds seemed to be favourable. Most noteworthy were China, Indonesia, and Iran, where broad reform movements, though repressed, exposed popular longing for change.

From the standpoint of the current day, however, the early 1990s seem like a golden age. It is now clear that the path to an open polity is strewn with obstacles and twists. Indeed, one of the most pronounced trends of the first decade of the twenty-first century is the reversal of democratization. This chapter aims to explain why some democratizers slid backwards while others did not. It further considers how to reduce the hazards of democratization's reversal. To investigate failed democratization, we analyse all countries with a population of at least half a million.

To assess the progress of democratization, we use the Freedom House Index (hereafter FHI). The scores range from 1 for the most open polity to 7 for the least open polity (see Ch. 3 for details). Our time frame is 1975–2007. When referring to the FHI for particular years, we use the data that reflect conditions in the country. Thus, when we refer to 2002, we mean the scores that Freedom House released in 2003, which represent conditions in 2002.[1]

Categorizing Countries

We sort countries into five categories. Two categories—*established democracies* and *established autocracies*—contain countries that have not experienced regime change since 1975. Established democracies have had an FHI of 2.5 or better each year since 1975. Established autocracies lie on the other end of the spectrum. Their annual FHI was never better than 4, the midpoint on the FHI scale. The established democracies were always open polities; the established autocracies never came close to being open polities. Of the 158 countries under examination, 23 count as established democracies and 45 as established autocracies.

The other three categories consist of three different kinds of *democratizers*. Democratizers are defined as countries that both failed to reach the 2.5 level in at least one year and that had a score of 3.5 or better in at least one year during the period 1975–2007. Among these countries we distinguish among *robust democratizers* (39 countries), *tenuous democratizers* (31 countries), and *failed democratizers* (20 countries). In this chapter we focus on the democratizers, and especially on the failed democratizers and what makes them different.

Robust democratizers

The robust democratizers are the successful cases. Each failed to reach the 2.5 level in the FHI in one or more years between 1975 and 2004, but subsequently attained that level (or better) in all three consecutive years from 2005 to 2007. Some of the robust democratizers had relatively favourable scores throughout the

three decades between 1975 and 2004, but in one year or a small set of years failed to meet the 2.5 threshold in the FHI. Cyprus, the Dominican Republic, India, Mauritius, Portugal, and Trinidad and Tobago are the cases. Other robust democratizers—Argentina, Brazil, El Salvador, Peru, and Slovakia—experienced substantial ups and downs, but the general trajectory of regime change was nevertheless positive and the countries ranked at the 2.5 level or better in 2005–07. Still others once laboured under autocratic regimes, but after an antiauthoritarian breakthrough exhibited linear movement to democracy and rated 2.5 or better in 2005–07. Benin, Bulgaria, Chile, Croatia, the Czech Republic, Estonia, Ghana, Hungary, Indonesia, Latvia, Lesotho, Lithuania, Mali, Mexico, Mongolia, Namibia, Panama, Poland, Romania, Senegal, Serbia, Slovenia, South Africa, South Korea, Spain, Taiwan, Ukraine, and Uruguay fit this description.

Tenuous democratizers

The tenuous democratizers are the intermediate cases. They are countries that in at least one yearly survey scored 3.5 or better, but that also failed to score as favourably as a 2.5 between 2005 and 2007. These countries also have avoided autocracy in the recent past; the FHI for each averages better than 4 over the three years from 2005 to 2007.

A broad range of countries falls in this category. Some have a history of open politics but slipped in recent years. Bolivia, Columbia, Ecuador, Guyana, Honduras, Malawi, Papua New Guinea, and the

Philippines are the cases. Others lack a substantial history of democracy, but have exhibited a generally positive trend following an antiauthoritarian breakthrough, without reaching the 2.5 level between 2005 and 2007. These countries are Albania, Bosnia, Kenya, Liberia, Macedonia, Madagascar, Moldova, Mozambique, Nicaragua, Paraguay, Sierra Leone, and Tanzania. Still other cases resided in an intermediate zone for most of the time since 1975 but have generally been closer to closure than to openness and have resisted a democratizing impulse in the recent past. Malaysia and Morocco typify this pattern. Finally, some countries have been on a regime-change roller coaster. Comoros, Georgia, Guatemala, Guinea-Bissau, Niger, Sri Lanka, Thailand, Turkey, and Zambia fit that description.

Failed democratizers

The failed democratizers have an experience of political opening but subsequently underwent a major reversal. They scored a 3.5 or better in at least one year in the past, but over the past three years have averaged 4 or worse. These polities at one time showed promise as potential democracies or actually were democracies, but then moved toward **authoritarianism** and, as of this writing, have not recovered. Since failed democratization is the subject of this chapter, more detail on the countries in this category is in order.

Armenia achieved political opening in the early years of the post-Soviet period and rated 3.5 in 1992–94. It then became a more closed polity and received scores of 4.5 in 2005, 2006, and 2007.

Bangladesh rated as a free polity for two years, 1991 and 1992, but subsequently declined dramatically. It received a score of 4 for each survey during the half-decade covering 2002–06, and deteriorated further to 4.5 in 2007.

In the wake of dissolution of the USSR, Belarus experienced a spell of relatively open politics, receiving a score of 3.5 in 1992. But it subsequently made a slide to hard authoritarianism. In 2004 its FHI sunk to 6.5, where it has subsequently remained. Belarus has become home to one of the world's most repressive political regimes.

Burkina Faso experienced a short period of constitutional rule in the late 1970s. It ranked as a free

polity in 1978 and 1979, with a score of 2.5 in each year, but then lapsed into dictatorship. The country underwent a partial opening in the 1990s, but its FHI was not better than 4 in any given year since then.

The Central African Republic, after decades of dictatorship, liberalized in 1993. At that time its FHI improved to 3.5, where it stayed in 1994 and 1995. After a brief decline, it resumed its previous level of 3.5 in 1998–2000. After that, however, the country's score deteriorated. In 2005 and 2006 it stood at 4.5, and in 2007 it further worsened to 5.

Congo-Brazzaville underwent an opening in the early 1990s. In 1992 it received a score of 3. It subsequently degenerated dramatically. In 2005 the country's FHI stood at 5, and in 2006 and 2007 fell further, to 5.5.

Djibouti began its post-independence existence in 1977 as a relatively open polity. Between 1977 and 1980, it rated 3.5. The country then moved toward authoritarianism and has remained a mostly closed polity for the past quarter century. It received a score of 5 over the past half-decade.

Fiji was a democracy from 1975 to 1986, but yielded to autocracy in 1987. It subsequently recovered and in 1999 regained status as a free polity. But the island nation again reverted to authoritarianism. Its FHI for 2005, 2006, and 2007 were 3.5, 5, and 5, respectively.

Gabon had a partial opening in the early 1990s, rating 3.5 in 1991. It then reverted to authoritarianism. The country received a score of 5 in each of the surveys for 2005, 2006, and 2007.

The Gambia has a tortuous political history. From 1975 to 1980 it was the most democratic country in Africa. Democracy eroded in the 1980s, though the Gambia still remained a partially open polity. Between 1989 and 1993 it experienced another political opening and recovered its status as Africa's most open political regime. In 1994 it fell into dictatorship. The country subsequently experienced some liberalization, but never returned to democracy. It rated 4 in 2005 and 2006 and 4.5 in 2007.

Jordan has known much more autocracy than democracy. It did, however, undergo a noteworthy opening in the early 1990s, scoring 3 in the FHI in 1992. The kingdom subsequently reverted to less open politics, and its score stood at 4.5 for each of the surveys for 2005–07.

Kuwait is included in the category of failed democratizers rather than established autocracies by virtue of its relatively favourable score in a single year—1975, the first year in the period under consideration. Thereafter Kuwait's FHI deteriorated and never recovered. It stood at 4.5 in each of the surveys for 2005–07.

Kyrgyzstan underwent a dramatic opening following the demise of the USSR, attaining a score of 3 in 1992. Its level of political openness subsequently declined precipitously. Though it underwent a slight recovery in the wake of the 'Tulip Revolution' in 2005, its FHI has not advanced beyond the 4.5 level, where it remained between 2005 and 2007.

Nepal has a topsy-turvy political history. It achieved status as a free polity in 1991 and 1992, with a FHI of 2.5 in each year, but subsequently declined. The country rated 5.5 in 2005 and 4.5 in both 2006 and 2007.

Between 1979 and 1983 Nigeria was a democracy, receiving scores of 2.5 in each year during this interval. The country subsequently succumbed to autocracy. While it experienced another opening at the end of the 1990s, it never recovered its status as a democracy. It rated 4 in each of the past three surveys.

Pakistan had a spell of relatively open politics in the late 1980s, rating 3 in 1988 and 1989. Its subsequent history has been one of greater political closure. Pakistan received scores of 5.5 in each of the three years between 2005 and 2007.

Russia's recent history of political openness resembles that of Pakistan. Its FHI was 3 in 1991, but it then steadily slunk toward autocracy. The country received scores of 5.5 over the past three annual surveys.

Tajikistan, like Russia, had a short-lived breakthrough in 1991, when its FHI was 3. Unlike Russia, which returned to authoritarianism gradually, Tajikistan reverted immediately; its FHI was 6 in 1992. The authoritarian regime has remained in place ever since.

Venezuela was a democracy for most of the period under consideration. During 1975–1991, it rated as a free polity, with an annual FHI of 2.5 or better. During this era, it was an exception to the autocracy that prevailed in Latin America. But in the 1990s its level of democracy declined. In 1999 Venezuela's FHI was 4, placing it at a much lower level of openness than it had historically enjoyed. It held this score in 2005–07.

Zimbabwe was never a full-blown democracy, but it did achieve a score of 3.5 in 1980. It subsequently tumbled. It scored 6.5 during each of the surveys for 2005–07, marking it as one of the world's harshest autocracies.

What Undermines Democracy?

In order to unearth the conditions that precipitate democratic failure, we use a statistical analysis that treats the three categories of countries as the dependent variable, i.e. as the phenomenon to be explained by other factors or variables. To be able to calculate statistical effects, we code the established democracies as 4, the robust democratizers as 3, the tenuous democratizers as 2, the failed democratizers as 1, and the established autocracies as 0. These five categories run from most to least success with democracy. We then test the influence of factors that scholars normally consider to be causes of cross-national variation in democratic attainment. We also consider several variables that are less frequently examined. Our aim is to figure out which major situational conditions influenced where countries ended up in terms of regime change.

High economic development is widely seen as democracy's fastest friend and poverty its biggest foe. Higher levels of development are typically associated with more sophisticated populations, larger middle classes, and less desperate lower classes (see Ch. 8). To assess development, we use gross national income (GNI) at purchasing power parity (PPP) in the year 2000, measured in thousands of US dollars.

To measure economic reliance on hydrocarbons, which is sometimes regarded as a bane to open government, we use the proportion of export income generated by oil and gas. Oil may distort modernization, finance repression, fuel corruption, promote economic statism, and reduce economic stability—among other pathologies (see Ch. 8). All these effects of oil wealth may hinder democratization. Data on this factor are scarce for many countries. Locating numbers for this variable for each country for each year, or for any given year, is impossible. We therefore construct the best set of data we can, drawing on the figures for years that are as close to 2000 as we can find.

Some observers believe that ethnic heterogeneity hinders democratization. They hold that diverse societies are more prone to conflict and less able to generate the compromise that is integral to democratic practice (Rabushka and Shepsle 1972). We assess this factor using the ethnic fractionalization scores that Alberto Alesina and colleagues (2002) have constructed. Among scholars who regard cultural context as significant, some focus on religion (see Ch. 9). Some recent studies have shown that Islam may pose special challenges (Fish 2002). A close association between sacred and secular authority, a strong distinction between believers and non-believers, and a lower status for females have been regarded as features of Islamic societies that may lower the prospects for open politics. We measure this variable using the percentage of the population that adheres to Islam.

Longevity of statehood may also affect democratization's chances. How long a country has enjoyed independence may influence national identity and political psychology, among other factors that can, in turn, affect the political regime (see Chs 2 and 9). In a blunt but useful way to capture this difference, we include a dummy variable for whether a country enjoyed national independence by the year 1900. Countries that existed as independent states at the advent of the previous century are scored as 0; those that gained independence only after 1990 are coded as 1. Finally, we include a measure for sex inequality. Greater sex equality may be conducive to popular rule by promoting a less hierarchical cultural milieu for decisionmaking, among other advantages (Fish 2002; Inglehart, Norris, and Welzel 2002, see also

Ch. 10). We measure this variable using the sex literacy gap, which is the male literacy rate minus the female rate. Figures are for the year 2000. A higher number is a sign of greater inequality between the sexes. This indicator measures deep demographic conditions. It is largely stable from year to year and even decade to decade. The **correlation** between the literacy gap in 1980 and in 1990, for example, is .96; virtually the same correlation obtains between the figures for 1990 and 2000 ('Summary Gender Profile,' 2002).

In the terminology of the 'bathtub model', introduced in Chapter 4, each of the variables assessed here may be regarded as *objective* geopolitical and social structural conditions. All are background conditions, and none normally changes quickly. The correlation between income per capita across recent decades, like that for the sex literacy gap, is over .9.[2] Numbers for relatively recent years are used because the data are more plentiful and there are fewer missing cases. The results do not change appreciably when data for earlier decades are substituted. While each factor considered here may itself be affected by democracy in the long run, the hazards of endogeneity—meaning that what is treated as the dependent variable actually causes what are treated as the causal variables—are not acute. None of the causal variables are institutions (e.g. voting rules), events (e.g. wars), trends (e.g. economic performance), or policies (e.g. level of economic openness). The last two factors may be worth considering, but assessing their effects without risking endogeneity is more difficult. In this section, we measure only the effects of the objective factors just reviewed.

Table 17.1 presents the results of a series of ordered **probit** models. The idea behind these models is to assess the independent effects of each hypothesized factor, contingent on the inclusion of the other factors, when the outcome consists of ordered discrete possibilities. In this case, these ordered possibilities are the probability of becoming an established autocracy, a failed democratizer, a tenuous democratizer, a robust democratizer, or an established democracy. Model 1 includes all the factors that we hypothesized would determine the category a country ends up in; to test the robustness of the findings we also present alternative specifications, for a total of five models.

Table 17.1 Ordered Probit Regressions of Political Regime Type on Hypothesized Determinants

Variable	Model 1	Model 2	Model 3	Model 4	Model 5
Economic development	0.13***	0.11***	0.13***	0.13***	0.14***
	(0.02)	(0.02)	(0.02)	(0.02)	(0.02)
Fuels dependence	-0.02***		-0.03***	-0.02***	-0.02***
	(0.004)		(0.004)	(0.004)	(0.004)
Ethnic fractionalization	1.12*	0.39	1.10*		
	(0.47)	(0.42)	(0.47)		
Percentage Muslim	-0.008**	-0.01***		-0.01***	
	(0.003)	(0.003)		(0.003)	
Late national independence	-0.48		-0.61*		
	(0.25)		(0.24)		
Sex inequality	-0.03**	-0.02*	-0.04***		
	(0.01)	(0.01)	(0.01)		
Pseudo R^2	.32	.24	.31	.29	.26

Note: N = 158 countries. Standard errors in parentheses. *p < .05; **p < .01; ***p < .001. Standard errors are a measure of our uncertainty in the estimates. The larger the ordered probit regression coefficient relative to the standard error, the more confident we are in a factor's effect. Conventionally confidence is indicated through the use of asterisks. The more asterisks there are, the more confident we are in the result.

Sources: For economic development, World Bank 2002b; for fuels dependence, World Bank 2002a and annual reports for other years; for ethnic fractionalization, Alesina *et al.* 2002; for percentage Muslim, *Muslim Population Worldwide* 2003; for sex inequality, United Nations Development Programme 2002.

Economic development, fuels export dependence, percentage Muslim, colonial heritage, and sex inequality are all statistically significant and the signs are in the expected direction. Higher economic development is good for democracy; more economic dependence on fuels is bad for it. Likewise, a higher proportion of Muslims is bad for democracy, as are late national independence and sex inequality. The only possible surprise is ethnic fractionalization, which does not hinder democratization. The sign on the coefficient is positive, indicating that higher fractionalization may help rather than hurt the prospects for democracy, but it is not statistically significant in all three of the models in which it is included. The results suggest that we cannot say whether or not higher ethnic fractionalization is good for democracy, but we can infer that it is not bad for it.

Comparison of the failed democratizers and the robust democratizers fleshes out the picture. The importance of economic development is evident. Annual income per person in the 20 failed cases

averages roughly US$3,700; in the 39 successful cases, US$8,100. In only two of the failed democratizers, Kuwait and Russia, are incomes higher than the average income in the robust democratizers. Poverty is democracy's antagonist. We can also illustrate how poverty reduces the prospects for democratization by computing the predicted probabilities of failed democratization at different levels of economic development. These probabilities are shown in Figure 17.1. To generate the lines in the figure we set the values of all the explanatory variables in our model except gross national income per capita to their average values in the data. We then computed, for values of gross national income per capita varying from 0 to 40,000 dollars, the predicted probabilities of failed democratization given our model. The solid line represents these predicted probabilities; the dashed lines indicate the associated 95 per cent confidence intervals. All statistical estimates have some uncertainty associated with them. Ninety-five per cent confidence intervals indicate the range within which we are 95 per cent confident that the

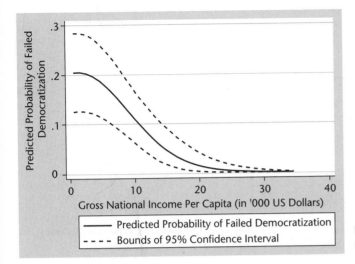

Fig 17.1 The Relationship between Economic Development and Failed Democratization

true value lies, in this case the true probability of failed democratization. As in clear from the downward trend in the figure, economic development is an excellent way to maximize the chances of successful democratization.

The relationship between fuels dependence and democracy is even more unequivocal. In 6 of the 20 failed cases (Congo-Brazzaville, Gabon, Kuwait, Nigeria, Russia, and Venezuela) fuels account for over half of exports, while in only one of the 39 robust democratizers, Trinidad and Tobago, do they account for more than one-quarter of exports. Democracy knows no greater foe than oil.

Islam may also complicate democratization. The proportion of the population that adheres to Islam in the failed democratizers averages 44 per cent; in the robust democratizers it is 11 per cent. Predominantly Muslim countries make up half of the failed democratizers but only 8 per cent of the robust democratizers. Countries that did not exist as independent states prior before 1900 may also have a disadvantage. Only 2 of the 20 failed democratizers, Russia and Venezuela, enjoyed an independent national existence prior to the year 1900, while 10 of the 39 robust democratizers did so.

Sex inequality may hinder democratization as well. Among the failed democratizers, the gap between male and female literacy rates favours males by 13 percentage points on average; among the robust democratizers, the gap is only 4 percentage points. The damaging effects of literacy gaps on democratization's prospects are illustrated in Figure 17.2. To generate the lines in the figure we set the values of all the explanatory variables in our model except sex inequality in literacy (defined as male minus female literacy) to their average values in the data. We then computed, for values of sex inequality in literacy ranging from -20 per cent to 40 per cent, the predicted probabilities of failed democratization given our model. As in Figure 17.1, the solid line represents these predicted probabilities; the dashed lines indicate the associated 95 percent confidence intervals. Figure 17.2 shows that, all other things being equal, as the gap between male and female literacy increases, the probability of failed democratization also increases.

Box 17.1 **Key points**

- The level of economic development is positively related to successful democratization.

- Fuels dependence, a large Muslim share of the population, and sex inequality are all negatively related to successful democratization.

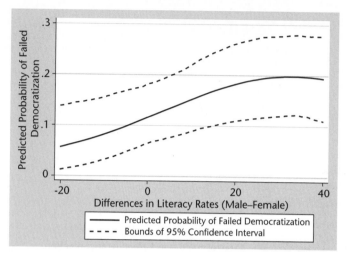

Fig 17.2 The Relationship between Literacy Rates and Failed Democratization

Who Undermines Democracy?

The limits of situational factors

The above analysis gives us a handle on the underlying conditions that affect how countries fare in regime change. But how far does it take us toward understanding why democratization fails in specific places? In order to delve into specific countries, we focus on the three categories in which some regime change took place (the robust democratizers, the tenuous democratizers, and the failed democratizers). We now drop the established democracies and established autocracies from the analysis and look only at the democratizers, which number 90 countries.

We are especially interested in the 20 failed democratizers. Zeroing in on them, let us ask: How well did our model predict that they would fail? How well can it account for the fact that these countries became failed—rather than tenuous or robust—democratizers? To determine this, we estimate, for each actual failed democratizer, the expected probability (conditional on the values of all the variables in our statistical model) of being a failed, tenuous, or robust democratizer.[3] Table 17.2 presents these expected probabilities, with 95 per cent confidence intervals in parentheses below each estimate. The left-hand

column shows the probability, given a country's scores on the six causal variables used in the analysis, of that country becoming what it became, meaning a failed democratizer. The middle column shows the chance of it becoming a tenuous democratizer, and the right-hand column of becoming a robust democratizer.

For the countries that had a 40 per cent or greater chance of ending up where they did in fact (meaning as failed democratizers), we may say that our statistical model worked reasonably well. This condition obtains for 10 of the 20 countries. For example, in Bangladesh, given the country's scores on the causal variables we used above, the chances that democratization would fail were 57 per cent. Bangladesh's export profile includes no oil or gas, which is a big plus for democracy's prospects. But it is poor (annual income per capita is US$1,650), Islamic (88 per cent of the people are Muslims), recently decolonized (in 1971), and highly unequal in terms of sex (the literacy gap is 22 per cent). So too does our model work well for predicting the trajectory of regime change in Nigeria, where the chances of democratization failing were an overwhelming 98 per cent. Nigeria is impoverished (annual income per capita is US$790),

Table 17.2 The Failed Democratizers and the Probabilities of Their Fates, in Percentages

Country	Chance of Becoming a Failed Democratizer	Chance of Becoming a Tenuous Democratizer	Chance of Becoming a Robust Democratizer
Armenia	22 (5–47)	45 (29–58)	33 (11–61)
Bangladesh	57 (21–87)	33 (12–52)	10 (1–34)
Belarus	7 (2–17)	33 (19–49)	60 (39–79)
Burkina Faso	32 (18–49)	46 (33–58)	21 (10–35)
Central African Republic	20 (7–40)	45 (31–58)	35 (15–56)
Congo–Brazzaville	91 (60–100)	8 (0–32)	1 (0–6)
Djibouti	41 (19–63)	43 (28–56)	16 (4–33)
Fiji	6 (2–13)	32 (20–45)	62 (45–77)
Gabon	73 (31–97)	22 (3–48)	5 (0–23)
Gambia	44 (21–67)	42 (26–56)	14 (4–32)
Jordan	30 (13–53)	46 (32–58)	24 (9–44)
Kuwait	36 (3–86)	39 (11–56)	25 (1–75)
Kyrgyzstan	41 (19–66)	43 (28–57)	16 (4–35)
Nepal	22 (4–50)	44 (27–57)	34 (9–66)
Nigeria	98 (84–100)	2 (0–14)	0 (0–1)
Pakistan	51 (26–73)	39 (22–53)	11 (2–26)
Russia	39 (13–69)	42 (26–57)	19 (3–47)

(*continued*)

Table 17.2 The Failed Democratizers and the Probabilities of Their Fates, in Percentages *Continued*

Country	Chance of Becoming a Failed Democratizer	Chance of Becoming a Tenuous Democratizer	Chance of Becoming a Robust Democratizer
Tajikistan	45	41	14
	(18–74)	(22–56)	(2–35)
Venezuela	76	20	4
	(35–98)	(2–47)	(0–22)
Zimbabwe	**12**	**41**	**47**
	(4–24)	**(27–54)**	**(28–65)**

Note: Entries are probabilities of each country falling in the designated category, given the values for that country in each of the causal variables presented in Model 1 of Table 17.1. 95 per cent confidence intervals in parentheses are below each estimate. Bolded entries indicate countries whose expected probability of being a failed democratizer was under 40 per cent, indicating a poor fit to our model.

all of its export income derives from oil, half its population is Muslim, it achieved independence late (in 1960), and sex inequality is considerable (the literacy gap is 17 per cent).

In 10 of the failed democratizers, however, our model offers predictions of failure that are lower than 40 per cent. These are the cases of failure that our model did not do a good job of predicting. They appear in bold in Table 17.2. In Belarus, for example, the probability of failure was only seven per cent, and there was as 60 per cent chance of success. In neighbouring Russia, the odds of succeeding were not as high, but those of failing were still only 39 per cent. Thus, in Belarus, Russia, and the other eight cases where our model yields predications of less than a 40 per cent chance of failure, something besides the factors we included in our models above must be at work. Our analyses, after all, only tested the effects of big background conditions. They did not include the *subjective* dimension of politics, i.e. the political actions of key actors. What other factors might help explain the failure of democratization? The question requires us to look beyond structural factors and to consider specifically who brought democratization to grief.

Agents of democratization's derailment

The first possible culprit for democratization's reversal is the masses, who may carry out an uprising or a revolution. The second are insurgents, who can sabotage democratization by instigating civil war. The third is a foreign power, which may thwart political opening by launching an invasion or sponsoring proxies who do their dirty work for them. Fourth, the armed forces may be at fault, as they may intervene in politics and throw elected civilian leaders out of power. Fifth, the chief executive may bury democratization by engaging in despotic action. One or some combination of these agents usually authors the reversal of political opening. Here we consider which of them has been active in undermining democratization since 1975. We focus on the 10 cases of failed democratization that our model did not do a good job of predicting.

In Armenia, the President and the armed forces have been democratization's biggest rivals. Independent Armenia's first President, Levon Ter-Petrosian, undermined his opponents and presided over a re-election effort that he won, possibly fraudulently, in 1995. He was succeeded in 1998 by Robert Kocharian, who only intensified his predecessor's high-handed ways and penchant for enforcing his authority thorough flawed elections. The military, by successfully putting pressure on Ter-Petrosian to resign and yield to Kocharian, also played a role in democratization's degradation.

In Belarus, the author of democracy's demise was the President. Shortly after assuming office in 1994, Aleksandr Lukashenko commenced what would become a relentless campaign to muzzle the media and undertake other measures that left Belarus in the company of the world's most closed polities.

Burkina Faso's experiment with democracy in the late 1970s was brought to a halt by the army's intervention. In 1987, Blaise Compaoré came to power in a coup and assumed the presidency, an office he has held ever since. Compaoré has sought **legitimacy** through partially open elections and has not emasculated open politics with the zeal that Belarus's Lukashenko has. But he has stood in the way of re-democratization. In Burkina Faso, both military intervention and presidential imperiousness have produced failure in democratization.

In the Central African Republic, insurgencies and the armed forces have been democratization's main antagonists. Early in the current decade, government forces loyal to the then-President, Ange-Félix Patassé, battled insurgents commanded by General François Bozizé, who managed to depose Patassé. As of this writing, Bozizé's government forces are fighting insurgents, many of them thugs and soldiers of fortune.

In Fiji, the military has been the main culprit. It staged coups in 1987, 2000, and 2006. Underlying the military's actions are grievances between Indo-Fijian and indigenous Fijian groups. While our analyses showed that higher ethnic fractionalization per se is not associated with worse performance in democratization, in Fiji ethnic divisions clearly bred conflict and underlay the armed forces' interventions.

Jordan's reversal of liberalization of the early 1990s, and the current enforcement of the authoritarian regime, owes to executive despotism. King Hussein, who reigned until his death in 1999, allowed liberalization by fits and starts, but consistently rolled back reforms as quickly as introduced them. His son, King Abdullah, has promised democratization but continued his father's tradition of using limited reforms more to shore up the authoritarian regime than to democratize it.

The limiting factor in Kuwait's democratization is also the monarch. Kuwait enjoyed a degree of political openness in 1975, but the emir has regularly shut down parliament, which he did in 1976–81 and 1986–92. Even with parliament now open, the emir remains in charge. He shows little interest in subjecting his own rule to popular scrutiny or in turning the reigns of power over to elected officials.

Nepal also has a monarch problem. The relatively open politics of the 1980s and early 1990s gave way to arbitrary rule by the monarch, King Gyanendra, who ascended the throne in 2001. An armed insurgency that Maoist rebels launched in 1996 shares culpability for the degradation of open politics.

In Russia, democracy's derailment has been the doing of the chief executive. After the high water mark of the early post-Soviet period, Russian politics moved toward closure. During the 1990s, the then-President, Boris Yeltsin, gradually undermined democratization. His successor, Vladimir Putin, accelerated the reversion to authoritarianism.

The President similarly engineered Zimbabwe's reversion to authoritarianism. Robert Mugabe served as Prime Minister in a parliamentary system between the time of formal independence in 1980 and 1987, when constitutional change created a presidential system and Mugabe took over as President. Zimbabwe was a reasonably open polity, albeit not a democracy, in 1980. But since that time Mugabe has dragged the country to ever greater depths of despotism.

The most remarkable finding that emerges from this review is the culpability of chief executives. In five of the 10 cases they were clearly the agents of democratization's failure. In another three cases they shared responsibility with another actor. In five of the eight cases in which democratization was foiled by in part or wholly by the chief executive, the latter took the form of a president. In the three other cases, he was a monarch. The next most frequently involved actor was the military, which was the sole offender in one case and one of two offenders in three cases. Insurgencies are not shown as the sole author of democratization's demise, but were one of two actors in two countries. A pattern is discernible. Over the past several decades the chief executive has been the main perpetrator of democratization's reversal. It follows that constraining the president or the monarch may be crucial to safeguarding democratization. How might this be done?

Box 17.2 **Key points**

- Objective structural conditions predict abut half of democratic failures with a reasonable degree of accuracy.

- Beyond that, we have to look at political actors; the role of the chief executive being particularly important.

What Can Be Done?

Strengthening legislatures and curtailing executive power

A—perhaps *the*—key to reducing the potential for presidential or monarchical abuse of power is a strong legislature. Much of the debate on the effect of political institutions on democratization has focused on the relative merits of presidential versus parliamentary systems (Linz and Valenzuela 1994; Cheibub 2006). Until recently, however, we have been limited to observing these highly aggregated categories, which do not really specify where power resides and in what measure. We have lacked data measuring the powers of the legislature (and the presidency). Recently, however, a study has been issued that offers useful quantitative data (Fish and Kroenig, 2008). The data take the form of the Parliamentary Power Index (PPI), and are based on an extensive survey. Scores range from 0 (powerless legislature) to 1 (all-powerful legislature). We may tap the numbers to see how the strength of the legislature may affect the probability of democratization's failure. Scores are available for all of the democratizers (robust, tenuous, and failed) except for Djibouti.

The correlation between the powers of legislatures and the fate of democratization is substantial. The weaker the legislature, the greater the chance that democracy fails. The average score for the failed democratizers is .42; for tenuous democratizers, .50; and for robust democratizers, .62. We need to be careful about attributing causal force to the power of legislatures, since the level of political openness might have affected the powers of the legislature. Among the 10 cases of failed democracy about which our original model does not produce good predictions, Burkina Faso, Fiji, and Nepal fit this description. Each of these underwent its departure—or, in Fiji and Nepal, one of its several departures—from open politics before the constitutional orders that are currently in place were adopted. Thus, we cannot readily use the PPI as a causal explanation for why democracy failed.

In the other seven countries, however, the powers of the legislatures were established before the

countries moved toward authoritarianism. In these cases we may ask whether having a stronger legislature might have reduced the risk of democratic reversal. The PPI scores for the seven countries are the following: Armenia .56; Belarus .25; Central African Republic .34; Jordan .22; Kuwait .38; Russia .44; and Zimbabwe .31. With the exception of Armenia, these are low scores. In global perspective, they range between medium-low (e.g. Russia) and very low (e.g. Jordan). For these seven countries, we can estimate what the probability of democratic failure would have been had we included the PPI as an independent variable in our statistical models. So too can we make counterfactual statements about what the probably of democracy's failure would have been had the powers of the legislature been different than they were in fact.

As shown in Table 17.2, our statistical model yielded results that would predict that the probability of Armenian democracy failing was 22 per cent. When we take into account Armenia's PPI, the probability rises to 28 per cent. The addition of this variable therefore yields only a mildly better prediction. Clearly, factors other than what we include contributed to the reversal of Armenia's democratization. The same may be said of the Central African Republic. Its probability of suffering reversal is 20 per cent in the initial model and 26 per cent when we take the PPI score into account. As recounted above, however, an overweening presidency was not the main culprit for the Central African Republic's bad experience with democratization. Rather, insurgencies and the army, which normally are much harder for the legislature to countervail than an overreaching president or monarch, were the main culprits. Kuwait provides another instance where including the PPI in the analysis yields a mildly higher prediction of failure (and therefore a more accurate prediction). In the initial model, Kuwait's chance of failing was 36 per cent; including the measure for the powers of the legislature increases the chances to 39 per cent.

The improvement in predictive power is greater in the remaining four cases. Our initial model predicts that democratization in Belarus had only a seven per cent chance of failing. Belarus had a lot going for it, including a decent standard of living, an economy that is not based primarily on oil and gas, and a miniscule sex literacy gap. Yet, when we factor in Belarus's (low) score on the PPI, the probability of failure jumps to 35 per cent. These numbers jibe with the story we know: faced with a toothless legislature under a fresh constitution that provided for a powerful presidency, Aleksandr Lukashenko easily defied—and ultimately silenced—his opponents and put an end to Belarus's short-lived experiment with open politics.

The numbers and the story for Zimbabwe, where Robert Mugabe has played the role of Lukashenko in Belarus, are similar. Democratization 'should have' worked; Zimbabwe's chances of failure were only 12 per cent. But when we include the PPI in the analysis, the probability of failure in Zimbabwe nearly triples, to 35 per cent.

In Jordan, the chances of failure in the initial model were 30 per cent. Including the PPI in the analysis raises the probability to 52 per cent. Indeed, the monarch has been able to quash opponents in part because the parliament does not have the capacity to counterbalance the palace.

In Russia, the likelihood of failure shifts from 39 per cent in the original model to 55 per cent when we account for the country's PPI. Indeed, since Russia adopted its post-Soviet constitution in 1993, the legislature has lacked the capacity to stand up to the president. Counterfactually, we can assess what Russia's probability of failing would have been were its PPI higher. If we set it to .78, the score for Bulgaria, which opted for a strong legislature in its postcommunist constitution, Russia's probability of failure would have been just 18 per cent.

The policy prescription is obvious: would-be democratizers should take special interest in strengthening the legislature. Constitutions' drafters who seek to maximize the chances of democracy's success should vest expansive powers in parliament. The success of democracy, of course, does not depend solely on a strong legislature, and a strong legislature is no guarantee of democratic stability. Fiji's strong legislature (its PPI is .63) did not prevent the military from junking democracy in 2006.

In many cases, however, bolstering the legislature may promote open politics. Let us take a look at Jordan and Kuwait. Their prospects for democracy have often seemed brighter than those of their neighbours (Mufti 1999; Tétreault 2000). Still, robust democratization, decade after decade, has proven elusive in both countries. According to our calculations, however, if we set the set Kuwait's PPI at .78, the figure for Turkey, the probability of democracy failing in Kuwait falls from 36 per cent to only 10 per cent. In Jordan, it would have been a mere 6 per cent instead of 30 per cent. In these countries, monarchs who stand in the way of the expansion of the legislature's power may be democratization's greatest antagonists (Herb 2002; Lucas 2005). Both countries have predominantly Muslim populations, both were decolonized only in the twentieth century, Jordan is relatively poor, and Kuwait's economy is based on hydrocarbons, but each country still should have succeeded in democratization. The chances of them failing would have been much lower if they had legislatures that were as strong as Turkey's.

The powers of the legislature are, of course, institutions. Institutions are the products of human volition and behaviour and can be altered, sometimes quickly. What, though, of the deeper structural factors that we analysed above? Is their any possibility for changing them in a manner that reduces the risk of democratization's failure?

Altering the structural factors

A country's level of economic development can change, but usually this takes decades. Its effects on the prospects for democratization may take generations to materialize. Sustained, rapid economic growth such as happened in post-war South Korea may have contributed to the success of democratization there. Some observers consider China's spectacular development a harbinger of democratization. Still, such explosive modernization is unusual. When it comes to the effects of economic development on democratization, the best source of hope may be the substantial number of exceptions to the general rule. Like the other relationships explored here, the tie between development and democracy is probabilistic, not absolute. Some poor countries have been successful democratizers. Benin, Ghana,

Mali, Mongolia, and Senegal each have an annual per capita income below US$2,000, yet each falls in the category of robust democratizers.

Countries' histories of national independence are, of course, fixed. But a history of late independence is the rule in the world. A long history of statehood may provide distinct advantages, but a majority of even the robust democratizers obtained independent statehood only in the past century. The ravages of colonialism are real, but they need not block democratization.

The proportion of the population that is made up of Muslims (or any other faith community) is normally stable across time, though it may change over generations. Yet it bears note that three Muslim-majority countries are found among the robust democratizers. One, Indonesia, is the world's largest Muslim-majority country, and two, Mali and Senegal, are major West African nations. In each country over four-fifths of inhabitants are Muslims and levels of religious observance are high. In Indonesia and Senegal, Islamic mass organizations are the mainstays of civil society and have played constructive roles in democratization (Ramage 1995; Villalón 1995). Furthermore, six of the robust democratizers—Benin, Bulgaria, Cyprus, Ghana, India, and Mauritius—have substantial Muslim minorities. Thus, Islam should be regarded as the source of special challenges, rather than an insuperable barrier, to successful democratization.

Fuels dependence normally changes slowly or hardly at all. But it *can* change quickly and in a manner that facilitates robust political opening. Mexico and Indonesia furnish examples. In 1990, hydrocarbons accounted for 44 per cent of Indonesia's export income and 38 per cent of Mexico's; in 2004, the figures were down to 18 and 12 per cent, respectively. This transformation, which is rare, may help explain the success of political regime change. Among the robust democratizers, Indonesia and Mexico are the two great latecomers. Each experienced a major improvement in its FHI only at the end of the 1990s, later than all of the other robust democratizers. But both have weathered formidable challenges in recent years without reverting to authoritarianism. Democracy came late, but stuck after it arrived, and the sharp decline in fuels dependence may have facilitated this auspicious outcome.

This result prompts us to speculate about what might happen if fuels-dependent countries whose democratization failed manage to 'outgrow' oil as Mexico and Indonesia did. To assess this, we estimate the probability of democracy failing for different levels of oil dependence. In Venezuela, 86 per cent of export income comes from hydrocarbons, and Venezuela's probability of landing among the failed democratizers was, according to our statistical model, 76 per cent. But if we set the proportion of export income derived from fuels down to 25 per cent, the probability of open politics failing in Venezuela would have been a mere 16 per cent. The practical implications are obvious: a reduction in oil dependence is a great—perhaps the best—hope for democracy's prospects in oil-dominated economies, from Congo-Brazzaville and Gabon to Venezuela and Russia.

What about sex inequality? Our models show that it matters for democratization. If we set the sex literacy gap from its actual 30 per cent down to zero in Pakistan the chance of democratization failing would have been 39 per cent rather than the 51 per cent that it was in fact. Lower sex inequality reduces the risk of failure in democratization. Inequalities between the sexes change slowly. Still, as with fuels dependency, there are exceptions; in some places rapid change has occurred. Examining the data on youth literacy (defined as people aged 15–24) provides a potentially telling glimpse into future prospects. In some places we find marked short-term improvements. Between 1990 and 2004, for example, the gap between male and female youth literacy rates in Tunisia fell from

---

Box 17.3 Key points

- Strong legislatures can act as important bulwarks against relapses into authoritarianism.

- Although difficult to manipulate in the short term, reductions in fuel export dependence would reduce the likelihood of democratic breakdown.

- Gender inequalities are more amenable to political engineering; their reduction would greatly aid democratic consolidation.

18 per cent to 4 per cent; in Saudi Arabia, from 13 per cent to 4 per cent; and in Albania, from 6 per cent to zero. Such trends are heartening, from the standpoint of human welfare as well as for democra-

tization's prospects more specifically. These numbers show that public policy can, under certain circumstances, make a difference in the level of sex inequality even in the short run.

Conclusion

The reversal of democratization is one of the central dramas of contemporary world politics. While many antiauthoritarian breakthroughs held fast, fewer than half of the countries that underwent regime change over the past three decades have really succeeded. In most countries democratization has been tenuous or has failed. What is more, among the three major countries that seemed ripe for political opening at the beginning of the 1990s, only Indonesia experienced a sustained breakthrough. China and Iran remain as closed as they were two decades ago.

As this chapter has shown, several major structural factors influence whether democratization succeeds fully, succeeds partially, or fails. Poverty increases the probability of democratization's failure. So too does a late history of national independence, a large Muslim population, economic reliance on oil and gas, and sex inequality. Yet the relationship between the each of these factors and the outcome of political regime change is only probabilistic. It is not absolute. For example, some countries that are poor, predominantly Muslim, and latecomers to national independence have undergone robust democratization. What is more, structural does not always mean immutable. History of national independence is fixed and religious composition of society very nearly so. But poverty, dependence on hydrocarbons, and sex inequalities can diminish over time, thereby mitigating the risk of democratization's failure.

One structural factor, ethnic fractionalization, is virtually fixed but is also unrelated to democratization. This finding bucks conventional wisdom but matches the conclusions of recent empirical studies (Fish and Kroenig 2006). It is good news for many fledgling democracies with diverse populations. Sometimes conflict among ethnic groups occurs and contributes to democracy's demise, as in Fiji. Still, ethnic conflict is the exception and cooperation the

norm, and fractionalization per se is not correlated with democratization's failure. We find also that a particular institution, the power of the legislature, may mould democracy's prospects. The legislature is important because it may check the arbitrariness of the president or the monarch, who we found to be common culprits in democratization's reversal.

We further found that the other agents that may take part in reversing democratization are not common threats. The military remains a potential problem, but it is less of a threat than are chief executives. Our finding is consistent with other recent works that have noted a diminution of the hazard that armed forces pose to open politics in recent decades (Clark 2007; Hunter 1997). Insurgencies may pose a danger, but among the 10 cases we examined closely, they were the sole culprits for democratization's reversal in no cases and one of two major actors in only two cases.

Interestingly, two agents that are often considered potential threats, the masses and a foreign power, were, in none of the cases we focused upon, a driving force in democratization's derailment. The spectre of popular uprisings, common in the wake of the interwar mass movements in Europe, is not a contemporary problem. Mass uprisings are not uncommon. But in the present-day world they normally push for democracy rather than against it, as in the Philippines in 1986, Ukraine in 2004, and Burma in 2006 (Bermeo 2003; Schock 2005). Similarly, foreign powers were not the central agent in any of the cases reviewed here. To be sure, outsiders have done some meddling. Some of the insurgents in the Central African Republic are from Sudan and Chad. Some of the chief executives who presided over democratization's demise in other countries enjoyed the backing of foreign governments. American support for Jordan's monarchs and Russia's support for Belarus's President are examples. But in no case was foreign intervention the central agent of backsliding toward authoritarianism. The fact is remarkable given how frequently outside intervention blocked democratization in times past, as in the US-and-British-sponsored coup in Iran in 1953, the US-sponsored coup in Guatemala in 1954, the US invasion of the Dominican Republic in 1965, and the Soviet invasion of Czechoslovakia in 1968. Recent decades include such heavy-handed foreign interventions, but usually not against countries undergoing political opening and not for the purpose of reversing such an opening. Perhaps mass uprisings, foreign intervention, insurgencies, and the armed forces posed the greatest immediate threat to open politics during the interwar period or at the height of the Cold War. But in recent times, democratization's chief antagonists are more likely to be clad in cravats than in workshirts, guerrilla garb, or epaulets.

What do our findings imply for democracy's advocates? Acknowledge that economic development, history of national independence, and religious tradition may be important, but they are not destiny. There are enough exceptions to general tendencies in the effects of these variables never to lose heart. Oil is poison; reduce the importance of it in the country's economy or face likely failure in any attempt to democratize. Reduce sex inequalities, even if doing so requires long-term effort and cannot be expected to produce short-term miracles. Fear not the masses or foreign powers. Minimize the political power of the military and the danger of insurgencies, but do not suppose that those with the guns will necessarily be your biggest threat. Fear instead your presidents and monarchs; build strong legislatures to constrain them.

QUESTIONS

1. What does a failed democratizer look like? How might we characterize it?

2. How does a failed democratizer differ from an established autocracy?

3. How might economic dependence upon oil and gas affect the prospects for democratization?

4. How might gender equality reduce the risk of democratization failing?

5. How might a long history of national independence and statehood decrease the probability that democratization will fail?

6. What factors, other than those discussed in this chapter, might affect the probability that democratization will succeed or fail?

Visit the Online Resource Centre that accompanies this book for additional questions to accompany each chapter, and a range of other resources: <www.oxfordtextbooks. co.uk/orc/haerpfer/>.

FURTHER READING

Åslund, A. (2007), *Russia's Capitalist Revolution: Why Market Reform Succeeded and Democracy Failed* (Washington, DC: Peterson Institute for International Economics). This book furnishes a provocative explanation for one of the most momentous cases of democratic failure of modern times, and provides a welcome evaluation of economic as well as political transformation.

Linz, J. J. (1978), *The Breakdown of Democratic Regimes: Crisis, Breakdown, and Reequilibration* (Baltimore, MD: Johns Hopkins University Press). This slim volume remains the starting point for all studies on the failure of democracy. Though it focuses largely on interwar cases, its acute theoretical insights remain relevant for contemporary circumstances.

Posusney, M. P. and Penner Angrist, M. (2005) (eds), *Authoritarianism in the Middle East: Regimes and Resistance* (Boulder, CO: Lynne Rienner). This edited volume provides a wealth of insights on why democratization fails. Its focus on the Middle East, given that the region is often overlooked in studies of regime change, makes the volume particularly useful.

Smith, P. H. (2005), *Democracy in Latin America: Political Change in Comparative Perspective* (Oxford: Oxford University Press). This engaging book holds up theories of regime change to the experience of Latin America. Exemplary in its use of theory to understand cases, and of cases to refine theory, the book provides a wealth of information as well as insights into various theories of democratization. It also probes the possible limits of democratization and the factors that may impose those limits.

Villalón, L. A. and VonDoepp, P. (2005) (eds), *The Fate of Africa's Democratic Experiments* (Bloomington, IN: Indiana University Press). Focusing largely on the effects and the limits of the effects of institutions on democratization, this edited volume provides much insight into the difficulty and tenuousness of many of Africa's experiments with open politics.

IMPORTANT WEBSITES

<http://hdr.undp.org/en/> The Human Development Report, issued annually by the United Nations Development Programme, contains a wealth of data for nearly all of the world's countries on factors related to socioeconomic development and living standards.

<http://genderstats.worldbank.org> GenderStats is an electronic database run by the World Bank that contains data broken down by sex for most of the world's countries.

<www.womanstats.org> The WomanStats project contains qualitative and quantitative information on several hundred indicators of women's status in 172 countries.

NOTES

1. The only countries we do not include are East Timor and Montenegro, which achieved independence only in the current decade.

2. The correlation coefficient (Pearson's r) is a measure of the linear relationship between two variables. Values range between 0 and 1, and a score of .9 indicates a very close relationship.

3. All probabilities and standard errors are computed using CLARIFY (King, Tomz, and Wittenberg 2000; Tomz, Wittenberg, and King 2003).

Part Four

Regions of Democratization

Southern Europe

Richard Gunther

Overview

How does the type of transition affect the prospects for success of a democratization process? The transitions to democracy in Southern Europe in the 1970s followed greatly different trajectories. In this chapter we will undertake an analysis of the political consequences of different types of **regime** change by comparing transitions via 'elite pacts' or 'elite convergence' with those involving much higher levels of mass-level mobilization. We will also determine the extent to which international actors and events, economic factors, as well as social-structural and cultural characteristics were relevant to processes of regime change. We will see that several of these characteristics had a significant short- to intermediate-term impact on democratization, while the impact of others was negligible. In the end, however, all three of these processes culminated in stable and consolidated democratic regimes.

Introduction

The latest global wave of democratization began in Southern Europe in the mid-1970s following the breakdown of dictatorships in Portugal, Greece, and Spain. In each case, the previous non-democratic system was a conservative (if not reactionary) authoritarian regime that sought to depoliticize society at the mass level—in contrast with the totalitarian regimes of Nazi Germany and Stalin's USSR, which penetrated deeply into society in an effort to mobilize the population in support of its revolutionary objectives. These three democratic transitions began at almost the same time, beginning with a coup against the Salazar/Caetano regime on 25 April 1974, closely followed by the demise of the 'colonels' regime' in

Greece on 20 July 1974, and by the death of Francisco Franco on 20 November 1975. And they all culminated in the **consolidation** of stable, democratic regimes by the 1980s.

Aside from these similarities, however, regime transformations in these three countries were remarkably different from one another. Two of them were characterized by the abrupt collapse of an authoritarian regime (that in the case of Portugal was accompanied by a socioeconomic and political revolution), while the Spanish transition unfolded over a period of four years largely within the political institutions established by the former dictator. The consolidation of democracy in Greece took a remarkably short period of time (being completed in 1977 or 1981), while that of Portugal took a relatively long time (ending in 1989). And the Spanish transition continues to be marked by only partial democratic consolidation in one region (the Basque Country), although throughout the rest of the country democracy had been fully consolidated since the early 1980s.

The distinct characteristics of these three transitions and consolidation processes preclude a generic description of a particular 'regional type' of transition, and requires separate consideration of each of them. At the same time, however, differences among these regime-transformation trajectories make possible a comparative analysis that can generate or test hypotheses about the impact of differing patterns of political change on the subsequent style politics in that newly democratic country. This is particularly true with regard to causal claims about the long-term effects of 'pacted' transitions, since Spain is the very prototype of that kind of regime change, while political change in Portugal and Greece unfolded in distinctly different ways.

This chapter will begin with overviews of the distinguishing features of the transitions to democracy in these three countries, including some observations about how the processes of regime transformation affected the conduct of politics for several years after democracy was established. It will conclude with lessons from these transitions with regard to the broad theoretical issues raised in the introductory chapters of this book.

Portugal

First transition to democracy

The starting point for any examination of the transition to democracy in Portugal must be the realization that there was not one regime transformation, but two. The first was triggered by a coup undertaken on 25 April 1974 led by middle-ranking left-wing officers of the Portuguese army. This led to the swift demise of the authoritarian regime initially established in the late 1920s by Antônio Salazar and continued in the late 1960s and early 1970s under Marcelo Caetano (both of whom were university professors by training). Over the following year and a half, however, political developments did not appear to be moving toward the establishment of a democracy, but rather a revolutionary dictatorship under a junta of extreme left-wing military officers.

During that period, political change was accompanied by a full-blown socioeconomic revolution in which large-scale seizures of agricultural properties and nationalization of industries took place. By the end of this revolutionary phase of political change, the **state**'s share of gross fixed capital increased from 18 per cent of GDP to 46 per cent. This was also a period of extreme social and political instability. In the south, landless peasants seized many of the huge agricultural estates predominant in that region and established collective farms, often under the leadership of cadres of the unrepentantly Leninist Portuguese Communist Party (*Partido Comunista Português*—PCP) or groups even farther to the left than the PCP. In the north, in contrast, most farmers owned their own lands, were conservative in their social, economic, and political views, and strongly opposed the revolution. Political violence and repression were common in both north and south, typically manifested in purges and intimidation of political opponents, and the destruction of the offices of rival parties. The summer of 1975 was characterized by extreme polarization between leftist revolutionaries in the south and conservative peasants who were mobilizing in the north. And there was no progress towards democratization. Indeed, at that time there were four or five times as many political prisoners as had occupied Portuguese jails under Caetano (Robinson 1979: 220).

Second transition to democracy

The second transition was initiated on 25 November 1975 by a coup by more moderate, high-ranking military officers under the leadership of General Antônio Ramahlo Eanes. It must be noted that this was not a counter-coup by right-wing officers; the new government was dominated by military officers who wished to preserve 'the conquests of the revolution,' rather than revverse the expropriation of agricultural and industrial properties by returning them to their former owners. Nonetheless, the new military government quickly stabilized the political atmosphere, ended the revolutionary turmoil, and entered into a series of pacts with civilian party leaders that made possible the establishment of a democratic system. While this was a decisive step toward the establishment of public order and a democratic regime, this coup can also be interpreted as the restoration of the proper military 'chain of command' by what political scientist Alfred Stepan calls the 'hierarchical military' over a military junta made up largely of colonels (see Linz and Stepan 1996). As in the case of Greece (which follows), it was easier to topple an authoritarian regime led by middle-level officers (whose political authority over higher-ranking officers must have been deeply resented) than would be the case of several Latin American authoritarian regimes (especially in Chile and Argentina) whose governing elites were generals at the top of the military hierarchy.

Nonetheless, in both the Southern Cone of Latin America and in Portugal, 'extrication of the military' from politics would prove to be a difficult aspect of the democratization process. Over the first seven years following the November 1975 coup, the military continued to exercise a tutelary role (through the Council of the Revolution, which had the authority to rule on the constitutionality of all legislation) that violates our definition of democracy (see Chs 2 and 3 above). Moreover, provisions in the 1976 constitution imposed by the outgoing Armed Forces Movement placed important sectors of public-policy making 'off limits', in an attempt to make permanent the 'conquests of the revolution'.[1] Accordingly, the transition to democracy could not be regarded as fully completed until two important steps were taken: the first of these was a constitutional reform in 1982 that eliminated the military-dominated Council of the Revolution, and the second was another round of constitutional reforms in 1989 that made it possible for democratically elected governments to denationalize properties that had been confiscated during the revolution. It is important to note that this final step also coincided with the full consolidation of Portugal's democracy. With this constitutional revision, all major parties except the rapidly declining and increasingly irrelevant Communist Party accepted the regime and all of its key institutions as fully legitimate frameworks for democratic contestation.

Reasons for democratic transition

How can we explain this democratic transition? And what were some of its consequences? Clearly, answers to these questions must differentiate between the revolutionary phase and that which followed Eanes's counter-coup of November 1975. With regard to the revolutionary period, there were multiple consequences, some of which continue to characterize Portuguese politics today. The most important is that the major parties today are not ideologically distinctive, and the social-structural anchoring of partisanship is very weak (see Gunther and Montero 2001). These features are the consequences of the revolution's disruption of the normal processes of party development. Following nearly five decades of authoritarian rule, only the PCP (which existed in clandestinity under Salazar and Caetano) was institutionalized and had a clear-cut ideology (Marxist-Leninist). All the other parties were passing through critical stages of institutional development as the revolution was raging on. Most important of these were the Socialist Party (*Partido Socialista*) and the conservative Party of the Social and Democratic Centre (*Centro Democrático Social*, CDS)—both founded in 1974—and the centre-right Popular Democratic Party (*Partido Popular Democrático*, PPD), which grew out of the more liberal segments of Salazar's *União Nacional* following the partial regime liberalization initiated by Caetano.

Several aspects of the revolution influenced party development. The first is that no parties of the right would be tolerated. An embryonic Christian Democratic Party (Partido da Democracia Cristã, PDC) was banned outright by the military junta, and the other parties shifted their ideologies and public images much farther to the left than their founders had intended or their electoral clienteles would have liked. In particular, both the PPD and CDS presented themselves as parties much farther to the left than their subsequent behaviour would justify. As Richard Robinson (1979: 228) writes, '[t]he PPD sought to project a more leftist image to avoid marginalization in Lisbon and therefore survive as a national grouping offering shelter to conservatives'. Accordingly, it remained within a government coalition with both the Socialist and the Communist Party until mid-July 1975. Even more remarkably, it applied for membership in the Socialist International—which was rejected because the Socialist Party had already been recognized by that body. In 1976, the PPD renamed itself the Social Democratic Party (PSD), even though its subsequent programmatic orientation would be of the centre-right. Similarly, the CDS adopted a centrist and somewhat social-democratic name (the Social and Democratic Centre) despite the fact that it received electoral support from many right-wing refugees from Portugal's former overseas colonies, and would subsequently adopt much more conservative political stands. In short, even though the Portuguese electorate is the most conservative and religious of the four southern European countries, its **party system** lacks a Christian democratic party and, initially at least, even any conservative party options. By the time the revolutionary turmoil had subsided, and these parties would take up their current ideological orientations, the left-right division within Portuguese politics had been substantial-ly blurred. A long-term consequence would be a low barrier between the principal party of the left (the Socialist Party) and of the right (the PSD), and Portuguese voters shift across that bloc boundary much more frequently and extensively than the voters of any other west European country.

The temporary circumstances of the revolution also blurred the partisan image and the cleavage anchoring of support for the Socialist Party. Despite the fact that the religious cleavage had been deeply divisive in Portuguese politics throughout the nineteenth and early twentieth centuries, there is virtually no religious cleavage that affects electoral behaviour in Portugal today. In part, this is because the Catholic church collaborated with the Socialists as the principal bulwark against the revolutionary turmoil of the far left. Similarly, the close collaboration between the Socialists and the centre-right PSD further undermined the image of the Socialist party as of the left. This not only included collaboration in coalition governments, but it also even affected the development of a non-communist trade union. In most other west European countries, Socialist and communist parties would form their own trade unions, at least in part to function as a 'transmission belts' of electoral support from the working class. The hegemonic position of the Communist Intersindical, the PCP-dominated labour union federation, however, combined with fear of a working-class revolution, led the principal parties of the centre-left and centre-right—the PS and the PSD—to jointly establish a single trade union. Thus, a usually important institutional link between the Socialist party and the working-class is very weak in the case of Portugal.

Characterizing the post-revolutionary phases of the Portuguese transition is somewhat more complex. As will become clear when we deal with the case of Spain, Portugal's democratic transition is hardly an example of a 'pacted transition'. Nonetheless, close collaboration among rival parties and the negotiation of a number of crucial political agreements played an important role in establishing Portugal's democracy. Political scientist Lawrence Graham (1992) views the Portuguese transition as moving forward through a series of partial pacts or 'elite settlements'.

The first of these was signed during the course of the revolution itself, on 11 April 1975. This

Box 18.1 Consensually Unified Elites and Elite Convergence

A 'consensually unified elite' (as defined by John Higley) is one in which there are overlapping and interconnected communication networks encompassing all or most elite factions; no single faction is dominant; and most elites have substantial access to decisionmaking (Burton, Gunther, and Higley 1989: 11). When this structural integration and value consensus supports a democratic political system, this consensual unity constitutes a core element in democratic consolidation. How is this achieved? One way is via 'elite settlements' or inclusionary pacts, as described above. Another pathway to democratic consolidation is via 'elite convergence,' in which a formerly anti-system party or movement in a new democracy concludes that pragmatic adjustments in its ideology and behavioural norms are necessary in order to come to power through peaceful, democratic means. Realizing that the majority of voters will oppose the party, as long as it retains its anti-system stance and radical ideology, the party moderates those positions and fully embraces the legitimacy of the existing democratic regime, its core institutions, and its behavioural norms.

agreement between the Armed Forces Movement and the major parties established the notion that civilian and military affairs should be kept separate. A second agreement was signed on 16 February 1976 which recognized a single national assembly composed of democratically elected political party representatives, committed the signatories to electing a president by means of universal and direct suffrage, and confined military influence to a Council of the Revolution in which counsellors elected by the Armed Forces were given constitutional oversight authority. Perhaps the most important of these pacts were signed in the early 1980s. One of these culminated in the 1982 constitutional revision that abolished the Council of the Revolution, transferring its constitutional oversight functions to a new, civilian Constitutional Tribunal. In that same year a national defence law was promulgated that established civilian supremacy over the military. Finally, an agreement was reached in 1989 among all major parties except the PCP that eliminated the constitution's clauses prohibiting the privatization of firms

Box 18.2 Key points

- Portugal underwent two very different transitions: one from a right-wing authoritarian regime to left-wing revolutionary turmoil, and the other to a stable democratic system.

- This complex process of change delayed and complicated the completion of the transition and consolidation processes.

- A series of 'partial pacts' contributed to the successful outcome of this process.

and properties nationalized during the revolution. As noted above, this completed Portugal's transition to democracy by placing all sectors of public policy under the control of electorally accountable officials, while removal of these objectionable clauses from the constitution eliminated all doubts or other sources of semi-loyalty towards the regime on behalf of the major political parties.

Greece

The second of these Southern European democratic transitions was the shortest, and the democratic regime brought into existence was the most quickly consolidated. In part, this is a reflection of the weakness of the regime established by 'the colonels' following their coup. Among all of the authoritarian regimes of Southern Europe, the Greek colonels' was the shortest lived—seven years (1967–74) instead of the nearly four or five decades, respectively, of the Franco and Salazar/Caetano regimes. It also had the narrowest and weakest base of support, and faced the most uniformly hostile citizenry of any of these countries. Not only was it a non-hierarchical military regime established and led by junior officers (which threatened and alienated many senior officers through a wave of purges in 1967–68), but it also relied on a power base strictly limited to the army. Many officers in the navy and airforce even participated in an abortive counter-coup in December 1967. It was not supported by any civilian political parties. Its appeal for unity in the face of an alleged communist threat failed to attract any prominent civilian politicians or parties, despite the intense anticommunism of the previous exclusionary democratic regime (1945–67). And it was increasingly opposed by those on the centre and left, particularly in the aftermath of the brutal suppression of students at the Athens Polytechnic in 1973. Indeed, following that event the regime shifted even farther toward the right, further alienating the regime from society and even the military high command.

The Cyprus conflict as trigger of transition

The trigger for the collapse of the colonels' regime was a major international crisis surrounding the Turkish invasion of Cyprus. Following decades of tension and conflict between Greek and Turkish Cypriots, the Turkish army invaded Cyprus in July 1974, swiftly overrunning much of the country. In response, Brigadier General Ioannides (the hardliner who had assumed leadership of the Greek junta the previous year) ordered a general mobilization of the Greek army to prepare for war with Turkey. At this point, the military high command—fully aware that the Greek army would be destroyed in a major war with Turkey—stepped in and dismissed Ioannides. Rather than seeking to establish a military dictatorship following this coup, it sought out a civilian political figure who might more effectively stabilize and reunify Greece.

The role of Karamanlis in transition

Konstantin Karamanlis (a former Prime Minister and leader of the right-wing National Radical Union party in the 1950s and 1960s) was invited to form a government and lead the transition to a new regime. Karamanlis had impeccable anti-communist credentials, and the military rulers who had overthrown Ioannides thought that he would restrict the scope of political change. Instead, Karamanlis went far beyond what the military high-command had intended (Diamandouros 1986: 157), and radically transformed the political system, establishing a fully open and democratic regime.

Karamanlis was given bargaining leverage in his dealings with the military by the grave threat posed by the prospects of war with Turkey. He refused to accept his new appointment unless the military agreed to return to their former military duties and desist from further interference in government. Faced with the dire alternative of a military disaster at the hands of the Turks, the military accepted his conditions. Karamanlis moved rapidly to establish a new democratic regime. He immediately proclaimed that the 1952 constitution was re-established on an interim basis (with the exception of those articles pertaining to the discredited monarchy—which was swiftly eliminated through a 1974 referendum), and that there would soon be elections to a constituent assembly that could revise that document. Reactivating the 1952 constitution accelerated the process of change, which would have been much slower if it had been necessary to draft and ratify an entirely new constitution.

While Karamanlis acted unilaterally, he took care to assuage the concerns of key actors on both the left and the right. He gained the support (or at least passive acquiescence) of the military elite by restoring to their positions most of the former senior officers who had been purged in 1967/68 by the colonels. But the most remarkable transformation of Greek politics resulted from a number of steps taken by Karamanlis that secured support from the left for the new democratic regime. The regime that came into existence in the aftermath of the Greek civil war (1946–49), following the defeat of the communist insurrection, was an exclusionary regime that fell short of being fully democratic. While elections were regularly held, the regime effectively ostracized and marginalized all of those who were suspected of harbouring sympathies for the left. Basic political and civil rights were regularly infringed through such practices as requiring police approval for employment in Greece's large public sector and even for receiving a passport. Clearly, a simple restoration of the *status quo ante* would not only have culminated in establishment of a regime whose **legitimacy** would have been questioned by parties of the left, but would also have violated our definition of a fully democratic system. Instead, Karamanlis quickly freed political prisoners and legalized all political parties, making it possible for the Communist Party of Greece (*Kommounistikó Kómma Elládas*, KKE) and other parties of the left to participate openly in Greek political life for the first time since the end of World War II. Most strikingly, he rescinded all of those restrictions on civil and political liberties that had been imposed in 1948 as a means of excluding communists and the left from participating in politics.

This policy of national reconciliation thus facilitated both the prompt completion of the transition to democracy and its consolidation, particularly among those on the left. But Karamanlis (a politician with origins on the right) took additional steps that precluded rejection by those on the right who might have sympathized with the colonels' regime. While leaders of the junta were tried and convicted for their crimes against democracy and basic civil rights, Karamanlis made sure that the former leaders of the junta would not be so harshly punished as to emerge as martyrs in the eyes of future opponents of the regime: the death sentences for the top three officials in the colonels' regime (Papadopoulos, Pattakos and Makarezos) were commuted to life in prison. This avoided a repetition of the vengeful purges and executions of political leaders that had so greatly polarized Greek politics in the 1920s (paving the way for establishment of the Metaxas dictatorship).

Founding elections and first democratic government

Thus, the new democratic regime got off to an excellent start. It was fully democratic and, for the first time since the early twentieth century, it was inclusionary of all political options, thereby encouraging acceptance of the regime by all politically significant groups. With regard to full regime consolidation, however, there were some problems. The first democratic elections were convened very quickly—which did not allow the long-repressed parties of the left sufficient time to organize—and were conducted under a strongly majoritarian electoral law. Accordingly, the communist KKE and the newly created PASOK (*Panellinio Sosialistikó Kínima*, the Pan-Hellenic Socialist Movement), founded by Andreas Papandreou, son of the former Centre Union Prime Minister George Papandreou) received just 6.7 per cent of the seats in the constituent assembly, while Karamanlis's *Néa Dimokratía* (New Democracy) party benefited enormously from the electoral law's magnification of its 54 per cent vote share into 73 per cent of the seats in the assembly. In reaction to the electoral law's powerful representational biases, as well as to certain constitutional provisions that some regarded as authoritarian and illegitimate, the two main parties of the left occasionally made anti-system statements and initially embraced some extreme policy stands. Moreover, the new constitution was passed with the parliamentary support of only *Néa Dimokratía* deputies.

The left's reservations concerning the new regime were substantially reduced over the following few years. The impeccably democratic and tolerant behaviour of the Karamanlis government contributed greatly to democratic consolidation among those on the left. So, too, did election of a PASOK government in 1981, when it was that party's turn to benefit from the majoritarian biases of the electoral law. By 1981, only the ambiguous stance of the KKE and its Marxist-Leninist rhetoric continued to reflect a lack of complete democratic consolidation. These reservations diminished in significance as the KKE's electoral support declined, and they completely disappeared (symbolically, at least) with the formation of a *Néa Dimokratía*–KKE coalition government in 1989—one which not only stretched from one end of the political continuum to the other, but also included representatives of the two sides in the civil war of the 1940s.

It is difficult to characterize the Greek transition and democratic consolidation in terms of the standard typologies. It was certainly not a 'pacted' transition, since Karamanlis acted unilaterally, without extensive consultation or any explicit agreements struck with any rival political forces. It is noteworthy, however, that extensive discussions among political elites on the left and the right took place in clandestinity throughout the colonels' regime, and the conciliatory stands taken by once rival political groups would help to forge 'consensual unity' in support of the new democracy after the initial stages of the transition (see Karakatsanis 2001). There are clear signs, however, of 'elite convergence' between parties of the left and right following the first elections.

In the first democratic election, ideological maximalists inside of PASOK held sway, and the party adopted a 'Third World' orientation toward foreign policy, regularly denouncing both NATO and the European Community (now European Union). The party also adopted a semi-loyal stance, challenging the legitimacy of the electoral law and some provisions of the constitution. It was resoundingly defeated in both the 1974 and 1977 elections. Following that second electoral disaster, PASOK leader Papandreou decided to adopt the electoral strategy advanced by the more moderate factions of the party (many of whom had origins in his father's Centre Union party) and take the 'short road to power.' Consistent with an 'elite convergence' characterization of the party's behaviour after 1977 (Karakatsanis 2001), the decision to abandon radicalism and

> ### Box 18.3 **Key points**
>
> - Like the second Portuguese transition, the first steps towards democratization involved the reassertion of authority by top military commanders over a non-hierarchical military junta.
>
> - Decisions of a single political leader, Konstantin Karamanlis, made decisive progress in re-establishing democracy and bridging a deep cleavage between the once-dominant right and the marginalized left.
>
> - 'Elite convergence' contributed to a full embrace of the new regime by the parties of the left.

semi-loyalty was taken in large measure to enhance the party's appeal to the majority of Greek voters. The success of this strategic reorientation can be seen in its 1981 electoral triumph (in which it won 48 per cent of the vote and 58 per cent of parliamentary seats). This not only entailed the adoption of a fully loyal stance toward the new regime, but it also reflected the party's conversion into a moderate, catch-all party, which continues to characterize PASOK today.

Spain

Elite pact as main feature of transition

There can be no doubt about how to categorize the transition to democracy in Spain. It was 'The Very Model of the Modern Elite Settlement' (Gunther 1992), the clearest manifestation of which could be seen in the process of drafting and ratifying a new democratic constitution during the period August 1977 to September 1978. Inclusion of all nationwide parties—from the communists on the left, to their former Franquist enemies in *Alianza Popular* on the right—within what Spaniards called 'the politics of consensus' not only led to overwhelming popular support for the new democracy, but also cemented patterns of mutually respectful and, indeed, cordial

elite interactions that greatly facilitated the laying to rest of historically divisive cleavages. These same co-optive procedures were employed in negotiations over regional autonomy statutes for Catalonia and the Basque Country in 1979, but only with partial success in the latter case. This has culminated in a fully consolidated democracy nationwide, except for the partial exception of the Basque region. Aside from the political party linked to the Basque terrorist organization ETA (*Euskadi Ta Askatasuna*, Basque Homeland and Freedom), whose name has been repeatedly changed following its banning for illegal activities, no party is disqualified as an untrustworthy contender in politics. Indeed, with the exception of the supporters of that anti-system party, no politically significant organization or sector of the Spanish public denies the legitimacy of the regime or regularly violates its rules of the game. In short, the Spanish transition was of intermediate length (beginning with Franco's death in November 1975 and ending with ratification of the Basque and Catalan autonomy statutes in October 1979), and it was highly successful, leading to nearly complete democratic consolidation by about 1982. As we shall see, the frequent reliance on elite pacts clearly differentiated this transition from the two others that unfolded in Southern Europe at about the same time.

However, this is not the only distinguishing feature of the Spanish transition. Unlike the abrupt collapse of the right-wing authoritarian regimes of Portugal and Greece, the most decisive decisions in Spain's democratization process were made within the institutions and procedures established by Franco himself. His hand-picked successor, King Juan Carlos I, served as Head of State throughout this process, and the crucial, initial decisions that culminated in the convening of the first democratic election (in June 1977) were ratified within Franco's corporatist Cortes and by a popular referendum, both of which were established within the legal framework of the Fundamental Laws of the Franco regime. It is noteworthy that this outcome is hardly what the aged dictator had in mind; indeed, he had stated that following his death things would remain 'well tied up' [atado y bien atado].

No one could have anticipated that crucial roles in dismantling the old regime and establishing a democratic system in its place could have been performed by individuals with such strong roots in the Franco regime. Aside from the King, these included Adolfo Suárez (appointed Prime Minister by Juan Carlos in July 1976 after having served as secretary general of the National Movement [the Franco regime's single party] and, under Franco, head of the national radio and televisions networks) and Torcuato Fernández-Miranda (appointed President of the Cortes and of the Council of the Realm by Juan Carlos shortly after Franco's death, and whose previous service to the authoritarian regime included leadership of the National Movement, 1969–73, and brief service as Prime Minister following the assassination of Franco's close collaborator Luis Carrero Blanco in December, 1973). Nonetheless, the three of them exercised impressive political skill in dismantling

the authoritarian system using its own rules, procedures and institutions.

Backward legitimacy

This institutional continuity has several positive implications for the success of the transition and consolidation processes. Overall, as described by Giuseppe Di Palma (1980), the transition effectively inherited 'backward legitimacy' and its propriety could not be challenged by those on the right. Indeed, survey data found that respondents who were sympathetic to the Franco regime—even those who described themselves as *Falangistas*—strongly supported Suárez's political reform project, with over 93 per cent of them voting 'yes' in the 1976 referendum on the Law for Political Reform. Similarly, the acquiescence of the military (whose officer corps had been socialized in military academies to oppose liberalism and democracy) was secured through their obedience to their duly authorized commander in chief, the king. This particular role proved to be of extraordinary importance in February 1981, when an attempted coup initially succeeded in capturing nearly the entire elected political elite at gunpoint in the Congress of Deputies; all but one of Spain's regional military commanders obeyed Juan Carlos's orders to remain in their barracks (delivered through a series of telephone calls and over television), and that one rebellious Captain General quickly surrendered following the collapse of the coup.

Aside from overcoming resistance to the transition from the military and the far right, this institutional continuity contributed to the legitimation of the new regime among conservative sectors of the polity. Endorsement of the new constitution by Manuel Fraga (founder of the right-wing *Alianza Popular*) was particularly crucial in this respect. Finally, continuity of personnel and procedures within the judiciary and state administration (which were not purged, since the Franco regime had not overtly politicized them) meant that this uncertain process of regime change could unfold within a relatively stable environment and under generally competent and efficient performance of government institutions.

But while this backward legitimacy may have helped to enlist support for the regime on the part of those on the right, it was necessary to reach out to the formerly clandestine parties of the left (*Partido Comunista de España*, PCE, and the *Partido Socialista Obrero Español*, PSOE), as well as once harshly suppressed Catalan and Basque nationalists. The 'politics of consensus', through which consensual agreements were reached over a new constitution and statutes of autonomy for Catalonia and the Basque Country, culminated in an elite settlement that not only consolidated the new democracy, but also laid to rest traditionally divisive cleavages over the monarchy, church-state relations, the structure of the state, and other matters that had given rise to a terrible civil war earlier in the twentieth century.

This particular style of pact-making included several crucial features: (1) tactical demobilization of street protests and unnecessary strike activity in order to avoid potentially polarizing street confrontations and to give elite negotiations a chance to succeed; (2) inclusion of representatives of all politically significant parties in face-to-fact negotiations; (3) at the same time, keeping the number of participants in these negotiations down to a manageable number; (4) deliberation behind closed doors; (5) restraint and mutual respect among elites; and (6) a modified version of the 'mutual veto'.[2] What is interesting to note is that the exception to these patterns 'proves the rule': Basques were not included in the initial negotiations over a new constitution, and there was no tactical demobilization of protests in the Basque region; accordingly, the mainstream Basque Nationalist Party abstained from parliamentary and referendum votes on the constitution and has maintained a semi-loyal stance ever since, while other Basque nationalist groups overtly opposed the new constitutional order. Polarization, only partial regime consolidation, and political violence in that region were the ultimate results.

Inclusion of all politically significant groups in direct face-to-face negotiations facilitates conflict resolution in several ways. First, it makes it possible for all relevant positions to be articulated in the negotiation process. Exclusion of a significant point of view might lead to a decision that is out of keeping with true majority preferences on important issues, thereby increasing the probability that the excluded group might reject the outcome of the deliberations on substantive grounds. Moreover, direct involvement in face-to-face negotiations gives the bargainers a sense of 'ownership' of the resulting decision, while exclusion may lead to a rejection of the process as illegitimate as a matter of principle. **Participation** in these negotiations also helps to convince representatives of the various groups that compromise was the only way to attain even some of their initial demands. Finally, a successful outcome of these talks can forge amicable personal ties among participants.

The new democratic constitution

All of these dynamic processes were at work throughout the negotiations over the first draft of the constitution (August 1977 through April 1978) by an ad hoc sub-committee of the Congress of Deputies' Constitutional Committee, which included representatives of the right wing *Alianza Popular*, the Spanish Communist Party, the Socialists, the governing centrist *Unión de Centro Democrático* (UCD), and the principal Catalan nationalist party. In the end, those groups all enthusiastically supported the constitution and have maintained full loyalty to the new constitutional order ever since. Moreover, warm interpersonal ties were developed among most of them, including across formerly deep ideological divides.

No representative of the Basque Nationalist Party (*Partido Nacionalista Vasco*, PNV), however, was included in these sub-committee deliberations, and that otherwise centrist party has maintained a semi-loyal stance ever since. One could further speculate that exclusion from this crucial decision-making arena implied that parliamentary channels for the articulation of Basque demands had been restricted, so that street protests would be the logical alternative means of influencing the transition. Unfortunately, that set the stage for a self-reinforcing series of confrontations that contributed to polarization of a wide array of political attitudes in the Basque Country. In short, the dialectic of rocks, clubs and tear gas that unfolded in the streets—with ETA sympathizers as *agents provocateurs* and sometimes heavy-handed police as their unwitting partners—often swept up formerly apathetic or moderate observers into the fury of angry conflicts. Continuing ETA assassinations of political and military elites outraged citizens and political leaders in other parts of Spain, further poisoning the political atmosphere.

While inclusion of all politically significant groups in face-to-face negotiations is important, the number of participants should not become excessive. Decision-making is easier when the number of participants is reasonably small, as numerous experiments in social psychology have demonstrated. Larger groups tend to dissolve into debating societies and reach decisions only with great difficulty. The seven-member constitution-drafting sub-committee, as well as the eight party representatives who deliberated over unresolved and potentially explosive articles of the constitution on 22 May 1978, both conform to this norm. Conversely, public deliberations in the plenary session of the much larger Constitutional Committee of the Congress nearly undid the carefully crafted compromises that had been forged by the sub-committee, necessitating the emergency deliberations of 22 May.

Politics of consensus

Other things being equal, negotiations conducted in private rather than in public facilitates the making of concessions, which are essential for the compromise resolution of divisive conflicts. Privacy helps to shield politicians from criticism by their constituents for 'selling out' their interests to the opposition. Conversely, politicians who are being directly observed by journalists or live on television will be inclined toward intransigence (if not empty 'gestures to the galleries') as a means of shoring up their base of support. The private sub-committee negotiations of August through November 1977 reached broad inter-party agreement over most of the constitution. Following a leak to the public of that document in December, however, various interest groups and ideological factions within parties (particularly within the governing UCD) were mobilized, and 'the problems began', as described by the Socialist representative on that sub-committee. The governing UCD, in particular, backed away from some of its previous concessions to the left, siding with the more conservative *Alianza Popular* in what was shaping up to be a straightforward clash between left and right. Resumption of private negotiations in January 1978 after the first of the year helped to restore many compromise agreements, but when public deliberations

in the full Constitutional Committee began in the spring of 1978, polarizing conflicts erupted and majoritarian voting by the two parties to the right of centre threatened to undo the broad interparty agreements that democratic consolidation would require. Only the restoration of consensus in another round of private negotiations on 22 May, and a decision to conduct all subsequent negotiations over serious matters in private, made possible the overwhelming consensual endorsement of the constitution in both the Cortes and the December 1978 referendum by parties of the left (including the communists) and of the right (including *Alianza Popular*).

There were many critics who strongly disapproved of these private negotiations as a means of addressing potentially divisive political issues. Some have even regarded foundational pacts as efforts to establish a democracy through undemocratic means. I strongly disagree. As long as elected representative are held publicly accountable for their historical decisions, it does not make much difference how they make them. What matters is that the substantive outcome of these decisions is acceptable to all politically significant groups and that the resulting democratic regime is widely regarded as legitimate.

The last two elements of 'the politics of consensus' involve behavioural norms among politically significant elites. Most importantly, these included restraint and mutual respect, as well as an understanding that the constitution should not include any provisions that would be unacceptable to a significant group or sector of Spanish society. Both of these crucial elements were a product of the ways in which Spanish elites chose to use 'historical memories' of failures of the past, particularly the polarization and collapse of the Second Republic (1931–36) which plunged Spain into a tragic civil war (1936–39) from which an authoritarian dictatorship emerged. The elites, ranging from leaders of the Communist Party to officials in the church, were well aware that a repetition of past patterns of behaviour (characterized by partisan rancour and an extreme form of majoritarianism, in which even governments that fell far short of receiving a majority of popular votes implemented maximalist versions of their ideological and policy preferences) could culminate in a stillborn democracy, or worse. This awareness of the past was reflected in two key characteristics of elite behaviour.

The first of these is quite paradoxical. It is the *pacto del olvido*—a de facto 'pact of forgetting' the horrible acts performed by the two sides in the 1930s (Aguilar 2001). In sharp contract with the 'truth and reconciliation' processes that some scholars and politicians believe essential for establishing democratic regimes in societies emerging from a period of violence and/or repression, Spanish elites consciously and explicitly chose to avoid digging up old horror stories and blaming the other side for past deeds. There was a general understanding that both sides were responsible for plunging Spain into a brutal civil war, and that pardon should be magnanimously extended by all to their former enemies. This greatly facilitated the creation of an elite sub-culture of tolerance and mutual respect across traditionally divisive political lines.

The second manifestation of this interpretation of history is more obvious and straightforward: elites exercised great restraint in expressing themselves and articulating the defence of their respective interests. The church was the first to signal a major change: it went so far as to adopt a resolution (at a 1971 conference of bishops and priests) formally apologizing for the polarizing role it had played in the 1930s, and the Episcopal Conference made an explicit decision to abstain from active involvement in politics—by avoiding any institutional ties to political parties or direct involvement in negotiations over the new constitution. At the other end of the political spectrum, the Communist Party was extraordinarily restrained and cautious, both in pressing its constitutional demands and in the rhetoric it adopted in the course of electoral or more generally partisan conflict. Finally, there was a widespread understanding that no party should push its maximalist demands, but should be prepared to make concessions in the interest of securing broad consensual support for the new regime. As described by the Socialist representative on the constitution-drafting sub-committee (Gregorio Peces-Barba [quoted in *El Socialista*, 7 May 1978]), the overall goal of the constituent process was 'not in being in agreement with everything, but that the constitution would not contain any aspect which would be absolutely unacceptable to any political group'.

In the aftermath of the overwhelming success of 'the politics of consensus' in securing nearly universal support for the new democracy that the 1978 constitution brought into existence, these same principles were used to address crucial issues relating to the 'second transition' following the end of the Franco regime—decentralization of the state. While the Catalan and Basque regions (among others) had enjoyed considerable self-government authority at various points in the past, the Franco regime eliminated all vestiges of local autonomy, culminating in one of the most rigidly centralized states in the world. He also harshly suppressed all manifestations of Catalan or Basque nationalism, even extending to the banning of the public use of those languages and of dancing the Catalan *sardana*. This only served to intensify regional-nationalist sentiments and resentment of the crude Spanish nationalism that the Franco regime sought to foster. But the structure of the Spanish state has been a frequent source of polarizing political conflict (culminating in no less than six civil wars), and there was widespread concern that reopening these issues in the late 1970s could lead to a resumption of violent conflicts between centre and periphery (as political developments in the Basque Country clearly suggested). Given the seriousness of these issues, representatives of the Suárez government, and, on numerous occasions, the Prime Minister himself, chose to negotiate the most crucial aspects of granting the Basques and Catalans statutes of autonomy through private meetings with the highest-ranking leaders of the major Basque and Catalan national-

---

Box 18.4 **Key points**

- The initial stages of the transition to democracy unfolded within the institutions of government of the authoritarian regime itself.

- 'Elite pacts' forged in accord with procedures and norms referred to as 'the politics of consensus' resolved many historic conflicts and culminated in a full embrace of the new democratic regime by nearly all political forces, from far left to right.

- Only the continuing challenge to the Spanish state by an active and sometimes violent minority of Basques represents a regional exception to full democratic consolidation.

ist parties. Once again, the 'politics of consensus' proved to be successful. The resulting two autonomy statutes were embraced by substantial majorities in referenda conducted in both regions, and the somewhat unbalanced *Estado de las autonomías* ['state of the autonomies'—the awkward term used to describe the current decentralized state] has been regarded as legitimate by all Spanish parties, from left to right. Even in the Basque Country, one of the two par-

ties linked to ETA concluded that this was a viable means of realizing Basque nationalist aspirations; it renounced violence, fully supported the legitimacy of the Spanish state and its new constitutional order, and eventually merged with the PSOE. Overall, both with regard to the drafting and enactment of a new constitution and in the course of decentralizing the Spanish state, elite pacts played crucial roles in establishing a consolidated democratic regime in Spain.

Explaining Democratization in Southern Europe

What lessons can be learned from this review of the transitions to democracy in Portugal, Greece and Spain? In this section of this chapter, I will address the major themes set forth in the introductory chapters of this volume, as well as other issues that have featured prominently in the now extensive literature on democratization.

The international context

In one important way, the impact of the international context on all three of these democratic processes was direct and significant. In contrast with the previous wave of democratization (when varieties of fascism, Communism and other non-democratic forms of government had not yet been discredited), by the early 1970s democracy was by and large 'the only game in town'. The three authoritarian regimes of southern Europe stood out as bizarre anachronisms in an otherwise democratic Western Europe. Moreover, given the massive migration of Southern European labourers to more developed affluent economies in the 1960s and early 1970s, a substantial segment of these populations (especially those of Portugal and Spain) were directly exposed to these democratic systems and the comfortable, affluent societies in which they were established. This direct exposure undermined the credibility of the anti-liberal, anti-democratic propaganda of the Franco, Salazar/Caetano and colonels' regimes. A democratic *zeitgeist* was predominant in western Europe, and substantial

segments of the populations of these three countries wanted to be 'like other Europeans', and therefore democratic. This vague longing for change underpinned the transition processes in all three countries, and in general terms helped to channel popular preferences away from potentially authoritarian alternatives. In addition, among informed elites who were aware of the sweeping processes of European integration that promised—and delivered—considerable economic benefits, the fact that the European Community explicitly refused to admit non-democratic countries added an economic incentive to the will to democratize.

In the cases of Portugal and Greece, other international factors played decisive roles in triggering the breakdown of the former authoritarian regimes. In Portugal, the blood-letting and massive economic costs of decade-long wars of liberation in the colonies of Angola and Mozambique made a continuation of the Salazar/Caetano regime, which offered no alternative to continued war, unacceptable. In a more direct sense, these colonial wars transformed the Portuguese army into the agent that toppled the authoritarian regime: since the number of young men who had emigrated in order to avoid the draft seriously depleted the pool for military recruitment, the army drafted many college students directly into the officer corps. They brought with them their radical political ideologies (Marxist-Leninist and beyond), and eventually served as the core of middle-ranking officers who executed the coup on 25 April 1974 coup. Similarly, the Greek transition was triggered by an international event—impending war with Turkey—that moved the military high command to reassert its authority by liquidating the colonels' regime.

Aside from the vaguely pro-democratic sentiments that grew out of the desire to be more like their west European neighbours and the peculiar ways in which international events triggered the collapse of authoritarian regimes in Portugal and Greece, international actors were of marginal relevance in these three transitions. To be sure, the German social-democratic Friedrich Ebert Stiftung gave some assistance to the rebirth of the Socialist parties of Spain and Portugal, but this was largely in the form of strategic advice that had much greater impact on their ability to compete electorally than on the process of regime transformation. In general, none of these three transitions were significantly affected by international democracy-promotion efforts. Indeed, in the case of Greece, continued collaboration between NATO and the colonels' regime was bitterly resented—especially by parties of the left—and this contributed to the temporary embrace of an anti-American, anti-European, Third-World orientation by PASOK in the late 1970s and early 1980s.

Business and the economy

Similarly, there was little positive impact of business elites or economic factors on the democratization processes of these countries. In none of them did economic elites play a prominent visible role during the transition. And unlike the post-Soviet transitions in Eastern Europe, the transition to democracy was not inextricably linked to a far-reaching transformation of the economy.

This is not to say that economic factors were irrelevant to democratic transition or consolidation. In Portugal, the enormous economic costs of the colonial wars contributed to the sense of dissatisfaction that culminated in the 1974 coup. Economic crisis also most likely exacerbated class tensions, eventually contributing to the socioeconomic revolution of the first year and a half following that coup. But in the case of Portugal, once that revolutionary phase of the transition had ended, parties and economic elites

increasingly turned their attention to the complex task of undoing the excesses of the revolution. And in this respect, constitutional prohibitions against reversing the 'conquests of the revolution' prevented duly elected democratic governments from addressing resulting structural problems with the economy, especially those related to inefficient and heavily subsidized nationalized or para-state industries. This resulted in a complex multi-level game, in which international economic forces were used to achieve domestic policy objectives. In a 1984 conversation with a former Portuguese Prime Minister (at a time when negotiations were under way regarding entry into the European Community), it became clear that Portugal was only competitive with other European producers in a handful of sectors of the economy (wine, olive oil, and textiles), and these would be kept out of the Common Market for several transitional years. When asked if under these circumstances a large number of inefficient and uncompetitive firms might be driven out of business by competition from EC firms, the former Prime Minister smiled broadly and said, 'that's precisely the point'. In other words, since the government could not close down or privatize inefficient nationalized industries through its own actions, the EU's prohibition of government subsidies to such firms, coupled with intense competitive pressures that would accompany integration into the Common Market, could achieve the same results.

In the case of Spain, the often posited causal relationship between economic reform and democratization (see Ch. 8) was reversed. Under the corporatist Franco regime, a sizable para-state sector of the economy emerged. Large numbers of firms (especially in declining heavy-industrial sectors like steel and shipbuilding) were partially or fully owned by the state's corporatist holding company, INI (*Instituto Nacional de Industria*). Their inefficiency and the heavy government subsidies needed to sustain them gave rise to a widespread awareness that far-reaching economic reforms were needed, especially if Spain were to be accepted for integration within the European Common Market. However, it was also understood that such economic reforms would generate considerable social tensions, as tens of thousands of workers would have to be laid off and large numbers of industrial plants would be closed down. Prime Minister Adolfo Suárez wisely chose to postpone economic reforms until after the consolidation of democracy had been completed. He believed that an increase in class tensions could increase instability and intensify political conflict over economic issues, thereby undermining the transition to democracy. Indeed, since the transition happened to coincide with a severe economic downturn in the late 1970s, his government chose to *increase* the subsidization of para-state industries and nationalize business firms that were on the verge of bankruptcy. By the time the Socialist government of Felipe González came to power in late 1982, Spain's new democratic regime had been consolidated, so concerns over the political impact of increased unemployment were somewhat abated. In addition, unlike the minority UCD governments of Suárez (1977–80) and Leopoldo Calvo Sotelo (1981–82), the PSOE had a substantial parliamentary majority and was therefore not threatened by parliamentary opposition to its bold reform plans. Accordingly, in 1983 the González government introduced an 'industrial reconversion' programme that restructured the industrial sector by closing down inefficient firms and making the somewhat reduced para-state sector of the economy more efficient and internationally competitive. As expected, this led to a substantial increase in unemployment and intensified class tensions. This did have political repercussions, but these took the form of a divorce between the PSOE and its trade union ally, the UGT (*Unión General de Trabajadores*) and did not threaten the stability of Spanish democracy.

Political culture and society

Political culture and religion were, indeed, important factors in these transitions to democracy, but the roles that they played differed substantially from one country to another. The absence of a tradition of stable democratic **governance** in Spain has often been attributed to political conflict over deep social cleavages (especially religion and regional nationalisms) and the absence of a unifying political culture supportive of democracy. Some classic works have referred to 'the two Spains', although in reality it would be more accurate to speak of 'many Spains'.

Some scholars have partially attributed the polarization and violent demise of the Second Republic more specifically to an elite sub-culture characterized by intransigence, rancour and a lack of commitment to democracy. And Francisco Franco claimed that 'family demons' were embedded within Spain's culture that could only be suppressed by strong authoritarian rule.

While Franco's regime was repressive and caused considerable human suffering (particularly in its early years), it did succeed in demobilizing and depoliticizing Spanish political culture. One negative long-term consequence of this is that political disaffection is widespread, and levels of active involvement with secondary associations are much lower than it is in other West European societies. A positive consequence, however, is that by the time of his death in 1975, the polarization of the past had been greatly reduced. One public opinion survey revealed that about 15 per cent of the population supported the Franco regime, about one quarter were opposed to the regime, while over half of the population—the 'indifferent majority'—was passive, uninformed, and uninterested in politics. At the same time, however, most Spaniards were vaguely predisposed toward a transition to some kind of democratic regime. But they were even more concerned over a breakdown of law and order, as was occurring in neighbouring Portugal, in the throes of its revolution. This lack of polarization and clear definition of political preferences, coupled with vaguely pro-democratic aspirations and a strong desire to avoid a repetition of the violent past, fit well with Spain's predominantly elite-driven transition to democracy. While protest demonstrations during the first six months following Franco's death clearly indicated that a continuation of the authoritarian regime was unacceptable, once the newly appointed Prime Minister Adolfo Suárez indicated his clear intention to democratize, and once inter-party negotiations with representatives of the formerly clandestine opposition began, there was a general 'tactical demobilization' that allowed the elite-level 'politics of consensus' to unfold (Tarrow 1995; Fishman 1990).

Attitudinal support for democracy as gauged by cross-national surveys grew steadily as democracy consolidated, with the percentage of Spaniards agreeing that 'democracy is preferable to any other form of government' increasing from 49 per cent in 1980 to 70 per cent by 1985, and finally in the 1990s to levels that equalled or exceeded those found in most other West European countries. A cross-national comparative analysis in Spain and a number of other young democracies (Gunther, Montero, and Torcal 2007) clearly suggests that support for democracy at the mass level is developed in accord with cues given by partisan elites: in countries such as Chile or Bulgaria, where the outgoing authoritarian elite resisted democratization, supporters of parties with origins in the former regime strongly tend not to hold pro-democratic attitudes; conversely, where the outgoing authoritarian elite constructively participated in the democratization process (e.g. Spain and Hungary), there is no political cultural cleavage rooted in fundamental attitudes toward democracy. In short, support for the new constitution among the full array of Spain's partisan elite (again, except in the Basque Country) appears to have played a crucial role in forging a political culture strongly supportive of democracy. At the same time, and contrary to the 'social capital' hypothesis initially set forth by Robert Putnam, the same cross-national survey analysis found no **correlation** between support for democracy and affiliation with secondary associations— except for explicitly political secondary associations, like political parties (see Ch. 11).

Political cleavages based upon religiosity, regional nationalism, and, to a much lesser extent, social class, continue to influence electoral behaviour. Here, again, these attitudes are to some extent influenced by cues emanating from political elites. This can clearly be seen with regard to the correlation between preferences regarding the structure of the state and stands on that issue taken by various political parties. Not only do survey data reveal a sharp difference between supporters of regional-nationalist parties and nationwide Spanish parties, but even among supporters of the various regional-nationalist parties subtle differences in preferences for the structure of the state (and even in one's own national identity, pitting multiple and overlapping identities against exclusionary and nationalist ones) closely parallel the specific stands taken by political elites. While questions of direction of causality in this relationship make it impossible to determine whether, on the one hand, voters select parties that most closely

accord with their national identities and preferences for the state, or, on the other hand, party elites help to mould such attitudes, an examination of another cleavage gives clearer indications of the significant role of political elites.

Religion has long been a powerful determinant of political behaviour in Spain. To a considerable degree, the civil war of the 1930s pitted anticlericals and non-believers against defenders of the traditional role of the Catholic church. And in the first democratic elections, religiosity re-emerged as the strongest predictor of the vote (after party identification and attitude towards the party's candidate for prime minister). Over the course of the following two decades, however, religiosity greatly declined as a predictor of the vote for parties of the left or right. To some extent, this is the product of a substantial secularization of Spanish society that has taken place since the mid 1970s, with the percentage of Spanish survey respondents describing themselves as 'very good Catholics' or 'practicing Catholics' declining from 64 per cent in 1970 to 32 per cent in 2002. But it was also the result of the strict avoidance of potentially divisive religious issues by Spanish party elites throughout that period. Following the 2000 elections, however, the governing *Partido Popular* (PP) explicitly used religious issues for partisan purposes and the PP government of José María Aznar reinstitutionalized mandatory religious instruction in public schools for the first time since the transition to democracy. Survey data collected in 2004 indicate that this elite-level shift has been mirrored by voters in making their electoral choices: the percentage of the variance in the vote (after the impact of the standard sociodemographic factors have been controlled for) explained by two religious-values variables increased from 0 in 1993 to 15 per cent in 2004. In short, after a long period of decline, the religious cleavage was revived. This provides some evidence that the conciliatory stands on religious issues taken by party elites during the 'politics of consensus', coupled with the political neutrality of the church at that crucial phase of the transition, played important roles in the consolidation of democracy in Spain.

The case of Greece is the least problematic with regard to political culture and democratization. Greek society is largely devoid of politically relevant cleavages over class and religion. Land reforms undertaken in the early twentieth century and the relative absence of heavy industries (most conducive to class formation and working-class organization) are largely accountable for the absence of an electoral impact of class, while the mutual 'ethnic cleansing' that accompanied the massive expulsions and resettlement of Greeks and Turks in the early 1920s made Greece religiously homogeneous. Entering into the current democratic era, however, an ideological cleavage between left and right deeply divided the Greek electorate. This inheritance of the civil war was further deepened by the exclusion of the left from the parliamentary regime of the 1950s and 1960s. Had those exclusionary policies been revived following the ouster of the colonels in 1974, it is likely that whatever parliamentary regime might have been established would have been rejected as illegitimate by a substantial number of Greeks on the political left. Fortunately, as discussed earlier, the national reconciliation policy implemented by Karamanlis from the very earliest days of the transition laid to rest that potential obstacle to democratic consolidation. Finally, Greece leads virtually all other political systems with regard to mass-level support for democracy. While this may be a reflection of Greece's historical role as the ancient birthplace of democracy, it is also most likely a consequence of the brevity of the colonels' regime and its complete lack of credibility and support from the Greek population.

Finally, with regard to Portugal, a clear distinction must be drawn between the early years following the revolution and the more recent period following the transition to democracy. For two reasons, support for democracy was weaker at the outset than it was in the other southern European countries and than it would be in later decades. The first is that the Portuguese Communist Party (which played a key role in the revolution) was explicitly antidemocratic. In the 1970s through mid 1980s it received a significant share of the vote—between 15 and 20 per cent of the total. This stands in sharp contrast with the pro-democratic stance of the Spanish Communist Party and its electorate. The second is that Portugal's democratic institutions at that time were weak and inefficient. Not only did the military continue to exercise tutelage over the political system until 1982, but governments were unstable, fragmented,

and often programmatically incoherent. While survey data of the kind presented for Spain and Greece are lacking for this early period, other attitudinal measures clearly imply a lack of support for the new regime. In a 1980s survey, 39 per cent of respondents said that the changes that occurred after 1974 (i.e. since the collapse of the Salazar/Caetano regime) were 'for the worse', while only 18 per cent regarded them as 'for the better' (with 15 per cent saying there was no change, while the rest were undecided, (Bruneau 1981). Similarly, when asked which was the best government Portugal had up to that time, 35 per cent said either Caetano or Salazar, while a total of only 21 per cent gave the names of all of the other government leaders since the collapse of the authoritarian regime. In sharp contrast, in a 2005 public opinion poll (Portuguese data set, posted on <www.cnep.ics.ul.pt>), 94 per cent of respondents either agreed or strongly agreed with a statement that 'democracy may have its problems, but it is better than any other form of government.' These data clearly suggest that, at the mass level, democracy in Portugal today is fully consolidated.

Finally, with regard to the political impact of cleavages on electoral behaviour and support for democracy, it should be noted that both Portugal and Greece lack any regional or regional-nationalist challenges to the legitimacy of these highly centralized states. And like Greece, Portugal lacks a deep anchoring of partisan preferences in either class or religious cleavages (Gunther and Montero 2001). Unlike Greece, however, this is not the product of mass-level social-structural characteristics. Until very recently, Portugal was characterized by a markedly inegalitarian class structure and by a long tradition of conflict between religious believers and secular or anticlerical segments of society. As described above, however, the behaviour of the two principal parties of the left and right during and in the first decade after the revolution has meant that neither of them has roots in either the class or religious cleavages. Both the Socialist Party and the centre-right CDS are moderate catch-all parties, and voters more frequently shift their support between these two rivals for government power than is found in any other west European democracy. Only the Portuguese Communist Party has an electorate that is anchored in the class and religious cleavages, but its significant decline in electoral support make

---

Box 18.5 **Key points**

- Rather than determining the course of political developments, cultural and social-structural factors represented the sources of problems to be overcome in the course of democratization.

- Business elites, economic factors and (except for serving as triggers for the collapse of the authoritarian regimes in Greece and Portugal) international forces did not play prominent roles in these democratization processes.

- While pressures from 'civil society' in Spain and Greece made clear the extent of public support for political change, mass-level social forces did not play the key roles in those two countries' successful transitions. In the case of Portugal and the Basque Country of Spain, mass mobilizations hindered the democratization process.

---

its vacillating stand toward democracy and the legitimacy of the regime increasingly irrelevant.

Actors: the role of elite pacts

As we saw in the case of Spain, pacts played a crucial role in establishing and consolidating a new democratic regime and in restoring self-government rights to the Basques and Catalans. While there was no comparable 'elite settlement' that simultaneously addressed and resolved all major issues in the Portuguese transition, a series of 'partial pacts' among military and party elites progressively moved Portugal through a complex transition from government by an undemocratic revolutionary junta to consolidation of a fully democratic regime. Conversely, the democratization process in Greece was devoid of formal negotiations among representative elites that culminated in a pact or elite settlement of historically divisive issues. Nonetheless, in all three cases, a fully democratic, consolidated political regime emerged. From this, one obvious conclusion emerges: pacts are not a necessary precondition for the success of democratic transitions and consolidation.

Pacts can, however, contribute significantly to the prospects for success of such efforts. They can stabilize the political environment at times that by their very nature are beset with uncertainty, if not potential polarization and instability. They constitute clear evidence of the firm commitment of relevant political elites to the democratization process (in contrast with the ambiguity that characterized the early stages of reform [*glasnost* and *perestroika*] in the former Soviet Union). This, in turn, can encourage contending forces to demobilize their mass bases of support, therefore reducing the prospects that violent clashes in the streets can further polarize an already divided polity.[3] Finally, they increase the probability that decisions made by political elites will be endorsed and respected by their followers.

However, several scholars argue that pacts constrain subsequent political development in ways that are detrimental to the quality of democracy. In the words of Guillermo O'Donnell and Philippe C. Schmitter (1986: 38)

Pacts move the polity toward democracy by undemocratic means. They are typically negotiated among a small number of participants representing established … groups or institutions; they tend to reduce competitiveness as well as conflict; they seek to limit accountability to wider publics; they attempt to control the agenda of policy concerns; and they deliberately distort the principle of citizen equality.

Other scholars, including Terry Karl (1990), Frances Hagopian (1990), and Adam Przeworski 1991), further argue that pacted transitions result in corporatist or consociational democracies in which party competition is constrained by collusion among political elites who had been the authors of the foundational pacts, that they retard social and economic progress, that they foster clientelism and corruption, and that they limit political competition and access to the policy arena.

Analyses of political developments in Spain, Portugal and Greece over the three decades that followed their respective transitions to democracy yield no support for these assertions. No significant political groups have been excluded from full democratic participation. The only exception is Spain, where those that have actively collaborated with ETA have been barred from the political establishment. There has been no 'freezing' of any particular style of democracy or subsequent output of its decision-making processes. In Spain, immediately after enactment of the Basque and Catalan autonomy statutes in 1979, the 'politics of consensus' was immediately replaced by a markedly majoritarian style of politics (Bruneau *et al.* 2001). Moreover, the decentralization process advanced steadily throughout the following three decades, transforming one of the most rigidly centralized states in the world into a one of the most decentralized states in Europe. In Portugal, unstable, fragmented, multi-party governments of the first decade following the revolution were abruptly replaced by majoritarian competition between one large party on the left (the Socialist Party) and one large party on the right (the PSD). And in the aggregate, despite their common starting-points as right-wing authoritarian dictatorships, all three of these political systems have evolved substantially since the end of their respective transitions. They are now structurally and procedurally about as divergent from one another as the full array of Western democracies (Bruneau *et al.* 2001).

Conclusion

In this chapter, we have seen evidence that the type of regime transition can have a significant impact on the success of the democratization process, at least over the intermediate term. Setting aside the regional exception of the Basque Country, the Spanish transition was initiated within the very governmental institutions established under the former dictator. There was no institutional vacuum that characterized any stage of this regime change. This institutional continuity helped to stabilize political interactions among contending elites, but did not preclude full democratization and the complete dismantling of the former authoritarian regime. More important for the success of the Spanish transition were the norms and procedures adopted by political elites during the course of negotiating the creation of a new constitutional order. Sharing many elements with 'consociational democracy', which several prominent scholars have argued can help to regulate if not resolve conflict in deeply divided societies, the forging of a broadly inclusive elite pact via private negotiations among representatives of all politically significant groups (except the Basques) directly contributed to their prompt and full embrace of the new democratic regime that they thereby created. Evidence of the impact of these quasi-consociational norms and procedures on the course of the transition can be seen in the Basque Country. Not only were Basque political elites not included within the important early stages of negotiating a new constitution, but the principal

arena for political interactions in the Basque region was in the streets, where seemingly incessant confrontations between Basque nationalist demonstrators and Spanish police, all of this accompanied by ETA's campaign of terrorist violence, led to extreme polarization and the absence (to this day) of democratic consolidation within the region.

The Portuguese transition was entirely different, particularly over the course of the first year and a half following the coup that toppled the Salazar/Caetano regime. The widespread mobilization of leftist forces in Lisbon and the latifundist zones of the rural south quickly led to the collectivization or nationalization of agricultural and industrial properties, but it did not move the country towards democracy. Instead, extreme political polarization, harassment of political opponents by both sides, and government by a left-wing military junta greatly complicated and delayed the democratization process, which was made possible only by a counter-coup by high-ranking military officers. Once the revolutionary process had subsided, however, the Portuguese case came to more closely resemble the Spanish, particularly insofar as key steps towards the establishment of a democratic regime involved 'partial pacts' negotiated among party elites. Undoing some of the excesses of the revolution, however, would take well over a decade. Paradoxically, one of the long-term consequences of this revolutionary transition has been the lack of polarization between the two major parties, which had collaborated with each other in the struggle to democratize.

The Greek case is the most unusual, insofar as a resolution of historic divisions (rooted in the civil war of the late 1940s) was achieved largely through the initiatives undertaken by one man. Despite his background as a prominent right-wing politician in the exclusionary regime of the 1950s and early 1960s, Konstantin Karamanlis exercised the nearly unlimited powers handed him by the military high command (which had overturned 'the colonels' regime') to eliminate the discriminatory policies that had marginalized the Greek left from normal social and political life. This, coupled with the dynamics of 'elite convergence' following Karamanlis's overwhelming electoral victory in 1975, led the largest party on the left, PASOK, to fully embrace the new regime within a quickly consolidated democracy.

Strikingly absent from these three analyses is evidence of a substantial impact of economic factors (except insofar as the deep recessions of the mid 1970s to early 1980s further complicated the processes of political change), or of international forces (except for the military confrontations that triggered the collapse of the right-wing authoritarian regimes in Portugal and Greece). And, while all three of these societies had surpassed the threshold level of socio-economic modernization that many scholars regard as a prerequisite for successful democratization, democratic consolidation could by no means be regarded as an automatic outgrowth of the social structures or cultures of these countries. Indeed, in previous decades they had contributed to the polarization and instability that brought about the authoritarian predecessor regimes in the first place. Instead, we must conclude that the success of democratization in Southern Europe is largely explained by the patterns of interaction among political elites—especially party elites—at crucial stages in the process of regime transformation.

QUESTIONS

1. Political elites were extremely important in the Southern European transitions, while mass-level social forces were of secondary importance at best, or, in Portugal and the Basque Country, complicated or impeded democratic consolidation. In Eastern Europe, in contrast, the fall of most non-democratic regimes would not have happened in the absence of massive popular mobilization. What does this tell us about these two different sets of actors? Under what circumstances might one or the other be more important or essential for success?

2. Support for democratization or the development of 'civil society' by international agencies is regarded as important in many parts of the world today, but in Southern Europe governmental or non-governmental international actors were largely irrelevant to the democratization process. Discuss reasons why this might be the case, as well as the implications for international democratization efforts.

3. Some would argue that economic reforms (especially those relevant to the creation or strengthening of market economies) are essential prerequisites for successful democratization, and yet such reforms played no significant role in the democratization of these three countries. Why? And what does this tell us about the relationship between economic and political change?

4. Elite pacts, secretly negotiated, are inherently undemocratic. Discuss.

5. Why is incorporation of all politically significant groups in elite pacts so important for their success?

6. The non-democratic predecessor regimes in Greece, Portugal, and Spain were authoritarian, and not totalitarian or post-totalitarian. Why do you think that would make a difference with regard to the processes of political change in these countries?

Visit the Online Resource Centre that accompanies this book for additional questions to accompany each chapter, and a range of other resources: <www.oxfordtextbooks. co.uk/orc/haerpfer/>.

FURTHER READING

O'Donnell, G., Schmitter, P. C. and Whitehead, L. (1986), *Transitions from Authoritarian Rule: Southern Europe* (Baltimore, MD: Johns Hopkins University Press). This early classic includes overviews of the transitions to democracy in southern Europe by a number of leading scholars (P. Nikiforos Diamandouros on Greece, Kenneth Maxwell on Portugal, and José María Maravall and Julián Santamaría on Spain).

Gunther, R., Diamandouros, P.N. and Puhle, H-J. (1995), *The Politics of Democratic Consolidation: Southern Europe in Comparative Perspective* (Baltimore, MD: Johns Hopkins University Press). Analyses the consolidation of these new democratic regimes, focusing on the roles played by the military, by international actors, by mass mobilizations, by interest groups, by political parties, and by core democratic institutions (with chapters written by Juan Linz, Alfred Stepan, Sidney Tarrow, Philippe Schmitter, Leonardo Morlino, José Ramón Montero, Gianfranco Pasquino and others).

Linz, J. and Stepan, A. (1996), *Problems of Democratic Transition and Consolidation* (Baltimore, MD: Johns Hopkins University Press). Expands upon the arguments they initially set forth in their contribution to the Gunther, Diamandouros and Puhle volume, and place the southern European transitions in a comparative context alongside those of Eastern Europe and Latin America.

Morlino, L. (1998), *Democracy Between Consolidation and Crisis* (Oxford: Oxford University Press). This book further elaborates on the roles played by parties, interest groups and the mass publics in subsequent political developments in these countries.

Diamandouros, P.N. and Gunther, R. (2001), *Parties, Politics and Democracy in the New Southern Europe* (Baltimore, MD: Johns Hopkins University Press). Studies the evolution of parties and electoral politics over the first two decades following these democratic transitions, and pays special attention to both the roles played by parties in the transition and consolidation of southern European democracies and the ways in which the transitions left lasting or transitory impacts on parties and electoral behaviour.

Gunther, R., Diamandouros, P.N. and Sotiropoulos, D. (2006), *Democracy and the State in the New Southern Europe* (Oxford: Oxford University Press). Analyses the impact of democratization on key state institutions (the judiciary, the bureaucracy, sub-national levels of government), as well as public-policy processes and outputs (including social welfare, environmental, and fiscal policies).

Karakatsanis, N. (2001), *The Politics of Elite Transformation: the Consolidation of Greek Democracy in Theoretical Perspective* (Westport, CT: Praeger). This presents the most comprehensive analysis of the transition to and consolidation of democracy in Greece.

Bermeo, N. (1986), *The Revolution Within the Revolution* (Princeton, NJ: Princeton University Press). Presents the most thorough analysis of the Portuguese revolution.

Numerous studies of the Spanish transition include José María Maravall (1982), *La politica de la transición* (Madrid: Taurus), and R. Gunther, G. Sani and G. Shabad (1986), *Spain After Franco* (Berkeley, CA: University of California Press).

NOTES

1 Article 83 of the constitution, for example, states that '[a]ll nationalizations effected since 25 April 1974 are irreversible conquests of the working class'.

2 Arend Lijphart (1977) includes as a key element in 'consociational' conflict management in divided societies the 'mutual veto', in which a single minority group can block a proposal.

3. However, in situations where the incumbent authoritarian elite rejects all prospects of regime transformation, pacts are not feasible, and continued mobilization in the streets may be the only means of initiating democratization.

19

Latin America

Andrea Oelsner and Mervyn Bain

Overview

This chapter looks at the main features of the undemocratic **regimes** that were in power in Latin America from the late 1960s, and the democratization processes that followed since the 1980s. The nature of the non-democratic governments varied throughout the region, and consequently the types of transition and the quality of the resulting democracy varied too. This chapter concentrates on four cases that reflect these differences—Argentina, Chile, Mexico, and Venezuela. For each country, the chapter reviews a number of dimensions that have been relevant in the democratization processes: the historical and international contexts, the role of economic factors, political culture and society, political parties and **social movements**, and the institutional challenges that still lie ahead. Contemporary Latin American democracies face numerous limitations and flaws, but no case of failed democracies currently exist. Moreover, it remains highly unlikely that military regimes will return to the region.

Introduction

Since the wave of democratization started in Latin America in 1978, almost every country in the region has undergone the transition from **authoritarianism** to democracy—the most noticeable exception being Cuba. Before that, by the late 1960s, non-democratic governments ruled Argentina, Bolivia, Brazil, Ecuador, Peru, Paraguay, Mexico, and most of Central America. Although a significant number of these were military regimes, the nature of the authoritarian governments was not the same throughout the region. Neither are the types of transition or the quality of the resulting democracies.

To review the different aspects of the democratic transitions in Latin America, this chapter concentrates on four cases: Argentina, Chile, Mexico, and Venezuela. Argentina offers a case of democracy following the collapse of the military government in 1983. The failure of the military regime in almost every front gave the newly elected democratic government **legitimacy** and room for manoeuvre to carry out trials for human right abuses and introduce a number of domestic reforms and foreign policies aimed to consolidate democracy at home and encourage it throughout the region.

The Chilean military government was similar in nature to that of Argentina. Its approval ratings, however, were higher and the transition to democracy was a longer, more gradual process where former regime members retained much power. Also, Chile was one of the latest countries in the region to move away from a military dictatorship towards a civilian government in 1990—only Paraguay democratized later, in 1993.

The cases of both Argentina and Chile, as well as Uruguay, are typical examples of what Guillermo O'Donnell called **bureaucratic-authoritarian** regimes (O'Donnell 1973). According to O'Donnell, in the Southern Cone of Latin America the military seized power with the proclaimed mission of overcoming economic crises produced by the exhaustion of the model of industrialization via import substitution (ISI) and restoring political order. They charged communism, populism and the organized working classes that emerged under these regimes with hindering economic progress and threatening national security. Thus, political repression and financial discipline were among the recipes implemented by bureaucratic-authoritarian governments. The main features of the bureaucratic-authoritarian **state** are political and

economic exclusion by means of repression and adoption of neoliberalism, and the depoliticization of social and political problems and their reduction to 'technical' issues to be dealt with by bureaucrats, who become top governmental officials.

In 1991, after the disintegration of the Soviet Union, the Institutional Revolutionary Party (*Partido Revolucionario Institucional*, PRI) in Mexico became the world's single longest serving political party. The Mexican experience was somewhat different from those in Argentina and Chile as it was a political party and not the military that held power. Mexico has only moved towards a more transparent system in 2000, ending the PRI's 71-year rule.

As with Mexico, and unlike the cases of Argentina and Chile, power was not in the hands of the military in the Venezuelan experience, but instead after the *Punto Fijo* agreement of 1958 it was shared between two political parties. This situation ended with the electoral victory of Hugo Chávez in 1998. However, in the years since Venezuela appears to be following a very different route not only to Argentina, Chile, and Mexico but also to the rest of the region.

Although there is no clear case of failed democratization in Latin America, this chapter highlights some of the most serious deficiencies that the region's democracies suffer from. Overall, the region remains one of weak political institutions, significant levels of corruption, unequal distribution of wealth, social exclusion, deficient justice systems, and high rates of social violence and criminality, all of which undermine the **consolidation** of democracy. This led Philip Oxhorn (2003: 36) to state there is always the danger that growing levels of social frustration will be vented in either a resurgence of demagogic populism or the re-emergence of extremism on both the Right and Left'.

Argentina + Chile military Rule

Historical Overview

Throughout Latin American history there has been a tradition in many countries for a strong leader or *caudillo* to rule. Despite this, by the middle of the twentieth century elections had been present in Argentina, Chile, Mexico, and Venezuela among

other countries. However, over the next two decades this situation began to change, and while elections continued to be held in Mexico and Venezuela, the systems were anything but democratic. In Argentina and Chile the military had taken courses of action

[handwritten: What made it dark?]

which had not only removed the incumbent presidents from power and replaced them by members of the military, but also resulted in the complete abolition of formal democratic institutions.

The historical impact of the Cuban Revolution

[handwritten: ???]

The victory of the Cuban Revolution and its aftermath was vital, as it resulted in a seismic change in the dynamics of Latin American politics in the late 1950s and early 1960s. A variety of people, not least members of the US administration, were extremely concerned that the ideas underpinning this development might become increasingly popular throughout the region as issues of underdevelopment and poverty continued to affect the lives of many. These concerns were only further increased by both Havana's burgeoning relationship with the Soviet Union—which led to fears of Cuba acting as a bridgehead for possible communist penetration in the region—and the radical foreign policy pursued by the Castro administration throughout the 1960s. It very much appeared as if the status quo in Latin America was being fundamentally challenged.

Argentina

This was most certainly the case in Argentina, where the military had a history of intervening in politics. However, the situation was abruptly changed in the 1970s with the death of Juan Domingo Perón, who had been a popular nationalistic figure throughout the second half of the twentieth century. His death left a power vacuum with the activities of both left-wing groups such as Montoneros and right-wing ones like the Triple A death squad[1] leading to increasing political violence. The situation continued to deteriorate and in conjunction with fears that left-wing ideas may even reach the Presidential palace, especially after Salvador Allende's presidency in Chile which will be detailed later, the armed forces acted on 24 March 1976 to replace Isabel Perón as President with a junta led by General Jorge Rafael Videla, launching seven years of what the military

[handwritten: power vacuum]

coined the 'Process of National Reorganization', or simply, the *Proceso*. Similar action had already taken place in both Brazil in 1964 and Peru in 1968, and although it was taken on the pretence of restoring order, it marked the beginning of the darkest stage of Argentine history.

This period only came to an end in the aftermath of Argentina's defeat in the Falklands/Malvinas war. In 1982 facing increasing economic pressure the junta attempted to rally national support by invading these islands. However, despite the widespread repression, the disastrous defeat in this war only increased this pressure to near breaking point, which led the military government to grant the population their wish of elections, resulting in the electoral victory of the civilian Raúl Alfonsín in 1983.

Chile

On 11 September 1973 the military violently overthrew the incumbent Chilean President Salvador Allende. He had been elected in 1970, with this victory making him the first elected socialist President in the Western Hemisphere. Over the following three years his economic policies and relations with both the Soviet Union and Cuba caused great concern not just for many within Chile but also in the USA. Washington was worried about the appearance of the second socialist regime in the region, as well as about the economic investments of US firms in Chile, which it was feared would be expropriated. In light of this, US President Richard Nixon instructed the CIA to 'make the economy scream', resulting in the implementation of various policies designed to topple Allende's regime (Kornbluh). At the same time, Allende's radical policies had split Chilean society with the Chamber of Deputies in August 1973 calling for his removal. The situation continued to deteriorate until the army acted on 11 September to remove Allende from power. Allende did not survive the attack on the Presidential palace, with great mystery surrounding the actual events leading to his death. The coup heralded a non-democratic stage in the country's history that was to last 17 years.

[handwritten: U.S. tried to undermine socialism]

Ironically it was the military's desire to have a mandate from the Chilean population that led to their eventual downfall. A plebiscite had already been held in 1980, which was to lead Chile towards a protected democracy. In a similar manner to Argentina, despite widespread repression, pressure on the government increased in the early 1980s as a result of economic problems. Protests ceased in 1986 as the opposition instead focused on the 1988 plebiscite, designed to ratify Pinochet as President until 1997, by forming the Coalition of the Parties for No. In effect they made this a vote on the merits of Pinochet's years as President and by defeating him they triggered the staging of presidential elections in 1989, which were won by Patricio Aylwin.

Mexico

Unlike both Argentina and Chile, the Mexican President has always been a civilian rather than a member of the military. Furthermore, Mexico has been characterized by the existence of a unique and distinctive political system. In the aftermath of the 1910 revolution various policies were implemented that were diametrically different from those later pursued by either the Argentine or Chilean military regimes but similar to the ones implemented in the 1970s by Allende's socialist government. This included, among others, agrarian reform and the nationalization of the oil industry. The *Partido Revolucionario Institucional* (PRI) took its heritage from the revolution and it very much appeared as if democracy was flourishing in Mexico, as not only were opposition parties allowed to exist, most noticeably the *Partido Acción Nacional* (PAN) and after 1989 *Partido de la Revolución Democrática* (PRD), but elections took place every six years, which signalled the inauguration of a new president, as constitutionally an incumbent president could not stand for re-election.

However, the reality was notably different. A clientilistic system existed which extended to the presidency, with the outgoing president being able to pick his successor as the leader of the PRI. As the PRI did not even lose a state election until 1989 it meant that he effectively chose the next Mexican president. This, in conjunction with a variety of different methods to manipulate the outcome of elections—the most infamous of which were the events surrounding the malfunction of the computer counting the votes in the 1988 presidential election when the PRI was losing—explains why the Peruvian writer and politician Mario Vargas Llosa described the PRI as 'the perfect dictatorship'.

The PRI came under increasing pressure from this point onwards not least due to an increase in international focus after democratic transitions elsewhere in Latin America in the 1980s and Eastern Europe at the end of this decade. Moreover, the signing of the North American Free Trade Agreement (NAFTA) only brought further attention, making a repeat of the 1988 events unlikely due to the international condemnation that it would receive. The PRI may have won the presidential election in 1994 but its grip on power was lessening as a result of both external and internal pressures and, without being able to revert to its 'traditional' methods, it lost the election in the year 2000 with Vicente Fox of PAN becoming the President of Mexico.

Venezuela

The case of Venezuela has similarities with Mexico, but in many ways is distinctive from the other three case studies. The similarity with Mexico is that democracy would have appeared to have existed in the twentieth century as elections were present, but as with Mexico a closer look may call that into question. In 1958 political instability increased after the electoral defeat of Marcos Pérez Jiménez with a number of attempted military coups being staged throughout the year. In order to quell this unrest and increase stability the *Pacto de Punto Fijo* was signed originally between the *Acción Democrática* (AD), *Partido Social Cristiano de Venezuela* (COPEI) and *Unión Republicana Democrática* (URD) on 31 October 1958. Over time the URD lost influence and in reality a two-**party system** was created whereby power would always remain in the hands of either the AD or COPEI.

This was distinct from the other cases as the pact was signed before the victory of the Cuban Revolution and the impact that it had on Latin American politics. In many ways it can be seen to have been successful, given that for the rest of the twentieth

[handwritten: democratic facade — president able to pick his successor]

Box 19.1 **Key points**

- Since the time of independence Latin America has had a tradition of strong leaders or *caudillos*.

- The Cold War setting and fear after the victory of the Cuban Revolution in 1959 of a 'second Cuba' appearing in Latin America resulted in many militaries seizing power to preserve the status quo, as in Argentina and Chile.

- Mexico and Venezuela may not have been governed by the military in the second half of the twentieth century but their political systems were far from democratic with both providing guaranteed winners.

century the military were mainly kept out of politics, with the noticeable exception of the attempted coup led by Hugo Chávez in February 1992. The result was that Venezuela enjoyed levels of stability not seen elsewhere in the region. This, however, had only been achieved at the expense of the existence of effective and accountable democracy.

As in the case of Mexico after the 1988 election, normality appeared to return to Venezuela after this but internal pressure continued to increase throughout the 1990s. This was despite political reforms, most noticeably direct elections being held for governorships, being implemented by Andrés Velásquez. This in conjunction with continued economic problems resulted in the Venezuelan population becoming increasingly disillusioned with both the AD and COPEI. Chávez, already perceived by many as a national hero after he took sole responsibility for the events of early 1992, took advantage of this desire for change by winning the presidential election in 1998 with over 50 per cent of the vote, ending at a stroke *puntofijismo*.

The International Context

The fact that a global wave of democratization was already underway (see Ch. 5 in this volume) when the Latin American transitions started in 1978 added momentum to them. Yet its influence was by no means decisive. The most influential international factor in the region is the USA, but up until the 1990s its role in its Southern neighbours' democratization was rather ambiguous. A regional contagion effect had a stronger positive impact, whereby political liberalization in some countries encouraged and supported similar demands in others. Additionally, international and regional actors helped strengthen the region's democratization. These include the UN, the Organization of American States (OAS), the Common Market of the South (Mercosur), and to some extent the North Atlantic Free Trade Association (NAFTA), as is discussed below.

During the first few decades of the Cold War, the USA was more concerned with the possible rise of left-wing movements in Latin America than with the democratic records of the region's governments, especially after the Cuban Revolution. Indeed, the promotion of democracy was seen to be less important than security, and it was assumed that military regimes would be more sympathetic to, and effective in, the goal of repressing insurgency. Yet in the 1970s a period of détente followed, when relations between the USA and the Soviet Union improved. During this the US Congress grew increasingly concerned about countries that violated human rights, passing a series of legislations aimed at limiting military and economic assistance to them. Presidents Nixon and Ford succeeded in circumventing Congress' pressure, yet Jimmy Carter proved more responsive to it.

Many West European states also condemned Latin American military dictatorships. For instance, Sweden, the UK, and Belgium temporarily broke or downgraded diplomatic relations with Chile after the 1973 coup, and Chancellor Helmut Schmidt (West Germany), President Giscard d'Estaing (France) and King Juan Carlos (Spain) all repeatedly

Box 19.2 The Ambiguous Role of US Foreign Policy in the Promotion of Latin American Democracy

As it became clear that a Soviet invasion was less likely than socialist revolutions in Latin America, in the 1950s the USA began to promote bilateral military cooperation seeking to strengthen the domestic policing roles of the region's armed forces. After the 1959 Cuban Revolution, weakening anti-US movements and ending the spread of left-wing guerrillas became an even more salient goal for the USA. On a number of occasions the USA resorted to indirect and even direct political intervention, such as the failed 1961 Bay of Pigs operation in Cuba, the deployment of American troops in the Dominican Republic in 1965, the 1983 invasion of Grenada, political and military support to the Salvadorian right-wing regime and to Nicaragua's 'Contras' in the 1980s, as well as to a number of military coups throughout the region—notably in Guatemala (1954), Chile (1973) and Panama (1989).

A change came with the Carter administration's human rights policy (1977–81). This policy ranged from condemning undemocratic regimes to withdrawing military and economic aid. For instance, the USA discontinued military aid to Chile and Uruguay in 1976, and to Argentina,

Nicaragua, and El Salvador in 1978. Such was the change in foreign policy that in 1977 Guatemala and Brazil rejected US aid as a way to repudiate the new American policy. However, Carter's policy failed to make Latin American dictatorships more respectful of human rights and democracy, not least because it did not last long enough to become effective. Ronald Reagan returned to the old policy of endorsing anticommunist regimes regardless of their democratic credentials, only rhetorically promoting human rights. When the region began the trend towards democracy, however, Washington seemed to welcome it.

Since the 11 September 2001 terrorist attacks on the USA, American promotion of democracy may have once again become ambiguous. In April 2002 Hugo Chávez, president of Venezuela, was ousted from power for 48 hours. While the OAS and most regional leaders immediately condemned the coup, not only did the USA fail to reject it but it rather welcomed the new government. Later, US officials even admitted to having had contacts with anti-Chávez leaders and indirectly channelling funds to opposition groups via the National Endowment for Democracy.

---

omitted Santiago de Chile from their visits to the region. However, most were reluctant to take stronger action, as illustrated by the case of Argentine Naval Captain Alfredo Astiz's detention by Britain after the Falklands War (1982). Both Sweden and France could have sought his extradition on charges of torture, disappearance, and murder of a Swedish girl and two French nuns, but by deciding not to do this they forwent the opportunity to further weaken the military junta.

The detention of former Chilean dictator Augusto Pinochet in London at the request of a Spanish court in 1998, when the Cold War was over, shows how things had changed. Due to ill health, Pinochet was eventually not extradited but returned to Chile, yet his detention in London helped to lift 'psychological, political, and juridical barriers to justice by weakening the powerful forces that had blocked trials in Chile since the return to democracy' (Lutz and Sikkink, 2001: 290). Indeed, once back in his own country Pinochet's immunity was revoked several

times (although also repeatedly restored). He faced charges of kidnapping, torturing and killing political opponents, was repeatedly declared fit to stand trial (after being declared unfit on a number of occasions), and was put under house arrest three times between 2000 and his death in 2006. Although he died without being convicted for the crimes committed during his rule, the pressure exerted from abroad and the effects this had on Chileans' attitude towards Pinochet are noteworthy.

International and regional organizations also contributed to democratization in the region, especially in the 1990s. From 1989 onwards, the UN took a central role in peace and democratization in Central America, particularly in Nicaragua, El Salvador, and Guatemala, where virulent and protracted civil wars had taken place. UN activities involved monitoring elections and promoting national reconciliation efforts, as well as mediating between opposing civil war parties, deploying international observers, and sponsoring peace accords.

During the Cold War the OAS had fallen into disrepute in the eyes of Latin American countries due to its inability to restrain the increasing unilateralism of the USA. Throughout the 1990s it started to take action to put democracy back onto its agenda and regain legitimacy, as three key documents reflect. First, Resolution 1080, which established an institutional procedure in the case of 'sudden or irregular interruption of the democratic political institutional process' in a member state (OAS 1991); second, the 1991 Santiago Commitment to Democracy and the Renewal of the Inter-American System; and third, the 1992 Protocol of Washington, which amended the OAS Charter to allow the suspension of member states that suffer a coup. Despite this normative change, the organization's role was only marginal in the cases of the 1991 military coup in Haiti, and the self-coups in Peru (1992) and Guatemala (1993). Its reaction was more decisive during the 1996 Paraguayan attempted coup, when the OAS Secretary General rushed to the capital Asunción and organized an OAS emergency meeting to condemn the event.

Mercosur also played an important part in the satisfactory resolution of the Paraguayan crisis by strongly repudiating the coup attempt and threatening to marginalize Paraguay from regional organization if there was to be an internal constitutional failure. Following this crisis, Mercosur adopted a 'democratic clause', showing that although the organization is mainly a trade association, the preservation and **consolidation** of democracy have been among its early objectives too.

Another regional organization that had a positive, albeit indirect, impact on democracy was NAFTA. Until the 1990s the lack of democracy in Mexico

> ## Box 19.3 **Key points**
>
> - Domestic factors were vital in the democratization process in Latin America, but international ones were also significant, not least the global wave of democratization, which created a positive international environment.
>
> - During the Cold War, the USA's human rights and democracy policy towards the region was characterized by ambiguity.
>
> - International and regional organizations, such as the UN, the OAS, Mercosur, and NAFTA had a positive influence in the spread of democracy in Latin America.

raised little international attention. After all, there had been no military coups, and the country regularly ran elections. However, it was increasingly feared that its weak democratic and human rights record could negatively influence the negotiations on Mexico's **participation** in NAFTA. In this context, and under growing domestic and regional pressure, the government introduced electoral reforms and created a National Commission on Human Rights. Partly as a result of these changes, in the year 2000 the PRI lost presidential elections for the first time in 71 years. More recently, the arguable setback of democracy in Venezuela can be partly explained as a rejection of **globalization**. Faced with increasing political dissent, Chávez has frequently mobilized support by resorting to an anti-globalization, populist and nationalist discourse.

Economic Factors

In August 1982 Mexico defaulted on its external debt. This event not only marked the beginning of the debt crisis, but also caused great concern in Western banking institutions due to the levels of money which they had lent to Latin American countries. In January 1983 Mexico was joined by Brazil with the debt crisis quickly engulfing the whole region. The

effects of this would be felt for a number of decades, but it would also impact on the return of democracy within Latin America in the rest of the 1980s.

Among the variety of different reasons lying behind the debt crisis, the slowdown in the 1970s of the ISI model, which most Latin American countries had employed since the 1950s, was key. In an attempt to reinvigorate this developmental strategy, regional governments had borrowed heavily from Western banks. The 1970s were an ideal time for this as these institutions were very keen to recycle their 'petro-dollars', which they had accumulated since the surge in oil prices prompted by the 1973 Yom Kippur war. The situation was further helped by low interest rates, and thus the majority of Latin American countries borrowed money on floating interest rates, which were considerably lower than fixed rates at this time. This advantageous situation received a further boost from the fact that the loans were conducted in US dollars, which in the 1970s were very weak. The context was so favourable that even Venezuela, blessed with huge oil reserves, borrowed heavily during this period.

However, by the end of the decade the world situation began to change and turn against Latin America. Interest rates increased dramatically—indeed they almost tripled between 1979 and 1982—and new Western leaders emerged; most noticeably Ronald Reagan, Margaret Thatcher, and Helmut Kohl, whose predominant economic goal was to keep a tight control on inflation. Moreover, the US dollar began to increase in value and a world recession reduced the demand for Latin American goods. This scenario, in conjunction with some of the loans not being spent in the most profitable manner and an upsurge in capital flight, resulted in a deterioration of the region's economies. As a result, not only could the original loans not be repaid but Latin American countries could no longer even afford to service them. In an attempt to deal with this situation a further round of borrowing commenced in the early 1980s. The terms of these loans, however, were not nearly as favourable as those of the 1970s. This situation continued to deteriorate until the Mexican government's announcement of August 1982, which marked the beginning of the regional debt crisis.

During the 1980s a number of attempted solutions were implemented, including both the Baker and Brady Plans, and the International Monetary Fund (IMF) and World Bank became increasingly involved in the region. These institutions imposed a variety of pre-requisites for their help, above all the implementation of so-called structural adjustment programmes. The foundation of the programmes was the neoliberal economic model, whereby government spending was drastically cut and trade barriers removed. These policies usually resulted in socioeconomic indicators falling dramatically, but due to gravity of the economic situation governments had few alternatives. Peru under Alan García did try and follow a different route but this was ultimately unsuccessful. Thus, by the late 1980s the neoliberal economic model was the predominant one throughout the region.

In the case of Chile, as mentioned earlier, the neoliberal economic model had been implemented at a much earlier stage than in the rest of the continent. Perhaps as a consequence of many disliking the economic policies pursued by Salvador Allende between 1970 and 1973 the military junta, who certainly disliked it for ideological reasons, instigated this model soon after coming to power in September 1973. Moreover, a number of the government's economic advisers had studied at the University of Chicago, where they had been heavily influenced by the ideas of Milton Friedman. They became known as the 'Chicago boys' and were essential to Chile following a very different economic path from the rest of the

> **Box 19.4 Key points**
>
> - Vast amounts of money were borrowed in the 1970s in an attempt to reinvigorate the Import Substitution Industrialization (ISI) model, which may have been highly successful from the 1950s, but by the 1970s had slowed down markedly.
>
> - As a result of a variety of reasons the 1970s were an excellent time to borrow money as the Western Banking system was awash with 'petro-dollars' from the effects of the Yom Kippur War in 1973.
>
> - World events began to turn against Latin America in the late 1970s and early 1980s, not least the new wave of Western leaders whose primary goal was to curb inflation by increasing interest rates. The upshot was that Latin American countries could not afford to service their loans.
>
> - In the aftermath of the 1982 debt crisis neoliberalism became the predominant economic model in Latin America—in line with the ideas of the 'Washington Consensus'.

↑ interest rates on loans

region. These economic policies also partly explain the high regard which many in Reagan's and Thatcher's governments held Pinochet in. The significance of this would become apparent once he was no longer the President of Chile.

Neoliberal economics is often closely associated with the spread of democracy (see Ch. 8). This combination, which Francis Fukuyama celebrated in his book *The End of History and the Last Man* (1992), was vital in the case of Latin America. Although the 1980s has been described as the 'lost decade' in terms of economics (Roddick 1988) it was most certainly not lost with respect to democracy. As detailed

above, after 1982 the region found itself immersed in the debt crisis. To some extent, the failure to overcome it debilitated some undemocratic regimes and was one of the reasons behind the wave of democratization in Latin America. However, it also debilitated the newly restored democracies. This lack of economic success eventually led international crediting institutions to draft the '**Washington Consensus'**, the conditions of which were attached to new loans of the 1990s. Yet neoliberal economics has also resulted in a number of problems for democracy as amongst other things unequal distribution of wealth has increased within the region.

'Neoliberal economics'

Political Culture and Society

During the various occasions that the military intervened in politics civil society was silenced and excluded from public debate, let alone the decision-making process. The **bureaucratic-authoritarian** regimes of the Southern Cone, for instance, saw organized labour as the cause of economic stagnation and even the source of Marxist insurgency, and consequently embarked on their brutal repression with the aim of depoliticizing, if not dismantling them. Nonetheless, trade unions in Argentina, Brazil, and Chile succeeded in re-organizing themselves and mounted a series of strikes and protests that were key in weakening and destabilizing military juntas.

Other groups also made important attempts to make themselves heard. Some of these succeeded in putting through an agenda that impacted on the processes of democratization. One such group was the *Madres de Plaza de Mayo* in Argentina—the mothers of the 'disappeared' who had been victims of military repression. In 1977 a group of women whose sons and daughters had been abducted by agents of the military government met to organize weekly demonstrations in the Plaza de Mayo, Buenos Aires' central square, demanding information about their missing children. The organization's claims, activities, and overall role during and after the authoritarian rule contributed significantly to pushing the

military out of power and uncovering the extent to which the junta had abused human rights. Probably taking inspiration from the *Madres*, in 2003 a group of Cuban women began to protest against the imprisonment of their dissident relatives. The *Damas de Blanco* (Ladies in White), as they came to be known, can still be seen walking through Havana in white dresses.

Despite the contribution of labour unions and the *Madres* to bringing down the dictatorship, Argentine civil society emerged from the military rule years fragmented and weakened. While organized labour (dominated by the Peronist party) staged a series of general strikes that paralyzed the first democratic government of Raúl Alfonsín and facilitated the victory of Peronist candidate Carlos Menem in 1989, the neoliberal economic model implemented by the latter only weakened their power and that of civil society more generally. The market reforms of the two successive Menem administrations resulted in the privatization of state enterprises and services and deregulation of economic activities, yet also in further deindustrialization, mass redundancies of public employees, growing unemployment, and a dramatic reduction of the middle class. After years of recession, unemployment and corruption, a full-blown economic collapse in 2001 triggered a brief upsurge of new kinds of civil society

Mothers of the disappeared

movements. Ordinary people banging pans and pots in the cities' squares and streets prompted the fall of De la Rúa's short-lived tenure and of a succession of interim presidents in 2002. During that period there were also neighbourhood assemblies putting direct democracy into practice, road blockades by unemployed *piqueteros* who soon organized themselves into a national movement, and the taking over of abandoned factories by former workers, who transformed them into cooperatives.

In Chile, the neoliberal economic model had been applied much earlier. Already by 1975 the government of General Pinochet had successfully implemented it, aided by the open repression of those who opposed it. Indeed, widespread repression prompted the Catholic Church, inspired in the teachings of the Liberation Theology, to create the Vicariate of Solidarity with three main objectives: defend the lives of political prisoners, obtain their release, and help the destitute and the oppressed.

In 1982–83 Chile, along with the rest of Latin America, was beset by an economic crisis resulting from the regional foreign debt crisis. Soaring unemployment figures and a rapidly shrinking middle class gave rise to a powerful opposition movement led by the Copper Workers' Federation, which between 1983 and 1986 mounted a number of mass demonstrations that seriously damaged the military government. Although their force had worn out by 1986—partly explained by the economic recovery that started in 1984—their actions paved the road for political parties' demanding free and fair elections for the 1988 plebiscite. The 'protected democracy' that ensued, where conservative political forces retained extraordinary powers, guaranteed political stability and economic prosperity during the transitional period. Yet by ensuring a favourable business environment, Chilean democracy was unable to effectively address the demands of (admittedly weakened) social groups such as urban and rural labour. However, other groups have felt the benefits of the newly restored democracy. Women's movements have had a number of victories with the creation of the National Women's Service aiming to reduce discrimination in society, the passing of a divorce law in 2004, and the access of women to high political posts—not least the presidency, which Michelle Bachelet won in 2006. Also indigenous peoples, who make up about 3 per cent of the population, saw their situation improve with democratization. After suffering abuse, discriminatory policies, poverty and exploitation during the military government, the main indigenous group, the Mapuches, organized themselves, achieving recognition and protection of their indigenous communities and ancestral lands, as well as the creation of a National Corporation of Indigenous Development that administers indigenous affairs.

Indigenous identity also remains strong in other parts of Latin America. In Ecuador and Bolivia, as well as Central America, it has been at the centre of civil and political mobilization. But perhaps the best-known indigenous organization is the *Ejército Zapatista de Liberación Nacional* (EZLN, the Zapatista National Liberation Army) in Mexico, and the social movement around them. For decades PRI policy towards indigenous minorities sought their assimilation and cultural homogeneity across the country, since this was believed to be a condition for socio-economic development. In the 1980s indigenous groups became more vocal and won some concessions from the government, but it was not until 1994 that their demands for political and cultural autonomy and control over their own resources and land became vociferous—with the appearance of the Zapatista rebellion in Chiapas. Indeed, the debt crisis and the implementation of neoliberal economic policies proved especially hard on indigenous communities. Thus, when Mexico joined NAFTA in 1994 the Zapatistas launched their armed campaign—an anti-globalization rebellion of mainly Mayan peasants resorting to guerrilla methods as well as to the media and internet to gain national and international support. Some argue that it was the Zapatista movement, rather than opposition parties, that has been the driving force behind Mexico's democratization by pushing civil society to demand democracy from the bottom up (Gilbreth and Otero 2001). By contrast, more traditional civil society groups, such as trade unions, played only a limited role due to the corporate structure of the PRI and thus of the state, which controlled the labour movement by exchanging considerable resources for political support.

Box 19.5 Brazil and the Rural Landless Workers' Movement (MST)

Unequal wealth and land distribution remains an important problem in Brazil today. According to the latest published census data, in 1998, 43 per cent of the land was owned by 0.8 per cent of the farmers, whereas the bottom 32 per cent of the farmers owned just 1.3 per cent of the land. Land concentration, mechanization of agriculture, and expulsion of workers from rural areas caused unemployment and mass migration to the cities. In the late 1970s—during Brazil's *abertura* or political liberalization process, which eventually ended 21 years of military government—rural workers in southern Brazil began isolated peaceful occupations of unused land. In 1984 they succeeded in coordinating their efforts and the MST was

officially founded with the aim of fighting for more equitable land ownership. Inasmuch as this has been its aim and it has achieved some of its goals, it can be said that the MST has been a movement that contributed to democratic consolidation across Brazil. The MST has helped to create about 400 associations and cooperatives that deal with agricultural production, commercialization and services, emphasizing the need to develop a sustainable socioeconomic model. In recent years, the MST has expanded its agenda, also campaigning against the neoliberal economic model and the Free Trade Area of the Americas (FTAA). See <www.mstbrazil.org>.

In Venezuela, following the *Punto Fijo* pact, the two main political parties virtually became the sole actors through which relations between the state and society were channelled. Large labour, business, and peasant associations existed, but they were controlled and penetrated by the political parties. In the 1960s and 1970s thousands of autonomous urban groups started to form around neighbourhoods', environmental or women's concerns. During the 1980s economic stagnation hit large parts of the population, and in February 1989 the government announced a sharp economic adjustment package. The result was a wave of popular protests, riots and looting—known as the *Caracazo*—in the capital Caracas and across the country, which was only quelled by the government's use of the Army. The number of dead remains unclear to this day, but estimates range from 300 and 3,000. While political instability and two coup attempts in 1992 can be seen as consequences of the protests, the *Caracazo* also led to the creation of an important human rights organization, the Commission of Relatives of the Victims of February 27.

More recently, the presidency of Chávez has caused such political polarization in Venezuela that civil society has become increasingly divided between organizations closely identified with the government and those hostile to it. The latter ultimately

mount a more effective opposition to governmental policies than the weak opposition parties. While an active civil society is usually proof of a healthy democracy, in the Venezuelan case this has resulted in its politicization rather than non-partisan, independent civil organizations.

Box 19.6 Key points

- Even in those countries where civil society organizations had been strong, they were severely weakened during the rule of undemocratic regimes. Many, however, succeeded in reorganizing themselves and played an important role in the democratization processes, as was the case of the trade unions and human rights organizations.

- The consolidation of democracy in Latin America has facilitated the empowerment of previously marginalized groups, such as indigenous communities and women.

- New types of civil society activism has emerged in the past few years, such as the Argentine *piqueteros* and the anti-globalization *Zapatistas*, a social movement exceeding indigenous demands.

Political Parties and Social Movements

As already observed, if any one feature has characterized Latin American politics—aside from its instability—it has been the presence of strong *caudillos* and charismatic populist leaders. From Perón in Argentina, Cárdenas in Mexico and Vargas in Brazil, to Castro in Cuba, Velasco Ibarra in Ecuador and Chávez in Venezuela, almost all Latin American countries have had theirs. Along with these leaders, or perhaps in spite of them and the recurrent democratic failures, strong political parties emerged and developed, and played an important role during the democratic transitions.

Historically, Argentine ideological cleavages have not run between the left and the right but rather between Peronism and anti-Peronism. Those who followed the charismatic leader supported the *Partido Justicialista* (PJ, Justicialist Party) that he created in 1946, a popular and broad movement that by the 1970s included within itself union leadership, women's and youth organizations, and armed guerrilla movements ranging from the far right to the far left. Those who fiercely opposed Perón traditionally joined the *Unión Cívica Radical* (UCR, Radical Civic Union), a moderate, middle-class centre party founded in 1891 demanding the opening and democratization of the then-reining oligarchic system.

Rather than pressure from political parties, the main reason for the demise of the Argentine military dictatorship was the Falklands/Malvinas defeat. Yet after 1983, political parties became the main political actors of the transition. The elections were won by the UCR candidate, Raúl Alfonsín, after he denounced a pact between the Peronist trade unions and the armed forces to grant the latter an amnesty if Peronism won. After seven years of repressive regime, the electorate went for the option with strongest democratic credentials. Alfonsín contributed greatly to consolidating democratic institutions and, inspired by the Nuremberg and Tokyo trials, promoted trails against the juntas for their human rights abuses. Later, however, his government sent to Congress two unpopular bills setting limits to the trials. In addition, economic crisis and hyperinflation spiralled out of control, forcing Alfonsín to step down five months before the end of his term. While it took the UCR many years to recover, by 1999 it was again in power as part of the centre-left coalition that ended 10 years of *Menemism*. The collapse in 2001 of the De la Rúa administration, though, proved very costly for the country in general, and for the UCR in particular, which saw splits and flight of votes. It still retains, however, some popularity at the local and congressional level.

On the other hand, by the end of the 1980s Peronism had recovered its traditional popularity aided by Menem's nationalistic and populist rhetoric. Once in government, he betrayed his promises, implemented neoliberal reforms in line with the Washington Consensus, granted pardon to the military, and pushed for a constitutional amendment to allow his own re-election, damaging the democratic process. The economic crisis that began during his term resulted in the colossal economic implosion of 2001 and the people's rejection of political parties and politicians. The popular protests which followed were not just demanding De la Rúa's resignation, but the removal of the entire political elite.

Two developments are worth highlighting here. First, the political crisis of 2001/2002 was ultimately resolved within constitutional provisions and institutional continuity was maintained. The fact that military intervention was unthinkable, unlike for much of Argentine history, shows a certain maturity on the part of the democratic system. Second, despite the apathy that dominated the 2003 election and the hostility towards traditional politicians, the main contenders for the presidency were two Peronists with a long political trajectory—former President Carlos Menem and Néstor Kirchner, Governor of a Patagonian province between 1991 and 2003, who eventually prevailed. Since Kirchner's term in office democracy has 'normalized'. However, Peronism has also become the undisputedly dominant party, fragmenting and co-opting political opposition, and consequently compromising the party system's ability to provide real alternatives to voters.

While not important in Argentina, the division between left and right has historically been key in Chile. Nonetheless, by 1988 parties ranging from the Socialist to the Christian Democratic succeeded in building a broad coalition to defeat Pinochet in the plebiscite for his permanence in power. Although the opposition prevailed, the 'yes' vote for Pinochet's continuity was still endorsed by 44 per cent of the electorate. The coalition *Concertación de Partidos por la Democracia* went on to win in 1989 the first presidential election in 19 years. The Chilean armed forces, however, had not suffered from the discredit of their Argentine colleagues and were therefore able to impose conditions on the democratic transition, to which the *Concertación* agreed in order to guarantee the success of the process. Additionally, the pro-Pinochet candidate received nearly a third of the votes, showing that society continued to be politically polarized.

The *Concertación* won four consecutive elections, leading two Christian Democrats (Aylwin 1990–1994; Frei 1994–2000), and two Socialists (Lagos 2000–2006; Bachelet 2006–present) to the Presidency of Chile. In all these elections right-wing candidates, some of whom were openly pro-Pinochet (such as Büchi and Lavín), came in second (see Table 19.1), illustrating the continued divide running through Chilean society. Moreover, in the 1999 election Ricardo Lagos defeated Joaquín Lavín, a former close aid of Pinochet, in the first and second rounds, but only by a very narrow margin. Despite the right being a

relatively powerful force, it has never questioned electoral results and proved not to be destabilizing. Thus, it has contributed to ensuring the democratic consolidation and the maturity of the Chilean party and political systems.

Like in Argentina, the main political split in Mexico has not been between the left and the right, but rather between adherence and opposition to the PRI. The party controlled the whole political system between 1929 and 2000, mostly by resorting to fraudulent elections and co-opting or neutralizing dissent, and fiercely repressing less docile opposition. This being the case, there was no need to ban other parties, which indeed existed. For instance, in 1939 the conservative, pro-Church PAN was founded, and eventually won the elections in 2000. During the 1980s the effects of the foreign debt crisis, which had originated in Mexico, coupled with disarray within the PRI led to a faction splitting from the party and creating a coalition of left-wing parties, social movements and grassroots organizations around Cuauhtémoc Cárdenas; the *Partido de la Revolución Democrática* (PRD). Although the 1988 election involved massive and blatant fraud, it also demonstrated that popular discontent and the force of the opposition had become impossible to ignore.

During the 1990s, the PRD constituted the main opposition to the PRI, as PAN tended to support the government's neoliberal reforms. Throughout the decade, corruption scandals, drug-traffic related violence, human rights violations, politically motivated assassinations, and further economic crisis combined to weaken the government, forcing it to recognize political defeat in local, state and legislative elections, and eventually in the presidential election

Table 19.1 Chilean Presidential Elections, 1989–2006

Election year	*Concertación* candidate		Candidate of the right	
1989	P. Aylwin	55.17%	H. Büchi	29.40%
1993	E. Frei Ruiz-Tagle	57.99%	A. Alessandri Besa	24.42%
1999 (first round)	R. Lagos Escobar	47.89%	J. Lavín Infante	47.57%
2000 (second round)	R. Lagos Escobar	51.31%	J. Lavín Infante	48.69%
2005 (first round)	M. Bachelet	44.27%	S. Piñera	24.47%
2006 (second round)	M. Bachelet	51.98%	S. Piñera	45.19%

Source: Chile—Tribunal Calificador de Elecciones <www.tribunalcalificador.cl>

of 2000 at the hands of Vicente Fox and PAN. While this seemed a major step towards democratization and a multi-party system, attempts by the PRI and PAN to prevent PRD candidate López Obrador from running in the 2006 elections and claims of fraud after they had taken place cast serious doubts about the Mexican democratic consolidation.

As previously outlined, Venezuela was different from the other cases. There were no military dictatorships nor a single hegemonic party, but rather a system of power-sharing between the AD and the COPEI that effectively excluded more radical left and right-wing options for forty years. During this time, opposition groups and even armed guerrilla emerged, yet they were faced with repression and the electoral legitimacy that the government enjoyed. Up until the early 1980s, the *Punto Fijo* governments benefited from an economic bonanza that came to an end in 1982–83. This, coupled with generalized corruption and a deepening economic crisis in the following years increased the general discontent with the *Punto Fijo*. In 1992, a group of young officers in the armed forces led by Lieutenant Colonel Hugo Chávez launched a coup against the government of Carlos Andrés Pérez. Although the coup was unsuccessful, widespread support for it became evident. The political and economic crises, as well as the general discontent with the neoliberal reforms deeply affected the *Punto Fijo* parties to the extent that by the 1998 elections COPEI and the AD supported the candidate of a third party rather than running with their own candidates.

In more recent years, the Venezuelan political system started to resemble the Argentine system of the 1950s when Perón was a dividing and polarizing figure. In the 1998 election Hugo Chávez and his *Movimiento Quinta República* (MVR, Fifth Republic Movement)—inspired by the values of Simón Bolívar, one of South America's liberators against the

> ## Box 19.7 **Key points**
>
> - Despite the instability that has characterized Latin American politics, strong political parties, and social movements have played an important role during the democratic transitions.
>
> - While in Chile the ideological division between left and right has always been strong, it has historically been difficult to apply it to Argentina, Mexico, and Venezuela. In Argentina that division was represented by Peronism and anti-Peronism, and in Mexico by pro-PRI and anti-PRI supporters. By contrast, Venezuela developed a system of power sharing that prevented the emergence of left-right cleavages and single party dominance.
>
> - In recent years, Argentina's and Venezuela's political systems have been characterized by one party's electoral dominance and the fragmentation of political opposition. The Mexican democratic consolidation has been questioned by claims of fraud in the 2006 presidential election. Conversely, since democratization Chile has developed into a stable political system.

Spaniards in the nineteenth century, and promising a democratic Bolivarian Revolution—won a 56 per cent majority. Nonetheless, the MVR itself has proved to lack democratic procedures to nominate its own candidates, and Chávez has shown a preference for—and some success in—strengthening his personal powers rather than democratic institutions. While opposition groups have formed a coalition, this is too disparate to pose any real threat to the MVR—except for the short-lived, US-sponsored coup of 2002. Yet *Chavismo* may also be proving to rely too heavily on patronage, corruption and clientelism to bring about the democratic revolution it propagates.

Institutional Challenges

Democracy swept through swathes of Latin America in the 1980s with military dictatorships being removed from power in Argentina, Chile, Brazil, Bolivia, Ecuador, Paraguay, and Peru. This is reflected in the region's average democracy scores, which dropped below -2 in the second half of the

1970s but have been consistently above +2 from 1985 onwards. Despite this, the region still faces a number of questions with regards to the state of democracy. Since the end of military government, Argentina has been ruled by decree on various occasions, particularly under Carlos Menem, a mode of **governance** that is far removed from the democratic norm. Moreover, Menem even changed the constitution so he could run for a third term as President. And while democracy and the neoliberal economic model are often closely associated, in December 2001, despite following the ideas of the IMF and World Bank, Argentina underwent considerable democratic strain when the country had five presidents in a two week period—it very much appeared that the economy was about to implode.

Since the return of democracy in Argentina accusations of corruption in general, and even extending as far the presidency, most noticeably under Menem, have existed. In a not dissimilar manner accusations have appeared in 2007 that Cristina Kirchner's presidential campaign funds were boosted by money sent covertly from Hugo Chávez's Venezuelan government. This suggests that Argentina still faces a number of institutional challenges. It seems that a much more robust system of checks and balances is still required since it is highly problematic from a democratic perspective for campaign funds to not only come from outside the country but even from a foreign government.

Military rule ended in Chile in 1989 but its legacy continued to cast a long shadow over the country

---

Box 19.8 Uruguay's Pacted Transition to Democracy

Uruguay had been considered a role model of democracy in the region until 1972, when years of economic crisis and political chaos resulted in a civil-military coup. The military took control, leaving the civilian President Juan María Bordaberry only formally in charge. The new regime shared the features of the bureaucratic-authoritarian regimes of the better known neoconservative military dictatorships in Argentina and Chile—repression and imprisonment of political activists, anti-communism, censorship, closing down of Congress and political parties, banning of trade unionism, and implementation of a neoliberal economic programme. Between 1976 and 1985 the military took direct power of the executive branch too.

Yet when in 1980 the military sought to institutionalize their rule through a referendum for a new constitution, they were faced with a solid 'No' vote of 57 per cent. This result, coupled with the military government's inability to address economic problems and growing popular discontent, led them later to begin secret negotiations with representatives of the political parties. The long process took two rounds of negotiations; at the Parque Hotel in 1982 and more famously at the Naval Club in 1984.

The negotiations lasted for several months, and representatives of the three branches of the armed forces as well as of three political parties—the centrist *Colorados* and *Unión Cívica*, and the leftist *Frente Amplio* coalition—took part in them. A fourth political party, the *Partido Nacional* (also known as the *Blancos*), withdrew from the talks as they rejected the military's demand that certain candidates and parties should be banned from the election. On 3 August 1984, the negotiations concluded with the signing of the Naval Club Pact. The Pact was agreed between moderate factions within each of the military and the parties, successfully excluding more hard-line sectors.

What exactly was discussed at the Naval Club meetings remains a matter of debate among historians. For instance, it is not clear whether negotiators agreed not to conduct trials against the military for human rights violations or whether the issue was not even on the agenda. At any rate, while human rights were not part of the text of the Pact, in 1986 the new democratic government passed a law declaring the expiration of the state's prerogative to prosecute members of the armed forces for the crimes committed during their regime ('*Ley de Caducidad*'). Not only did trials not take place, but the civilian government decided that abuses would not be investigated at all. As David Pion-Berlin (1994: 114) argues, 'those negotiations insured that neither side would enjoy a decisive advantage once the elected government had been installed. A relative balance of power between the two sides resulted, where neither had a dominant strategy to deploy nor realistic hopes of imposing its preferred outcomes in the short term'.

throughout the 1990s, and in some respects this remains the case even today. The military believed that the loss of the 1988 plebiscite, which eventually led to their electoral defeat in 1989, was a personal defeat for Augusto Pinochet and not for the system which his regime had imposed. As a result, by passing the so-called '*leyes de amarre*' during its final year in power, the military made sure that this system could not suddenly be changed. This appeared very much to follow the ideas of a 'pacted transition' (O'Donnell, Schmitter, and Whitehead 1986). Amongst the conditions demanded by the military were that Pinochet and another eight of his junta colleagues became senators for life, that the new President could not appoint the heads of the military, and that the constitution was altered so that the neoliberal economic model was safeguarded and would remain in place. These arrangements are examples of the high price that had to be paid at times to achieve a pacted transition.

Throughout the 1990s it proved increasingly difficult for the Chilean authorities to prosecute members of the military regime for human rights violations perpetrated during their time in power, as the case of Pinochet discussed earlier clearly shows. It was only his finances that the authorities were allowed to investigate at the time of his death in December 2006. However, in the 1990s cases of illegal phone tapping by the military surfaced and in 1993, when President Aylwin was out of the country, the army even returned to the streets in an act of intimidation. Electoral democracy has returned to Chile but the country still faces a number of questions, not least the continuing legacy of military rule, which must be addressed. The country's democratic institutions need to be strengthened so that some citizens are not elevated above the law, in order that this dark period of its history can finally be laid to rest and democratic consolidation be completed.

Elections have been present in Mexico throughout the twentieth century but due to the undemocratic nature of the political system during most of this period, the country has faced a number of institutional challenges since the PRI was finally defeated by PAN in the year 2000. This was most graphically illustrated in the aftermath of the bitterly fought 2006 presidential election. Many of the peculiarities of the Mexican political system under the PRI may

have been removed, yet Andrés López Obrado. PRD did not only dispute the election results but ev proclaimed himself to be President. His followers held mass demonstrations protesting the result, which even prevented the outgoing President, Vicente Fox, from making his final speech to Congress. International observers seemed to be happy with the way in which the 2006 election was conducted, but some Mexicans still appear to distrust the electoral system to produce an honest and fair result. This may be a legacy from the PRI era, but the system must be beyond reproach so that the events of 2006 are not repeated. Moreover, violence continues to haunt Mexican society—most noticeably concerning the international drugs trade, with a number of policemen having been murdered throughout 2008.

The electoral victory of Hugo Chávez in December 1998 ended the bipartisan system created under the *Punto Fijo* pact and heralded the beginning of a very different era of Venezuelan politics. While it can be said that democracy had only been very limited in Venezuela, the system created stability and the army remained largely absent from politics, unlike in many other Latin American countries. This dramatically changed in April 2002 when the military staged a coup against Chávez and he was removed from power for 48 hours.

The coup was staged because many within Venezuelan society were deeply concerned about the implications of Chávez's 'Bolivarian Revolution'. They felt that democracy was being threatened, that the country was headed towards a one-party state and a political model not dissimilar to the Cuban one. On his part, Chávez claimed that he could not implement his policies within the traditional political system, which he believed favoured the country's elite, with the National Assembly in particular doing this. Thus, Chávez created the Constitutional Assembly that met in the summer of 1999 and began rewriting the constitution, which amongst a variety of things increased its own power by changing legislature from a two-chamber system to a single-chamber one. In addition, and no differently from the changes in Argentina under Menem, the power of the president was also increased and his terms of office extended from five to six years.

International observers were unhappy about the transparency in the July 2000 general election

'Enabling Act', which allowed …ecree for one year. As this year …Chávez passed 49 decrees which …essary in order to radically change …itical system, and make Venezue- …qual. Chávez has not only survived the 200~ ~~ ~~, ~ut also a recall vote in June 2004 when the opposition collected enough signatures to set this in motion. Moreover, in December 2007 a referendum was called which would allow further changes to the constitution and, in particular, would remove the two-term presidential limit. Some believe that this was the precursor for Chávez remaining in power for a number of decades. While it appeared that this was a further attack on democracy, Chávez lost this vote, to the surprise of many. He has since said that the pace of his reforms will have to be slowed. Significantly, the result of this referendum also illustrates that Venezuela has not, as many had

---

Box 19.9 Key points

- Elections may have returned to Latin America but the region continues to face a number of related issues, chiefly that of weak institutions. Despite elections political instability continues to sporadically appear most noticeably in Argentina in late 2001, Venezuela in April 2002, and Mexico in the aftermath of 2006 presidential election.

- The Chilean military attempted to protect the system which they had imposed by passing the *'leyes de amarre'*—the effects of which can still be felt on contemporary Chile.

---

feared, in effect become a one-party state and that democracy may in fact be more consolidated than it would appear at first glance.

Conclusion

A wide variety of factors, including domestic, regional, and international, explain the wave of democracy that swept through Latin America in the 1980s. Economic reasons were particularly significant as a result of the close association of neoliberal economics and democracy. Conversely, the regional economic crisis also increased public discontentment as many economies did not appear as if they would survive the shock of the debt crisis. In the case of Argentina this, in conjunction with the legacy of the Falklands/Malvinas War, resulted in the military junta simply imploding. Military regimes may now appear to be confined to history but the region still faces a number of different and difficult problems with relation to the state of democracy. This is most certainly the case with regards to economic disparity, corruption, deficient justice systems, and high rates of violence and crime. The continuing impact of the international drugs trade is significant in this, as has been seen in the outbreak of violence in Mexico throughout 2008. The case of Mexico is not unique, as similar drugs-related violence exists elsewhere in Latin America, adversely impacting on the state of democracy in the region.

Latin America's political institutions on the whole remain weak, not least with regard to minority rights. This has received increasing international attention in no small part due to the appearance of the Zapatistas in Mexico. Throughout the region indigenous groups have mobilized, highlighting challenges that democracy continues to face in terms of access to justice, recognition, rights, and integration. Although much remains to be done, the rise of indigenous leaders like Evo Morales in Bolivia may be a reflection of a stronger and politically more dynamic civil society.

As the case studies of Argentina, Chile, Mexico, and Venezuela have illustrated, contemporary Latin America faces a wide variety of issues with regard to the quality and state of democracy, but what can be conclusively said is that in comparison to 30 years ago military regimes have disappeared from the region's political landscape and are unlikely to return.

QUESTIONS

1. Is the Bolivarian Revolution antidemocratic?

2. How might the Venezuelan situation unfold?

3. Has the PRI's power suffered a terminal blow?

4. With the 2006 presidential election appearing to illustrate the divided nature of Mexican society could the PRI in the future assume the position of 'kingmaker' in Mexican politics?

5. What does the situation regarding Augusto Pinochet in the 2000s say about Chilean democracy?

6. Has Argentine civil society been strengthened or weakened by the 2001–2002 crisis?

Visit the Online Resource Centre that accompanies this book for additional questions to accompany each chapter, and a range of other resources: <www.oxfordtextbooks. co.uk/orc/haerpfer/>.

FURTHER READING

Kingstone, P. R. (2006), *Readings in Latin American Politics: Challenges to Democratization* (Boston, MA: Houghton Mifflin). Provides a good up to date account of the various challenges that continue to face Latin America with regards to the state of democracy within the region.

Lewis, P. H. (2006), *Authoritarian Regimes in Latin America: Dictators, Despots, and Tyrants* (Lanham, MD: Rowman & Littlefield). An excellent historical account of the history of non democratic governments within Latin America.

Nagy-Zekmi, S. and Leiva, F. (2005) (eds), *Democracy in Chile: the Legacy of September 11, 1973* (Brighton: Sussex Academic Press). This book examines the effects that Pinochet's years as Chilean President has had, and continues to have, on the state of democracy within Chile.

Oxhorn, P. (1998), *What kind of Democracy? What kind of Market? Latin America in the Age of Neoliberalism* (University Park, PA: Pennsylvania State University Press). The very important connection between the effects of the debt crisis, the imposition of the neoliberal economic model and democracy are thoroughly examined and explained.

Wiarda, H. J. (2005), *Dilemmas of Democracy in Latin America: Crises and Opportunity* (Lanham, MD: Rowman & Littlefield Publishers). The continuing questions which Latin America faces with regards to democracy after more than two decades since the return of elections are analysed at great depth.

Borzutsky, S. and Oppenheim, L. (2006) (eds), *After Pinochet. The Chilean Road to Democracy and the Market* (Gainesville, FL: University Press of Florida). Pinochet's colossal legacy, both politically and economically, is detailed with regards to contemporary Chilean society.

IMPORTANT WEBSITES

<http://lanic.utexas.edu> Latin American Network Information Center, University of Texas at Austin. An excellent website with links to numerous Latin American and related websites that are in both Spanish and English.

<www.nuncamas.org> Never Again (Nunca Más) Report of the National Commission on the Disappearance of Persons, Argentina. Important report on human rights abuses during the darkest period in Argentina's history.

<www.mstbrazil.org> Brazil's Landless Workers Movement (Movimento dos Trabalhadores Rurais Sem Terra). The official website of the Landless Workers Movement, with good information about their organization, history, campaigns, and news.

<www.latinobarometro.org> Latinobarómetro is a non-profit NGO that carries out annual public opinion surveys in 18 Latin American countries on the development of democracy, economies and societies.

NOTES

1. Triple A stood for 'Argentine Anticommunist Alliance'.

Post-Communist Europe and Post-Soviet Russia

Christian W. Haerpfer

Overview

This chapter describes and explains the democratic revolutions which occurred between 1989 and 2008 in post-communist Europe and post-Soviet Eurasia. It analyses the beginning of the decline of communism and the failed attempts to reform communist one-party **states** in the period between 1970 and 1988 as stage one of democratization. The next section deals with the end of communist **regimes** as the second stage of democratization—between 1989 and 1991. The following part is devoted to stage three of the democratization process, which focuses on the creation of new democracies. The dynamics of post-communist democratization is differentiated into three separate paths of development: the path towards consolidated and liberal democracies, the second path to partial and electoral democracies, and finally the transformation of post-Soviet countries into illiberal autocracies. The conclusions present the main drivers of successful democratization in post-communist Europe.

Introduction

From Stettin in the Baltic to Trieste in the Adriatic an iron curtain has descended across the Continent. Behind that line lie all the capitals of the ancient states of central and eastern Europe, Warsaw, Berlin, Prague, Vienna, Budapest, Belgrade, Bucharest and Sofia; all these famous cities and the populations around them lie in what I must call the Soviet sphere, all are subject, in one form or another, not only to Soviet influence but also to a very high and in some cases increasing measure of control from Moscow.

This famous speech by Winston S. Churchill, on the occasion of accepting an Honorary Degree at Westminster College in Fulton, Missouri on 5 March 1946, is regarded as the commencement date of the Cold War between a democratic Western world and the communist Eastern bloc. Between 1946 and 1989, the iron curtain forced many Central and Eastern European countries to join the communist block of countries under the control of the Soviet Union in general and Moscow as centre of communist power in particular.

The Iron Curtain was finally lifted on 27 June 1989 at the border between Austria and Hungary, by the foreign ministers Gyula Horn (Hungary) and Alois Mock (Austria), who took down the barbed wired fence in a joint symbolic political action with historical consequences. This first crack in the long border of concrete walls and barbed-wired fences between the free world and the communist world in mid-summer 1989 was the beginning of the final collapse of communism in November and December 1989, and the first sign of the final fall of the Soviet Union in December 1991. The end of the Iron Curtain coincides with the termination of the Cold War, signifying the end of this crucial and dramatic period of European and World history since the end of World War II in 1945. In November 1989 those communist political regimes in Central and South-East Europe, which have been dominated and controlled by the Soviet Union, commenced their journey towards democracy. The end of global bipolar conflict in international relations, the Cold War between 1946 and 1989, contributed to the beginning of widespread democratization within the sinking world of communist political regimes in politics.

Following the political and ideological climate change of the student revolution in May 1968, the global wave of democratization began in Southern Europe in the early 1970s (see Ch. 18). The process of democratic change in former communist Europe and Eurasia forms an important sub-wave which has not ended yet. The complex transformation from communist regimes towards alternative democratic and autocratic forms of government and political order took place during the 19 years between 1989 and 2008, and has not been concluded as a historical process. In terms of contemporary European history, democratization in Central and Eastern Europe and Eurasia is still a work-in-progress—we are still far away from the final victory of democracy and any form of 'end of history' (Francis Fukuyama 1992) in that important geographical area between Prague and Bishkek.

The process of democratization in post-communist Europe and Eurasia can be structured along a series of subsequent stages of political transformations. The first stage of democratization in Central Eastern Europe consists of long-lasting stagnation and steady decline of the old communist regime in the course of the 1970s and 1980s. Some innovative communist leaders like Mikhail Gorbachev in the Soviet Union, or János Kadar in Hungary attempted to reform the political and economic system of communist rule to ensure its survival, but failed to rescue the faltering communist Empire in the long run. The second stage is relating to the period of revolutionary regime change form communist regimes to democratic or autocratic regimes. This next period is characterized by the collapse of communist systems between Warsaw and Vladivostok and took place between November 1989 and December 1991. The third stage of democratization is constituted by the creation of a new political regime out of the ashes of communism, in most cases a new democracy (Christian Haerpfer 2002). The specific characteristics of post-communist change in comparison with other forms of democratizations—like those in Southern Europe—is that we are confronted with a tri-fold revolution, a political revolution from a communist one-party state, a economic revolution from a centrally planned command economy to a free market economy, and finally a social revolution from a communist society with a small political upper class (*nomenklatura*) to a modern society with a broad middle class.

The fourth stage within the overall process of democratization is opening the dynamics of regime change and democratization in the direction of three different paths of political transformations. The first path relates to those new democracies which achieved the transition to a consolidated democracy. The second path of democratization is dealing with those new democracies which achieve the status of an electoral democracy. Finally, the third path of regime dynamics is characterized by mainly post-Soviet systems, which transformed into some form of autocracy and cannot be considered part of the group of new democracies in Central Eastern Europe or Eurasia.

Decline and Failed Reforms of Communist Regimes, 1970–88

In the history of the communist political systems four attempts of political and economic reform have been made in Central Europe. The first partial attempt for political reform took place in 1953 in the German Democratic Republic, the second full attempt happened in Hungary in 1956. Both reforms failed completely, the Hungarian uprising ended with violence and bloodshed. Within the context of the May Student Revolution in Western democracies like France, Germany and the USA, the 'Prague Spring' of 1968 tried to develop a third way of political and economic regimes. Like the Hungarian revolt, the Czechoslovak concept of a 'socialism with a human face' was destroyed with the military power of the Warsaw Pact armies in Autumn 1968. The last revolt against Soviet-communist rule happened in Poland in 1980, when the Catholic trade union Solidarity under the leadership of Lech Walesa tried to challenge the Polish communist regime. The Polish Unified Workers' Party and the Polish army suppressed this reform attempt with a hybrid regime between communist and army rule, thus preventing an invasion by the Warsaw Pact armies, on a comparable scale as the previous military interventions in 1956 in Hungary and 1968 in Czechoslovakia.

The failure of large-scale reforms of the communist regime in Hungary and Czechoslovakia caused the introduction of small-scale reforms, which did not openly threaten the main principles and doctrines of orthodox Marxism-Leninism. Such early and minor reforms, mainly in the field of the economy, were planned and implemented in the course of the 1980s in Hungary, Yugoslavia, and Poland. In Hungary, the communist leader János Kadar allowed private ownership of farms and small enterprises, and freedom of travel to other parts of the world. In Yugoslavia, the communist leader Josip Broz Tito tried a 'third way' between communism and capitalism with cooperative ownership of enterprises, and travel outside the Eastern bloc allowed. In Poland, the communist leaders Edward Gierek and Wojciech Jaruzelski implemented small-scale capitalist reforms in the agricultural sector, including private ownership of farm land. These early economic and political reforms in Hungary, former Yugoslavia, and Poland formed a positive path-dependency, which facilitated accelerated economic transition after the end of communism. These small-scale entrepreneurs, in capitalist islands within the centrally planned economy, form a group of proto-capitalists which can contribute at a later stage to a take-off of a new 'capitalism without capitalists' (Szeleni et al. 2001).

The 1970s and early 1980s within the Soviet Union have been characterized by political stagnation, together with a modest, but stable, economic standard of living for the Soviet citizens. The concept of stagnation is very closely associated with the historical era of Leonid Brezhnev, the Communist Party leader of the Soviet Union during the 1960s and 1970s (1964–82). The elderly successors of Brezhnev,

Yuri Andropov, and Konstantin Chernenko, died after around one year in office. After long periods of older men as leaders of the Soviet Empire, a young-ish Mikhail Gorbachev (in his early fifties) became the leader of the communist world and began the 'seven years that changed the world' (Brown 2007)—the period between 1985 and 1991. He tried to reform the Soviet political and economic system by introducing an extremely ambitious programme of reform. That programme had three main pillars, *perestroika* (=restructuring of society and politics), *glasnost* (=openness and transparency), and *uskore-nie* (=acceleration). Mikhail Gorbachev wanted to reform the Soviet Union, the biggest country in the world, and to ensure a sustainable political, military, and economic future for communism as an alterna-tive to democracy and capitalism. The ambitious project of *perestroika*, which started in 1985, col-lapsed in August 1991, when orthodox communist political actors attempted a coup and put Gorbachev under house arrest in his holiday residence ('dacha') in Foros on the Black Sea.

> ## Box 20.1 Key points
>
> - In Central Europe, there have been four failed attempts to reform the communist system: German Democratic Republic 1953, Hungary 1956, Czecho-slovakia 1968, and Poland 1980.
>
> - During the 1980s the Hungarian communist state introduced small-scale capitalist reforms in agricul-ture and business, which facilitated the economic transformation from a planned economy to a free market economy after 1989.
>
> - In Yugoslavia and Poland modest forms of proto-capitalism developed within a communist economy, mainly in agriculture and industry.
>
> - The most ambitious and wide-ranging reform in politics and economy was perestroika in the Soviet Union under Mikhail Gorbachev between 1985 and 1991. Its failure triggered the collapse of the Soviet Union in December 1991 and the end of commu-nism in Europe and Eurasia.

End of Communist Political Regimes, 1989–91

This stage is analysing regime change per se, and many theories of democratization are focusing on that specific stage of the historical process of regime change, thereby neglecting the previous and later stages. The first collapse of communist regimes occurred in November 1989 in many Central East-ern European countries. They had been dominated and controlled by the Soviet Union since the estab-lishment of the Iron Curtain in 1946 and the begin-ning of the Cold War between the 'First World' in the West and the 'Second World' in the Eastern bloc of communist countries. One critical factor for 'the fall' of communism (Saxonberg 2001) in Central and Eastern Europe was that the Soviet leader Mikhail Gorbachev, who was concentrating on his ambitious domestic reform programme *perestroika* within the Soviet Union, decided to exclude voluntarily the military option of open intervention by the Warsaw Pact army in other communist states as a strategic

political option to stabilize the Communist Empire. The lack of this military option, and of direct politi-cal orders from Moscow, caused a political paralysis within the national communist political elites, which have been used to obey the central power in Mos-cow since 1946. This absence of international armed and security forces took away a military umbrella and security 'insurance' from many national com-munist elites. Their military and political weaponry to respond to democratic challenges was reduced. This historical time-window of non-intervention by the Soviet Union created the opportunity for regime change in many communist Central and East Euro-pean states. The regime change from communist one-party states to new democracies occurred in most countries without physical violence and in a peaceful manner. A strong dissident movement and previously suppressed civil society achieved a 'vel-vet revolution' in Czechoslovakia, the communist leadership left their offices of power and government in Prague silently and without open resistance. Another form of regime change and regime transition took place in the form of so-called 'roundtable agreements', especially in Hungary and Poland. These roundtables transferred the political conflict between the 'old communist elite' and the 'new democratic elite' from the streets of capital cities like Budapest and Warsaw into conference and meeting rooms. Sometimes, respected authorities from the areas of religion and science acted as moderators of these roundtable talks. The strategic, and sole, aim of these roundtable talks was to ensure a peaceful, non-violent, and orderly hand-over of power from the communist power elite to the emerging democratic elite. The non-violent end of the rule of the Bulgarian communist leader Todor Schivkov was the result of a non-violent coup within the communist elite in Sofia. The violent end of the regime of the Romanian Dictator Nicolae Ceausescu and his wife Elena was a coup within the communist elite in Bucharest. The President of Yugoslavia, Slobodan Milosevic—in stark contrast to the Soviet leader Gorbachev—decided to keep the military option as a political option in order to preserve communism and the Federal Republic of Yugoslavia. This use of military power by the central government in Belgrade caused a prolonged, bloody, and bitter war between Serbia and Slovenia, Croatia, and Bosnia-Herzegovina. The process of democratization and national independence for Slovenia, Croatia, and Bosnia-Herzegovina was extremely violent and cost thousands of lives in the former Yugoslavia. In August 1991, an attempted coup by orthodox communist forces was smashed by

---

Box 20.2 Key points

- The communist political regimes in Central and Eastern Europe collapsed in November 1989.

- One main factor for the success of these democratic revolutions in the former 'Satellite states' of the Soviet Union had been the decision of the Soviet leader Gorbachev not to intervene militarily in those countries to stop the beginning of democratization.

- Most of European democratic revolutions, e.g. in Czechoslovakia, Poland, and Hungary, happened without the use of force or violence.

- Violent democratic revolutions occurred in Yugoslavia—in the form of a prolonged domestic, and later international, war—and Romania.

- The 'Second Russian Revolution', after the First Russian Revolution in 1917, commenced on 8 December 1991.

Boris Yeltsin, who later became the first President of the Russian Federation. That violent suppression—of an attempted communist-Stalinist restoration—by Boris Yeltsin involved casualties and deaths, but the final collapse of the Soviet Union in particular, and the Soviet Empire in general, was not violent. This Second Russian revolution (after the First Russian Revolution in 1917) began on 8 December 1991, when the leaders of Russia (Boris Yeltsin), the Ukraine (Leonid Kravchuk), and Belarus (Shushkevich) signed a declaration which officially dissolved the Soviet Union (USSR).

Creation of New Democracies

The collapse of the communist one-party states at the second stage of democratization produces a dangerous vacuum of political institutions and values. The new regime has to be established quickly and in an orderly manner. The particular difficulty for post-communist regime change was based in the fact that three transformations had to be achieved, from a communist one-party state to a pluralist democracy, from a collective command economy to a free market economy, and finally from a communist society to an open society. The historical advantage of democratization in Spain, Portugal, and Greece has been that they required only political transitions—because a market economy and modern society was already in place. The historical need for a tri-fold transformation required a full-scale destruction of the three old areas of politics, economy, and society and a simultaneous construction of a new democracy, a new economy, and a new society. This put the millions of post-communist and post-Soviet citizens under enormous pressure and produced a high level of transition stress, which resulted in a very deep and catastrophic demographic and health crisis, especially in the former Soviet Union. There was a dramatic decrease of life expectancy amongst post-Soviet citizens.

From New Democracies towards Consolidated Democracies

The optimal path of democratization in post-communist Europe is from a new democracy towards a 'consolidated democracy' (see Table 20.1). A new democracy can be described as consolidated when it fulfils the criteria for a complete or liberal democracy: a new democracy has to have the rule of law, a clear separation of powers, a vibrant civil society independent from the state, a democratic constitution and associated constitutionalism, pluralism of political actors and institutions, full respect of human and political rights, and freedom of media and political association. In addition to these criteria, a new democracy has to fulfil the minimum criterion of free, fair, competitive multi-party elections, as well as a successful **consolidation** of its political and legal institutions. Finally, an absolute majority of the citizens have to support democratic rules and principles as the only game in town.

The process of democratization can be measured by a variety of empirical indicators and indices (see Ch. 3). In order to analyse the progress of democratization in post-communist Europe and post-Soviet Eurasia, three such indicators of democratization have been selected: The Polity IV democracy scale, the Freedom House Index of Political Rights, and the Freedom House Index of Civil Liberties (Table 20.1). Of the Polity IV scale, only the 11-point democratic component is used. To facilitate easy comparison with the Freedom House Indices, the scores have been reversed, so that 11 means 'no democracy' and 1 means 'full democracy'.

In order to have a point of reference, regarding the current state of democracy in a variety of post-communist political systems, we use the state of democracy in two mature democracies—the USA and the UK—as benchmark political systems. Both the USA and the UK have the top index value of 1 regarding Political Rights (1), Civil Liberties (2), the overall performance of democracy in 2006 (4), as well as a mean value for the period between 1993 and 2006 (3). The most successful examples of democratization are Slovenia and Hungary. Both are post-communist countries, which are located in Central Europe and display the top index value of '1' in all dimensions of measurement of democratic change. Other examples of successful transformations are the neighbouring countries Poland and Lithuania, which also show excellent ratings regarding their democratic

---

Box 20.3 Key points

- The first and optimal path of democratization is from a new democracy towards a consolidated democracy.

- The best achievements of democratization in post-communist have been found in Slovenia, Hungary, Poland, Lithuania, and Slovakia.

- A cluster of consolidated democracies at the Black Sea consists of Bulgaria, Romania, and Moldova.

- Another group of consolidated democracies at the Adriatic Sea: Croatia, Macedonia, and Albania.

Table 20.1 Consolidated Democracies in Post-Communist Europe, 1993–2006

	Freedom House		Polity IV Index	
Country	Political Rights 2005	Civil Liberties 2005	Polity IV Democracy 1993–2006	Polity IV Democracy Index 2006
Full democracies:				
USA	1	1	1	1
UK	1	1	1	1
1. Slovenia	1	1	1	1
2. Hungary	1	1	1	1
3. Poland	1	1	2.2	1
4. Lithuania	1	1	1	1
5. Slovakia	1	1	3.4	1
6. Czech Republic	1	1	2.9	3
7. Bulgaria	1	2	3.4	2
8. Romania	2	2	4.6	2
9. Moldova	3	4	4.4	3
10. Croatia	2	2	7.6	2
11. Albania	3	3	5.4	2
12. Macedonia	3	3	4.1	2
13. Latvia	1	1	3	3

performance and structures. Poland is lagging within that top group because there have been delays of democratic change during the early stages. The same is true for Czech Republic and Slovakia, which are consolidated democracies regarding political rights and civil liberties, but do not fulfil all criteria of the Polity IV Democracy Index yet. The next group of consolidated democracies could be located on the Western part of the Black Sea: Bulgaria, Romania, and Moldova are consolidated democracies in 2006 according to the Polity IV Democracy Index, but have only recently joined the top group of post-communist democracies after difficult political transformations since 1990 in the cases of Bulgaria and Romania, and since 1992 in the case of Moldova.

The same is true for three Southern European countries: Croatia, Albania, and Macedonia still have minor problems with political rights and civil liberties, but they are—after violent transformations during the blood-stained break-up of Yugoslavia in the 1990s—now consolidated democracies and can be described as success stories of democratization. Latvia finally has an improving record regarding civil liberties and political rights, especially after coping with the political integration of minority groups, but achieved only a third class rating from the Polity IV Democracy Index. It is at the lower end of this top category of successful democracies. One might argue that the democratic revolution has been fully successful in the Central European countries of Slovenia, Hungary, Poland, Lithuania, Slovakia, and Czech Republic. Most of these countries have a democratic path-dependency of previous periods in their history, when they experienced already early forms of democracy and democratic culture, of democratic behaviour and proto-structures of civil society. All consolidated democracies within this first group of successful democratization commenced a process of deep democratization.

From New Democracies towards Electoral Democracies

The second path of political transformations and democratic revolutions refers to those countries which have not yet managed to achieve the top status of a consolidated democracy, but have been able nevertheless to reach the middle status of an electoral democracy. A political regime can be described as an electoral democracy when it is fulfilling a minimum definition of democracy. When a political system is holding competitive and multi-party elections it can achieve the status of an electoral democracy. This concept of electoral democracy is restricted to the institutions and processes of nationwide elections and does not account for the democratic character of political institutions. It is not considering the democratic performance of actors and institutions, e.g. the national government, in the period between nationwide parliamentary and presidential elections. An electoral democracy is not obliged to fulfil any of the criteria for full or consolidated democracies, such as the rule of law, separation of powers, civil society, constitutionalism, pluralism, human and political rights, or freedom of media and opinion. The comparative study of democratic revolutions has resulted in six post-Soviet countries which followed the second path of democratization from a new democracy towards an electoral democracy (see Table 20.2). Until 1991 these six electoral democracies were Republics of the Soviet Union. The leading electoral democracy in that second group has been found in Estonia, which has an excellent rating regarding political rights and civil liberties from Freedom House, but only a value of 4 on the Polity IV Democracy Index. Being embedded as new member state within the European Union Estonia has very good chances to improve its democratic rating and to move up to the top group of consolidated democracies in a mid-term perspective. Other electoral democracies in that middle group of political change are Ukraine, Georgia, and the Russian Federation. The mean Polity IV Democracy Index regarding Ukraine and Georgia for the period between 1993 and 2006 is very low, which is due to the fact that both countries had strong autocratic structures under President Leonid Kuchma in Ukraine and President Edvard Shevardnaze in Georgia. The Orange Revolution in Ukraine

and the Rose Revolution in Georgia improved the democratic rating to a Polity IV value of 4 in 2006. Russia is an example of a failed full democratization, but has still the status of an electoral democracy, albeit with very strong anti-liberal and semi-autocratic elements. The recent 'Tulip Revolution' in Kyrgyzstan helped to allocate the status of an electoral democracy at the lower end of this group with a Polity IV value of only 7. A second country from the Southern Caucasus, Armenia, is also a member of the group of post-Soviet electoral democracies.

The so-called 'Coloured Revolutions' in Ukraine (Orange), Georgia (Rose) and Kyrgyzstan (Tulip) constitute secondary democratic revolutions after the primary revolutions between 1989 and 1991. These countries are in a process of shallow democratization—

Box 20.4 Key points

- The second path of democratic revolutions is used by those post-Soviet political systems which achieved the status of an electoral democracy.

- Estonia is an electoral democracy, with high levels of political rights and civil liberties, but is the only new member state of the European Union which has not reached the status of a consolidated democracy.

- The Orange Revolution achieved the status of an electoral democracy for Ukraine.

- The Rose Revolution did the same for Georgia in the Southern Caucasus.

- The Tulip Revolution kept Kyrgyzstan at the lower end of the group of electoral democracies.

- These coloured revolutions have the historic effect of transforming competitive autocracies into electoral democracies.

- Russia currently has the status of an electoral democracy and has the choice of moving either up, towards fuller forms of democracy, or down, to become an autocracy like Belarus.

Table 20.2 Electoral Democracies in Post-Communist Europe, 1993–2006

Country	Freedom House		Polity IV Index	
	Political Rights 2005	Civil Liberties 2005	Polity IV Democracy 1993–2006	Polity IV Democracy Index 2006
1. Estonia	1	1	4	4
2. Ukraine	3	2	5.4	4
3. Georgia	3	3	6.8	4
4. Russia	6	5	5	4
5. Armenia	5	4	7.9	6
6. Kyrgyzstan	5	4	10.4	7

democracy is not developing deep roots in society nor amongst the elites. Their historic function is not to achieve consolidated democracies, but to lift autocratic regimes to the status of electoral democracies.

From New Democracies towards Autocracies

The third path of democratic revolutions in post-Soviet Eurasia is finally relating to those post-Soviet countries which failed completely on the road to democracy, and ended up as autocratic regimes without any significant democratic elements, principles, or institutions (see Ch. 2). The least autocratic regime has been identified as Tajikistan with a Polity IV Democracy Index value of 10, a small extent of political rights and civil liberties (see Table 20.3). All other regimes represent full autocracies with a value of 11. Kazakhstan and Azerbaijan show a minimum support for citizens' freedom and political rights, with

Box 20.5 **Key points**

- Belarus under president Alexander Lukashenka constitutes the last full dictatorship in Europe.

- All post-Soviet states in Central Asia—with the recent exception of Kyrgyzstan—did choose the third path of transformation from communist Soviet Republics to autocracies.

- Complete and non-competitive autocracies have been found in Uzbekistan and Turkmenistan.

Table 20.3 Autocracies in Post-Communist Europe-Asia, 1993–2006

Country	Freedom House		Polity IV Index	
	Political Rights 2005	Civil Liberties 2005	Polity IV Democracy 1993–2006	Polity IV Democracy Index 2006
1. Tajikistan	6	5	10	10
2. Belarus	7	6	10.3	11
3. Kazakhstan	6	5	10.6	11
4. Azerbaijan	6	5	10.1	11
5. Uzbekistan	7	7	11	11
6. Turkmenistan	7	7	11	11

a Freedom House value of 5 regarding civil liberties and 6 regarding political rights. Belarus is the last full autocracy in post-communist Europe amongst these authoritarian regimes in the Caucasus and Central Asia. Democratic values and principles are completely absent in Uzbekistan and Turkmenistan. The latter Asiatic regimes are at the very bottom of post-Soviet democratization and constitute full autocracies without any hope for democratic improvements in a mid-term perspective.

Conclusion

The most important outcome of this chapter is that democratization is not an inevitable and necessary quasi-natural transition from a communist one-party state towards a democracy. On the contrary, democratization is dealing with an open process of political transformation, which can take the form of three different paths of democratization. The first path of successful democratization leads from a new democracy towards a consolidated democracy—a full member of liberal democracies of the world. The best examples of such a successful democratization are Slovenia, Hungary, Poland, Lithuania, and Slovakia.

Regarding the main and critical drivers of successful democratization this study identified the main factors which are supporting and facilitating the process of democratization in post-communist Europe and post-Soviet Eurasia:

- Historical experience of democratic systems and institutions as form of path-dependency in the past.
- Absence of international military threats by the Warsaw Pact troops during the transition from the old communist regime to the new democratic regime.
- Historical experience of a modern economy before the period of communist rule and a strong economy within the communist economy.
- High levels of human capital.
- Historical experience of civil society institutions.
- International integration into European Union.
- Non-violent regime change.

The second path of post-communist democratization consists of the political transformation of a new democracy towards an electoral democracy, which can be described as a partial democratic system without a variety of elements and institutions of a complete liberal democracy. This path of development has been noticed especially amongst post-Soviet countries like Estonia, Ukraine, Georgia, and Russia. The Orange Revolution in Ukraine, the Rose Revolution in Georgia, and the Tulip Revolution in Kyrgyzstan had the main historical function to keep these transforming systems on the way to democracy and away from the cul-de-sac of an autocratic regime. Despite many pessimistic comments about current and future politics of Russia, the Russian Federation is still fulfilling the criteria of an electoral democracy and still has the chance to become a democracy in the long run of history.

The third path of post-Soviet political transformations is mainly used by states in Central Asia, like Uzbekistan and Turkmenistan. These third group of post-Soviet countries have to be characterized as competitive, or full autocracies, or authoritarian dictatorships. These countries, like Azerbaijan and Belarus, as the last dictatorships in Europe have left the historical path towards democracy at the beginning of the twenty-first century and are proof of the fact that not all processes of democratization are successful. They are also clear scientific evidence that we are still far away from the end of political history.

QUESTIONS

1. What are the main elements and historical effects of perestroika in the Soviet Union between 1985 and 1991?

2. Why did the democratic revolution in November 1989 succeed?

3. Why did the coup d'état in the Soviet Union in August 1991 fail?

4. What have been the main factors for the end of the Soviet Union in 1991?

5. Which path of democratization best characterizes current Belarus?

6. Taking into account the dynamics of democratization in Central and Eastern Europe and Eurasia, what are the main reasons for failed democratizations and transformations towards autocracies?

Visit the Online Resource Centre that accompanies this book for additional questions to accompany each chapter, and a range of other resources: <www.oxfordtextbooks.co.uk/orc/haerpfer/>.

FURTHER READING

Ágh, A. (1998), *The Politics of Central Europe* (London: Sage). This leading Hungarian political scientist describes the initial transformation to democracy in Hungary, Poland, Czech Republic, Slovakia, Slovenia, Croatia, Serbia, Bulgaria, Romania, and Albania. An excellent and detailed historical account of democratization in these countries.

Dawisha, K. and Parrott, B. (1997), *The Consolidation of Democracy in East-Central Europe* (Cambridge: Cambridge University Press). Outstanding comparative analysis of democratization in Hungary, Czech Republic, Slovakia, Latvia, Lithuania, and Estonia.

Dawisha, K. and Parrott, B. (1997), *Politics, Power, and the Struggle for Democracy in South-East Europe* (Cambridge: Cambridge University Press). Regional analysis of democratization in Croatia, Bosnia-Herzegovina, Serbia, Slovenia, Macedonia, Albania, Bulgaria and Romania.

Dawisha, K. and Parrott (1997), *Democratic Changes and Authoritarian Reactions in Russia, Ukraine, Belarus, and Moldova* (Cambridge: Cambridge University Press). Authoritative account of post-Soviet political transformations in Russia, Ukraine, Belarus, and Moldova.

Derleth, J. W. (2000), *The Transition in Central and Eastern European Politics* (Englewood Cliffs, NJ: Prentice Hall). Systematic comparative analysis of democratization in an historical and contemporary perspective regarding Russia, Bulgaria, Hungary, and Poland.

Kaldor, M. and Vejvoda (1999), *Democratization in Central and Eastern Europe* (London: Pinter). Excellent account of democratization in Estonia, Latvia, Lithuania, Poland, Czech Republic, Slovakia, Hungary, Slovenia, Romania, and Bulgaria by Central and Eastern European scholars.

Zielonka, J. (2001), *Democratic Consolidation in Eastern Europe. Volume 1: Institutional Engineering* (Oxford: Oxford University Press). Comparative study of the role of new constitutions and constitutionalism in Estonia, Latvia, Lithuania, Bulgaria, Romania,

Ukraine, Russia, Belarus, Czech Republic, Slovakia, Slovenia, Hungary, and Poland, mainly by Central and Eastern European scholars.

IMPORTANT WEBSITES

<www.cepsa.cz> The Central European Political Science Association (CEPSA) was established in 1994 as a common forum of Central European political scientists.

<www.russiatoday.com> Russia Today is an English-language television programme. It reports daily about politics and international relations in the Russian Federation and many other states which have been Republics in the former Soviet Union.

<www.abdn.ac.uk/cspp> The Centre for the Study of Public Policy (CSPP) has been conducting academic surveys in post-communist Europe and post-Soviet Eurasia since 1991. It is an invaluable data-source for scholars and students of post-communist and post-Soviet politics.

21 The Middle East and North Africa

Francesco Cavatorta

Overview

With the exception of Israel and Turkey, the region comprising the Middle East and North Africa remains a bulwark of authoritarian rule. But the persistence of **authoritarianism** in the Arab world does not mean that countries in the region have remained unchanged since the **consolidation** of authoritarian rule soon after de-colonization. Arab polities have gone through considerable political, social, and economic changes over the last three decades, with most of them experiencing different degrees of liberalization and, in some cases, even democratization for a limited amount of time. The global wave of democratization had a profound influence in the Middle East and North Africa, although democratic openings eventually failed to consolidate. This chapter explores the reasons behind these failures.

Introduction

The Middle East and North Africa is often identified as the region of the world where democratic **governance** has made the least progress. Scholarship (Brownlee 2002; Bellin 2004; Gambill 2003) on the region therefore tends to focus on the persistence of authoritarian rule and on the ability of the post-colonial ruling elites to remain in power for such a long time in spite of their decreasing popular **legitimacy** and the periodic crises they have had to endure. At first glance, it is true that the majority of the countries in the region do not seem to have changed much since they first achieved independence, when small democratic advances were quickly overturned in favour of authoritarian rule. This seems to be particularly true for the Arab countries where the same ruling elites and, in some instances, the same families have been in power for decades. This picture of a static region, which has not kept up with the political, social and economic developments that occurred in the rest of the world, is partially misleading. First of all, while authoritarian rule is the dominant form of governance, the region is also the host of democratic countries such as Israel and Turkey and while both have serious deficiencies in relation to minority rights and role of the military in politics, the democratic nature of their political and electoral contests cannot be overlooked. In addition, Lebanon, with its consociational arrangements, does not belong to the category of authoritarian **states** and Iraq, despite the enormous problems it faces, is also no longer in the authoritarian camp, although it is not in the democratic one either for the moment. Thus, democratic governance is present in the region. The picture of authoritarian stasis is also misleading because it does not take into account the profound changes that the global wave of neo-liberal democratization provoked in these polities. The vast majority of the Arab world has gone through sweeping neo-liberal reforms, which have transformed economic relationships and created a new middle class linked to the global economy. The social transformation of the Arab world has had a profound impact on the political system. In addition, technological innovations partly dismantled the monopoly on information that Arab states had enjoyed over their population, leading to a much more significant contestation of the legitimacy of the ruling elites. Finally, countries in the Arab world have not been immune to wider liberalizing trends and the democratic discourse has penetrated the region, forcing **regimes** to at least introduce *façade* democratic reforms and institutions.

But none of this should hide the fact that authoritarianism is the dominant form of government in the region. Explaining the durability of authoritarian rule is one of the most challenging intellectual enterprises. The first point to deal with is that there is no other region of the world where democratic governance has progressed so little. This leads some to point to an Arab 'exceptionalism' when it comes to democracy (Stepan and Robertson 2003). The notion of 'Arab exceptionalism' is contested, but it influences the scholarly debate about democratization in the Arab world. A second reason why explaining authoritarianism is so crucial has to do with policy-making, as the absence of democracy is perceived to be the most significant obstacle to international peace and stability. This seems particularly urgent with respect to international terrorism, which is believed to be intimately linked to the absence of institutionalized channels for dissent. It is therefore no surprise that significant academic effort is made to find explanations for the survival of authoritarian rule when both domestic and international conditions seem to be detrimental to it and when important internal and external actors place democracy and democracy promotion at the heart of their discourse and actions.

Explanations for the survival of authoritarian rule in the Arab world range from grand cultural theories to institutional factors. Within this range, scholars identify a large number of explanatory variables. Some scholars such as Lakoff (2004) concentrate their attention on the predominance of Islam in society, while others (Kedourie 1992; Garfinkle 2002) blame an inherently authoritarian Arab political culture. When institutions are included in the analysis, the absence of civil society emerges as a powerful explanation, as does the lack of an autonomous middle-class that could push for democratization and fulfil its historical role as an agent of democratic change. International variables are also very much part of the analysis, with some arguing that the international community, despite its rhetorical commitment to democracy, supports authoritarian rulers because it would be adversely affected if regime change were to empower anti-western political actors (Ghalioun 2004). Other scholars still contend that the presence of Israel in the region, and the almost permanent state of conflict that this generates, allow regimes to preserve their authoritarian prerogatives in the name of unity and steadfastness against the Zionist enemy, with all the consequences that derive from having domestic institutions geared towards permanent confrontation with a foreign power. This chapter will analyse the validity of such explanations, keeping in mind that the region and the countries within it are very diverse. This diversity can be seen in the institutional structures, the party systems, the degree of openness of society, international affairs, and the degree of integration with the global economy. This should lead one to be aware of the difficulties that exist to account for the phenomenon of authoritarianism through sweeping regional explanations when each country is so diverse and peculiar. At the same time, the authoritarianism they all share should not preclude one from seeking precisely such explanatory commonalities. As will become apparent in the course of this chapter, scholarship tends to fluctuate between these two approaches.

Authoritarian Persistence in the Arab World

While only Turkey seems to have emerged from authoritarianism and consolidated its democratic institutions, the vast majority of countries in the region also experienced processes of liberalization during the last three decades. Even before the collapse of the Iron Curtain in Europe, in the late 1980s, Tunisia and Algeria had liberalized the political system and begun a significant process of democratization. To a certain extent, some Arab countries could count on the fact that they had a brief experiment with democratic politics during the period of the mandate, and immediately after independence. In addition, the democratic rhetoric of the late 1980s did not leave ruling elites unstirred. Thus, in the late 1980s and early 1990s liberalizing measures were also introduced in Egypt, Morocco, Libya, and Jordan, indicating that the discourse and practice of democracy were not alien concepts in the Arab world. Even Saudi Arabia and the Gulf states were pressured into introducing some changes in the direction of increasing consultation with wider social groups and constituencies if not the entire population. Syria was a latecomer that experimented with political liberalization only with the arrival to power of Bashar Assad in 2000. In fact only Iraq avoided introducing even a *façade* of democratic institutions and remained solidly authoritarian. These experiments with liberalism and democratic governance were implemented to seek renewed legitimacy for the ruling elites and were not intended to be the beginning of a radical political transformation. Thus, they ultimately failed to consolidate and by the mid 1990s authoritarian rule strongly re-asserted itself. A new generation of leaders came to power at the end of the 1990s in a number of countries including Jordan, Morocco, and Syria and revived hopes for change, but such hopes were short-lived. However, the democratic discourse and the economic changes of the late 1980s profoundly affected Arab societies as well as Iran, and the new authoritarianism was substantially different from the one preceding it, with different social constituencies and groups now providing the necessary support to the ruling elites (Schlumberger and Albrecht 2004). Thus, if one examines the region in a superficial manner, the persistence of authoritarian rule does indeed emerge as the single most important feature in the Middle East and North Africa. But this fundamental fact should not distract attention from the different experiences the various countries made during the global wave of democratization.

The penetration of the democratic discourse and the international pressure to conform, at least on paper, to the requirements of liberal democracy profoundly affected all Arab regimes, which adapted to this new environment by modifying the institutional structure of the state and by finding new strategies through which they could guarantee their own survival while creating *façade* democracies that would satisfy the international community and some democracy-aspiring sectors of domestic society. Some countries, such as Morocco, went much further than others in terms of liberalization and can still claim today to be on the road to democratization—although for most commentators the process has virtually stalled (Cavatorta 2005; Willis 2006). Other countries, such as Algeria, even

Box 21.1 **The Mandate**

The Middle East and North Africa experienced a significant degree of external penetration and control since the mid 1800s and until the late 1940s and 1950s. Algeria acquired independence from France as late as 1962, and some Gulf states such as Oman obtained it only in the early 1970s. These experiences differed quite substantially in terms of how Western imperial power was exercised, and while there were very few actual colonies (Algeria, Libya, and Aden), imperial powers directly controlled the entire region through institutions such as the mandate and the protectorate. The break-up of the Ottoman Empire led to the creation of a number of rather artificial states and the institution of the mandate allowed France and Great Britain in particular to divide the region according to their own strategic interests and balance of power. In legal terms the mandates were created through the League of Nations and allowed the imperial powers to 'assist' the newly independent states like Iraq, Syria, Lebanon, Jordan, and Palestine until they could stand on their own. The mandate was effectively colonialism in disguise and this is the reason why Roger Owen (2000: 11) convincingly argues that post-World War I political systems in the region can be analysed using the concept of 'colonial state'. It is during this period that countries in the Middle East and North Africa saw the creation of a centralized bureaucracy and fixed borders, while experiencing a transformation of domestic political dynamics. Notions and institutions associated with liberal-democracy were introduced in the region and although they were not practiced by the imperial power, they nevertheless made their way into the political system, leading to the creation of political parties, parliaments and liberal legislation. These institutions survived for a short period of time after the end of the mandate, but the strength of the domestic nationalist discourse, with its emphasis on unity, anti-imperialism, and modernization, quickly asserted itself and led to the installation of authoritarian rule.

went through a significant democratic period between 1988 and 1992 before democratization was forcefully halted with the intervention of the military in the democratic process. Other countries still, such as Jordan, Tunisia, and Egypt, made a number of cosmetic changes—introducing nominally liberalizing laws and concepts to satisfy powerful Western allies. Finally, countries such as Saudi Arabia and Syria remained quite solidly authoritarian and illiberal, although both experienced a short-lived 'spring' in terms of civil society activism and social mobilization in opposition to the incumbent regimes. While political democratic changes failed to consolidate throughout the Arab world, a neo-liberal economic agenda has been implemented more successfully throughout the region, contributing to significant economic and social changes, which in turn have had a dramatic impact on the respective polities. Similar trends have characterised the political and economic developments of Iran, where, upon the death of Khomeini, a rather significant degree of liberalization took place, culminating with the election of the pro-reform candidate Khatami to the post of President. While Khatami's reformist and democratizing agenda was eventually defeated by the more conservative elements within the regime, Iranian society is today fundamentally different from the early revolutionary one of the 1980s and the reform movement is still very active. However, the current international climate is not conducive to experimenting with political change and, thanks to reinvigorated patriotic discourse, Iranian conservatives have placed liberal reforms firmly on the backburner.

The progressive integration of Arab countries and Iran in the world economy has transformed their political economies and their social structures, increasing

Box 21.2 **Key points**

- While democratization has transformed countries around the world, authoritarianism managed to survive in North Africa and the Middle East.

- Authoritarian regimes have survived through their ability to adapt to a new set of domestic and international circumstances, this enabled them to fend off political competition.

the gap between the upper strata of society, who have benefited from the openings, and the masses of people whose livelihoods have become more difficult as subsidies were cut, social services privatized, and the costs of living increased. The implementation of economic reforms was seriously flawed (Dillman 2001). It ben-efited mainly those with connections to the regime, leaving the latter even more exposed to criticism from genuine opposition actors. The following sections offer a number of explanations for the durability of authoritarian rule in the face of both domestic and international pressures for democratic governance.

The International Context

Studies of democratization have traditionally analysed regime change as a product of domestic variables and internal dynamics. The international dimension was perceived to be at times a trigger for transitions or a facilitating factor in producing a successful outcome, but it was rarely treated as a central explanatory variable (see Ch. 7 for an overview). When it comes to the Middle East and North Africa, however, it is quite difficult to exclude international factors from the analysis, given the geo-strategic and economic centrality that the region has in global affairs. Scholars such as Burhan Ghalioun (2004) and Mohammed Ayoob (2005) have highlighted how the most powerful states in the global system support authoritarian rule in the region in the name of regional and international stability. In the complex game between domestic actors with radically different objectives, each side can count on a set amount of resources.

The role of Islamist political actors

Thus, the opposition, including the Islamists, may enjoy a considerable degree of support among the population for its anti-regime stances but the ruling elites can also count on extensive support, especially among those social constituencies that enjoy security and privileges under the authoritarian regime. It is always very difficult to gauge the precise amount of support that political actors in the region have, but the rare times when the population was called to express its ideas in free and fair elections, opposition parties—Islamist ones in particular—performed extremely well (Algeria in 1991, Egypt in 2005, and Palestine in 2006), defeating the ruling parties in the process. Irrespective of these electoral results, the existing regimes managed to survive, but popular dissatisfaction has become much more difficult to hide, as Fattah (2006) also indicates in his survey work in the region.

The distribution of material and legitimacy resources among political agents is crucial to determine the outcome of a domestic game where political actors are aware of their strengths and weaknesses. In this game, the international community, despite its rhetorical commitment to democratization, provides the ruling regimes with both legitimacy (i.e. **participation** to international forums and the shunning of genuine opposition parties and figures) and material resources (i.e. military and economic aid), which allow them to survive.

The absence of significant pressure to democratize, the refusal to deal with Islamists in opposition, the provision of economic and military assistance, and the acceptance of authoritarian interlocutors at international forums, are all instruments through which the international community strengthens authoritarianism. In return, the ruling elites maintain regional stability and avoid pursuing policies that might be perceived as anti-Western. Thus, they implement economic policies favouring foreign investors, refrain from taking a confrontational stance on the Arab-Israeli conflict, and generally avoid challenging Western dominance. More specifically, Arab countries are increasingly drawn into the neo-liberal frameworks that Western countries have put in place, including the signature of bilateral free trade agreements with the USA and the participation in the Euro-Mediterranean Partnership, which calls for the liberalization of trade between the European Union and partner countries. In addition, the vast majority of Arab countries are called on to acquiesce to the US military and diplomatic dominance in the region. Among other things, this results in the inability to challenge the Israeli-Palestinian peace process and the US presence in Iraq. The joint fight against terrorism further strengthens Arab authoritarian elites, whose security and intelligence services have become a privileged interlocutor for Western countries. At the core of this is the perception of the international community that the arrival to power of Islamist political forces would undermine the policies described above and result in increased instability, if not direct confrontation.

Thus, the role of international actors in augmenting the resources available to the ruling elites and their supportive domestic constituencies is believed to be crucial in explaining how authoritarianism survives. Perhaps the clearest example of this is the failed consolidation of Algerian democracy. After the liberalization of the country's political system in early 1989 Algeria experienced the revival of civil society activism and multi-party politics. This could have led to the creation of a genuinely democratic society where ordinary citizens would be able to elect their most preferred candidates and hold them accountable for their work, replacing the one-**party system** the country had known since independence. The country went through a round of reasonably free and fair local elections in the summer of 1990, which the newly formed Islamist party *Front Islamique du Salut* (FIS) dominated. The outcome was repeated in the crucial legislative elections of December 1991. The FIS electoral march to power was stopped when the army, at the instigation of some domestic liberal and secular political forces, intervened to halt the experiment with democracy. Far from expressing severe criticism and 'punishing' the generals who had carried out the coup through a number of targeted sanctions, the international community, following the lead of France, threw its support behind the new regime and effectively sanctioned the return to authoritarian rule. Some go as far as to claim that the Algerian military was encouraged to take action by the French authorities, with which they had a

privileged relationship (Aggoun and Rivoire 2004). In any case, the support of the international community for the Algerian regime never wavered and it is also thanks to the aid of key international actors that the regime was able to remain in place (Cavatorta 2004). The attitude of the international community towards authoritarian rulers in the region is best summed up by Zakaria (2003: 2) who states: 'the Arab rulers of the Middle East are autocratic, corrupt, and heavy-handed. But they are still more liberal, tolerant, and pluralistic than those who would likely replace them.'

All this does not necessarily indicate that the international community is entirely responsible for the persistence of authoritarian rule, and that there are no significant domestic factors at play. It should be noted that countries very inimical to the West, and considered pariahs of the international community—such as Syria and Iran—have also remained authoritarian throughout the last three decades. If it were true that key international actors support current ruling regimes in the Arab world because they ensure the protection of Western interests, it would be legitimate to expect that, at the same time, the international community would attempt to undermine those regimes that have anti-Western policies. This is indeed what happens as authoritarian regimes in Syria, Libya, Iran, and Iraq all came under significant pressure to democratize. These regimes however survived and remained authoritarian, even in the face of significant pressure—with the obvious exception of the use of military force recently employed in Iraq to remove Saddam Hussein. How is one then to reconcile the power ascribed to the international community to provide for the persistence of authoritarian rule in some contexts and its inability, bar the use of overwhelming military force, to provoke regime change in others?

The role of Israel

Any answer to this question has to take into account the role of Israel in the region. The conflicts that the presence of Israel generates do not only have an international dimension in the form of wars, invasions, and periodic disputes, but have a very significant domestic dimension for the countries in the Arab world and, more recently, for Iran. In particular, the state of almost permanent conflict with Israel allows a number of Arab regimes and the Iranian ruling clerics to keep a very tight control on domestic politics in order not to weaken the resistance against the Zionist enemy. The claim of rulers like the Syrian President Bashar Assad is that Syria cannot afford political pluralism because this would undermine the country when it faces an enemy with whom hostilities are a permanent possibility. This permits ruling elites to maintain a very powerful security and military apparatus, which, with the excuse of having to face Israel, can be used to control the local population and keep it in line. In addition, the presence of Israel allows for the continuation of special laws that impede political pluralism.

Box 21.3 **Key points**

- In the Middle East and North Africa the international community is very much at ease with authoritarian rule.

- The possibility that democratization would benefit Islamist parties or movements likely to challenge the international status quo makes international support for democratization in the region unlikely in the future.

- International factors are not the principal explanation for the persistence of authoritarianism, but are a contributing factor to the loss of appeal of 'liberal democracy' amongst Arab citizens, as Western states are perceived to espouse hypocritical stances in their support for authoritarian rulers.

Political Culture and Society

When analysing the persistence of authoritarian rule in the region there is no escaping a discussion of the relationship between Islam and democracy. A number of scholars (Lewis 2002) contend that Islam is an inherently un-democratic religion because it did not have to confront the European Enlightenment and consequently generates an authoritarian political culture. In the past this was assumed to be the case because Islam demands submission from believers. From a political point of view, this submission was translated into political quietism, whereby Muslims were compelled never to question their political leadership because this would have created the conditions for internal divisions that, in turn, would have undermined the unity of believers living under the same political authority. The lack of political pluralism is the logical outcome of this belief. Thus, political quietism characterized Muslim polities, fundamentally opposing the requirements of democracy, which demands both questioning of authority and pluralism. However, political quietism is increasingly questioned through the emergence of a number of political movements, both Islamist

and secular, which clearly indicate that Muslims are divided on issues related to how to govern a society as much as their counterparts belonging to other cultures and political traditions.

This has not stopped some scholars from insisting on the incompatibility between Islam and democracy (Kedourie 1992). It is argued that such incompatibility exists as Islamist parties and movements are perceived to be inherently antidemocratic (Khalil 2006) because the creation of an Islamic state, their ultimate objective, can only be achieved through violence and authoritarian behaviour (Ben Mansour 2002). This view assumes that Islamist parties are highly ideological and unable to come to terms with the requirements of political pluralism because their positions would always enjoy God's support as they interpret it, cutting off avenues of criticism for other political actors. This framing of Islamist parties is an *a priori* assumption that halts any discussion or analysis about them. The problem is that it is impossible, as Brumberg (2002a) convincingly argues, to determine the true essence or nature of any political party or movement, including the Islamists. Political movements

Box 21.4 **Political Islam**

The growth and the popularity of Islamist movements across the region constitute a significant political phenomenon that has often been referred to as the resurgence of political Islam or Islamism. The term refers to the use of Islamic symbolism and discourse in order to promote a political programme of radical changes. Islamist political movements adapt religious teachings and injunctions to serve specific political purposes and are usually much more interested in bringing about political change than in promoting religion per se. It follows that the doctrinal body of Islam is interpreted to underpin a plurality of strategies and objectives. While it can be argued that the fundamental goals of Islamist movements are the instauration of an Islamic state and the introduction of religious law, the methods to achieve such objectives and the legislative and political content with which to 'fill' the Islamic state are profoundly different and conflicting. Islamist movements and figures differ sharply on the interpretation of the doctrinal teachings of Islam because they have very different views on what an Islamic state should look like, and how movements should operate in order to achieve its creation. This multiplicity of interpretations is evidence of the neutral nature of Islam, which does not per se support any particular form of government and does not sanction any specific method of political activism. The social, economic, and institutional constraints in any given political environment shape how Islamist political actors will read the message that religion provides. In turn this explains why Islamist movements are often in open conflict with each other on issues such as democracy, human rights, sovereignty, violence, and social activism. The popularity of Islamism and of religious discourse is largely the product of the failures of imported ideologies. Through the utilization of a very familiar and indigenous ideological framework, Islamist movements are able to occupy the terrain of political opposition in the region.

should be seen in the institutional context within which they operate and should therefore be judged on how they interact with other political actors and how their policies and actions are shaped by the surrounding institutional environment. The presence and support for Islamist movements should not be seen as the confirmation that Islam and authoritarian rule are inextricably linked, as Islam per se can support and legitimize any type of political action, movement, and system of government (Esposito 2002).

The debate on the relationship between political Islam and democracy is crucial to understand the many ways in which civil society is analysed in the Arab world. Civil society is often regarded as a crucial factor in democratization studies, as a strong and active civil society can become a de-legitimizing force for authoritarian rule (see Chs 6, 9, and 11 above). Broadly speaking, there are four views regarding the role and importance of civil society in the Arab world. From a theoretical perspective, the first view treats the concept of civil society as being exclusively a liberal normative one. From this it follows that civil society in the Arab world appears weak and incapable of playing the same positive pro-democratization role that it played in other transitional contexts. As Sean Yom (2005) argues, there are only very few civil society organizations that promote and defend democratic and liberal values and the state is able to dismantle or co-opt them quite easily. This is quite correct for most countries if only the secular and liberal organizations are considered to be part of civil society. While the number of civil society groups engaged in issues related to democratization and human rights has significantly increased, their appeal and popularity is quite limited because their conceptual and intellectual apparatus is perceived to be a foreign import by the vast majority of the population, which is unable to relate to such issues and tends to focus its attention on crucial services delivery rather than on political issues.

The second view conceptualizes civil society in more neutral terms, avoiding normative judgments about it. This school argues that civil society activism is strong when organizations with an Islamist *ethos* are included in the definition. The argument is that civil society organizations do not have per se any normative liberal-democratic traits and do not necessarily promote liberal values. Civil society can be therefore strong and non-liberal at the same time and this is precisely what Sheri Berman (2003) argues with respect to Arab civil society given the overwhelming presence of Islamists, who are considered to have an antidemocratic *ethos* by definition.

The third view suggests that civil society has indeed been strengthened over the last decade, with a significant surge in the numbers of organizations being created. The case of Morocco illustrates this trend quite well. With the arrival to power of King Mohammed VI, Moroccan society has been permitted to organize and liberate itself from the suffocating legislation that had hitherto impeded their creation and curtailed their activities. Today, Morocco boasts an active and large civil society sector with organizations involved in all kinds of social and political work. However, this is not necessarily a sign that the ruling elites are losing control of their own society. Quite the contrary is true, as many civil society organizations are largely creations of the state itself, while others are either beholden to the state or fully co-opted, ceasing to be autonomous civil society actors. This generates an artificial civil society where independence of action is limited and therefore civil society activism becomes another means of social control (Wiktorowicz 2000).

The fourth view also holds that civil society should be treated as a neutral explanatory category, but it also suggests that Islamism should not be *a priori* treated as possessing an authoritarian nature (Brumberg 2002a). This perspective implies that the strength of civil society should be examined through the dynamics that occur between its different sectors, with particular attention paid to the relations between the Islamist camp and the secular/liberal one. In this view, authoritarian rule might benefit from 'the paradox of strength' of civil society. In the face of similar authoritarian constraints, it would seem logical that all opposition groups within civil society would cooperate to bring about political change. The vibrancy of associational life and the widespread criticism of authoritarianism should theoretically lead to an increase in democratic attitudes and behaviour, which, in turn, should lead to political reforms. However, cooperation and alliance-building between the two sectors of civil society on the basis of shared objectives and values occurs only rarely because of the sharp ideological conflicts that exist between Islamist and secular/liberal groups, which translate into radically conflicting policy preferences.

This division is based on a fundamentally opposing objective. While Islamists wish to make Islam the central reference for policy-making, secular/liberal groups wish to take Islam completely out of politics. This means that there is no shared democratic discourse that can unite these groups because they have conflicting views on the values, if not the procedures, that should underpin the new society each hopes to create. The further paradox of this difficult relationship is that both factions make a rhetorical commitment to the values of democracy and human rights, but fill these concepts with very different content. Ultimately, this division allows authoritarian regimes to use 'divide and conquer' strategies in order to remain in power (Cavatorta 2007).

To conclude, the literature on civil society postulates that democratic change stems from the close relationship that exists between a vibrant associational life, the generation of social capital and the growth of democratic values and attitudes. While civil society in the Arab world is indeed vibrant, it is ineffective in producing democratic change because, despite using the same rhetoric of democracy, justice, rights and **accountability**, the Islamist sector and the secular-liberal one are in profound disagreement as to how these terms should be translated into institutional practice and, more crucially, into policy-making. This obviously calls into question the universalistic claims of the positive role of civil society for democracy. As Amaney Jamal (2007) argues, the role of associational life in authoritarian contexts is distinct from that in established democracies. The dynamics that are produced in the relationships between authoritarian regimes and civil society organizations are fundamentally different despite the fact that similar trends, such as the increase in interpersonal trust among association members, exist in both authoritarian and democratic contexts. The argument is that the authoritarian constraints the regime put in place make it necessary for associations to decide which side they are on. If the association wants to achieve some of its objectives, it may have to play by the rules of the authoritarian regime. It is then only through corrupt networks of patronage that the association will be able to satisfy the basic needs of its members and achieve its goals because only the regime can deliver the goods. These networks reinforce the central role of the authoritarian regime because they strengthen non-democratic access to decision-makers. Paradoxically, social capital increases within these pro-regime associations because their members, by playing within the constraints provided, can reasonably expect positive outcomes for the group, which then has no interest in dismantling such networks in favour of fairer and more democratic ways of access to decision-makers as doing so would diminish their benefits. The flipside of this logic is that anti-regime organizations, which do not utilize or do not have patronage networks available to them, have lower levels of social capital as a result of their more democratic values, which do not allow them to obtain the same level of benefits. Jamal (2007) does not write off the difficult work of many autonomous anti-regime organizations, but civil society in the end does not produce democratization because authoritarian dynamics provide a very rigid structure of incentives for associational life and do not permit the emergence of democratic attitudes. This occurs, as mentioned earlier, despite the fact that, at least rhetorically, all politicised civil society groups are committed to democracy and human rights. The difficulty is that the Islamist sector and the secular one are very suspicious of each other because they have a significantly different understanding of what democracy is, what

> ### Box 21.5 Key points
>
> - Islam and Arab political culture are not good explanations for the persistence of authoritarianism in the region.
>
> - There is a rather significant division between Islamists and liberals within civil society, which stops them from building coalitions that could challenge the authoritarian regimes.
>
> - The behaviour of political actors, particularly Islamist ones, should be examined by understanding the environment within which they operate.

it should do and how it should be practised. These deep ideological differences and these divisions over the degree of liberalism that should be introduced undermine the possibility of coalition-building rendering civil society ineffective in bringing about change. This scenario is quite different from the one that occurred in Eastern Europe and Latin America where civil society groups, irrespective of their differences, managed to build short-term alliances in order to achieve their common goal: ridding the country of authoritarianism.

Business and the Economy

When it comes to the Arab world it is very difficult to avoid the importance of economic factors in stifling democratization. One of the most relevant findings in the literature on transition to democracy postulates that the creation and strengthening of an autonomous middle class will generate significant pressure on the authoritarian regime to democratize. The progressive integration of Arab countries into the global economy and the expansion of the private sector have created a substantial middle-class, which has benefited from programmes of privatization, increasing interaction with foreign investors and increased opportunities for trade and commerce. However, a significant push for democratization has not occurred and according to some scholars this is

due to the role of rents, which affect the domestic economy and the political systems. For a number of years, a popular explanation for the presence of authoritarianism was pinned on *rentierism*. Hazem Beblawi and Giacomo Luciani (1987) argue that the externally-generated rents that regimes enjoy have a significant impact on the political system of the country because they permit authoritarian ruling elites to buy off political dissent through the provision of essential services for the population. This 'democracy of the bread' (Sadiki 1997) is possible because the resources that the state has at its disposal come from the exploitation of natural resources, which do not require productive mobilization of vast sectors of society. The absence of this sector makes entire social categories dependent on the state for economic success and advancement, leading to the development of a very large state apparatus and the creation of a class of businessmen, whose position and wealth depend on the distributive powers of rents.

With such an economic structure in place, the control of political dissent is facilitated because the state is not only the main employer, but because the resources available through rents can be invested in constructing a security apparatus tasked with suppressing such dissent when it arises (Bellin 2004). Thus, the absence of significant personal taxation and the provision of essential services in exchange for political acquiescence form the basis of an unwritten **social contract**, which isolates ruling elites from the necessity of political pluralism. As a result, the region is largely authoritarian because of the presence of oil and gas, which constitute the most important natural resources for the world economy, and their impact on the political systems of the country of the region (see also Ch. 8).

There are two addendums to this theoretical approach. First, a cursory look at the countries in the Arab world shows quite clearly that not all of them possess natural resources, which could generate sufficient rents to qualify them as *rentier states*. However *rentierism* affects every country in the region because foreign aid, workers remittances and investments from oil rich countries to oil-poor ones are considered to be externally generated rents (Brynen 1992). More specifically, the geo-strategic centrality of the region provides some countries with the opportunity to generate external rents by relying on international patronage. This means that through privileged links with the dominant powers in the international system, countries like Egypt can partially fill the state coffers and avoid popular pressure to reform. In addition, the regional oil economy permits the wealthier countries with large oil and gas revenues to create a large labour market whose needs are filled by regional migrant workers from countries devoid of natural resources. The remittances of these workers generate income for the families left behind and contribute to heighten their purchasing power while, at the same time, limiting the state's necessity to have a domestic productive apparatus. Finally, oil and gas generated wealth is invested across the region and serves to shore up the economies of oil deprived countries and maintain political stability.

The second addendum to *rentierism* has to do with the impact that economic crises have on the economic and political system. The over-reliance on natural resources exposes *rentier states* to the fluctuations of the global market, and therefore to forces beyond their control. This means that when there is a significant drop in external revenues, the state finds itself unable to meet its end of the bargain with the population, leading to a questioning of political authority. Thus, as Sadiki (19997) argues, at times of severe economic crisis the demands for a move towards a 'democracy of the vote' increase significantly. Within the context of liberalization and democratization in the region, this means that the pervasiveness of *rentierism* keeps countries authoritarian and that it is only at times of economic crisis that opportunities for change arise. The Algerian case would be the best example. During the 1980s Algeria was dependent on its oil and gas sector for 98% of its foreign revenues and the Algerian economy worked around the distribution of oil and gas rents. When the drop in the price of oil significantly reduced the resources available, the ensuing economic crisis hit the population very hard and the cost-cutting measures the regime had to undertake to face the recession made the situation even worse, leading to widespread demands for change (Ruf 1997).

Thus, a number of scholars explain the survival of authoritarian rule in the Arab world with the ability of the ruling elites to take advantage of *rentierism*. The current re-assertion of authoritarian rule is therefore due to the surge in oil and gas prices, which allows ruling elites to hold on to power by using the tried and tested strategy of redistribution and domestic investments in order to generate both support for, and dependency on, the state among the population. Steven Heydemann (2007) talks about the 'bounded adaptiveness' of regimes and the social pacts they put in place. However, the central idea that financial autonomy from the productive forces of the country insulates the regime from social pressures is not without critics. Gwenn Okruhlik (1999) argues quite convincingly that *rentier* states, through the political choices they make when spending rent money, 'engender their own opposition'. *Rentierism* places structural economic factors at the centre of its analysis, but the marginalization of political factors is not conducive to understanding. It is precisely the state's strategies in place and the decision-making processes behind the decisions on how to spend the rents that generate political opposition because of the manners in which the rents are distributed and allocated. The generation of political opposition does not occur only when there is a significant economic crisis that the state cannot deal with, but is a constant feature of rent distribution. Further studies seem to confirm that the importance of *rentierism* in determining political and social outcomes has been overemphasized. Benjamin Smith (2006) in particular postulates that oil busts rarely lead to authoritarian breakdowns. The survival of Arab *rentier* states during the years of crisis in the late 1980s can be explained by the fact that 'oil wealth facilitates building robust regime coalitions and powerful institutions, enabling rulers to ride out oil-induced crises that undercut other governments' (Smith 2006: 55).

Thus, the role of oil and gas wealth is mainly a facilitating one. The robustness of the institutions and the strength of the governing coalition are in place before the discovery of profitable natural resources, which then simply make the task of these institutions and coalitions to survive easier. This would explain why the oil busts of the late 1980s did not have a long-lasting democratizing effect in the region. Nevertheless, it remains quite difficult

---

> **Box 21.6 Key points**
>
> - The exploitation of natural resources is a very important aspect of economic life in the region.
>
> - *Rentierism* is a facilitating factor in the survival of authoritarianism.
>
> - Severe economic downturns intensify demands for political change, but regimes are able to manage such demands by redrawing the terms of the unwritten social contract with the population.

---

to explain the survival of authoritarian rule in the region without making references to the availability of external rents that regimes have at their disposal. As mentioned above, Algeria seemed to fit the profile of a *rentier* state paying the price for over-reliance on natural resources. When the severe economic downturn hit the country a period of political liberalization and even democratization ensued, but the authoritarian ruling elites eventually halted the experiment and reasserted themselves in power. This occurred despite the growing economic crisis, pointing to the validity of Smith's analysis. The post-colonial institutions and ruling coalitions, while severely tested, managed to survive even at a time when the distribution of rents was no longer a feature of the state.

Agents of Democratization and Democratic Failure

One of the most salient features of the political developments in the Arab world over the course of the last two decades has been the emergence of a substantial number of political parties. Before the wave of *façade* liberalizations of the late 1980s most Arab countries did not display multi-party systems, with some countries in fact having a one-party system in place. The necessity to adapt to new international requirements and domestic pressures led a number of regimes to permit the formation and re-emergence of political parties with the intent of providing the regime with increased legitimacy. As a result, the vast majority of the countries can now claim to have functioning multi-party systems. These political parties are permitted to operate in the open, can hold congresses and can stand for elections, both legislative and local. But the emergence of multiple political parties should not be confused with the arrival of genuine political pluralism. Far from playing the same role that they play in established democracies, political parties in the Arab world are not the main wielders of power. Real policy-making power is in the hands of unaccountable and often unelected groups of people who are isolated from the pressures that political parties could exercise. This leads Michael Willis (2002: 4) to conclude that 'rather than controlling the state, [political parties] are controlled by the state.' Political parties are therefore simply another means through which the ruling elites exercise control over society and over the political system. This does not mean that some political parties in the region do not attempt to perform the tasks of genuine opposition parties, but they are impeded from properly fulfilling their role by the repressive legislation in place and the tight control that the ruling elites exercise on the electoral process.

Weak multi-party systems under state control

Furthermore, political parties are frequently discredited in public opinion. This is due to the fact that some of them are indeed simply instruments of the regime and therefore do not truly represent social or economic groups, but there is also a more fundamental problem that has to do with the institutional set-up. While elections do take place, the institutions for which elections are held carry very little policy-making power. In traditional monarchies such as Morocco and Jordan, the King is the dominant executive player and decision-maker, while elected parliaments simply function as debating chambers. In the Arab republics, the President is the main decision-maker and therefore a similar pattern is at work, whereby parliament is emasculated of any real power. This *façade* political pluralism with the participation of a number of political parties does very little in the long term for the legitimacy of the system and for the parties themselves. Popular disenchantment with political parties is captured by the decreasing **turnout** at elections. Thus, rather than becoming founding moments for a new liberalizing and democratizing *élan*, elections are perceived as empty exercises destined to provide some form of international legitimacy to incumbents who do not enjoy, with very few exceptions, a significant degree of popularity and domestic legitimacy as studies examining popular attitudes towards incumbents show (Fattah 2006).

Thus, in much of the region, political parties and legislatures are largely discredited. The example of Morocco illustrates this point. King Mohammed

VI has invested a lot of resources in attempting to present Morocco as being on the way to democracy and the September 2007 elections should have represented, at least rhetorically, the culmination of such democratizing efforts. This was even more the case given that the Islamist party was not only permitted to run, but was encouraged to present candidates in all constituencies. The elections results in the end were quite disappointing for the Islamist party, beaten by the nationalist party, but, more significantly, voter turnout was very low at 37 per cent (Storm 2008). In addition, the number of spoiled votes was considerable. Popular indifference toward the electoral process is largely due to the lack of trust and belief in the ability of elected institutions to actually implement changes and provide a credible alternative to the overwhelming executive power of the monarchy. A general trend of declining voter turnout is evident throughout the region.

Islamist social movements and political parties

With respect to political parties, Islamist movements seem to constitute an exception in terms of popular support and legitimacy. When elections have been held, Islamist parties performed quite well, demonstrating that they constitute a genuine alternative to the incumbent regimes. However, political Islam is treated very differently across the region. Syria and Tunisia do not permit the political participation of Islamists in the political process and Islamist parties are effectively banned. This does not mean that Islamist formations and movements are not present in the country, but they have no access to the system. In Algeria, the Islamist party FIS was the most popular opposition force in the late 1980s and 1990s and was bound to take over power before the Algerian Army intervened to stop it. Since then Islamist parties, except the FIS, have been licensed and have been able to win seats in parliament and hold ministerial posts. This is part of the regime's strategy of gaining legitimacy among Islamist supporters. In Algeria the party system is shaped by the state, and official political Islam is the expression of state concerns rather than popular ones (Volpi 2006). In Egypt the Muslim Brotherhood is at times permitted to participate in

elections by presenting candidates running as independents, and it has been able to win a considerable
number of seats when the results were not rigged *ex
post*. But the organization has very little influence on
the policy-making process, which is largely in the
hands of the presidency and its ruling party. In Jordan the Islamic Action Front (IAF) swings from participation to boycott when it comes to elections, but
is a considerable opposition force and certainly more
popular than any other political formation. In spite
of this popularity, the IAF does not have any influence on policy-making. The same is true in Morocco
where the Party of Justice and Development (PJD)
enjoys a significant degree of popularity, but despite
winning seats in parliament, it does not have the
opportunity to shape policies and implement its programme because of the executive powers of the King
and its choice to sit in opposition, rather than participating in a weak coalition government. Even in the
Gulf monarchies, Islamist parties poll ahead of all the
other political movements, but the executive emirs
are the ones responsible for running the country.

The participation of Islamist parties in political
institutions devoid of real power demonstrates their
willingness to play by the rules and to try to exercise a modicum of influence, but in the longer term
they run the risk of losing popularity for lending
legitimacy to authoritarian practices and discredited
leaders. This is already happening in Morocco where

the Islamist PJD is progressively losing influence
and popularity in favour of the more radical, openly
anti-monarchical and semi-legal Islamist Justice and
Spirituality Group. In order to withstand the pressure of authoritarian regimes and take full advantage of the limited openings being created, political
parties of all ideological persuasions have tended at
times to coalesce in an attempt to win more seats in
parliament and therefore become a stronger force.
This coalition-building strategy among opposition
parties for both electoral purposes and for everyday contestation of the political system is a crucial
aspect of the game of liberalization and democratization because through the creation of a united
front stronger democratic demands can be made
on the regime. Unfortunately, in the Middle East
and North Africa, these coalition building strategies
among political actors tend to fail to be successful
because of the inability to sustain this coalition over
the long-term. This dynamic is very similar to the
one that characterizes civil society. This is due to
the ideological and strategic differences that characterize the relationships between Islamist political
actors and secular/liberal ones. While opposition to
the regime in place should function as the unifying link, the widespread ideological differences that
underpin, respectively, the Islamist project and the
secular-liberal one impede the sustainability of coalition building. In fact, fear and mutual suspicions
characterize the relationships between the two sets
of regime opponents.

In addition to almost irreconcilable ideological
differences, there are strategic divergences. The
popularity of the Islamist political project is anticipated by the other opposition actors, who believe
that a full democratization of the system will inevitably lead to the victory of the Islamist parties at
the polls with negative repercussions on the newly
established democratic rules, which, they believe,
would be eliminated in order to proceed to the creation of an Islamic state. Given this expectation, the
secular/liberal parties prefer to be co-opted by the
regimes in place, while attempting to win concessions from them. Ultimately, it is the incumbent
authoritarian regime that benefits most from these
divisions.

Box 21.7 **Key points**

- Electoral multi-party competitions do exist in the
  region, but they are largely emptied of any significance because they are stage-managed events.

- Islamist parties and movements are generally
  responsive to changes in their structure of incentives and when given the opportunity they usually
  participate to institutional politics.

- Divisions between popular Islamist parties and
  generally discredited liberal-secular parties allow
  the regime to benefit from a lack of coherent
  opposition.

Institutional Challenges

There are two fundamental challenges for the region's chances to become more democratic. First and foremost, there is the necessity to reduce the powers of the executive. Throughout the region, be they monarchs or elected presidents, heads of the executive concentrate an enormous amount of discretionary power, which enables them to bypass the rather weak checks put in place to guarantee a modicum of vertical accountability, namely elected parliaments. This is not an objective that will be easily achieved. The heads of these neo-patrimonial states still enjoy the support of key social and economic constituencies and a reduction of their powers is unlikely to be voluntary. The international environment, which could theoretically constitute a pressurizing force for reform, refrains from interfering and effectively supports the continuation of authoritarian rule. Thus, the costs of domestic repression are lowered and significant institutional changes are unlikely to occur. The second challenge that the states of the region face is the integration of Islamist parties into the political system. While most countries allow for the participation of Islamists to selected electoral competitions, this occurs with the knowledge that they will not be permitted to have any significant policy-making role. This is a major obstacle to democratization, but it also constitutes, over the longer term, a security problem. As John Entelis (2004: 210) points out, 'in blocking the rise of moderate Islamism, incumbent regimes have unleashed a much more virulent form of Islamic radicalism, one that cares little for co-operation or compromise.' The international situation, with the US occupation of Iraq, the flare up of hostilities between Israel and Lebanon, and the failure of the peace process between Israelis and Palestinians, further increases the appeal of radicalism.

From a formal point of view the countries in the region display all the institutions and trappings of democracies, from elections to parliaments to courts. However, they are emptied of substantive content and simply function as a *façade* for authoritarianism. When it comes to electoral competition, over the last few years multi-party and multi-candidate elections have become the norm throughout the region, but the recourse to elections in order to gain a degree of domestic and international legitimacy should not obscure the fact that such elections are still very much stage-managed by the regimes themselves and do not necessarily reflect popular preferences. Ruling parties in countries like Tunisia and Egypt not only benefit from state resources and wider access to the media, but can also count on state institutions to intervene and 'fix' the results. Opposition parties have little, if any, recourse when this occurs. Even in countries where elections are generally considered to be relatively free and fair, as in Morocco, the quality of the electoral process is quite low given the poor turnout, the 'buying' of votes and the heavy patronage. Overall, it can be argued that elections in the region are usually sham polls. While this is more the case in countries like Syria and Tunisia and less so in the case of Morocco and Egypt, meaningful electoral competition is largely absent. This does not mean that analysing such competition under authoritarian constraints is not important, but in terms of democratization, such elections simply contribute to the disenchantment of ordinary citizens towards the political system and the institutions of the state. When popular will was freely expressed, the FIS in Algeria was banned from government and Hamas in Palestine has been shunned by the international community. This does not do any service to the popularity of the concept of democracy.

A similar pattern is found when one analyses how the courts operate and how civil society is structured. The authoritarian constraints weigh heavily on all of these institutions, making the durability of authoritarianism the salient feature of the region. This does not mean that democratic discourse and the value of democracy have not penetrated the region. Quite the opposite is true and Fattah (2006) demonstrates that the attachment and support for democratic values and procedures in the region is quite high, but it is extremely difficult to translate such support into mechanisms of change and reform. A similar study by Tessler and Gao (2005: 84), examining citizens' attitudes to democracy in the Arab world, found that the region 'stands out on account of its high degree of popular support for democracy.'

> ### Box 21.8 Key points
>
> - Blocking the rise of moderate Islamist parties and movements led to a radicalization of political Islamism.
>
> - Popular support for democracy in the Arab world is high among ordinary citizens, irrespective of their degree of religiosity.

Conclusion

The most salient feature of the Middle East and North Africa is the persistence of authoritarian rule. Aside from Turkey and Israel, there are no other democracies in the region, given that the future of both Lebanon and Iraq is still very uncertain. However, the survival of authoritarian rule should not lead one to assume that Middle Eastern and North African polities have not changed over the last few decades. Quite the contrary is in fact the case and the consequences of neo-liberal market reforms, the impact of new technologies, and significant international events have all contributed to radically change these polities from a social and an economic point of view. But these changes have not been translated into effective democratization. While most states in the region have introduced a degree of liberal reforms, the ruling elites have been able to avoid the central issue of transfer of power and popular involvement in politics. While adopting the trappings of democratic societies, most regimes in the Middle East and North Africa still have unaccountable decision-makers at the heart of their political systems. It is therefore no surprise that much of the current scholarship focuses on attempting to explain the survival of authoritarian rule. While the focus on the presence of Islam as an obstacle to democratization seems misplaced, just as the focus on the authoritarian nature of Arab culture is misleading, there are a number of factors that can help understand how the ruling elites of the region have been able to effectively stave

off demands of democratization from their societies. There is no doubt that the considerable external rents the regimes enjoy are helpful in solidifying their security apparatuses and buying a degree of political acquiescence, but *rentierism* cannot be the sole explanation for authoritarianism. When examining the region, there is one factor that sets it apart. Contrary to many other transitional contexts, the most popular opposition does not enjoy any degree of domestic and international credibility in terms of its democratic commitments and credentials. The Islamists are perceived as inherently inimical to democracy and liberalism, leading the international community and liberal sectors of domestic society to reluctantly support the authoritarian rulers in place. This stalls any move towards greater democratization, allowing uncompromising opposition groups to emerge and challenge the stability of the state and of the international system through violence. The region's weak potential to democratize is not due to Islam or Arab political culture per se, but there is no doubt that the controversial role of political Islamism is a major stumbling bloc because of its perceived irreconcilability with the tenets of liberal-democracy. Islamism is a response to poverty, patrimonial repression and Western dominance of the international system, and while it might be incorrect to entirely blame the absence of democratic change for the emergence of political violence in the region, the lack of institutionalized access for dissenting voices articulating such response certainly favours the discourse of extremists. Given the extremely tense regional situation with the conflicts in Palestine and Iraq affecting the regimes of the area, it is quite difficult to see where democratic reforms could come from. It is likely that authoritarian rule, or at best liberalized authoritarianism (Brumberg 2002b), will remain a regional feature for the foreseeable future.

QUESTIONS

1. How does the international dimension affect authoritarian regimes in the Arab world?

2. What are the effects of *rentierism* on the political systems of Arab countries?

3. What are the main characteristics of the relationship between Islam and democracy?

4. What can explain the absence of effective coalition-building between Islamist and secular opposition groups?

5. Why does civil society activism seem not to have the same pro-democratic influence in the Arab world as it does in other regional contexts?

6. What steps should opposition groups undertake to limit the predominance of executives in the political system?

Visit the Online Resource Centre that accompanies this book for additional questions to accompany each chapter, and a range of other resources: <www.oxfordtextbooks. co.uk/orc/haerpfer/>.

FURTHER READING

Saikal, A. and Schnabel, A. (2003), *Democratization in the Middle East* (New York, NY: United Nations University Press). This small edited volume deals with the very important debate on the relationship between secularization and democracy. In addition, there are a number of chapters on national and regional experiences with democracy.

Schwedler, J. (2006), *Faith in Moderation. Islamist Parties in Yemen and Jordan* (Cambridge: Cambridge University Press). While focusing specifically on the Islamist movements in Yemen and Jordan, the book provides a number of very useful insights on the wider question regarding the inclusion of Islamist movements in the democratic process.

Wiktorowicz, Q. (2004), *Islamic Activism. A Social Movement Theory Approach* (Bloomington, IN: Indiana University Press). This edited collection provides a very solid overview of how Islamist movements in the region can be better understood through the theoretical frameworks offered by social movement theory. Contributors deal in depth with a vast number of Islamist movements and explain their activism and methods of action in great detail.

Volpi, F. and Cavatorta, F. (2007), *Democratization in the Muslim World. Changing Patterns of Power and Authority* (London: Routledge). This is another edited collection of writings detailing how processes of liberalization and democratization occur and how they are played out in a number of different countries in the Arab world and beyond.

Schlumberger, O. (2007), *Debating Arab Authoritarianism: Dynamics and Durability in Nondemocratic Regimes* (Stanford, CA: Stanford University Press).

This edited collection offers an analysis of the factors that explain the durability of authoritarian rule in the Arab world. Through an in-depth examination of state-society relations, the political economy of the region, the international dimension and the resources available to the different ruling elites, the volume constitutes one of the best overviews of the debate on the survival of non-democratic regimes in the Arab world.

IMPORTANT WEBSITES

<www.merip.org> The Middle East Research and Information Project (MERIP) is an excellent magazine, which provides 'news and perspectives about the Middle East not available from mainstream news sources.' The analysis is highly sophisticated and topical.

22 Sub-Saharan Africa

Michael Bratton

Overview

This chapter looks at efforts to introduce multi-party politics into Sub-Saharan Africa during the 1990s. A variety of **regimes** resulted, ranging from liberal democracy (as in South Africa), through electoral democracy (for example, Ghana), to electoral autocracy (Nigeria and Zimbabwe, among others). Still other autocracies remained unreformed. While certain structural conditions were conducive to political change (like the end of the Cold War, economic crisis, and a culture of nationalism), transitions to democracy only occurred where key political actors (such as opposition protesters or perceptive leaders) took the initiative. Few of Africa's limited number of democratic regimes have since consolidated. While African citizens welcome the introduction of competitive elections, powerful executive presidents still evade **accountability**, a situation abetted by the continent's persistent poverty and weak institutions.

Introduction

It may seem odd to couple the words 'democracy' and 'Africa' in the same sentence. After all, the international news media portray the Sub-Saharan subcontinent as a terrain of autocratic government and failed **states**. We have all seen disturbing pictures of child soldiers, ethnic riots, and civil wars splashed across our television screens. But these images tell only part of the complex story of Africa's recent political evolution. Closer examination reveals a more mixed reality. As a result of converging internal and external pressures, there have been encouraging developments in recent African politics. Several long-standing civil conflicts have been resolved peacefully, for example in Angola, Sierra Leone, Liberia, and Burundi. The rate of successful military coups has declined drastically from five per year in some years before 1990 to only five in total since then (Clark 2007). Almost all African governments have liberalized politically by releasing political prisoners, allowing greater press freedoms, and re-legalizing opposition political parties. And, most importantly, multi-party elections are now the modal method of choosing African leaders.

This turnabout in political direction has been so drastic as to support an extraordinary claim: since 1990, the rate of democratization has been faster in Sub-Saharan Africa than in any other region of the world except the communist bloc. Figure 5.2 in this volume shows mean levels of democracy for all world regions between 1972 and 2004. Two regions stand out as having strong upward trajectories in demo-cratic freedoms during the 1990s: the former Soviet Union (including Central and Eastern Europe) and Sub-Saharan Africa. Admittedly, the erstwhile com-munist countries attained somewhat higher average level of democracy and a faster rate of democratiza-tion by 2004 than the African countries. But both regions began at extremely low starting points and Sub-Saharan Africa progressed at a relatively faster rate than North America, Western Europe, Latin America, Asia, and the Middle East. Because African countries had much more room to improve, their average *rate* of democratization has been superior by recent world standards.

By the same token, much of Africa's apparent democratization reflects form rather than substance. While almost all regimes now go through the motions of elections, the quality of electoral procedures—are

they free and fair?—is highly variable. For example, while South Africa and Ghana have held exemplary contests, the quality of elections is in steep decline in Nigeria and Zimbabwe. The December 2007 balloting in Kenya captures—within the boundaries of a single country—both a successful parliamentary election that displaced many incumbents and a failed presi-dential election, whose overt rigging of a close con-test led to a paroxysm of ethnic violence.

This chapter seeks to explain these facts. The first part examines regime transitions and makes the following points. Transitions result from the 'conjuncture' of various forces (Berg-Schlosser, this volume). Some of these forces are structural—such as the decline of Afri-can economies, the end of the Cold War—but political actors produce others, like incumbents' concessions, opposition protests, and military withdrawals from politics. With reference to various African examples, it will be shown that certain structural conditions were necessary for democratic transitions in the 1990s, but that outcomes more often hinged on purposive politi-cal action. The second part of the chapter examines the quality of resultant African regimes. While few of the continent's democracies are consolidated, the range of other regime types is extremely diverse. To capture variety, we concentrate on the uneven quality of democratic developments noting, for example, that elections are often more widely accepted and deep-ly entrenched than other political institutions. The chapter concludes by identifying several fundamen-tal constraints on further democratization including endemic poverty and weak states.

Africa's Democratic Wave

A period of transition

The 1990s were a decade of democratization in Sub-Saharan Africa. A wave of transitions to multi-party rule began with Namibia's decolonization in 1990 and subsided only after Nigeria returned to civil-ian government in 1999. At the crest of the wave, the world witnessed a landmark transition from racial oligarchy to multiracial democracy in South

Africa in 1994. The political changes that unfolded in Africa during the 1990s were the most far reach-ing since the era of political independence some 30 years earlier. By the end of the 1980s, one-party or military regimes were entrenched in most African countries; in fact, multi-party electoral competition was allowed in only six out of 47 countries. And only two of these—Botswana and Mauritius—were con-sidered by Freedom House (1989) to be 'free', that is, liberal democracies.[1] Yet, just 10 short years later in 1999, some 43 countries had introduced competitive multi-party elections,[2] and six more countries—Benin, Cape Verde, Malawi, Namibia, Sao Tome and Principe, and South Africa—were certified as 'free' (Freedom House 2000).

What happened? Why did a large number of closed political systems begin to open up to electoral competition? And why did some of these liberalizing regimes go on to make a transition to democracy via free and fair elections? The principal argument in this chapter is that democratization occurred mainly because ordinary Africans began to demand greater accountability from their political leaders. At the time of independence, the nationalist founding fathers had promised their followers not only liberty from colonial rule but also higher standards of living. But neither of these promises was kept. Instead, after 30 years of post-colonial rule, Africans found themselves worse off economically and shorn of basic liberties of speech, association and assembly. As a consequence, they took to the streets to demand the ouster of corrupt and unresponsive leaders.

To be sure, other factors apart from mass political action were at play in Africa's democratic wave. There were rare historical conjunctures in which international and economic conditions converged to create the conditions in which protest could momentarily succeed. A pervasive economic crisis undercut African leaders' ability to distribute patronage rewards to their supporters and the end of the Cold War meant that petty dictators (except those in the Arab world) could no longer rely on superpower patrons to prop them up. Thus protesters faced severely weakened governments that were ripe for overthrow. These various strands of explanation will be elaborated below. But the thrust of the argument is that democratization occurred where domestic political actors took the lead: either perceptive incumbent leaders launched pre-emptive liberalization reforms or opposition forces were able to marshal a cohesive movement, preferably with the military on its side, that could exert pressure for genuinely free elections. Under these circumstances, a handful of fragile new democracies emerged on the African continent during the 1990s.

Although the pace of political change slowed after 2000, the democratic wave did not reverse, at least not through 2006. During this later period, four more countries—Ghana, Lesotho, Mali, and Senegal—graduated into the ranks of 'free' regimes and, overall, more African countries moved towards than away from the goal of a functioning democracy. The signal events in this period were the convocation of the first open elections in strife-torn countries like Rwanda (2003) and the previously inaptly named Democratic Republic of Congo (2006). These elections provided an alternative channel for the resolution of disputes that remained unavailable in other conflict zones like Eritrea, Somalia, and Sudan. Along with Swaziland, the latter unreformed autocracies had yet to hold competitive national elections by 2006.

Features of transition

Several features distinguish recent regime transitions in Africa. First, the continent has enjoyed meagre previous experience with democracy. In the pre-colonial era (before 1885), Africans governed themselves through patrimonial customs that concentrated power in the hands of hereditary chiefs, headmen, and elders. These systems had some democratic features: communal discussion was allowed and a group consensus was invited. But the oldest males held office until they died. Their style of **governance** hardly distinguished familial and political roles since rulers treated the polity as if it were a personal kinship network.

The colonial experience (1885–1960) did little to offset these less-than-democratic precedents. The European overlords were openly authoritarian, being more concerned with effective administration than political representation. Either they ruled directly through coercion (army, police and courts) or they devised indirect control by piggybacking Western laws on existing systems of traditional authority. Only in belated reaction to mass African nationalism did the departing colonial authorities try to install institutions of (British) parliamentary or (French) presidential democracy. In this respect, newly independent African nations briefly partook in the second global wave of democratization that accompanied the break-up of European empires in the middle twentieth century (Huntington 1991).

Not surprisingly, however, Western institutions hastily transplanted from abroad did not readily take root in Africa. Within a decade of independence, indigenous leaders either replaced multi-party systems with one-party regimes that outlawed opposition organizations or were swept away in military coups. Whether civilian or military, Africa's top leaders deployed the regulations and resources of the state to bolster their own political power. In this regard, a *neo*-patrimonial form of rule characterized the postcolonial period in Africa (1960–89) in which leaders co-opted the formal institutions of the state to serve their personal needs (Clapham 1982). A key feature of neo-patrimonial rule was that citizens found it impossible to remove the big man at the top who, for all practical purposes, was a president for life. In short, legacies of authoritarian rule—pre-colonial, colonial, and post-colonial—condemned Africans to embark on a quest for democracy from a low starting point and with little previous acquaintance with democratic forms of rule.

Second, the African regime transitions of the 1990s were rapid. The length of any political transition can be measured from the date of the first demands for a new political order to the installation of a regime that is observably different to the one that went before. For the African countries that first experienced regime change, the median interval between the onset of political protest and the accession to office of a new government was only 35 months, and just nine months in Cote d'Ivoire (Bratton and van de Walle 1997: 5). Compared with the trajectories of Poland, where trade union protests began a decade before the Berlin Wall came down, or Brazil, where the military gradually introduced reforms at a leisurely pace, the African regime changes seemed frantically hurried. Some later African transitions were protracted, as in Nigeria where the military repeatedly hesitated to surrender control, or in the Democratic Republic of Congo (DRC), where the death of strongman Mobutu Sese Seko was followed by a period of armed conflict that delayed elections. But, insofar as democratization requires the institutionalization of popular government, precious little time was available in African transitions for people to practice operating new political procedures. One implication was that the **consolidation** of democratic institutions in Africa would be problematic in years to come.

Third, regime transitions had diverse, and not always democratic, outcomes. Just 11 African countries were scored as 'free' democracies by 2006. Thus, by Freedom House criteria, less than one quarter of the continent's 48 countries actually consummated a democratic transition.[3] Moreover, because democratic transitions were disproportionately concentrated in countries with small populations, fewer than 15 per cent of all African people could be counted as politically free in 2006 (less than 10 per cent if South Africa is excluded). More commonly, many African transitions fell short of democracy: either competitive elections were never held, or elections were less than free and fair, or the losers of elections refused to accept the election results.

Regime transitions in Africa most often led to 'electoral autocracy', a type of political regime in which rulers adhere to the form of elections but manipulate the rules to ensure that opposition forces have little or no chance of winning (Schedler 2006). Africa's electoral autocracies are somewhat more liberal than the one-party or military regimes they replaced, not least because opposition parties are now allowed to operate. But political continuities undergirded African regime transitions. For example, the continent has seen relatively little electoral alternation of ruling parties: just 20 turnovers in 96 post-transition elections through 2006 (Lindberg 2006). While the frequency of such peaceful turnovers increased compared with the period before 1989, they still only occurred in one out of five post-transition elections. Rather than being displaced at the polls, dominant

---

Box 22.1 Key points

- While reversals and setbacks were less frequent than advancements towards democracy, they were common enough to demonstrate that Africa's transitions to open and competitive politics were tentative at best.

- Regime changes via free and fair elections did not guarantee that a set of high quality democratic institutions would subsequently survive, let alone consolidate.

- Democratization remains a fragile work in progress in many of Africa's poor and unstable states.

political parties in Africa have more often been able to secure re-election in a multi-party setting, even when they have failed to deliver on promises of economic development.

Finally, the attainment of democracy was short-lived in certain African countries. In 1994, a military coup ejected the democratic regime in Gambia, which at the time was one of the only five African countries—along with Botswana, Mauritius, Senegal, and Zimbabwe—to have retained a multi-**party system** since independence. In 1997, the former dictator in the Republic of Congo was reinstalled by the military following factional competition that escalated into civil war. In the following year in Lesotho the opposition rejected the results of national elections that had denied them a share of parliamentary seats. Extremist elements torched the business district of the capital city of Maseru, leading to an externally imposed interim authority charged to design a more proportional electoral system. In 2000 Malawi slipped back from a 'free' to 'partly free' due to deterioration in the management of elections and rising official corruption. And by 2002, Zimbabwe had regressed from 'partly free' to 'not free' as the dominant party embarked on violent campaigns to seize farmland and control elections.

Key Cases of Regime Transition

Because Africa is politically diverse it is inadvisable to over-generalize about the status of the continent's current regimes. This chapter therefore selects particular country cases to illustrate some major patterns of attempted democratization (see Table 22.1). The outcomes of these transitions run the gamut from an emerging liberal democracy (South Africa) and a promising electoral democracy (Ghana), through an ambiguous hybrid regime (Nigeria), to a downward spiralling electoral autocracy (Zimbabwe). Without ignoring each country's distinctive history, the cases provide a contrast between success stories (South Africa and Ghana) and problematic paths (Nigeria and Zimbabwe). The narratives provide an empirical base for subsequently analysing the factors that help to distinguish success from failure in democratization.

South Africa

As is well known, South Africa is a complex, divided society. Historically, the original Khoisan inhabitants experienced waves of Bantu immigration (from

Table 22.1 Political Regime Types in Sub-Saharan Africa, 1980–2006

	Liberal Democracy	Electoral Democracy	Ambiguous Hybrid	Electoral Autocracy
	South Africa	Ghana	Nigeria	Zimbabwe
Date of regime transition	1994	1996	1999	1980
Political Rights, at transition	2	4	4	4
Civil Liberties, at transition	3	4	3	4
FH Status at transition	Free	Partly Free	Partly Free	Partly Free
Political Rights, 2006	1	1	4	7
Civil Liberties, 2006	2	2	4	6
Status of Freedom, 2006	Free	Free	Partly Free	Not Free

Source: Freedom House, various years

the north) followed by the arrival of Dutch and British settlers (from the south). Encounters between these ethnic groups have long driven politics in South Africa. Until 1994 the government was racially exclusive. A small white minority used vast mineral wealth to industrialize the economy and build a modern bureaucratic state. While whites adopted a full array of democratic institutions for their own community (including multi-party elections, an independent judiciary, a free press) they denied the same to others. Independent from Britain after 1910, and ideologically committed to the complete separation of ethnic groups after 1948 (a policy known as **apartheid**), white settler governments were always dead set against black majority rule.

But the influx of African workers into South Africa's cities made a mockery of any attempt at social segregation and, in a context of the indignities imposed by apartheid, African political aspirations grew apace. Even after the National Party (NP) Government banned the African National Congress (ANC) in 1960 and imprisoned its leader, Nelson Mandela, in 1962, new forms of resistance arose: a guerrilla insurgency, a militant labour movement, and a coalition of civic groups. This succession of African political organizations mounted an intermittent but escalating sequence of political protests: demonstrations against 'pass' (identity document) laws in the 1950s and 1960s; a student uprising against language policy in the 1970s; and industrial strikes and consumer boycotts in the 1980s. Given the hard-line position adopted by the government—and, in reaction by protesters—race-based confrontation seemed destined to end in bloodshed.

Remarkably, leaders from both sides ultimately pulled back from the brink. In 1990 incoming President F. W. de Klerk released Mandela from jail, allowing him to walk free for the first time in 27 years. Along with other parties the ANC and NP entered constitutional negotiations in 1991 and, propelled in part by further protest, accepted the principle of a government of national unity. Pressured from abroad, but also recognizing a shared interest in South Africa's productive economy, political leaders crafted a political pact that protected white property rights in return for political rule by the black majority. For their foresight and moderation, de Klerk and Mandela were jointly awarded the Nobel Peace prize in 1992.

The transition from authoritarian rule was consummated in an April 1994 election in which all South Africans, regardless of background, participated as political equals in the democratic ritual of choosing their own rulers. The election did not run entirely smoothly: a key Zulu leader withheld his endorsement of the pact until the eleventh hour; voting had to be extended for several days in order to satisfy voter demand; and the reliability of election results was questionable in some pockets of the country. Nevertheless, the Independent Electoral Commission declared the contest substantially free and fair, an outcome that all parties came to accept and to celebrate. For the first time, South Africans had attained a multiracial government based on majority rule (the ANC won 63 per cent of the vote) with Mandela as the country's first democratically elected President.

Ghana

The contemporary state of Ghana occupies a territory on the West African coast previously governed by the centralized Ashanti Kingdom and the communities it conquered. Authority in the pre-colonial period was strictly hierarchical, but the Ashanti King could be removed from his golden stool if he ceased to rule in the public interest. As such, the traditional political system included expectations of political accountability that remain embedded in Ghanaian political culture today.

Reflecting this political sophistication, Ghana played a leading role among African countries in the independence era. Under the leadership of Kwame Nkrumah, the former Gold Coast was one of the first colonies to develop a militant mass nationalist movement, to win self-government in colonial legislative councils, and to secure the departure of the British colonial authorities in 1957. This early experiment with modern democracy, however, was short lived. Within a few years of independence, Nkrumah had formed a repressive one-party state under the banner of African socialism and imprisoned most of his opponents. Increasingly unpopular, he was ousted from power in 1966 by elements in the armed forces.

A series of subsequent military coups occurred through 1981, the last of which brought to power (for a second time) Flight-Lieutenant Jerry Rawlings—a radical populist who harboured aspirations of citizen empowerment and the redistribution of wealth. Faced with the imminent collapse of the Ghanaian economy, however, Rawlings had no choice but to accept conditions of economic structural adjustment required by the International Monetary Fund and World Bank. Economic reforms in the early 1980s in turn paved the way for political liberalization in the early 1990s. In 1990, Rawlings surprised even his own followers by announcing a two-year timetable to release political detainees, promulgate a multi-party constitution, and hold competitive elections. Even so, this military-led and tightly managed program of political transition was designed to maximize every advantage for the incumbent.

The elections of 1992 therefore fell short of installing a democratic regime. Although international observers declared presidential elections generally free and fair, opposition political parties charged rigging, refused to accept results, and boycotted the subsequent parliamentary polls. Thus Rawlings, who had won the presidential race, saw his National Democratic Congress (NDC) take almost all legislative seats without contest. By 1996, however, the opposition had concluded that boycotts were self-defeating and had joined the next regularly scheduled electoral campaigns. Rawlings and NDC won again, but with a lowered share of 57 per cent of the presidential vote and with less than two-thirds of the parliamentary seats. With the introduction of a meaningful degree of political competition in elections broadly accepted by all parties, Ghana made a transition to democracy.

Nigeria

With the largest population in Africa, and an economy second in size only to South Africa, Nigeria is the dominant state in the West Africa region. But its political development has been more problematic than that of Ghana, its smaller neighbour. The ethnic diversity of Nigeria's population—divided between western Yoruba, eastern Ibo, northern Hausa-Fulani, and a host of minority language groups in the middle belt and Niger Delta—has posed a challenge to all who have sought to govern the country as a unified entity.

During the colonial period, the British authorities adopted a system of indirect rule that ceded powers over local affairs to traditional rulers, especially in the north. After independence in 1960, and as a consequence of a debilitating civil war during 1967–70, Nigerian leaders experimented with a series of federal formulas, which expanded the number of states in the federation from 3 to 36. Complicating the division of political authority was the discovery of oil in the Niger Delta, which unleashed fierce competition over government revenues. Windfall profits from the oil industry also fuelled corruption by political elites and the emergence of huge wealth gaps between rich and poor.

Against this background, Nigerians have encountered difficulty in establishing stable democratic government. For the first four decades of independence, Nigeria was ruled mainly by the military. The First Republic, a parliamentary system, succumbed to ethnic and regional contention and was displaced by an army coup within six years. A brief experiment with a civilian presidency during the Second Republic of 1979–83 led to growing corruption and rigged elections, and again ended in a military takeover. In each instance, many Nigerians welcomed the intercession by soldiers, although the public also nurtured hopes that a viable democracy would soon be restored.

But the coup of 1983 gave way to a protracted period of military control that lasted until 1999. Political instability reached a peak when General Ibrahim Babangida abrogated his own promises of democratic reform by annulling presidential elections in 1993 and imprisoning the winner. The regime of Babangida's successor, General Sani Abacha, was marked by a crackdown against protest by oil workers and political activists and the spectacular personal enrichment of the ruler and his family. At a time when South Africa and Ghana had both undergone a political transition via competitive elections, Nigeria looked like a democratic laggard. An opening occurred only with the sudden death of Abacha in 1998 and the inauguration of a phased transition to civilian rule by a more progressive military leader.

The democratic regime inaugurated in May 1999, headed by Olusegun Obasanjo (himself a former military leader but now elected as civilian president) faced daunting challenges. Declining to accept the authority of the country's first president from the south, governors of several northern states invoked Islamic Sharia law. Resisting the extraction of oil revenues by the federal government, armed separatist movements disrupted oil supplies from the Niger Delta. With the military still lurking in the wings, ordinary Nigerians wondered whether civilian politicians could install the institutions and procedures of lasting democratic rule.

Zimbabwe

Zimbabwe's name (as Ghana's) recalls a pre-colonial African empire—in this case the Kingdom of the Monomatapa, the historic homeland of the Shona-speaking peoples. Colonized in the 1890s, Southern Rhodesia (as Zimbabwe was then known) followed in several important respects the political trajectory of South Africa. European settlers seized the best arable land and denied political rights to blacks. Self-governing from 1923, a white minority government broke away illegally from Britain in 1965 in an effort to avert independence under African majority rule.

A war of national liberation ensued (1972–79) in which rural guerrilla forces ultimately drove the settler government to the negotiating table. A constitutional settlement hammered out at Lancaster House in London granted votes to all adults, regardless of race, in return for a guarantee of compensation payments for any land reform. In the country's founding democratic election of April 1980, Robert Mugabe became the first Prime Minister of Zimbabwe when his party won 63 per cent of the votes on a common roll. At first, Mugabe extended a hand of reconciliation to the settler community, inviting them to stay in order to build the country for the benefit of all.

But the independence war revealed a deep cleavage between Shona and Ndebele-speakers. Each ethnic community had formed its own political party and armed wing, which operated from separate rear bases (in Mozambique and Zambia respectively). Clashes broke out between these factions during the war itself and intensified into a pogrom by the new government of the Zimbabwe African National Union (ZANU) against Ndebele-speakers in the 1980s. By 1987, the latter's Zimbabwe African Peoples' Union (ZAPU) was forced to accept a junior partnership in a merged national political party known as the Zimbabwe African National Union-Patriotic Front (ZANU-PF).

The paradox of Zimbabwe's political regime is that it retained a multi-party constitution while gradually becoming a repressive de facto one-party state. True, opposition parties could contest elections, but they rarely won parliamentary seats: for example, just two (against ZANU-PF's 118) in 1995 elections. Moreover, election campaigns became increasingly violent and results increasingly rigged after Mugabe unexpectedly lost a referendum on presidential powers in 2000 to a new labour-based opposition known as the Movement for Democratic Change (MDC). Charging that his political opponents represent colonial and settler interests, Mugabe has since employed a battery of coercive instruments—restrictive laws, political imprisonment, extrajudicial violence—in an effort to destroy the MDC. Thus, over the past decade, one of Africa's earliest and most promising democracies deteriorated into an intolerant and autocratic police state.

Explanatory Factors

What factors help us to understand Africa's contrasting political outcomes? What common or distinctive features underlie the above narratives of regime transition? In this section, we explore three structural possibilities—namely international, economic, and cultural contexts—plus the initiatives of political leaders and their interactions with opponents. As intimated earlier, our preferred explanation grants greater weight to specific political actions and reactions—by incumbents, protesters, and the military—rather than to broader international, economic, or cultural forces.

International influences

It would be foolish to deny that changes in the international environment, like the end of the Cold War, had no effect on African regime transitions. After all, the spurt of democratic experiments across the continent began immediately after the fall of the Berlin Wall in 1989. The timing of these events suggests that transitions were a response to external stimuli, such as the withdrawal of superpower support to Africa's authoritarian governments, the introduction of political conditions for Western development assistance, or the diffusion of mass pro-democracy protests from Central and Eastern Europe.

Indeed without international pressures political transition would have been considerably delayed in key African cases. In Southern Rhodesia (as Zimbabwe was then), the white minority regime was driven to concede a transfer of power in good part by international trade sanctions in the 1970s. The old regime survived only so long as South Africa provided an economic lifeline to the wider world; but it collapsed when South Africa joined the rest of the international community in demanding a transition to majority rule. In South Africa itself the economy began to shrink in the 1980s as international investors withdrew capital, forcing the government to seek political accommodation with the West. At the same time, the collapse of communism in the Soviet Union and Central and Eastern Europe deprived the ANC of its main sources of political, military, and economic support. Because both sides lacked the means to win an outright victory, each began to see virtue in coming to terms.

International influences shaped transitions elsewhere on the continent too. Foreign donors were able to push incumbent presidents in Benin and Zambia toward open elections in good part because these aid-dependent African governments were bankrupt. Other presidents, for example in Zaire (now DRC) and Tanzania, quickly conceded political reforms after they observed these events, plus the death of their ally, Romanian President Nicolae Ceausescu, at the hands of his own citizens. In Togo and Malawi, a domino effect of democratization in neighbouring states (Benin and Zambia respectively) prompted citizens to take to the streets to demonstrate for their own political transitions. And the image of Nelson Mandela walking free from a South African jail in 1990 inspired Africans across the continent to pluck up the courage to demand lost liberties.

Economic conditions

By the end of the 1980s, African countries had endured two decades of stalled growth and faced deepening economic crisis. The living standards of the average African were lower by 1989 than at independence. Material hardship thus formed a ubiquitous backdrop to political reform and, before protest movements took up a pro-democracy banner, they often began as a reaction against economic austerity.

In Ghana, for example, the radical Rawlings regime had discouraged private entrepreneurship, leading to capital flight and shortages of basic consumer goods. Needing investment, the government had no option but to accept loans from international financial institutions, whose conditions required cutbacks in public employment and social services. In Nigeria, the discovery of oil meant that the country was far less dependent than Ghana on foreign economic assistance. But successive governments overspent the proceeds from the oilfields, forcing the government to introduce its own homegrown policies of economic contraction. Yet efforts at economic recovery in Nigeria were severely distorted by corruption and, by the time of Abacha's death in 1998, the government had abandoned any effort at systematic economic management. As poverty trickled up in both countries, political constituencies emerged for good governance, economic deregulation, and social justice. Ghanaians and Nigerians alike began to clamour for a capable government that could deliver these things.

To a greater or lesser extent, a scenario of economically induced unrest unfolded across much of the continent. In Benin and Kenya, among other places, demonstrations started among university students protesting the declining purchasing power of government scholarships. In Mali and Tanzania, informal street traders demanded the removal of restrictions on where and how they could sell their goods. In Congo, Guinea, and Zambia, labour unions organized general strikes that shut down commercial and government operations in African capital cities. Anti-corruption was a unifying theme, illustrated by the placards declaring 'Mobutu, voleur!' carried by striking civil servants in Zaire. As people began to attribute their own economic hardships to theft by political elites, so protest turned political and people were poised to follow leaders who proclaimed a pro-democracy message.

Political culture and society

For democratic transition to occur, a measure of cultural homogeneity is required (Rustow 1970). Before people can agree to accept democratic rules for a political regime, they must first reach consensus that they belong to the same political community. Stated differently, nationhood is often a precondition for democracy.

Yet the construction of a shared sense of nationhood is an incomplete project in all the culturally diverse country cases we have considered so far. South Africa's society is still riven by the deep divisions of apartheid, which established largely impermeable institutional barriers between whites, Africans, Indians and Coloureds. While the settler population in Zimbabwe dwindled after 1980, Mugabe's ideology of permanent liberation war still stokes the historical embers of racism. Moreover, new tensions between Shona and Ndebele-speakers have arisen since Zimbabwe became independent. In Ghana ethnic divisions are relatively less politicized, but social and voting cleavages can be seen between the Akan and Volta heartlands, and between the Muslim north and Christian south. Finally, Nigeria stands as the paradigm of a culturally complex African country. Multiple ethnic divisions are accompanied by regional, religious, and class differences, leading to a polyglot society in which every identity group struggles first and foremost for its own share of national political and economic pie.

In some African countries, the promise of democracy induced political actors to set aside their cultural differences, at least temporarily. In Ghana, for example, the 1996 transition was accomplished without shifting the centre of political gravity away from the incumbent's Volta home base. In Zimbabwe, black ethnic factions were able to subdue their struggles long enough to accomplish a larger goal, namely removing white settlers from political power. And in South Africa, the 1994 transition represented a moment when estranged communities came to the realization that they could not go it alone and that all racial groups needed each other. Even in Nigeria, the 1999 transition represented a conciliatory power shift in which Obasanjo, a southern Christian, ascended to the presidency after a long string of northern Muslim leaders. Implicit in this transition, however, was the understanding that the presidency in Nigeria would in the future continue to circulate between different religious and ethnic communities and between the north and south.

The roles of political actors

The analysis so far would seem to suggest that certain structural conditions—like international pressure, economic crisis, and an emergent nationalism—contribute to democratic transitions. But such an account leaves out an essential additional element: the behaviour of political actors. After all, it is people who make regime change, even if they do so within the constraining circumstances in which they find themselves. But which people? Here we consider three sets of actor: incumbent political elites, opposition movements, and the armed forces.

The choices made by African political leaders were often decisive. It is hard to imagine a peaceful democratic outcome in South Africa, for example, without the decisions of F.W. de Klerk to gamble on political reform or Nelson Mandela to adopt policies of economic moderation and political reconciliation. Often unappreciated in Nigeria was General Abdulsalami Abubakar's break with a past mould of military repression and his determination to press for a quick and orderly transition to civilian elections in 1999. Indeed, incumbents often set the pace for transition, not only from military rule (as in the gradual steps mandated by Rawlings in Ghana) but also from long-standing one-party regimes, such as Tanzania under Nyerere in 1995 and Uganda under Museveni in 2006. In the latter cases, incumbent leaders actually persuaded their own people to consider multi-partyism. More commonly, however, incumbents embarked on political liberalization as a defensive strategy to pre-empt mounting popular protest and remain in control, an approach that worked well for, among others, Paul Biya in Cameroon and Omar Bongo in Gabon. At the time of writing both still held office after 25 and 40 years respectively.

Opposition movements comprised the other major players in the game of transition. Unlike incumbents, they always lacked access to the financial and coercive resources of the state. But they held the advantage of appealing ideologies of anti-corruption, human rights protection, and democratic change. Whether opposition movements were able to translate these resources into a successful bid for power via elections depended in turn on the emergence of capable leaders and unified followings. Contrast Zambia with Kenya. In Zambia, trade unionist Frederick Chiluba managed to pull together the Movement for Multiparty Democracy (MMD), a multi-ethnic, cross-class coalition that decisively defeated incumbent Kenneth Kaunda at the polls in 1991. In Kenya, however, the opposition remained split among a bevy of small ethnic and personal parties that lost 1992 and 1997 elections to Daniel Arap Moi, even though the incumbent could command votes from only about one-third of the electorate. A democratic transition was completed in Kenya in 2002 only after smaller parties were able to rally behind a single candidate, Mwai Kibaki of the National Rainbow Coalition (NaRC). It is notable, however, that once in power, both MMD and NaRC were unable to sustain a unified front; both parties governed narrowly and suffered defections, which suggests that opposition coalitions in Africa have been little more than alliances of convenience.

Finally, the military were a wild card in the game of transition. Whether military forces remained loyal to the incumbent or defected to the opposition had a decisive impact on the course of political events. Take two of our key cases: in South Africa, the transition outcome was sealed when the defence forces resisted any temptation to rebel and pledged their loyalty to the incoming government of national unity headed by Nelson Mandela. By contrast, an attempted democratic transition in Nigeria was aborted when military leaders refused to recognize the results of the reasonably free and fair elections in 1993. In short, as went the military—to support or oppose democratization—so went the transition. This robust finding has major implications for democratic prospects in Africa because it demonstrates that the fate of political regimes still indirectly rests in the hands of men with guns.

Conjuncture and causality

We are now in a position to piece together a comprehensive explanation. It can be argued that all of the above factors, *both* structural *and* contingent,

---

Box 22.2 **Key points**

- While certain structural background conditions may have been necessary for transition, no single or combined set of cultural, economic, or international factors was sufficient.

- In order to effect a democratic transition a country also required an organized constituency for democratic reform with sufficient resources to challenge incumbents.

- The explanation has to be *conjunctural*: structural circumstances created a given set of political resources; but the critical consideration is whether political actors made use of the opportunities thereby presented.

---

are necessary for a full understanding. But in what order? We give primacy to political action, by suggesting that democratic transitions could not be consummated unless some combination of key actors—incumbent, opposition or military—willed free and fair elections into effect and accepted the results.

Deep structural conditions, like ethnic diversity and economic crisis, may have influenced the prospects for democratization—the former usually negatively, the latter often positively. These are necessary background considerations. The end of the international superpower rivalry (the Cold War) was clearly a powerful precipitating condition. But all these structural factors were common to virtually *all* African countries. Hence, a purely structural analysis cannot distinguish the diversity of transition outcomes, whether liberal democracy, electoral democracy, electoral autocracy, or unreformed autocracy. To distinguish resultant regimes, reference is also needed to the strategic political interactions of key actors during the transition period. We need to know what sort of resources were available to incumbents and opposition—for example, state repression versus political protest—and how confrontations between incumbents, opposition, and the military played themselves out.

Institutional Challenges

The democratic regimes recently installed in Africa are young and fragile. To deepen democracy, the fundamental challenge is to establish institutions of political accountability which, in Africa, mainly means imposing checks on the powers of 'big man' executive presidents. Political accountability is the core operating code of a functioning democracy because it establishes the principle that rulers should answer to the ruled.

Accountability can be exercised in various ways: 'vertically' by citizens over rulers, 'horizontally' over the executive by other branches or units of government, or 'obliquely' by institutions in political and civil society, such as political parties, voluntary organizations and the mass media (O'Donnell 1994). In Africa, a particular form of vertical accountability—competitive multi-party elections—has recently begun to take root. But, within other parts of the democratic regime, institutions of horizontal accountability—like independent judicial bodies to uphold civil liberties and a rule of law—are much less developed. Hence the most common form of democracy in the region is the electoral (rather than the liberal) version. By the same token, the quality of recent African elections often leaves a lot to be desired, notably in the region's electoral autocracies. In this section, we review the challenges of institution building, beginning with elections but including other governmental, political, and civic institutions.

Elections

Competitive multi-party elections have become an established norm of African politics. Almost every African president now finds it necessary to wrap himself in the legitimating mantle of elections.[4] On the rare occasion that the military still intervenes (as in Niger in 1999), coup makers nowadays immediately issue assurances that they are temporary caretakers who plan to remain in control only long enough to organize civilian elections (Nugent 2004). Among ordinary citizens, 82 per cent of Africans interviewed in 18 countries in 2005 believe that regular, open, and honest elections are the best way to choose leaders (Afrobarometer 2006).

Because elections are now widely valued, they occur in all sorts of regimes. But their quality varies. In South Africa's liberal democracy, elections are professionally managed and conducted in an atmosphere of free speech. In Ghana's electoral democracy, the calibre of the electoral contests has gradually improved over time: campaign irregularities are kept to a minimum, as are challenges to the results. In Nigeria, however, electoral conduct has steadily deteriorated as evidenced by increasing levels of vote buying and violent intimidation. Whereas in 1999, observers could announce that the election results roughly represented the will of the Nigerian people, by 2007 no such pretence was possible. By that time the quality of elections in Nigeria approached the low levels of those in Zimbabwe's electoral autocracy, where ZANU-PF incumbents blatantly stole the 2005 parliamentary and 2008 presidential polls by preventing opposition campaigning and manipulating the count.

In the absence of a fully developed set of political institutions, the openness of elections serves as a reliable shorthand guide to the quality of democracy. As illustrated above, free and fair contests are associated with liberal democracy, whereas sham polls are a feature of electoral autocracy. Ordinary Africans make precisely these connections. In public opinion surveys, people express levels of satisfaction with democracy based on the degree to which they think the last national election was free and fair (Bratton 2007). And popular judgments about the extent of democracy prevailing in any given country are in turn affected by a turnover of the ruling party at the polls. Wherever such alternations have occurred—as in Ghana in 2000, Senegal in 2001, and Mali in 2002—popular commitments to democracy have grown, probably because citizens see elections as an effective mechanism for holding leaders accountable. And vice versa: the more timr that has elapsed without a change of government, the more that people begin to wonder whether elections and democracy are working well.

Political parties

The outcome of elections depends in part on the degree of pluralism in political society. African countries seldom possess competitive, two-party systems. Opposition groups that are adequately prepared to assume office exist in only a handful of countries, including Botswana, Cape Verde, Ghana, and Senegal. And coalition governments composed of many minority parties—as in Mali and Niger—are also rare. Instead, the modal situation is a single, dominant ruling party surrounded by multiple, small, satellite parties. The persistence of de facto one-party governments—including in South Africa, Zimbabwe, Namibia, Zambia, Tanzania, and Uganda—represents continuity with previous post-colonial practices. Indeed, in Tanzania, which has been governed continuously by the same political party since 1961, it is hard to discern meaningful differences in the regime type under old one-party and new multi-party constitutions.

The power imbalance between ruling and opposition parties has economic and cultural roots. Ruling parties enjoy an incumbent's advantage of access to the budgetary and regulatory resources of the state. In African societies, the state is the principal provider of jobs, benefits, scholarships, licenses, and other perquisites, which rulers employ to reward followers and punish opponents. For their part, challengers must draw resources from the private sector which is usually modest and often informal. Thus opposition parties tend to form, if at all, around the interests and ambitions of wealthy individuals, a process that tends to reproduce pathologies of personal rule and patronage. Culturally, incumbent elites usually promote an ideology of national unity, which can be used all too easily to brand legitimate opposition as disloyal. Most ordinary Africans also regard opposition parties in a negative light, granting them among the lowest levels of popular trust of any national political institution (see Table 22.2). And while citizens are gradually coming to accept the desirability of having more than one viable political party, they still worry that multi-party competition can lead to political violence (Afrobarometer 2006).

Civil society

The institutions of civil society have occasionally been more effective than opposition parties in ensuring governmental accountability—recent political openings have allowed the expression of independent African voices, including many that were previously silent. Private newspapers, magazines, radio stations, and even television channels have proliferated since 1990 and some now challenge the orthodoxies propagated by the official press and broadcast media (Hyden *et al.* 2003). Indigenous non-governmental watchdog agencies have sprung up in space beyond the state to monitor human rights abuses, promote an anti-corruption agenda, and conduct civic education.

But these gains, and the political accountability they promise, have been uneven. For example, a grass-roots Treatment Action Campaign forced the South African Government to belatedly begin distributing

Table 22.2 Popular Trust in Political Institutions, Selected African Countries, 2005

	South Africa	Ghana	Nigeria	Zimbabwe
Trust in ruling political parties	62	67	22	31
Trust in opposition parties	29	51	24	47
Trust in national assembly	54	68	22	35
Trust courts of law	67	62	37	53

Note: Cell entries are percentage of randomly selected survey respondents saying they trust this institution 'somewhat' or 'a lot' (weighted N = 4,800).

Source: Afrobarometer, Round 3, 2005

affordable anti-retroviral drugs to AIDS patients. And segments of the independent press in Nigeria have relentlessly exposed corruption among senior officials, especially state governors. But in Zimbabwe, ruling party thugs have stopped non-governmental organizations engaged in civic education or emergency food relief programs from operating in opposition areas. And, in a context where foreign journalists are prevented from reporting from within Zimbabwe, the opposition *Daily News* was firebombed under suspicious circumstances. As such, civic and media organizations operate freely only if authorities permit. As demonstrated by the ban on live media broadcasts in the aftermath of Kenya's disputed 2007 elections, governments can strike down civil liberties with impunity, even in countries that had previously been on an upward democratic trajectory.

Legislatures and courts

The effectiveness of political and civic demands for accountability often depends on whether state institutions play their constitutionally mandated roles. Do legislatures and courts act independently, especially to restrain the executive branch? Take legislatures first. Although weak in relation to the executive, these institutions of horizontal accountability are arguably more effective today than at any time since independence (Barkan *et al.* 2004). In Ghana, the National Assembly gained credibility as a forum for public policy debate and for amending budget bills, especially after the 1996 elections reduced the ruling party's majority. And in Nigeria (as well as Zambia and Malawi), parliamentarians voted against presidents who sought constitutional amendments to overturn term limits.

Even so, all African parliaments remain underfinanced to the point that elected representatives can hardly afford to perform legislative research or constituency service. And when legislators do obtain control over public budgets, as in Nigeria and Kenya, they routinely boost their own salaries and benefits before attending to public business. The independence of the legislature remains compromised to the extent that the executive branch holds the purse strings. In Zimbabwe's electoral autocracy, President Mugabe appoints a proportion of assembly members,

created a second senate chamber in 2005, and has packed these institutions with generously rewarded patronage appointees. Beholden to the president, these loyalists provide a 'rubber stamp' endorsement to any legislation, however draconian, that the executive branch wishes to propose.

The independence of the judiciary also varies across political regimes. In South Africa's liberal democracy an independent constitutional court has sometimes ruled against the ANC Government, including in the AIDS drug case mentioned above. In Nigeria, the judiciary stemmed some of the worst abuses in the 2007 election, for instance preventing the disqualification of Obasanjo's principal rival from contesting the presidency. In South Africa many blacks still harbour reservations about courts staffed by white judges from the old regime, and in Nigeria, the judicial system is far from immune from the country's pervasive corruption. Once more, however, Zimbabwe provides an egregious example of abuse. In 2001, the Mugabe Government forced an uncooperative chief justice into retirement and replaced him with a compliant political ally.

Because of uneven performance in some countries, institutions of horizontal accountability have yet to win universal popular trust. According to 2005 Afrobarometer surveys, the judiciary usually enjoys more trust than the legislature (Table 22.2). The courts attract most trust in South Africa and least in Nigeria, and the legislature attracts most trust in Ghana and least in Nigeria. Trust in the legislature is also restricted to a low one-third of the citizenry in Zimbabwe. Thus, while an independent judici-

---

Box 22.3 Key points

- Competitive multi-party elections are now institutionalized in African politics, even though the quality of some such contests leaves much to be desired.

- Institutions of horizontal accountability—such as parliaments and courts—rarely enjoy enough capacity or independence to limit executive power.

- Political and civil society—including political parties, voluntary associations, and the mass media—are maturing, but remain weak in relation to the state.

ary may be consolidating in some of Africa's liberal and electoral democracies, legislatures probably fail to attract the confidence of citizens in many of the continent's hybrid regimes and electoral autocracies.

And the construction of solid democratic institutions—within state and society alike—remains an unfinished project in most African countries.

Conclusion

Contemporary Africa possesses few, if any, consolidated democracies. Its newly reformed political regimes remain flimsy and incomplete. Even promising liberal and electoral democracies (like those in South Africa and Ghana) are not immune from backsliding into hybrid or autocratic systems (presently typified by Nigeria and Zimbabwe). This assortment of African polities highlights the wide variations in the quality of democracy that Africans are constructing in different parts of the continent.

Yet underneath such flourishing diversity—which is a boon to scholars of comparative politics—lie certain harsh regularities. Powerful structural constraints pose challenges that confront all would-be democrats. Whereas African political actors were able to influence the course of events during the heady moments of regime transition in the 1990s, they encounter much greater difficulty in exercising effective human agency during the longer-term tasks of consolidating democratic institutions in a new century.

In the first place, the international environment has changed since the post-Cold War moment when the USA was an unrivalled superpower and an unambiguous advocate for democracy. Since September 11, 2001, the USA has calibrated its foreign policy as much in terms of national security as of democratization, for example by backing a non-democratic anti-jihadist regime in Ethiopia. At the same time, the Peoples' Republic of China has extended its reach into Africa in search of the oil and raw materials needed to sustain its own economy's breakneck expansion. African authoritarian governments, including those in Zimbabwe and Sudan, find it easy to do business with this like-minded regime that does not demand democratization as a condition of aid or trade. Indeed, the global boom in democratization—from which Africa benefited as much as any world region—may

now have given way to a period of international democratic recession (Diamond 2008).

Second, the endemic weakness of African states constitutes a structural obstacle to the deepening of democracy. As several scholars have noted, the democracy project often commenced in Africa before state building was complete. Central governments that cannot project authority throughout their own territories—as in Somalia, the DRC, and other failed or failing states—offer flawed foundations on which to create democracy. Indeed, new African democracies have only ever emerged in the continent's stronger states and never in those places that suffer from political instability, governmental ineffectiveness, or uncontrolled corruption (Bratton and Chang 2006). The limitation of weak states need not be taken as an admonition to delay democratization until the groundwork of effective authority can be laid. Rather, it requires that political order be accompanied by a rule of law by which any claim to political authority is legitimate from the outset.

Third, Africa remains the world's poorest continent. Historically, modern democracies first emerged in the wealthy, industrial world. The precondition of economic development has seemingly been relaxed, however, since extremely low-income African countries like Mozambique and Liberia made transitions to electoral forms of democracy (Przeworski *et al.* 2000). But how long can democracy survive in poor countries? Sooner or later, or so goes the argument, elected governments will surely have to deliver the benefits of economic development to deprived populations. Otherwise, ordinary people are likely to lose faith in democracy. To date, however, most Africans appear to be content to enjoy the political freedoms of a democratic regime even if unaccompanied by improved material standards of living. This political honeymoon has lasted longer than most analysts expected. But the patience of Africa's long-suffering masses cannot be infinite.

Finally, political cultures are slow to change. In most African countries, social relationships, including between leaders and followers, remain highly personal. Formal political rules frequently take second place to cultural norms like kinship, reciprocity and redistribution. When perverted, these norms fuel pathologies like nepotism and corruption. Indeed, African state elites—even those who are freely and fairly elected—invariably act as political patrons whose main goal is to attract a loyal group of clients. More so than in other world regions, they manipulate the structures of the state and the procedures of democracy in order to distribute benefits in return for votes. In this climate of informal exchange, democracy takes on new and often unrecognizable forms in which ordinary citizens find great difficulty in holding their leaders accountable.

This last discussion brings us back to human agency. It is often said by casual observers of African politics that the continent needs better leaders. While there is a germ of truth to this insight, it places agency in the wrong place. Unless they are selfless public servants, political leaders are unlikely to voluntarily submit themselves to a rule of law, to strengthen formal political institutions, or to invest in economic growth rather than political patronage. In short, democratic leaders rarely emerge of their own accord. They have to be held accountable by an active citizenry. And this is where democracy comes in.

QUESTIONS

1. Compared to other world regions, how slowly or rapidly has Sub-Saharan Africa democratized?

2. How widespread were democratic transitions across African countries in the 1990s?

3. Using country examples, distinguish various types of contemporary political regime in Sub-Saharan Africa.

4. With reference to South Africa and Zimbabwe, contrast the regime trajectories of former white settler states in Southern Africa.

5. With reference to Ghana and Nigeria, contrast the regime trajectories of former military governments in West Africa.

6. Which structural factors were conducive to democratic transitions in Africa in the 1990s? Were they necessary, sufficient, or neither?

Visit the Online Resource Centre that accompanies this book for additional questions to accompany each chapter, and a range of other resources: <www.oxfordtextbooks. co.uk/orc/haerpfer/>.

FURTHER READING

Afrobarometer (2006), 'The Status of Democracy, 2005–2006: Findings from Afrobarometer Round 3 for 18 Countries', *Afrobarometer Briefing Paper*, 40 (available at <www. afrobarometer.org>). A snapshot of African public opinion on democracy issues.

Bratton, M. and van de Walle, N. (1997), *Democratic Experiments in Africa: Regime Transitions in Comparative Perspective* (Cambridge: Cambridge University Press). Expands on many of the arguments presented in this chapter.

Nugent, P. (2004), *Africa Since Independence* (London: Palgrave Macmillan). Probably the best overview of modern African political history.

Posner, D. and Young, D. (2007), 'The Institutionalization of Political Power in Africa,' *Journal of Democracy*, 18/3: 126–40. An argument about the emerging strength of formal institutions.

Schedler, A. (2006) (ed.), *Electoral Authoritarianism: The Dynamics of Unfree Competition* (Boulder, CO: Lynne Rienner). A useful framework for viewing African politics.

IMPORTANT WEBSITES

<www.africanelections.tripod.com> A trove of African electoral data.

<www.afrobarometer.org> Shows what ordinary Africans are thinking.

<www.commissionforafrica.org> Makes a case for expanded aid to Africa.

NOTES

1. *Freedom in the World, 1988–89* (New York: Freedom House, 1989). In the other multiparty regimes—Gambia, Madagascar, Senegal and Zimbabwe—political competition was constrained, causing Freedom House to dub them only 'partly free'.

2. Under Uganda's 'no party' regime, elections were competitive but not multi-party. The source of data on first competitive contests is Staffan Lindberg, 'Elections in Africa, 1989–2006', kindly provided by the author.

3. Eritrea, the newest (and 48th) Sub-Saharan country, gained independence form Ethiopia in 1993.

4. Or herself: Ellen Johnson-Sirleaf was elected as Africa's first female president in Liberia in 2005.

East Asia

Doh Chull Shin and Rollin F. Tusalem*

Overview

This chapter offers a comprehensive and dynamic account of democratization in East Asia over the past two decades. It first traces the history of democratic transitions in the region, and thereafter examines their contours, modes, and sources from a comparative perspective. It then considers the extent to which third-wave democracies have consolidated by appraising the quality of their performances. Finally it explores the prospect of democratic **regime** change in China and Singapore. Analyses of Freedom House and the World Bank data reveal

that the East Asian region has been slow in responding to the surging wave of global democratization in terms of not only transforming authoritarian regimes into electoral democracies, but also consolidating electoral democracies into well-functioning liberal democracies. Analyses of the Asian Barometer surveys, on the other hand, suggest that the mass citizenries of China and Singapore endorse their current regime as a well-functioning democracy, and are not much in favour of democratic regime change in their country.

Introduction

Asia, the world's largest continent, is also the most populous continent on earth. More than 60 per cent of the world's population lives on the mass of land stretching from the Middle East to the South Pacific islands and as many as 60 countries have their

homes there. Asia's cultural contributions include the birth of Buddhism, Confucianism, Hinduism, Islam, Shintoism, and Daoism, and it is also home to the largest Muslim population in the world. Economically, Asia encompasses countries of great wealth, including Japan and Singapore, and countries of extreme poverty, including Bangladesh and Myanmar. Politically, it covers a startling range of regimes, from the oldest non-Western democracies of India and Japan to the world's most oppressive regimes of Myanmar and North Korea. All in all, it is hard to overstate the enormous differences among countries in Asia in terms of their natural resources, cultural and religious heritages, socioeconomic development, and political legacies.

Indeed, Asia is so large and so diverse that it is difficult to compare all of its countries and identify even a few general patterns of Asian democratization. In an attempt to ascertain such patterns, we follow the customary practice of separating the continent into regions and focus on the region known as East Asia, which covers the north-eastern and south-eastern parts of the continent. In this chapter, we analyse the process of democratization that has taken place within this particular region since the mid-1970s. Of the 14 countries in the region, much of our analysis presented below focuses on the seven countries that have undergone democratic regime change over the past two decades, namely Cambodia, Indonesia,

Mongolia, the Philippines, South Korea, Taiwan, and Thailand. In addition to these countries, we examine the prospects of democratic regime change in China and Singapore, two of the world's most notable non-democratic countries.

To offer a comprehensive and dynamic account of democratization in East Asia, the chapter begins with a brief discussion of the three forces—economic development, Confucianism, and elite conceptions of democracy—that have shaped the contours of democratization in East Asia, followed by an overview of the diffusion of the global wave of democratization in East Asia, which began with the demise of the personal dictatorship in the Philippines in 1986. In the following three sections, we analyse how East Asian countries have democratized institutionally and substantively. After these multi-dimensional analyses of democratization in East Asia, we examine the prospects China and Singapore have of joining in the global wave. The final section highlights the distinguishing characteristics of East Asian democratization and discusses their implications for the ongoing debate about the sources and consequences of democratization.

East Asia as a Region of Democratization

A multitude of forces, including domestic and international contextual factors, shape democratization, and political leaders and ordinary people participate in its process. In the words of Samuel P. Huntington (1993), the former constitute 'causes' and the latter 'causers' of democratization. Of the various causes reported to have shaped the process of democratization in East Asia over the past two decades, economic development and Confucian Asian cultural values constitute the two most unique contextual forces. Of the people involved in the democratization process, political elites are known to be the most powerful causers (Friedman 1995). In this section, we explore how these two structural and cultural forces shape the actions of political leaders and ordinary people in the context of democratic regime change.

Economically, East Asia is vastly different from the rest of the democratizing world. Unlike their peers in other regions, a number of countries in this region achieved unprecedented economic growth and social modernization under authoritarian rule. Prior to their transitions to democracy, East Asian countries, with a few exceptions such as Mongolia and the Philippines, experienced rapid and sustained economic growth for decades and freed millions of people from poverty and illiteracy. This pattern of rising economic prosperity and expanding social modernization under authoritarian rule contrasts sharply with that of incessant economic stagnation and social decay that Central and Eastern Europe experienced under communist rule, and Latin America under military rule (Haggard and Kaufman 1995; Linz and Stepan 1996). Growing prosperity under authoritarian rule meant ordinary citizens of new democracies in East Asia had fewer incentives to abandon authoritarian rule in favour of democracy than their counterparts in other authoritarian regimes.

Culturally, East Asia is a region infused with the core values of Confucianism, even in Malaysia and other countries in non-Confucian South-Eastern Asia (Inoguchi and Newman 1997). These Confucian values, once promoted as 'Asian values', have historically played a significant role in prioritizing and justifying the rights and duties of individual citizens and the power and authority of their political leaders (Bell 2000). Besides the distinct makeup of political institutions and their practices, these values have also shaped the formulation and implementation of political order and national security as goals of national development. They are also known as the major source of delegative democracy with the concentration of powers within the executive (Im 2004).

As Huntington (1993) and many others point out, these values emphasize family and community over individuals, discipline and hierarchy over freedom and equality, and consensus and harmony over diversity and conflict. Many theorists have argued that these cultural values of collectivism, hierarchism, and conformism are likely to detract from the process of cultural democratization by discouraging East Asians from rejecting the norms of authoritarian rule and accepting those of democracy (e.g. Chang, Chu, and Tsai 2005; Linder and Bachtiger 2005; Park and Shin 2006).

The same Confucian authoritarian values are also known to have affected East Asians' intellectual understanding of democratization by promoting non-liberal or undemocratic conceptions of good government and politics, especially among political leaders in these countries. Specifically these values motivated some East Asian political leaders, such as former Prime Ministers Lee Kuan Yew of Singapore and Mahathir Mohamad of Malaysia, to develop a model of authoritarian **governance** under the name of 'Asian democracy' (Neher 1994). Placing the peace and prosperity of the community above the rights and freedom of its individual citizens, these leaders equated democracy with benevolent or soft authoritarian rule and defended it as a viable

alternative to western liberal democracy, which is based on the values of individualism and pluralism. By invoking East Asia's cultural differences from the west, they sought to fend off pressure for the democratization of their authoritarian political systems (Foot 1997).

Confucian values have not only affected the leaders of East Asia's authoritarian regimes but also the first-generation leaders of new democracies in the region (Shin 1999). As democratically elected Presidents, for example, Kim Young Sam and Kim Dae Jung of South Korea recognized the installation of free, fair, and competitive elections as an essential component of democratic politics. Being inculcated in the Confucian norm emphasizing virtuous leadership above the rule of law, however, they themselves oftentimes failed to obey the basic laws and rules of democratic politics. Kim Dae Jung secretly transferred 500 million dollars to North Korea for the first summit meeting between the two Koreas, which earned him a Nobel Peace Prize. In the other East Asian countries too, leaders are known to have a minimal conception of democracy, limited to free and competitive elections (Kurlantzick 2007).

The global wave of democratization reached the shores of East Asia in 1986 with the removal of the dictator Ferdinand Marcos through the bloodless people power movement in the Philippines. One year later, South Korea ended military rule and elected a new President in a free and competitive election for the first time in nearly three decades. In the same year, after ending more than three decades of the Kuomintang's one-party rule, Taiwan lifted martial law and ushered in an era of highly competitive multi-party democracy. In 1990, Mongolia became a third-wave democracy by abandoning its 60-year-old communist one-**party system** and holding competitive multi-party elections. The October 1991 Paris Accord made it possible for Cambodia to begin its transition to democracy. In 1992, Thailand re-established democratic rule after massive protests ousted the military-backed Government. In 1999, Indonesia ended three decades of Suharto's personal dictatorship and thereafter held democratic elections to become the largest democracy in the region. By the end of the 1990s, the global wave had brought about seven new democracies in East Asia.

Table 23.1 Changing Characters of Political Systems in East Asia

Country	Year				
	1985	1990	1995	2000	2007
Cambodia	7 (7/7)	7 (7/7)	6 (6/6)	6 (6/6)	5.5 (6/5)
	Not free	Not free	Not free	Not free	Not free
China	6 (6/6)	7 (7/7)	7 (7/7)	6.5 (7/6)	6.5 (7/6)
	Not free	Not free	Not free	Not free	Not free
Indonesia	5.5 (5/6)	5.5 (6/5)	6.5 (7/6)	3.5 (3/4)	2.5 (2/3)
	Partly free	Partly free	Not free	Partly free	Free
North Korea	7(7/7)	7(7/7)	7(7/7)	7(7/7)	7(7/7)
	Not free	Not free	Not free	Not free	Not free
South Korea	4.4 (4/5)	2.5 (2/3)	2 (2/2)	2 (2/2)	1.5 (1/2)
	Partly free	Free	Free	Free	Free
Japan	1 (1/1)	1 (1/1)	1.5 (1/2)	1.5 (1/2)	1.5 (1/2)
	Free	Free	Free	Free	Free
Malaysia	4 (3/5)	4.5 (5/4)	4.5 (4/5)	5 (5/5)	4 (4/4)
	Partly free	Partly free	Partly free	Partly free	Partly free
Mongolia	7(7,7)	4 (4, 4)	2.5 (2, 3)	2.5 (2, 3)	2 (2, 2)
	Not Free	Partly Free	Free	Free	Free
Myanmar	7 (7/7)	7 (7/7)	7 (7/7)	7 (7/7)	7 (7/7)
	Not free	Not free	Not free	Not free	Not free
Philippines	3.5 (4/3)	3 (3/3)	3 (2/4)	2.5 (2/3)	3.5 (4/3)
	Partly free	Partly free	Partly free	Free	Partly free
Singapore	4.5 (4/5)	4 (4/4)	5 (5/5)	5 (5/5)	4.5 (5/4)
	Partly free	Partly free	Partly free	Partly free	Partly free
Taiwan	5 (5/5)	3 (3/3)	3 (3/3)	1.5 (1/2)	1.5 (2/1)
	Partly free	Partly free	Partly free	Free	Free
Thailand	3.5 (3/4)	2.5 (2/3)	3.5 (3/4)	2.5 (2/3)	5 (6/4)
	Partly free	Free	Partly free	Free	Partly free
Vietnam	7 (7/7)	7 (7/7)	7 (7/7)	6.5 (7/6)	6 (7/5)
	Not free	Not free	Not free	Not free	Not free
Free (%)	7.1	21.4	21.4	42.9	35.7
Partly Free (%)	50.0	42.9	35.7	21.4	28.6
Not Free (%)	42.9	35.7	42.9	35.7	35.7

Notes: Cell entries are combined Freedom House scores (separate scores for political rights and civil liberties are in parentheses); free: 1–2.5; partly free: 3–5; not free: 5.5–7.

Source: Freedom House 2008

As this history shows, democratization in East Asia has been a gradual movement. Today, more than three decades after democratization began to spread from Southern Europe, nearly half the countries in East Asia have yet to undergo democratic regime change (see Table 23.1). Moreover, two of these new democracies, Cambodia and Thailand, have reverted to authoritarian rule. The Philippines, also, is no longer rated an electoral democracy due to political killings targeting left-wing political activists. As a result, the 2008 report by Freedom House (2008) designates a minority of five countries in the region as liberal democracies: Japan, South Korea, Mongolia, Indonesia, and Taiwan. All in all, the democratic transformation of authoritarian regimes in East Asia has virtually stalled for more than a decade.

Why has East Asia been slower than other regions in responding to the surging wave of global democratization? One reason is lack of precedent for change. In most of East Asia's history, governmental or regime change, not to mention democratic regime change, has been rare. In Singapore, for example, the People's Action Party has ruled since 1959. In Japan, except for a brief span of 11 months in the early 1990s, the Liberal Democratic Party has ruled since World War II. In Malaysia, the United Malays National Organization of former Prime Minister Mahathir Mohammed is still in power after more than 50 years. Indonesia's Golkar party ruled from

> ### Box 23.1 Key points
>
> - Material improvements under authoritarian rule restrained ordinary East Asians from endorsing new democratic governments unconditionally until these began to deliver tangible benefits.
>
> - Confucian notions of good government and leadership in terms of harmony and the virtuous example were likely to have motivated the old generation of political leaders to embrace the notion that democracy brings chaos.
>
> - These notions are also likely to have dissuaded leaders from accommodating citizen demand for democratic regime change and for expanding partial democracy into full democracy.
>
> - Democracy in the region spread late, and slowly, and democratization came to a halt in the late 1990s.

1967–2001, and Taiwan's Kuomintang governed for more than 40 years. Many scholars attribute East Asians' unyielding allegiance to one-party rule and their general aversion to political turnovers to a Confucian value system that emphasizes deference to authority and antipathy to political change (Robinson 1996).

Democratic Transition

Modes of democratic regime change

The first step in transforming authoritarian governments into full democracies is to exchange the authoritarian regime for a democratic one, even a limited democratic one. What role did ordinary East Asians and their political leaders play in this transition process? Huntington (1993) classified transition processes into three broad types in terms of who plays the leading role in those processes. When opposition groups play such a role, *replacement* occurs. When ruling elites play the lead role, *transformation* occurs.

When ruling elites and opposition groups together play an equally important role, *transplacement* occurs. Of these three modes, replacement and transformation represent, respectively, the most radical and least radical modes of democratic transition.

Table 23.2 lists the recently democratized East Asian countries with their modes of transition and their combined Freedom House ratings of political and civil rights at the cusp of transition and their most recent score in 2007. Also included in this table is an indication of what forces drove each Asian country's transition, and whether the transition involved significant violence between the **state** and opposition

Table 23.2 Modes of Transition and Democracy Ratings in East Asia

Country	Method of Transition	Year of Transition	Strength of Non-violent Civic Associations	Level of Violence	Source of Violence	Force Driving the Transition	Pre-Transitional Rating	2007 Rating	Change in Compositing Rating
Cambodia	Intervention/ Transplacement	1991	Weak	Significant Violence	State and Opposition	External Intervention	7	5.5	+1.5 (increase)
Indonesia	Transplacement	1998	Strong	High Violence	State and Opposition	Civil Society and Political Elites	6	2.5	+3.5 (increase)
Mongolia	Transplacement	1990	Strong	Non-violent	None	Civil Society and Political Elites	7	2	+5.0 (increase)
Philippines	Replacement (unpacted)	1986	Strong	Significant Violence	State	Civil Society	3.5	3	+0.5 (increase)
South Korea	Transplacement	1987	Strong	Significant Violence	State and Opposition	Civil Society and Political Elites	4.5	1.5	+3.0 (increase)
Taiwan	Transformation	1992	Moderate	Non-violent	None	Civil Society and Political Elites	5	1.5	+3.5 (increase)
Thailand	Transplacement	1992	Moderate	Significant Violence	State	Civil Society and Political Elites	2.5	5.5	-3.0 (decrease)

Sources: Transition data obtained from Karatnycky and Ackerman (2005); Freedom House data obtained from <www.freedomhouse.org>. Mode of transition is classified according to Huntington's (1993) classification scheme.

forces. In East Asia, the Philippines was the only case of installing democracy by violent replacement, while Taiwan was the only transformation case of gradual democratic regime change in which the ruling elite played the initial and leading role.

The Philippines

The Philippines' move to democracy began with the presidency of Ferdinand Marcos, who ruled for more than two decades, from 1965 to 1986. During this period, he suspended and replaced the 1935 democratic constitution so that he could be elected for a term of six years with no term limits. He entrusted key positions in the Government to his wife, children, and relatives or close friends. He also imposed martial law to solidify his power and allowed state security agencies to torture and kill more than 30,000 people, including Senator Benigno Aquino, Jr, the main opposition figure, in 1983. At the same time, Marcos and his family were enriching themselves through open and widespread corruption. During his entire tenure as a civilian dictator, Marcos legally earned no more than an annual salary of US$5,700. When he left the country in 1986, his personal fortune was estimated to be in excess of US$5 billion.

Increasingly rampant corruption and widespread political violence alienated every segment of the population, including Marcos's former supporters. In February 1986, he ran against Corazon Aquino for his fourth term. Though declared the winner of the highly fraudulent Presidential elections, Marcos was forced to leave the country for Hawaii on the day of his swearing in by a people's uprising known as the 'People Power Revolution', which involved as many as 500,000 ordinary Filipinos as well as a number of religious, political, and military leaders. With Marcos's departure, Corazon Aquino, the leader of the opposition movement, became the President of the first third-wave democracy in East Asia.

South Korea

From the Philippines, the global wave of democratization spread to other countries in East Asia and triggered a negotiated transition in South Korea.

For nearly two decades beginning in 1961, General Park Chung Hee ruled the country ruthlessly, while developing its economy rapidly by promoting export industries. Less than two months after Park was assassinated, on 26 October 1979, General Chun Doo Hwan assumed power through another coup to suppress the awakening of the democracy movement after the death of Park Chung Hee. On 17 May 1980, Chun extended martial law over the entire country and disbanded the National Assembly. On 18 May he dispatched troops to quell growing protests against martial law in Kwangju; those troops killed 207 people and injured 987. This event is symbolic of despotism and to this date is remembered as the infamous Kwangju massacre.

From 10 to 29 June 1987, street demonstrations, often referred to as the 'June Popular Uprising', drew increasingly larger crowds and overwhelmed police forces. The Chun Government confronted a painful choice. Should it bring in the army to quell those demonstrations just a few months before the scheduled Summer Olympics, or accept the demands of anti-Government forces for the direct election of the President by the people? After 17 consecutive days of demonstrations and under intense pressure from the USA and the International Olympic Committee, the Government agreed to popular demands for democratic reforms. This agreement, dubbed as the 'June 29 Declaration of Democratic Reform', served as the foundation for South Korea's peaceful transition to democracy. It also served as a transplacement model of democratic transition in other East Asian countries.

Taiwan

Taiwan became a third-wave democracy after five years of gradual liberalization initiated by Chang Ching-Kuo, the leader of the ruling Kuomintang (KMT). Since Taiwan's break from China in 1949, the KMT ruled the island as a one-party state under martial law. For nearly four decades, opposition parties were banned and political dissidents were not allowed to contest national elections. From 1980 onward, however, the opposition movement against martial law gradually gained momentum, especially in the aftermath of the Philippines' People Power

Revolution and South Korea's June Popular Uprising. In September 1986, the movement illegally formed the Democratic Progressive Party (DPP) as the first opposition party in Taiwan to counter the KMT. On 12 June 1987, the DPP sponsored a rally to protest against the National Security Law in front of the Legislative *Yuan*. Realizing unmanageable consequences of growing protests and under increasing pressure from the US Congress to build a framework for democracy, President Chiang Ching-Kuo lifted martial law on 14 July 1987, more than a year after he informally indicated the need to lift it.

With the lifting of martial law, the Taiwanese were formally allowed to engage in protests and demonstrations against the KMT Government. More new political parties, like the Chinese New Party and the Taiwanese Independence Party, were formed to demand the end of one-party rule. These parties demanded more political liberalization and challenged the KMT in every important policy arena, as well as about its close relationship with mainland China. Finally, the KMT and opposition forces agreed to a series of constitutional amendments, which provided for holding free, fair, and competitive elections to the national assembly in 1992, and the election of a President and Vice President by direct popular vote in 1996. Compared to South Korea's transition, Taiwan's democratic regime change moved more slowly and gradually while the leaders of the ruling party played greater leadership roles.

Thailand

Thailand followed a path similar to South Korea's in that the country had been under military rule for decades prior to its democratization. Beginning with a 1932 coup that transformed the absolute monarchy into a constitutional monarchy, the army ruled periodically. In 1986, General Prem, who was once the junta leader, began to liberalize the political system by allowing civil society forces and opposition groups to form. In 1988, the country conducted fully democratic parliamentary elections and formed a coalition Government under General Chatichai Choonhaven. While the economy was booming under his Government, Prime Minister Choonhaven was arrested in

a military coup on 23 February 1991 on charges of corruption and incompetence.

The new military junta led by Generals Sunthorn and Suchinda initiated draconian measures aimed at undoing the political liberalization reforms of Generals Prem and Choonhavan. This led to massive demonstrations in the streets. The junta responded with aggressive force, shooting protesters in Bangkok who demanded the return of civilian rule. This did not deter the public from massing in the streets. After three weeks of significant violence in May 1992, the military junta and opposition forces entered into a binding agreement that the constitution would be amended to minimize the role of the military in politics. It was also agreed that the Prime Minister should be elected from among the members of the parliament instead of being selected by the military establishment. The 'People's Constitution' of 1997, the region's most democratic constitution, created three new democratic institutions and mandated the direct election of the Senate; as a result, Thailand was well on its way toward the **consolidation** of its nascent democratic regime. However, the military staged another coup to oust the democratically elected Thaksin Government on 19 September 2006, claiming as a reason endemic corruption in his Government.

Mongolia

Mongolia began its transition to democracy as the Soviet Union began to fragment. In early 1989, civic groups, mostly led by members of the middle class, began to demand democratic reforms and formed opposition parties such as the Mongolian Democratic Union. In response, soft-liners of the Mongolian People's Revolutionary Party, the former communist party known as the MPRD, entered into protracted negotiations with the opposition forces to pass democratic reforms and to draft a new democratic constitution. In July 1990, Mongolia held its first free and fair parliamentary elections, which led to the restoration of the MPRD to power under a democratic system. In July 2003 the first election was held under the new constitution guaranteeing political rights and civil liberties. To date, Mongolia has the distinction of being the only country outside

Eastern Europe to have made a successful transition from communist rule to a highly competitive multi-party capitalist democracy.

Cambodia

Like Mongolia, Cambodia began its transition to democracy from communist one-party rule. But unlike Mongolia, its history was blighted by an ongoing conflict with Vietnam, which necessitated the international community to play a major role in its transition to democracy. In October 1991, four rival groups (the Khmer Rouge, the royalist Funcinpec, the pro-Vietnamese CCP of Hun Sen and a very small republican-bourgeois faction) together with 18 countries, signed the Treaty of Paris, which began the transition process. The goal of the treaty was to make Cambodia a truly sovereign state with limited Vietnamese influence in its domestic politics. The installed democracy, therefore, did not emanate from a strong grassroots movement of middle-class segments. With the consociational agreements among pro-monarchy and pro-Hun Sen forces, the May 1993 parliamentary elections created a multi-party democracy, which became highly unstable. In July 1997 a bloody and brutal coup restored the dictatorial power of Hun Sen, a former Khmer Rouge soldier. Cambodia is unique among newly emerging Asian democracies primarily because its democratic constitution and free elections resulted from a peace settlement and the direct involvement of the United Nations.

Indonesia

Indonesia's transition to democracy marks the most recent civilian authoritarian regime to collapse in the East Asian region. The transition, which began in 1998, was mostly a result of a protracted economic crisis fuelled by the Asian economic crisis which broke out in late 1997. Food and medicine shortages led university students and other ordinary citizens to wage waves of protests against President Suharto, who ruled the country for more than 30 years from 1967 to 1998. On 21 May 1998, facing growing mass mobilizations against his regime, Suharto handed his power over to Vice President Habibie, a loyalist who also belonged to the Golkar party. For months, the new Golkar party negotiated with opposition parties and the military about a new democratic constitution and the holding of free, fair, and competitive elections. The successful negotiations between the ruling and opposition forces led to Indonesia's first democratic parliamentary elections in 1999 and a Presidential election in 2004, which created the largest Muslim democracy in the world.

As we have documented above, six of the seven democratic transitions in East Asia involved a series of negotiations between the ruling and opposition forces and required compromises from each of them. The only exception to this mode of transplacement was the Philippines, where the people forced the authoritarian leaders to depart. Five of the seven transitions overturned authoritarian regimes that were not ideologically based (The Philippines, South Korea, Taiwan, Thailand, and Indonesia). Only two were transitions from states built on the ideology of communism (Cambodia and Mongolia).

The literature on the global wave of democratization shows that the mode of transplacement, which required political pact-making before the advent of transition, has consistently produced stable democracies that are less susceptible to reversals or breakdowns than those that follow other modes (Linz and Stepan 1996). In Portugal, Spain, and Greece, for example, such pacted transitions produced stable and consolidated democracies in less than a decade by facilitating conciliation, compromise-building, and consensus-seeking between the democratic opposition and authoritarian elites. In sharp contrast, unpacted transitions, from either above or below, have yielded either authoritarian reversals or unstable democratic regimes because either democratic or authoritarian forces were excluded from the process of installing a new democratic system.

The Philippines fit this pattern. As a case of replacement, the Philippine transition to democracy has been highly unstable. The country has seen a series of unsuccessful coup attempts and mass protests. However, all other new democracies in East Asia, which were built on pacts, have also been unstable. In Indonesia, the National Assembly impeached President Abdurahman Wahid and elected Vice President Megawati Sukarnoputri as his successor. In South

Korea, the National Assembly impeached President Roh Moo Hyun and suspended his executive powers. In Taiwan, the loser of a Presidential election tried to bring down the democratically elected Government through the extralegal means of mass protests. Coups overthrew the democratically elected Governments in Cambodia and Thailand. By dissolving parliaments and banning all political activities, these two countries reverted to authoritarian rule. Regardless of the mode of transition, new democracies in East Asia have been unstable. Evidently, the mode of transition is not determinative in the process of democratic consolidation in East Asia.

Causes of democratic transitions

What propelled seven East Asian countries to join the global wave of democratization? The existing literature has identified two sets of facilitating factors as the most probable causes of the worldwide current wave. The first set concerns political and other changes that occurred within each country, whereas the second set deals with developments in neighbouring or other foreign countries (Diamond 2008; Huntington 1993). The particular mix of these two sets of factors varies significantly from region to region and from country to country (Shin 1994). The domestic set played a more powerful role in Latin America, while the international set predominated in Europe. In East Asia, as in Latin America, domestic factors have been more influential than international factors in propelling democratic transitions.

In Europe and Latin America, region-wide international organizations and individual governments promoted democracy. In East Asia, there were no such organizations or governments. The USA remained the single most powerful external actor. Until the collapse of the Berlin Wall, moreover, the international context of the Cold War severely constrained democratic development in East Asian countries by giving their authoritarian governments a rationale for repressing political opposition. The USA supported those repressive regimes to stop the spread of communism and thus 'created an unfavourable balance of power between the state and civil society for democratization' (Shelley 2005: 143). Only after dec-

ades of rapid economic development did civil society actors become powerful enough to challenge those in power. Then the USA intervened directly to constrain authoritarian regimes from using force against the budding democracy movement.

There is no doubt that the interventions of the USA contributed to peaceful democratic transitions especially in the Philippines, South Korea, and Taiwan. As Diamond (2008) and others point out, it is also clear that the desire of authoritarian rulers to see their countries accepted as developed countries in an international event, such as the Summer Olympics, contributed to peaceful transitions in these countries. The Philippines' transition by the 'People Power Revolution' also affected subsequent transitions in other East Asian countries by spreading methods and techniques of democratic change across borders (Diamond 2008, Ch. 5). With the exception of Cambodia, however, such international interventions or snowballing effects cannot be considered the direct or primary cause of democratic transitions in East Asian countries.

As in other regions, a variety of domestic factors facilitated democratization in East Asia. Among these factors, which included the rise of the middle class and shifts in cultural values in favour of democratic rule, the expansion of civil society is generally considered the direct and primary cause of East Asian democratization (Alagappa 2001; Quadir and Lele 2005). The growth in civil society groups alone produced the balance of power between authoritarian rulers and democratic opposition. In six of the seven recent democratizations in East Asia, such a power balance led to successful negotiations between the two rival forces and produced democratic transition by the mode of transplacement or transformation. In South Korea, for example, religious institutions played a prominent role by promoting human rights and civil liberties. In Taiwan and Thailand, a variety of **social movements** organized by civil rights and environmental groups mostly from the urban middle class challenged repressive regimes and demanded democratic reforms.

According to Junhan Lee (2002), colonial legacies and external factors had no direct influence in spurring democratic regime change. It is the civic movements that spurred democratic changes in East Asia. Across the region, these movements weakened authoritarian elites by engaging in waves of demonstrations, boycotts, and strikes, and inculcated the spirit of democracy in ordinary citizens by demanding the election of new rulers and the establishment of their political rights. From Catholic Philippines to mainly Buddhist Taiwan and Thailand and multireligious South Korea, civic movements were the most decisive and powerful force that drove authoritarian rules in a democratic direction.

The activities of civic organizations during the process of democratic transition are known to have long-term consequences for deepening and expanding limited democracy. A recent analysis of the Freedom House data by Karatnycky and Ackerman (2005) has confirmed the long-term beneficial effect of civic activism on liberal democratization in the world. According to this analysis, of 67 countries that underwent democratic transitions over the past three decades, 75 per cent of the transitions driven by strong civic coalitions became liberal democracies. Only 18 per cent of the transitions that lacked active involvement of civic coalitions turned into liberal democracies. The more vigorous civil society is, the likelier the progress toward full democracy is. Where there is violence and less vigorous civil society, reversal to non-democratic rule is more common. Is this generalization applicable to the East Asian region?

Contrary to inferences from the analysis of the Freedom House data, improvements in political rights and civil liberties in post-transition East Asia have little to do with either the levels of civic activism

> ## Box 23.2 **Key points**
>
> - The importance of civil society associationalism in increasing freedoms and liberties is not as highly salient in East Asia as it is in other regions.
>
> - Almost all of the pacted, transplacement transitions received improved Freedom House ratings for many years after the transition.
>
> - In East Asia, transitions based on replacement hurt more than help the subsequent stage of democratic consolidation.
>
> - In East Asia, the mode of transition matters more than the level of civic activism.

or those of violence (see Table 23.2). For instance, the Philippines had strong civic associations pre-transition, but their political systems failed to enlarge freedom even after more than a decade of democratic rule. Taiwan had only a moderate level of civic activism but formally became a liberal democracy. Indonesia and South Korea also formally became liberal democracies despite the fact that they experienced significant levels of violence during their processes of democratic transition. Of the seven third-wave democracies in East Asia, only Mongolia fits the earlier finding that strong non-violent civic activism leads to liberal democratization.

Substantive Democratization

Democratic governance

All new East Asian democracies, except the collapsed one in Cambodia, hold competitive and free elections regularly to choose political leaders for the national and local levels of government. In institutional terms, therefore, they have been successfully transformed into electoral democracies. In substantive terms, however, they became well-functioning, full democracies only when electoral and other political institutions perform according to the rules and norms of democratic politics, and as these institutions become

increasingly responsive to the preferences of the citizenry (Diamond and Morlino 2005). To monitor progress in this dimension of substantive democratization an increasing number of scholars have attempted to evaluate improvements in democratic regime performance in other regions. Francis Hagopian (2005), for example, has analysed the World Bank (2007) Governance Indicators (WBI) to assess and compare the changing quality of democratic **governance** in 12 Latin American countries.

How well do new East Asian democracies perform? How much progress have they made in consolidating democratic institutions and responding to the electorate? The WBI provides numerical measures on six dimensions of governance for the 10-year period of 1996–2006. As Hagopian (2005) points out, the first two dimensions—voice and accountability, and political stability—capture the strength of democracy; the second two—government effectiveness and regulatory quality—its effectiveness; and the last two—rule of law and control of corruption—constitutionalism. Indicator values for each country are weighted averages of what is available from a variety of sources for that country. Countries can range from a low of -2.5 to a high of +2.5. Negative scores indicate a sub-standard or relatively worse performance, while positive scores indicate a relatively better performance. For each East Asian country that recently underwent a process of democratization, Table 23.3

(Panel A) reports the 2006 scores for all six dimensions of democratic governance and the differences between these scores and the 1996 scores.

A look at the 2006 scores for each dimension across the seven recently democratized East Asian countries reveals that none of the dimensions received consistently positive or consistently negative average ratings. In each dimension, the seven countries divide into two groups, one with positive ratings and the other with negative ratings. In three domains—voice and accountability, government effectiveness, and control of corruption, for example, four of the seven countries rated positively, while three countries rated negatively. In the dimensions of political stability, regulatory quality, and rule of law, on the other hand, four countries rated negatively, while three countries rated positively. Among the new East Asian

Table 23.3 The Shifting Qualities of Democratic Governance

A. 2006 WBI Scores

Country	Voice and Accountability	Political Stability	Government Effectiveness	Regulatory Quality	Rule of Law	Corruption Control
Japan	0.91	1.11	1.29	1.27	1.40	1.31
Cambodia	-0.98	-0.48	-1.01	-0.63	-1.11	-1.19
Indonesia	0.25	-1.11	0.38	-0.26	-0.82	0.77
South Korea	0.71	0.42	1.05	0.70	0.72	0.31
Mongolia	0.10	0.78	-0.46	-0.31	-0.32	-0.54
Philippines	-0.18	-1.26	-0.01	-0.06	-0.48	-0.06
Taiwan	0.79	0.51	1.11	0.94	0.77	0.53
Thailand	-0.50	-0.99	0.29	0.37	0.03	0.26

B. Changes in WBI Scores over the 1996-2006 period

Country	Voice and Accountability	Political Stability	Government Effectiveness	Regulatory Quality	Rule of Law	Corruption Control
Japan	+0.06	+0.22	-0.05	+0.71	-0.06	+0.10
Cambodia	0.00	+0.93	+0.11	-0.66	-0.02	-0.08
Indonesia	+1.38	-0.30	+0.24	-0.69	-0.46	+1.32
South Korea	+0.24	+0.31	+0.13	+0.18	+0.01	-0.21
Mongolia	-0.37	+0.20	+0.07	-0.38	-0.39	-0.22
Philippines	-0.40	-0.77	+0.02	-0.70	-0.45	-0.22
Taiwan	-0.19	-0.48	+0.32	+0.06	-0.04	-0.21
Thailand	-0.80	-0.71	-0.15	-0.22	-0.55	+0.13

Source: World Bank Governance Indicators, available at <www.govindicators.org>

democracies, therefore, there is no single dimension of democratic governance that performs consistently better or consistently worse as compared to the other dimensions considered in the WBI study. In every dimension, the quality of democratic performance is of a mixed nature.

Each country's average ratings, when compared across the six dimensions, reveal the three patterns of fully negative, mixed, and fully positive ratings. Cambodia and the Philippines belong to the fully negative pattern, while South Korea and Taiwan belong to the fully positive pattern. Indonesia, Mongolia, and Thailand, meanwhile, belong to the mixed pattern of positive and negative dimensional ratings. In East Asia as a whole, the countries that scored positive ratings in all six performance dimensions constitute a small minority of less than one-third. Moreover, even the two countries with fully positive ratings failed to score above +1.0 on the 5-point scale ranging from -2.5 to +2.5 in all or most of the performance dimensions. Only in the governmental effectiveness dimension did South Korea and Taiwan score above +1.0. In this respect, the recently democratized East Asian countries contrast markedly with Japan, Spain, and other fully consolidated democracies, which score above +1.0 in all or most of six performance dimensions.

Altogether these findings make it clear that the new democracies in East Asia are far from being well-functioning consolidated democracies.

How much progress did these countries make in improving the quality of their democratic governance over the 10-year period between 1996 and 2006? To address this question, we examined changes in each country's dimensional ratings as reported in the second panel (B) of Table 23.3. The panel shows that over the 10-year period, more performance dimensions changed for the worse in a majority of the seven countries—Cambodia, Mongolia, the Philippines, and Thailand. Only in one country, South Korea, did more performance dimensions change for the better. In Indonesia and Taiwan, an equal number of dimensions experienced negative and positive changes. On balance, a larger number of new East Asian democracies did not substantially improve their performances over the past decade. Their failures appear to have little to do with any of the independent variables considered, including the

mode of transition, the magnitude of civic activism, the form of government, and the level of socioeconomic development.

We now compare scores indicating changes in each dimension of governance across the seven countries. In a majority of four performance dimensions—political stability, regulatory quality, the rule of law, and corruption control—more countries experienced negative changes than positive changes. Only in the dimension of governmental effectiveness did more countries experience positive changes than negative ones. By a large margin of four to one, deteriorations outnumber the improvements. In the case of the rule of law dimension, all countries except South Korea experienced negative changes. Also in controlling corruption, five of the seven countries registered negative changes. These negative changes indicate *a clear trajectory toward illiberal democracy during the past decade.*

The mostly negative current ratings of the six dimensions indicate that a majority of the seven East Asian countries do not perform as well as most of the other countries examined by the World Bank. Meanwhile, declines in their average ratings over the past 10 years indicate that a large majority of these

---

Box 23.3 **Key points**

- According to World Bank Governance indicators measuring the rule of law and corruption control, most East Asian third-wave democracies remain illiberal or malfunctioning liberal democracies.

- Their movement to broaden and deepen limited democracy into well-functioning liberal democracy remains stalled.

- Only South Korea and Taiwan maintain consistently positive ratings in the realm of rule of law, control of corruption, regulatory quality, voice and accountability, political stability, and governmental effectiveness over the past 10 years.

- Higher levels of socioeconomic development and longer experiences with democratic rule together contribute to the improved quality of democratic governance.

democracies have failed to improve their performance over the period. When these findings are considered together, it is evident that stalled progress in democratic governance is a notable characteristic of substantive democratization in East Asia (Chang, Chu, and Park 2007). The relatively poor quality of democratic governance and its downward trend have very little to do with the modes of democratic transition, the forms of government, or the levels of civic activism prior to the transition. The distinguishing factors of relatively better performing democracies are high levels of socioeconomic development and longer periods of democratic rule, as shown in South Korea and Taiwan.

Prospects of Democratization in China and Singapore

In the world today, China and Singapore represent two of the most notable non-democratic regimes. China is the largest and most populous autocracy that has successfully mixed capitalism with authoritarian rule. Singapore, on the other hand, represents the most affluent of all authoritarian regimes in the world. For all remarkable socioeconomic development in recent decades, these two countries have failed to democratize. What are their near-term prospects of joining the current wave of global democratization?

For millennia, China has been the centre of Eastern civilization. As the birthplace of Confucianism, it constitutes the core state of this civilization. Economically, this country has outperformed other so-called 'Asian tigers' to become the world's fastest growing economy and in so doing has freed nearly half of its population from extreme poverty. Today, more than 90 per cent of the population is able to read and write. Internationally, as well, China has successfully integrated into the global economy. As the third largest trader, it holds more than US$1.4 trillion in foreign currency reserves. Despite these structural changes that are known in the literature to facilitate democratization, China remains the largest and most dynamic one-party dictatorship in the world, defying the long standing theory that links modernization and **globalization** to democratization.

Situated at the apex of East Asian civilization and atop a long stretch of undemocratic countries from Myanmar through Vietnam to North Korea, China's transition to democracy could trigger similar transitions in North-East and South-East Asia. China's continuing rise as an economic and military powerhouse under authoritarian rule, on the other hand, could inspire other non-democratic countries in the region and elsewhere to follow its model of capitalism without democracy (Dickson 2007). As the centre of East Asian civilization and a rising economic and military powerhouse, China unquestionably holds the key to further democratization of the region and other parts of the world (Diamond 2008).

In 1988, the National People's Congress passed a law requiring all villages to hold competitive elections for their village committees, and all candidates were to be nominated by villagers. Since then, China has experimented with competitive elections at the lowest level of its civil administration to introduce the so-called 'four democracies': democratic election, democratic decision-making, democratic management, and democratic supervision. Members of all village committees have been elected directly by their residents, and experiments with direct elections have occurred at the township and other high levels of civil administration on a selective basis. At the same time, people's congresses at various levels have become increasingly competitive and independent as their deputies have been allowed to assert their own views in deliberating policy and personnel matters, independent of the ruling party (Guo 2007).

All of these changes can contribute to building electoral democracy in China. Nonetheless, it is fair to say that after more than two decades of electoral experiments, China is still in an early stage of political liberalization, not to mention democratization.

Judging by the 27 December 2007 decision of the National People's Congress to put off the popular election of Hong Kong's leader and the entire legislature for a minimum of one more decade, it is highly unlikely that President Hu Jintao and other fourth-generation leaders will soon allow the Chinese people to choose directly their political leaders, beyond the village and township levels, on the basis of free and competitive multi-party elections (Fewsmith 2004). Through a continuing crackdown on political dissent and independent associations, these leaders seem determined to avoid the fate of the Soviet Union. What continues to concern these leaders most is 'political order and technocratic governance rather than popular **participation** and regime transformation' (Yang 2007a: 251). Consequently, China's one-party dictatorship, often called 'democracy with Chinese characteristics', is not likely to be transformed into a fully electoral democracy unless the leaders are forced to meet an increasing demand for democratization from the people.

There is no doubt that the rapid growth of China's economy has expanded the capitalist or middle class known to have played a key role in the development of democracy in the West. This has led to expectations that China's capitalists or middle class would become the leading agent of democratic regime change (Gilley 2007). Contrary to these expectations, an increasing number of these capitalists have been co-opted into the process of one-party rule and became 'red capitalists'. Even those who

are not members of the party have 'little interest in challenging the status quo that has allowed them to prosper' (Dickson 2007: 243). To date, China's growing capitalist and middle class as a whole has failed to become an agent promoting democratic regime change (Solinger 2006).

Are other groups in Chinese society more interested in democratizing the country than the conservative wealthier segments? To explore this question, we analysed the first round of the Asian Barometer Survey (ABS) conducted in China in 2003. The survey asked Chinese respondents to rate their current regime on a 10-point scale, where a score of 1 indicates complete dictatorship and a score of 10 indicates complete democracy. It also asked them to rate on a 4-point scale the extent to which they were satisfied or dissatisfied with the way the regime was performing. We considered positive responses to these two questions to determine the proportion of the Chinese who endorsed the current regime as a well-functioning democracy. We compared this proportion across five levels of socioeconomic resources, composed of the respondent's own education and family income. Table 23.4 reports the results of this analysis.

As expected, given a lack of experience with democratic politics and limited exposure to a college education, a relatively high proportion (25 per cent) of the Chinese respondents failed to answer one or both questions evaluating their country's democratization. Of those who answered the questions, a large majority

Table 23.4 How the Chinese Assess the Current Regime and its Performance

Assessments of the Current Regime	Entire sample	Socioeconomic Resources Levels					
		lowest	low	middle	high	Test of highest	Difference (eta)
As a democracy	82	86	85	82	80	82	(.00)
As satisfying	79	90	84	81	77	73	(.01)
Both (WFD)	70	81	76	70	68	67	(.08)
None (MFA)	10	6	7	9	11	12	(.07)
N	3,180	291	592	829	778	690	

Note: Cell entries are percentages of respondents classifying their country as democratic, satisfying, both or none. WFD = well-functioning democracy; MFA = malfunctioning autocracy

Source: Asian Barometer (I)

of more than four-fifths (82 per cent) rated their current regime as a democracy. A near equal proportion (79 per cent) also expressed satisfaction with its performance as a democracy. When positive responses to both questions are considered together, a substantial majority of 70 per cent embraced the current regime as a well-functioning democracy. Only a small minority, 10 per cent, of Chinese fully rejects the current regime as an ill-functioning dictatorship.

Equally notable is the finding that democratic perceptions of the current regime vary little across different segments of the Chinese population. In each of the five segments, defined by respondents' levels of formal education and family income, a large majority of more than 80 per cent classifies the current regime as a democracy. As is the case in other Asian countries, the level of satisfaction with the regime's performance is significantly lower among those better-off than those worse-off. In classifying China as a democracy rather than a dictatorship, however, the former are not much different from the latter. Regardless of their exposure to social modernization, the overwhelming majority of Chinese people perceive their country as democratic. This can be considered one piece of evidence indicating a low level of popular demand for democratization (Shi 2008).

Thanks to rapid socioeconomic development over the past three decades, China today stands on a structural foundation that has been expected to favour democratic regime change (Rowen 2007). Yet elite and mass political cultures remain highly unfavourable to such regime change. A lack of basic knowledge about democracy among the mass public and the unwillingness of the ruling elite to embrace the democratic norms of public participation and competition in the political process is keeping China in an equilibrium between low levels of popular demand for and institutional supply of democracy. Given this low-level equilibrium and its proven ability to adapt to various predicaments (Nathan 2003), the existing authoritarian regime is likely to endure for many years to come. This view does not accord with the claim that China will become a liberal democracy with the next 15 to 20 years (Inglehart and Welzel 2005).

Another notable democratic holdout in the East Asian region is Singapore. Since it was granted independence by the British in 1951, Singapore has been ruled by the People's Action Party (PAP) as a de facto one-party dictatorship. Even if opposition parties like the Worker's Party of Singapore and the Singapore Democratic Party are allowed to compete in periodic elections, there is no chance for an alternation in power. Opposition parties who are vocal about the perceived clientelism, cronyism, and corruption by the PAP are usually slapped with libel and slander charges. Individual citizens critical of the PAP's corrupt or malfeasant activities face imprisonment. Public protest and demonstrations are banned, and there is rigid press censorship. As a result, there are no effective opposition parties that can make Singapore democratic. In 2006, the Economist Intelligence Unit typified Singapore as a hybrid democracy, while Freedom House has continuously classified Singapore as a 'partly free' country.

Despite increasing modernization and the growth of a robust middle class, Singapore, like China, has remained an illiberal polity, defying the theory that economic development spurs democratic transitions. The PAP has maintained its dominance of the political system by capitalizing on the fear that, if the PAP is out of power, Singapore's ethnic fragmentation would produce a weak and unstable regime like the one in place during the early 1960s. The emphasis that Lee Kuan Yew and other leaders of the PAP have placed on public order and social virtue may have emanated from the country's historical experience with ethnic violence. On the other hand, many believe that the Singaporean focus on law and order, morality, and ethics (for example, banning chewing gum, public lashings for those who commit vandalism, and the death penalty for transporting illegal narcotics), stems from the Asian value system that places a high premium on collectivism and the preference of greater communal good rather than on the Western values of individualism and liberalism.

To determine the extent to which Singaporeans support the current authoritarian regime, we analysed responses to the questions from the second round of the ABS survey that tap the democratic perception of the current regime and satisfaction with it. Nearly three-quarters perceived the current regime as a democracy, and a larger majority of 85 per cent expressed satisfaction with it (see Table 23.5). When these two ratings of the current regime are considered together, two-thirds endorsed the current regime as a well-functioning democracy while

Table 23.5 How Singaporeans Assess the Current Regime and its Performance

Assessments of the Current Regime	Entire sample	Socioeconomic Resources Levels					
		lowest	low	middle	high	Test of highest	Difference (eta)
As a democracy	73	70	74	77	76	69	(.01)
As satisfying	85	85	87	84	85	89	(.00)
Both (WFB)	67	63	65	67	65	69	(.00)
None (MFA)	8	6	7	9	8	0	(.00)
N	933	114	205	249	278	87	

Note: Cell entries are percentages of respondents classifying their country as democratic, satisfying, both or none. WFD = well-functioning democracy; MFA = malfunctioning autocracy

Source: Asian Barometer (II)

less than one-tenth reject it as a malfunctioning non-democracy. Supporters of the existing authoritarian regime outnumber its opponents by a large margin of more than eight to one. As in China, there is little variance in the percentages of such regime supporters and opponents across respondents' levels of education and income. Regardless of their exposure to social modernization, Singaporeans appear to see little need to transform their authoritarian regime into a democracy.

Recent developments indicate that there is little change in the illiberal conceptions of politics and governance among the leaders of the PAP. On 12 August 2004, Lee Hsien Loong, the oldest son of Senior Minister Lee Kuan Yew, took over as the Prime Minister of Singapore from Goh Chok Tong. Since then, the PAP has lost none of its dominance. In the May 2006 parliamentary elections, the younger Lee led the PAP to win 82 of the 84 seats by a variety of means including the handing out of cash bonuses to the electorate. Although he expresses an international outlook, he remains steadfastly attached to the Asian values of maintaining law and order and national consensus. In Singapore, recent leadership change is not likely to democratize de facto one-party rule in the foreseeable future. Nor is a majority of its citizens likely to demand its transformation into a competitive multi-party democratic system. These assessments also run counter to the prediction that Singapore will become a liberal democracy before 2015 (Inglehart and Welzel 2005).

Majorities of ordinary Chinese and Singaporeans are alike in perceiving their country's regime as a democracy and in expressing satisfaction with its performance. Besides remaining attached to the Confucian value of political stability, they prefer the illiberal and authoritarian to a more liberal and democratic mode of governing. From these findings, it is apparent that the mass citizenries of the two countries demand as little democracy as their elites provide. Trapped in the low-level equilibrium of democratic supply and demand, the near-term prospects for democratic regime change in these two countries are not bright.

Box 23.4 Key points

- Even after two decades of electoral experiments at the local level, China still remains at an early stage of political liberalization.

- In China today there is a low-level equilibrium between popular demand for democracy and elite supply of democracy.

- Even in Singapore, one of the richest non-democracies in the world, there is a low-level equilibrium between democratic demand and supply.

- The continuous presence of such an equilibrium trap poses a serious obstacle to democratic regime change in these countries.

Conclusion

This chapter has examined the East Asian contribution to the global wave of democratization. For the past two decades, this wave has transformed seven of the thirteen autocracies in the region into democracies. Of these seven, two were driven back to autocratic rule by the military. Even with the election of a civilian government in one of these two (Thailand) on 23 December 2007, there are more autocracies than democracies in the region. Included in this group of autocracies is the largest and most populous country and the core state of Confucian civilization. In view of the slow pace of democratic regime change and its limited range, it is fair to conclude that there has been no truly region-wide movement towards democracy. It is also fair to say that, together with North Africa and the Middle East, East Asia remains a region markedly resistant to the global wave of democratization. On the whole, democratization in East Asia has been more like an ebb-and-flow tide than a surging wave. Moreover, there is little prospect for the further democratization of authoritarian regimes in the near term, mainly because citizens of East Asian countries and their political leaders are trapped in an equilibrium of low levels of democratic supply and demand.

Why is it that a region blessed with rapid economic development remains cursed with a democratic deficit? Prominent theories of democratic transitions contribute little to the explanation of this conundrum. The theories of modernization and culture cannot explain why South Korea and Taiwan successfully transitioned to democracy while Singapore and Malaysia failed to do so. Likewise, past regime experience cannot explain why Mongolia joined the global wave, while China, North Korea, and Vietnam failed to do so. And diffusion theory cannot explain why Indonesia and Mongolia became liberal democracies, while neighbouring Malaysia and China failed to become even electoral democracies. Unquestionably, these domestic contextual factors, known to be democratic regime facilitators in other regions, all fail to solve the democratic puzzle set forth in East Asia.

As a region, East Asia is different from Europe and Latin America in that there is no regional organization promoting democracy and human rights (Shelley 2005). The region is also geographically distant from the clusters of powerful democracies in the West. Even within the region, its core state of Confucian civilization remains a powerful authoritarian state resisting the spread of democracy. Authoritarian states in the region have been, by and large, immune from democratic reform impulses generated from the external environment. Due to the absence of such external impulses, democratic transitions have primarily had to emerge out of democratic demand from the mass citizenry in the form of a vigorous civic movement. This may explain why East Asia remains a democratically underdeveloped region. Another possible explanation points to the illiberal conceptions of democracy and good governance among both citizens and political leaders and their unwillingness to submit to the democratic norms of pluralism and diversity. The illiberal cultural values and norms do not prevent the birth or emergence of democratic regimes, but they do determine how its institutions function on a daily basis. For this reason, democracies in East Asia may never resemble the liberal democracies of the West.

Substantively, despite growing experience with democratic politics, all new democracies in East Asia have failed to become effective liberal democracies. While the new democracies in southern Europe became consolidated within the first decade of democratic rule, new East Asian democracies remain defective or illiberal even in their second or third decade of democratic rule (Croissant 2004).

East Asian experiences to date provide a number of insights into the ongoing debates about the contours, dynamics, sources, and consequences of current global democratization. Contrary to modernization theory, which claims democracy is economically preconditioned, democracy has blossomed in one of the world's poorest countries (Mongolia). Contrary to the notion that democracy requires a Judeo-Christian or liberal political culture, it has also successfully emerged in Buddhist (Mongolia and Thailand),

Confucian (South Korea and Taiwan), and Muslim (Indonesia) countries. The successful emergence of democracies in culturally, economically, and politically diverse countries appears to support the *universalist* claim that the whole world can become democratic (Diamond 2008; Friedman 1995).

Nonetheless, the failure of nearly two-thirds of East Asian countries to become and remain fully democratic appears to support more strongly the *preconditionalist* claim that democracy is not suitable for any and every type of society (Dahl 1971; Huntington 1993; Sartori 1995). Moreover, the enduring illiberal mode of democratic governance in all of the remaining democratic countries in East Asia supports the *sequentialist* claim that the introduction of democracy prior to the establishment of modern political institutions, such as the rule of law and multiple groups of civil society, leads to incomplete democracy (Rose and Shin 2001). The persistent and pervasive embrace of illiberal political norms by the East Asian mass citizenries also supports the widely discredited

Asian values thesis in the West that the liberal mode of democratic governance will not become a universal phenomenon (Bell *et al.* 1995; Zakaria 1994). It also undermines the characterization of Asian exceptionalism as an illusion (Fukuyama 1997).

Over the next two to three decades, East Asia is not likely to become a region of liberal democratic miracles. Instead, this region of amazing economic progress is likely to unfold the illiberal or a-liberal patterns of democratization hidden by Occidentalism, a tendency of the West to see other parts of the world from the perspective of its own values. The democratic transformation of authoritarian regimes and the enrichment of illiberal democracies will continue to evolve very slowly and in different ways in the various nations of East Asia. The specific evolutionary paths the different countries will take will depend upon how political leaders and the mass citizenries understand and perceive democratic politics and how they interact through democratic institutions.

QUESTIONS

1. What constitutes democratization? Why is it often conceptualized as a multi-level and multi-dimensional phenomenon? In what specific level and dimension of democratization do you think the East Asian region is most deficient?

2. What contextual factors distinguish East Asia from other regions in democratization?

3. Much has also been said about the influence of Confucian values in promoting conflict avoidance during the transition process. Is this a unique feature in Asia or have other regions also been influenced by predominant cultural forces?

4. In East Asia, modes of transitions, either pacted or unpacted, have had relatively little effect in promoting democratic stability and consolidation. Is this the same for other regions?

5. The Asian values thesis argues that some East Asian countries may not be amenable to democracy because their Confucian value system promotes a mindset of deference to authority and the preservation of political order at all costs. Do you agree or disagree with this thesis? Why?

6. Why is civil society viewed as essential to democratization? What specific roles has civil society played in the processes of transition and consolidation in the region?

Visit the Online Resource Centre that accompanies this book for additional questions to accompany each chapter, and a range of other resources: <www.oxfordtextbooks.co.uk/orc/haerpfer/>.

FURTHER READING

Chu, Y., Diamond, L., Nathan, A. and Shin, D. C. (2008) (eds), *How East Asians View Democracy* (New York, NY: Columbia University Press). The first volume of the Asian Barometer project monitoring the dynamics of cultural and political democratization in China, Hong Kong, Japan, South Korea, Mongolia, the Philippines, Thailand, and Taiwan. It is a seminal piece exploring the contours of democratic support among East Asians.

Dalton, R. and Shin, D. (2006) (eds), *Citizens, Democracy, and Markets Around the Pacific Rim* (Oxford: Oxford University Press). A collection of articles examining popular reactions to political democratization and economic liberalization in East Asian countries, Australia, Canada, and the USA from the perspective of congruence theory. It is based on the latest wave of the World Value Survey.

Dalton, R., Shin, D.C. and Chu, Y. (2008) (eds), *Party Politics in East Asia* (Boulder, CO: Lynne Rienner). This edited work is the first of its kind analysing electoral systems and the contours, sources, and consequences of partisanship in East Asia. Using the most recent waves of the Comparative Study of Electoral Systems, the East Asia Barometer, and the World Value Survey, it examines the determinants and effects of party polarization, and value cleavages that political parties have elicited in an understudied region.

Diamond, L. and Plattner, M. (1998) (eds), *Democracy in East Asia* (Baltimore, MD: Johns Hopkins University Press). A collection of articles examines the current state and future prospects of democratization in East Asian countries. It also explores the validity of the Asian values debate.

Friedman, E. (1994) (ed.), *The Politics of Democratization: Generalizing East Asian Experiences* (Boulder, CO: Westview Press). This edited work emphasizes the importance of politics in the general process of democratization and examining their role in the democratization of Japan, Korea, Hong Kong, Taiwan, and China. Its central claims are that there are no historical, cultural, and class preconditions for democracy, and there is nothing in Europe or the West that was peculiarly conducive to democracy.

Hsiao, H.-H. M. (2006) (ed.), *Asian New Democracies: The Philippines, South Korea and Taiwan Compared* (Taipei: Foundation for Democracy). In-depth analyses of institutional and cultural democratization in the Philippines, South Korea, and Taiwan.

Laothamatas, A. (1997) (ed.), *Democratization in Southeast and East Asia* (New York, NY: St. Martin's Press). A collection of case studies of modernization and its effects on democratization in six southeast and two East Asian countries.

Lynch, D. C. (2006), *Rising China and Asian Democratization* (Stanford, CA: Stanford University Press). An analysis of successful democratization in Thailand and Taiwan and the prospect of democratic regime change in China from the perspective of elite socialization to a liberal global culture. It introduces a new theory on why China resists international efforts to democratize the country.

Ravich, S. (2000), *Marketization and Democratization: East Asian Experiences* (Cambridge: Cambridge University Press). Quantitative and case studies of how economic liberalization affects the process of political democratization in China, Taiwan, Indonesia, and South Korea.

Rich, R. (2007), *Pacific Asia in Quest for Democracy* (Boulder, CO: Lynne Rienner). Comparative analyses of democratic institutions and their performances in Indonesia, the Philippines, South Korea, Taiwan, and Thailand, and other countries in Pacific Asia. It explores the important question of how and why democracies in the region remain defective.

IMPORTANT WEBSITES

<www.asianbarometer.org> The website of the Asian Barometer (ABS), an applied research programme on public opinion on political values, democracy, and governance in the region.

NOTES

* The authors gratefully acknowledge the helpful comments and suggestions from Aurel Croissant, Yun-han Chu, Larry Diamond, Edward Friedman, Baogang He, Choong Nam Kim, Andrew Nathan, Chong-Min Park, Benjamin Reilly, Conrad Rutkowski, Doris Solinger, and Jack Van Der Slik.

24 Conclusions and Outlook: The Future of Democratization

Christian W. Haerpfer, Patrick Bernhagen, Ronald F. Inglehart, and Christian Welzel

WHAT have we learned from the foregoing chapters about how societies attain and sustain democracy? The first part of the book taught us how to tell a democratic **regime** when we see one, and gave an overview of how societies struggle to become and remain democratic. We learned that democracy is not complete without the rule of law (Ch. 2) but also that democracy does not include every political, social or economic condition that people consider desirable (Ch. 3). Chapter 4 demonstrated that democracy has expanded to dominate the global political landscape in major waves and conjunctures, but that it is inaccurate to think of all of the democratic transitions since the early 1970s as forming one continuous 'third wave'. We speak of a 'global wave of democracy' instead, emphasizing the diverse causes and discontinuities of different clusters of democratization since 1970. Chapter 5 outlined the contours of this wave in broad strokes, anticipating some of the problems subsequently addressed in greater detail in the regional chapters in Part Four of the book. Reviewing the major theoretical perspectives from which democratization has been analysed, Chapter 6 proposed that human empowerment constitutes the underlying theme of democratization. The two middle sections of the book demonstrated how a variety of causal and contextual factors affect the process of democratization and the **consolidation** of new democracies. The international environment, the economy,

business elites, mass beliefs, **gender**, social capital, **social movements** and **transnational advocacy networks**, voter behaviour, political parties, electoral systems, party systems, forms of government, and the media all condition and help shape whether countries democratize and how successful they are in doing so. Chapter 18 explored the factors responsible for less successful democratization.

How easily these insights can be turned into practical recommendations for democratizers depends on whether one focuses simply on the adoption of democratic institutions or whether one widens one's view as to how democratic institutions become anchored in a society: it involves the difference between *shallow democratization* and *deep democratization*. Shallow democratization is a tactical matter that is relatively easy for elites to shape, something political scientists like to focus on. For this task, one can give precise advice and identify successful actor strategies. By contrast, deep democratization is a developmental task that requires broadly coordinated, long-term strategies to initiate a far-ranging process of human empowerment through which ordinary people acquire the means and the will to struggle to attain and sustain democratic freedoms. This process is less easily amenable to human intervention aimed at immediate success.

The remainder of this chapter identifies and discusses a series of facilitating and impeding factors of democratization, moving from *tactical* to *strategic* to *developmental* factors. As we move along this path, we also move from factors shaping shallow democratization to factors shaping deep democratization, and from short-term to long-term processes. Our analysis assumes that, as power maximizing actors, authoritarian elites are unlikely to surrender their power unless they are pressured to do so. Thus, a crucial question is how to mount and sustain democratizing pressures on elites.

Tactical and Strategic Factors

One of the conditions that helps initiate a transition to democracy in an authoritarian regime, is if the ruling regime elite splits into factions with opposing interests. This is more likely to happen in developed societies whose complexity creates multi-faceted regime coalitions that are not as easily held together. Rifts within the ruling elite are also more likely when there is a mounting **legitimacy** crisis, due to economic setbacks, unfulfilled policy promises, and failures in crisis management.

In heterogeneous regime coalitions, legitimacy crises encourage elite splits because they create an opportunity for some elite groups to try to strengthen their position in the regime coalition by pursuing a reform strategy that they hope will bring them popular support—thus regaining legitimacy. Accordingly, many transitions to democracy have been instigated by the emergence of a reform camp within the regime elite. Typically, the reformers initiate a liberalization programme that opens a space for criticism and alternative voices. As a result, opposition groups surface from the underground and in many cases advance further claims for democratization. If the opposition groups remain moderate in their methods (avoiding violence), demonstrate their readiness for compromise but at the same time muster widespread public support, a negotiated transition to democracy becomes possible.

The emergence of a regime opposition does not always result from an elite-initiated opening process. Sometimes, policy failures lead to spontaneous manifestations of widespread mass opposition, launching a legitimacy crisis that impels an intra-elite reform camp to surface and engage in negotiations with the opposition. Again, this configuration of events often leads to 'pacted transitions'.

The institutional basis of a given authoritarian regime is an important factor in this context because different types of authoritarian regimes show different vulnerabilities to democratizing pressures. For instance, the weakness of military regimes is that they lack an ideological mission that legitimates them on a long-term basis. Usually, they take power as crisis managers, so their justification is—often explicitly—only temporary. The legitimacy of military regimes is relatively easily questioned, either because the junta fails to manage the crisis, in which case its justification lacks credibility, or because things run smoothly, in which case the need for crisis management becomes obsolete. One obvious advantage of military regimes is that they control the means of coercion, so they can silence emerging opposition by brute force. But confronted with widespread mass opposition that proves resilient even in the face of oppression, the loyalty of the troops may erode if they are ordered to turn on peaceful protestors. On the other hand, even though military regimes sometimes exit quickly from power, they also easily return, as the repeated oscillations between military and civilian rule in such countries as Turkey, Pakistan, or Thailand demonstrate.

Personalistic regimes put all their eggs into the basket of the central ruler's charisma. Accordingly, when the ruler dies, there is an opportunity for political change, as Chapter 18 demonstrated in the Spanish case. Whether or not this opportunity is used for a transition to democracy then depends on the power balance between pro-democratic and antidemocratic forces and their relative support among the population.

One-party regimes, whether leftist or rightist, profit from a more strongly institutionalized power basis. These regimes usually have an ideological mission that inspires their existence and provides legitimation. It generally takes longer, and is a bigger challenge, for a potential regime opposition to erode the ideological basis of one-party regimes. One strategy that proved successful in the former communist bloc is to demonstrate that the regime betrays its very own ideals. When communist countries signed the human rights declaration in the Final Act of the Conference on Security and Co-operation in Europe (CSCE), while refusing to respect these rights in practice, civil rights movements like the Charta 77 effectively publicized this contradiction—and in doing so helped to erode the regimes' legitimacy. Eventually, the legitimacy crisis went so deep that even within the communist parties no one believed any longer in the regime's ideals. The only remaining reason to support the party was given individuals' desire for power. In this situation, reform camps surfaced in a number of communist parties (most notably in the Soviet Union and Hungary) together with regime opposition organizations outside the party, once Gorbachev's nullification of the **Brezhnev Doctrine** in 1988 eliminated the threat of intervention in Central and Eastern Europe.

Rightist one-party regimes, most notably in Taiwan, moved through a similar process of intra-party reform camp formation after their ideological credibility had been exhausted. Renewing the credibility of its ideological ideals is the major challenge for a one-party system, and it becomes difficult to handle when after decades in power the leadership turns corrupt. The future will show how communist China manages to cope with this challenge.

Splits in the ruling elite are important because they give leverage to domestic as well as international actors, enhancing their bargaining options to push a democratization agenda through. The leverage that international actors have in pushing for democracy increases in so far as a country depends on international aid. In some cases, dependence on international assistance can be so strong that external powers can trigger democratization, even in the absence of a pro-democratic regime opposition within the country. In the extreme case, democratic powers can enforce democratic institutions by military intervention, as was attempted in Afghanistan and Iraq. But externally triggered processes of democratization are unlikely to penetrate very deep unless there are strong domestic forces inside a country. Internationally isolated countries, such as Iran, North Korea, or Myanmar, are less susceptible to international democracy promotion, while China

may simply be too powerful to be forced to respond to international pressures. In these countries, the question of whether and when they democratize depends mainly on domestic developments.

This does not make it impossible for outside forces to try to influence developments in a positive way. But it is important to identify the appropriate strategy for dealing with countries that cannot be forced to respond to democratizing pressures from outside. The surest way to keep an authoritarian regime in power that is not vulnerable to outside pressures is to isolate and sanction it. Such a strategy is likely to help authoritarian rulers present themselves as stalwart fighters for their people's well-being in a hostile world. It also helps to foment threat perceptions, rally the people around the flag and create loyalty pressures that make it very difficult for a regime opposition to criticize government. This prevents the opening up of a legitimacy gap that a potential regime opposition could credibly fill. Iran is a current example of inappropriate strategy. Even though democratic powers should not hesitate to criticize human rights violations and other malpractices in authoritarian regimes, staying on moral high ground alone is not very helpful. Along with criticism, pro-democratic powers should attempt to integrate authoritarian regimes into international exchange, exposing these regimes to the transnational flow of information, ideas, and people. Inspired by awareness of alternative possibilities through inflows from outside, it is possible that pro-democratic forces within these countries will gain ground and that an incumbent regime's legitimacy gaps will become apparent.

When regime elites are unified to sustain an authoritarian system, a transition to democracy is less easily achieved, particularly if the regime is able to isolate itself from international democratizing pressures. In such cases, the chances to democratize depend very strongly on whether a pro-democratic regime opposition emerges, how massive it grows, and how skilfully it uses its repertoire of elite-challenging actions. If the regime opposition can mobilize support from all layers of the population, if it is able to demonstrate this support, and if it remains resilient even in the face of oppression, loyalty to the regime elite erodes, thereby undermining the regime's repressive capacities. Thus, massive, determined, and well organized regime opposition can overcome elite resistance to democratize. If, however, the regime opposition remains limited to isolated sectors of society, is unable to demonstrate popular support across the country, and cannot stay resilient in the face of repression, its chances of success will be limited.

To a considerable extent, then, democratization is a matter of the skills and virtues of mass opposition leaders. It matters how willing and able they are to advance claims that resonate with many people, to mobilize resources for popular campaigns, and to make use of the full set of elite-challenging actions even in the face of repression. Tactical and strategic factors, such as the presence of skilful political dissidents, benevolent reform elites, and international assistance, are important but when it comes to deep democratization these factors can hardly compensate for deficiencies in the development of ordinary people's capabilities and motivation to struggle for democracy. Here we leave the realm of tactical political action and enter the world of developmental factors.

Developmental Factors

Mounting and sustaining pro-democratic regime opposition against authoritarian rulers requires that societies embark on a process of human empowerment that gives people the resources that make them capable and the ambitions that make them willing to struggle for democratic freedoms. Ordinary people's readiness to struggle for democratic freedoms is necessary for deep democratization to be attained, for authoritarian leaders are unlikely to surrender their powers unless they are pressured to do so.

The processes that contribute to making wider parts of a population capable and motivated to struggle for democratic freedoms have been discussed in the various chapters of this book. But paramount among them is a type of economic development that is knowledge-driven and distributes action resources widely throughout society rather than concentrating them in small minorities of the population. The rise of the knowledge society equips growing segments of the population with the material means, intellectual skills, and social opportunities needed to mount effective pressures on elites. As a consequence, ordinary people's action repertoires expand in ways that make the value of democratic freedoms intuitively obvious, giving rise to emancipative worldviews that value freedoms highly. These long-term developmental factors enhance a society's ability and willingness to struggle for democracy.

External Threats and Group Hostilities as Impediments to Democracy

Various factors can hinder developmental factors in actualizing their pro-democratic tendencies. Perceptions of external threats and internal group hostilities are such factors because they diminish tolerance of opposition—a basic principle of democratic organization. External threats help leaders' to conduct 'rally around the flag' strategies that silence inner opposition. Group hostilities do the same within groups, closing ranks around leaders and silencing opposing views.

Involvement of a country in an enduring international conflict can undermine democratic institutions because conflicts provide a sense of being threatened that allows skilful leaders to present suppression of the opposition as crucial to the nation's survival. Chapter 21 provided ample evidence of this pattern. But even among democracies the operation of this pattern is manifest, as is illustrated by the excesses of the McCarthy era in the 1950s and more recently the Homeland Security Act of 2002 in the USA. External threats, whether attributed to a communist world conspiracy or to Islamic terrorism, can legitimate authoritarian rule and undermine civil liberties.

Although, internal group divisions are not necessarily threatening to democracy, ethnic, linguistic, religious and other easily discernible group divisions can be manipulated to foment support for authoritarian leaders. Extremist leaders almost always mobilize support by playing on group hostilities. Thus,

democracy has historically been more easily established and consolidated in societies that are relatively homogenous culturally and relatively egalitarian economically.

Regardless of whether such hindering factors are present, deep democratization requires that a society's people acquire the capability and motivation to struggle for the freedoms that define democracy. This is because democracy is a socially embedded phenomenon, not just an institutional machine that operates in a vacuum. Shallow democratization involves crafting institutions but deep democratization involves the development of empowering ambitions and skills among large segments of a society.

An Evolutionary Perspective

Most social scientists failed to predict the democratic trend of recent decades, especially in the communist world. By contrast, in a largely-forgotten article, Talcott Parsons (1964) predicted the democratic trend, arguing that the democratic principle is sufficiently powerful that, in the long run, non-democratic regimes, including the communist regimes, will either adopt it or they will fail. Theoretical considerations led Parsons to this view. He understood something that many political scientists do not recognize: that evolutionary dynamics exist that work beyond the horizon of elite actors' intentions and that political development, in particular the survival and diffusion of regime types, is driven by dynamics that lack a central agent.

Thus, Parsons argued that in the global system of nation **states** there is an uncoordinated process of regime selection going on, such that regime characteristics that bestow on states an advantage diffuse at the expense of regime characteristics lacking that advantage. Parsons called such advantageous regime characteristics 'evolutionary universals'. Along with market organization and bureaucratic organization, he claimed the democratic organization was such an evolutionary universal, especially in the age of mass politics. The advantages of the market principle and

the bureaucratic principle are obvious. They nurture economic productivity and administrative efficiency, respectively. But what are the advantages of the democratic principle? For Parsons the democratic principle bestowed on political systems a unique capacity that is of crucial value for their survival when the masses are involved in politics—which is true of all modern industrialized societies, whether democratic or not. The capacity Parsons had in mind is the capacity to generate regime legitimacy, or more precisely, to generate regime legitimacy in a reliable and credible way.

This is not to say that democratic systems are *always* legitimate, nor that authoritarian systems are *never* legitimate. Nevertheless, because democratic procedures are the only means to measure authentic popular support, how legitimate a regime is in the eyes of the population can only be known under democracy. In the age of mass politics it is the most crucial weakness of authoritarian regimes, that it is never exactly known how much genuine support they have in the population. This is responsible for what Kuran (1991) called the 'element of surprise' when authoritarian regimes that lacked any obvious sign of regime opposition for decades are suddenly confronted with mounting mass opposition.

Legitimacy is a crucial resource for regime survival because it eliminates a major source of regime failure: anti-regime mass upheaval. Regimes considered legitimate by the population can mobilize resources of support that are unavailable to illegitimate systems. Illegitimate systems can, to some extent and for some time, silence open mass resistance by repression. But they suffer passive resistance, withholding of support, and sabotage. Illegitimate regimes can only mobilize as much human support as can be controlled by external rewards and coercion. But the most creative and productive aspects of human activity are not mobilized by external sanctions and gratifications but by intrinsic motivations. These aspects of human activity are outside an illegitimate regime's reach. They can create and mobilize extrinsic motivations, not intrinsic ones.

How can we understand the fact that democratization processes in separate countries cluster into coherent and sweeping international waves, behaving as if they were centrally coordinated by a master agent when in fact neither that master agent nor central coordination of the international waves exist? The answer is that evolutionary forces are at work that go beyond the awareness and control of even the most powerful elites. These evolutionary forces bestow a systematic selective advantage on democracies over autocracies. To the extent that such selective advantages exist, it is essential to understand them in order to assess the future potential of democracy and in order to understand the limits and opportunities within which agents pursuing a democratic agenda are acting.

In an era of mass politics, democracies enjoy three distinct selective advantages over autocracies. First, there is a selective advantage by a tendency to win *international confrontations*. States have been involved in international conflicts and wars and often the winning states' political regimes replaced the loosing states' ones. Success in international confrontations has been related to regime type. Democracies usually won the wars they were engaged in, partly because in the long run, they could mobilize their people and resources more effectively. Moreover, democracies tend not to fight each other, avoiding extinguishing their own kind. Autocracies do not have this tendency.

Second, there is a selective advantage by *economic performance*. For reasons explained in Chapters 6 and 8, democracies have emerged and persisted in technologically and economically more advanced and powerful states, which partly explains their superiority in international confrontations with autocracies. Democracies have been established in more prosperous economies from the start. In addition, democracies continued to outperform autocracies economically, greatly increasing their initial prosperity advantage over time. Equally important, autocracies repeatedly lost their more prosperous members to the democratic camp.

The third selective advantage of democracies is an advantage by *popular support*, which is a truly selective force. Because they grant power to the people and because their rulers are selected by the population, democracies tend to have more popular support than autocracies, which makes them less vulnerable to mass regime opposition. Even autocracies that seem stable on the surface, lacking obvious signs of mass opposition, are vulnerable to the 'element of surprise' that becomes apparent in democratic revolutions when massive regime-opposition suddenly emerges and persists, toppling a regime that may have lasted for decades. Democracies are less vulnerable to extinction by popular revolutions. They simply change their rulers through elections.

The most fundamental selective advantage of democracy, however, is its deep rootedness in human nature. Democracy reflects a human aspiration for freedom (Sen 1999), making it the most demanded system for all people who have acquired the means and ambition to raise their voices. To be sure, specific democratization processes always reflect the actions of specific actors in specific transition situations, which vary greatly from country to country. But in order to understand why such transitions occur in relatively developed societies far more often then in less developed ones; and why they cumulate into an international trend that goes beyond what specific actors seek, one has to see the broader selective forces that operate in favour of democracy. One must be aware of these forces in order to adequately assess democracy's future.

The Democratic Agenda of the Future

The selective advantages of democracy are of such a long term nature and so deeply rooted in basic developmental processes that there is no reason to assume that the odds will fundamentally turn against democracy in the foreseeable future. Setbacks will occur in specific countries, but the achievements of the global wave of democracy are unlikely to be reversed. But this does not mean that there are no future challenges. Instead, we see a number of challenges on the democratic agenda, which can be formulated in the following questions: (1) Will democracy continue to spread geographically? (2) Will the deficiencies of new democracies, such as those in the former Soviet Union, be overcome? (3) Will the democratic qualities of established democracies be further deepened?

One might also question the viability of the democratic principle in an era in which the major organizational frame of democracy, the nation state, is said to lose its significance. And one might question the viability of the democratic principle in a world in which decisive ecological measures seem to be unpopular, though they may be necessary to save our planet. However, as these questions go beyond the scope of this book, we limit ourselves to the first three.

Spreading Democracy to New Regions

Three important geographical areas have, so far, proved relatively immune to the democratic trend: China and the predominantly Islamic Middle East and North Africa (see Ch. 21). Anchoring democracy in these areas would without doubt constitute a major breakthrough for the democratic principle. As far as the Middle East and North Africa are concerned, a sweeping democratic trend throughout the region does not seem likely in the near future. The terror and violence nurtured by the Israeli-Palestinian conflict, Islamic fundamentalism, and the predominance of patrimonial states based on oil rents all amount to powerful obstacles to democratization. In addition, we find throughout much of the Islamic world, but especially in the Middle East, a cultural self-appraisal of Islam as the West's counter-civilization—an understanding that is sometimes mirrored in Western views of Islam as its counter-civilization. On this basis, democracy is considered to be a Western product in much of the Islamic world, which might disqualify it in the eyes of many people. Evidence from the World Values Surveys indicates that even among those segments of Islamic populations that overtly support democracy, there is often a fundamental misunderstanding of democratic principles. Evidence from the World Values Surveys also suggests that patriarchal-authoritarian values, which are incompatible with democracy, are prevalent in much of the region, particularly the Arab-speaking countries. These factors hinder the emergence of democracy, and are partly misunderstood in most historically Islamic societies.

China is the superpower of the future, having the largest population in the world and moving toward becoming the second largest economy and second strongest military power. In coming decades, China may replace the USA as the world's most powerful nation. Given its paramount importance, China's future political order is of crucial relevance. The socioeconomic transformations China is undergoing may give rise to emancipative values, which in the long run will fuel mass pressures to democratize. At the same time, Asian cultures are distinctive and the socioeconomic transformations may not result in the same democratizing pressures as they produced in the west. Nevertheless, it is clear that Asian cultures are not immune to global trends of human development, as is obvious from the fact that as they reached high levels of development, both Taiwan and South Korea made transitions to democracy and have emerged as consolidated democracies.

Consolidating and Improving New Democracies

Many new democracies in Latin America, Sub-Saharan Africa, and Central and Eastern Europe show serious deficiencies concerning the rule of law, **accountability**, and transparency. Not surprisingly then, there is widespread popular cynicism about the integrity of representatives, the trustworthiness of institutions, and the policy performance in these new democracies. This popular cynicism often leads to political apathy rather than mass political activism, weakening civil society and placing corrupt leaders under little popular pressure to behave more responsively. But in those new democracies where cynical citizens become 'critical citizens' who sustain a high level of elite-challenging mass activities, government is consistently more effective, transparent, and accountable. Civic action matters: both within new and old democracies, relatively widespread civic action helps increasing accountable **governance**. This insight is important. It shows that the quality of democracy is not solely a matter of elites. It is also, and very markedly so, a matter of the citizens. When they are motivated to put elites under popular pressure and actually do so, they can improve the quality and effectiveness of governance. There is no reason for civic defeatism.

Deepening Old Democracies

The most obvious aspect of the global democratic trend is the geographical spread of democracy. But the global democratic trend has a second, often forgotten aspect: the deepening of democracy. This occurs even where democracy has been in place for many decades. This trend is well documented in a book by Cain, Dalton, and Scarrow (2005), showing that over the past 25 years most post-industrial democracies have widened elements of direct democracy, have opened channels of citizen participation in policy planning, have extended the scope of civic rights and have improved accountability to the public. These institutional changes have been accompanied and driven by cultural changes that gave rise to emancipative values and high levels of sustained elite-challenging actions. In fact, a major reason why long established democracies show high levels of accountable governance is because they are constantly exposed to popular pressure by increasingly 'critical citizens'. This should affect our views of what kind of citizenry is needed to consolidate democracies and keep them flourishing.

In *The Civic Culture*, Gabriel Almond and Sidney Verba (1963) assumed that in order for democracy to flourish, citizen participation should be limited to the institutional channels of representative democracy, focusing on elections and the activities around them. This view was reinforced by Samuel Huntington's (1968) influential work *Political Order in Changing Societies*, contributing to deep-seated suspicions of non-institutionalized, assertive citizen action. This suspicion is so deeply ingrained in political science that, even today, prevailing concepts of social capital and civil society still focus on institutionally channelled participation, emphasizing membership and participation in formal associations. By contrast, non-institutionalized forms of assertive citizen action are rarely recognized in prevailing conceptions of civil society. As Chapter 12 suggests, the essentially fruitful role of elite-challenging mass actions in improving democratic governance is unjustifiably neglected.

The dominant view of what sort of citizenry makes and keeps countries democratic, needs to be revised. Democracy flourishes with an uncomfortable citizenry that makes life difficult for their rulers, exposing them to constant popular pressure. Democracy requires a citizenry who place a high value on democratic freedoms and are capable of struggling for them—to attain them when they are denied and to sustain them when they are challenged.

Unfortunately, such a citizenry cannot be ordered into existence by elite decree, nor can it be crafted by institutions. Its emergence reflects a more basic process of human empowerment through which people acquire the resources and skills to demand responsive government and the ambitions that motivate them to do so. Democratic institutions can be imposed from outside, but if these conditions are absent, it is likely to be a flawed version of democracy if it survives at all. Sustainable democracy is not just about crafting institutions. It is about shaping development.

Glossary

Accountability: The ability of citizens to reward or sanction political leaders so as to induce them to act in the interest of citizens. Absolute monarchs claimed to be accountable only to god; in fact, they were often subject to checks by non-elected elites. Democracy involves the accountability of governors to the mass of the citizenry through free elections.

Authoritarianism: Authoritarian regimes are non-democratic regimes that suppress political opposition and limit political participation to relatively meaningless acclamation rituals. Authoritarianism is sometimes contrasted with **totalitarianism**.

Brezhnev Doctrine: A principle of Soviet foreign policy from the late 1960s onward that laid claim to the Soviet Union's right to define socialism and its violations among member states of the Warsaw Pact and justified soviet military intervention in these countries.

Bureaucratic authoritarianism: Model developed by Guillermo O'Donnell (1973) to characterize and explain the type of repressive state that resulted from the military seizing power in the Southern Cone of Latin America in the 1960s–1980s with the aim of restoring political order and economic stability following the exhaustion of ISI.

Business associations: Long-term organizations with formal statutes, including chambers of commerce, national and international trade associations, and business think tanks. Their members can be individual business people, firms, or other associations.

Conference on Security and Co-operation in Europe (CSCE): During the Cold war, The CSCE was an agreement between both eastern and western countries that common security was important to avoid another third world war. Symbolizing détente, the CSCE included limitations on troop movements as well as economic and human cooperation. It was this later dimension that characterizes the OSCE, which is a more permanent structure focussing on the issues of the post-cold war order: democracy, human rights, and ethnic conflict.

Consociational democracy: Defined by Arend Lijphart (1969: 216) as 'government by elite cartel designed to turn a democracy with a fragmented political culture into a stable democracy', consociational democracy is an institutional framework to ensure that all relevant groups in society (e.g. ethnic groups) are always influential to some degree.

Consolidation: A consolidated regime is a regime that has sufficiently strong institutions so that the pressures for change that arise can be dealt with within its existing framework, whether by responses that maintained the regime unaltered, for example, changing leadership through an election or by agreement among a military junta or the central committee of a one-party state.

Contentious politics: Episodic, collective interactions between claimants and their targets (usually at least one government) involving conflictual claims and covering phenomena such as social movements, revolutions, strike waves, nationalisms, and democratization.

Correlation: A measure of co-variation between two variables. Variation is a measure of dispersal, indicating how much the values of a variable fluctuate around the average value. Co-variation exists when positive/negative deviations from the mean in one variable are systematically linked with positive/negative deviations from the mean in another variable. Correlation is a standardized way to express co-variation. For metrically scaled variables, *Pearson's r* is the standardly used correlation coefficient. The closer its values approach 0, the weaker the co-variation. Values of *r* approaching -1 or +1 denote stronger co-variation.

Cycles of protest: Phases of heightened conflict and contention characterized by a rapid diffusion of collective action among different social and political actors, with innovation in the forms of protest and intense interactions between challengers and authorities.

Disproportionality: The extent to which the vote share and the seat share of parties diverge.

Effective number of parties: A measure to calculate the number of parties taking into account their relative size, so that bigger parties weight more than smaller parties.

Gender: The difference between male and female as perceived by individuals' in a social context. The concept is distinct from biological differences of sex, which may or may not correspond to gender differences.

Global civil society: Refers to the community of transnational advocacy networks that operate beyond the national boundaries and at a planetary level.

Global justice movements: Networks of groups and individuals that mobilize at various geographical levels for global justice, having been identified, in different countries, as alter-global, no global, new global, global justice, *Globalisierungs-skritiker*, *altermondialists*, globalizers from below, and so on.

Globalization: A process by which the economies, political regimes, cultures, security systems, and peoples of the different nations and regions of the world become more interlinked and interdependent; the boundaries that separate them become more permeable or they disappear altogether; and the people of the world are unified into a single global society.

Governability: The ability of the government to make decisions and have them approved by parliament.

Governance: The interactive process through which the state influences the lives of its citizens arbitrarily or through bureaucratic institutions, and through which a small or large fraction of citizens influence the state.

Idealism: In the context of international relations, idealism holds that a state should base its foreign policy on ethical and philosophical principles. A radical version of idealism holds that a state's foreign policy should never betray its declared principles even if these principles clash with its economic and military interests. Idealism is marked by the prominent role played by international law and international organizations in its conception of policy formation.

Institutional learning theory: This theory holds that positive attitudes towards democracy take root through the exposure to and the practice of democracy. After Dankwart Rustow (1970) this theory is also called 'habituation theory'.

Institutionalization of accountability: Democratic regimes vary greatly in their institutional forms. The chief representative institution can be a parliament or a president. Elections can be held by proportional representation or on first-past-the-post rules. The system of government can be unitary or federal. There is no one best way to organize a democratic system of government.

Kondratieff waves: Pattern of recurring structural change in the modern world economy. Thought of as spanning across some 60 years, they encompass an alternation of periods of high sectoral growth with periods of slower growth.

Legitimacy: In political sociology, legitimacy means the popular acceptance of a political system. A regime is legitimate if the people think it is.

Legitimation: The process of developing legitimacy, that is, the unfolding of a set of positive societal attitudes towards an institution.

Multi-level analysis: A variant of **regression analysis** designed to identify the extent to which the characteristics of an observation unit (e.g. an individual) are determined by other characteristics of this unit and by higher-level characteristics of its context, respectively. In political science, multi-level analysis is used to distinguish individual-level effects from country-level effects as well as analyzing the interaction between these two levels.

Multiple regression: Regression analysis is a tool to explain and predict variation in a dependent variable Y by variation in an independent variable X. When more than one independent variable X (X_1, X_2, X_3 and so on) are involved, we refer to multiple regression. Multiple regression isolates the part of the variation in each independent variable that is independent (unexplained) by all other independent variables and calculates the isolated effect of each of the independent variables on the dependent variable. This is a helpful tool to identify the relative explanatory importance of variables that are theoretically contested.

National Endowment for Democracy (NED): A government-funded organization in the USA designed to promote democracy by means of financing democracy promotion as well as research on democratization in the form of the *Journal of Democracy* and the International Forum for Democratic Studies.

Necessary condition: A condition that has to be present for an effect to occur.

New institutionalism: The rediscovery in the 1980s of the importance of institutions for social, political and economic life.

Ostpolitik: Aimed at sustained reconciliation between Eastern and Western Europe, *ostpolitik* was designed by the West German foreign minister and later chancellor Willy Brandt in the late 1960s. The strategy included an agreement with the Soviet Union accepting the frontiers of Berlin and, in 1972, the commitment by the two German states to developing normal relations on the basis of guaranteeing their mutual territorial integrity and sovereignty.

Participation: Political participation refers to the activities of citizens intended to influence state structures, authorities, and the making of collectively binding decisions regarding the allocation of public goods by means of political action such as voting or protesting. This can be restricted to an oligarchy that may claim entitlement to influence based on birth, wealth, guns or expertise, or involve universal suffrage in which all adult citizens have the right to vote in elections.

Party system: The pattern of interactions resulting from competition between political parties. Different patterns of interaction form different types of party system.

Party system function: The way in which the party system functions as an intermediary between society and government.

Political engineering: The deliberate attempt to reform or build political institutions with the aim of achieving particular objectives, such policies or other political outcomes.

Polyarchy: First introduced by Robert Dahl and Charles Lindblom in their book *Politics, Economics, and Welfare* (1953), polyarchy denotes a political system in which non-leaders exert a high degree of control over leaders. The concept's main raison d'être is to maintain a distinction between an ideal of democracy and the imperfect approximations of that ideal found in the real world.

Power-sharing democracy: Encompassing term that captures a wide variety of non-majoritarian types of democracy in which power is shared or dispersed instead of concentrated.

Probit: A probit model is a type of regression analysis model suitable for situations in which the phenomenon of interest, the dependent variable, can take on only two possible values (such as democracy or autocracy, or war and peace). An ordered probit model applies a similar estimation technique to situations in which the dependent variable can take on a number of different values that represent distinct categories and can meaningfully be put into an order (e.g. uncountable autocracy, constitutional oligarchy, and effective democracy).

Realism: In the context of international relations, realism holds that states base their foreign policies on their national interest, which is generally understood to be of an economic and military nature. Realists deny the importance of ethical and philosophical principles in the relations between nations.

Regime: A set of institutions by which political authority is exercised within a state. Regimes can come and go while the state remains.

Relevant parties: The number of parties that have either coalition or blackmail potential.

Rentier state: A state with a high dependence on external rents produced by a relatively small number of economic actors. Rents are often generated from the exploitation of natural resources rather than from production or investment. Because they have a reduced need to levy taxes, rentier states tend to be autonomous vis-à-vis civil society and hence less accountable to the public.

Representativeness: The extent to which different groups and tendencies in society gain parliamentary representation in accordance with their numerical strength in the electorate.

Rule of law: An essential pre-condition of democratic governance. Without it, governors cannot be held accountable for their actions by the courts or by the electorate.

Social contract: The result of a process in which the people of a country or other social or geographical entity decide upon the fundamental principles of their common existence. In practical terms, this decision can be taken directly by the people themselves, as in a public debate and a final referendum on a constitution. Alternatively, the decision can be taken as a result of debates and negotiations between the elites, such as party leaders, leaders of ethnic and religious groups, civic leaders, media figures, business managers, and heads of labour unions.

Social movements: networks of organizations and individuals that share a distinct collective identity and intervene in political conflicts, mainly relying upon protest action.

State: An organization that exercises authority within a given geographical region and claims a monopoly of the physical means of coercion to protect these boundaries and itself against external or internal challenges. A state that lacks this authority is subject to being overthrown.

Sufficient condition: When this condition is present, an effect occurs.

Supranationalism: A decision making process in a community of national-states, in which member states delegate part of their decision making powers in certain policy areas to the governing organs of the community. The opposite method of decision-making in international organizations is inter-governmentalism where every decision is taken by a committee of the representatives of the member states.

Thick description: In the methodology of the social sciences, thick description denotes the idea that the context of human behaviour is as important to understanding and explaining social life as is the behaviour itself. Without context, in this view, behaviour remains meaningless to outsiders.

Totalitarianism: Totalitarian regimes are undemocratic regimes that suppress political opposition and limit political participation. In addition, they restrict the sphere of citizens' private life and emphasize mass mobilization in pursuit of national goals. The latter aspects are sometimes held to distinguish totalitarian regimes from **authoritarian** ones hat lack these features.

Transnational advocacy networks: Alliances of social movement organizations, political parties, interest groups, non-governmental organizations, and representatives of governments from different countries, which act transnationally for the promotion of specific concerns and values (such as human rights, environmental protection, etc.).

Transnationalism: A process that denoted the growing interconnectivity and interdependency between the economies, political systems, cultures and people around the world and the loosening of boundaries between countries. Transnationalism refers to cooperation between sub-state actors and points to activities that transcend national boundaries; it should be distinguished from internationalism, which refers to cooperation and relations between nation-states.

Turnout: The percentage of eligible voters who cast a ballot in an election. Calculations of turnout are made in different ways. US studies tend to base calculations on those voting as a proportion of the voting age population because in the US a large proportion of this latter group is not even registered to vote. Elsewhere it has been more common to take as the denominator the numbers registered.

United States Agency for International Development (USAID): A US federal government organization respon-sible for most of the country's non-military foreign aid. Its official goals are to further US foreign policy interests through expanding democracy and free markets as well as improving the lives of people in the developing world.

Urban movements: Social movements active in urban environments. They often combine an interest for social issues, with demands for participatory democracy and territorial identity.

Washington consensus: Consensus among the Washington-based international monetary institutions (World Bank, International Monetary Fund) and the Reagan administration to tie credits to conditions of 'good governance', which include abidance to structural re-adjustment programs (cutting back public spending and implementing de-regulation and privatization measures), enforcing the rule of law, respecting civil rights and holding contested elections.

Bibliography

Acemoglu, D. and Robinson, J. A. (2006), *Economic Origins of Dictatorship and Democracy* (Cambridge: Cambridge University Press)

Acuña, C. H. (1995), 'Business Interests, Dictatorship and Democracy in Argentina', in E. Bartell and L. Payne (eds), *Business and Democracy in Latin America* (Pittsburgh, PA: University of Pittsburgh Press), 3–48

Addis, C. (1999), *Taking the Wheel: Auto Parts and the Political Economy of Industrialization in Brazil* (University Park, PA: Pennsylvania State University Press)

Afrobarometer (2006), 'The Status of Democracy, 2005–2006: Findings from Afrobarometer Round 3 for 18 Countries', *Afrobarometer Briefing Paper*, 40. Available at <www.afrobarometer.org>

Aggoun, L. and Rivoire, J.–B. (2004), *Françalgérie. Crimes et mensonges d'Etats* (Paris: Ed. La Découverte)

Aguilar, P. (2001), *The Politics of Memory: Transitional Justice in Democratizing Societies* (Oxford: Oxford University Press)

Alagappa, M. (ed.) (2001), *Civil Society and Political Change in Asia* (Stanford: Stanford University Press)

Almond, G. A. and Verba, S. (1963), *The Civic Culture: Political Attitudes and Democracy in Five Nations* (Princeton, NJ: Princeton University Press)

Altman, D. and Peréz–Liñan, A. (2002), 'Assessing the Quality of Democracy: Freedom, Competitiveness and Participation in Eighteen Latin American Countries', *Democratization* 9/2: 85–100

Alverez, S. E. (1990), *Engendering Democracy in Brazil: Women's Movements in Transition Politics* (Princeton, NJ: Princeton University Press)

Anderson, B. (1991), *Imagined Communities* (London: Verso)

Andeweg, R. (2000), 'Consociational Democracy', *Annual Review of Political Science*, 3: 509–36

Aristotle (1962 [350 BC]): Aristotle (1984 [350 BC]), *Politics: Books III and IV*, translated with introduction and comments by Richard Robinson (Oxford: Clarendon Press)

Armony, A. C. and Schamis, H. E. (2005), 'Babel in Democratization Studies', *Journal of Democracy*, 16/4: 113–28

Arrow, K. J. (1963), *Social Choice and Individual Values*, 2nd edn (New York, NY: Cowles Commission)

Åslund, A. (2007), *How Capitalism Was Built: The Transformations of Central and Eastern Europe, Russia and Central Asia* (Cambridge: Cambridge University Press)

Ayoob, M. (2005), 'The Future of Political Islam: the Importance of External Variables', *International Affairs*, 81/5: 951–61

Baeg Im, H. (1996), 'Globalization and Democratization: Boon Companions or Strange Bedfellows?', *Australian Journal of International Affairs*, 50/3: 279–91

Bahry, D. and Silver, B. D. (1990), 'Soviet Citizen Participation on the Eve of Democratization', *American Political Science Review*, 83: 821–47

Baiocchi, G. (2005), *Militants and Citizens: The Politics of Participatory Democracy in Porto Alegre* (Stanford, CA: Stanford University Press)

Baker, G. (1999), 'The Taming Idea of Civil Society', *Democratization*, 6/3: 1–29

Barber, B. R. (1984), *Strong Democracy: Participatory Politics for a New Age* (Berkeley, CA: University of California Press)

Barkan, J. *et al.* (2004), 'Emerging Legislatures: Institutions of Horizontal Accountability', in B. Levy and S. Kpundeh (eds), *Governance and Public Sector Management in Africa* (Washington DC: The World Bank), 211–55

Barnes, S. H. and Kaase, M. *et al.* (1979), *Political Action: Mass Participation in Five Western Democracies* (Beverly Hills, CA: Sage)

Barrera, C. and Zugasti, R. (2006), 'The Role of the Press in Times of Transition: The Building of the Spanish Democracy (1975–78)', in K. Voltmer (ed.), *Mass Media and Political Communication in New Democracies* (London: Routledge), 23–41

Bartolini, S. and Mair, P. (1990), *Identity, Competition and Electoral Availability: The Stabilisation of European Electorates 1885–1995* (Cambridge: Cambridge University Press)

Beblawi, H. and Luciani, G. (1987) (eds), *The Rentier State* (London: Croom Helm)

Beetham, D. (1994), *Defining and Measuring Democracy* (London: Sage)

Bell, D. A. (1973), *The Coming of Postindustrial Society* (New York: Basic Books)

Bell, D. A. (2000), *East Meets West: Human Rights and Democracy in East Asia* (Princeton, NJ: Princeton University Press)

Bell, D. A. (2006), *Beyond Liberal Democracy* (Princeton, NJ: Princeton University Press)

Bell, D. A., Brown, D., Jayasuriya, K. and Jones, D. (1995) (eds), *Towards Illiberal Democracy in Pacific Asia* (New York, NY: St. Martin's Press)

Bellin, E. (2000), 'Contingent Democrats: Industrialists, Labor, and Democratization in Late–Developing Countries', *World Politics*, 52/2: 175–205

Bellin, E. (2004), 'The Robustness of Authoritarianism in the Middle East', *Comparative Politics*, 36/2: 139–58

Ben Mansour, L. (2002), *Frères Musulmans, Frères Féroces: Voyage dans L'enfer du Discours Islamiste* (Paris: Editions Ramsay)

Bennett, W. L. (1998), 'The media and democratic development. The social basis of political communication', in P. H. O'Neil (ed.), *Communicating Democracy: The Media and Political Transitions* (Boulder, CO: Lynne Rienner), 195–207

Berg–Schlosser, D. (2004a), 'The quality of democracies in Europe as measured by current indicators of democratization and good governance', *Journal of Communist Studies and Transition Politics*, 20/1: 28–55

Berg–Schlosser, D. (2004b), 'Concepts, Measurements and Sub–Types in Democratization Research', in D. Berg–Schlosser (ed.), *Democratization* (Wiesbaden: VS Verlag), 52–64

Berg–Schlosser, D. (2004c), 'Indicators of Democracy and Good Governance as Measures of the Quality of Democracy in Africa', *Acta Politica*, 39/3: 248–78

Berg–Schlosser, D. and Mitchell, J. (eds) (2000), *Conditions of Democracy in Europe, 1919–39: Systematic Case–Studies* (London: Macmillan)

Berg–Schlosser, D. and Mitchell, J. (eds) (2002), *Authoritarianism and Democracy in Europe, 1919–39: Comparative Analysis* (London: Palgrave Macmillan)

Berman, Bruce J. (1998), 'Ethnicity, Patronage, and the African State: The Politics of Uncivil Nationalism', *African Affairs*, 97, 305–41

Berman, S. (1997), 'Civil Society and the Collapse of the Weimar Republic', *World Politics*, 49/3: 401–29

Berman, S. (2003), 'Islamism, Revolution and Civil Society', *Perspectives on Politics*, 1/2: 258–72

Bermeo, N. (1997), 'Myths of Moderation: Confrontation and Conflict during Democratic Transition', *Comparative Politics*, 29/2: 205–322

Bermeo, N. (2003), *Ordinary People in Extraordinary Times: The Citizenry and the Breakdown of Democracy* (Princeton, NJ: Princeton University Press)

Bernhagen, P. (2007), *The Political Power of Business: Structure and Information in Public Policymaking* (London: Routledge)

Bernhard, M. (1993), 'Civil Society and Democratic Transition in East-Central Europe', *Political Science Quarterly*, 108/2: 307–26

Bill, J. A. and Leiden, C. (1984), *Politics in The Middle East* (Boston, MA: Little, Brown and Company)

Birch, S. (2003), *Electoral Systems and Political Transformation in Post-Communist Europe* (London: Palgrave)

Birch, S. (2005), 'Single–member District Electoral Systems and Democratic Transition', *Electoral Studies*, 24/2: 281–301

Blais, A. and Carty, K. (1991), 'The Psychological Impact of Electoral Laws: Measuring Duverger's Elusive Factor', *British Journal of Political Science* 21: 79–93

Bogaards, M. (2004), 'Electoral Systems and the Management of Ethnic Conflict in the Balkans', in A. Mungiu–Pippidi and I. Krastev (eds), *Nationalism after Communism: Lessons Learned* (Budapest: CEU Press), 247–68

Bogaards, M. (2007), 'Electoral Systems, Party Systems, and Ethnic Conflict Management in Africa', in M. Basedau, G. Erdmann, and A. Mehler (eds), *Votes, Money and Violence: Political Parties and Elections in Africa* (Uppsala: Nordiska Afrikainstitutet), 168–93

Boix, C. (2003), *Democracy and Redistribution* (Cambridge: Cambridge University Press)

Boix, C. and Posner, D. N. (1998), 'Social Capital: Explaining Its Origins and Effects on Governmental Performance', *British Journal of Political Science*, 294: 686–93

Boix, C. and Stokes, S. L. (2003), 'Endogenous Democratization', *World Politics*, 55: 517–49

Bollen, K. A. (1980), 'Issues in the Comparative Measurement of Political Democracy', *American Sociological Review*, 45/3: 370–90

Bollen, K. A. (1990), 'Political Democracy: Conceptual and Measurement Traps', *Studies in Comparative International Development*, 25: 7–24

Bollen, K. A. and Jackman, R. W. (1985), 'Political Democracy and the Size Distribution of Income', *American Sociological Review*, 50/4: 438–57

Bollen, K. A. and Jackman, R. W. (1989), 'Democracy, Stability, and Dichotomies', *American Sociological Review*, 54/4: 612–21

Bollen, K. A. and Paxton, P. (2000), 'Subjective Measures of Liberal Democracy', *Comparative Political Studies*, 33/1: 58–86

Boudreau, V. (2004), *Resisting Dictatorship: Repression and Protest in Southeast Asia* (Cambridge: Cambridge University Press)

Bowles, S. and Gintis, H. (1986), *Democracy and Capitalism: Property, Community, and the Contradictions of Modern Social Thought* (London: Routledge and Kegan Paul)

Bracher, K. D. (1971 [1955]), *Die Auflösung der Weimarer Republik* (Königstein: Deutsche Verlagsanstalt)

Brady, H. E., Verba, S. and Schlozman, K. L. (1995), 'Beyond SES: A Resource Model of Political Participation', *American Political Science Review* 89/2: 271–94

Brambor, T., Clark, W. and Golder, M. (2007), 'Are African Party Systems Different?' *Electoral Studies*, 24: 315–23

Bratton, M. (2007), 'Formal versus Informal Institutions in Africa', *Journal of Democracy*, 18/3: 96–110

Bratton, M. and Chang, E. (2006), 'State Building and Democratization in sub-Saharan Africa', *Comparative Political Studies*, 39/9: 1059–83

Bratton, M. and Mattes, R. (2001), 'Support for Democracy in Africa', *British Journal of Political Science*, 31: 447–74

Bratton, M. and van de Walle, N. (1997), *Democratic Experiments in Africa. Regime Transitions in Comparative Perspective* (Cambridge: Cambridge University Press)

Bratton, M., Mattes R. and Gyimah–Boadi, E. (2005), *Public Opinion, Democracy, and Market Reform in Africa* (Cambridge: Cambridge University Press)

Bratton, Michael and van de Walle, Nicolas (1994), 'Neopatrimonial Regimes and Political Transitions in Africa', *World Politics*, 46 (4), 453–89

Brennan, G. and Buchanan, J. M. (1980), *The Power to Tax: Analytical Foundations of a Fiscal Constitution* (Cambridge: Cambridge University Press)

Brinks, D. and Coppedge, M. (2006), 'Diffusion is No Illusion: Neighbor Emulation in the Third Wave of Democracy', *Comparative Political Studies*, 39: 463–89

Brown, A. (2007), *Seven Years that Changed the World. Perestroika in Perspective* (Oxford: Oxford University Press)

Brownlee, J. (2002), 'And Yet They Persist: Explaining Survival and Transition in Neopatrimonial Regimes', *Studies in Comparative Development*, 37/2: 35–63

Brumberg, D. (2002a), 'Islamists and the Politics of Consensus', *Journal of Democracy*, 13/3: 109–15.

Brumberg, D. (2002b), 'The trap of liberalized autocracy', *Journal of Democracy*, 13/4: 56–68

Bruneau, T. (1981), 'Patterns of Politics in Portugal Since the April Revolution', in J. Braga de Macedo and S. Serfaty (eds), *Portugal Since the Revolution* (Boulder, CO: Westview), 1–24

Bruneau, T. *et al.* (2001), 'Democracy, Southern European Style', in Diamandouros and Gunther (eds), 16–82

Bryce, J. A. (1921), *Modern Democracies* (London: Macmillan, 2 volumes)

Brynen, R. (1992), 'Economic Crisis and Post–Rentier Democratization in the Arab World: the case of Jordan', *Canadian Journal of Political Science*, 25/1: 69–97

Brysk, A. (1993), 'From Above and Below: Social Movements, the International System, and Human Rights in Argentina', *Comparative Political Studies*, 26/3: 259–85

Brysk, A. (2000), 'Democratizing Civil Society in Latin America', *Journal of Democracy*, 113: 151–65

Bueno de Mesquita, Smith, B. A., Siverson, R. M. and Morrow, J. D. (2003), *The Logic of Political Survival* (Cambridge, MA: MIT Press)

Bunce, V. (2001), 'Democratization and Economic Reform', *Annual Review of Political Science*, 4: 43–65

Burdick, J. (1992), 'Rethinking the Study of Social Movements: The Case of Christian Base Communities in Urban Brazil', in Escobar, A. and Álvarez, S. (eds), *The Making of Social Movements in Latin America. Identity, Strategy and Democracy* (Boulder, CO: Westview), 171–84

Burkhart, R. E. and Lewis–Beck, M. S. (1994), 'Comparative Democracy: The Economic Development Thesis', *American Political Science Review*, 88: 903–10

Burnell, P. J. (2008), 'International democracy promotion: a role for public goods theory?', *Contemporary Politics*, 14/1: 37–52

Burnell, P. J. and Calvert, P. (eds) (2004), *Civil Society in Democratization* (London: Frank Cass)

Burton, M. Gunther, R. and Higley, J. (1992), 'Introduction', in Higley and Gunther (eds)

Cain, B. E., Dalton, R. J. and Scarrow, S. E. (2005) (eds), *Democracy Transformed? Expanding Political Opportunities in Advanced Industrial Democracies* (Oxford: Oxford University Press)

Campbell, D. and Wolbrecht, C. (2006), 'See Jane Run: Women Politicians as Role Models for Adolescents', *Journal of Politics*, 68/2: 233–47

Caramani, D. (2004), *The Nationalization of Politics* (Cambridge: Cambridge University Press)

Carlson, M. (2007), 'Public Opinion on Dimensions of Governance', *Japanese Journal of Political Science* 8: 285–303

Carothers, T. (2006), 'The Backlash Against Democracy Promotion', *Foreign Affairs*, 85/2: 55–68

Carothers, T. (2007), *U.S. Democracy Promotion During and After Bush*. Washington, D.C.: Carnegie Endowment, Carnegie Endowment Report, September 2007. Available at <www.carnegieendowment.org>

Casper, G. and Taylor, M. M. (1996), *Negotiating Democracy: Transitions from Authoritarian Rule* (Pittsburgh, PA: University of Pittsburgh Press)

Cavatorta, F. (2004), 'Constructing an Open Model of Transitions. International Political Economy and the Failed Democratisation of North Africa', *Journal of North African Studies*, 9/3: 1–18

Cavatorta, F. (2005), 'The International Context of Morocco's Stalled Democratization', *Democratization*, 12/4: 549–67

Cavatorta, F. (2007), 'More than repression: the Significance of *Divide et Impera* in the Middle East and North Africa', *Journal of Contemporary African Studies*, 25/2: 187–203

Cerny, P. G. (1999), 'Globalization and the Erosion of Democracy', *European Journal of Political Research*, 36/1: 1–26

Chalaby, J. K. (1998), *The Invention of Journalism* (London: Macmillan)

Chalmers, D. A. (1993), 'Internationalized Domestic Politics in Latin America. The Institutional Role of Internationally Based Actors', unpublished paper. Department of Political Science, Columbia University

Chang, Y. C., Chu, Y. and Park, C.-M. (2007), 'Authoritarian Nostalgia in Asia', *Journal of Democracy*, 18/3: 66–80

Chang, Y. C., Chu, Y. and Tsai, F. (2005), 'Confucianism and Democratic Values in Three Chinese Societies', *Issues and Studies* 41/4: 1–33

Chebel d'Appolonia, A. and Reich, S. (eds) (2008), *Immigration, Integration, and Security. America and Europe in Comparative Perspective* (Pittsburgh, PA: University of Pittsburgh Press)

Cheibub, J. A. (2006), *Presidentialism, Parliamentarism, and Democracy* (Cambridge: Cambridge University Press)

Chhibber, P. and Kollman, K. (2004), *The Formation of National Party Systems: Federalism and Party Competition in Canada, Great Britain, India, and the United States* (Princeton, NJ: Princeton University Press)

Chua, A. (2002), *Globalization and Democratization–A Combustible Mix? World on Fire: How Exporting Free Market Democracy Breeds Ethnic Hatred and Global Instability* (New York: Doubleday)

Chuchryk, P. (1991), 'Feminist Anti–authoritarian Politics: the Role of Women's Organizations in the Chilean Transition to Democracy', in J. S. Jaquette (ed.), *The Women's Movement in Latin America: Feminism and the Transition to Democracy* (Boulder, CO: Westview Press), 149–84

Churchill, W. (1947), *Hansard* (London: Her Majesty's Stationery Office), 11 November, column 206

Claibourn, M. P. and Martin, P. S. (2007), 'The Third Face of Social Capital: How Membership in Voluntary Associations Improves Policy Accountability', *Political Research Quarterly*, 60/2: 192–201

Clapham, C. (1982), *Private Patronage and Public Power: Political Clientelism in the Modern State* (London: Pinter)

Clark, J. (2007), 'The Decline of the African Military Coup', *Journal of Democracy*, 18/3: 141–55

Cohen, J. and Arato, A. (1992), *Civil Society and Political Theory* (Cambridge, MA: MIT Press)

Cohen, M. R. and Nagel, E. (1934), *An Introduction to Logic and Scientific Method* (New York, NY: Harcourt)

Coleman, J. S. (1988), 'Social capital in the creation of human capital', *American Journal of Sociology*, 94: 95–120

Coleman, J. S. (1990), *Foundations of Social Theory* (Cambridge, MA: Harvard University Press)

Collier, D. and Adcock, R. (1999), 'Democracy and Dichotomies: A Pragmatic Approach to Choices About Concepts', *Annual Review of Political Science*, 2: 537–65

Collier, D. and Levitsky, S. (1997), 'Democracy with Adjectives: Conceptual Innovation in Comparative Research', *World Politics*, 49/3: 430–51

Collier, R. B. (1999), *Paths toward Democracy: The Working Class and Elites in Western Europe and South America* (Cambridge: Cambridge University Press)

Collier, R. B. and Mahoney, J. (1997), 'Adding Collective Actors to Collective Outcomes: Labor and Recent Democratization in South America and Southern Europe', *Comparative Politics*, 29/3: 285–303

Colomer, J. (2004a) (ed.), *Handbook of Electoral System Choice* (London: Palgrave Macmillan)

Colomer, J. (2004b), 'The Strategy and History of Electoral System Choice', in Colomer, J. (2004a) (ed.), *Handbook of Electoral System Choice* (London: Palgrave Macmillan), 3–78

Compton, R. (2000), *East Asian Democratization: Impact of Globalization, Culture, and Economy* (New York, NY: Praeger)

Conge, P. J. (1988), 'The Concept of Political Participation: Toward a Definition', *Comparative Politics*, 20/2: 241–9

Coppedge, M. and Reinicke, W. H. (1991), 'Measuring polyarchy', in A. Inkeles (ed.), *On Measuring Democracy: Its Consequences and Concomitants* (New Brunswick, NJ: Transaction Publishers), 47–68

Cox, G. (1997), *Making Votes Count: Strategic Coordination in the World's Electoral Systems* (Cambridge: Cambridge University Press)

Cox, M., Ikenberry, G. and Inoguchi, T. (2000), *American Democracy Promotion: Impulses, Strategies, and Impacts* (Oxford: Oxford University Press)

Croissant, A. (2002), 'Electoral Politics in Southeast and East Asia'. Available at <http://library.fes.de>

Croissant, A. (2004), 'From Transition to Defective Democracy: Mapping Asia Democratization', *Democratization* 11/5: 156–78

Cronin, T. (1989), *Direct Democracy: The Politics of the Initiative, Referendum, and Recall* (Cambridge, MA: Harvard University Press)

Cross–National Time–Series Data Archive. Available at <www.databanksinternational.com> (accessed 2 June 2008)

Crouch, C. (2004), *Post–Democracy* (Cambridge: Polity Press)

Curran, J. and Park, M.-J. (2000), 'Beyond Globalization Theory', in J. Curran and M.-J. Park (eds), *De–Westernizing Media Studies* (London: Routledge), 3–18

Curtis, G. (1997), 'For Democratic Development: The East Asian Prospect', *Journal of Democracy* 8/3: 139–45

Daalder, H. (1983), 'The Comparative Study of European Parties and Party Systems: An Overview', in H. Daalder and P. Mair (eds), *Western European Party Systems: Continuity and Change* (London: Sage), 1–27

Dahl, R. A. (1970), *After the Revolution? Authority in a Good Society* (New Haven: Yale University Press)

Dahl, R. A. (1971), *Polyarchy: Participation and Opposition* (New Haven, CT: Yale University Press)

Dahl, R. A. (1989), *Democracy and its Critics* (New Haven, CT: Yale University Press)

Dahl, R. A. (1997), 'A Brief Intellectual Biography', in H. Daalder (ed.), *Comparative European Politics: The Story of a Profession* (London: Pinter), 68–78

Dalton, R. J. (1988), *Citizen Politics in Western Democracies* (Chatham, NJ: Chatham House)

Dalton, R. J. (2004), *Democratic Challenges, Democratic Choices* (Oxford: Oxford University Press)

Dalton, R. J., Shin, D.C. and Jou, W. (2007), 'Popular Conceptions of the Meaning of Democracy', Centre for the Study of Democracy Paper Series, Irvine, CA

Dalton, R. J. and Wattenberg, M. (2000), *Parties Without Partisans: Political Change in Advanced Industrial Democracies* (Oxford: Oxford University Press)

Dalton, R. J. and Weldon, S. (2007), 'Partisanship and Party System Institutionalization', *Party Politics* 13/2: 179–96

Davenport, C. (2005), 'Introduction', In C. Davenport, H. Johnston and C. Mueller (eds), *Repression and Mobilization* (Minneapolis, MN: University of Minnesota Press)

David, P. A. (1985), 'Clio and the Economics of QWERTY', *American Economic Review*, 75/1: 332–7

de Smaele, H. (2006), 'In the Name of Democracy', The Paradox of Democracy and Press Freedom in Post–Communist Russia', in K. Voltmer (ed.), *Mass Media and Political Communication in New Democracies*, (London: Routledge), 42–58.

del Carmen Feijoo, M. and Gogna, M. (1990), 'Women in the Transition to Democracy', in E. Jelin (ed.), *Women and Social Change in Latin America* (London: Zed Books), 79–114

della Porta, D. and Mattina, L. (1986), 'Ciclos políticos y movilización étnica. El caso Vasco', *Revista Española de Investigaciones Sociológicas*, 35: 123–48

della Porta, D. and Tarrow, S. (2005) (eds), *Transnational Protest and Global Activism* (Lanham, MD: Rowman and Littlefield)

Di Palma, G. (1980), 'Founding Coalitions in Southern Europe: Legitimacy and Hegemony', *Government and Opposition*, 15: 162–89

Di Palma, G. (1990), *To Craft Democracies: An Essay on Democratic Transitions* (Berkeley, CA: University of California Press)

Diamond, L. (1999), *Developing Democracy: Toward Consolidation* (Baltimore, MD: Johns Hopkins University Press)

Diamond, L. (2003), 'How People View Democracy', Center for the Study of Democracy Paper Series, Irvine, CA

Diamond, L. (2008), *The Spirit of Democracy: The Struggle to Build Free Societies throughout the World* (New York, NY: Times Books)

Diamond, L. and Gunther, R. (2001a), 'Types and Functions of Parties', in L. Diamond and R. Gunther (eds.), *Political Parties and Democracy* (Baltimore, MD: Johns Hopkins University Press), 3–39

Diamond, L. and Gunther, R. (2001b) (eds), *Political Parties and Democracy* (Baltimore, MD: Johns Hopkins University Press)

Diamond, L. and Kim, B. (2000) (eds), *Consolidating Democracy in South Korea* (Boulder, CO: Lynne Rienner)

Diamond, L. and Morlino, L. (2005) (eds), *Assessing the quality of Democracy* (Baltimore, MD: Johns Hopkins University Press)

Diamond, L. and Plattner, M. (1998) (eds), *Democracy in East Asia* (Baltimore, MD: Johns Hopkins University Press)

Diamond, L., Hartlyn, J. and Linz, J. J. (1999) 'Introduction: Politics, Society, and Democracy in Latin America', in L. Diamond, J. Hartlyn, J. J. Linz and S. M. Lipset (eds), *Democracy in Developing Countries: Latin America*, 2nd edn (Boulder, CO: Lynne Rienner), 1–70

Diamond, L., Linz, J. J. and Lipset, S. M. (1990) (eds), *Politics in Developing Countries: Comparing Experiences with Democracy* (Boulder, CO: Lynne Rienner)

Diamond, L., Plattner, M., Chu, Y. and Tien, H. (1997) (eds), *Consolidating the Third Wave Democracies. Regional Challenges* (Baltimore, MD: Johns Hopkins University Press)

Diamandouros, P. N. (1986), 'Regime Change and the Prospects for Democracy in Greece: 1974–1983', in G. O'Donnell, P. Schmitter and L. Whitehead (eds), *Transitions from Authoritarian Rule: Southern Europe* (Baltimore, MD: Johns Hopkins University Press)

Diamandouros, P. N. and Gunther R. (eds), *Parties, Politics and Democracy in the New Southern Europe* (Baltimore, MD: Johns Hopkins University Press)

Dickson, B. (2003), *Red Capitalists in China* (Cambridge: Cambridge University Press)

Dickson, B. (2007), 'The Future of China's Party–State', *Current History*, 243–5

DiFranceisco, W. and Gitelman, Z. (1984), 'Soviet Political Culture and "Covert Participation" in Policy Implementation', *American Political Science Review*, 78/3: 603–21

Dillman, B. (2001). 'Facing the Market in North Africa', *Middle East Journal*, 55/2: 198–215

Dimitrova, A. and Pridham, G. (2004), 'International Actors and Democracy Promotion In Central And Eastern Europe: The Integration Model And Its Limits', *Democratization*, 11/5: 91–112

Diskin, A., H. Diskin and Hazan, R. Y. (2005), 'Why Democracies Collapse', *International Political Science Review*, 26: 291–309

Dobry, M. (1986), *Sociologie des Crises Politiques. La Dynamique des Mobilisations Multisectorielles* (Paris: Presses de la Fondation Nationale des Sciences Politiques)

Domhoff, G. W. (1998), *Who Rules America? Power and Politics in the Year 2000* (Mountain View, CA: Mayfield)

Doner, R. F., Schneider, B. R. and Wilson, E. J., III (1998), 'Can business associations contribute to development and democracy?', in A. Bernstein and P. L. Berger (eds), *Business and Democracy: Cohabitation or Contradiction?* (London: Continuum), 126–47

Doorenspleet, R. (2000), 'Reassessing the Three Waves of Democratization', *World Politics*, 52/3: 384–406

Doorenspleet, R. (2005), 'Electoral Systems and Democratic Quality: Do Mixed Systems Combine the Best or the Worst of Both Worlds? An Explorative Quantitative Cross–national Study', *Acta Politica,* 40/4: 28–49

Downing, B. M. (1992), *The Military Revolution and Political Change* (Princeton, NJ: Princeton University Press)

Downs, A. (1957), *An Economic Theory of Democracy* (New York, NY: Harper and Row)

Durand, F. (1995), 'From Fragile Chrystal to Solid Rock: the Formation and Consolidation of a Business Peak Association in Peru', in E. Bartell and L. Payne (eds) *Business and Democracy in Latin America* (Pittsburgh, PA: University of Pittsburgh Press), 141–77

Duverger, M. (1954), *Les Partis Politiques* (Paris: Librarie Armand Colin)

Duverger, M. (1964), *Political Parties: Their Organization and Activity in the Modern State* (New York, NY: Wiley)

Duverger, M. (1986), 'Duverger's Law: Forty Years Later', in B. Grofman and A. Lijphart (eds), *Electoral Laws and Their Political Consequences* (New York, NY: Agathon Press), 69–84

Easton, D. (1965), *A Framework for Political Analysis* (Englewood Cliffs, NJ: Prentice-Hall)

Eckstein, H. (1966), *A Theory of Stable Democracy* (Princeton, NJ: Princeton University Press)

Eckstein, H. (1998), 'Congruence Theory Explained', in H. Eckstein *et al.* (eds), *Can Democracy Take Root in Post-Soviet Russia? Explorations in State-Society Relations* (Lanham, MD: Rowman & Littlefield), 3–33

Eckstein, H. and Gurr, T.R. (1975), *Patterns of Authority* (New York, NY: John Wiley)

Eckstein, S. (2001) (ed.), *Power and Popular Protest: Latin American Social Movements*, 2nd edn (Berkeley, CA: University of California Press)

Eckstein, S. and Wickham–Crowley, T. (2003), *What Justice? Whose Justice? Fighting for Fairness in Latin America* (Berkeley, CA: University of California Press)

Edwards, B. and Foley, M. W. (2001) (eds), 'Civil Society and Social Capital: A Primer', in B. Edwards, M. Foley and M. Diani (eds), *Beyond Tocqueville. Civil Society and the Social Capital Debate in Comparative Perspective* (Hanover, NH: Tufts University Press), 1–16

Eisinger, P. (1973), 'The Conditions of Protest Behavior in American Cities', *American Journal of Political Science*, 67: 11–28

Ekiert, G. and Kubik, J. (1999), *Rebellious Civil Society: Popular Protest and Democratic Consolidation in Poland, 1989–1993* (Ann Harbor, MI: University of Michigan Press)

Elkins, Z. S. (2000), 'Gradations of Democracy? Empirical Tests of Alternative Conceptualizations', *American Journal of Political Science*, 44/2: 293–300

Elster, J. (1989), *Nuts and Bolts for the Social Sciences* (Cambridge: Cambridge University Press)

Elster, J., Offe, C. and Preuss, U. (1998), *Institutional Design in Post–Communist Societies: Rebuilding the Ship at Sea* (Cambridge: Cambridge University Press)

Emerson, D. (1996), 'Singapore and "the Asian Value" Debate', *Journal of Democracy* 6/4: 95–105

Encarnación, O. G. (2003), *The Myth of Civil Society: Social Capital and Democratic Consolidation in Spain and Brazil* (London: Palgrave Macmillan)

Entelis, J. (2004). 'Islamist Politics and the Democratic Imperative: Comparative Lessons from the Algerian Experience', *The Journal of North African Studies*, 9/2: 202–15.

Epstein, D. L., Bates, R., Goldstone, J., Kristensen, I. and O'Halloran, S. (2006), 'Democratic Transitions', *American Journal of Political Science* 50/3, 55–69

Escobar, A. and Álvarez, S. (1992) (eds), *The Making of Social Movements in Latin America. Identity, Strategy and Democracy* (Boulder, CO: Westview)

Espindola, R. (2002), 'Political Parties and Democratization in the Southern Cone of Latin America'. *Democratization*, 9/3: 109–30

Esposito, J. (2002). *Unholy War: Terror in the Name of Islam* (Oxford: Oxford University Press)

Esser, H. (1993), *Soziologie: Allgemeine Grundlagen* (Frankfurt am Main: Campus)

Evans, P. (1987), 'Class, State, and Dependence in East Asia: Lessons for Latin Americanists', in F. C. Deyo (ed.), *The Political Economy of the New Asian Industrialism* (Ithaca, NY: Cornell University Press), 203–26

Fattah, M. A. (2006), *Democratic Values in the Muslim World* (Boulder, CO: Lynne Rienner)

Fewsmith, J. (2004), 'China's New Leadership: a One–Year Assessment', *Orbis*, 205–15

Finer, S.E. (1999), *The History of Government* (3 vols) (Oxford: Oxford University Press)

Fish, M. S. (2002), 'Islam and Authoritarianism', *World Politics* 55/1: 4–37

Fish, M. S. and Kroenig, M. (2006), 'Diversity, Conflict, and Democracy: Some Evidence from Eurasia and East Europe', *Democratization* 13/5: 828–42

Fish, M. S. and Kroenig, M. (2009), *The Handbook of National Legislatures: A Global Survey* (Cambridge: Cambridge University Press)

Fish, M. S. (2001), 'The Inner Asian Anomaly: Mongolia's Democratization in Comparative Perspective', *Communist and Post–Communist Studies*, 34/3: 323–38

Fisher, J. (1989) *Mothers of the Disappeared* (London: Zed Books)

Fishkin, J. S. (1991), *Democracy and Deliberation: New Directions for Democratic Reform* (New Haven, CT: Yale University Press)

Fishman, R. (1990), *Working–Class Organization and the Return to Democracy in Spain* (Ithaca, NY: Cornell University Press)

Flora, P., Kuhnle, S. and Urwin, D. W. (1999), *State formation, nation–building, and mass politics in Europe: the theory of Stein Rokkan: based on his collected works* (Oxford: Oxford University Press)

Foley, M. and Edwards, B. (1996), 'The Paradox of Civil Society', *Journal of Democracy*, 7, 38–52

Foot, R. (1997), 'Human Rights, Democracy and Development', *Democratization* 4/2: 139–53

Foweraker, J. (1989), *Making Democracy in Spain: Grassroots Struggle in the South, 1955–1975* (Cambridge: Cambridge University Press)

Foweraker, J. (1995), *Theorizing Social Movements* (London: Pluto Press)

Foweraker, J. and Krznaric, R. (2000), 'Measuring Liberal Democratic Performance: an Empirical and Conceptual Critique', *Political Studies*, 48/4: 759–78

Foweraker, J. and Landman, T. (1997), *Citizenship Rights and Social Movements* (Oxford: Oxford University Press)

Fowler, M. S. and Brenner D. L. (1982), 'A Marketplace Approach to Broadcast Regulation', *Texas Law Review*, 60/2: 207–57

Fox, R. L. and Lawless, J. L. (2004), 'Entering the Arena? Gender and the Decision to Run for Office', *American Journal of Political Science*, 48/2: 264–80

Fraenkel, J. and Grofman, B. (2006a), 'Does the Alternative Vote Foster Moderation in Ethnically Divided Societies: The Case of Fiji', *Comparative Political Studies* 39/5: 623–51

Fraenkel, J. and Grofman, B. (2006b), 'The Failure of the Alternative Vote as a Tool for Ethnic Moderation in Fiji: A Rejoinder to Horowitz', *Comparative Political Studies*. 39/5: 663–6

Fraile, M. (2002), 'The Retrospective Voter in Spain During the 1990s', in H. Dorussen and M. Taylor (eds), *Economic Voting* (London: Routledge), 284–302

Francisco, R. A. (1995), 'The Relationship between Coercion and Protest', *The Journal of Conflict Resolution*, 39: 263–82

Francisco, R. A. (2005), 'The Dictator's Dilemma', in C. Davenport, H. Johnston and C. Mueller (eds), *Repression and Mobilization* (Minneapolis, MN: University of Minnesota Press)

Franklin, M. N. (2004) *Voter Turnout and the Dynamics of Electoral Competition* (Cambridge: Cambridge University Press)

Franzese, R. J. (2002), *Macroeconomic Policies of Developed Democracies* (Cambridge: Cambridge University Press)

Freedom House (1978ff), *Freedom in the World* (New York, NY: Freedom House). Available at <www.freedomhouse.org>

Freedom House (1989), *Freedom in the World, 1988–1989* (New York, NY: Freedom House)

Freedom House (2000), *Freedom in the World, 1999–2000* (New York, NY: Freedom House)

Freedom House (2006), *Freedom in the World 2006: The Annual Survey of Political Rights and Civil Liberties* (New York, NY and Washington, DC: Rowman and Littlefield)

Freedom House (2008a), 'Methodology'. Available at <www. freedomhouse.org> (accessed June 2008)

Freedom House (2008b), 'Freedom in the World'. Available at <www.freedomhouse.org> (accessed June 2008)

Friedman, E. (1995) (ed.), *The Politics of Democratization: Generalizing East Asian Experiences* (Boulder, CO: Westview Press)

Friedman, E. (2003), 'A Comparative Politics of Democratization in China', *Journal of Contemporary China* 12/24: 103–23

Friedman, M. (1962), *Capitalism and Freedom* (Chicago, IL: University of Chicago Press)

Fukuyama, F. (1992), *The End of History and the Last Man* (New York, NY: Avon Books)

Fukuyama, F. (1995), *Trust: The Social Virtues and the Creation of Prosperity* (London: Hamish Hamilton)

Fukuyama, F. (1997), 'The Illusion of Exceptionalism', *Journal of Democracy*, 8/3: 146–9

Gallagher, M. and Mitchell, P. (2005) (eds), *The Politics of Electoral Systems*. (Oxford: Oxford University Press)

Gallie, W. B. (1964), 'Essentially Contested Concepts', in *Philosophy and the Historical Understanding* (London: Chatto and Windus)

Gambill, G. (2003), 'Explaining the Arab Democratic Deficit: Part I', *Middle East Intelligence Report*, 5/2.

Garfinkle, A. (2002), 'The Impossible Imperative? Conjuring Arab Democracy', *The National Interest* (Fall)

Gasiorowski, M. J. (1996), 'An overview of the Political Regime Change Dataset', *Comparative Political Studies*, 29/4: 469–83

Gates, R. (2007), 'The future of democracy', speech delivered to the World Forum on the Future of Democracy Conference hosted by Colonial Williamsburg and the College of William and Mary, on 19 September 2007. Available at <http://hnn.us>

Geddes, B. (1999), 'What Do We Know about Democratization After Twenty Years?' *Annual Review of Political Science* 2: 115–44

Geddes, B. (2007), 'What Causes Democratization?' in C. Boix and S. Stokes (eds), *The Oxford Handbook of Comparative Politics*, 316–39

Gélineau, F. (2007), 'Presidents, Political Context, and Economic Accountability: Evidence from Latin America', *Political Research Quarterly*, 60/3: 415–28

Gerring, J., Bond, P., Barndt, W. T. and Moreno C. (2005), 'Democracy and Economic Growth', *World Politics*, 57: 323–64

Ghaliuon, B. (2004), 'The persistence of Arab Authoritarianism', *Journal of Democracy*, 15/4: 126–32

Gilbreth, C. and Otero, G. (2001), 'Democratization in Mexico: The Zapatista Uprising and Civil Society', *Latin American Perspectives*, 28/4: 7–29

Gillespie, R. and Youngs, R. (2002), 'Themes in European Democracy Promotion', *Democratization*, 9/1: 1–16

Gilley, B. (2007), 'Democrats Will Emerge', *Current History*, 245–47

Ginsburg, T. (1995), 'Political Reform in Mongolia: Between Russia and China', *Asian Survey,* 35/5: 459–71

Ginsburg, T. (2008), 'Lessons from Democratic Transitions: Case Studies from Asia', *Orbis*, 91–105

Gleditsch, K. S. and Ward, M. D. (2006), 'Diffusion and the International Context of Democratization', *International Organization*, 60: 911–33

Gleditsch, N. P. and Sverdrup, B. O. (2003), 'Democracy and the Environment', in E. Paper and M. Redclift (eds), *Human Security and the Environment: International Comparisons* (London: Elgar), 45–70

Glenn, J. (2003), 'Contentious Politics and Democratization: Comparing the Impact of Social Movements on the fall of Communism in Eastern Europe', *Political Studies*, 55: 103–20

Global Forum on Media Development (2007) (ed.), *Media Matters. Perspective on Advancing Governance and Development* (Internews Europe)

Gomez, E. (2002), *Political Business in East Asia* (London: Routledge)

Goodhart, M. (2005), *Democracy as Human Rights: Freedom and Equality in the Age of Globalization* (New York, NY: Routledge)

Goodin, R. (1996), *The Theory of Institutional Design* (Cambridge: Cambridge University Press)

Graham, L. (1992), 'Redefining the Portuguese Transition to Democracy', in Higley and Gunther (eds), 282–99

Gray, M. and Caul, M. (2000), 'Declining Voter Turnout in Advanced Industrial Democracies, 1950–1997: The Effects of Declining Group Mobilization', *Comparative Political Studies*, 33/9: 1091–122

Green, D. M. (1999), 'Liberal Movements and Democracy's Durability: Comparing Global Outbreaks of Democracy – 1918, 1945, 1989', *Studies in Comparative International Development*, 34/1: 83–120

Grugel J. (1999) (ed.), *Democracy without Borders: Transnationalization and Conditionality in New Democracies* (London: Routledge)

Gunther, R., (1992) 'Spain: The Very Model of the Modern Elite Settlement', in Higley and Gunther (eds), 38–80

Gunther, R. and Montero, J. R. (2001), 'The Anchors of Partisanship', in Diamandouros and Gunther (eds), 83–152

Gunther, R., Montero, J. R. and Torcal, M. (2007), 'Democracy and Intermediation: Some Attitudinal and Behavioural Dimensions', in R. Gunther, J. R. Montero and H.-J. Puhle (eds), *Democracy, Intermediation, and Voting on Four Continents* (Oxford: Oxford University Press), 29–74

Gunther, R. and Mughan, A. (2000) (eds), *Democracy and the Media: A Comparative Perspective* (Cambridge: Cambridge University Press)

Guo, D. (2007), 'Chinese Model of Political Development: Comparative Perspective', *Journal of East Asian Affairs* 21/2: 117–38

Gurr, T. R. (1974), 'Persistence and Change in Political Systems', *American Political Science Review*, 68: 1482–504

Gurr, T. R. (2000), 'Ethnic warfare on the wane', *Foreign Affairs*, 79: 52–64

Gyimah–Boadi, E. (1996), 'Civil Society in Africa', *Journal of Democracy*, 7/2: 118–32

Habermas, J. (1984), *The Theory of Communicative Action* (Cambridge: Polity)

Hadenius, A. (1997) (ed.), *Democracy's Victory and Crisis* (Cambridge: Cambridge University Press)

Hadenius, A. and Teorell, J. (2005), 'Cultural and Economic Prerequisites of Democracy', *Studies in Comparative International Development*, 39: 87–106

Haerpfer, C. W. (2002), *Democracy and Enlargement in Post–Communist Europe: The Democratization of the General Public in Fifteen Central and Eastern European Countries, 1991–1998* (London: Routledge)

Haggard, S. and Kaufman, R. R. (1995), *The Political Economy of Democratic Transition* (Princeton, NJ: Princeton University Press)

Hagopian, F. (1990), 'Democracy by Undemocratic Means? Elite, Political Pacts, and Regime Transition in Brazil', *Comparative Political Studies*, 23: 147–170

Hagopian, F. (2005), 'Conclusions: Governmental Performance, Political Representation, and Public Perceptions of Contemporary Democracy in Latin America', in F. Hagopian and S. Mainwaring (eds), *The Third Wave of Democratization in Latin America* (Cambridge: Cambridge University Press), 319–62

Hall, P. and Taylor, R. (1996), 'Political Science and the Three New Institutionalisms', *Political Studies*, 44/5: 936–57

Hannam, J., Auchterlonie, M. and Holden, K. (2000), *International Encyclopaedia of Women's Suffrage* (Santa Barbara, CA: ABC–CLIP)

Harriss, J. (2002), *Depoliticizing Development: The World Bank and Social Capital* (London: Anthem Press)

Held, D. (1995), *Democracy and the Global Order: From the Modern State to Cosmopolitan Governance* (Stanford, CA: Stanford University Press)

Held, D. and Pollitt, C. (1986) (eds), *New Forms of Democracy* (London: Sage)

Herb, M. (2002), 'Emirs and Parliaments in the Gulf', *Journal of Democracy* 13/4: 41–7

Hermet, G., Rose, R. and Rouquié, A. (1978) (eds), *Elections Without Choice* (London: Macmillan)

Heydemann, S. (2007), 'Social Pacts and the Persistence of Authoritarianism in the Middle East', in O. Schlumberger (ed.), *Debating Arab Authoritarianism* (Stanford: Stanford University Press), 21–38

Higley, J. and Burton, M. (2006), *Elite Foundations of Liberal Democracy* (Lanham, MD: Rowman and Littlefield)

Higley, J. and Gunther, R. (1992) (eds), *Elites and Democratic Consolidation in Latin America and Southern Europe* (Cambridge: Cambridge University Press)

Hipsher, P. (1998), 'Democratic Transitions as Protest Cycles: Social Movements Dynamics in Democratizing Latin America', in D. Meyer and S. Tarrow (eds), *The Social Movement Society: Contentious Politics for a New Century* (Lanham, MD: Rowman and Littlefield), 153–72

Hobbes, T. [1996 (1651)], *Leviathan* (Cambridge: Cambridge University Press)

Hofferbert, R. I. and Klingemann, H.-D. (1999), 'Remembering the Bad Old Days: Human Rights, Economic Conditions and Democratic Performance in Transitional Regimes', *European Journal of Political Research*, 5/2: 30–44

Hoffman, K. and Centeno, M. A. (2003), 'The Lopsided Continent: Inequality in Latin America', *Annual Review of Sociology*, 29: 363–90

Hood, S. (1998), 'The Myth of Asian–Style Democracy', *Asian Survey*, 38/9: 853–66

Horowitz, D. (1991), *A Democratic South Africa? Constitutional Engineering in a Divided Society* (Berkeley: University of California Press)

Horowitz, D. (2006), 'Strategy Takes a Holiday: Fraenkel and Grofman on the Alternative Vote', *Comparative Political Studies*, 39/5: 652–62

Howard, M. M. (2002), *The Weakness of Civil Society in Post–Communist Europe* (Cambridge: Cambridge University Press)

Huber, E., Stephens, J. D. and Rueschemeyer, D. (1992), *Capitalist Development and Democracy* (Chicago: University of Chicago Press)

Hunter, W. (1997), *Eroding Military Influence in Brazil: Politicians against Soldiers* (Chapel Hill, NC: University of North Carolina Press)

Huntington, S. P. (1965), *Political Order in Changing Societies* (New Haven, CT: Yale University Press)

Huntington, S. P. (1968), *Political Order in Changing Societies* (New Haven, CT: Yale University Press)

Huntington, S. P. (1984), 'Will More Countries Become Democratic?', *Political Science Quarterly*, 99/2: 193–218

Huntington, S. P. (1991), *The Third Wave: Democratization in the Late Twentieth Century* (Norman, OK: University of Oklahoma Press)

Huntington, S. P. (1996), *The Clash of Civilizations and the Remaking of the World Order* (New York, NY: Simon and Schuster)

Huntington, S. P. (1997), 'After Twenty Years: The Future of the Third Wave', *Journal of Democracy* 8/4: 3–12

Hyden, G., Leslie, M. and Ogundimu, F. (2003) (eds), *The Media and Democracy in Africa* (London: Transaction Publishers)

Hyland, J. L. (1995), *Democratic Theory: The Philosophical Foundations* (Manchester: Manchester University Press)

Im, H. B. (2004), 'Faltering Democratic Consolidation in South Korea', *Democratization*, 11/5: 179–97

Inglehart, R. (1997), *Modernization and Postmodernization: Cultural, Economic, and Political Change in 43 Societies* (Princeton, NJ: Princeton University Press)

Inglehart, R. (2003), 'How Solid is Mass Support for Democracy – And How Do We Measure It?' *PS Political Science and Politics*, 36: 51–7

Inglehart, R. and Welzel, C. (2005), *Modernization, Cultural Change and Democracy: The Human Development Sequence* (Cambridge: Cambridge University Press)

Inglehart, R., Norris, P. and Welzel, C. (2002), 'Gender Equality and Democracy', *Comparative Sociology* 1/3–4: 321–45

Inglehart, R., Foa, R., Welzel, C. and Peterson, C. (2008), 'Social Change, Freedom and Rising Happiness: A Global Perspective, 1981–2007', *Perspectives on Psychological Science* 3/4: 264–85

Inoguchi, T. and Newman, E. (1997), 'Introduction: 'Asian Values and Democracy in Asia'. Available at <www.unu.edu>

International Federation of Journalists (2008), 'Nigeria: Legislators delay passage of Freedom of Information Bill' (press release 12 May 2008). Available at <http://allafrica.com> (accessed June 2008)

Jackman, R. W. and Miller, R. A. (1998), 'Social Capital and Politics', *Annual Review of Political Science* 1: 47–73

Jaggers, K. and Gurr, T. R. (1996), *POLITY III: Regime Change and Political Authority, 1800–1994*, 2nd ICPSR version

Jamal, A. (2007), *Barriers to Democracy. The Other Side of Social Capital in Palestine and the Arab World* (Princeton, NJ: Princeton University Press)

Jaquette, J. S. (1989) (ed.), *The Women's Movement in Latin America: Feminism and the Transition to Democracy* (Boulder, CO: Westview Press)

Jaquette, J. S. and Wolchik, S. L. (1998), 'Women and Democratization in Latin America and Central and Eastern Europe: A Comparative Introduction', in J. S. Jaquette and S. L. Wolchik (eds), *Women and Democracy: Latin America and Central and Eastern Europe* (Baltimore, MD: Johns Hopkins University Press), 1–28

Jayawardena, K. (1986), *Feminism and Nationalism in the Third World* (London: Zed Books)

Jelin, E. (1987) (ed.), *Movimientos Sociales y Democracia Emergente*, 2 vols. (Buenos Aires: Centro Editor de América Latina)

Jones, D. M. (1998), 'Democratization, Civil Society and Illiberal Middle Class Culture in Pacific Asia', *Comparative Politics* 30/2: 147–69

Jones, E. L. (1985), *The European Miracle* (Cambridge: Cambridge University Press)

Jorgensen–Earp, C. R. (ed.) (1999), *Speeches and Trials of the Militant Suffragettes: The Women's Social and Political Union, 1903–1918* (London: Associated University Presses)

Kaldor, M. (2003), *Global Civil Society: An Answer to War* (Cambridge: Polity Press)

Kant, I. (1996 [1788]), *Kritik der praktischen Vernunft: Grundlegung zur Metaphysik der Sitten* (Frankfurt a. M.: Suhrkamp)

Kant, I. (2006 [1796]), *Toward Perpetual Peace and Other Writings on Politics, Peace, and History* (New Haven, CT: Yale University Press)

Karakatsanis, N. (2001), *The Politics of Elite Transformation: The Consolidation of Greek Democracy in Theoretical Perspective* (Westport, CT: Praeger)

Karatnycky, A. and Ackerman, P. (2005), *How Freedom is Won: From Civic Resistance to Durable Democracy* (Washington DC: Freedom House)

Karl, T. L. (1990), 'Dilemmas of Democratization in Latin America', *Comparative Politics*, 23/1: 1–23

Karl, T. L. (2000), 'Electoralism', in R. Rose (ed.), *The International Encyclopedia of Elections* (Washington DC: Congressional Quarterly Press), 96–97

Karp, J. A. and Banducci, S. A. (2007), 'Party Mobilization and Political Participation in New and Old Democracies', *Party Politics* 13/2: 217–34

Katz, R. S. and Crotty, W. J. (2005) (eds), *Handbook of Party Politics* (Beverly Hills, CA: Sage)

Kaufmann, D., Kraay, A. and Mastruzzi, M. (2006), *Governance Matters V: Governance Indicators for 1996–2005*, Available at <www.worldbank.org>

Keane, J. (1988), *Civil Society and the State* (New York, NY: Verso)

Keane, J. (2003), *Global Civil Society?* (Cambridge: Cambridge University Press)

Keck, M. and Sikkink, K. (1998), *Activists beyond Borders: Advocacy Networks in International Politics* (Ithaca, NY: Cornell University Press)

Kedourie, E. (1992), *Democracy and Arab Political Culture* (Washington DC: Washington Institute for Near East Policy Studies)

Kelley, D. and Donway, R. (1990), 'Liberalism and Free Speech', in J. Lichtenberg (ed.), *Democracy and the Mass Media* (Cambridge: Cambridge University Press), 66–101.

Key, V. O. (1955), 'A Theory of Critical Elections', *Journal of Politics*, 17/1: 3–18

Khalil, M. (2006), 'Egypt's Muslim Brotherhood and Political Power: Would Democracy Survive?', *Middle East Review of International Affairs*, 10/1: 44–52

Kihl, Y. W. (2004), *Transforming Korean Politics* (New York, NY: M. E. Sharpe)

King, A. (1969), 'Political parties in western democracies: some skeptical reflections', *Polity*, 2/2: 111–41.

King, G., Keohane, R. O. and Verba, S. (1994), *Designing Social Enquiry: Scientific Inference in Qualitative Research* (Princeton, NJ: Princeton University Press)

King, G., Tomz, M. and Wittenberg, J. (2000), 'Making the Most of Statistical Analyses: Improving Interpretation and Presentation', *American Journal of Political Science* 44/2: 347–61

Kitschelt, H. and Wilkinson, S. I. (2007) (eds), *Patrons, Clients, and Policies. Patterns of Democratic Accountability and Political Competition* (Cambridge: Cambridge University Press)

Klingemann, H. D. (1999), 'Mapping Political Support in the 1990s', in P. Norris (ed.), *Critical Citizens* (Oxford: Oxford University Press)

Klingemann, H. D., Fuchs, D. and Zielonka, J. (eds) (2006), *Democracy and Political Culture in Eastern Europe* (London: Routledge)

Klingemann, H. D., Fuchs, D., Fuchs, S. and Zielonka, J. (2006), 'Support for Democracy and Autocracy in Central and Eastern Europe', in H. D. Klingemann, D. Fuchs and J. Zielonka (eds), *Democracy and Political Culture in Eastern Europe* (London: Routledge)

Knack, S. (2004), 'Does Foreign Aid Promote Democracy?' *International Studies Quarterly*, 48: 251–66

Koh, T. (1993), 'The 10 Values Which Undergird East Asian Strength and Success', *The International Herald Tribune* (December 11), 6

Kondratieff, N. D. (1979), 'The long waves in economic life', *Review of Economics and Statistics*, LVI/3: 573–609

Kopecký, P. and Mudde, C. (2003), 'Rethinking Civil Society', *Democratization*, 10/3: 1–14

Kornbluh, P. (no date), 'Chile and the United States: Declassified Documents Relating to the Military Coup, September 11, 1973', National Security Archive Electronic Briefing Book No 8. Available at <www.gwu.edu> (accessed June 2008)

Kostadinova, T. (2003), 'Voter Turnout Dynamics in Post–Communist Europe', *European Journal of Political Research*, 42/6: 741–59

Kuran, T. (1991), 'Now out of Never', *World Politics* 44/1: 7–48

Kurlantzick, J. (2007), 'Going Down', *New Republic* (December 5)

Laakso, M. and Taagepera, R. (1979), '"Effective" Number of Parties: A Measure with Application to West Europe', *Comparative Political Studies*, 12/1: 3–27

Lakoff, S. (2004), 'The Reality of Muslim Exceptionalism', *Journal of Democracy*, 15/4: 133–9

Lal, B. and Larmour, P. (1997), *Electoral Systems in Divided Societies: The Fiji Constitution Review* (Canberra: Australian National University, National Centre for Development Studies)

Landes, D. S. (1998), *The Wealth and Poverty of Nations* (New York, NY: W.W. Norton)

Lasswell, H. D. (1951), *The Political Writings of Harold D. Lasswell* (Glencoe, IL: Free Press)

Lavrin, A. (1994), 'Suffrage in South America: Arguing a Difficult Case', in C. Daley and M. Nolan (eds), *Suffrage and Beyond: International Feminist Perspectives* (Auckland: Auckland University Press), 184–209

Lazarsfeld, P. F. (1966), 'Concept formation and measurement in the behavioral sciences: some historical observations', in G. J. DiRenzo (ed.), *Concepts, Theory and Explanation in the Behavioral Sciences* (New York, NY: Random House)

Lee, J. (2002), 'Primary Causes of Democratization', *Asian Survey*, 42/6: 821–37

Lerner, D. (1958), *The Passing of Traditional Society* (New York, NY: Free Press)

Letki, N. (2004), 'Socialization for Participation? Trust, Membership and Democratization in East–Central Europe', *Political Research Quarterly*, 57/4: 665–79

Letki, N. and Evans, G. (2005), 'Endogenizing Social Trust: Democratization in East–Central Europe', *British Journal of Political Science*, 35/3: 515–29

Levitsky, S. and Way, L. (2002), 'The Rise of Competitive Authoritarianism', *Journal of Democracy*, 13/2: 51–65

Lewis, B. (2002). *What Went Wrong? Western Impact and Middle Eastern Responses* (London: Phoenix Press).

Lewis-Beck, M. S. and Stegmaier, M. (2000), 'Economic Determinants of Electoral Outcomes', *Annual Review of Political Science* 3: 183–219

Li, Q. (2005), 'Does Democracy Promote or Reduce Transnational Terrorist Incidents?', *Journal of Conflict Resolution*, 49/2: 278–97

Li, Q. and Resnick, A. L. (2003), 'Reversal of Fortunes: Democratic Institutions and Foreign Direct Investment Inflows to Developing Countries', *International Organization*, 57/1: 175–211

Li, Q. and Reuveny, R. (2006), 'Democracy and Environmental Degradation', *International Studies Quarterly*, 50: 935–56

Lijphart, A. (1969) 'Consociational democracy', *World Politics*, 21/2: 207– 25

Lijphart, A. (1977), *Democracy in Plural Societies* (New Haven, CT: Yale University Press)

Lijphart, A. (1985), *Power–Sharing in South Africa* (Berkeley, CA: Institute of International Studies)

Lijphart, A. (1992), *Parliamentary versus Presidential Government* (Oxford: Oxford University Press)

Lijphart, A. (1994), *Electoral Systems and Party Systems: A Study of Twenty–Seven Democracies, 1945–1990* (Oxford: Oxford University Press)

Lijphart, A. (1999), *Patterns of Democracy: Government Forms and Performance in Thirty–Six Countries* (New Haven, CT: Yale University Press)

Lijphart, A. (2002), 'The Wave of Power–Sharing Democracy', in A. Reynolds (ed.) *The Architecture of Democracy: Constitutional Design, Conflict Management, and Democracy* (Oxford: Oxford University Press), 37–54

Lijphart, A. and Grofman, B. (1986) (eds), *Choosing an Electoral System: Issues and Alternatives* (New York, NY: Praeger)

Lindberg, S. (2006), *Democracy and Elections in Africa* (Baltimore, MD: Johns Hopkins University Press)

Lindblom, C. E. (1977), *Politics and Markets: The World's Political–Economic Systems* (New York, NY: Basic Books)

Lindner, W. and Bachtiger, A. (2005), 'What Drives Democratization in Asia and Africa?', *European Journal of Political Research*, 44: 861–80

Ling, L. H. M. and Shih, C. (1998), 'Confucianism with a Liberal Face: the Meaning of Democratic Politics in Postcolonial Taiwan', *The Review of Politics*, 60/1: 55–82

Linz, J. J. (1978), 'Crisis, breakdown and reequilibration' in J. J. Linz and A. Stepan (eds), *The Breakdown of democratic regimes* (Baltimore, MD: Johns Hopkins University Press)

Linz, J. J. (1980), 'Political Space and Fascism as a Late–Corner', in S. U. Larsen, B. Hagtvet and J. P. Myklebust (eds), *Who were the Fascists? Social Roots of European Fascism* (Oslo: Universitetsforlaget), 153–89

Linz, J. J. (1997), 'Democracy Today: An Agenda for Students of Democracy: Lecture Given by the Winner of the Johan Skytte Prize in Political Science, Uppsala, September 28, 1996', *Scandinavian Political Studies*, 20/2: 115–34

Linz, J. J. (2000), *Totalitarian and Authoritarian Regimes* (Boulder, CO: Lynne Rienner)

Linz, J. and Stepan, A. (1996a), *Problems of Democratic Transition and Consolidation: Southern Europe, South America, and post–Communist Europe* (Baltimore, MD: Johns Hopkins University Press)

Linz, J. J. and Stepan, A. (1996b), 'Toward consolidated democracies', *Journal of Democracy*, 7/2: 14–33

Linz, J. J. and Valenzuela, A., eds. (1994), *The Failure of Presidential Democracy* (Baltimore, MD: Johns Hopkins University Press)

Lipset, S. M. (1959) 'Some Social Requisites of Democracy: Economic Development and Political Legitimacy', *American Political Science Review*, 53/1: 69–105

Lipset, S. M. (1960), *Political Man: The Social Bases of Politics* (Garden City, NY: Doubleday)

Lipset, S. M. (1983 [1960]), *Political Man: The Social Bases of Politics*, 3rd edn (London: Heinemann Education)

Lipset, S. M. and Rokkan, S. (1967), 'Cleavage Structures, Party Systems, and Voter Alignments', in S. M. Lipset and S. Rokkan (eds), *Party System and Voter Alignments: Cross-National Perspectives* (New York, NY: Free Press), 1–64

Livingston, S. (1997), 'Clarifying the CNN Effect: An Examination of Media Effects According to Type of Military Intervention', The Joan Shorenstein Center, Harvard University, Research Paper r–18

Lovitt, J. (2004), 'Promotion of Pluralism and Good Governance Through Media Development'. Available at <http://portal.unesco.org> (accessed June 2008)

Lowden, P. (1996), *Moral Opposition to Authoritarian Rule in Chile, 1973–1990* (London: Macmillan)

Lucas, R. E. (2005), *Institutions and the Politics of Survival in Jordan* (Albany, NY: SUNY Press)

Lutz, E. L. and Sikkink, K. (2001), 'The International Dimension of Democratization and Human Rights in Latin America', in A. M. Garretón and E. Newman (eds), *Democracy in Latin America: (Re)constructing Political Society* (New York: United Nations University Press), 278–300

Macpherson, C. B. (1973), *Democratic Theory: Essays in Retrieval* (Oxford: Clarendon Press)

Magen, A. and Morlino, L. (2008) (eds), *International Actors, Democratization and the Rule of Law: Anchoring Democracy?* (London: Routledge)

Mainwaring, S. (1987), 'Urban Popular Movements, Identity, and Democratization in Brazil', *Comparative Political Studies*, 20/2: 131–59

Mainwaring, S. (1999), *Rethinking Party Systems in the Third Wave of Democratization: The Case of Brazil* (Stanford, CA: Stanford University Press)

Mainwaring, S. and Peréz–Liñan, A. (2005), 'Latin American Democratization Since 1978. Democratic Transitions, Breakdowns, and Erosions', in F. Hagopian and S. P. Mainwaring (eds), *The Third Wave of Democratization in Latin America. Advances and Setbacks* (Cambridge: Cambridge University Press), 14–59

Mainwaring, S. and Scully, T. (1995) (eds), *Building Democratic Institutions: Party Systems in Latin America* (Stanford, CA: Stanford University Press)

Mainwaring, S. and Shugart, M. S. (1997a) (eds), *Presidentialism and Democracy in Latin America* (Cambridge: Cambridge University Press)

Mainwaring, S. and Shugart, M. S. (1997b), 'Juan Linz, Presidentialism, and Democracy', *Comparative Politics*, 29/4: 449–71

Mair, P. (1997), *Party System Change. Approaches and Interpretations* (Oxford: Clarendon Press)

Mansfield, E. D. and Snyder, J. (2006), 'Prone to Violence', *National Interest*, 82 (Winter): 39–45

Mansfield, E. D. and Snyder, J. (2007), *Electing to Fight* (Cambridge: Cambridge University Press)

Manza, J. and Uggen, C. (2002), 'Democratic Contraction? The Political Consequences of Felon Disenfranchisement in the United States', *American Sociological Review*, 67: 777–803

Maravall, J. M. (1982), *The Transition to Democracy in Spain* (London: Croom Helm)

Markoff, J. (1996), *Waves of Democracy. Social Movements and Political Change* (Thousand Oaks, CA: Pine Forge Press)

Markoff, J. (1997), 'Really Existing Democracy: Latin America in the 1990s', *New Left Review*, 23: 48–68

Markoff, J. (2004), 'Who Will Construct the Global Order?', in B. W. Morrison (ed.), *Transnational Democracy in Critical and Comparative Perspective: Democracy's Range Reconsidered* (London: Ashgate), 19–36

Marshall, M. and Jaggers, K. (2005), 'Polity IV Project. Political Regime Characteristics and Transitions, 1800–2004. Dataset Users' Manual', <www.cidcm.umd.edu>

Marshall, M. G. and Jaggers, K. (2007), *Polity IV Project: Political Regime Characteristics and Transitions, 1800–2006, Dataset Users' Manual* (MD: Center for International Development and Conflict Management, University of Maryland). Available at <www.systemicpeace.org> (accessed 26 June 2008)

Marx, K. and Engels, F (1977 [1848]), 'The Communist Manifesto', in D. McLellan (ed.), *Karl Marx: Selected Writings* (Oxford: Oxford University Press), 221–47

Massicotte, L. and Blais, A. (1999), 'Mixed Electoral Systems: A Conceptual and Empirical Survey', *Electoral Studies* 18/3: 341–66

Mattes, R. and Bratton, M. (2007), 'Learning about Democracy in Africa: Awareness, Performance, and Experience', *American Journal of Political Science*, 51/1: 192–217

Mattes, R. and Gyimah–Boadi, E. (2005), 'Ghana and South Africa', in L. Diamond and L. Morlino (eds), *Assessing the quality of Democracy* (Baltimore, MD: Johns Hopkins University Press), 238–73

Mayer, A. J. (1959), *Political Origins of the New Diplomacy, 1917–1918* (New Haven, CT: Yale University Press)

McAdam, D. (1986), 'Recruitment to High–Risk Activism: The Case of Freedom Summer', *American Journal of Sociology* 92/1: 64–90

McAdam, D., Tarrow, S. and Tilly, C. (2001), *Dynamics of Contention* (Cambridge: Cambridge University Press)

McAllister, I. and White, S. (2007), 'Political Parties and Democratic Consolidation in Postcommunist Societies', *Party Politics* 13/2: 197–216

McAllister, I. and White, S. (2008), 'Voting "Against All" in Postcommunist Russia', *Europe–Asia Studies* 60/1: 67–87

McFaul, M. (2002), 'The Fourth Wave of Democracy and Dictatorship: Noncooperative Transitions in the Postcommunist World', *World Politics*, 54/2: 212–44

McNair, B. (2000), 'Power, Profit, Corruption, and Lies: The Russian Media in the 1990s', in J. Curran and M.-J. Park (eds), *De–Westernizing Media Studies* (London: Routledge), 79–94

McNeill, W. (1968), *The Rise of the West* (Chicago, IL: University of Chicago Press)

McQuail, D. (1992), *Media Performance: Mass Communication and the Public Interest* (London: Sage)

Meltzer, A. H. and S. F. Richard (1981), 'A Rational Theory of the Size of Government', *Journal of Political Economy*, 89/5: 914–27

Merkel, W. (2004), 'Embedded and Defective Democracies', *Democratization*, 11/5: 33–58

Meyer, T. (2002), *Media Democracy: How the Media Colonize Politics* (Cambridge: Polity)

Mickiewicz, E. (1999), *Changing Channels: Television and the Struggle for Power in Russia* (Oxford: Oxford University Press)

Midlarsky, M. I. (1997) (ed.), *Inequality, Democracy and Economic Development* (Cambridge: Cambridge University Press)

Mill, J. S. (1974 [1843]), *A System of Logic: Collected Works of J.S. Mill*, vol. 7/8 (London: Routledge and Kegan Paul)

Mill, J. S. (1974 [1859]), *On Liberty* (London: Penguin)

Mishler, W. and Rose, R. (2001), 'Political Support for Incomplete Democracies: Realist vs. Idealist Theories and Measures', *International Political Science Review*, 22/4: 303–20

Mitchell, N. J. (1997), *The Conspicuous Corporation: Business, Public Policy, and Representative Democracy* (Ann Arbor, MI: University of Michigan Press)

Mkandawire, T. (2005), 'Maladjusted African Economies and Globalisation', *Africa Development*, 30/1 and 2: 1–33

Moene, K. O. (1993), 'Contested Power', in D. Copp, J. Hampton and J. Roemer (eds), *The Idea of Democracy* (Cambridge: Cambridge University Press), 400–8

Montesquieu, C. de (1989 [1748]), *The Spirit of the Laws* (Cambridge: Cambridge University Press)

Moore, B. (1966), *Social Origins of Dictatorship and Democracy: Lord and Peasant in the Making of the Modern World* (Boston, MA: Beacon Press)

Moravcsik, A. (1993), 'Introduction: Integrating International and Domestic Theories of International Bargaining', in P. B. Evans, H. K. Jacobson and R. D. Putnam (eds), *Double–Edged Diplomacy: International Bargaining and Domestic Politics* (Berkeley, CA: University of California Press), 5–9

Morlino, L. (1998), *Democracy between Consolidation and Crisis. Parties, Groups and Citizens in Southern Europe* (Oxford: Oxford University Press)

Morlino, L. (2001), 'Constitutional Design and Problems of Implementation in Southern and Eastern Europe', in J. Zielonka (ed.), *Democratic Consolidations in Eastern Europe*. Volume 1: *Institutional Engineering* (Oxford: Oxford University Press), 48–108

Morlino, L. (2003), *Democrazie e Democratizzazioni* (Bologna: Il Mulino)

Morlino, L. (2004), 'What is a "Good" Democracy?', *Democratization*, 11/5: 10–32

Moser, R. (2001), *Unexpected Outcomes: Electoral Systems, Political Parties, and Representation in Russia* (Pittsburgh, PA: University of Pittsburgh Press)

Mozaffar, S., Scarritt, J. and Galaich, G. (2003), 'Electoral Institutions, Ethnopolitical Cleavages, and Party Systems in Africa's Emerging Democracies', *American Political Science Review*, 97/3: 379–390

Mudde, C. (2003), 'Civil Society in Post–communist Europe: Lessons from the "dark side"', in P. Kopecký and C. Mudde (eds), *Uncivil Society? Contentious Politics in Post–Communist Europe* (London: Routledge), 157–10

Mufti, M. (1999), 'Elite Bargains and the Onset of Political Liberalization in Jordan', *Comparative Political Studies* 32/1: 100–29

Muller, E. N. (1995), 'Economic Determinants of Democracy', *American Sociological Review*, 60/6: 966–82

Muller, E. N. and Seligson, M. A. (1994), 'Civic Culture and Democracy: The Question of Causal Relationships', *American Political Science Review*, 88/3: 635–52

Munck, G. L. and Verkuilen, J. (2002), 'Conceptualizing and Measuring Democracy: Evaluating Alternative Indices', *Comparative Political Studies*, 35/1: 5–34

Munck, R. (2006), 'Global Civil Society: Royal Road or Slippery Path?', *Voluntas – International Journal of Voluntary and Non–profit Organisations*, 6/3: 325–32

Myers, M. (1998), 'The Promotion of Democracy at the Grassroots: The Example of Radio in Mali, *Democratization*, 5/2: 200–16

Nathan, A. (2003) 'Authoritarian Resilience', *Journal of Democracy*, 14/1: 6–17

Nathan, A. J. and Link, P. (2001), *The Tiananmen Papers* (London: Little, Brown)

Navarro, M. and Bourque, S. C. (1998), 'Fault Lines of Democratic Governance: A Gender Perspective', in F. Agüero and J. Stark (eds), *Fault Lines of Democracy in Post–Transition Latin America* (Miami, FL: North–South Center Press at the University of Miami), 175–202

Neher, C. D. (1994), 'Asian Style Democracy', *Asian Survey* 34/11: 949–61

Newton, K. (2001), 'Social Capital and Democracy', in B. Edwards, M. Foley and M. Diani (eds), *Beyond Tocqueville: Civil Society and the Social Capital Debate in Comparative Perspective* (Hanover, NH: Tufts University Press)

Nodia, G. (1996), 'How Different Are Postcommunist Transitions?', *Journal of Democracy* 7/4: 15–29

Noonan, R. K. (1995), 'Women Against the State: Political Opportunities and Collective Action Frames in Chile's Transition to Democracy', *Sociological Forum* 10/1: 81–111

North, D. C. and Weingast, B. R. (1989), 'Constitutions and Commitment: The Evolution of Institutions Governing Public Choice in Seventeenth–Century England', *Journal of Economic History*, 49/4: 803–32

Nugent, P. (2004), *Africa Since Independence* (London: Palgrave Macmillan)

O'Donnell, G. (1973), *Modernization and Bureaucratic Authoritarianism: Studies in South American Politics* (Berkeley, CA: Institution of International Studies, University of California)

O'Donnell, G. (1988), *Bureaucratic Authoritarianism: Argentina 1966–1973 in Comparative Perspective* (Berkeley, CA: University of California Press)

O'Donnell, G. (1993), 'On the State, Democratization and some Conceptual Problems (A Latin American view with Glances at some post–Communist Countries)'. Working Paper Series No. 92 (Notre Dame, IN: The Helen Kellogg Institute for International Studies, University of Notre Dame)

O'Donnell, G. (1994), 'Delegative Democracy', *Journal of Democracy*, 5/1: 55–69

O'Donnell, G. (2004), 'Why Rule of Law Matters', *Journal of Democracy*, 15(1): 5–19

O'Donnell, G. (2007) 'The Perpetual Crises of Democracy', *Journal of Democracy*, 18/1: 5–11

O'Donnell, G., Schmitter, P.C. and Whitehead, L. (1986), *Transitions from Authoritarian Rule: Latin America* (Baltimore, MD: Johns Hopkins University Press)

O'Donnell, G., Vargas C. J. and Iazzetta, O. (2004) (eds), *The Quality of Democracy. Theory and Applications* (Notre Dame, IN: University of Notre Dame Press)

O'Donnell, G. A. and Schmitter, P. C. (1986), *Transitions from Authoritarian Rule: Tentative Conclusions About Uncertain Democracies* (Baltimore, MD: Johns Hopkins University Press).

O'Dwyer, S. (2003), 'Democracy and Confucian Values', *Philosophy East and West*, 3/1: 39–61

O'Leary, B. (2005), 'Debating Consociational Politics: Normative and Explanatory Arguments', in S. Noel (ed.) *From Power–sharing to Democracy: Post–Conflict Institutions in Ethnically Divided Societies* (Montreal: McGill–Queen's University Press), 3–43

O'Neil, H. 1998. *Communicating Democracy: The Media and Political Transitions* (London: Lynne Rienner)

OAS (1991), AG/RES. 1080 (XXI–O/91) Representative Democracy, Resolution adopted at the fifth plenary session held on June 5, 1991. Available at <www.oas.org> (accessed January 2008)

Oates, S. (2006), 'Where's the Party? Television and Election Campaigns in Russia', in K. Voltmer (ed.), *Mass Media and Political Communication in New Democracies* (London: Routledge), 152–67

Oberschall, A. (1996), 'Opportunities and Framing in the Eastern European Revolts of 1989', in D. McAdam, J. D. McCarthy and M. N. Zald (eds), *Comparative Perspectives on Social Movements* (Cambridge: Cambridge University Press), 93–122

Oberschall, A. (2000), 'Social Movements and the Transitions to Democracy', *Democratization*, 7/3: 25–45

Offe, C. (1999), 'How can we trust our fellow citizens?', in Mark Warren (ed.), *Democracy and Trust* (Cambridge: Cambridge University Press), 42–87

Okruhlik, G. (1999). 'Rentier Wealth, Unruly Law, and the Rise of the Opposition', *Comparative Politics*, 31/3: 295–315.

Olson, M. (1965), *The Logic of Collective Action: Public Goods and the Theory of Groups* (Cambridge, MA: Harvard University Press)

Olson, M. (1982) *The Rise and Decline of Nations: Economic Growth, Stagflation, and Social Rigidities* (New Haven, CT: Yale University Press)

Olson, M. (1993), 'Dictatorship, Democracy, and Development', *American Political Science Review*, 87/3: 567–76

Onis, Z. (1999), 'Turkey, Europe and Paradoxes of Identity: Perspectives on the International Context of Democratization', *Mediterranean Quarterly*, 10/3: 107–136

Opp, K. D. (1994), 'Repression and Revolutionary Action', *Rationality and Society*, 6: 101–38

Osa, M. (2003), 'Networks in Opposition: Linking Organizations Through Activists in the Polish People's Republic', in M. Diani and D. McAdam (eds), *Social Movements and Networks: Relational Approaches to Collective Action* (Oxford: Oxford University Press), 77–104

Oxhorn, P. (2003), 'Social Inequality, Civil Society, and the Limits of Citizenship in Latin America' in S. E. Eckstein and T.P. Wickham–Crowley (eds), *What Justice? Whose Justice?: Fighting for Fairness in Latin America* (Ewing, NJ: University of California Press), 35–63

Page, B. I., Shapiro, R. Y. and Dempsey, G. R. (1987), 'What Moves Public Opinion?', *American Political Science Review*, 81/1: 23–44

Pagnucco, R. (1995) 'The Comparative Study of Social Movements and Democratization: Political Interaction and Political Process Approaches', in M. Dobkowski, I. Wallimann and C. Stojanov (eds), *Research in Social*

Movements, Conflict and Change (London: JAI Press), 18: 145–183

Paletz, D. L. and Jakubowicz, K. (2003) (eds), *Business as Usual. Continuity and Change in Central and Eastern European Media* (Cresskill, NJ: Hampton Press)

Pallinger, Z. T., Kaufmann, B., Marxer, W. and Schiller, T. (2007) (eds), *Direct Democracy in Europe. Developments and Prospects* (Wiesbaden: VS Verlag)

Park, C.–M. and Shin, D. C. (2006), 'Do Asian Values Deter Popular Support for Democracy?', *Asian Survey* 46/3: 341–61

Park, H. W. and Lee, Y. (2008), 'The Korean Presidential Election of 2007. Five Years on from the "Internet Election"', *Journal of Contemporary Eastern Asia*, 7/1: 1–4

Parsons, T. (1964), 'Evolutionary Universals in Society', *American Sociological Review*, 29/3: 339–57

Pateman, C. (1970), *Participation and Democratic Theory* (Cambridge: Cambridge University Press)

Pateman, C. (1989), *The Disorder of Women: Democracy, Feminism, and Political Theory* (Stanford, CA: Stanford University Press)

Patterson, T. E. (1993), *Out of Order* (New York, NY: Knopf)

Paxton, P. (2000) 'Women's Suffrage in the Measurement of Democracy: Problems of Operationalization', *Studies in Comparative International Development* 35/3: 92–111

Paxton, P. (2002), 'Social Capital and Democracy: An Interdependent Relationship', *American Sociological Review*, 67/2: 254–77

Paxton, P. and Hughes, M. (2007), *Women, Politics, and Power: A Global Perspective* (Thousand Oaks, CA: Pine Forge Press).

Paxton, P., Hughes, M. and Green, J. (2006), 'The International Women's Movement and Women's Political Representation, 1893–2003', *American Sociological Review*, 71/6: 898–920

Pedersen, M. (1980), 'On Measuring Party System Change: A Methodological Critique and a Suggestion', *Comparative Political Studies*, 12/4: 387–403

Pei, M. (2007), 'How Will China Democratize', *Journal of Democracy*, 18/3: 53–57

Petras, J. and Morley, M. (1990), *U.S. Hegemony Under Siege. Class, Politics and Development in Latin America* (London: Verso).

Pevehouse, J. C. (2005), *Democracy from Above–Regional Organizations and Democratization* (Cambridge: Cambridge University Press)

Pharr, S. J. and Putnam, R. D. (2000), *Disaffected Democracies: What's Troubling the Trilateral Countries?* (Princeton, NJ: Princeton University Press)

Phillips, A. (1991), *Engendering Democracy* (University Park, PA: Pennsylvania State University Press)

Phillips, A. (1995), *The Politics of Presence: The Political Representation of Gender, Ethnicity and Race* (Oxford: Clarendon Press)

Pion–Berlin, D. (1994), 'To Prosecute or to Pardon? Human Rights Decisions in the Latin American Southern Cone', *Human Rights Quarterly*, 16/1: 105–30

Pitkin, H. F. (1972), *The Concept of Representation* (Berkeley, CA: University of California Press)

Plattner, M. (2004), 'The Quality of Democracy: A Skeptical Afterword', *Journal of Democracy*, 15: 106–10

Poe, S. and Tate, C. (1994), 'Repression of Human Rights to Personal Integrity in the 1980s: A Global Analysis', *American Political Science Review*, 88/4: 853–72

Polanyi, K. (2001 [1944]), *The Great Transformation: The Political and Economic Origins of Our Time* (Boston, MA: Beacon Press)

Polity IV Project (2007). Available at <www.cidcm.umd.edu>

Posusney, M. P. (2004), 'Enduring Authoritarianism: Middle East Lessons for Comparative Theory' *Comparative Politics*, 36/2: 127–38

Powell, G. B. (2000), *Elections as Instruments of Democracy: Majoritarian and Proportional Visions* (New Haven, CT: Yale University Press)

Powell, G. B. (1980), 'Voting Turnout in Thirty Democracies: Partisan, Legal, and Socio–Economic Influences' in R. Rose (ed.), *Electoral Participation: A Comparative Analysis* (Beverly Hills, CA: Sage), 5–34

Price, M. E. and M. Thompson (eds) (2002), *Forging Peace. Intervention, Human Rights and the Management of Media Space* (Edinburgh: Edinburgh University Press)

Pridham, G. (1991), 'International Influences and Democratic Transition: Problems of Theory and Practice in Linkage Politics', in G. Pridham (ed.), *Encouraging Democracy: The International Context of Regime Transition in Southern Europe* (New York, NY: St. Martin's Press), 1–29

Pridham, G. and Vanhanen, T. (1994) (eds), *Democratization in Eastern Europe: Domestic and International Perspectives* (London: Routledge)

Przeworski, A. (1991), *Democracy and the Market: Political and Economic Reforms in Eastern Europe and Latin America* (Cambridge: Cambridge University Press)

Przeworski, A. (1999), 'Minimalist Conception of Democracy: A Defence', in I. Shapiro and C. Hacker–Cordón (eds), *Democracy's Value* (Cambridge: Cambridge University Press), 23–55

Przeworski, A. and Limongi, F. (1997), 'Modernization: Theories and Facts', *World Politics* 49 (January), 155–83

Przeworski, A., Alvarez, M., Cheibub, J. and Limongi, F. (2000), *Democracy and Development: Political Institutions and Well-Being in the World, 1950– 1990* (Cambridge: Cambridge University Press)

Przeworski, A. *et al.* (1995), *Sustainable Democracy* (Cambridge: Cambridge University Press)

Putnam, R. D. (1993), 'Diplomacy and Domestic Politics: The Logic of Two-Level Games', in P. B. Evans, H. K. Jacobson and R. D. Putnam (eds), *Double-Edged Diplomacy: International Bargaining and Domestic Politics* (Berkeley, CA: University of California Press), 431–68

Putnam, R. D. (1993), *Making Democracy Work: Civic Traditions in Modern Italy* (Princeton, NJ: Princeton University Press)

Pye, L. (1997), *Asian Power and Politics: the Cultural Dimension of Authority* (Cambridge, MA: Harvard University Press)

Quadir, F. and Lele, J. (2005) (eds), *Democracy and Civil Society in Asia* (London: Palgrave)

Rabushka, A. and Shepsle, K. A. (1972), *Politics in Plural Societies* (Columbus, OH: Merrill)

Rae, D. (1971), *The Political Consequences of Electoral Laws*, revised edition (New Haven, CT: Yale University Press)

Ramage, D. (1995), *Politics in Indonesia: Democracy, Islam, and the Ideology of Tolerance* (New York, NY: Routledge)

Randall, V. (1987), *Women and Politics: An International Perspective* (Chicago, IL: University of Chicago Press)

Randall, V. and Svasand, L. (2002), 'Political Parties and Democratic Consolidation in Africa'. *Democratization, 9/3:* 30–52

Raniolo, F. (2006), 'Un'analisi organizzativa dei partiti politici', in L. Morlino and M. Tarchi (eds), *Partiti e caso Italiano* (Bologna: Il Mulino), 19–52

Rawnsley, G. D. (1996), *Radio Diplomacy and Propaganda* (London: Macmillan)

Reilly, B. (2001), *Democracy in Divided Societies: Electoral Engineering for Conflict Management* (Cambridge: Cambridge University Press)

Reinares, F. (1987), 'The Dynamics of Terrorism during the Transition to Democracy in Spain', in P. Wilkinson and A. Stewart (eds), *Contemporary Research on Terrorism* (Aberdeen: Aberdeen University Press), 453–65

Reporters Without Borders (2008), Seven leading dailies appear with blank front pages in protest against new media law (press release of 11 April 2008). Available at: <www.rsf.org> (accessed June 2008)

Reynolds, A. (1999), *Electoral systems and democratization in Southern Africa* (Oxford: Oxford University Press).

Reynolds, A. (2005), 'Building Democracy After Conflict: Constitutional Medicine', *Journal of Democracy, 16/1:* 54–68

Reynolds, A., Reilly, B. and Ellis, A. (2005), *Electoral System Design: The New International IDEA Handbook* (Stockholm: IDEA)

Riker, W. (1982), 'The Two-Party System and Duverger's Law: An Essay on the History of Political Science', *American Political Science Review,* 76/4: 753–66

Robinson, R. (1979), *Contemporary Portugal: A History* (London: George Allen and Unwin).

Robinson, R. (1996), 'The Politics of Asian Values' *The Pacific Review* 9/3 215–36

Roddick, J. (1988), *The Dance of Millions: Latin America and the Debt Crisis* (London: Latin America Bureau)

Roeder, P. and Rothchild, D. (2005), *Sustainable Peace: Power and Democracy after Civil Wars* (Ithaca, NY: Cornell University Press)

Roeder, P. G. (1989), 'Electoral Avoidance in the Soviet Union', *Soviet Studies,* 41/3: 462–83

Rokkan, S. (1970), *Citizens, Elections, Parties: Approaches to the Comparative Study of the Processes of Development* (Oslo: Universitetsforlaget)

Rokkan, S. (1975), 'Dimensions of State Formation and Nation-Building: A Possible Paradigm for Research on Variations within Europe', in C. Tilly (ed.), *The Formation of Nation States in Western Europe* (Princeton, NJ: Princeton University Press), 562–600

Rokkan, S. (1983), 'The Territorial Structuring of Western Europe', in S. Rokkan and D. Urwin (eds), *Economy, Territory, Identity: Politics of Western European Peripheries* (London: Sage), 19–65

Rose, R. (2001), 'When Government Fails. Social Capital in an Antimodern Russia', in B. Edwards, M. W. Foley and M. Diani (eds), *Beyond Tocqueville. Civil Society and the Social Capital Debate in Comparative Perspective* (Hanover, NH: Tufts University)

Rose, R. (2007), 'Learning to Support New Regimes in Europe', *Journal of Democracy* 18/3: 111–25

Rose, R. (2008), 'Evaluating Democratic Governance: a Bottom Up Approach to European Enlargement', *Democratization,* 15/2: 1–21

Rose, R. and Shin, D. C. (2001), 'Democratization Backward', *British Journal of Political Science,* 31/2: 331–75

Rose, R. and Davies, P. (1994), *Inheritance in Public Policy: Change without Choice in Britain* (New Haven, CT,: Yale University Press)

Rose, R. and Mishler, W. (2002), 'Comparing Regime Support in Non-Democratic and Democratic Countries', *Democratization,* 9/2: 1–20

Rose, R., Mishler, W. and Haerpfer, C. W. (1998), *Democracy and Its Alternatives. Understanding Post–Communist Societies* (Baltimore, MD: Johns Hopkins University Press)

Ross, M. L. (2001), 'Does Oil Hinder Democracy?' *World Politics*, 53: 325–61

Ross, M. L. (2006), 'Is Democracy Good for the Poor?' *American Journal of Political Science*, 50:4: 860–74

Ross, M. L. (2008), 'Oil, Islam, and Women', *American Political Science Review*, 102/1:107–24

Rossi, F. (2007), 'Movimientos Sociales', in L. Aznar and M. De Luca (eds), *Política: Cuestiones y Problemas*, 2nd edn (Buenos Aires: Emecé), 265–304

Rossteutscher, S. (2002), 'Advocate or Reflection? Associations and Political Culture', *Political Studies*, 50/4: 514–28

Rostow, W. W. (1961), *The Stages of Economic Growth: A Non–Communist Manifesto* (Cambridge: Cambridge University Press)

Rowen, H. (2007), 'When Will the Chinese People Be Free?', *Journal of Democracy*, 18/3: 38–52

Rueschemeyer, D. (2005), 'Addressing Inequality', in L. Diamond and L. Morlino (eds), *Assessing the Quality of Democracy* (Baltimore, MD: Johns Hopkins University Press), 47–61

Rueschemeyer, D., Stephens, E. H. and Stephens, J. D. (1992), *Capitalist Development and Democracy* (Chicago, IL: University of Chicago Press)

Ruf, W. (1997), 'The Flight of Rent: the Rise and fall of a National Economy', *Journal of North African Studies*, 2/1: 1–15.

Russett, B. (1993), 'The Fact of Democratic Peace', in B. Russett (ed.), *Grasping the Democratic Peace* (Princeton, NJ: Princeton University Press), 3–23

Rustow, D. (1970), 'Transitions to Democracy: Towards a Dynamic Model', *Comparative Politics*, 2/3: 337–63

Sadiki, L. (1997). 'Towards Arab liberal governance: from the democracy of bread to the democracy of the vote', *Third World Quarterly*, 18/1: 127–48

Salisbury, R.H., Johnson, P., Heinz, J. P., Laumann, E. O. and Nelson, R. L. (1989), 'Who You Know versus What You Know: The Uses of Government Experience for Washington Lobbyists', *American Journal of Political Science* 33/1: 175–95

Sandoval, S. (1998), 'Social Movements and Democratization. The Case of Brazil and the Latin Countries', in Giugni, McAdam and Tilly (1998), 169–201

Santos, B. S. (2005) (ed.), *Democratizing Democracy: Beyond the Liberal Democratic Canon* (London: Verso).

Sartori, G. (1968) 'Political development and political engineering', in J. D. Montgomery and A. O. Hirschmann (eds.), *Public Policy* (Cambridge: Cambridge University Press), 261–98

Sartori, G. (1976), *Parties and Party Systems: A Framework for Analysis* (Cambridge: Cambridge University Press)

Sartori, G. (1986), 'The Influence of Electoral Systems: Faulty Laws or Faulty Methods?', in B. Grofman and A. Lijphart (eds), *Electoral Laws and Their Political Consequences* (New York, NY: Agathon Press), 43–68

Sartori, G. (1987), *The Theory of Democracy Revisited* (Chatham, NJ: Chatham House)

Sartori, G. (1994), *Comparative Constitutional Engineering: An Inquiry into Structures, Incentives and Outcomes* (London: Macmillan)

Sartori, G. (1995), 'How Far Can Free Government Travel?', *Journal of Democracy,* 6/3: 101–11

Saxonberg, S. (2001), *The Fall: A Comparative Study of the End of Communism in Czechoslovakia, East Germany, Hungary and Poland* (London: Routledge)

Scarrow, S. E. (1996), *Parties and Their Members* (Oxford: Oxford University Press)

Schedler, A. (2006) (ed.), *Electoral Authoritarianism. The Dynamics of Unfree Competition* (Boulder, CO: Lynne Rienner)

Schedler, A. and Sarsfield, R. (2006), 'Democrats with Adjectives: Linking Direct and Indirect Measures of Democratic Support', *European Journal of Political Research*, 46/5: 637–59

Schlumberger, O. and Albrecht, H. (2004). 'Waiting for Godot: Regime Change Without Democratization in the Middle East', *International Political Science Review*, 35/4: 371–92

Schmitt-Beck, R. and Voltmer, K. (2007), 'The Mass Media in Third-Wave Democracies: Gravediggers or Seedsmen of Democratic Consolidation?', in R. Gunther, J. R. Montero and H.-J. Puhle (eds), *Democracy, Intermediation, and Voting in Four Continents* (Oxford: Oxford University Press), 75–134

Schmitter, P. C. (2001), 'Parties are not what they once were', in L. Diamond and R. Gunther (eds), *Political Parties and Democracy* (Baltimore, MD: The Johns Hopkins University Press), 67–89

Schmitter, P. C. and Brouwer, I. (1999), 'Conceptualizing, Researching and Evaluating Democracy Promotion and Protection'. EUI (European University Institute) Working Paper SPS No 99/9

Schmitter, P. C and Karl, T. L (1991), 'What Democracy Is . . . and Is Not', *Journal of Democracy*, 2/3: 75–88

Schneider, C. (1995), *Shantytown Protests in Pinochet's Chile* (Philadelphia, PA: Temple University Press)

Schneider, C. Q. and Schmitter, P. C. (2004) 'Liberalization, Transition and Consolidation: Measuring the Components of Democratization', *Democratization*, 11/5, 59–90

Schock, K. (2005), *Unarmed Insurrections: People Power Movements in Nondemocracies* (Minneapolis, MN: University of Minnesota Press)

Schumpeter, J. A. (1943), *Capitalism, Socialism and Democracy* (London: George Allen and Unwin)

Seligson, M. (2002), 'The Renaissance of Political Culture or the Renaissance of the Ecological Fallacy', *Comparative Politics*, 34/3: 273–92

Seligson, M. (2007), 'The Rise of Populism and the Left in Latin America', *Journal of Democracy*, 18/3: 81–95

Sen, A. (1999), *Development as Freedom* (Oxford: Oxford University Press)

Sened, I. (1997), *The Political Institution of Private Property* (Cambridge: Cambridge University Press)

Shelley, B. (2005), *Democratic Development in East Asia* (London: Routledge)

Shi, T. (2008), 'China: Democratic Values Supporting an Authoritarian System', in Y. Chu, L. Diamond, A. Nathan and D. C. Shin (eds), *How East Asians View Democracy* (New York, NY: Columbia University Press)

Shin, D. C. (1994), 'On The Third Wave of Democratization: A Synthesis and Evaluation of Recent Theory and Research', *World Politics* 47/1: 135–70

Shin, D. C. (1999) *Mass Politics and Culture in Democratizing Korea* (Cambridge: Cambridge University Press)

Shin, D. C. (2007), 'Democratization: Perspectives from Global Citizenry' in R. Dalton and H.–D. Klingemann (eds), *The Oxford Handbook of Political Behaviour* (Oxford: Oxford University Press), 259–282

Shin, D. C. and Lee, J. (2003), 'Comparing Democratization in the East and the West', *Asia Pacific Perspectives* 3/1: 40–9

Shin, D. C. and Tusalem, R. F. (2007), 'The Cultural and Institutional Dynamics of Global Democratization', *Taiwan Journal of Democracy*, 3/1: 1–28

Shin, D. C. and Wells, J. (2005), 'Is Democracy the Only Game in Town?', *Journal of Democracy*, 16/2: 88–101

Shugart, M. (2001), '"Extreme" Electoral Systems and the Appeal of the Mixed–Member Alternative', in Shugart and Wattenberg, 25–51

Shugart, M. (2005), 'Comparative Electoral Systems Research: The Maturation of a Field and New Challenges Ahead', in M. Gallagher and P. Mitchell (eds), *The Politics of Electoral Systems* (Oxford: Oxford University Press), 25–55

Shugart, M. and Carey, J. (1992), *Presidents and Assemblies: Constitutional Design and Electoral Dynamics* (Cambridge: Cambridge University Press)

Shugart, M. and Wattenberg, M. (2001) (eds), *Mixed–Member Electoral Systems: The Best of Both Worlds?* (Oxford: Oxford University Press)

Siaroff, A. and Merer, J. W. A. (2002), 'Parliamentary Election Turnout in Europe Since 1990', *Political Studies*, 50/5: 916–27

Skocpol, T. (1979), *States and Social Revolutions. A Comparative Analysis of France, Russia, and China* (Cambridge: Cambridge University Press)

Slater, D. (1985), *New Social Movements and the State in Latin America* (Amsterdam: CEDLA)

Smith, B. (2006). 'The Wrong Kind of Crisis: Why Oil Booms and Busts Rarely Lead to Authoritarian Breakdown', *Studies in Comparative International Development*, 40/4: 55–76

Smith, M. A. (2000), *American Business and Political Power: Public Opinion, Elections, and Democracy* (Chicago, IL: University of Chicago Press)

Smith, T. (1978), 'Decolonization and the Response of Colonial Elites: A Comparative Study of French and British Decolonization', *Comparative Studies in Society and History*, 20/1: 70–102

Smith, T. (1994), *America's Mission. The United States and the Worldwide Struggle for Democracy in the Twentieth Century* (Princeton, NJ: Princeton University Press).

Snow, D. E. and Benford, R. (1988), 'Ideology, Frame, Resonance and Participant Mobilization', In B. Klandermans, H. Kriesi and S. Tarrow (eds), *From Structure to Action* (Greenwich, CT: JAI Press), 197–217

Solinger, D. (1993), *China's Transition from Socialism: Statist Legacies and Market Reforms, 1980–1990* (Armonk, NY: M.E. Sharpe)

Solinger, D. (2006), 'The Nexus of Democratization: Guanxi and Governance in Taiwan and the PRC', presented at a conference 'Democratization in Greater China' held at Stanford University on 20–21 October 2006

Splichal, S. (1994), *Media Beyond Socialism. Theory and Practice in East-Central Europe* (Boulder, CO: Westview).

Stark, D. and Bruszt, L. (1998), *Postsocialist Pathways: Transforming Politics and Property in East Central Europe* (Cambridge: Cambridge University Press)

Stepan, A. and Robertson, G. (2003). 'An Arab more than a Muslim electoral gap', *Journal of Democracy*, 14/3: 30–44

Stigler, G. J. (1975), *The Citizen and the State: Essays on Regulation* (Chicago, IL: University of Chicago Press)

Stolle, D. and Rochon, T. R. (2001), 'Are All Associations Alike? Member Diversity, Associational Type, and the Creation of Social Capital', *American Behavioral Scientist*, 42/1: 47–65

Streeck, W. and Schmitter, P. C. (1985), *Private Interest Government: Beyond Market and State* (London: Sage)

Storm, L. (2008), 'The parliamentary election in Morocco, September 2007', *Electoral Studies*, 27/2: 359–364

Strom, K. (1990), 'A behavioral theory of competitive political parties'. *American Journal of Political Science*, 34/2: 565–98

Sükösd, M. (2000), 'Democratic Transformation and the Mass Media in Central and Eastern Europe: From Stalinism to Democratic Consolidation in Hungary', in R. Gunther and A. Mughan (eds), *Democracy and the Media: A Comparative Perspective* (Cambridge: Cambridge University Press), 122–64

Sunstein, C. (2001), *Designing Democracy: What Constitutions Do* (Oxford: Oxford University Press)

Szeleni, I. *et al.* (2001), *Making Capitalism without Capitalists: The New Ruling Elites in Eastern Europe* (London: Verso)

Taagepera, R. (1999), 'Supplementing the Effective Number of Parties', *Electoral Studies*, 18/4: 497–504.

Taagepera, R. (2007), *Predicting Party Sizes: The Logic of Simple Electoral Systems.* (Oxford: Oxford University Press)

Taagepera, R. and Shugart, M. (1989), *Seats and Votes. The Effects and Determinants of Electoral Systems* (New Haven, CT: Yale University Press)

Tarrow, S. (1995), 'Mass Mobilization and Regime Change: Pacts, Reform, and Popular Power in Italy (1918–1922) and Spain (1975–1978)', in R. Gunther, P. N. Diamandouros, and H.-J. Puhle (eds), *The Politics of Democratic Consolidation: Southern Europe in Comparative Perspective* (Baltimore, MD: Johns Hopkins University Press), 204–30

Tarrow, S. (1998), *Power in Movement* (Cambridge: Cambridge University Press)

Tavits, M. (2005), 'The Development of Stable Party Support: Electoral Dynamics in Post–Communist Europe', *American Journal of Political Science*, 49/2: 283–98

Tessler, M. and Gao, E. (2005), 'Gauging Arab support for Democracy', *Journal of Democracy*, 16/3: 83–97.

Tétreault, M. A. (2000), *Stories of Democracy: Politics and Society in Contemporary Kuwait* (New York, NY: Columbia University Press)

Therborn, G. (1977), 'The Rule of Capital and the Rise of Democracy', *New Left Review*, 103: 3–41

Thomas, G. M., Meyer, J. W., Ramirez, F. O. and Boli, J. (1987), *Institutional structure: Constituting state, society, and the individual* (Newbury Park, CA: Sage)

Thompson, A. (ed.) (2006), *The Media and the Rwanda Genocide* (London: Pluto Press)

Thompson, J. (2000), 'The Survival of Asian Values as 'Zivilisationskritik', *Theory and Society* 29/5: 651–86

Thompson, M. (2001), 'Whatever happened to Asian Values?' *Journal of Democracy*, 12/4: 145–65

Thompson, M. R. (2004), *Democratic Revolutions* (London: Routledge)

Tien, H. (1997), 'Taiwan's Transformation', in L. Diamond, M. Plattner, Y. Chu and H. Tien, (eds), *Consolidating the Third Wave Democracies. Regional Challenges* (Baltimore, MD: Johns Hopkins University Press), 123–61

Tilly, C. (1997), *Coercion, Capital, and European States, AD 990–1992* (Oxford: Blackwell)

Tilly, C. (2001), 'When Do (and Don't) Social Movements Promote Democratization?', in P. Ibarra (ed.), *Social Movements and Democracy* (London: Palgrave Macmillan), 21–45

Tilly, C. (2004a), *Contention and Democracy in Europe, 1650–2000* (Cambridge: Cambridge University Press)

Tilly, C. (2004b), *Social Movements, 1768–2004* (Boulder, CO: Paradigm)

Tironi, E. and Sunkel, G. (2000), 'The Modernization of Communication and Democratization: The Media in the Transition to Democracy in Chile', in R. Gunther and A. Mughan (eds), *Democracy and the Media: A Comparative Perspective* (Cambridge: Cambridge University Press), 165–94

Tocqueville, A. de (1994 [1837]), *Democracy in America* (London: Fontana Press)

Tomz, M., Wittenberg, J. and King, G. (2003), CLARIFY: Software for Interpreting and Presenting Statistical Results. Version 2.1. Available at <http://gking.harvard.edu>

Touraine, A. (1981), *The Voice and the Eye: An Analysis of Social Movements* (Cambridge: Cambridge University Press)

Treier, S. and Jackman, S. (2008) 'Democracy as a Latent Variable', *American Journal of Political Science*, 52/1: 201–17

Tremblay, M. and Pelltier, R. (2000), 'More Feminists or More Women? Descriptive and Substantive Representations of Women in the 1997 Canadian Federal Elections', *International Political Science Review*, 21/4: 381–405

Tu, W. (1996) (ed.), *Confucian Traditions in East Asian Modernity* (Cambridge, MA: Harvard University Press)

Ulfelder, J. (2005), 'Contentious Collective Action and the Breakdown of Authoritarian Regimes', *International Political Science Review*, 26/3: 311–34

Ulfelder, J. and Lustik, M. (2007), 'Modelling Transitions To and From Democracy', *Democratization*, 14/3: 351–87

UNCTAD (2002), *World Investment Report 2002: Transnational Corporations and Export Competitiveness* (New York/Geneva: United Nations)

United Nations Development Programme (2002), *Human Development Report 2002* (Oxford: Oxford University Press)

Vanhanen, T. (1997), *Prospects of Democracy: A Study of 172 Countries* (Routledge: London)

Vanhanen, T. (2000), 'A new dataset for measuring democracy, 1810–1998', *Journal of Peace Research*, 37/2: 251–65

Vanhanen, T. (2003) *Democratization: A Comparative Analysis of 170 Countries* (London: Routledge)

Verba, S. and Nie, N. H. (1972), *Participation in America* (Chicago, IL: University of Chicago Press)

Verba, S., Nie, N. H. and Kim, J. O. (1971), *The Modes of Democratic Participation: A Cross–National Comparison* (New York: Sage)

Verba, S., Nie, N. H. and Kim, J.-O. (1978), *Participation and Political Equality: A seven–nation comparison* (Cambridge: Cambridge University Press)

Verba, S., Schlozman, K. L. and Brady, H. E. (1995), *Voice and Equality: Civic voluntarism in American politics* (Cambridge, MA: Harvard University Press)

Verbitsky, H. (2005) *El Silencio: De Paulo VI a Bergoglio. Las Relaciones Secretas de la Iglesia con la ESMA* (Buenos Aires: Sudamericana)

Villalón, L. A. (1995), *Islamic Society and State Power in Senegal: Disciples and Citizens in Fatick* (Cambridge: Cambridge University Press)

Villegas, B. M. (1998), 'Business in the Philippines: A self–conscious business actor', in A. Bernstein and P. L. Berger (eds), *Business and Democracy: Cohabitation or Contradiction?* (London/New York: Continuum), 157–9

Volpi, F. (2006). 'Algeria's Pseudo–Democratic Politics: Lessons for democratization in the Middle East', *Democratization*, 13/3: 442–455.

Voltmer, K. (2008), 'Comparing Media Systems in New Democracies: East Meets South Meets West', *Central European Journal of Communication*, 1/1

von Beyme, K. (1987), *I Partiti Nelle Democrazie Occidentali* (Bologna: Zanichelli)

von Beyme, K. (1996), *Transition to Democracy in Eastern Europe. Advances in Political Science* (London: Macillan)

von Beyme, K. (1999), 'Institutional Engineering and Transitions to Democracy', in J. Zielonka (ed.) *Democratic Consolidation in Eastern Europe, Volume 1* (Oxford: Oxford University Press), 3–24

Waisbord, S. (2000), 'Media in South America: Between the Rock of the State and the Hard Place of the Market', in J. Curran and M.-J. Park (eds), *De–Westernizing Media Studies* (London: Routledge), 50–62

Wallerstein, I. (1974), *The Modern World System I: Capitalist agriculture and the origins of the European world–economy in the 16th century* (New York, NY: Academic Press)

Ware, A. (1996), *Political Parties and Party Systems* (Oxford: Oxford University Press)

Wasserman, H. and De Beer, A. (2006), 'Conflicts of Interests? Debating the Media's Role in Post–Apartheid South Africa', in K. Voltmer (ed.), *Mass Media and Political Communication in New Democracies* (London: Routledge), 59–75

Waylen, G. (1994), 'Women and Democratization: Conceptualizing Gender Relations in Transition', *World Politics* 46/3: 327–54

Weber, M. (1958 [1904]), *The Protestant Ethic and the Spirit of Capitalism* (New York, NY: Charles Scribner's Sons)

Welzel, C. (2006), 'Democratization as an Emancipative Process', *European Journal of Political Research*, 45: 871–96

Welzel, C. (2007), 'Are Levels of Democracy Influenced by Mass Attitudes?' *International Political Science Review* 28/4: 397–424

Welzel, C., Inglehart R. and Klingemann, H.–D. (2003), 'The Theory of Human Development', *European Journal of Political Research*, 42/2: 34–79

Welzel, C. and Inglehart, R. (2006), 'The Human Development Model of Democracy: East Asia in Perspective', In R. Dalton and D. C. Shin (eds), *Citizens, Democracy and Markets around the Pacific Rim* (Oxford: Oxford University Press), 21–49

Welzel, C. and Inglehart, R. (2008), 'Democratization as Human Empowerment', *Journal of Democracy*, 19/1: 126–40

White, S. and McAllister, I. (2007), 'Turnout and Representation Bias in Postcommunist Europe', *Political Studies* 55/3: 586–606

White, S., Rose, R. and McAllister, I. (1997), *How Russia Votes* (Chatham, NJ: Chatham House)

Whitehead L. (2001) (ed.), *The International Dimensions of Democratization: Europe and the Americas* (Oxford: Oxford University Press)

Whitehead, L. (1991), 'Democracy by Convergence and Southern Europe: A Comparative Politics Perspective', in G. Pridham (ed.), *Encouraging Democracy: The International Context of Regime Transition in Southern Europe* (New York: St. Martin's Press), 1–29.

Whitehead, L. (2002), *Democratization: Theory and Experience* (Oxford: Oxford University Press)

Whitehead, Laurence (2002), *Democratization. Theory and Experience* (Oxford: Oxford University Press)

Wickham–Crowley, T. (1992), *Guerrillas and Revolution in Latin America. A Comparative Study of Insurgents and Regimes since 1956* (Princeton, NJ: Princeton University Press)

Wiktorowicz, Q. (2000). 'Civil Society as Social Control: State Power in Jordan', *Comparative Politics*, 33/1: 43–61.

Williams, M. S. (1998), *Voice, Trust, and Memory: Marginalized Groups and the Failings of Liberal Representation* (Princeton, NJ: Princeton University Press)

Willis, M. (2002). 'Political Parties in the Maghrib: The Illusion of Significance?', *The Journal of North African Studies*, 7/2: 1–22.

Willis, M. (2006). 'Containing Radicalism through the Political Process in North Africa', *Mediterranean Politics*, 11/2: 137–150

Wilson, W. (1917), 'The World Must Be Made Safe for Democracy', address of US President Woodrow Wilson to Congress on 2 April 1917, Sixty–Fifth Congress, 1 Session, Senate Document No 5. Available at <http://historymatters.gmu.edu>, Centre for History and New Media, George Mason University

Wintrobe, R. (1998), *The Political Economy of Dictatorship* (Cambridge: Cambridge University Press)

Wolbrecht, C. and Campbell, D. (2007), 'Leading by Example: Female Members of Parliament as Political Role Models', *American Journal of Political Science* 51/4: 921–39

Wood, E. (2000), *Forging Democracy from Below: Insurgent Transitions in South Africa and El Salvador* (Cambridge: Cambridge University Press)

Wood, E. M. (2003), *Empire of Capital* (London: Verso)

World Bank (2002a), *World Development Indicators* (Washington, DC: The World Bank)

World Bank (2002b), *World Development Report* (Washington, DC: The World Bank)

World Bank (2005), *East Asia Decentralizes—Making Local Government Work* (Washington DC: The World Bank)

World Bank (2007), *Governance Matters 2007*. Available at <www.govindicators.org>

Wright, T. (2007), *State Terrorism in Latin America: Chile, Argentina and International Human Rights* (Lanham, MD: Rowman and Littlefield)

Yang, D. (2007a), 'Trying to Stay in Control', *Current History* (September), 249–51

Yang, D. (2007b) 'China's Long March to Freedom', *Journal of Democracy*, 18/3: 58–64

Yilmaz, H. (2002), 'External–Internal Linkages in Democratization: Developing an Open Model of Democratic Change', *Democratization*, 9/2: 67–84

Yom, S. (2005), 'Civil Society and Democratization in the Arab world', *Middle East Review of International Affairs*, 9/4: 14–33

Young, I. M. (1990), *Justice and the Politics of Difference* (Princeton, NJ: Princeton University Press)

Zakaria, F. (1994), 'Culture is Destiny: A Conversation with Lee Kuan Yew', *Foreign Affairs*, 73/2: 109–26

Zakaria, F. (1997), 'The Rise of Illiberal Democracy', *Foreign Affairs*, 76/6: 22–43

Zakaria, F. (2003), *The Future of Freedom: Illiberal Democracy at Home and Abroad* (New York, NY: Norton)

Zartman, W. I. (1995), *Collapsed states: the disintegration and restoration of legitimate authority* (Boulder, CO: Lynne Rienner)

Zhao, D. (2000), *The Power of Tiananmen* (Chicago, IL: Chicago University Press).

Index